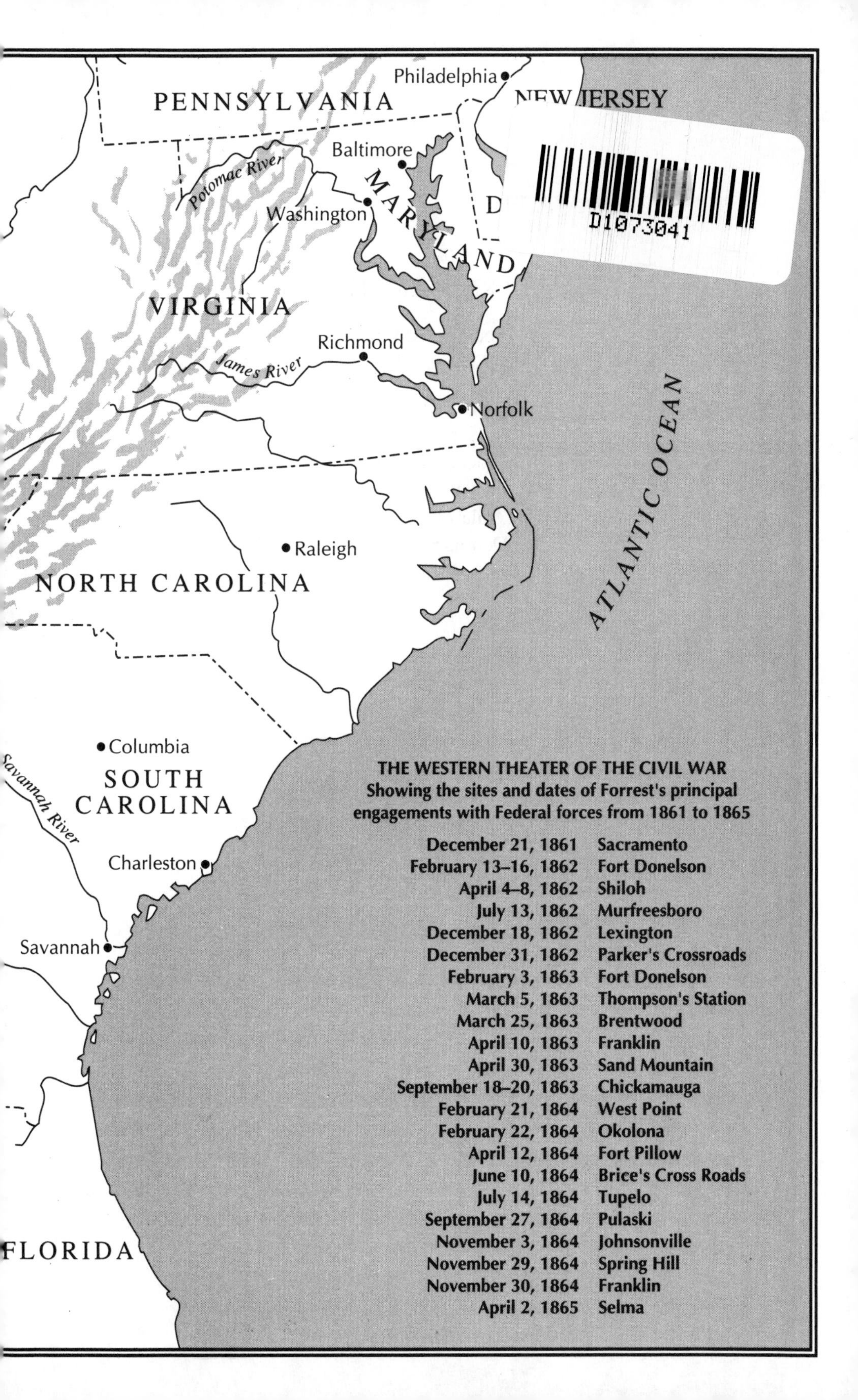

THE WESTERN THEATER OF THE CIVIL WAR
Showing the sites and dates of Forrest's principal engagements with Federal forces from 1861 to 1865

December 21, 1861	Sacramento
February 13–16, 1862	Fort Donelson
April 4–8, 1862	Shiloh
July 13, 1862	Murfreesboro
December 18, 1862	Lexington
December 31, 1862	Parker's Crossroads
February 3, 1863	Fort Donelson
March 5, 1863	Thompson's Station
March 25, 1863	Brentwood
April 10, 1863	Franklin
April 30, 1863	Sand Mountain
September 18–20, 1863	Chickamauga
February 21, 1864	West Point
February 22, 1864	Okolona
April 12, 1864	Fort Pillow
June 10, 1864	Brice's Cross Roads
July 14, 1864	Tupelo
September 27, 1864	Pulaski
November 3, 1864	Johnsonville
November 29, 1864	Spring Hill
November 30, 1864	Franklin
April 2, 1865	Selma

MODERN WAR STUDIES

The Confederacy's Greatest Cavalryman

Nathan Bedford Forrest

Brian Steel Wills

Foreword by Emory M. Thomas

University Press of Kansas

Frontispiece and Battle of Brice's Cross Roads maps by Paul Pugliese based on maps in *Life of General Nathan Bedford Forrest* by John Allan Wyeth. All other maps are reproduced from that work.

Published by the University Press of Kansas (Lawrence, Kansas 66049), which was organized by the Kansas Board of Regents and is operated and funded by Emporia State University, Fort Hays State University, Kansas State University, Pittsburg State University, the University of Kansas, and Wichita State University

Library of Congress Cataloging-in-Publication Data

Wills, Brian Steel, 1959–
[Battle from the start]
The Confederacy's greatest cavalryman : Nathan Bedford Forrest / Brian Steel Wills : foreword by Emory M. Thomas
p. cm.
Originally published : A battle from the start. New York : HarperCollins, © 1992.
Includes bibliographical references and index.
ISBN 0-7006-0885-0 (pbk. : alk. paper)
1. Forrest, Nathan Bedford, 1821–1877. 2. Generals—United States—Biography. 3. Confederate States of America, Army—Biography. 4. United States—History—Civil War, 1861–1865—Cavalry operations. I. Title.
[E467.1.F72W55 1998]
973.7'13'092—dc21
[B] 98-11044

British Library Cataloguing in Publication Data is available.

Printed in Canada

10 9 8 7 6 5 4 3 2 1

The paper used in this publication meets the minimum requirements of the American National Standard for Permanence of Paper for Printed Library Materials Z39.48-1984.

To my parents,
Curtis and Harriet Wills,
and Lauren

Contents

Maps

Foreword

TOO OFTEN WE FAIL to see the Forrest for the Lees.

Historians of the American Civil War, and presumably their readers, have tended to treat Nathan Bedford Forrest and other quasi-guerrilla commanders as colorful supporting characters in the great drama of sectional conflict. While Forrest was having his little fun at Brice's Crossroads in Mississippi, back at the "real" war in Virginia, Ulysses Grant was preparing to cross the James and march on Petersburg. Even Forrest's biographers have allowed themselves to emphasize derring-do at the expense of larger themes and more expansive visions.

Of course Forrest was a colorful figure, and his exploits were indeed exciting. Perhaps the wealth of Forrest lore has led his biographers, despite their protestations to the contrary, to focus on many isolated adventures rather than ask a few ambitious questions about his whole life and Confederate career.

Before this book six serious biographies have confronted Forrest. The best of these was one of the first.

At age sixteen John Allan Wyeth joined a regiment of Alabama cavalry and during the middle years of the American Civil War (he was captured shortly after Chickamauga) rode with men who had ridden with Nathan Bedford Forrest. It was from these veterans that Wyeth heard stories about Forrest and victory:

> His escape from Fort Donelson: the desperate charge which saved Beauregard's army from Sherman's vigorous pursuit after

> Shiloh, in which he was severely wounded; the capture of Murfreesborough [*sic*] with its entire garrison of infantry and artillery, with his small brigade of cavalry without cannon; the charge on and capture of Coburn's infantry at Thompson's Station; the capture of the garrison at Brentwood; and the relentless pursuit of Streight's raiders which ended in the surrender of these gallant Union soldiers to Forrest with less than one-half of their number, had already attracted wide attention and had made him famous.

After the war, and after Forrest's death, Wyeth determined to write Forrest's biography to "place him in history not only as one of the most remarkable and romantic personalities of the Civil War, but as one of the ablest soldiers of the world."

Wyeth, a physician by profession, became a historian, too, and worked long and hard to get the facts of Forrest right. Finally, in 1899 Wyeth published the *Life of General Nathan Bedford Forrest,* and this book through newer editions and reprintings has become the "classic" life of Forrest.

Bedford Forrest alive blessed the work of Thomas Jordan and J. P. Pryor, published in 1868, *The Campaigns of Lieutenant-General N. B. Forrest*—"For the greater part of the statements of the narrative I am responsible." However, the availability of Forrest and eyewitnesses to his exploits proved a mixed blessing; Wyeth and others discovered inaccuracies and instances of rose-colored reminiscence in this "first-draft" biography.

Another early biography is *General Forrest* by J. Harvey Mathes (1902). Like that of Wyeth, Jordan, and Pryor, Mathes's focus was military, and his goal was to get the story told accurately.

Bedford Forrest: The Confederacy's Greatest Cavalryman, by Eric William Sheppard (1931), is an attempt to demonstrate the validity of the subtitle. Sheppard also claimed license to create dialogue and characters to enhance his narrative.

Southern agrarian "fugitive" Andrew Nelson Lytle wrote *Bedford Forrest and His Critter Company* (1931) and dedicated the book to his grandmother, "who has heard on the hard turn-pike the sudden beat of his horses' hoofs and the wild yell of his riders." Lytle also dedicated his work to the proposition that Forrest was "the most typical strong man of the Agrarian South" and "a symbol of Southern Feudalism." Forrest, Lytle contends, would have won the war had it not been for Braxton Bragg's incompetence and Jefferson Davis's failure to fathom his genius. Even so, Lytle argues, Forrest saved the "Culture of the South" via the Ku Klux Klan, "the last brilliant example in Western Culture of what feudalism could do." Thus, in the cause of unreconstructed apology, Lytle manages to thrash Western culture, Southern culture, feudalism, and Forrest all at once.

The most recent biography of Forrest appeared in 1944: Robert Selph Henry's *"First With the Most" Forrest*. Henry retells the old stories without Lytle's Agrarian baggage. The result is a good book but less than an analytical one. Though Henry makes a case for the importance of the western theater in the Civil War and for Forrest as a dashing character in the martial drama, for the most part he is content to revive the facts of Forrest one more time.

The facts of Nathan Bedford Forrest have little changed since 1944, and, for that matter, the history Forrest made has remained relatively unchanged since Forrest died in 1877. But the world of the living has changed considerably since 1877 and significantly since 1944. Consequently the questions historians and others ask about the record of Forrest's life have changed. And, accordingly, the answers are different.

Brian Wills knows more about Forrest than any previous biographer. He has sought the scraps of Forrest's record in county courthouses, newspapers, private correspondence, and oral tradition, and he offers here previously unknown information, especially about Forrest before and after the war. The true significance of Wills's work, however, lies in what he does with the facts of Forrest's life.

Wills takes Forrest seriously as a person and understands him as an offspring of the Southern frontier. Before Forrest was a soldier, he spent forty years scratching and clawing his way from backcountry oblivion to wealth and power in Memphis. Wills recites, indeed invigorates, the incidents of Forrest's life and military career. He tells the old stories with a fresh voice.

Following Forrest to war, Wills watches him learn to be warrior. Then the action accelerates as Forrest rides to battle after campaign after raid. Wills never lets the narrative escape his analysis, however; he offers insight even while he and his reader canter with Forrest into combat.

At Fort Pillow, for example, Wills reveals Forrest out of control as his troopers vent blood lust on African-American Federal soldiers and white Tennessee Unionists. Yet Forrest himself had instilled the savagery that motivated the massacre.

In 1865 Forrest gave up because he and his horsemen were used up. Wills traces Forrest's failures during the postwar period, fully implicates him in the infamy of the Ku Klux Klan, and illumines his attempt at redemption.

Having offered Forrest in context, Wills concludes by placing him in perspective as a Confederate general. The contrast with Robert E. Lee is important. The "conventional" war that Lee fought relegated Forrest to a secondary role. In a sense Forrest and other "freaks" played the sideshows, while Lee and commanders like him worked the center ring. But Lee and generals like him lost. Could Forrest have won?

He was a primitive in the mid-nineteenth century, when warfare was evolving toward struggles between whole peoples, fought by massive armies in which relatively small bands of armed horsemen would seem unimportant. But no circumstance is inevitable simply because it happened; people choose, and in this case Jefferson Davis chose Lee's way of warfare.

When "total war" continued to evolve, primitive behavior again became successful. Bedford Forrest may have seemed slightly out of step in the American Civil War; but he seems ideally suited for combat in Vietnam, Afghanistan, or Croatia. Our "modern" world appreciates the primitive. So again the question—could Forrest have won?

Thanks to Brian Wills, we can see the whole Forrest and Forrest whole.

EMORY M. THOMAS
Athens, Georgia, 1991

Acknowledgments

I remember the balmy summer nights when my brothers and I slipped onto the old battleground at Shiloh ... half fearful of the ghosts of the 23,000 casualties who everyone said roamed the field by night. I can remember the many campfires we burned and the phantom Rebels we conjured up.

—THOMAS LAWRENCE CONNELLY

ANY PROJECT OF THIS KIND is heavily dependent upon others for their assistance along the way. I would particularly like to express my appreciation to some of my professors and friends at the University of Georgia. This study is better than it would have been because of them.

Emory Thomas spent long hours working with me on the manuscript, first listening to my ideas about Bedford Forrest and later helping me to shape those ideas into written form. He deserves and has my fullest appreciation and gratitude. We have spent many pleasant hours discussing everything from Forrest to football, and I have been many times confirmed in my judgment to come to Athens to study under him years ago. He is truly a mentor, colleague, and friend.

I cannot fully express the importance of having studied under and with Numan V. Bartley. My debt to him, in matters far greater than just this book, is a heavy one. F. Nash Boney used his enormous skills as a writer to improve mine. Robert A. Pratt, Jean E. Friedman, and William S. McFeely provided excellent suggestions and criticisms at various stages in this long process. I am grateful that they read the document so closely and critically.

I would like to thank the staff members of the following institutions, who helped make my research efforts much easier than they would otherwise have been: Southern Historical Collection, University of North Carolina; William R. Perkins Library, Duke University; Tennessee State Library and Archives; Memphis Public Library; Mississippi Valley Collection, Memphis State University Libraries; Memphis Pink Palace Museum; Cossitt-Goodwyn Library, Memphis; Hargrett Rare Book and Manuscript Library, University of Georgia; U.S. Army Military History Institute, Carlisle Barracks, Pennsylvania; Birmingham Public Library; Chicago Historical Society; Auburn University Library; Western Reserve Historical Society, Cleveland; Henry E. Huntington Library, San Marino, California; Georgia Department of Archives and History; Georgia Historical Society; Alabama Department of Archives and History; Mississippi Department of Archives and History; Carnegie Public Library, Clarksdale, Mississippi; and the courthouses in Hernando and Clarksdale, Mississippi.

Michele Fagan and Margaret Witt greatly assisted me in several research jaunts to Memphis. Steve Daniels took time from his busy schedule to show me around the battlefield at Parker's Crossroads, and Harry Abernathy was especially generous with his time and research during my visit to Clarksdale, Mississippi.

Although I cannot properly thank everyone who has helped make this book possible, I wish specifically to thank my two graduate school officemates and close friends, Randy Patton and Leann Grabavoy Almquist, for putting up with me. Glenn Eskew, Jim Cobb, John Inscoe, Sheree Dendy, Russ Duncan, Lesley Gordon, Chris Phillips, Keith Bohannon, Stan Deaton, Dan Carter, Reid Mitchell, and Edward F. Williams, III, offered their ideas and assistance to me in a variety of ways. M. S. Wyeth, Jr., and his associates at HarperCollins have been enormously helpful, supportive, and patient. Production editor Susan H. Llewellyn suggested the title for the book based upon Forrest's own assessment of his life. My colleagues at Georgia Southern University, particularly Jay Fraser, Frank Saunders, Anne Bailey, Don Rakestraw, Jamie Woods, Craig Roell, Charlton Moseley, and Ray Shurbutt, generously offered their support and friendship, for which I am grateful. Tracy Revels, Carolyn Malone, Buck Melton, Elmer Clark, and Michael Justus also did everything they could to help keep me sane in the year that I spent turning the dissertation into a book, while trying to remain a credible teacher. Thank you.

Finally, to my father, who seems to be proud, despite his bafflement at what I do for a living; to my mother, whose love of history and encouragement have been my foundation for doing what I do; and to Lauren, who has taught me that life and love endure, I have dedicated this book.

Like Thomas Connelly, I remember spending many of my days on a farm in Virginia riding with Bedford Forrest or marching with Robert E. Lee and Patrick Cleburne. The stories I read of Forrest's pursuit and capture of Streight's raiders, his confrontation with the gunboats at Johnsonville, and many other of his wartime feats sparked my imagination. For five summers I tried my hand at soldiering, to some extent, as a Confederate artilleryman in the "Living History" program at Petersburg National Battlefield. I, too, have felt the ghosts.

In undertaking this study, it has been my intention to break through the myths and stories that have surrounded Forrest, to understand him better as a man, and to place him in the context of his times. He was an enormously complicated individual and like all human beings had his failings. There is much to dislike about Nathan Bedford Forrest; there is also a good deal to admire.

INTRODUCTION

Git Thar Fustest with the Mostest

Well, I got there first with the most men.

—NATHAN BEDFORD FORREST

Forrest! Forrest! Here he comes! Get out of the way!

—GRANDPAP, IN WILLIAM FAULKNER, "SHALL NOT PERISH"

"GIT THAR FUSTEST WITH THE MOSTEST MEN." The enigma of Nathan Bedford Forrest is wrapped up in that widely disseminated phrase. Although he never uttered the famous statement in this form, it has come to symbolize his life. The man who allegedly spoke in this manner has been depicted as the untutored genius, the homespun hero, the rough-hewn cavalry raider. Contemporaries and others knew him as the Wizard of the Saddle. When asked to name the greatest soldier produced on either side during the war, Robert E. Lee was said to have replied, "A man I have never seen, sir. His name is Forrest."[1] One of Forrest's former soldiers wrote that his commander's "commission as General, was signed not only by Mr. Jefferson Davis, but by the Almighty as well."[2]

Bedford Forrest's ferocity as a warrior was also legendary. Confederate General Richard Taylor doubted that "any commander since the days of lion-hearted Richard has killed as many enemies with his own hand as Forrest."[3] The fact that Forrest liked to say that he had slain one more enemy soldier than the twenty-nine horses killed beneath him only added to the legend.[4] Such was the stuff of literature, and former comrades, writers, and biographers lost little time enshrining the man in myth.[5]

Southern novelist William Faulkner chose Bedford Forrest as one of his tainted heroes. Faulkner referred to the cavalry commander in nine of his novels and eight of his short stories and essays.[6] Certainly Forrest's prewar and postwar connections with the slave trade and the Ku Klux Klan, respectively, and his controversial encounters with black Union troops during the war made him an ideal character for Faulkner's fiction. According to one scholar, Faulkner believed that although the inhabitants of the Deep South lived "single-mindedly by a fixed code," they also labored under the curse of slavery, which plagued them with guilt and civil war.[7] For instance, in *Go Down, Moses,* it was Forrest, "while he was still only a slave-trader and not yet a general," who sold the McCaslin family a slave on March 3, 1856, thereby bringing the guilt of the slave taint on the McCaslins.[8]

Yet, however tainted men like Forrest and Faulkner's heroes were, they were still unwilling, or at least unable, to rid themselves of their code, and they distanced themselves from other Southerners who broke it. The Snopes family, generally portrayed by Faulkner as amoral figures motivated solely by self-interest, had no place with the Forrests.[9] As one character observed in *Sartoris:* "General Johnston or General Forrest wouldn't have took a Snopes in his army at all."[10] And "old man" Falls explained that when horse thief Zeb Fothergill could not sell the horses he had gathered on one of "them trips of his'n," he "turned 'em loose and requisitioned to Joe Johnston's haid quarters [for payment] fer ten hosses sold to Forrest's cavalry." Falls concluded, of the attempted fraud, "I don't know ef he ever got air answer. Nate Forrest wouldn't 'a' had them hosses."[11] For Faulkner, Bedford Forrest represented the ambiguity—the unique mixture of honor and curse, fantasy and reality—of the Southern experience.

Forrest was an appropriate choice for Faulkner to make as one of his tainted heroes. One suspects that as the Reverend Gail

Hightower peered through the haze, the vision that he saw on the dusty street might have included the Wizard of the Saddle:

> Hungry, gaunt, yelling, setting fire to the store depots of a whole carefully planned campaign and riding out again. No looting at all: no stopping for even shoes, tobacco. I tell you, they were not men after spoils and glory; they were boys riding the sheer tidal wave of desperate living. Boys. Because this. This is beautiful. Listen. Try to see it. Here is that fine shape of eternal youth and virginal desire which makes heroes. That makes the doings of heroes border so close upon the unbelievable that it is no wonder that their doings must emerge now and then like gunflashes in the smoke....[12]

CHAPTER 1

Young Bedford

(July 13, 1821–1842)

With him life was at best an uncertain game, and he recognized the usual percentage in favor of the dealer.

—BRET HARTE

Bedford had plenty of sense, but would not apply himself. He thought more of wrestling than his books; he was an athlete.

—JOHN LAWS

THE NEW ENGLAND transcendentalist surveyed his audience of eager, young faces. They were the cream of New England, indeed American, society. On this day, August 31, 1837, Ralph Waldo Emerson would challenge them to become "Man Thinking." He would admonish these young men—members of Harvard's chapter of Phi Beta Kappa—to cast off the restricting bonds "of dependence [upon] ... the learning of other lands" and thus free themselves from the "courtly muses of Europe." But he considered a threat from within their own country even more insidious. In his closing remarks he specifically warned the Phi Beta Kappas not to allow themselves "to be reckoned in the gross, in the hundred, or the thousand, of the party, the section, to which we belong" and, therefore, have their "opinion predicted geographically, as the north, or the south."[1]

A little over a month later, Emerson recounted in his journal an evening spent in the company of the Reverend and Mrs. Samuel Ripley. Since Ripley and his wife ran a boarding school for boys that assisted a number of young Southerners in their preparations for Harvard, the conversation surely touched upon the transcendentalist's recent address. In any event, Emerson used the opportunity to express himself further concerning Southern students in New England. "The young Southerner," he explained,

> comes here a spoiled child with graceful manners, excellent self-command, very good to be spoiled more, but good for nothing else, a mere parader. He has conversed so much with rifles, horses and dogs that he has become himself a rifle, a horse and a dog, and in civil, educated company, where anything human is going forward, he is dumb and unhappy, like an Indian in a church. Treat them with great deference, as we often do, and they accept it all as their due without misgiving. Give them an inch, and they take a mile. They are mere bladders of conceit. Each snipper-snapper of them all undertakes to speak for the entire Southern States.... They are more civilized than the Seminoles, however, in my opinion; a little more. Their question respecting any man is like a Seminole's, How can he fight? In this country, we ask, What can he do? His pugnacity is all they prize in man, dog, or turkey. The proper way of treating them is not deference, but to say as Mr. Ripley does, "Fiddle faddle," in answer to each solemn remark about "The South."[2]

And so, in one great sweep of his pen, the Sage of Concord dismissed Southerners "in the gross." As historian, Lewis P. Simpson observed of the entry, "Indeed, it seems clear that in his description of Southern students Emerson had discovered an absolute cultural contrast between the South and New England: the one was a culture of no mind, the other a culture of mind."[3] From this and other writings emerged a sense, for Emerson, that far from the hallowed halls of Harvard lay a dark and sinister land, an immoral and barbarous place—the American South.[4]

Four years later, a Virginia-born writer of short stories and poetry sat at his desk, poised to assault the New England transcendentalists with his pen. Edgar Allan Poe determined to answer his critics and strike a blow at men like Emerson with a short story.[5] Entitled "Never Bet the Devil Your Head," the story first appeared in *Graham's Magazine* in September 1841.[6] Poe's tale chronicled the misadventures of a young braggadocio named Toby Dammit.

Although ostensibly a New England transcendentalist, young Dammit labored under rather Southern handicaps. He was passionate to a fault, often unwilling or unable to control his passions. As the narrator relates, this fault manifested itself early in Toby's life: "The fact is that his precocity in vice was awful. At five months of age he used to get into such passions that he was unable to articulate. At six months, I caught him gnawing a pack of cards," an early indication of his propensity for gambling. Other vices followed, for at "eight months he peremptorily refused to put his signature to the Temperance pledge."

Despite his friend's efforts to rechannel his energies to more constructive pursuits, Toby regressed, until he was no longer able to govern his passions. This shortcoming left him vulnerable. His friend found Toby's desire to "bet the Devil my head" on almost every occasion particularly distasteful and potentially destructive. A warning provoked only an angry response. Then, one day, as the two friends walked, they encountered a covered bridge.

At length the two young men reached a turnstile at the opposite end of the bridge. The narrator quietly went through it, but Dammit insisted that he could leap it and do so gracefully enough to "cut a pigeon-wing over it." Thinking the boast impossible to fulfill, the friend challenged Toby, who retorted that he bet the devil his head he could do it. Immediately a lame old man appeared and accepted the rhetorical bet. Toby had no choice but to comply. With a running start he cleared the turnstile; however, instead of continuing over the obstacle, he fell back onto the same side from which he began. In the meantime, the old man caught an object in his leather apron as it dropped from the darkness above.

His curiosity piqued, the friend hastened to the place where Toby lay and was astonished to find "that he had received what might be termed a serious injury. The truth is, he had been deprived of his head." Throwing open a window, the friend revealed a flat iron brace that had caused Toby such grief. It is not surprising that Toby "did not long survive his terrible loss ... [and] in the end he grew worse, and at length died, a lesson to all riotous livers."[7]

Even in a tale so obviously meant to display his talents as a humorist, Poe could not escape his darker side. According to Dickson Bruce, this inclination toward pessimism was not unusual for Poe in particular or Southerners in general. Bruce considered Poe the "one Southern figure" who embodied in his fiction the struggle between passion and restraint, violence and control. It was Poe, he insisted, who demonstrated "the darkest streaks of the antebellum Southern world view in their most general form." Thus, when Toby Dammit proved incapable of exercising control over his passions, the result was violent death. He had literally and figuratively lost his head. As Bruce noted generally of Poe's work: "Passion was grown so obsessive as to overcome all restraint and control." And in a world fraught with insecurity, Southerners saw such displays of passion, and the violence that so frequently resulted, as an almost natural part of life.[8]

Both Emerson and Poe were partially correct in their assertions about the South and the Southerners' character, for sixteen years before Emerson's discourse on Southerners and twenty years before Poe's tale of a passionate youth's violent demise, a man was born who embodied many aspects of character suggested by the two literary giants. Unlike the students who listened to Emerson at Harvard, his education was limited. Furthermore, he had already spent much of his life with rifles, horses, and dogs. He was a man who judged others, among other means, by the way they fought. He was also a man who frequently displayed the darker side of Poe's ill-fated protagonist. He struggled with passion and for control throughout his life. Honor and violence remained constants for him. However, he did not exist in a world of "no mind." His culture had "a mind," shaped by its own peculiar heritage and worldview. His life was neither fiction nor life "in the gross." In short, this man combined aspects of these generalizations and much more, to form a hard reality—a flesh-and-blood human being named Nathan Bedford Forrest.

Forrest began his life in the backwoods of Tennessee on July 13, 1821. Named for his grandfather, Nathan, and the county of his birth, Bedford (the name by which he was usually called), he and his twin sister Fanny were the first children born to William and Mariam Beck Forrest. He was not the scion of a great and wealthy family. His parents were simple folk, inured to hardship by seemingly endless labor. Both were large, strapping individuals. William stood over six feet, while Mariam was nearly that tall. By trade William was a blacksmith, and he boasted a good reputation in the community. Mariam performed all the tedious chores that were necessary to keep a growing family clothed and fed on the frontier.

The fledgling family lived in a log cabin that fronted the public road. The cabin consisted of one and a half rooms, the half room being a loft that provided sleeping quarters for the family. It was awkwardly constructed of rough-hewn cedar logs, chinked to keep out the wind and the elements. William cleared several acres of land and fenced in a yard, a garden, and an orchard of fruit trees. His blacksmith shop sat across the road from the house. The Forrests lived in a state of semisubsistence, relying largely upon William's skills to support them. They grew enough crops to eat and to provide seed for the next year, supplementing their diet with the produce of their orchard or from game hunted in the nearby forests.

The earliest reference to the Forrests was to Shadrach, Bedford's great-grandfather, who moved from western Virginia to Orange County, North Carolina, in 1740. Shadrach's second son, Nathan, moved to Tennessee in 1806, taking with him Shadrach and his own family, including eight-year-old William. The Forrests continued to follow the frontier westward until 1808, when they finally settled in the Duck River country in what was then Bedford County, within a half mile of the present hamlet of Chapel Hill, Tennessee. Here the sons of Nathan Forrest grew and established themselves in their own careers. All of them, except William and one other brother, a tailor, engaged in the livestock trade. Here also, William met and in 1820 married Mariam Beck.[9]

William's family grew steadily; Mariam bore eleven children. Aside from Nathan, there were seven sons and three daughters. Of these children, six boys—Bedford, John, William, Aaron, Jesse, and Jeffrey—lived to adulthood. Even so, there were plenty of children to help around the house and to provide each other with playmates. And although largely secluded in the backwoods, Bedford occasionally found a friend in the community. As might be expected of a boy growing up in a rural, relatively isolated setting, he enjoyed an active, robust life. A local resident recalled that no child in the neighborhood made more noise when playing or being punished.[10]

Bedford also exhibited a fearlessness that few of his companions possessed. On one occasion he was picking berries with some friends when they happened suddenly upon a rattlesnake. As the snake coiled, the rest of the children ran. Bedford called for the others to come back, but they left him to fend for himself. Perhaps because he was as angry at his friends for deserting him as he was at being frightened by the snake, Bedford refused to run; instead, he looked for a stick. When he had found a suitable weapon, he proceeded to pummel the reptile.[11] In other situations such as this, young Bedford remembered the dangers of the wilderness and prepared himself to meet them head on.

Bedford and a younger friend, McLauren, enjoyed every opportunity to ride their horses on errands or strictly for pleasure. Once, while riding through the woods, they stopped at a stream to water their horses. McLauren owned a prized Barlow knife, and when he leaned forward, he dropped it into the murky water. Understandably upset, the young fellow began to wail his displeasure. At first Bedford tried to comfort McLauren, but when he could not, he acted. Stripping off his clothes, he dived into the water repeatedly until he came to the surface clutching the knife.[12]

Frequently, these horseback rides took the youths past a cabin with two vicious dogs. The boys thoroughly enjoyed baiting the animals with words and stones. The dogs obliged by racing after the riders, barking with all their might. Bedford became so self-confident and complacent that on one occasion, he rode a young colt past the dogs, expecting the encounter to be no different from usual. However, this time he miscalculated, for when the dogs sprang at the horse, the colt bolted and tossed him to the ground. Terrified at the prospect of confronting his four-legged enemies at close hand, the boy immediately sprang to his feet, prepared to be torn to shreds but go down fighting. To his surprise, he realized that the animals were racing for safety. It seems that they, too, had been unprepared for the change in the routine and were as unsure of how to react as he was. Forrest would later admit that he had never been as frightened as he was at that instant.[13]

Presumably, this admission included an incident at his uncle's tailor shop, where Bedford used a pair of shears to disperse a group of rowdies who were harassing him. The boys had come into the shop to pass the time, saw Forrest, and began to badger him. Urged on by alcohol, peer pressure, and Bedford's initial refusal to respond, the boys became more vehement in their taunting. Finally, Forrest warned them to stop. Their ringleader, a young man named Adams, took exception and came at Forrest. Although Adams was larger than he was, Bedford sprang from his seat, the shears poised menacingly to strike. Adams froze, then turned, and taking his cohorts with him, stumbled out the door. Forrest's uncle rushed over to restrain his angry nephew from pursuing his antagonists.[14] Undoubtedly, the encounter taught Bedford a lesson in self-reliance and self-defense: Through his own quick and decisive actions, he could intimidate and disarm an apparently superior opponent.

Such lessons proved valuable, for despite the joys of childhood play, life in the Tennessee backwoods was difficult and demanding for everyone who lived there. Bedford's father William struggled to support his family, but business in the neighborhood was not sufficient for the blacksmith, and his prospects in Bedford County dimmed. The promise of new lands and new opportunities to the west beckoned. Finally, in 1834, he yielded to the urge to better his situation, sold what he could not move, and left for Mississippi. Bedford was thirteen at the time and must have regretted leaving the friends he had made and the woods and fields he had explored as a boy.

William and the growing Forrest family settled in Tippah County, in northern Mississippi, on lands recently vacated by Chickasaw Indians. Here William hoped to improve his family's fortunes and status. Unfortunately, he had scarcely settled there and begun wresting a homestead from the wilderness when he died, early in 1837. William's sudden death left Bedford the oldest male in a family to which another son, Jeffrey, was born four months later.[15]

This untoward circumstance quickly forced young Forrest to accept more serious responsibilities. His father's death left a void that he, the eldest son, would have to help fill. Thus, the task of raising a family fell to Bedford and his mother. According to John Allan Wyeth, one of Forrest's principal biographers, the other boys assisted him in this effort as they grew older. "He and the oldest of the brothers which came after him labored hard in clearing new land, and in cultivating that which had already been opened up while the father was still alive."[16] Together they functioned in a manner similar to the "thousands of small-scale farmers who came to work the land" on the frontier.[17] They raised such crops as corn, wheat, oats, and cotton and accumulated "a drove of cattle and a goodly supply of horses and mules and other stock."[18] As Malcolm J. Rohrbough explained, "Some members of this group [small-scale farmers] were making the upward transition to the economic and social status of a plantation society. Others were simply holding their own."[19] At this point, Bedford and the Forrest clan were decidedly among the latter.

Forrest never forgot the struggles he endured during these early trying years. According to Wyeth, he later proudly recalled how "after being deprived of his father" and having responsibility for his mother and the children devolve upon him, "he would labor all day in the field and then at night sit up and work until it was late making buckskin leggings and shoes and coon-skin caps for his younger brothers."[20]

Bedford's opportunities for an education had already been greatly limited by his father's desperate need for his help in supporting the family. Before the Forrests left Tennessee, Bedford had attended only three months of school. He received little more than that amount in Mississippi. For people in the Southern backcountry, formal education was at best an expendable luxury, possible only during the period between planting and harvesting, when crops required the least attention. Therefore, Bedford had to educate himself, using the wilderness and frontier life as his teacher. Thus, his education came largely from practical experience, not from the classroom.

Yet, even when the classroom opened to him, he often seemed preoccupied with other matters, which caused his attention to wander. As a former teacher explained to one of Forrest's wartime subordinates when the latter asked him if the general had been a good student: "Bedford had plenty of sense, but would not apply himself. He thought more of wrestling than his books; he was an athlete." As for the teacher, Bedford recalled that he should remember his pupil, since "you have whipped me often enough."[21] Forrest later admitted, "I never see a pen but what I think of a snake."[22]

Ray Allen Billington, historian of the American frontier experience, found this attitude toward education to be common among frontiersmen. These people understandably had little time to devote to such a luxury when other concerns, not the least of which were food and shelter, occupied most of their time. Nevertheless, Billington observed, they developed a practical-mindedness that served them well in their circumstances.[23]

Whatever his educational limitations, young Bedford found ample opportunity to test his mettle on the frontier. The caprices of nature and the struggles of subsistence living defined his world. He learned that both cooperation and self-reliance were essential to survival. The wilderness forced him to overcome fear and to rely on his instincts and his wits. Thus, he learned to trust himself and his judgment and to insist that others do the same. But the teacher was harsh. Typhoid fever struck the Forrests and took the lives of two of Bedford's brothers and all three of his sisters, including his twin sister, Fanny. Bedford himself was severely ill for a long time. He struggled mightily with the disease, but eventually made a full recovery.[24]

Despite the long hours of toil he endured, Forrest found occasional diversions. For a young man on the frontier, it is not surprising that he particularly enjoyed hunting and horse racing. As biographers Thomas Jordan and J. P. Pryor noted, "his only relaxations were found in the recreation of hunting and an occasional horse-race: for, in common with his whole family, as far back as they are known, an ardent taste for horses and dogs possessed him."[25] Violence was an important element in the Southern experience. It was especially important on the Southern frontier, where the environment encouraged the early development of skills in marksmanship and horsemanship. Thus, Forrest acted naturally in sharing a love of hunting and horse racing with others like himself. He enjoyed gambling as well. These activities honed necessary skills and provided welcome diversions from the hardships of everyday life. They also became matters of honor. Public approbation accompanied one's success in horse racing and skill in shooting.[26]

Molded as he was by the frontier and the early death of his father, Bedford understood the limitations he faced. The life of a blacksmith or a yeoman farmer in the backwoods held little promise of security for a struggling family. Yet, it was this sense of security and the element of control over his fate that it embodied that Forrest most craved. He was not one to face life passively.

Shortly after the death of his father, young Bedford encountered the uncertainties and insecurities of the wilderness in an incident that was not uncommon for his time and place. His mother and her sister had ridden out one day to visit a distant neighbor. Near dusk the two women returned from their visit, carrying a basketful of chickens given them by their neighbor. They rode along without incident for much of the return trip when a panther's cry suddenly rent the air. Wisely, the riders spurred their horses, hoping to reach the safety of their home. They succeeded in eluding the cat until they arrived at a creek near the cabin. They slowed the pace to navigate the hazard safely, but doing so allowed the animal to reach them. Leaping from the bank, the panther buried its claws into Mariam Forrest and her horse. She struggled to stay atop the horse and dislodge the panther. Finally, the cat slid off, allowing her to ride to safety.

Fiercely defensive of his family, particularly of his widowed mother, Bedford responded predictably to the attack. He determined to track the animal and kill it. Gathering his dogs, he set out in the dark. He realized the danger of his actions, but wanted to start the dogs on the track while it was still warm. The strategy succeeded. The dogs soon trapped the animal in a treetop. Here Bedford gained control of his passions. He would wait for dawn and light to finish the cat.

The boy waited patiently in the dark. His face and hands stung with the scratches from the briers and thickets he encountered during the chase. Although bone tired, he remained alert.

He kept his eyes fixed upon the spot where the panther crouched. It was not in his nature to let his quarry rest; he would have preferred to finish the task and be done with it. But darkness prevented him from being sure of success. And in the wilderness, failure could mean death.

As the sunlight slowly filtered through the trees, the young lad readied himself. He fingered his flintlock, nimbly replacing the damp powder with a fresh supply from his powder horn. There was no room for error. He would have to make the shot count. Alone in the wilderness, nothing was more dangerous than a wounded animal.

The hounds the boy had used to track the beast leapt anxiously about the tree. The panther grew increasingly restless. Bedford was now ready to act. He lifted the gun, took careful aim, and squeezed the trigger. The report echoed in the early morning air, followed by the thud of the animal dropping from its perch. Bedford strode over to the carcass, trimmed off the ears as proof of his conquest, and headed home.[27]

In the next few years, new settlers began to fill the surrounding region. One family moved next to the Forrests. Unfortunately, relations between the neighbors quickly soured. An ox belonging to the neighbor repeatedly broke down the fence that protected the Forrests' property and rummaged through their corn crop. After a while Bedford tired of the annoyance and called upon the owner to warn him that should the animal encroach in such a manner again he would shoot it. The neighbor responded indignantly. If Bedford harmed the ox, he assured him, the lad would suffer likewise.

Shortly thereafter, the two neighbors had an opportunity to test their mutual resolve, when the animal once again crashed through the fence and plundered through the Forrests' cornfield. Seeing this development, Bedford went inside the cabin to fetch his flintlock. He then calmly strode toward the culprit, pausing only to aim and fire his weapon. Hearing the sound of gunfire, the neighbor correctly deduced that the young man had fulfilled his threat. He grabbed his gun and marched angrily to the scene. By this time, Bedford had reloaded. He stared at the man, insisting that he meant him no harm but advising him to approach no closer. The neighbor ignored Bedford's admonition and began to climb the fence. Forrest watched his adversary reach the top rail. Here he was the most vulnerable and presented the clearest target. He fired, and the man tumbled to the ground unsettled, but unharmed. The shaken neighbor retreated quickly, not wishing to test further Bedford's determination to defend his family's interests and protect their property.[28]

As such incidents suggest, Nathan Bedford Forrest was a product of the frontier. And this frontier heritage shaped his entire life. Characteristically, he was a man of action, prepared to defend his family and his interests, often through violent means. A crude code of honor informed his life. In the words of John Hope Franklin, a man like Forrest would have "insisted on the right to defend his own honor."[29] Nevertheless, this sense of honor also imbued him with a sense of social status and a corporate identity.[30]

Forrest was the embodiment of the Jacksonian mystique—the notion, as David G. Pugh expressed it, that "manliness" in the nineteenth-century popular mind could be "traced to the Jacksonian belief that direct action, rather than thoughtful consideration, was the best response to almost any situation and that men could be measured not by their deepest motivations, but by what they did based on those motivations."[31] Certainly Bedford believed in direct action. Besides, circumstances limited the opportunities he might have had for learning contemplation rather than action. Moreover, reason might hamper resolution. Therefore, every man had to be prepared to defend himself and his interests by whatever means he had at his disposal. Bedford lived by Andrew Jackson's maxim: "Take time to deliberate; but when time for action arrives, stop thinking."[32] His experience often suggested that success came not to those who waited, but to those who acted.

Forrest engaged in an almost continuous defense of himself and his family. He displayed a willingness to do so violently, if necessary. For him, violence was an essential fact of life. The frontier created the sort of atmosphere in which such a penchant for violence could flourish. As W. J. Cash observed, "However careful they might be to walk softly, such men as these of the South were bound to come often into conflict. And being what they were—simple, direct, and immensely personal—and their world being what it was—conflict with them could only mean immediate physical clashing, could only mean fisticuffs, the gouging ring, and knife and gun play."[33] In the backwoods, the "plain folk" were usually armed and the "folkways" were often dangerous.[34]

Not only were these frontier folk willing to employ violence against each other, they saw such activity as a natural part of social life. According to Emory Thomas, the people of the Old South, particularly those of the southern backcountry, engaged in violence that "tended to be more personal and more socially acceptable than elsewhere."[35] They were used to more direct and immediate means of settling difficulties.[36]

Forrest's experience certainly supports John Hope Franklin's assessment that "a Southerner might be called upon to defend his life against some beast of the forest or some intractable human being. [And] if this did not happen, it was always within the realm of possibility; and it was best to be prepared."[37] Of course, Forrest needed little encouragement to believe that the wilderness could be, and often was, a harsh environment in which to live.

Perhaps the most important trait that Forrest developed from his early years on the frontier was the art of intimidation. In a world of arbitrary violence, he learned to use any means at his disposal to disarm and defeat his foes. Exacerbated by a quick temper and an assertive personality, this intimidating element became a decisive part of Forrest's personal arsenal. He learned that he could obtain desired results in this manner, often without fighting, simply by overwhelming an opponent or potential opponent with his reputation. His willingness to support his words with force strengthened this aspect of his character. Few people tested Forrest's resolve twice, for his first reaction was usually sufficient to make his point. Yet, as James C. Curtis observed of Andrew Jackson, this trait contained the seeds of excess: "Anger was his most effective weapon for it bore the imprint of conviction; but when angry, he had to guard against the excesses of temper," as manifested in a range of expressions from "blurted statements" and "rash remarks" to physical violence.[38]

Whether Forrest engaged in violence because he was a backcountry Southerner or because violence was part of his character, he undoubtedly embodied the struggle between "passion" and "control" that Dickson Bruce discussed in *Violence and Culture in the Antebellum South.*[39] He struggled for control over his emotions throughout his life. Consequently, he emphasized discipline and order, both as a civilian and as a military commander.

Control (or the lack of it) was a crucial element in his life. Forrest grappled with a violent temperament that frequently won its bouts with him. Yet displays of emotion undoubtedly annoyed him, for as Bruce explained: "The violent man was the passionate man, the man who, for whatever reason, tended to let his passions go out of control."[40] Often circumstances warranted Bedford's anger, but just as often they did not. In any case, the result was forbidding. Wyeth noted that during "these paroxysms of excitement or rage," Forrest assumed an almost savage appearance. His face became flushed and his voice became harsh.[41] Indeed, Forrest's personality propelled him into numerous confrontations throughout his life. As one newspaper reporter described him soon after his death, "He was simply one of those men who considered themselves bound to avenge an insult on the instant it was given, and a man so arbitrary and determined as General Forrest was certain to provoke insults, oftentimes unintentionally."[42]

Given the importance of honor on the Southern frontier, it is not surprising that displays of anger frequently led to violence. As Elliott Gorn ably demonstrated, Southern backwoodsmen were inordinately sensitive to slights and insults, real or imagined. Such insults led to backcountry "rough-and-tumbling" and gouging matches. Gorn noted that this fighting "grew out of challenges to men's honor—to their status in patriarchal, kin-based, small-scale communities—and were woven into the very fabric of daily life." For these people honor was "an intensely social concept, resting on reputation, community standing, and the esteem of kin and compatriots."[43]

One of the most volatile ingredients in the mixture of honor and violence in the South was alcohol. As Bruce explained, "The one thing that, more than temperament or age, led to passionate outbursts was drinking."[44] To W. J. Cash, "Great personal courage, unusual physical powers, the ability to drink a quart of whisky or lose the whole of one's capital on the turn of a card" were all elements of Southern frontier life.[45] Such abilities made one "a hell of a fellow," but they also suggested the dominion of passion over control. Bruce observed that "many Southerners, looking around, saw a close connection between drinking and disorder, including violence, in their society."[46] This relationship between "drinking and disorder" helps to explain the fact that alcohol had virtually no place in Forrest's life. One colleague later observed that Forrest "abhorred ... disorder" and recalled that "he did not know whiskey from brandy, but called everything liquor. He was often invited to take a drink, but always declined, and would at times, in refusing the invitation, remark with humorous suggestion and a mild reproof to his aides, 'My staff does all my drinking.'"[47]

Forrest's temperance seemed out of place in his life-style. One could expect to see drinking at the poker table or during a horse race, but early in life Bedford, after enduring one bout with alcohol, pledged that if he survived, he would drink no more. As he later explained, "I was never drunk but once in my life." Having seen "the antics of a drunken man," young Bedford thought "to try a spell of it" himself. "I got the liquor and drank it one afternoon," he recalled. "What happened as a consequence I do not know, but when I got over the spree I found myself with a burning case of typhoid fever. I promised 'Old Master' that if he would let me up from that bed I would never get drunk again." Whether he had a case of "typhoid fever," as he thought, Forrest added that he "never broke that pledge."[48]

If honor motivated Forrest to display his temper, even without the stimulus of alcohol, it also encouraged him to remain with his family until its members were sufficiently secure. By 1840, his efforts had proved successful. The family enjoyed comparative prosperity, unlike any they had previously known. And so, with affairs somewhat settled at home, Forrest became interested in the struggles of the Republic of Texas. Rumors circulated of an imminent Mexican invasion. In February 1841, Forrest joined a company formed at Holly Springs that was destined for service in Texas. Described by a local resident as "a tall, black-haired, and gray-eyed athletic youth, scarce twenty years of age," young Bedford must have looked forward to the adventure that lay before him.[49] Like any young man flushed with the excitement of the imagined glories of war, he was destined to be disappointed by its realities.

The company reached New Orleans, but could proceed no farther because of the lack of boat transportation to Galveston. Thwarted by this situation, the volunteers disbanded their organization. Most of them returned home, but Forrest persisted. His blood was up. He had come to fight, and by God he would do it. Determined to continue on to Texas, Bedford and a few other hardy souls went overland as far as Houston. There they received news that there was no invasion and, therefore, no need for their military services. Unfortunately, Bedford had no more money. And so he took a job as a rail splitter on a plantation for fifty cents per hundred rails and slowly saved the money necessary to make the return trip four months later.

When Bedford returned to Mississippi, he was once again battling illness. Eventually, he recovered sufficiently to accept an uncle's offer to join him in his horse-trading business. Undoubtedly, he saw this joint venture as the means by which he could improve the family's fortunes and provide them with greater security. He remained at home until 1842, presumably still helping his uncle and watching over the family. In that year he decided to leave the Forrest homestead. At the insistence of another uncle, Jonathan Forrest, Bedford traveled to the small Mississippi town of Hernando to join Jonathan in a limited business partnership.[50] This relocation marked the beginning of Bedford's rise to planter status.

Forrest had lived the hard life of frontier poverty. He had struggled to provide security for his mother, brothers, and sisters. At age twenty-one, he was now old enough to make his own way in the world and perhaps to raise his own family. The remarriage of his widowed mother to Joseph Luxton, in 1843, undoubtedly helped ease the burden of responsibility Bedford felt for her and his younger siblings, although the family remained close and Mariam's welfare continued to be one of her eldest son's chief concerns.[51]

Forrest's desire to go into business with his uncles suggests that he did not wish to remain a yeoman farmer, scratching out an existence where he was or following the frontier as his father had done. But escape from these familial responsibilities was no mean feat. Circumstances beyond his control thwarted his first attempt to make his own way, when the Texas expedition collapsed. His military career seemed at an end. The business partnership with his uncle Jonathan in Hernando offered him a second chance, and he availed himself of this opportunity. It was not that he did not love his family. It was not that he did not want the best for them. He had been their guardian and protector since his father's death. And this was a role he would never completely relinquish.

Rather, Bedford was a young man looking for his own path in life. As he plowed the fields as a lad in Mississippi, he might have wished for a different fate. No doubt such thoughts had accompanied him to Texas. And his travels to and from Texas revealed, for the first time, a world of which he knew little. He simply had no reason to know that greater world beyond his own everyday experience. Bedford had barely had the opportunity to learn to read and write, much less to learn of such exotic places as New Orleans and Houston. Yet, the glimpse he got of plantation life while he split rails in Texas made a lasting impression upon him. If he, too, could somehow acquire such vast holdings, he could finally gain a measure of control over his life that might guarantee security for himself and his loved ones.

Fortified with the experiences he gained in the Texas misadventure, determined to seek his own place in life, and offered an opportunity in the business world by his uncle, Forrest must have sensed that his "main chance" was at hand. He would have to leave the fold and make his own way. He understood that fact, and he was prepared.

CHAPTER 2

The Making of a Planter

(1842–1861)

Success often depends upon knowing how long it will take to succeed.

—MONTESQUIEU

You cuss and gamble and Mary Ann is a Christian girl.

—SAMUEL MONTGOMERY COWAN

HERNANDO, MISSISSIPPI, was an unlikely place to begin a career in business. Located approximately twenty-two miles south of Memphis, the little hamlet boasted few buildings aside from a post office, a courthouse, and some stores. Only four hundred people lived there.[1] Yet, for a young man born in a place where mail was a rarity and raised in a community with nothing but a post office, Hernando must have seemed cosmopolitan. Bedford had begun his life in the Tennessee backcountry, the son of a yeoman skilled laborer. However, his father had not been content to remain in Tennessee when better prospects appeared likely in a new location. Neither would Bedford. He was a practical individual, who, like his father before him, wanted more for himself and his family.

Forrest found success in the business association with his uncle. More important, his hard work soon began to pay him the desired dividends of increased financial security. According to one biographer, while living in Hernando, the young man succeeded in "acquiring year after year a more comfortable future."[2] With some money in his pockets, Bedford might even consider marriage and a family of his own. But these would come with time.

Nevertheless, Hernando was still a frontier community. Violence and honor continued to be much a part of daily life. Men fought over real and imagined grievances in the streets, usually settling their differences in blood, oblivious to innocent bystanders who might get caught in the way. These factors led to a confrontation in the square of the town that would involve Bedford and cause Jonathan Forrest's death.

On March 10, 1845, Bedford rode into the public square of Hernando. Heading his horse in the direction of his uncle's business establishment, he noticed the approach of four men—a planter, William Matlock; Matlock's two brothers; and their overseer—from another direction. These men harbored a grudge against the uncle and had come to settle the score.

Forrest stopped the men and explained that he had no quarrel with them, but would not stand idly by while the four of them attacked his uncle. One of the men responded to Forrest's statement by shooting at him. Then a hail of gunfire erupted. Passersby scurried for cover, leaving the combatants to blaze away at each other until one party triumphed. Blood would decide the matter now.

At this point, hearing the commotion in the street, Jonathan Forrest appeared in the doorway of his business. He had barely stepped forward when a shot intended for his nephew struck him and mortally wounded him. In the meantime, Bedford drew a pistol and felled two of his opponents before exhausting his ammunition. Wounded himself and out of ammunition, Bedford nevertheless determined to stand his ground. Fortunately, someone tossed him a bowie knife, and he charged his remaining opponents. They fled, no longer wishing to engage a man who lacked the good sense to know he was outnumbered. Bedford's audacity won both the day and the approval of the town.[3] The local newspaper observed that the "unfortunate and melancholy occurence" threw the community "into a great deal of excitement."[4]

Soon after the deadly fray with the Matlocks, Forrest became involved in another fatal incident. He was riding with a lawyer friend, James K. Morse, on the road from Hernando to Holly Springs. Ironically, Morse had been one of three men who witnessed Jonathan Forrest's final moments and helped record his last will and testament.[5] Now, as the two men rode along, Bedford unwittingly became entangled in another personal quarrel, this one between Morse and a local planter, James Dyson. An angry Dyson suddenly confronted them, and before any words passed, fatally shot Morse with a double-barreled gun. The planter instantly turned the gun on Forrest, threatening to blast him with the other barrel, since he was the only witness to the affair. Bedford reacted instinctively. He pulled a pistol from his pocket and took aim at the assailant, assuring Dyson all the while that if he intended to fire, he had "better make sure work, for it was now a game at which two could play." The threat sobered the planter, and he lowered his weapon. Later he would claim that only fear that the buckshot in the unfired barrel would not disable Forrest kept him from firing. Subsequently, Bedford participated in both murder trials as a witness for the prosecution.[6]

As Elliott J. Gorn has demonstrated, violence and honor were significant and descriptive elements in the mentalité of backcountry Southerners. Bedford's defense of his family and himself in the town square and his confrontation with Dyson appealed to that mind-set. Here was proof that this man could meet violence without flinching. Forrest became a local hero. The citizens of Hernando and of DeSoto County rewarded him by making him not only constable of the town, but coroner of the county. Public opinion, moved by his public displays of honor and courage, elevated Forrest to positions of responsibility in a community of which he had been a part for only three years.[7]

While these incidents brought local fame to young Forrest, allowing him to demonstrate his mettle publicly, they required him privately to evaluate his life as well. His propensity for violence battled his desire for control. Often the latter triumphed over the former, unless his temper weighed in and tilted the balance. But when he held his temper in check, Bedford made allies with a rough-hewn charisma.

Like others who were shaped by honor Southern style, Bedford paid particular attention to what others thought of him. Reputation mattered greatly if he was to continue in his rise to a higher status. He had to prove capable of belonging in this new community. He began to pay greater attention to his appearance; he combed his hair religiously and dressed immaculately.[8] This compulsiveness reflected his desire for order and control. At least one contemporary later recalled of him: "Few men were neater in personal appearance or in his surroundings than General Forrest. He abhorred dirt and disorder. To have papers scattered about the floor, or ashes on the hearth, brought a reproof from him, not always in words, for he would frequently take the broom himself and never stop until things were neat and clean."[9] Some people even thought him foppish.[10]

Perhaps his appearance paid important dividends, for the already eventful year of 1845 proved even more so when this dapper young man met a soft-spoken young lady from the neighborhood. The circumstances surrounding their meeting were hardly unusual in such a rural setting. Riding through the countryside on a Sunday morning, Forrest encountered a ford, swollen by recent heavy rains, and saw a carriage caught in the middle of the rushing brown water. A driver frantically whipped the horses in a vain attempt to wrest the vehicle from the mud. Two women passengers huddled inside watching the struggling driver and horses and the swirling water with equal apprehension. Two men watched from the bank with more amusement than a desire to help.

Bedford left his horse and plunged into the water. Wading to the carriage, he admonished the driver to stop beating the animals, since it was clear that this action would not free the vehicle, but might overturn it. He then waded to the carriage and offered his assistance to the women, which they quickly accepted. Lifting them from the carriage, he deposited each one safely on dry land. One can imagine that he gave special attention to the younger woman, nineteen-year-old Mary Ann Montgomery. Once he had carried them to dry ground, Forrest returned to the carriage and coaxed it out of the mud. The women soon continued on their way, but not before Forrest had exacted permission to call upon Mary Ann. Then he turned his attention to the would-be rescuers, chased them from the scene, and threatened to thrash them for their cowardly behavior.

True to his word and his heart, Bedford called upon Mary Ann the next day. Ironically, he found the two "gentlemen" from the previous encounter waiting to see her as well. Even though one of the men was studying for the ministry and Forrest wanted to make a good impression on Mary Ann in their first formal meeting, he bristled with anger as he caught sight of the men. Again he lost his composure and chased them away. By the time Mary Ann appeared in the parlor, only Bedford remained to greet her.

Bedford lost no time explaining the purpose of his mission. He wanted to marry her. He could care for her in a way the others could not—a fact proved by the ease with which he had run off the rival suitors. The suddenness of his pronouncement must certainly have taken Mary Ann by surprise; after all, they had just met. But Forrest was not one to stand on ceremony. Mary Ann managed to delay him briefly, but at their next (third) meeting, he repeated his intentions toward her, and this time she accepted.[11]

Having won Mary Ann's heart, Bedford faced the more formidable task of winning her uncle's, and guardian's, consent. This dual role belonged to Samuel Montgomery Cowan, pastor of the Cumberland Presbyterian Church. Cowan knew young Forrest's reputation and opposed the marriage on that account. According to a friend of Mary Ann, from whom she heard the story, Bedford approached the imperious preacher with his request only to meet with a sharp refusal. "Why, Bedford, I couldn't consent," Cowan explained. "You cuss and gamble and Mary Ann is a Christian girl." Forrest instantly retorted, "I know it, and that's just why I want her."[12]

Forrest's honest assertion may not have been enough to win the preacher's consent, but the young man had more of an advantage in his struggle than he realized. Cowan had nearly the same background as his ward's suitor. Orphaned from the time he was fourteen years old, Cowan had had to care for a widowed mother and five sisters and brothers, all younger than himself. Cowan managed to educate himself while he worked on his farm and supported his family, but he was familiar enough with the obstacles he had faced to understand the reasons for some of Bedford's social limitations.[13] In any event, Cowan eventually consented, and Forrest's whirlwind courtship led to marriage on September 25, 1845. A notice of the marriage in the Hernando paper suggested the degree to which Bedford had won the minister over: "Married—On Thursday evening, the 25th inst., by the Rev. S. M. Cowan, Mr. N. B. Forrest to Miss Mary Ann Montgomery, all of this county. The above came to hand accompanied by a good sweet morsel of cake and a bottle of the best wine."[14]

Forrest and his new bride settled into life in Hernando. He began his two-year term of office as coroner following the November elections with duties to "collect fines, forfeitures and amercements."[15] In the spring of 1846, he testified against Dyson, although that trial ended in acquittal, allegedly because of bribery.[16] Later in the year Forrest had happier news: He received an appointment as lieutenant in the DeSoto Dragoons, a local militia company, in the Fifty-first Regiment, Mississippi Militia. The appointment was dated October 23, 1846, although it is unclear how long Forrest remained in that post.[17]

During the busy year of 1846, one private event matched the intensity of Forrest's public life. On September 28, Bedford became a father, when Mary Ann bore a son, William Montgomery. Two years later, the couple rounded out their little family with a daughter, Frances A., or Fanny, probably named for Forrest's deceased twin sister. These were Bedford's and Mary Ann's only children, the latter destined to live only five years.[18]

His growing family and his own restless energy prompted Bedford to dabble in a variety of business enterprises. He remained in the mercantile business, but he also ran "a stage line" between Hernando and Memphis for a brief time. He sold cattle and horses and then tried his hand at selling slaves.[19] Forrest also established a local brickyard. Although generally prosperous in these efforts, he suffered his first business failure in Hernando in 1849. He had contracted with an agent to build a local academy. The entire scheme fell through when the agent, according to one biographer, "violated his trust."[20] Undaunted and educated by the experience, Forrest proceeded to expand his business interests. He would not make the mistake of so blindly trusting anyone associated with his financial transactions a second time.

By 1850, Bedford Forrest had risen to the rank of small-scale slaveholder. He owned three slaves, a woman and two children, and had, aside from his immediate family, other kinfolk living with him.[21] As his business interests and family responsibilities grew, Forrest began to think in larger terms. Hernando had given him his start. For that he was grateful, but now it was time to move to a more suitable location. His small-scale involvement in the slave trade had given him a sense of the capital he could raise in a larger operation. To this end, Bedford moved his family to Memphis in 1851. In that bustling river town he became active in real estate and slave trading. It was a relatively simple matter for Forrest to make the transition from trading mostly in livestock in Hernando to trading almost exclusively in slaves in Memphis.

Undoubtedly, such a transition appeared logical, practical, and profitable. He must have realized that providing such a service to the planter class would offer him one of the best opportunities to become rich. The fact that he would do so at the price of trading in human beings seems not to have concerned him. In this way, he could virtually guarantee that his family would be spared the hardship of the subsistence living he had endured on the Tennessee and Mississippi frontier.

Memphis was an ideal location for this business. It enjoyed direct water routes to the Deep South, particularly the lucrative New Orleans slave market. According to Frederic Bancroft, "Of the cities in the Central South, Memphis had by far the largest slave-trade."[22] Of course, Forrest was not alone in so favorable a marketplace. The 1855 *Memphis City Directory* listed five other dealers besides Forrest & Maples.[23] Furthermore, at first, he stood considerably behind his chief competition: Bolton, Dickins & Co.

Forrest's attempts to establish himself as a major player in the Memphis slave trade may have involved him in a spectacular steamboat accident in 1852. Having traveled to Texas, most likely in connection with his slave-trading interests, Forrest hoped to return to Memphis as quickly as possible. He boarded an old steamer, the *Farmer,* for the trip home. The voyage proceeded smoothly for awhile, and he retired to his cabin to rest. Sleep came fitfully. Gamblers in the saloon became more and more animated, no doubt stimulated by drink, as well as by the ebb and flow of the games. The increasing level of noise and the threatening tone of the group disturbed him. Angered by his inability to sleep in the midst of this turmoil, Forrest burst from his quarters without pausing to dress completely and stormed into the game room. He peremptorily warned the gamblers to settle their differences more quietly. Through both his tone and his determination, Forrest convinced the men to comply, but by now, sleep was out of the question. Instead, Bedford decided to go out on deck to get some fresh air.

As he walked the deck he noticed that the boilers were laboring under a greater strain than was normal. Indeed, they were. The captain of the *Farmer* had encountered another vessel and engaged in a race with it. The decision was foolhardy. Forrest watched as men with buckets of water splashed the smokestack and cabin roof. Even with such potential danger, the boat showed no sign of lessening its speed. Forrest quickly realized that something was amiss. Ever the man of action, he made his way to the bridge to question the skipper. He need not have bothered.

The captain stood drunkenly at the wheel, totally absorbed in the competition. Forrest urged him to quit the race before the boilers exploded. On this occasion Bedford's intimidating persona failed to have an impact. Bolstered by drink and stimulated by his vessel's performance in the race, the skipper roared that he would not relinquish the lead with the race so near its end (Galveston was then only six miles away). He would "get there first," he stated, "or blow the old tub and every soul on board to hell." Despite his best efforts, Forrest could make no headway with the stubborn captain. Finally, determining that any further protest would be useless, he left the cabin and went to the stern to await disaster.

It was not long in coming. A tremendous explosion suddenly shattered the night, and the boat shuddered as the blast ripped through it, raining debris on the decks. The stricken vessel foundered in the shallow water as the shrieks of the injured began to fill the air. Fortunately for the survivors, the other vessel came alongside to rescue them. Nursing a bruised shoulder, Forrest assisted more severely wounded people to safety aboard the other boat and helped recover some of the bodies, before seeking refuge. Some sixty people, including the captain, died in the accident. Before long, Forrest was again on his way home, arriving without further incident.[24]

By this time Forrest was heavily involved in the slave trade. He spent a good deal of time traveling to other states in the region to purchase or deliver slaves. He also began to employ agents, like James McMillan, to broaden his market potential. As Bancroft noted, "By January, 1853, he [Forrest] was a typical interstate trader, traveling extensively."[25] Bedford later explained that he had first met McMillan in Lexington, Kentucky, in January 1853, and that "he transacted business for me." Forrest had been "buying negroes there." Perhaps remembering his earlier experience in Hernando, he thoroughly investigated McMillan's character. Apparently satisfied with what he found, Forrest entered into an agreement whereby he supplied the money and promised McMillan one-fourth the profits made on those sales. According to Forrest, this arrangement lasted "about a year."[26]

During his slave-trading years in Memphis, Bedford had several different partners, including his brothers, John, William, Aaron, and Jesse.[27] In the beginning, he teamed with a man named Hill. Forrest and Hill had custody of a young slave, Nat Mayson. Sometime in May 1853, Nat succeeded in running away from the slave mart. The slave traders advertised for his return, explaining that he had run away "without a cause." Bancroft assumed that their failure to advertise the escape until July, two months after Nat had actually run away, was due to the traders "presumably hoping to recover him without letting the damaging fact be known that a slave could escape from them."[28] This interpretation is plausible, since Forrest had only been in the city for about a year. He had entered a highly competitive business and might have been inordinately sensitive to public perceptions of his competence.

If this were the case, he need not have worried. McMillan and other agents apparently met with success in their search for slaves. In January 1854, Forrest and Hill notified potential customers, "We will have a good lot of Virginia Negroes on hand, for sale, in the fall." But, since they could hardly rest on their laurels, the traders advertised "FIVE HUNDRED NEGROES WANTED—WE will pay the highest cash price for all good Negroes offered. We invite all those having Negroes for sale, to call on us, at our Mart, opposite Hill's old stand, on Adams street."[29] Throughout the summer of the next year, Forrest and a new partner observed that they had "agents in every market, on the lookout for good family servants."[30] Those agents were successful in supplying "fresh lots" of "likely Negroes" from as far away as Virginia, according to newspaper advertisements.[31]

The *Memphis City Directory* of 1855 listed Forrest with a new partner, Josiah Maples. But the change seems not to have adversely affected business. "Forrest & Maples, Slave Dealers" claimed to have "constantly on hand the best selected assortment of Field Hands, House Servants & Mechanics, at their Negro Mart." Listing the capacity of their mart as three hundred, the traders observed that they were "daily receiving ... likely Young Negroes" from Virginia, Kentucky, and Missouri. They invited prospective customers to "examine their stock before purchasing elsewhere." They also advised that they would sell slaves on commission, "the highest market price always paid for good stock."[32]

One part of the "stock" at the Forrest slave mart was a slave woman and her five-year-old son. The son later recalled that the yard consisted of "a square stockade of high boards." Barracks lined three sides of the stockade, in which the slaves remained until an auction was arranged. At that point the slaves would be "brought out and paraded two by two around a circular brick walk in the center of the stockade." Potential customers lined the walk, occasionally stopping a slave to inspect him or her. Often this inspection was quite thorough. Purchasers probed the teeth and limbs, particularly looking for signs of sickness or violence. Whip marks were indications of ill temper, laziness, or insolence.[33]

Forrest quickly established a widespread reputation as a good slave dealer. Contemporaries credited him with showing humanity, cleanliness, and care, but even if he did, it was due less to interest in the slaves than to self-interest. Whippings meant discipline. Discipline meant bad behavior. Bad behavior signaled trouble to potential customers. Self-interest demanded moderation. It was in Forrest's best interests to treat his "stock" with some care. He understood the value of reputation in any business or social endeavor, especially in the South. As Michael Tadman explained, "Those [slaves] who were exceptionally troublesome to owners might well show signs of having been sharply punished, and such signs, we know, would have tended to damage sale prices."[34] Every account of Forrest's dealings in this trade suggests that he was keenly aware of his slaves' physical well-being. His biographers attribute this attitude to kindness and humanity—in comparison to other slave traders.[35] Forrest, like most other traders, had to guarantee, usually in writing, that the slave being purchased was the property of that particular buyer against all other claims and, more important, that he or she was healthy at the time of purchase. The failure to deliver "sound" merchandise jeopardized any future dealings with that customer—a hazard that any trader in a highly competitive market like Memphis could ill afford.

In all likelihood, Forrest's advertisement claiming that "his regulations [were] exact and systematic, cleanliness, neatness and comfort being strictly observed and enforced" was no idle boast.[36] It is also possible that he meant what he said when he proclaimed, "Persons wishing to dispose of a servant may rest assured that, if left with us, a good home will be secured."[37] Although Forrest most likely failed to appreciate the irony of "disposing" of a servant to "a good home," his sentiments were probably sincere. As he frequently observed, his "aim [was] to furnish to customers A.1 servants, and field hands, sound and perfect in body and mind."[38]

For Forrest, then, slaves were commodities, to be bought and sold profitably. And if he took pains to ensure that they went only to those customers who would treat them reasonably well, he did so because he understood that reputation counted for a great deal in his business. Southern planters and, for that matter, Southerners in general were quick to condemn abusive traders. Whatever else he might be, Forrest was not stupid.

Because of his role in the marketplace, Forrest considered the slaves in his mart in commercial terms. As James Oakes noted, "It was inevitable that slaveholders would come to speak of their bondsmen in the language of the marketplace."[39] Traders used terms usually associated with animals in reference to their slaves.

In his newspaper advertisements, Forrest preferred the term *stock*, while others used *head* or similar market terms to describe the members of their slave gangs.[40] According to Oakes, even paternalists "stood with the slaveholding majority in their embrace of the free-market economy and of white supremacist values." They cited the close relationship of master and slave as mitigating the dehumanization that plagued the free labor system. "Yet," Oakes continued, "it was the racial basis of slavery, coupled with the bondsman's dual function as laborer and capital asset within a commercial market economy, that tended to dehumanize slaves."[41]

Money was at stake, and speculating in slaves was primarily a "nakedly commercial activity." Whatever one can say about their hearts, these traders were "hard-headed businessmen, seriously dedicated to the pursuit of profit."[42] Like good businessmen, they wanted most to maximize their profits, for they were motivated by their own economic self-interest.[43] As Oakes observed, "Slaveholding was the symbol of success in the market culture of the Old South."[44] At the least, speculating in slaves could be enormously profitable. In a two-year period, 1856–57, the firm of Bolton, Dickins & Co. grossed profits of $130,492 on the sale of 664 slaves.[45] Such profits meant that dealers like Forrest would certainly have subscribed to Oakes's assessment that "the slaveholders' chief defense of bondage focused upon the profitability of slavery and the white man's right to make money and accumulate property."[46]

Indeed, economic self-interest was the grease that kept the machinery of slavery in motion. It was the prime motivating factor in a capitalist system in which one section of the country willingly supplied raw materials, picked by slave laborers, supplied by men like Forrest, to another section that transformed these raw materials into finished products that they often sold back to the first section.[47] Profits could be had all around, except, of course, by the slave laborers themselves. But, then, the slaves got food, shelter, and clothing, which was all they wanted, according to their "paternalistic" masters. And the occasional fits of conscience aside, such speculation and exploitation meant that few participants had any reason, in their minds, to abhor their activities or to be unwilling to do business with participants in other aspects of the process.

According to the commonly held view of white Southerners concerning slave dealers, Forrest should have lived his life in obscurity, banished by people, particularly the slaveholders themselves, who detested him for what he did to make a living. The evidence contradicts this view. Bedford used his business to gain entree into the planter class, certainly with the knowledge of other planters and most likely with their approval. As Tadman ably demonstrated, "The logic of slavery therefore demanded that there be stereotyping of vicious traders as a class [both for propaganda purposes and for conscience's sake], but also that a place be made for the trader [particularly the "honorable" trader]." Contrary to the myth of the slave trader as a pariah, many slave traders were "citizens of standing, [who] like almost any other successful businessmen, could become leaders of the local and even the wider community." The slave trade need not, and in Forrest's case did not, "automatically lead to social ostracism, and a substantial section of the trading fraternity seems to have gained positions of real influence, respect, and leadership in the community."[48] This was certainly true of Nathan Bedford Forrest, who emerged from his days as a trader both wealthy and widely respected.

However, more than a profit motive propelled Forrest in his slave-trading business. He never lost the sense of his role as the protector and defender of his family and himself. He had known poverty. He knew he did not want poverty to be his legacy to his children. Slave trading was a way out of the trap of yeoman farming he had feared would be his lot. For more than one reason, then, he perceived himself as a businessman operating in a legitimate trade for potentially enormous returns. And he was doing so not for himself, he could say, but for his loved ones. To be sure, his business required him to work hard, to travel often, and to prevail in the marketplace. Running a successful slave-trading business required great amounts of time, energy, and attention. He was enduring these hardships and inconveniences so that his children need not do so.[49]

Despite the "humanity" with which he reputedly treated his "stock," Forrest usually focused upon his own hardships, not those of the slaves. His chief concern was mastery of the market—getting top prices, moving his merchandise, and replenishing his stock.[50] Bedford shared with other traders a "most settled complacency about the fact that their traffic was in people."[51] He was like other slaveholders who "recognized the tenuousness of their economic security" and worried most about themselves and their families.[52]

Forrest was unquestionably successful in his work. He described his slave mart at Eighty-seven Adams Street in Memphis as "one of the most complete and commodious establishments of the kind in the Southern country."[53] As an aspiring member of the planter class, Bedford understood that the money he was making was a means to that end. Furthermore, the money he gained would ensure his family a security they could not otherwise have attained.

Whatever else it meant, Forrest's success kept him busy. In 1856, he took a coffle of slaves to Louisiana for sale, remaining approximately two weeks.[54] In January 1857, Samuel Tate and Archibald Wright paid Bedford $1,250 for a twenty-year-old "negro boy named Cyrus."[55] About the same time, B. B. Mitchell, a Memphis resident, purchased a twenty-two-year-old slave named Bent. "Said boy was raised in Charleston, South Carolina, and brought from there some four months since by Mr. N. B. Forrest."[56] In May 1859 Forrest sold two young slaves to James Sheppard of Arkansas. Sheppard traveled to Memphis to make his purchases. On May 29, Forrest placed the slaves aboard a steamboat, sending a receipt with them for "two negro boys Dick & Emanuel" in the amount of $53.40 that included two days' board at the Forrest slave mart, at 40 cents each per day. He requested that the person who came for the slaves, probably Sheppard's overseer, "please pay the boat." The captain of the steamer *Jennie Whipple* added $14.00 for passage from Memphis to Pine Bluff, Arkansas, and $3.00 for "Boarde 2 days & fare."[57] Such sales guaranteed Forrest a significant accumulation of capital and demonstrated that, in his case at least, the idea that a yeoman farmer could gain wealth and join the economic elite was grounded in a measure of reality. Upward mobility in the slave South was indeed possible.

Forrest continued to ply his trade, thereby gaining the capital necessary to enter the planter class. He also began to act like a planter. He made large investments in cotton plantations and other real estate holdings. He bought uncleared and unimproved land along the Mississippi River that he transformed, with the use of a large number of slaves, into productive fields of cotton. At one time or another, he owned land in Tennessee, Mississippi, and Arkansas.[58]

According to Coahoma County land records, Forrest bought a plantation, consisting of 1,900 acres, from Henry C. Chambers in 1858. To this acquisition, he added another 1,445 acres just before the Civil War.[59] His obituary noted that he had been so successful as a slave trader that he had owned "a splendid plantation in Coahoma County, Mississippi [Green Grove], with two hundred field hands, and making upwards of 1,000 bales of cotton yearly."[60] One contemporary resident later remembered that Forrest's "six-room dwelling, not beautiful but well built and comfortable," at Green Grove stood in "a grove of magnificent oak trees." Nearby were two rows of slave cabins "facing each other, forming a sort of avenue."[61] According to the 1860 census, Forrest had thirty-six slaves, ranging in ages from five to thirty-five, living in twelve cabins on his Coahoma County property. Twenty-one of these slaves were male, aged twenty-three to thirty. In addition, Forrest owned seven slaves in Memphis, where he resided, most of whom were female. He listed his occupation as "Planter" and placed the value of his real estate holdings at $190,000 and his personal estate at $90,000.[62]

Like other Southern planters, Forrest exploited black laborers in his search for wealth. But his goal was not to accumulate wealth for its own sake. He was a seigneur, in the sense that historian Raimondo Luraghi used the term; capital was a means to an end, not an end in itself. Money brought with it status, power, and respect, and for planters who were motivated by honor—the opinions others held of them—these were the most desirable ends. Of course, such motivations did not exclude ambition as a motivating factor. And in Forrest's case, the ambition to enter a "better" class was certainly present. However, once he had attained this status, Forrest was less interested in simply accumulating more capital than in enjoying the benefits that accrued from the capital he had already accumulated.[63]

Despite his elevated status, Forrest lived at the edge of the frontier. Memphis was growing, but it had not yet lost its frontier flavor. This environment created the circumstances in which Forrest's principal competition, Bolton, Dickins & Co., would fall from the pinnacle of the Memphis market. The man who did much to precipitate that fall was James McMillan, Forrest's roving purchasing agent.

The sequence began when McMillan purchased the unexpired term of a free black apprentice, the rights to whom he sold to Washington Bolton. Bolton, Dickins & Co. then marketed and sold the man, as a slave, in Memphis. Subsequently, the apprentice brought suit and obtained his freedom. This turn of events compelled Bolton to refund the sale price to the buyer and threatened the reputation of the firm. Shortly thereafter, in May 1857, McMillan came to Memphis with a number of slaves. Another member of the Bolton family, Wade, sent word that he wanted to purchase a "house-boy" for his wife. He asked the agent to bring a slave boy to the Bolton mart for him to inspect. Despite some understandable reservations, McMillan went. When he arrived, he found two men waiting for him. One of them was Isaac Bolton, who had recently returned from Vicksburg and who McMillan did not know personally. Isaac condemned McMillan as a rascal for selling his kinsman the free black apprentice. He demanded that McMillan refund the purchase price and threatened to kill him if he did not. McMillan claimed not to have any money with him and protested that, in any case, Washington Bolton had known all the facts concerning the sale. Given the issues of honor at stake, this answer failed to satisfy Isaac Bolton. The two men could reach no accommodation, and when the other man with Bolton left the room, Isaac determined to settle the matter. He pulled a pistol out of his pocket and fired at McMillan, wounding him fatally. Then, Bolton drew a bowie knife and tossed it by the stricken man's side. Predictably, he claimed to have acted in self-defense, but made the error of not finishing off his victim. McMillan was still alive when several men, coming to investigate the shots, found him on the floor in a pool of blood. Bolton and his friend had left the scene, assuming that the agent was dead.

Some of the people who found McMillan put him into a van and took him to Forrest's house. Conscious, but aware that he was going to die, the agent recounted his version of the bloody confrontation. McMillan died later that afternoon. According to Bancroft, Isaac Bolton first fled, "but soon returned and gave himself up, realizing that flight was inconsistent with his pretense that he had acted in self-defense." The grand jury promptly issued an indictment against Isaac for murder.[64]

When the trial began in the spring of 1858, Forrest testified. He recounted his association with McMillan and recalled that in 1854, when the agent brought him some slaves, he told of trouble he had had with one of them. Forrest characteristically advised McMillan to "take something for such occasions," ostensibly to defend himself, but the agent had rejected the trader's advice. On the basis of this evidence, Bedford speculated that the victim had, in all likelihood, gone to the Bolton Mart unarmed.[65]

The trial cost the Boltons dearly. They won the case, but spent a sizable portion of their slave-trade profits in Isaac's defense—allegedly bribing the jury to obtain a favorable verdict. The publicity surrounding the trial played havoc with their business. The firm's sales declined, and family squabbling led to feuds that decimated the family. "Bedford Forrest thus became the big slave dealer of the middle Mississippi Valley."[66] Bancroft placed Forrest in an even more prominent position, noting that "since the decline of Bolton, Dickins & Co. he had become one of the best known and richest slave-traders in all the South."[67]

Bedford seemed to attract violence. In June 1857, a Memphis resident encountered one of his gambling companions, a shady character named John Able, in front of the Worsham House Hotel. Able apparently owed the man a sizable sum of money, and the man had come to collect. A heated argument ensued, and Able drew a gun and blasted his erstwhile friend in the chest, killing him. The sheriff arrested Able and placed him in jail.

This affair might have ended quietly had the Memphis judicial system demonstrated itself consistently capable of prosecuting and punishing such lawless acts. Indeed, John Able's father Joseph had escaped punishment for a similar crime earlier the same year. By the time the sheriff locked young Able in jail, a crowd had gathered in front of the Worsham House Hotel. As the crowd grew, so did its anger. Nearly two thousand people soon stood in front of the hotel, prepared to march on the jail, break into it, and lynch Able.

The crowd surged toward the prison. When they arrived, several individuals, including the mayor, attempted to calm the angry mob and dissuade them from carrying out their intentions. Finally, one of the men proposed that they post a special guard of twenty-five people to watch the jail, while everyone gathered at another location to discuss the matter and form a vigilance committee. But when the crowd reassembled at the Exchange Building, emotions remained high. They decided to hold a mock trial and elected thirty-six men to act as jurors. This "jury" listened to witnesses and retired to consider whether Able should stand trial for his crime. They returned approximately an hour and a half later to issue their "verdict." On the basis of the available evidence, they voted twenty-four to twelve to hold him for formal trial, convinced that any jury would reach the "proper" verdict in the case.

The crowd greeted the news with hostility. Perhaps most people did not really believe that justice would be served. Twelve of the jurors had voted to lynch Able then and there, and many in the house echoed those sentiments. Sensing that Able might be lynched, some of the more moderate leaders present suggested an alternative course. If the crowd was determined to punish someone, why not target Able's father, Joseph? He was also a gambler and had committed a similiar crime earlier without being punished for it.

They quickly passed a resolution to form a committee to instruct Joseph Able to leave town. A second resolution expanded the committee's charge to include "all gamblers." As part of the three-man committee, Forrest went to Joseph Able's house the following day and left word that his "immediate departure from the city is demanded." Able was to leave town by noon the next day. The committee also advised him "never to return to Memphis," warning that, "if you do, in our opinion, your life will be the penalty."

Except for this committee's activity, June 25 passed quietly.

However, on the following day, the crowd reassembled at the Exchange Building. The citizens elected officers, including Forrest as one of the vice presidents, and debated further measures by which law and order could be attained in Memphis. Despite attempts to maintain order, the crowd quickly disintegrated into a lynch mob. Rushing from the Exchange Building, they stormed the jail and pulled John Able from his cell, still in chains. They dragged the prisoner to the navy yard's rope walk. Someone lowered a noose over the boy's head, and he was about to be hanged when his mother raced to his side, begging the mob to spare her son. Finally, the mother's pleas prevailed. Forrest may or may not have witnessed all this activity, but he would recall the whole affair differently in later years.[68]

But the Nathan Bedford Forrest who got caught up in the Able affair in 1857 was not precisely the same man who had defended his uncle in Hernando fifteen years earlier. He had come a long way toward achieving respectability among the citizens of Memphis. He was now part of the city's efforts to improve its reputation and to enforce law and order. He was no longer the rugged, individualistic Jacksonian frontiersman; he was a businessman-planter in a rapidly developing and civilizing "frontier" town.

The people of Memphis confirmed their regard for Forrest when they elected him an alderman for the Third Ward. He served the Board of Aldermen as a member of the Finance Committee, forcefully, even vehemently, standing his ground on issues related to the city's finances. No matter involving business principles was too trivial for Forrest's attentions. Thus, when the board considered an offer from a job printer to publish the minutes at no charge, in 1858, and again in August 1859, Forrest balked. He argued that "the city can pay for the work it has done, and it is ready to do so." Perhaps he sensed that the generous "offer" might result in some quid pro quo later, or he might have worried that acceptance would imply that the city was financially insecure. In any case, he strenuously opposed the acceptance of "any offer of the kind."[69]

Although his vehemence over such issues might have irritated some of his colleagues, Forrest remained popular with most of his fellow aldermen. When he retired from his seat in 1859 to attend to his ever-widening planting interests in Coahoma County, the board met the announcement with at least a show of regret at his decision. One member offered a resolution expressing "our regret at parting with him, regarding him, as we do, as an active and efficient Alderman," adding that "he carries with him in retiring our warmest wishes for his prosperity." The board adopted the resolution without opposition, but some of the members were undoubtedly relieved to see him go.[70]

Forrest was destined to remain in Coahoma County for only a short while. He stayed long enough to settle his affairs, but then returned to Memphis and resumed his position on the Board of Aldermen.[71] Soon afterwards, in the fall of 1860, his strong convictions led him to a confrontation with a fellow alderman involving work on the city's wharf. Despite his hard-won respectability, Forrest still waged a constant battle to control his temper. On this occasion he lost the battle, but for good reasons.

The board had contracted with John Loudon to construct the wharf. Some difficulty arose in completing the project when the Mississippi River rose unexpectedly, damaging some of the stonework. Loudon requested the board to inspect the section and to recommend how he should proceed. And on the day of the inspection, Mayor R. D. Baugh and the board of Aldermen gathered for that purpose. As they marched along the completed (and undamaged) portion, an alderman from the front of the procession stopped to talk with his colleagues. Forrest, at the end of the line, remained out of earshot of the conversation. Presently, the alderman approached him and announced, "Mr. Forrest, we have concluded to condemn the whole of this work."

Bedford was astounded. Probably thinking that he had misunderstood the man, he asked, "For what reason do you condemn the whole of this wharf? The portion we have passed has stood and is standing the test admirably, and much better than I thought it would." And as if to confirm his statement, he added, "Why, I remember to have seen mule-drays sink in the quagmire here where we are walking, which is perfectly sound and safe; and remember we have not reached the sunken portion which we have been called upon to inspect."

The alderman decided to take Bedford into his confidence, and undoubtedly leaned forward conspiratorially to explain, "We have concluded to condemn the whole job." Then, finally and carefully revealing his real intent, "This will break up old man Loudon, and then we can give the work to one of our friends; and we want you to help us." Yet, no sooner were the words out than he had reason to regret having said them. Forrest's face flushed, and his eyes blazed. In a loud voice, urged on by anger, he blurted, "You infernal scoundrel! Do you dare to ask me to be as damned a rascal as yourself?" Bedford added, "I have a big notion to pitch you into the Mississippi River. Now, I warn you if you ever presume to address such a damnable proposition to me in future I will break your rascally neck."

By this point, everyone's attention riveted upon the debate. The astonished audience proceeded quietly to the damaged section and listened to the contractor as he explained the manner in which he intended to resolve the problem. Throughout, the alderman who had approached Forrest remained silent, and the matter passed.[72]

Obviously, not everyone, including the alderman just mentioned, was pleased at Bedford's return to the board, but Forrest continued to fulfill his role as the defender of the city's interests in his own simple, direct, and forceful manner. As Memphis Mayor R. D. Baugh later grandiosely observed, Alderman Forrest "never offered a resolution in the board on any subject, no matter how unpopular it be at first, that he did not stick to it and work at it until he carried it triumphantly through."[73]

Mayor Baugh's memory to the contrary, Forrest occasionally lost a vote. But even then he found a way to win. Once he attempted to convince his fellow aldermen not to sell the city's stock in the Memphis and Charleston Railroad, but they voted to proceed despite his protestations that the price was too low. Unperturbed by the rebuff, Forrest shrewdly purchased about fifty thousand dollars of the stock and resold it at a profit of twenty thousand dollars.[74]

In 1859–60, Forrest debated his future. At first, he decided to sell his business interests in Memphis and return to his Mississippi plantation. Then, after a brief hiatus at Green Grove, he chose to return again to Memphis. Thus, as the rumblings of division increased between the North and the South, Forrest sought to maintain what he had worked so hard to obtain. When he left Hernando, he wanted to improve his status, to gain financial security and the independence that would bring him. A restless, hard-nosed individual, conditioned by life on the Southern frontier to succeed in the pell-mell world of Memphis, Forrest nevertheless modified his roughest edges somewhat as he achieved success. He had gone from yeoman semisubsistence to planter affluence. By all accounts he was wealthy, successful, and respected. In 1871, he told a congressional committee that at the time he was worth "a million and a half dollars."[75] Forrest had reached the pinnacle of his career, or so it seemed. What he could not know was that in 1860, at age thirty-nine, he was about to embark upon an entirely new and equally successful career.

Nathan Bedford Forrest just prior to the Civil War, when he was approximately forty years old, had amassed a considerable fortune—largely through the slave trade—and was serving as an alderman in Memphis, Tennessee. *(Memphis Pink Palace Museum, Memphis, Tennessee)*

Bedford and Mary Ann Montgomery Forrest settled into this home in Hernando, Mississippi, in the first years of their married life. Here they raised two children, William Montgomery and Fanny. (Confederate Veteran 12, *June 1904)*

Forrest was still a colonel when this photograph was made in 1862, but he was already beginning to win fame for his exploits on the battlefield. *(North Carolina Division of Archives and History, Raleigh)*

A number of wartime photographs of Forrest exist, including this one of him as a major general. *(*Confederate Veteran 18, *June 1910)*

This photograph of Forrest was probably taken in late 1864. Despite his approximately four years of military service, he still maintained a striking bearing in uniform. *(Alabama Department of Archives and History, Montgomery)*

This is the best known of the wartime images of General Forrest.
(U.S. Military History Institute, Carlisle, Pennsylvania)

Forrest returned from the war "completely used up—shot to pieces, crippled up." By 1877, even his astounding physical prowess seemed to have left him. *(*Confederate Veteran *10, March 1902)*

Forrest's military family included *(clockwise from left)* his son, Captain William Montgomery Forrest; his brother, Colonel Jeffrey E. Forrest; and his chief surgeon and kinsman, Dr. John B. Cowan. *(Illustrations from the* Life of General Nathan Bedford Forrest, *by John Allan Wyeth)*

Clockwise from the top left: Colonel David C. Kelley; Major Charles W. Anderson, assistant adjutant and inspector general; Major J. P. Strange, assistant adjutant general; and Major G. V. Rambaut, chief of subsistence, were among Forrest's closest aides during the war. *(From the* Life of General Nathan Bedford Forrest*)*

When Forrest first met John Morton he wanted to know why Bragg had sent "that tallow-faced boy" to command his artillery, but Morton quickly earned his commander's respect and admiration, serving with distinction for the remainder of the war. *(From the* Life of General Nathan Bedford Forrest*)*

(From the Life of General Nathan Bedford Forrest*)*

Throughout General Forrest's military career, a number of capable and talented officers served under him. The photographs and sketches on the following three pages originally appeared in John Allan Wyeth's *Life of General Nathan Bedford Forrest.*

Colonel James W. Starnes, Fourth Tennessee Cavalry, commanding a brigade.

Brigadier General George G. Dibrell (from a photograph taken after the war).

Colonel W. L. Duckworth, Seventh Tennessee Cavalry.

Colonel A. A. Russell, Russell's Fourth Alabama Cavalry, commanding a brigade (from a photograph taken after the war).

Brigadier General W. H. Jackson, commanding a division of Forrest's cavalry.

Brigadier General Frank C. Armstrong.

Brigadier General A. Buford, commanding a division of Forrest's cavalry.

Brigadier General Tyree H. Bell, commanding "Bell's Brigade" of Forrest's cavalry.

Brigadier Hylan B. Lyon, commanding the "Kentucky Brigade" of Forrest's cavalry.

Colonel Edmund W. Rucker, commanding a brigade of Forrest's escort.

Colonel Robert McCulloch, Second Missouri Cavalry, commanding a brigade.

Colonel William A. Johnson, commanding a brigade of Forrest's cavalry.

Brigadier General James R. Chalmers. *(From the* Life of General Nathan Bedford Forrest*)*

Major General Earl Van Dorn (from a photograph). *(From* Battles and Leaders of the Civil War*)*

Forrest's combative personality often led to clashes with subordinates and superiors alike. He attempted to transfer Chalmers out of his command, very nearly engaged in a saber duel with Van Dorn, and promised to "be in my coffin" before he would serve again under Wheeler.

Lieutenant General Joseph Wheeler (from a photograph). *(From* Battles and Leaders of the Civil War*)*

Forrest's denunciation of General Bragg was his stormiest confrontation with a superior. Shaking his finger at his stunned commander, Forrest angrily observed: "You have played the part of a damned scoundrel, and are a coward, and if you were any part of a man I would slap your jaws and force you to resent it." *(From* Battles and Leaders of the Civil War*)*

Forrest enjoyed much smoother professional and personal relationships with *(clockwise from the left)* Lieutenant General S. D. Lee, Major General Dabney H. Maury, and Lieutenant General Richard Taylor, all of whom expressed their desire to allow Forrest a high degree of autonomy. *(From* Battles and Leaders of the Civil War*)*

CHAPTER 3

A Chance for Active Service

(June–December 1861)

Give Forrest a chance and he will distinguish himself.

—General Lloyd Tilghman

Forward, men, and mix with 'em!

—Nathan Bedford Forrest

Secession was not a new idea in 1860–61. New Englanders debated the issue at the Hartford Convention as a means of protesting the War of 1812. South Carolinians threatened it during the nullification crisis of 1828–32. Many Southern orators and politicians considered it in their calculations for the preservation of the institution of slavery. Indeed, some Southerners believed that secession might be the only means by which they could safeguard their "way of life." The series of compromises and half measures implemented in the 1850s had failed to placate people on both sides of the slavery question who disagreed widely and felt strongly about the fate of the South's "peculiar institution."

The talk of secession must have disturbed Bedford Forrest greatly. Such talk was at once equally powerful and distasteful. He had already spent the better part of the previous decade building his business interests and compiling his fortune. Now the heated atmosphere, stirred by the rhetoric of Southern fire-eaters like Robert Toombs, William Lowndes Yancey, Robert Barnwell Rhett, and others threatened to undo what he had so painstakingly achieved. Forrest was not inclined to fall sway to such oratory. He would not willingly surrender control of his affairs to others. He was used to making up his own mind on issues of importance to him. He had finally reached the point at which he could enjoy the benefits he had derived. Secession might preserve and protect these fruits, or it might endanger and even destroy them. Either way events threatened to bring change, and change was something Bedford no longer needed or wanted.

Although Forrest confined his political activity to the local arena, he certainly kept abreast of developments on the state and national levels as well. Biographers Thomas Jordan and J. P. Pryor described him as "a strong and decided States Rights Democrat in politics," adding that he was "deeply attached" to the Union. They insisted that Bedford remained "earnestly opposed to its dissolution" as long as some hope existed of a rapprochement between the sections on the issues that divided them. Of course, the chief issue was the institution of slavery, in which both the South and Bedford Forrest had a vested interest.[1]

More precisely, the problem involved expansion of the South's "peculiar institution." Southern slave owners defended their right to own property, in whatever form, and the capacity to carry their property with them wherever they pleased. They saw efforts to curtail the expansion of slavery not only as inimical to those rights, but as dangerous to the system as a whole. Slavery had to expand or die. However, Northerners, particularly those who supported the newly formed Republican party, opposed the expansion of slavery. A vocal minority wanted slavery abolished.[2] Forrest was certainly not disinterested in this debate, and undoubtedly he watched the election of the Republican candidate Abraham Lincoln in 1860 with concern.

If Lincoln's election worried Bedford Forrest, it alarmed South Carolina. On December 20, 1860, South Carolina voted overwhelmingly to leave the Union. Other lower-South states likewise seceded, eventually joining to form the Southern Confederacy.

The new nation's leaders quickly convened in Montgomery, Alabama, to elect a provisional government and to draw up a constitution. These actions breathed life into the Confederate States of America, but these first breaths were not without discomfort. President Jefferson Davis and his colleagues found the existence of one Federal installation—Fort Sumter, in Charleston Harbor—particularly disturbing. Davis planned to seize the fort, and Lincoln determined to resupply and hold it. The resulting Confederate bombardment of the fort on April 12, 1861, compelled Lincoln to answer the blow with a call for seventy-five thousand volunteers. The president's actions demanded that choices be made. States like Tennessee and individuals like Nathan Bedford Forrest now had to choose between the North and the South.

On June 8, the Tennessee legislature responded to Lincoln's call for volunteers to fight the Confederacy by voting to leave the Union. Forrest, who had chosen to bide his time when Mississippi seceded, despite his owning extensive properties there, now followed his native state. Then, having settled his affairs at home, he went to Memphis, where he expected to attach himself to one of the many military units being formed to defend the new nation. His long-standing love of horses prompted him to join the cavalry—Captain Josiah White's Tennessee Mounted Rifles, as a private, on June 14, 1861.[3]

Bedford was not the only Forrest to enlist in this cavalry company. His youngest brother, Jeffrey, and his fifteen-year-old son, William, joined as well. The Mounted Rifles shortly left Memphis to go to Camp Randolph, sixty-five miles up the Mississippi River, to drill and dig fortifications. However, Private Forrest was not destined to remain in White's command for long. He had earned a solid reputation among people of influence in Memphis, and they petitioned Tennessee Governor Isham G. Harris to offer him a field command. Harris concurred, as one person recalled, "knowing Forrest well and having a high regard for the man." Harris promptly ordered Forrest to Memphis and authorized him to raise a regiment of cavalry.[4]

Forrest undertook the responsibilities of raising a new command with energy and dedication. He issued his own call for volunteers, promising them "A CHANCE FOR ACTIVE SERVICE," and established a recruiting office and headquarters in the Gayoso House Hotel in Memphis. There Bedford hoped to enlist "five hundred able-bodied men, mounted and equipped with such arms as they can procure (shotguns and pistols preferable), suitable to the service." His preference for weapons used in close-hand fighting should have warned recruits of their commander's partiality for war at the most personal level. As was typical of such Southern mounted units, Forrest expected the men to supply their own mounts, although the government would credit them for the value of the horses and other equipment they provided.[5]

Of course, not every recruit could bring a horse or a weapon "suitable to the service" with him. So, Lieutenant Colonel Forrest soon faced the same dilemma that other commanders confronted throughout the South: He had too many men for the number of weapons on hand. Forrest had even fewer options open to him than did others who had gotten an earlier start organizing their units. The least satisfactory of these options was to wait for the new Confederate government to supply weapons, horses, and equipment. Waiting was not in Bedford's nature, so he sought his own source of supplies.

This quest for supplies immediately embroiled him in a cloak-and-dagger operation to rival the best spy story. The largely untapped resources in the state of Kentucky presented Forrest with the opportunity to supply his command. He called upon all the business acumen he had gained and the contacts he had made from his years as a slave trader. To accomplish this new goal, Forrest sought Southern sympathizers in Kentucky who lived in the vicinity of the Ohio River or in such towns as Lexington and Frankfort. With the slave-trading network to buttress him, Bedford and his handpicked agents scoured the region for weapons and other equipment with which to outfit his command. Given the number of Unionists who might try to thwart his efforts, Bedford had to take care to avoid detection.

Within a week after his authorization to raise troops, Forrest was in Kentucky seeking both recruits and equipment. On July 20, he purchased a large consignment of weapons and accoutrements, including "five hundred Colt's navy pistols, and one hundred saddles and other horse-equipments." He bought and paid for this equipment with his own funds, but buying and paying for it was just the beginning.

Forrest and his cohorts ran into trouble in Louisville. Unionists there maintained a close watch on anyone they suspected of Confederate sympathies. But Forrest proved equal to the challenge. With the help of two other men, he succeeded in eluding the Unionist net and escaping with the valuable weapons concealed "under their linen 'dusters.'" Secreting the pistols and other supplies in a local livery stable, Forrest and his compatriots packed the pistols in sacks marked "potatoes." They loaded these "potatoes" in an ordinary market wagon and drove them to a farm outside Louisville. The Confederate colonel and his men then piled the saddles in a wagon marked "leather" and sent them to a tanyard several miles south of the city. The Southerners stashed other supplies in bags marked "coffee" and smuggled them out in the same way.

At this point, a detachment of Forrest's men arrived at the tanyard with other wagons. About dusk, the colonel supervised the loading of the "leather" goods onto the waiting vehicles. The convoy subsequently picked up the "potatoes" and "coffee" as well, then started hastily toward the safety of the Confederate lines in Tennessee. In the meantime, Forrest rode off to complete the deception. He was sure that no unwanted witnesses had seen the operation, but knowing that the Unionists had watched him so closely, he decided to take no chances. As the sun dipped low in the western sky, Bedford rode slowly and deliberately into the outskirts of Louisville, in the opposite direction from the tanyard, the farm, and the wagons' route southward. He expected, even wanted, to be seen. Being seen would virtually guarantee that the precious cargo would reach Tennessee unmolested. Then, in the darkness of night, he rode around the city before speeding south, eventually overtaking the wagons.

A detachment of new recruits soon joined the wagon train, adding to the numbers with which Forrest could defend the supplies. Yet, despite all these precautions, the Confederates were not completely out of danger. Local residents informed Bedford that a strong company of Home Guards at Munfordville, Kentucky, intended to block his way to the Confederate lines. Aware that his detachment of cavalrymen was still relatively small and untested in combat, he resolved to fight his way through the obstacle if he had no other choice. But before he resorted to force, Forrest decided to try bluff. A fairly large number of relatives had accompanied the recruits, apparently prolonging their good-byes. Bedford immediately put them to good use. Informed that a train would pass on its way to Munfordville, he formed his troopers and their relatives into lines within sight of the railroad. As the train rolled past, passengers gazed from the windows at what appeared to be a formidable military force. They obligingly informed the leaders of the Home Guard of what they had witnessed, and the latter decamped, leaving the road open to the Confederates. Forrest easily brushed aside a small force of scouts and, in due course, the wagon train reached Southern lines safely.[6]

This expedition again established Bedford Forrest as a man of action. Not awaiting orders or the convenience of others, he sought to meet the needs of his new command. He demonstrated an aptitude for bluff and deception that would serve him well in the years ahead. Lieutenant Colonel Forrest fared well in these covert pursuits, and in other, more routine activities. He functioned efficiently and successfully in his administrative duties as a military commander. One future staff officer, the Reverend David C. Kelley, later recalled that he had little trouble competing for supplies with nearly every other Confederate officer, "except when I came in contact with the requisitions of N. B. Forrest."[7]

When Forrest and his roving band of warriors returned to Memphis, the Southern commander still needed soldiers to fill his ranks. Again he advertised for individuals seeking "ACTIVE SERVICE." On the same page of the *Memphis Daily Appeal,* the editors echoed the Confederate officer's call: "To Arms!—We invite attention to the call of Col. N. B. Forrest, in to-day's paper.... Those whose fancy inclines them to the cavalry service will find no better opportunity to enlist under a bold, capable and efficient commander. Now is the time."[8]

Early in September, the strategic situation changed for the opposing sides in the west. Confederate troops under General Gideon J. Pillow entered Kentucky on September 3, fearing preemptive action by the Federals. The movement precipitated a flurry of activity by both sides as the Southern forces sought to establish themselves more firmly in the state and the Northern forces prepared to move against them. Against this background of activity, Forrest rode into the no-man's land between the main lines, reconnoitering the region, scouting for enemy movement, and interrupting the flow of Union supplies on the Ohio River.

By late October Forrest's command was ready to take the field. Soon after, Colonel Samuel Tate informed General Albert Sidney Johnston, "Colonel Forrest's regiment [of] cavalry, as fine a body of men as ever went to the field, has gone to Dover or Fort Donelson." He added, "Give Forrest a chance and he will distinguish himself."[9] And in mid-November 1861, General Lloyd Tilghman ordered Forrest and his command to search the region northwest of Hopkinsville for enemy units. They reached Princeton, where the main body remained while a detachment under Major David C. Kelley proceeded to the northern bank of the Ohio River. Forrest knew that Union forces used the Ohio as a conduit for supplies, and he sent Kelley there to intercept a supply ship if possible. During the operation, the Confederates reached Ford's Ferry, a crossing on the river near Smithland, where they found a Union transport, loaded with supplies. Under cover of darkness, a small party slipped onto the vessel, captured the crew, and forced them to load the supplies onto wagons. By 2 A.M., the wagons were filled and moving away from the river. The Confederates set the empty transport afire and rode away. One participant recalled, "Some of the wagons were overloaded and stuck in the mud, and as a consequence the road was strewn with bacon, coffee, salt, etc., from Ford's Ferry to Princeton." The loss of supplies had no negative effect upon the morale of the men at this stage in the war. "When we got back to the camp at Hopkinsville," the trooper explained, "we were the proudest boys in the army."[10]

The men could be proud, for they brought back far more of the captured commissary and quartermaster supplies than they had lost. Perhaps most welcome, given the onset of winter, was a large supply of woolen blankets. One private in Forrest's cavalry wrote his family that Kelley returned to the command with "about $5,000

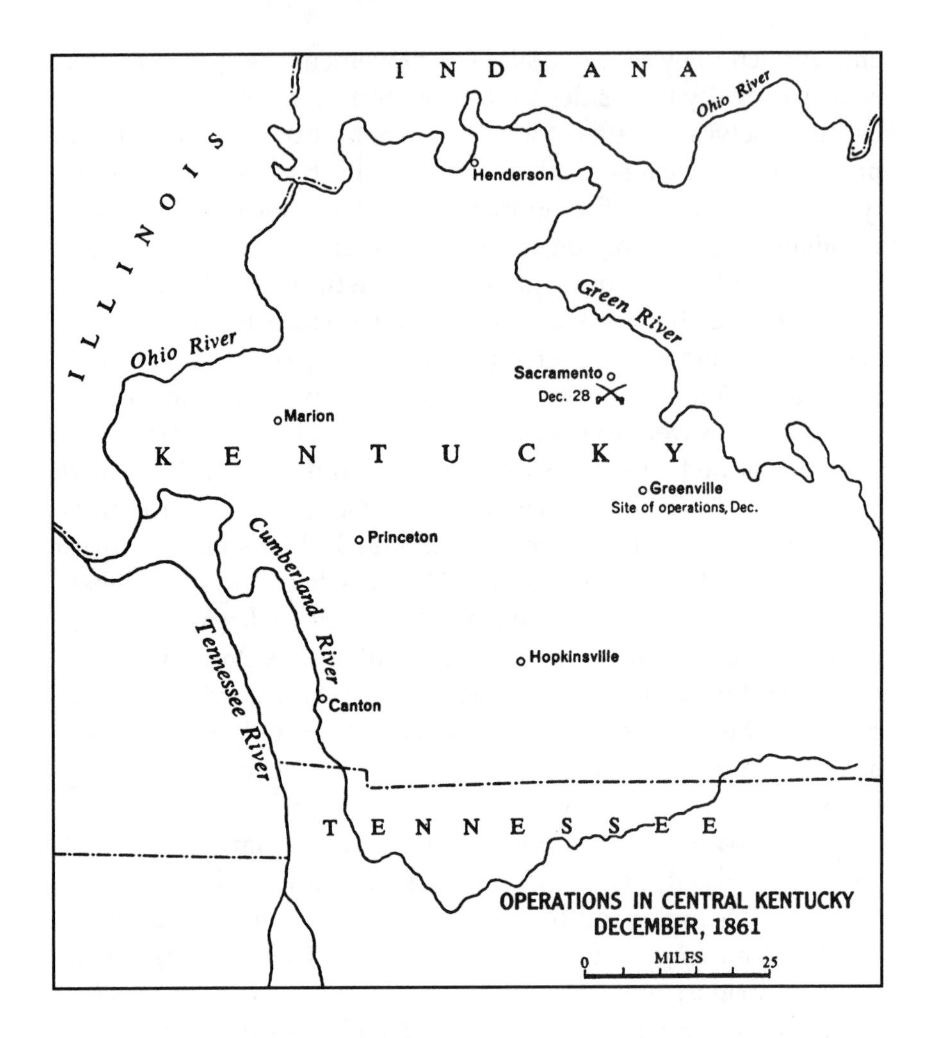

OPERATIONS IN CENTRAL KENTUCKY
DECEMBER, 1861

worth of ... goods they had taken from the enemy at a landing on the Ohio River, above Smithland. It consisted of bacon, sugar, coffee, molasses, whiskey, candles, etc. etc., of a good quality."[11]

Kelley had barely rejoined the command when Forrest received word that a Union gunboat, the USS *Conestoga,* was heading southward up the Cumberland River. Its apparent target was a cache of Southern supplies stored at Canton, thirty-two miles southwest of Princeton. Forrest raced his reunited command there through the night. He managed to arrive just before the Union vessel appeared, masked a four-pounder cannon, and concealed most of his men along the bank. Forrest hoped to lure the gunboat into range with a handful of men and then blast it with the forces he had waiting in ambush. However, the savvy Union commander wisely avoided the trap. One participant grumbled that the Southerners "fired on a gunboat passing down the Cumberland but could not get them to come on shore so that we could fight them." He noted that the Federals "returned the fire with cannon but did not *'hurt'* anybody but some of the boys on our side killed 4 of them and a *dog*, when the fun was broken up by our boys retiring and the boat going down the river at the same time."[12]

Forrest continued to be active in Kentucky in these early days of his military career. His command scouted the western part of the state through the remainder of the year. During one of these expeditions, he became involved in a couple of incidents that were typical of civil war. The operation started fairly routinely. Forrest and his troopers captured some arms and equipment, bagged an occasional stray Federal soldier, and scouted the area for Union concentrations of troops. Then, nearing the small town of Marion, the expedition took an ominous turn. A neighborhood woman rushed up to the Confederate commander, imploring him to free her husband, whom Federal troops had arrested as a Southern sympathizer with the aid of two local Unionists. Yet the captors compounded the problem by whisking their prisoner to another, safer location when word reached them that a force of Southern cavalry was nearby.

Forrest decided to retaliate by capturing the two Unionists. He apparently hoped to exchange the two Northern sympathizers for their pro-Southern counterpart. He succeeded in capturing one of the men, but, as he approached the house of the other, Jonathan Bells, the expedition ran into unexpected trouble. Forrest rode at the head of the detachment, with his aide and surgeon, Dr. Van Wick, at his side, dressed resplendently in a new Confederate uniform. Bells watched from inside the house as the column approached. He had already determined not to be taken and concocted a clever scheme to avoid capture. Perhaps understanding that confusion might allow him to escape, Bells leveled his weapon at the ornately dressed officer in the front ranks, assuming that he was the Southern commander. The shot broke the rhythm of jingling equipment and the staccato of horseshoes on the roadway. Van Wick fell. Bells fled. Forrest attended his fallen subordinate, before quickly turning his attention to an attempt to flush the Unionist from the nearby woods. The attempt failed. Forrest remained in the area for another day, nabbing another Union prisoner, but having no success finding Bells. He succeeded in striking a serious blow by killing the leader of a band of Unionists "who had sworn to shoot Southern men from their houses and behind trees, he [the band's leader] attempting it by wounding three horses with a shot-gun."[13]

This kind of war must have seemed familiar to Forrest, a man who had lived much of his life on the Southern frontier. Here was violence on the personal level, not unlike what he had seen in Hernando and Memphis before the war. He must have been struck by the arbitrary nature of life in war, so similar to the nature of life in the backcountry. Ironically, his instincts had not saved him; a simpler uniform had. The bullet meant for him had killed his aide instead. Forrest could not avoid fighting this war, as he would any fight in his life, on the most personal level. In the next engagement with the enemy, he would personally dispatch several Union opponents in hand-to-hand combat. Perhaps he remembered Van Wick; more likely, he became so absorbed in the act of combat that he did not think about the possibility of his own death. Certainly, those who knew him best observed that combat wrought a transformation in Forrest that seemed to affect his physical appearance and his personality.

Yet, Forrest was not finished with this awkward business. While searching for Van Wick's killer, one of the Southern detachments stumbled onto ten pro-Union clergymen returning from an annual conference in Illinois. They detained the ministers and brought them to the colonel. Already incensed at the surgeon's death and plagued by a desire to gain the release of a number of pro-Southern Kentuckians being held in Illinois, Forrest decided to keep them in custody against the safe return of the Kentuckians. He released two of the clergymen, explaining matter-of-factly that they had twenty-four hours to return to Marion with the Southern sympathizers or he "would hang the remainder all on one pole." Impressed by the warning, the ministers rushed off, returning in the allotted time with the Kentuckians. Forrest released the captured ministers unharmed and soon left the area.[14]

Lieutenant Colonel Forrest and his troopers continued to perform reconnaissance and outpost duties in Kentucky. This activity soon led them to their first real engagement with the enemy. The expedition began on December 26, when Forrest and three hundred of his men cut short their Christmas holiday to scout the Green River country north of Hopkinsville. The weather and the poor condition of the roads made the operation unpleasant. Then, early on December 28, outriders raced back to inform Forrest that a sizable Union force, which they estimated at five hundred, was some eight miles ahead of them. The effect was electric. Trooper James H. Hamner later recalled: "As soon as Col. Forrest heard it he gave the command to follow him. We started in a gallop and from that we went to a run for about 7 miles, when the advance guard came up with the enemy."[15]

News of the impending fight and the exhilaration of rushing at full gallop toward it stirred the horsemen along. There would finally be a fight—a chance for each man to prove himself in combat. This was no gunboat that would close its hatches and steam away. As the rebel horsemen approached the town of Sacramento, women urged them on from houses alongside the road. It was more than most of the men could stand. They spurred their horses on all the faster to reach the enemy, which also had the effect of badly scattering the command. Then Forrest, riding at the head of the column, suddenly confronted a rider from the town. He referred to the incident in an after-action report in rather uncharacteristic terms: "A beautiful young lady, smiling, with untied tresses floating in the breeze, on horseback, met the column just before our advance guard came up with the rear of the enemy, infusing nerve into my arm and kindling knightly chivalry within my heart." She had just ridden through the Union force and was coming to bring word of what she had seen to the Confederate commander.[16]

One cavalryman recalled how those with the fastest horses soon outdistanced the rest of their comrades. "The ride from here on was like a fox-chase, the best-mounted men in front, regardless of order or organization."[17] One mile outside Sacramento the

Southerners ran into the enemy rearguard. At first the Northerners seemed to be unable to determine if the Southerners were friends or foes. Bedford, his "knightly" ardor aroused, grabbed a Maynard rifle and shot at them, dispelling their doubt. As they turned to ride off, Forrest formed his men to charge, admonishing them to fire only when in range of their targets. One of Forrest's horsemen described the scene as he arrived: "I never saw so much excitement in my life as on this occasion. Some of the horses fell down, others gave out, some ran away, among them my little black."[18]

The Confederates lost all semblance of formation as they charged the Union position. The Union line erupted when the Southerners approached to within two hundred yards. As ordered, Forrest's men held their fire until within eighty yards. However, Bedford quickly realized that he did not have enough men on hand to carry the Union line. His men fired several rounds and fell back. At the same time, Major Kelley arrived with the remainder of the Confederates. Kelley was concerned that his commander had lost control of himself and the situation. He had watched the majority of his comrades gallop full tilt down the road. Thinking it might be necessary, he held his command in tight formation and followed the others at a slower pace. He expected to find Forrest in serious trouble and wanted to be in a position to help him.[19]

Forrest was indeed preoccupied with the enemy. Trooper Hamner saw the colonel "about 50 yards ahead of us ... fighting for his life." The combat was so fierce around Forrest that the astonished trooper thought "there was at least fifty shots fired at him in five minutes." He believed that his commander must have "killed 9 of the enemy."[20] By now, Forrest had decided to break off the fight. He returned to find Kelley on the field and immediately disposed his men to renew the attack. First Bedford dismounted a portion of his command to serve as sharpshooters. Then he dispatched small forces on both flanks to work their way around the Federals. Finally, he planned to make a frontal assault with the remainder.

Allowing a few moments for the flankers to reach their positions, Forrest launched his attack. The plan succeeded brilliantly.

The Union line broke and soon both sides raced along the road to Sacramento. Forrest's troopers pressed their counterparts, but found little opportunity to use their pistols, shotguns, or sabers until they reached the town. At that point, as Forrest stated in his report, "there commenced a promiscuous saber slaughter of their rear, which was continued at almost full speed for 2 miles beyond the village, leaving their bleeding and wounded strewn along the whole route."[21] Private Hamner observed, in a letter to his family, "We followed them about two and a half miles shooting them at every sight."[22]

On the other side of the town, several Union officers attempted to rally some of their troops. Once again, Forrest's horse carried him beyond immediate support and into personal danger. Captain C. E. Meriwether, riding just behind his chief, fell from his horse, shot through the head. Forrest suddenly became engaged in a desperate fight with three opponents—a private and two officers, Captains Bacon and Davis. As his horse carried him past, he shot the Union trooper and, leaning forward in his saddle, managed to elude the saber thrusts of the two officers. Riding on beyond them, he pulled up and swerved in the saddle. As Forrest turned, a Confederate private, W. H. Terry, rode up to help him, drawing Davis's attention. Terry's action gave his colonel the precious seconds he needed, but cost Terry his life. Forrest then sped back, mortally wounding Bacon and disabling Davis when his horse collided with the Union officer's, separating Davis's shoulder. The two officers apparently hoped to gain time for the rest of the Union force to escape. If this was their intention, they succeeded. The heap of horses, struggling to regain their footing on the roadway, effectively blocked further pursuit.[23]

Union casualties in the affair are difficult to determine. Union reports listed eight killed and eight to thirteen captured. Forrest placed the Union's losses at sixty-five killed and thirty-five wounded and captured,[24] but Private Hamner observed that the Confederates "left about 30 [Federals] killed on the field."[25] Both Lieutenant Colonel Forrest and Private Hamner recalled that many wounded Federals clung to their horses and got away. Union General T. L. Crittenden noted in a report to his superior, General Don Carlos Buell, that the Confederates "took away three wagon loads of dead and wounded."[26] These wagons were more likely filled with Union casualties. The only Confederate casualties were Meriwether and Terry killed and three others wounded. Ironically, Southern fire wounded one of the men, dressed in a blue uniform he had originally worn during the Mexican War. Hamner witnessed the incident, explaining, "We were all mixed up together and one of our men took him for a Yankee."[27]

The fight at Sacramento had an electrifying effect upon the Confederate troopers' morale. One Southerner explained that the engagement caused "men and officers to confide in and respect each other. We were convinced that evening that Forrest and Kelley were wise selections for our leaders."[28]

In this first significant military action of his career, Bedford Forrest demonstrated the traits that would characterize him as a soldier throughout the conflict. He employed the tactics of envelopment, striking simultaneously on the flanks while attacking the front. He also fought the war on the most personal level, as his combat with the Union officers attests. Forrest's actions were simple, direct, and effective. Sacramento was the first opportunity Forrest had to apply his standing rule for combat: "Forward, men, and mix with 'em."[29] He had learned that he could lead men into combat and that they would follow. He also demonstrated that he understood the fundamental truth of war—that it was at best a brutal business of killing or being killed. In these earliest stages of his military career, Forrest proved that he could cut to the core of warfare, without the qualms or subtleties that might affect or characterize the actions of other commanders.

CHAPTER 4

Riders on the Storm

(December 1861–July 1862)

Boys, these people are talking about surrendering, and I am going out of this place before they do or bust hell wide open.

—FORREST AT FORT DONELSON

I did not come here to make half a job of it. I mean to have them all.

—FORREST AT MURFREESBORO

LIEUTENANT COLONEL FORREST and his troopers had some time to celebrate their victory at Sacramento. Aside from the occasional scouting expedition, Forrest spent most of his time perfecting his military organization. Active service meant replacing worn-out mounts, refitting the men and animals, and performing other routine duties. Much of the work was mundane and administrative. But once again Bedford's years in business paid dividends. He knew the importance of detail. He also expected much from his subordinates.[1]

While Forrest looked to the needs of his men, the Federals looked longingly at two major Confederate fortifications: Fort Henry, on the Tennessee River, and Fort Donelson, on the Cumberland River. In early February, Union forces under General Ulysses S. Grant and Commodore Andrew H. Foote moved toward Fort Henry. The Confederate commander, General Lloyd

Tilghman, eyed the Union flotilla and the rising river apprehensively. Seeing that there was little hope of saving the fort, he opted to save most of his men by sending them to Fort Donelson. With a small contingent of artillerists to serve the fort's heavy guns, Tilghman waited for the inevitable. He did not have to wait long. By early afternoon on February 6, the Union flotilla's superior fire power had taken its toll on the Southern garrison. Tilghman watched as, one by one, the guns fell silent. Feeling that further resistance would be useless under the circumstances, he lowered his flag and surrendered the fort.[2]

Fort Henry's capture threatened the Confederates' forward line in Kentucky. Regional commander General Albert Sidney Johnston saw little else to do but abandon that line and retreat toward Nashville. In the meantime, he decided to augment Fort Donelson's garrison, apparently hoping to slow Grant's push against him. One of the commands Johnston sent to Donelson was that of Lieutenant Colonel Nathan Bedford Forrest. Forrest arrived in the area on the tenth and entered the fort early the next day. As the senior cavalry officer present, he assumed command of all the horsemen stationed there.

Forrest and his troopers were scarcely settled at the fort when General Gideon J. Pillow ordered them to scout the road from Fort Henry. Everyone expected the victorious Union forces to march across the thin strip of land separating the two forts. Indeed, Forrest ran into a force of Union cavalrymen, engaged in a brief running fight, and drove them off with some loss. Fresh from their conquest of Fort Henry, Commodore Foote and General Grant were moving on Donelson.

What followed was a medley of mishap and misunderstanding that would result in Donelson's surrender on February 16. In addition to Pillow, two other Confederate generals, John B. Floyd and Simon Bolivar Buckner, subsequently arrived at the fort, adding further haze to an already cloudy command structure. Floyd, as the senior officer, assumed command and considered abandoning the fort. But Pillow managed to convince him to concentrate his forces and make a stand. Throughout February 12, Floyd ferried his men into Fort Donelson, while Forrest attempted to slow, or at least harass, Grant's advance.[3]

Once back in the trenches, Forrest and some of his troopers performed different work. Union sharpshooters played havoc with the Southerners as they struggled to improve their entrenchments. To counteract the annoyance, Pillow ordered two companies of Forrest's men to drive them off. Forrest went to the front line with his men and soon became involved in the mission. He spotted a careless marksman in one of the trees. Grabbing a rifle from a nearby trooper, he took aim at the sharpshooter and sent the man tumbling headlong from his perch.[4] A Virginia artilleryman gratefully acknowledged that the cavalrymen "at once communicated with those fellows ... informing them that the position they occupied was totally at variance with our wishes," adding with evident satisfaction that the enemy sharpshooters "soon took in the situation."[5]

The front lines might have seemed a particularly dangerous place for Forrest to be under the circumstances. But this was his style of waging war. He preferred to be on the front lines, although such a preference often got high-ranking officers killed in this war. Nevertheless, here he could observe the terrain and watch the enemy's movements at close proximity—so close, in fact, that he rarely used field glasses. Too often scouts provided inadequate or even inaccurate reports that exaggerated the enemy's strength or failed to understand the enemy's dispositions. Forrest preferred to rely on his own eyes and his own judgment, as he had learned to do on the frontier. He understood the importance of accurate information. Besides, he wanted to participate in the action, as he did when he shot the Union sharpshooter.[6]

The Union ground forces tested the Confederate lines several times on February 13 and found them well defended. The Southerners repulsed each advance. But as night fell, both sides braced for an assault that neither could hope to resist. The weather had been extraordinarily mild; then it turned, radically. A cold north wind blew sleet and snow, pelting blue and gray alike. Soldiers who had impetuously discarded their heavier clothing now had ample reason to regret their decision.[7]

The next day, February 14, Grant called upon the navy to strike a blow at Donelson's water batteries. If Commodore Foote wished to convey Valentine's Day greetings, he certainly did not expect to receive them as well. By the time the Union flotilla slunk back down the Cumberland, it had sustained a brutal beating. All the mighty ironclads suffered damage, three of them drifting helplessly out of the fight when shots to the pilothouse or machinery disabled them.[8]

Despite the success of the Southern shore batteries in fending off the Union flotilla, the issue seemed much in doubt to at least one spectator early in the fight. Bedford Forrest had ridden through a ravine and into a clearing overlooking the Cumberland to get a better view of the spectacle below. He watched as the fighting grew more fierce and the shells from the gunboats ploughed into the earthworks. Soon, Major Kelley, a preacher in peacetime, rode up to find his commander greatly agitated. Amid the deafening roar of the cannonade, Forrest swerved in his saddle and shouted excitedly to his aide, "Parson! for God's sake, pray; nothing but God Almighty can save that fort!"[9]

Had he known to do so, Forrest might have asked the preacher to save his prayer for the next day. On the night of February 14, in the flush of the victory over the Union ironclads, Floyd, Pillow, and Buckner decided to attack the enemy's right flank at first light. Intelligence suggested that Grant had recently received substantial reinforcements. The three Southern commanders agreed that their best hope lay in blasting a hole in the Union line through which the majority of the Confederate troops could escape Grant's tightening noose around Donelson. They almost succeeded.

In "the early gray of the morning," Forrest led his men into position "on the left and in advance." Although the Confederates had hoped for surprise, Bedford "found the enemy prepared to receive us."[10] Union sharpshooters harassed the Southern cavalrymen as they waited for the main force of infantry to fall in line. By 5:30 A.M. the Confederates were ready to launch their offensive.

Slowly the Southerners pressed General John McClernand's Northerners back from the river. For a brief moment Lieutenant Colonel Forrest thought he saw an opening. The Union flank appeared exposed and unprotected, but when he attempted to exploit the opening, he found that a marsh effectively defended it

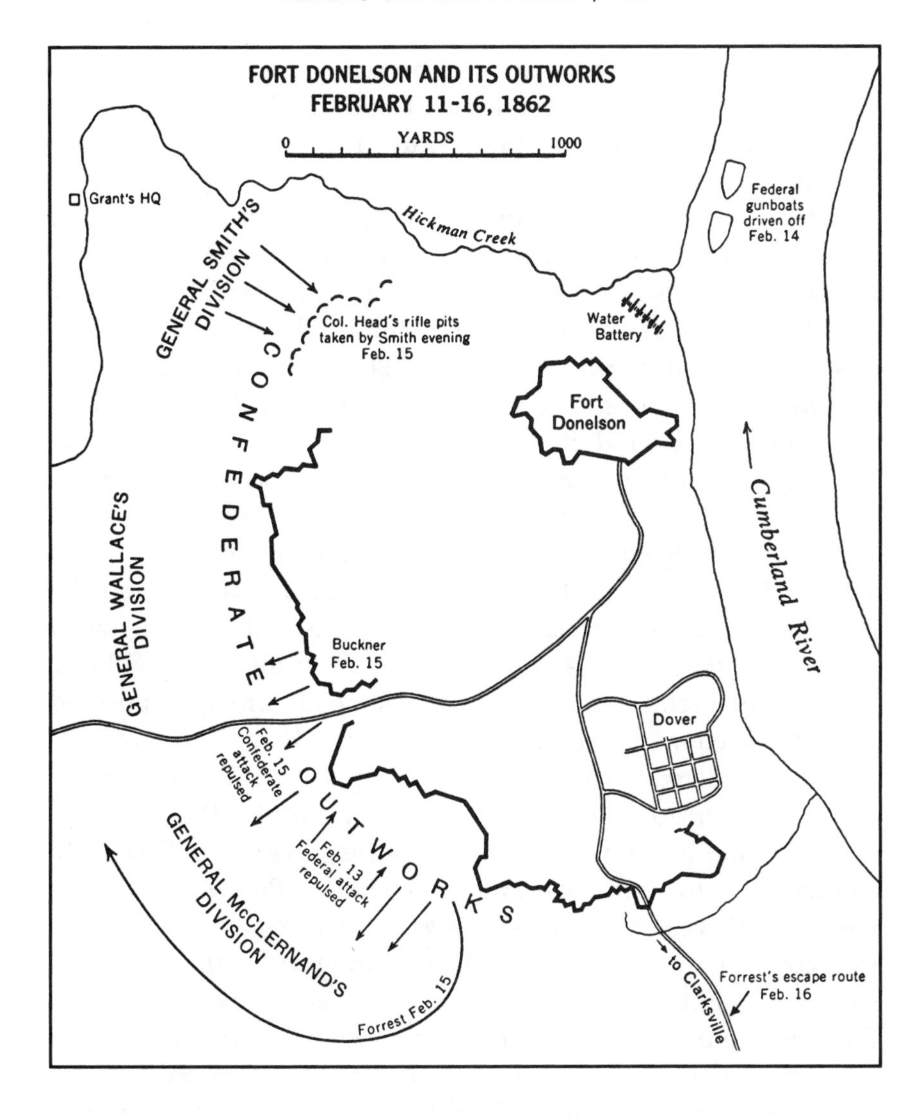

from attack. However, the Confederate assault continued to gain momentum, and soon the Union forces opposite Forrest's men retreated farther.

By now Forrest was operating essentially on his own. Thus, when he came upon a six-gun Union battery that had stubbornly stalled the Confederate advance for several hours, he attacked it. "I captured the battery," he noted in his report, "killing most of the men and horses." During this assault, both Bedford and his younger brother Jeffrey, lost their horses, Jeffrey badly injuring himself when he fell. Subsequently, Forrest and his men assisted the infantry in dislodging the enemy from their new position, "committing great slaughter."

Through the rest of the afternoon, Forrest engaged the Union forces he confronted in vicious fighting. He drove them from a ravine, "leaving some 200 dead in the hollow," and captured or ran off the guns of another battery, killing "about 50 sharpshooters, who were supporting the guns."[11] Forrest lost two more horses during the fighting, one when an artillery shell smashed into the animal, just behind the colonel's legs.[12]

The entire advance had been a great success. The Confederates had rolled their opponents back for miles, "having opened three different roads by which we might have retired if the generals had, as they deemed best in the council the night before, ordered the retreat of the army." Instead, the fighting ended at 2:30 P.M., when Pillow ordered the attacking units to return to their original lines. Forrest's men remained on the battlefield, collecting weapons and wounded men from among the dead and the dying. The task completed, he ordered his men back into camp to rest. He fully expected his superiors to renew the fighting in the morning.[13]

Sometime around midnight, a courier awakened Forrest to summon him to a conference of the generals at Pillow's headquarters in the Dover Inn. As he strode wearily through the door, Bedford could not believe what he was hearing. After the bitter and successful fighting of the previous day, this triumvirate of West Pointers were discussing surrender. They were convinced that Grant had again been heavily reinforced and that he used the new troops to reoccupy the lines. Forrest assured them that he had just recently ridden over the area and had found only wounded or dead men. But, in deference to his superiors, he agreed to send out scouts to survey the battlefield and check for possible escape routes. If the only avenues for escape lay under too much water from the back flow of the Cumberland, the infantry might not be able to march over them under the freezing conditions without suffering heavily from frostbite, pneumonia, or hypothermia.[14]

The three generals continued to debate the fate of their command. As one Confederate observer recalled, "a conforance tuck place at whitch was present Ginerril floyd, Pillow, Buckenor Col Forist ... and, bush Rod Johnson." Pillow argued "tha nesesity of cutting our way out or make a fite for a nother day," saying that in that time they "could get steam boats enouf to carrey tha hold command a cross the river and make our escape by way of Clarksville." Buckner disagreed. He believed that "the wornout and distrest condision of his men and the occupation of the riful pits by the Enimy" prevented him from holding his "posision for a half a nour if a tacked by the Enimy at day ligt whitch he sintainly would do."

The Federals had made inroads into Buckner's lines earlier in the day, but Pillow thought the lines would hold. In any case, he explained, the garrison "ought to cut our way out at all hazards." Buckner held fast, "saing [I] no my posision I can onley bring to bare a gainst the Enimy 4,000 men while he can oppose me with Eny given number," adding "that to attempt to cut our way through the linds would cost a sacrifice of Two thirds of the command and that no Gin had the rite to make such a sacrifice of human life." Floyd "concurd" with Buckner, and Pillow agreed that under the circumstances "thear was but one alternative"—surrender.

The fate of the garrison sealed, the commanders then began their personal posturing. Floyd, with an eye to his service as a former secretary of war, pointedly asked Buckner, "Gin if you ar put in command will you allow me to take out my brigade[?]" When Buckner agreed, provided Floyd leave before the surrender formalities began, the latter observed, "I will surrender the command[.] Pillow upon whome the command next devolved sed I will not Except it[.] Buckenor a mediatly replide I will Except it and shear the fate of my command." Pillow played out the string by asking and receiving permission to escape. "Col Forrist adrest him self to Gin Buckenor and sed I think theare is more fite in our men than you think for but if you wil let me I wil take out my command to whitch Buckenor and Floyd both conceded [and] turning to Pillow [Forrest] sed ginerril I fought under your command what shal I do—Pillow ancierd cut your way out to whitch forrist replide I will by G D."[15]

Forrest knew that he could escape from the trap before it

closed again. The others simply did not have the desire to break the rules. They waged war like they were playing chess. But Bedford refused to admit he was checkmated. He would ride out, taking those of his command who would go with him. As he had explained to the generals when they reached their decision: "I then stated that I had not come out for the purpose of surrendering my command, and would not do it if they would follow me out; that I intended to go out if I saved but one man."[16] Although he probably embellished this final statement, Forrest clearly had no interest in surrendering.

Bedford left the council of war infuriated at the turn of events. In the first of three reports he filed detailing his role at Fort Donelson, Forrest remarked, "I am clearly of the opinion that two-thirds of our army could have marched out without loss, and that, had we continued the fight the next day, we should have gained a glorious victory."[17] Although Bedford moderated this view in subsequent reports, he never discarded it.[18]

Forrest rode back to camp and angrily announced, "Boys, these people are talking about surrendering, and I am going out of this place before they do or bust hell wide open."[19] He met with his staff, and explained his plans. They roused the men and ordered them to prepare to ride out on short notice. By 4:00 A.M., all was ready. Forrest and five hundred of his men, plus numerous individuals from other units, started their trek out of Donelson. They left behind Colonel George Gantt's Tennessee battalion and two companies of Kentuckians, who failed to rendezvous with the rest of the command.[20] These soldiers' reasons for ignoring Forrest's repeated orders are unclear, but another soldier, from a different unit, declined the general's offer to take him along because he thought he should share the fate of his comrades. Forrest replied, "All right; I admire your loyalty, but damn your judgment!"[21]

Almost immediately, the expedition encountered grave danger. Scouts raced back to tell the colonel that a formidable array of Union infantrymen blocked their escape route. Forrest wanted to see for himself. He summoned his brother Jeffrey, still sore from his fall earlier in the day, and the two Forrests rode in the direction in which the scouts had seen the enemy line of battle. Just ahead, in the gray light of predawn, they caught a glimpse of what the scouts must have seen. They could detect no movement, and creeping forward, the two men soon found out why. The Union battle line in front of them was actually a rail fence, silhouetted against the early morning sky, so the posts appeared, from a distance, to be people standing. Bedford and Jeffrey remounted and rode farther, finding wounded men huddled about small fires, but nothing to hinder their progress. Forrest soon had his men on the road again—until they encountered a second potential obstacle.[22]

The backwater from the Cumberland River overflowed the road before them for some distance. It was impossible to determine the depth of the water and the bottom on which the soldiers would cross without sending a rider to test the crossing. Bedford called for volunteers. None came forward. So an exasperated Lieutenant Colonel Forrest plunged his horse into the water. Forrest wisely chose not to mention this reluctance or to censure his men for it in his report: "When about a mile out [the command] crossed a deep slough from the river, saddleskirt deep, and filed into the road to [the] Cumberland Iron Works." He left a small force to serve as a rearguard, while he pushed the others along. Despite Buckner's fears, in the two hours it took Forrest to get his men to this point, "not a gun had been fired at us. Not an enemy had been seen or heard."[23]

Bedford moved at a "slow march with my exhausted horses" away from Fort Donelson. He wanted to instill confidence in his men with his nonchalance. He also knew that the men had been through an ordeal and that both the troopers and their mounts were exhausted. He paused in a small village to rest his command and quickly had farriers working overtime to shoe the horses that were most in need. Forrest soon had the men back on the road, heading for Nashville.[24]

When the Confederate horsemen rode into the capital of Tennessee, they found the city in a state of panic. People expected the enemy to arrive at any moment. Inexplicably the citizens of Nashville had not fortified their city in the early days of the war. They translated the news of the massive Confederate attack at Donelson as the harbinger of victory. Subsequent news of the fort's surrender shocked them. According to one historian,

"Excitement spread instantly through the city, which straightway became electric with terrifying rumors of immediate disaster." The rumors left Nashville "in a perfect frenzy of terror."[25] The name given to this collective public reaction was The Great Panic.[26] It was a fitting description. People crammed the roads in every conceivable conveyance or surged onto trains heading South. Although the frenzy subsided somewhat by the next day, the crowds began clamoring for governmental supplies to be distributed. Johnston soon left the city with most of the troops, leaving Floyd to attend to the removal or dispersal and destruction of such supplies as he could not remove. Under Floyd's supervision, the operation quickly lost any semblance of order, and a mob looted the government's warehouses. The situation in Nashville had reached a crisis.[27]

Then, on Tuesday, February 18, Forrest and his weary troopers rode into the city. Floyd quickly passed the responsibility for saving supplies to the cavalry colonel and left town. Now it became Forrest's task to bring some order out of the chaos, and he approached the job with characteristic determination. First, he seized control of the warehouses. Next, he tackled the mob, appealing to them as Southerners. When that tactic failed, Bedford turned to force. He sent his cavalrymen into the mob and used icy water from the Cumberland to disperse them. Then he requisitioned every available vehicle and transferred all the stores he could to the railroad connection outside the city. In this way, Forrest saved vast quantities of foodstuffs, clothing, ammunition, and other vital supplies, including the rifling machinery from a local gun foundry. Finally, he distributed or destroyed the remaining goods, before evacuating the city as the Federals entered its outskirts.[28]

Forrest and his men moved on to Huntsville, Alabama. The Confederate commander generously issued furloughs to his entire command, allowing the men the opportunity to rest and recuperate while he recruited. A new company under his brother Jesse Forrest arrived to add to their numbers.[29] These and other new additions allowed Bedford to replace some of the losses his command had suffered because of battle casualties, disease, and desertion.

Typical of volunteer organizations in the Civil War, reorganization required the election of new officers, a right to which enlisted men clung throughout the early years of the war. As historian James M. McPherson noted, "citizen soldiers remained citizens even when they became soldiers."[30] Forrest shared none of the qualms that professional soldiers had concerning this practice, although he quickly learned that an officer had to demonstrate indispensable leadership qualities, especially when that officer applied firm standards of discipline to the men he expected to vote for him. The men promptly chose Bedford Forrest the unit's colonel in the accompanying elections.[31]

Confederate fortunes in the west had taken a severe beating. The fall of Forts Henry and Donelson opened the territory below them to invasion by Union troops. Grant lost little time preparing to press after the Confederates. By the end of March, he had roughly 40,000 men concentrated in camps near Pittsburg Landing in southern Tennessee, with 35,000 more under General Buell marching from Kentucky to unite with them there. In the meantime, 42,000 Southern troops assembled at Corinth, under the command of General Johnston, with General P. G. T. Beauregard as second-in-command. They planned to strike at Grant's command near Pittsburg Landing before Buell could arrive to augment the Union's forces.

Following the necessary rest and refitting, Forrest's cavalry command joined the Confederate march toward the Federal camps at Pittsburg Landing. His horsemen were part of Johnston's surprise offensive. Despite the Southerners' noisy approach and Beauregard's insistence that they had lost the vital element of surprise and should abandon the operation, the battle of Shiloh began auspiciously enough for the Confederates. The Southerners swept through the outlying Union camps with relative ease. The attack gathered momentum as Southern soldiers roused unsuspecting Northern soldiers from their sleep or interrupted their early efforts to cook breakfast. Little threatened to break this momentum, until the wave of attackers met General Benjamin M. Prentiss and the defenders of the "Hornet's Nest." In desperate fighting, these men bought General Grant the time he needed to regroup and rally his command. Although Prentiss eventually surrendered to the mass of Confederates who virtually surrounded him, his stand proved crucial.

Forrest had little to do that day. His cavalrymen guarded the fords across Lick Creek, from which they could hear the roar of the battle to the north. He grew impatient to join the fighting, finally riding in from the outposts. "Boys, do you hear that musketry and that artillery?" he wanted to know. "It means that our friends are falling by the hundreds at the hands of the enemy, and we are here guarding a damned creek! Let's go and help them. What do you say?" The regiment needed no encouragement; the men all hastened to the sound of the fighting. By succumbing to the lust of combat, Forrest had forsaken his role as a cavalry commander. Fortunately, the Confederates' advance meant that he would have no reason to regret his impetuosity.

Forrest swept to the front with his horsemen, found Confederate General Benjamin Cheatham, and asked for his authority to attack the Union lines. Cheatham replied that he could not give the cavalryman such orders and that if Forrest made the assault he would have to act on his own responsibility. Anxious to try his hand against the Federals, Forrest formed his command and charged. Several men and horses fell under the heavy fire, and the attack floundered in marshy ground just short of the battery. However, Cheatham's infantry quickly came up and forced the Union troops back. The cavalrymen paused only long enough to re-form before joining the final assault against Prentiss's Federals.[32]

Early in the afternoon a bullet struck General Johnston, severing an artery. Within half an hour the Confederate commander had bled to death. The responsibility for the army and the offensive devolved upon Beauregard. He succeeded in compelling the Union troops in the "Hornet's Nest" to surrender, but accomplished little else because Grant massed enough artillery to hold a final line near Pittsburg Landing. Rather than push on, the victorious Confederates settled into their hard-won positions for the night. But, for some, rest came fitfully. Grant slept little, with a shoulder that ached from a fall during the day and the anxiety of getting Buell's men across the Tennessee and into position for the morning. Forrest also rested little. He understood the desperate need of the moment, perhaps better than anyone else on the field. He wandered the battlefield through the night looking for someone who would authorize a continuation of the attack that had

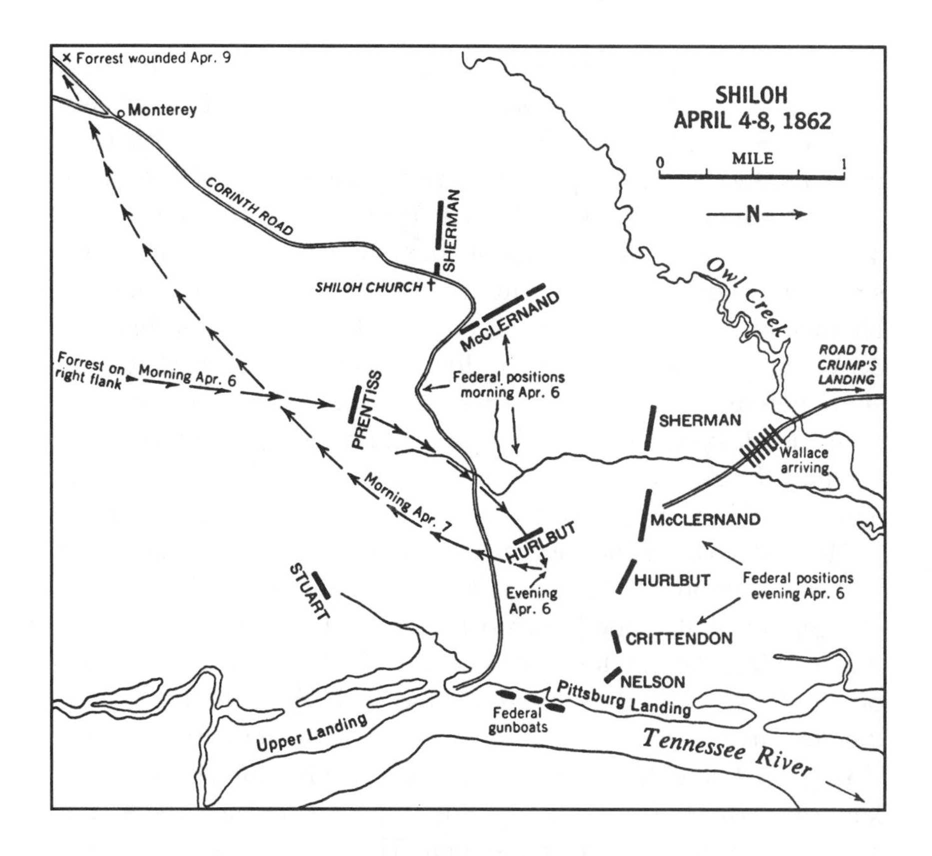

shown such promise through the day. His scouts had seen Buell's men as they crossed the river at Pittsburg Landing. He knew the importance of what they had seen. And when he finally found someone, General William J. Hardee, and failed to convince him to act, Bedford realized the significance, and expressed himself succinctly: "We'll be whipped like hell tomorrow." He was right.[33]

Early the next day, Grant launched an offensive with the fresh troops and steadily reclaimed the ground he had earlier lost. Beauregard began to search for a way, not to win the battle, but to save his army. He began a retreat and designated Forrest and his cavalry command part of the rearguard. Beauregard could not have made a better choice. The colonel had assured the three commanders of Fort Donelson that he could hold off the enemy while their troops pulled out of the fort; now at Shiloh, he demonstrated that he was as good as his word, defending the entire army as it retreated to Corinth.

General William Tecumseh Sherman was Forrest's adversary in this effort, and he steadfastly pushed his command after Beauregard's Southerners. On a patch of ground littered with trees from a prewar logging operation, appropriately called Fallen Timbers, Sherman and Forrest clashed. Typically, the Southern commander refused to wait while his opponent bore down upon his small force with overwhelming numbers. Instead, Forrest formed his men and impetuously charged the advancing Union line. He drove the pickets into the main line, causing considerable confusion, thereby masking his relatively weak force. He soon pushed the Federals back and forced Sherman to bring up more troops to stabilize the line. The operation gained time and allowed Beauregard and his wounded army to limp unmolested toward Corinth.

Forrest's Union opponent later recalled the skirmish in his postwar memoirs: "The enemy's cavalry came down boldly at a charge, led by [Colonel] Forrest in person, breaking through our line of skirmishers; when the regiment of infantry, without cause, broke, threw away their muskets, and fled."[34] As the Union line disintegrated before him, Forrest pressed the retreating enemy closely. He knew that the advantage rested with him as long as he kept the Federals from rallying. But, in his exuberance, the Southern officer raced ahead of his men. The men pulled up as the number of Federals swelled, and before Forrest realized it, he was surrounded. With shouts of "kill him" ringing in his ears, the Confederate commander began to search for a way out of his predicament. His own troopers would be of no use to him. They had seen the array of bluecoats and turned back. He was alone. In this moment of crisis, Forrest responded the only way he could—instinctively lashing from side to side with his saber or shooting his way through the labyrinth of Union troops.

One bold Union soldier pressed his rifle muzzle against Forrest's side and fired. The ball penetrated Forrest's side and lodged against his spine. But in an instant, the Confederate commander turned his horse and broke free of the pack of angry Federals. As he rode clear, he grabbed an unsuspecting opponent and hoisted him onto the horse behind him. With the soldier as a shield, Forrest rode back to his waiting men, dumping the hapless rider when he got out of range.[35]

Forrest's wound proved less serious than was initially feared, but it was serious enough to disable him and send him home to Memphis. Bedford convalesced briefly, making a quick recovery—perhaps too quick—cutting the recovery time prematurely. He simply was not a good patient, much preferring to return to the field to be with his command. Shortly after he returned, the wound reopened, and required a second operation in which a surgeon removed the bullet. He remained incapacitated for two weeks.

Ironically, while Forrest spent his time recuperating from his wound, he supervised efforts to recruit additional troops for his command. The regiment had diminished to approximately three hundred men.[36] An advertisement in the *Memphis Appeal* called for "200 able-bodied men ... by the first of June with good horse and gun." Noting that "I wish none but those who desire to be actively engaged," Forrest offered recruits one inducement: "Come on, boys, if you want a heap of fun and to kill some Yankees."[37] The returns for April 28 showed that Forrest's command had 463 men ready "for duty" and 842 on the rolls, compared to 679 and 863, respectively, the previous month, with the engagement at Shiloh accounting for the number of men unfit for duty or absent from the command.[38] Finally, the wounded cavalry commander healed sufficiently to return to his command, only to lose it.[39]

On June 11, 1862, Forrest left for Chattanooga under orders he had received to assume a new cavalry command.[40] Other than a few handpicked staffers and troopers to act as an escort, under his brother William Forrest, Bedford reluctantly left behind the men he had led in the early campaigns. He bade his old regiment farewell, apparently satisfied to leave the men under the command of Lieutenant Colonel Kelley and to move on to a wider field of operations, more troops, and the chance for promotion.[41]

His new command consisted of Terry's Texas Rangers, under Colonel John A. Wharton, and the Second Georgia Cavalry, under Colonel J. K. Lawton. Forrest seems to have left the training routine largely to his subordinates. Since he knew little of the manual of arms himself, he watched the drills and parade-ground maneuvers with great interest. On one occasion, the observations encouraged future tactics. One fellow Confederate officer remembered that Forrest was so impressed with the maneuvers of the men by bugle calls that he asked if they could be made to circle a given point in that manner. When the officer answered that they could, Forrest replied, "I will often have need of this manoeuvre, as it will be necessary from time to time for me to show more men than I actually have on the field."[42]

Despite his only basic knowledge of military exercises, Forrest became involved in the drills, sometimes with unintended results. One of Forrest's new troopers later recalled the humor that attended the veteran colonel's efforts to teach his sometimes raw cavalrymen the rudiments of horsemanship. He observed that "as soon as we saw Gen Forrest mount the 2nd Georgia and order them to fire their guns Shot guns and saw about fifty of the Regiment go tumbling over their horses heads and heard Forrest Cuss we were Satisfied that he would do to tie to."[43] Nevertheless, within a month, Forrest had his new troopers ready to launch their first raid into Union lines in Tennessee. The objective was to slow or stall the advance of Buell's Army of the Ohio against Chattanooga, now that it had finally started. The principal target was the garrison and depot at Murfreesboro, on the Nashville and Chattanooga Railroad.

The Confederates began their operation on July 9, when they crossed the Tennessee River, heading to McMinnville. There, they received some reinforcements and prepared for the final push to Murfreesboro late on July 12 and early on July 13. Forrest's men made short work of the Union pickets outside the town. They crept around the outposts and came in from the rear, capturing them without firing a shot. This would be the simplest task of the day. Next, Forrest formed his men into three groups in columns of fours. Each group had a specific job to perform: one each to attack two separate Union troop encampments, the other to attack the center of the town. Ironically, the recently arrived Union commander at Murfreesboro, T. T. Crittenden, played perfectly into Forrest's hands. The cavalry patrols he ordered onto the numerous roads that radiated from the town returned at dusk each day.

Southern scouting reports indicated that the major Federal infantry regiments in the garrison were camped at opposite ends of the town. Forrest could not have known that quarrels among

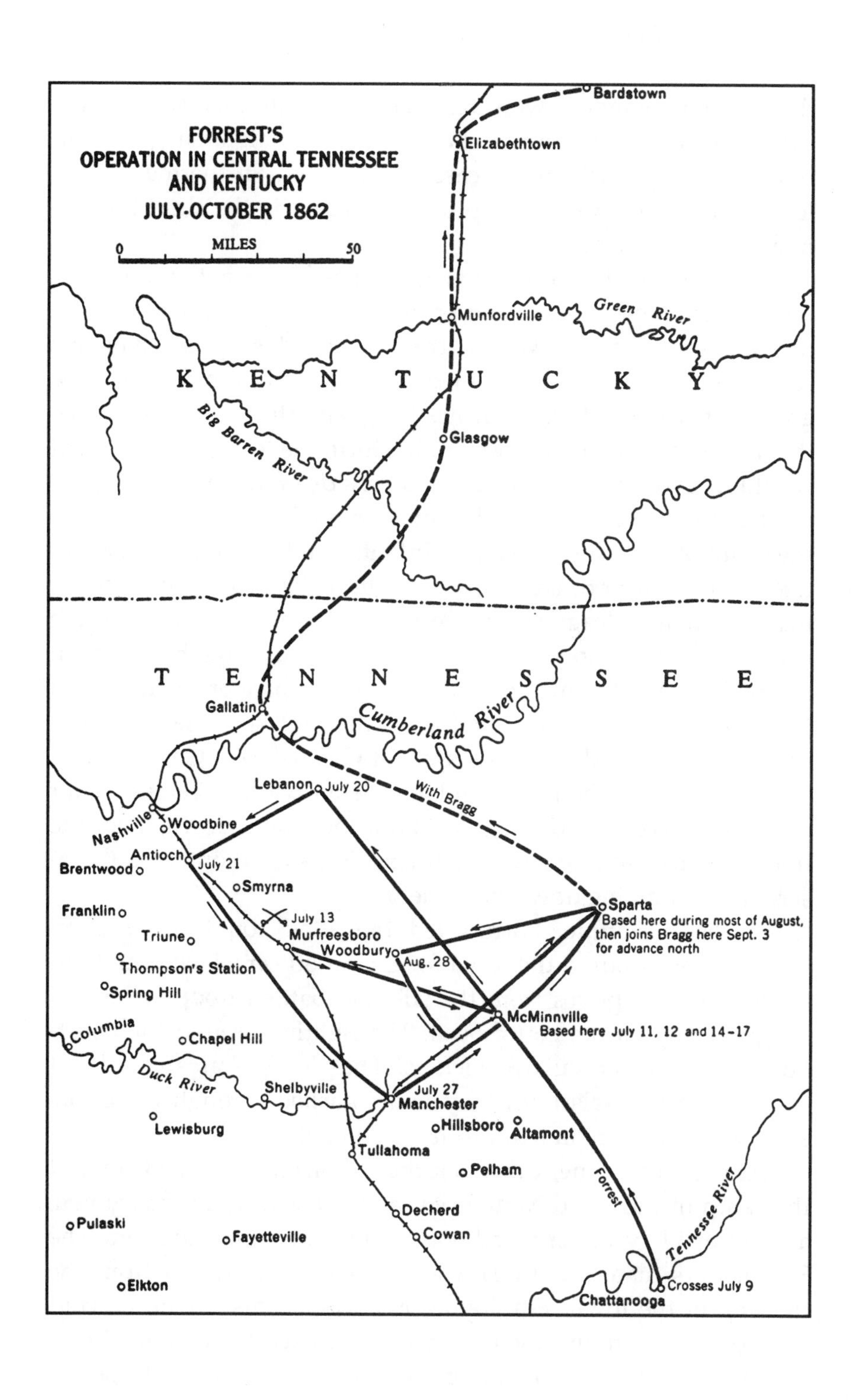
FORREST'S
OPERATION IN CENTRAL TENNESSEE
AND KENTUCKY
JULY-OCTOBER 1862
0
MILES
50
Bardstown
Elizabethtown
Munfordville
Green River
K E N T U C K Y
Big Barren River
Glasgow
T E N N E S S E E
Gallatin
Cumberland River
Lebanon
July 20
With Bragg
Nashville
Woodbine
Antioch
July 21
Brentwood
Smyrna
Franklin
July 13
Murfreesboro
Triune
Woodbury
Aug. 28
Thompson's Station
Spring Hill
Sparta
Based here during most of August,
then joins Bragg here Sept. 3
for advance north
McMinnville
Based here July 11, 12 and 14-17
Columbia
Chapel Hill
Duck River
Shelbyville
July 27
Manchester
Lewisburg
Hillsboro
Altamont
Tullahoma
Pelham
Forrest
Decherd
Cowan
Pulaski
Fayetteville
Tennessee River
Elkton
Crosses July 9
Chattanooga

the unit commanders were responsible for the dispersal of the camps. Soldiers who could not camp together might have difficulty cooperating efficiently in case of an attack. Furthermore, Crittenden had failed to patch up the difficulties in the short time he had been in Murfreesboro.[44]

However, if the Confederates expected to benefit from such intangibles, they would have been wise to expect their plans to develop problems as well. Forrest achieved surprise; then his scheme went awry almost immediately. He had expected the three groups of attackers to take on specific goals: The first would attack the nearest camp, the second would storm the town, and the third would race for the camp on the farthest side of Murfreesboro.

The first detachment, Wharton's Texas Rangers, crashed into the camp of the Ninth Michigan Infantry and Seventh Pennsylvania Cavalry. Unfortunately for their immediate hopes of success, many of their colleagues erroneously followed the others into the town. In the first moments, the Texans poured through the Union camp firing wildly and wounding the commander of the Ninth Michigan, Colonel William Duffield. Although surprised, the Federals quickly rallied under Lieutenant Colonel John G. Parkhurst. Soon they established a formidable defensive line behind cedar posts and overturned wagons. Wharton went down, and the fighting subsided into covering fire as the Texans contented themselves with pinning down the Federals.

In the meantime, Forrest led the attack on Murfreesboro. Detachments scoured the town for Union officers, including Crittenden, freed captives from the jail, and battled troops who had sought refuge in the courthouse. The fighting around the courthouse proved particularly vicious. The Confederates could not subdue the Federals until they had smashed through the doors and overcome them in hand-to-hand combat.

At the same time, other Southern horsemen dashed toward the camp of the Third Minnesota. Again the Union infantrymen, and an artillery battery, stubbornly defended their ground. The Southerners made little headway until Forrest arrived from the fighting in the town. Employing his favorite maneuver, he conducted a force around the enemy and attacked their camp. Twice repulsed, the irate commander led his men in a final desperate and successful charge. Combined attacks soon pushed the Federals out of their first line, but they rallied and appeared willing to contest any further Confederate offensives. Suddenly, Forrest halted his men, ordering them to pin down their stubborn opponents in their new line. He directed other troops to burn the enemy camp and start the prisoners and captured stores on the road to McMinnville.

Then Forrest raced off toward the fighting between the Texas and Michigan troops that was still raging on the other side of town. Some of his officers believed that they had already achieved enough. They suggested that he break off the fighting and run for safety. Bedford succinctly rejected the proposal. "I did not come here to make half a job of it," he explained, "I mean to have them all."[45]

That point firmly established, Forrest moved his men through town. Arriving before the makeshift Union barricade, he ordered his men to cease firing and sent in a flag of truce. He was prepared to gamble that bluff could do what bluster had as yet failed to do: compel the enemy forces to surrender. His note demanded "the unconditional surrender" of the Union troops. If they refused, he warned, "I will have every man put to the sword." He reminded Parkhurst that he had subdued the other Union units and concentrated a superior force that would decide the issue. Forrest concluded his note by saying that he simply wished to avoid further bloodshed.[46] Parkhurst received the message, consulted with his subordinates, and reluctantly agreed to surrender.

With one surrender achieved, the colonel again raced through Murfreesboro with all his spare troops in tow. One gamble had paid off, and he was not one to quit a winning streak. He wanted to break the bank and "have them all." To that end, he sent a second surrender note, similar to the first, to a second Federal force. This Union commander, Colonel Henry C. Lester, sought further assurances that his defense was untenable. He asked Forrest to allow him to meet with the wounded Colonel Duffield, and Forrest granted his request. Troops escorted Lester through Murfreesboro, making no attempt to prevent him from seeing the Southern command. If Lester was not suspicious, he should have been. Employing a tactic for which he would become famous a year later, Forrest moved his troopers through the streets so the Northern officer unwittingly saw the same soldiers several times. This strategy inflated the strength of the Confederate troops and magnified the reasons that would make surrender the most logical choice. Duffield and Lester's own staff advised him to capitulate, and Lester reluctantly agreed to do so.

Forrest's busy but successful day won him 1,200 prisoners, several pieces of artillery, numerous wagons, and great amounts of weapons and equipment. He inflicted casualties of 29 killed and 120 wounded, while sustaining losses of some 25 killed and 40 to 60 wounded. His troops dismantled the railroad and burned the depot and such supplies as they could not carry off. Murfreesboro had been a difficult but decisive victory for Forrest—a fitting birthday present for a man who cherished hard fighting.[47] As one soldier remembered, "old N. B. was every where it Seemed."[48] Forrest's omnipresence and willingness to bluff and fight with equal vigor won impressive results and ensured that his reputation would continue to rise.

There was, however, one ominous element in the events that occurred at Murfreesboro. Forrest had created a personal fortune through the slave trade. He considered black Southerners to be commodities or laborers. The war threatened his convictions. Although Lincoln's government had not yet armed blacks, Union forces in the field used them extensively in noncombat roles, just as the Confederates did. Forrest dictated his own policy about black men captured in combat; he considered blacks runaways and sought to return them to their masters.[49]

The record clearly indicates that Forrest personally killed one black man at Murfreesboro, although his biographers have presented the story with various degrees of detail and accuracy. The earliest of these biographers, Thomas Jordan and J. P. Pryor, described the incident more clearly. According to them, as Forrest rode through the camps of the Minnesota troops, a "negro campfollower" fired at least five times in an effort to kill the Confederate officer, before Forrest shot his assailant "with his pistol at the distance of thirty paces."[50] Subsequent biographers have glossed over the incident or failed to mention it.[51]

Later in the war, after Forrest's capture of Fort Pillow, Union

Major General D. S. Stanley suggested to readers of the *New York Times* that Forrest was involved in another killing at Murfreesboro that was more cold-blooded. Stanley attributed the story to "a rebel citizen of Middle Tennessee, a man of high standing in his community, who had it from his nephew, an officer serving under FORREST." Apparently, the incident occurred when the Federals surrendered to Forrest's troops:

> A mulatto man, who was the servant to one of the officers in the Union forces, was brought to FORREST on horseback. The latter inquired of him, with many oaths, what he was doing there. The mulatto answered that he was a free man, and came out as a servant to an officer, naming the man. FORREST, who was on horseback, deliberately put his hand to his holster, drew a pistol, and blew the man's brains out.
>
> The rebel officer stated that the mulatto man came from Pennsylvania; and the same officer denounced the act as one of cold-blooded murder, and declared that he would never again serve under FORREST.[52]

In a similar vein, a participant in the Murfreesboro raid remembered that

> in going out of a corn field into some timber the writer run out a fine big Buck Negro dressed in federal uniform[.] I took him and started to hunt up Gen Forest[.] I Soon found him Siting on his horse his eyes blazing fire and I called his attention to my capture and instead of complimenting me he gave me a Cussing that still amuses me when I think of it[.] I tried to reason that that was a Very Valuable nigger but *the general* reasoned that a Dead nigger in federal uniform was more valuable to the Confederacy than a live one but finally he ordered me to turn himover to Col Morrison who had charge of the prisoners and he finally Sent the Negro home to his owner Dr Rucker of Rutherford Co Tenn[.][53]

A month after the raid, one Southern civilian confided in his diary: "The negroes are rather afraid of familiarity with Yankees since they heard that Forrest hung quite a number that were taken in arms at Murfreesborough & also at Gallatin." The diarist quickly added, "This policy seems severe—but the Southern people can never consent to treat negroes as prisoners of war & exchange for them with white prisoners."[54]

All these incidents suggest that Bedford Forrest first confronted the issues of race and war at Murfreesboro. There can be no doubt that the participation of blacks in the Union war effort angered him. And he was certainly not averse to expressing that anger in a personal and violent manner. Whether Forrest actually executed a defenseless black prisoner is not clear. The Union officer who told it admittedly "heard" the story third hand and chose to relate it in the period of heated rhetoric following the "massacre" of blacks at Fort Pillow. Nevertheless, the other sources indicate that Forrest grappled with the issue and may have been intent on imparting lessons for future behavior among Southern blacks. He might easily have lost his battle for control over himself and his actions. One fact is certain: Murfreesboro was only the beginning of Forrest's dilemma.

If he had ever harbored any doubts, these early months of war demonstrated to Forrest that he was a capable military commander. More important, he inspired in his men a belief in his abilities. Riding with Bedford Forrest meant something. To be sure, it meant hardship and hard fighting, but it also meant the unit's pride in accomplishing tasks that other forces could not or would not carry out. Before he could prove to his opponents that he was a "wizard," Forrest realized that he had to prove it to his own men. Routing the Union force at Sacramento, riding out of Fort Donelson, bringing order from chaos at Nashville, personally supervising the rearguard at Shiloh, and conducting the successful raid on Murfreesboro were ample indications that he was well on his way to achieving his goal. Other campaigns and questions yet faced him, as Forrest and his troopers prepared to ride into Kentucky with General Braxton Bragg.

CHAPTER 5

Charge Them Both Ways!

(July 1862–February 1863)

I will have about 1,200 cavalry, and Mr. Forrest shall have no rest. I will hunt him down myself.

—General William Nelson

Charge them both ways!

—Forrest at Parker's Crossroads

I will be in my coffin before I will fight again under your command.

—Forrest to General Joseph Wheeler

Bedford Forrest's success at Murfreesboro impressed his superiors. General Braxton Bragg described the raid to General Edmund Kirby Smith as a "gallant, brilliant operation," adding, "Such successful efforts deserve immediate reward." Ironically, given future relations between Bragg and Forrest, the former offered to join Kirby Smith "in recommending Colonel Forrest." Bragg closed by observing, "This affair, added to his gallantry at Shiloh, where he was severely wounded, mark him as a valuable soldier."[1]

Understandably, the Federals were not so enamored with Forrest and his horsemen. Brigadier General William Nelson assured General Don Carlos Buell that he would soon "take the field and will try to clear out the country."[2] In the meantime, Forrest and his men pulled back to McMinnville, while the Federals swarmed about Nashville, expecting him to strike there next. Soon to be commissioned a brigadier general, Bedford obliged his opponents with short harassing slashes against the rail lines, bridges, and telegraph lines outside Nashville. He reveled in the stir he created, observing throughout his report on the operation the "excitement," the "great confusion and evident fright," and the "terror" his movements caused.[3] Indeed, Nelson became so exasperated with the Confederate cavalryman that he promised Buell that when his expected reinforcements arrived, "I will have about 1,200 cavalry, and Mr. Forrest shall have no rest. I will hunt him down myself."[4] It was the first of many such promises made by many Union commanders.

True to his word, Nelson remained on the hunt, but "Mr. Forrest" continued to elude him. Buell, chafing at the ordeal, begged his subordinate to "Destroy Forrest if you can."[5] Finally, at the end of July, after weeks of slogging his infantry along the dusty Tennessee roads on the Confederate cavalryman's trail, a thoroughly frustrated Nelson informed Buell, "To chase Morgan and Forrest, they mounted on race horses, with infantry [in] this hot weather is a hopeless task."[6] More Southern maneuvering and the reactions this maneuvering engendered among Union garrisons throughout middle Tennessee prompted Buell to observe to his commander in Nashville: "[Our guards] are gathered up by the enemy as easily as he would herd as many cattle."[7]

Typically, Forrest remained aggressive and offensive minded. In a dispatch to General Bragg, on August 6, he reported that according to "a reliable source" the "enemy is diligently engaged in running his heavy siege guns and artillery across the river from Nashville." To Forrest it looked like the beginning of a Union evacuation of the Tennessee capital, and he urged Bragg to act quickly. "I am of [the] opinion," Forrest explained, "that an energetic movement forward by our force would certainly result in overtaking the Federals before they could escape from Tennessee."[8] He hoped to persuade Bragg to retake Nashville, a move strongly endorsed by Isham Harris, the exiled governor and Forrest's friend.[9]

These efforts at persuasion were typical of Forrest's communications with his superiors. He thrust opinions, suggestions, and advice at them regularly. While there was certainly nothing wrong with a subordinate expressing his opinions and offering suggestions and advice to his superiors, Forrest seldom missed an opportunity to do so and often became angry and sullen when he thought they disregarded or ignored what he had to say. If the situation appeared sufficiently important to warrant it and he deemed his immediate superior too hesitant or too incompetent to meet the requirements of the moment, he sometimes went to a higher authority. One of Forrest's closest aides, David C. Kelley, later described his chief as "restless" when serving in "a subordinate position." On the battlefield, Kelley explained, Forrest was "constantly leaving his command when not actively engaged, for the purpose of observation," and he "did not hesitate to communicate the results of these observations and to make suggestions to the general commanding."[10] Such tendencies could be useful; they could also become annoying. Ironically, for the commander who always demanded accurate information from his subordinates, the repeated messages Forrest sent Bragg concerning the Union evacuation of Nashville were well meaning, but inaccurate.

Whatever the Federals might do in Nashville, Forrest intended to keep them occupied. He relished his role as a raider. He enjoyed weaving in and around the forces that were sent to destroy him. But this bold policy occasionally led to close calls and narrow escapes. Twice, Union columns of infantry nearly succeeded in trapping and punishing these pesky Confederates. At one point, Forrest's practice of sending out scouts well in advance of his main force saved him. Some of the advance party spotted a strong Union force and informed their leader in time for him to hurry the entire command off the main road and into some nearby woods. There they watched as the Federal infantry marched past, oblivious to their presence.[11] But, on another occasion, the Southerners were not nearly so fortunate. In that instance, Union troops, under the command of General Thomas J. Wood, caught the Confederates during a similar maneuver, with half already off the road. Rather than attempt to unite the two halves of his divided command and fight the numerically superior Union force, Forrest sped off with the half already clear of the road, while the other half hastily retreated out of range of the Federal artillery. The troops in this latter force forged their way across country and soon rejoined their comrades. Despite a great opportunity, the Federals came away with only a handful of horses and mules, and a "light spring-wagon."[12]

Having eluded the Union trap, Forrest then overtook Bragg's advance units at Sparta on September 3, 1862. But the weary horsemen had no time to rest. By late August, Bragg had transferred his command from Mississippi to Tennessee, in preparation for an invasion of Kentucky, in conjunction with Kirby Smith. The Confederate commanders planned to liberate the state and rally a significant number of bluegrass recruits to the Southern cause. Bragg needed the cavalry to scout the advance of his army, screen his movements, and harass Buell's attempt to pursue. He also expected Forrest to help him win his race with Buell to Louisville.

Forrest and his men performed admirably. The cavalry commander kept scouts out gathering information on enemy dispositions, and remained in close contact with Bragg's headquarters. He devoted most of September 3 to "shoeing many of my horses—which were in a bad condition," in anticipation of the hard riding that was ahead.[13] By the next day, Forrest was both anxious and ready to move. He forwarded the current intelligence on Union troop movements and positions, and asked for Bragg's orders "as to what course I shall persue." Forrest offered to "leave 3 or 4 new companies" at Sparta "to serve as pickets and couriers," but clearly preferred to "go forward with the balance of my command, about 1,500 strong."[14]

On September 7 and for several more days, Forrest reported that General Buell's Union forces were retreating from Nashville. On September 10, he informed his superiors that he thought "the enemy are still evacuating Nashville and I think in a few days the city will be left to us." Confirming his opinion through personal observation, Forrest explained, "I got near enough to the city on yesterday morning to have a full view of the city. There appeared to be great bustle and confusion. They are doing but little work on their defences—only enough to keep appearances."[15] Forrest was still attempting to influence Bragg to assault Nashville, but the army commander had other concerns, particularly his attempts to cooperate with Kirby Smith and to anticipate the Union army's intentions.

Despite his tendency to impose his opinions on strategy on his superiors and his anger when they did not always heed his advice, Forrest continued to work well in tandem with the Army of Tennessee. He could cooperate, as long as he retained relative control of his own forces and got some sense of the direction his superiors wanted him to take. Under the temporary command of General Leonidas Polk, the cavalry commander assisted in the capture of a Union infantry brigade at Munfordville, Kentucky, and cut the Louisville and Nashville Railroad line at several junctures. Reaching Bardsville late in September, Forrest received orders to report to Bragg's headquarters in Chattanooga. Arriving there, an astonished Forrest learned that Bragg no longer required his services in Kentucky. Instead, the commanding general directed his subordinate to raise a new command in middle Tennessee. Bragg seems to have harbored no ill will against Forrest. There is no clear evidence of an effort to deprive the rough-hewn cavalryman of his command out of spite. But Bragg had little respect for Forrest as a conventional cavalry commander, preferring to cast him in the roles he did best: raider and recruiter. For a second time, Forrest set out, with only his escort and a few companies of men to accompany him, to create a new command.[16]

General Forrest immediately established a headquarters at Murfreesboro and began to scrape together this new force, largely through recruitment. Because of the success he had already achieved, Forrest had little difficulty drumming up recruits. Among those who answered his call was Colonel James W. Starnes, who had ridden with him earlier at Sacramento. Bedford gave Starnes command of a cavalry regiment—the Fourth Tennessee. Three other regiments also formed: the Eighth Tennessee, under Colonel George G. Dibrell; the Ninth Tennessee, under Colonel Jacob B. Biffle; and the Fourth Alabama, under Colonel A. A. Russell. In accord with the practice in the Confederate army, the artillery acted as a separate entity, under the command of Captain Samuel L. Freeman.

Once again, assembling a command and a staff was just the

beginning. Like those first troops in Memphis, Forrest's newest recruits needed arms and equipment—items that the Confederacy had only in short supply at best. The lack of supplies meant that Forrest's troops had to arm themselves with a dizzying assortment of weapons. The wide variety, which included shotguns, Enfield rifles, muskets, and even flintlocks, promised to be a nightmare to supply with adequate amounts of ammunition.[17] But as Forrest was wont to do, he expected to spend minimal time preparing his command for the field. He preferred to break camp, set out into Union-occupied territory, and supply his needs from the enemy.

By the end of October, Major General John C. Breckinridge joined Forrest at Murfreesboro and assumed command of all the troops in the region. Forrest moved to a forward post at La Vergne. Having earlier failed to convince General Bragg of the propriety of attacking Nashville, Forrest sought to persuade General Breckinridge. On the evening of October 20, he speculated that his recent experiences at Nashville—driving the enemy pickets "in Great Confusion" and forcing the Union troops to remain in line of battle "for four days" with just his cavalry—suggested that "if you was Here with your force Nashville would fall in forty Eight Hours after Reaching it."[18] By the next day, Forrest's enthusiasm had tempered. He sent Breckinridge a telegram reporting an encounter with the Federals and asking him to "Come on as soon as possible," but noted, "I am Having chills," and complained that he was "too unwell to do much."[19]

By November 4, Forrest was feeling better and had succeeded in convincing Breckinridge to test the Nashville defenses. Forrest wired that he had "everything ready" and advised his commander, "I think you had better come up and bring on yours [Breckinridge's command.] now is our time[.]"[20] Breckinridge decided to send only a portion of his infantry, but Forrest cooperated with them in attacking Nashville. Lacking the strength to recapture the Tennessee capital, this combined force had to content itself with spreading alarm through the city and driving the Union pickets back into the defenses.[21]

In November, affairs in Tennessee returned to the pre-Kentucky status quo. Bragg and the new Federal commander,

William S. Rosecrans, repositioned their respective armies. When the Confederacy's western army concentrated, Forrest came under the command of General Joseph Wheeler, a West Pointer fifteen years his junior. But soon Forrest resumed independent operations, under orders from Bragg to strike the enemy supply lines in western Tennessee.

Striking the enemy's supply lines would be no simple task. The logistics of operating behind Federal lines, in winter, over poor roads, with an inadequately armed command might have proved daunting. However, Forrest characteristically undertook the new mission with enterprise and common sense. In mid-December, he sent a team of men to prepare flatboats for the command to use in crossing the Tennessee River. In the meantime, he readied his troopers for a fast-paced raid in which they would be constantly surrounded and hounded by larger enemy forces attempting to bring them to bay. As always, Forrest had a sense of urgency.

Having crossed the Tennessee, Forrest ordered the flatboats sunk in shallow water so they could be retrieved when the command later attempted to recross that barrier. Then the Confederates proceeded in the direction of Lexington, running into approximately 800 Federals under Colonel Robert G. Ingersoll. After a short fight most of Ingersoll's men broke and ran for Jackson, leaving the colonel, 147 of his men and a sizable amount of weapons, ammunition, and other supplies in Forrest's hands.[22]

Among the most prized captures of the day were two three-inch Rodman guns. These guns became the nucleus around which Lieutenant John Morton formed the artillery battery that would serve Forrest well for the remainder of the war. Ironically, Morton initially thought Forrest was an extremely difficult commander. The general apparently suspected that Bragg had sent Morton to keep an eye on him and his command. When the young artilleryman first approached the cavalryman, Forrest lashed out, "I have a fine battery of six guns under Captain Freeman and I don't propose to be interfered with by Bragg." Morton assured him that this was not the case, but as soon as the young officer was out of earshot, Forrest turned to his aide and remarked, "I'd like to know why in the hell Bragg sent that tallow-faced boy here to take

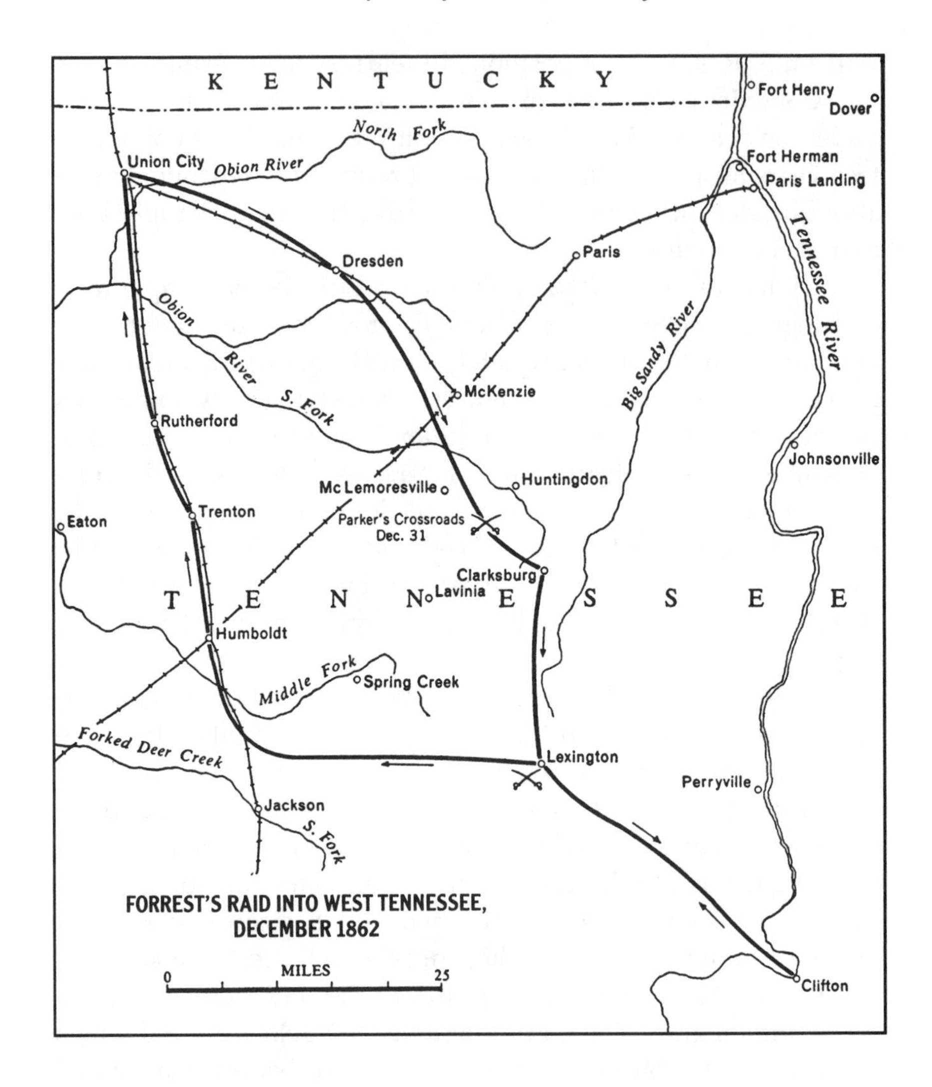

FORREST'S RAID INTO WEST TENNESSEE, DECEMBER 1862

charge of my artillery?" With emphasis, he added, "I'll not stand it. Captain Freeman shan't be interfered with!" However, Freeman generously lent the young officer two artillery pieces, which Morton returned when he took charge of the two captured Rodmans.[23]

Following their victory at Lexington, the Southerners quickly pressed on to Jackson. Union General Jeremiah Sullivan had 10,000 men concentrated there, but reports of Forrest's supposed superiority, brought in by the remnants of Ingersoll's men who straggled into town, and Forrest's elaborate efforts to deceive his enemy concerning the strength of his troops convinced Sullivan to hold his force for the defense of the town. Once again, Forrest proved a master of psychology and human nature. His force, variously inflated from 3,000 to 20,000, actually numbered 2,500, nearly half of whom were so badly armed as to be useless in a fight.[24] Confederate artilleryman Morton later remembered that his commander spared little opportunity to encourage these exaggerated estimates. "No device for creating this impression was too insignificant to be called into play," Morton explained. "The constant beating of kettledrums," to imply the presence of infantry marching along, "the lighting and tending of numerous fires, moving pieces of artillery from one point to another, the dismounting of cavalry and parading them as infantry—nothing was overlooked."[25] Forrest's misinformation campaign later included paroled prisoners, who spread the intelligence that the Southern commander carefully crafted for them.[26] The Confederate cavalryman's orchestrations paid handsome dividends. Instead of bringing his superior numbers to bear against the Confederate raider, General Sullivan concentrated his forces in Jackson, conceded the surrounding countryside, and awaited developments. Forrest could have asked for nothing more.

Ingersoll's capture gave the raid a good beginning. Forrest had eliminated a serious Federal force in the area and spread panic throughout the region. His various ploys to inflate his numbers added further to the Union commander's worries, prompting them to remain within their lines at Jackson and leaving him free to roam, at least for the moment. Grant had dispatched troops to help fend off the Southern blows at his rail lines and supply depots, but they had not yet arrived.

However, Forrest was not one to rest on laurels won. He wanted to isolate the strong outpost and rail junction of Jackson and wreak as much havoc on Grant's supply lines as he could. He ordered two detachments to accomplish that task, while he and the rest of the command prepared for a show of force before Jackson the next day. One of these detachments left at ten o'clock on the evening of December 18 and rode through the night to be in position to attack Carroll Station, north of the town. At first light, Colonel Dibrell and his men promptly charged; the garrison protecting the station quickly surrendered, and the Confederates began the systematic destruction of the post and the rail line. Dibrell's attack netted 101 prisoners and as many rifles. Many of his men carried flintlocks, which they exchanged for the better weapons they had captured.[27]

While Dibrell's men dealt with Carroll Station, another detachment, under Colonel Russell, sped off to the south and west to disrupt the railroads that led to Corinth and Bolivar, respectively. Forrest expected them to lay waste to that section of rail, destroying culverts, trestles, and bridges. At Jackson, Union General Sullivan attested to their success, reporting that word had arrived that "the bridges 12 miles south were burned, and that a large force had crossed going toward the railroad leading to Bolivar."[28] Russell's men spent the remainder of the day dismantling railroads, pausing only long enough to let a sizable force of Union infantry under Colonel John W. Fuller pass on the way from Oxford, Mississippi, to Jackson, where they arrived late in the afternoon of December 19.[29]

In the meantime, at dawn on December 19, Forrest launched his feint against Sullivan's forces in Jackson. Although he expected only to hold the Federals in place in the town while his men ravaged the nearby rail lines, Forrest accomplished much more than that. He deployed his troops and used his artillery so effectively that he succeeded in driving the Federal cavalry back into the fortifications. As the Union commander noted delicately in his report: "At this time the cavalry both on my right and left flanks, weary from the hardships to which they had been exposed for the two preceding days, and now under the fire of the enemy's battery, fell back about a mile towards Jackson without having first obtained any orders from me to that effect."[30] When Sullivan finally ventured out of Jackson the next day, reinforced by Fuller's men, he found that most of the Southerners were gone.

Forrest left only a thin screen of skirmishers to continue the ruse while he raced north toward Humboldt and Trenton. Again he divided the tasks at hand to cover the maximum ground and inflict the greatest damage. To Dibrell, he assigned the capture of the bridge over Forked Deer Creek. To Starnes, he gave the assault on Humboldt, while he allotted himself the strike against Trenton.

The first of these missions went badly. Dibrell arrived at

Forked Deer Creek to find that reinforcements had arrived from Jackson. He could do little more than annoy the Union garrison while the other columns attacked their respective targets. At the same time, Starnes and Forrest enjoyed considerably greater success. Starnes met little resistance and had no difficulty capturing Humboldt, its garrison, and large amounts of governmental property. But while he burned the depot and bridge and such supplies as he could not carry off, his commander was encountering much more stubborn resistance at Trenton. That garrison had taken great care with its defense, using bales of cotton and hogsheads of tobacco and constructing loopholes in the brick masonry of the train station. Thus, when Forrest's troopers rode into town, they encountered a withering fire that emptied several saddles. Rather than continue to test the defenses with frontal assaults, Forrest surrounded the garrison and ordered his artillery to blast his opponents into submission. It was a wise decision. By the third round, Colonel Jacob Fry had had enough and surrendered his seven hundred soldiers.[31]

Trenton further augmented Forrest's command with weapons, ammunition, and other supplies. Among the more useful items was a considerable quantity of counterfeit Confederate bills, printed too perfectly to be taken as real, that some of the Southerners used for poker money. Forrest, himself, obtained a handsome saber, which he characteristically sharpened on both edges for better use in close-hand fighting.[32] He then spent the remainder of the day and night paroling prisoners and destroying captured Union supplies and facilities. He could not afford the guards to watch these men, especially since he needed to move swiftly to elude his pursuers and continue his campaign of destroying the enemy rail and supply systems.

The next morning, he started his command toward Union City, destroying bridges and rails as he went. His various detachments rejoined him on the march. At Rutherford Station, Forrest easily captured two companies of Federals. Then, at nearby Kenton Station, he took more prisoners and destroyed more bridges and rails. The destruction of the vast trestlework over the Obion River required the rest of the day and part of the next.[33]

While teams of Confederates hacked and burned these structures, the rest moved on to Union City. Again, the Southerners were fortunate. They had barely arrived in front of the Union post and deployed to fire on it, when a flag of truce yielded the desired results, and the Federal garrison surrendered. However, Forrest's actions at Union City again pointed to the differences between the manner in which he and the regular army officers of both sides conducted the war. His straightforward and unsophisticated approach to war yielded results, but often ruffled feathers. In this case, the controversy centered on the use of the flag of truce. Forrest had earlier dispatched an officer, Lieutenant Colonel N. D. Collins, and all the paroled Union prisoners under such a flag toward the Union lines. Having obtained paroles, the prisoners were under obligation to wait until they were properly exchanged to rejoin their units and return to the war. The practice, commonly accepted and employed, allowed prisoners to return to their lines without requiring them to endure internment in a prisoner-of-war camp.

To this end, Collins and the prisoners marched northward, reaching Union City a short while (twenty minutes by the Federal commander's account) before Forrest arrived with the main force. Thus the main Southern column approached, surrounded the post, and sent in a second flag of truce, while the Union commander, Captain Samuel B. Logan, negotiated with Collins under the first one. As it happened, neither commander met initially under this second flag; both sent subordinates. However, Logan objected that Forrest had used the earlier flag of truce to gain an advantage over him. But, if the Union officer had hoped to buy time with his legalistic objection, he failed to understand Bedford Forrest. Forrest saw no connection between the two flags of truce and brushed the argument aside, insisting upon "the immediate and unconditional surrender" of the garrison. The Union commander had no choice but to comply. Logan later concluded of the whole episode, "I would do Lieutenant-Colonel Collins and General Forrest whatever justice there may be in their emphatic denial of collusion in the two flags of truce."[34]

However the Federal commander of Union City may have felt, Forrest was eminently satisfied with the work thus far, noting in his December 24 report: "We have made a clean sweep of the Federals and [rail]roads north of Jackson."[35] His presence harried

Union commanders even farther north. One general, Thomas A. Davies, ordered the troops at Island No. 10 and New Madrid to spike the heavy guns and dump their powder stores into the Mississippi, to prevent them from falling into Forrest's hands, even though Forrest had demonstrated no interest in advancing against those positions. Davies was so sure that he had actually accomplished something that he proudly boasted in his report, "I kept Forrest, however, for several days under the impression that I was going to give him battle outside, by the movement of trains and the circulating of rumors. He has been richly paid for his temerity and boldness."[36] One general became so alarmed at Davies's actions that he telegraphed General Grant describing Davies as "easily frightened" and concluded, "You will hardly endorse all this."[37] But if Forrest enjoyed the chaos he created, he still faced the much more difficult task of extracting his command from the Union vise that was beginning to close on it.

On Christmas Day, Forrest turned his command east from Union City toward Dresden and McKenzie, to continue his destructive work. Along the way, Lieutenant Colonel T. A. Napier and 430 men joined his command. Rain soaked the Southerners throughout the next day. That evening they arrived at Dresden, subdued the garrison, and destroyed the supplies and rails there. On December 27 Forrest moved on to McKenzie. There he learned that a significant force of Union troops was hot on his trail. He also learned that the Federals had destroyed the bridges across the Obion River, hoping to trap him. The rising waters of the river seemed to spell more trouble for the Confederate raiders. A confident General Sullivan wired Grant, "I have Forrest in a tight place.... The gunboats are up the river as far as Clifton and have destroyed all the bridges and ferries.... My troops are moving on him from three directions, and I hope with success."[38] At first reluctant to move, Sullivan now appeared on the verge of trapping and crushing Forrest's command.

Indeed, Forrest might have been in a serious predicament, except that he was ever alert to opportunities, and an unlikely one presented itself. The Federals had destroyed the best bridges over the Obion, but they had ignored an extremely rickety one, on the road midway between McKenzie and McLemoresville, perhaps thinking that it was too unsound to allow passage across it. In this bridge, Forrest saw salvation and immediately set his men to work shoring up the structure. Perhaps as a way of impressing the importance of this work on the men, Forrest "made a full hand" himself in the work. And, when they had finished, he drove the first team across personally, as he had done at Fort Donelson. Before long, the entire command had safely crossed the river and extricated itself from the trap.[39]

Having spent the night forcing their way across the makeshift bridge over the Obion, Forrest rested the bulk of his men, while others scoured the roads for enemy pursuit. After only a couple of hours rest, the general received word that a large Union force, estimated at ten thousand, was bearing down upon them. Thus warned, he started the command on the road to Lexington. On December 29 and 30, the Confederates camped at Flake's Store, only a few miles northwest of a tiny community called Parker's Crossroads, or Red Mound. Forrest continued to send out detachments to locate and advise him of Union movements. His brother Captain William Forrest led one, and late on December 30, William's detachment ran into a strong Union infantry command marching toward the crossroads. Realizing that the close proximity of the enemy meant that any subsequent crossing of the Tennessee would be a hot one, Forrest decided to fight there. If he could defeat the Union column, he could race toward Clifton, refloat the sunken barges, and effect a less harried crossing.

To that end, Bedford instructed his younger brother to harass the Union force and keep him informed of its progress. The general wanted to rest his command as much as possible before it took on the Federal infantry. At the same time, the Union commander, Colonel Cyrus L. Dunham, sent word back to his superior, General Sullivan, to hurry the rest of the command toward Parker's Crossroads, since he hoped to "coax or force a fight" out of Forrest early on December 31.[40]

Before daylight that day, both Dunham's Federals and Forrest's Confederates moved toward the crossroads. Dunham arrived first, chased off a small force of Southern pickets, deployed his men along the intersection, and waited for Forrest's main column to appear. Dispatching several companies to watch the road from

Huntington, under orders to report the approach of any Union reinforcements from that quarter, Forrest soon obliged Dunham. He threw Dibrell's and Russell's regiments forward as skirmishers with artillery support. Following a brief but intense artillery duel, the main Union line withdrew and repositioned itself beyond the crossroads, still blocking the road south.

Forrest dismounted the bulk of his troops and pushed them forward, placing his artillery in advance of his line and employing it at extremely close range. The dismounted men advanced slowly and deliberately, using all available cover. Forrest placed the greatest burden of the fight on his artillery, hoping to win the battle with his cannoneers, "and unless absolutely necessary was not pressing them with my cavalry." The strategy appeared to be working. "I had them entirely surrounded," he observed, "and was driving them before me, and was taking it leisurely, and trying as much as possible to save my men."[41]

Indeed, Forrest's artillerymen performed well. They helped drive the Union line behind a split-rail fence and pushed to within two hundred yards of this new defensive position. Undoubtedly expecting the fence to protect them, the Federals found that it added to their woes. The Confederate artillery continued to pour a galling fire into them, badly splintering the fence and turning its shards into deadly missiles. Forrest later recalled that "their position in the fence corners proved ... a source of great loss, as our shot and shell scattered them to the winds, and many were killed by rails that were untouched by balls."[42] Twice the Federals left their pseudoshelter to charge the Confederate guns only to meet repulse with even greater loss.

About this time, Colonel Napier, who had only recently joined Forrest's command, launched an unauthorized assault against the Union line. He fell mortally wounded at the rail fence, and his men retreated back to their original lines. Forrest had no desire for such gallantry. He had a different plan in mind. The general hoped to repeat the tactics he had used on earlier battlefields with great success. He divided his command, sending Starnes's regiment around the enemy's left flank and Russell's regiment and Colonel Thomas G. Woodward's battalion around the enemy's right. While these units maneuvered to their respective positions,

Forrest shifted his artillery to the Confederate's right, where it could work with greater effect against the Union left flank. In the meantime, Dunham's men left their defenses for a new assault against the Confederates' main line. Again, the concentration of artillery proved too much for them. Dunham's advance melted in the cross fire and fell back to the rail fence.

As the Federals withdrew, Forrest saw his opportunity and pressed home his assault. He ordered the entire line to advance. The murderous toll of shelling and the effect of the general Southern advance quickly shattered the Union line. The Thirty-ninth Iowa, positioned on the Union extreme left, broke and fled in disorder. The commander of the Thirty-ninth attempted to stem the rout, with little success, observing, "They then in more confusion fell back toward the fence, and received standing the fire of the enemy's artillery, and under it and the fire from the rear the confusion became worse."[43] As the Federal officer's report indicated, by this time, the combined forces of Russell and Woodward had struck the Union rear, capturing the Union supply train and causing even greater chaos in the Federal lines.

By now the fight was almost over. Dunham's line had disintegrated from the combined assaults and heavy artillery fire. He no longer had artillery with which to respond. With a typical touch of frontier zest, Forrest noted, "We drove them through the woods with great slaughter and several white flags were raised in various portions of the woods and the killed and wounded were strewn over the ground."[44] The fire quickly subsided as the two sides began to observe a truce to discuss the surrender of Dunham's Federals.

Then, almost as suddenly as the firing had stopped, it began again, but this time not between Forrest and Dunham. The firing came from the Confederates' rear. A thoroughly astonished Forrest, certain that he had protected himself against just such a development, "could not believe that they were Federals until I rode myself into their lines."[45] He got so close that some of the Union soldiers he encountered ordered him to surrender. He replied that he had already done so, adding shrewdly, "I'll go back and get what few men I have left."[46] With that, he wheeled his horse around and rode off to attempt to salvage the increasingly desperate situation.

Forrest remembered correctly. He had sent several companies to guard the Huntington road along which Union reinforcements were most likely to come. But the Confederates had taken the wrong road, missed the advance of Union Colonel John W. Fuller's regiment, and thus failed to warn Forrest of the Federals' advance. The first inkling the Confederate commander had that something was wrong was the sudden burst of musketry and the stampede of horses and horse holders who had been stationed in the rear of the lines. Approximately three hundred of his men became prisoners when they raced back to get their horses.[47]

Despite his surprise, a calm General Forrest is supposed to have responded to an excited staff officer's request for instructions: "Charge them both ways!"[48] Although the statement is probably apocryphal, Forrest had virtually no other choice, short of surrender, to save the bulk of his command. Without the possibility of coordinating their efforts, his subordinates acted promptly to assist him. Russell and Starnes, farthest from the new attack, immediately deciphered what had happened and ordered assaults of their own against Dunham's still-demoralized troops. These assaults ensured that Dunham's force remained busy while Forrest struggled to free his command from the trap.

At the same time, Forrest, his escort, and part of Dibrell's command gathered for an attack against Fuller's newly arrived Federals. If they could neutralize this force, they might be able to escape. The importance of the assault made it imperative that Forrest pull together as many men as possible for it. But when the general accosted one soldier, ordering him into line for the charge, the man protested that he did not have a weapon. Forrest instantly responded, "That doesn't make any difference; get in line and advance on the enemy with the rest; I want to make as big a show as possible."[49] With this force, the indefatigable cavalryman led a charge against Fuller's artillery, scattering the gunners and their infantry support. The bold maneuver bought him the time he needed to ride across the face of Dunham's command and race for safety.

Forrest was able to extricate most of his men from the battle at Parker's Crossroads. The men rested briefly at Lexington, before moving on to Clifton. On New Year's Day, 1863, General Forrest parried a final blow from his Union pursuers when he defeated and scattered a cavalry regiment that was attempting to keep him from crossing the Tennessee River. He paroled the prisoners who were still in his hands and set about recrossing the river. In approximately eight to ten hours the Confederates were safely across that final barrier, having rafted the men, artillery, and supplies and swum the horses to the other side. Forrest's eventful western Tennessee raid was over.[50]

Despite Forrest's rough handling at Parker's Crossroads, his western Tennessee raid was by any measure a success. Coupled with General Earl Van Dorn's dramatic attack, capture, and destruction of Grant's forward supply base at Holly Springs, Mississippi, Forrest's raid crippled Grant's initial assault on Vicksburg. Van Dorn eliminated the stockpiles of supplies that the Union general had accumulated nearby, while Forrest wrecked the railroads along which new supplies would principally have to come. Grant's determination to catch and punish Forrest and his raiders underscored the respect he had for that officer. As one contemporary explained: "He [Forrest] was the only Confederate cavalryman of whom Grant stood in much dread," adding that while the Union general usually dismissed news of other raiders, "if Forrest was in command he at once became apprehensive, because the latter was amenable to no known rules of procedure, was a law unto himself for all military acts, and was constantly doing the unexpected at all times and places."[51]

General Sullivan's elation after Parker's Crossroads may have temporarily taken the edge off Grant's apprehension. Indeed, Sullivan was so pleased with the outcome of the battle that he wired the latter on the evening of December 31: "We met Forrest seven thousand strong, and after a contest of four hours routed him with great slaughter."[52] Then on January 2, he concluded, "Forrest's army is completely broken up. They are scattered over the country without ammunition. We need a good cavalry command to go through the country and pick them up."[53] A relieved General Grant replied to the news with unconcealed joy: "You have done a fine job," he told Sullivan, "retrieved all lost at Trenton and north of you."[54] That this report was patently untrue did not matter to the Union general. He was happy to be rid of Forrest.

Forrest and his command were not quite so "broken up" as Sullivan and Grant believed them to be. To be sure, they were hurt; Sullivan noted that the Southern "dead, I have good reason to believe, is 200; their prisoners over 400. My loss will not exceed 100 killed and wounded; prisoners, 63."[55] Later returns showed the Union casualties to be slightly higher, at 167 killed and wounded and 70 captured.[56] On January 3, Forrest reported to Bragg, "I have not been able as yet to ascertain our exact loss, but am of the opinion that 60 killed and wounded and 100 captured or missing will cover it." Actually, his casualties were certainly far heavier.[57]

In the wake of Parker's Crossroads, Forrest moved his weary command to Columbia, Tennessee, where it anchored the left flank of Bragg's army and rested and refitted for the balance of the month of January. There was much to do. Horses needed shoes, wounded men needed attention, and tired troopers needed rest. But the recovery period, as badly desired as it might be, was short. In the meantime, Bragg clashed with the new Union army commander, William S. Rosecrans, in a monumental battle at Stones River (Murfreesboro) from December 31, 1862, to January 2, 1863. Although the battle was technically a draw, the Confederates finally retreated. On January 26 Bragg summoned Forrest to his headquarters at Shelbyville, to which he had withdrawn.

Bragg informed the Confederate cavalryman that a portion of his men were already marching toward the Cumberland River under General Joseph Wheeler, to interrupt navigation on that river, and that he should overtake the expedition and assume command of those troops. Forrest raced after them, joining the column after two days' hard riding.

Initially, the Confederates took up positions at Palmyra, where they expected to ambush any supply transports that attempted to pass. When it became clear that the Federals were aware of their presence and would send no vessels within range of them, the Southern commanders weighed the alternatives and opted for an attack against the fortified post of Dover, next to Fort Donelson. Wheeler noted in his report on the ensuing engagement, "After maturely considering the matter, we concluded that nothing could be lost by an attack upon the garrison at Dover, and, from the information we had from spies, citizens, and other sources, we had good reason to believe the garrison could be easily captured."[58]

Wheeler's use of the pronoun "we" is particularly interesting, given Forrest's apparent opposition to the scheme. According to biographers Thomas Jordan and J. P. Pryor, whose text Forrest examined and approved, the general registered his disapproval of the idea, noting the detriments of making such an attack and insisting that those negatives far outweighed any possible benefits to be derived from the post's capture.[59] Later, biographer John Allan Wyeth supported this contention, observing, "The premonition of disaster weighed upon Forrest so heavily that on the morning of the engagement he spoke of the matter in strict confidence to his chief-of-staff, Charles W. Anderson," and the surgeon. In the course of this private conversation Forrest explained, "I have protested against the move, but my protest has been disregarded, and I intend to do my whole duty, and I want my men to do the same." He proceeded to request of the two staffers, "If I am killed in this fight, you will see that justice is done me by officially stating that I protested against the attack, and that I am not willing to be held responsible for any disaster that may result."[60]

Thus, on February 3, 1863, when Generals Wheeler, Forrest, and Wharton arrived before the Union defenses at Dover, there was some difference of opinion regarding the propriety of the operation.[61] But in any event, the Southerners won the opening blow of the contest when they captured a small force of Union pickets outside the works. Then events turned against them. As overall commander, Wheeler dispatched a demand for the immediate surrender of the fort, also signed by Forrest and Wharton. The plucky Union commander, Colonel A. C. Harding, respectfully declined to "surrender the forces under my command or the post without an effort to defend them."[62]

Accordingly, Wheeler placed his batteries on ground overlooking the Union's defenses and hammered away at them. He expected to follow the bombardment with a general attack by dismounted cavalry. But despite his earlier reservations, Forrest suddenly warmed to the idea of attacking the fortified post when he saw enemy soldiers moving away from the works. As Wheeler later

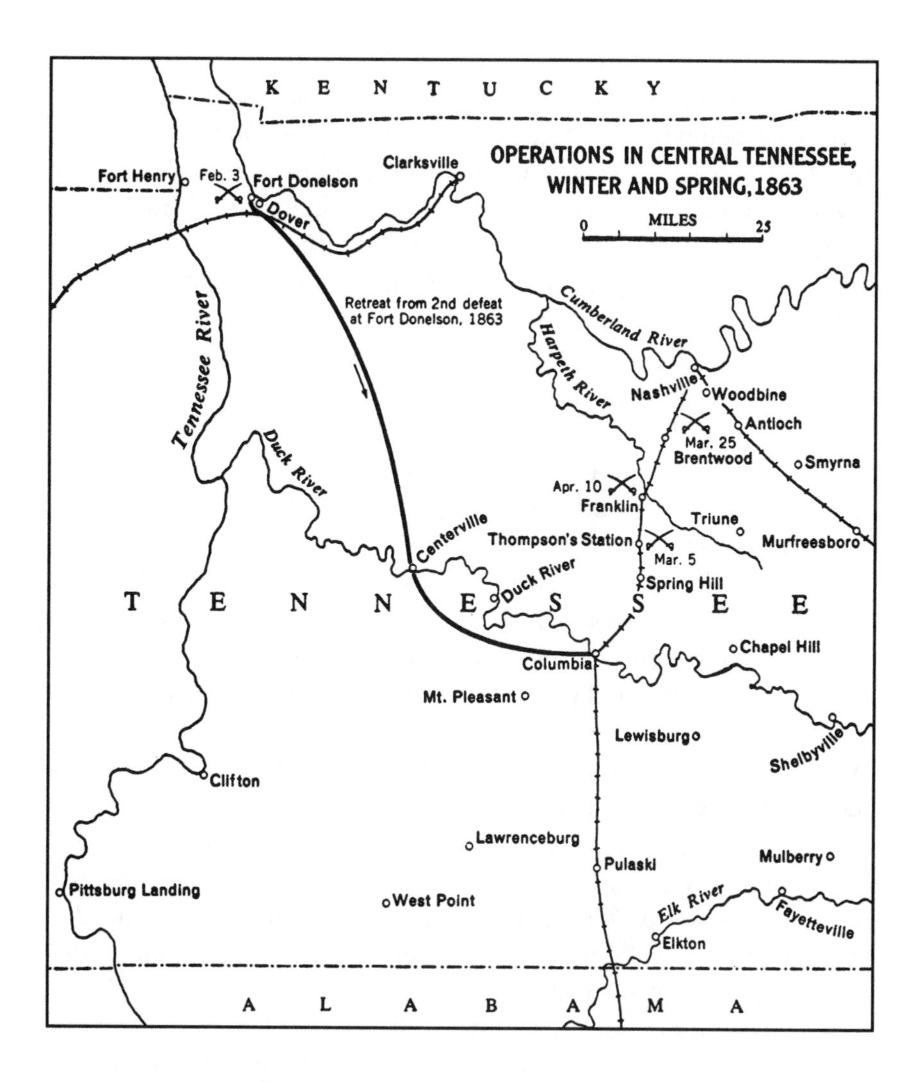

reported: "Just as I left General Forrest to assist General Wharton (in forming for the attack), General Forrest, thinking the enemy were leaving the place, and being anxious to rush in quickly, remounted his men and charged the place on horseback."[63]

Actually, the Union commander had no intention of abandoning his post, and Forrest's impetuous assault met serious resistance. When Forrest misread the enemy's movements, remounted, and attacked, he not only suffered a blistering repulse, but ruined Wheeler's chances for a coordinated general attack. The attacks became piecemeal, and even the relatively small number of Federals in the works had no real difficulty turning them back.

Other factors, aside from the desire to attack the enemy troops whom he believed to be abandoning their post, may have motivated Forrest to act so impulsively. Before arriving at Dover, the cavalry commander had insisted upon inspecting his men. The inspection revealed that they were dreadfully short of ammunition. Thus, Forrest may have hoped that by attacking quickly and capturing the garrison suddenly, he could mitigate that shortage and, at the same time, redeem the surprise and the resultant casualties he had suffered earlier at Parker's Crossroads. The attack was a gamble, but he thought it was worth trying. Forrest's ill-advised attack helped to deplete the limited stock of available ammunition and doomed the Confederates' attempt to take Dover to almost certain defeat.

Nevertheless, while Forrest's impetuous action might have been unwise, it did not lack for bravery. The mounted assault was short lived but furious, resulting in considerable loss to the Confederates. Harding had placed a 32-pounder siege gun, taken from the water batteries after Fort Donelson's fall the previous spring, at a critical point in his defense perimeter. Thus, when the wave of screaming Confederates, led by Forrest, crashed against the Union's works, this piece of heavy artillery proved particularly deadly. In his report, Harding noted: "In an instant the siege gun was double-shotted with canister, and turned upon them and discharged, tearing one man to atoms and two horses, within 10 feet of the muzzle."[64] Forrest had a horse killed beneath him, and when he fell momentarily out of sight, most of his men retreated, thinking their commander was dead. But the general, still very much alive and miraculously uninjured, managed to pull himself free from the animal and, in Wyeth's polite appraisal, "made his way to the rear with scant regard to the order of his going."[65]

Having dashed unceremoniously for safety, a slightly wiser Forrest gathered his men for a second charge, this time on foot. He also advanced in tandem with General Wharton's attack, but the result was little better. Forrest's men succeeded in driving some sharpshooters from houses in front of the works, but failed to carry the main Union lines. Again the casualties mounted in the face of severe resistance. For the second time, Forrest lost his horse to hostile fire, and he severely injured himself in this second fall. With the Southern attack floundering badly, many of the Confederate horsemen fell back to the houses to shield themselves from the galling fire. Short of ammunition themselves, the Federals launched an impromptu charge to reconnect their forward rifle pits, which contained several units and all their reserve ammunition, cut off by the fighting. The maneuver may have determined their fate, for when the Southerners saw the charge, they thought that it was an attempt to stampede their horses. They abandoned the houses and dashed to head the Federals off. Wheeler viewed this action as decisive: "But for this accident the garrison would have surrendered in a very few minutes."[66] Of course, whether Wheeler's assessment reflected military reality, the Confederates had to admit that they were soundly beaten, physically exhausted, and practically out of ammunition. They were certainly in no shape to renew the offensive.

Toward the end of the day, Wheeler tried one final time to bluff the garrison into a surrender that he had been unable to force upon them. He suggested that he had used only half his men in the fighting thus far and was now prepared to overrun the Union position with all his men. Again, Harding declined the offer. Wheeler met with Forrest and Wharton, and all agreed that further assaults would achieve nothing. Reports of the arrival of a substantial number of Union reinforcements made withdrawal even more imperative. Wheeler paused only long enough to send out detachments to burn a barge loaded with Federal supplies and to gather the wounded and the captured stores before retreating from the stubbornly defended town.[67]

That night the despondent Confederates camped four miles from the scene of their dismal repulse. Forrest had lost fully one-quarter of his men in two fruitless attacks at Dover. The Union commander estimated the Confederates' total losses at 150 killed, 600 wounded, and 105 prisoners, the bulk of which came from Forrest's command, while he placed his entire loss at only 13 killed, 51 wounded, and 46 captured.[68] The three Southern generals spent most of the night huddled around a fire attempting to figure out where they had gone wrong. There was much to discuss. Wheeler scribbled his report of the fiasco to Bragg, while

Bedford fumed. Forrest was in a fearful mood. Sore from his fall, angry at the repulse, and disturbed by the toll exacted by the fighting upon his command, he found little solace in the dancing flames on this cold night.

The arrival of Forrest's aide, Major Charles W. Anderson, momentarily interrupted their activities, but did nothing to cool the anger boiling inside the disgruntled general. According to Anderson, Forrest marched over to the only available bed, ordered the occupants to vacate it for his frozen staff officer, and returned to his place by the fireside. In the meantime Wharton gave his report orally while Wheeler wrote and Forrest listened. "As we fell back," Wharton recalled of the day's events, "I noticed the garrison from our side of the fort rush across to the other side to take part against General Forrest's attack, and, as his command caught the fire of the entire garrison, he must have suffered severely." Wharton had struck a nerve.

Forrest suddenly bolted upright and angrily insisted, "I have no fault to find with my men. In both charges they did their duty as they have always done." Wheeler interjected that his report assigned no such fault. "General Forrest, my report does ample justice to yourself and your men." But the commander's attempt to quell his subordinate's anger managed only to direct it upon himself. Forrest was in no mood to drop what he had already started. "General Wheeler," he snarled, "I advised you against this attack, and said all a subordinate officer should have said against it, and nothing you can now say or do will bring back my brave men lying dead and wounded and freezing around that fort tonight." His tenuous control already gone, Forrest ended with a flourish. "I mean no disrespect to you; you know my feelings of personal friendship for you; you can have my sword if you demand it; but there is one thing I do want you to put in that report to General Bragg—tell him that I will be in my coffin before I will fight again under your command." A weary General Wheeler waited patiently until the storm had passed and then responded quietly, "Forrest. I cannot take your saber, and I regret exceedingly your determination. As the commanding officer I take all the blame and responsibility for this failure." There was nothing more to be said. Even Forrest knew that.[69]

CHAPTER 6

A Streight Bluff

(February–May 1863)

Whenever you see anything blue, shoot at it, and do all you can to keep up the scare.

—NATHAN BEDFORD FORREST

Ah, Colonel, all is fair in love and war you know.

—FORREST TO COLONEL ABEL STREIGHT

BEDFORD FORREST'S RESPONSE to the events at Dover reveal a great deal. As an individual born and raised in the Southern backcountry, he understood war on its simplest level; yet, he also saw himself as the defender and protector of his men. His miscalculation of Union intentions at Dover led to an impulsive and disastrous initial attack. The assault lacked nothing of courage, but demonstrated the difficulty Forrest had acting in tandem with others. Part of this difficulty was that when called upon to act as a team player, he had to surrender (or share) control over himself and his troops to (or with) others. This need for absolute control allowed him to achieve some of his greatest military successes, but it also was his greatest failing or weakness as a soldier. In the case of Dover, once the operation proved a failure, he sought to shift the blame and berate his superior for squandering the lives of his men. This behavior was typical of Forrest, who found it difficult to admit, especially while his temper was up, that he was responsible for any of the negative results of his actions.

In any event, the next day, February 4, the Southern column continued its withdrawal. The troops avoided an encounter with a large Union force under General Jefferson C. Davis (no relation to the president of the Confederacy) and returned to Confederate lines. Forrest spent the next several weeks reorganizing his command. A. A. Russell's Fourth Alabama transferred out, and Forrest consolidated several battle-weakened units into the Tenth Tennessee under N. N. Cox and the Eleventh Tennessee under James H. Edmondson. Bedford wanted to return to the field as quickly as possible to exact some measure of revenge upon the enemy for his repulse at Dover, but he wanted his men in the best condition to march again. He was even willing to employ regular army techniques: "I am going to have my forces thoroughly organized before I go out into the field again. I have ordered dress-parade twice per week."[1]

General Forrest soon had the opportunity to test his command's readiness. On March 4, lead elements of Confederate cavalry, under the immediate command of General William H. Jackson and the overall command of General Earl Van Dorn, collided with a substantial Union force near Thompson's Station. The two forces exchanged long-range artillery fire before a Federal advance forced the Southern cavalry to fall back. By this point, Van Dorn had arrived with the remainder of his men and disposed them to await the Union advance the next day.

The Union commander, Colonel John Coburn, slowly marched out the next day. It was nine-thirty or ten o'clock before a reluctant Coburn finally moved against the Confederates' center and left. From his place at the extreme right end of the Southern line, Forrest watched as the Federals advanced, briefly held their ground, and finally fell back. At that juncture, General Forrest pushed his artillery half a mile in front of his main line, all the time adjusting his dismounted cavalry line forward. From this new vantage point, Captain Samuel L. Freeman's battery drove off their Union counterparts. Then Van Dorn instructed Forrest to go forward and attempt to attack the Federals from the rear.

In the meantime, the bulk of the Confederate forces, including two of Forrest's regiments, repeatedly assaulted the Union flank and front, while Bedford, with the remainder of his command, worked his way around to the enemy's rear. For the most part, the Federals stoutly defended against these maneuvers, driving back the Confederates' attacks with some loss. Forrest was able to crack through the stubborn Union resistance only after two charges, in one of which he lost yet another horse. When he finally did so, the way lay open to the Union column's only line of retreat. Although the end was now only a matter of time, Forrest encountered even heavier fighting. A final charge in the face of galling fire proved decisive. He broke through the Union line and forced Coburn to surrender.

While Forrest's men overran the last Union resistance, a portion of his command rode off to chase down the remnants of the Federals who had gotten away before the jaws of the trap slammed shut. The Southerners harassed these men until they had reached Nashville, capturing an additional seventy-five prisoners. Van Dorn's Confederates, largely through the timely actions of Forrest's cavalry, captured approximately 1,221 men. Forrest listed his casualties as 9 killed; 58 wounded, some mortally; and 2 missing. Van Dorn's total loss stood at 357 killed, wounded, and captured or missing.[2]

Forrest's men had fought as if they had something to prove. Artilleryman John Morton later remembered that the "command was eager for an opportunity to wipe out the disappointment of Dover."[3] Bedford, himself, was still inordinately sensitive from that experience and attempted to compensate in his Thompson Station report. He made sure that no negative connotation could remain attached to his men after this battle: "I cannot speak in too high terms of the conduct of my whole command. The colonels commanding led their regiments in person, and it affords me much pleasure to say that officers and men performed their duty well. I discerned no straggling or shirking from duty on the field. Every order was promptly obeyed, and the bravery of the troops alike creditable to them and gratifying to their commanders."[4]

Following the battle of Thompson's Station, Forrest's cavalrymen returned to their normal routine of picket duty and camp life. Occasional skirmishing broke out between the two armies. Sometimes it was fairly severe. Then, on March 15, Forrest received his assignment as head of a division of cavalry made up of his brigade and that of General Frank C. Armstrong. With these men, he marched out a week later to surprise and capture the Union troops garrisoned at Brentwood.

Through the night of March 24, Forrest and his men maneuvered into position. They struck at dawn the next day. The Southerners moved swiftly around the flank, again to cut off the enemy's line of retreat. Once they had done so, General Forrest sent in a demand for surrender. The Union commander initially rejected it, instructing the Confederate cavalryman to "come and get him." But his nerve proved somewhat weaker than his words, and he surrendered the command without a shot being fired. Ironically, these Federals, numbering 529 officers and men, had fought earlier at Thompson's Station and escaped to Nashville, only to be captured a few weeks later. Forrest's men suffered only one man killed and two wounded in the operation.[5]

Forrest left these prisoners to Starnes and took the rest of his men toward Franklin. They encountered a heavily defended bridge. Typically, the Confederate general sent his counterpart in the stockade a demand for surrender, which the latter promptly rejected. Then Forrest brought up his artillery and sent a shot into the stockade, whereupon the Federals accepted his offer and marched out as his prisoners. These 230 men had also been part of Coburn's ill-fated command at Thompson's Station.[6]

Forrest's men destroyed the captured stockade and bridge and began the return march to Confederate lines with their prisoners. As a precaution, the general sent a detachment in the direction of Nashville to watch for the approach of enemy pursuers. The detachment moved to within four miles of the Tennessee capital, capturing a few Federals. Its approach caused a stir in Nashville and diverted a good bit of attention from Forrest's withdrawal. However, a good bit was not all, for, in the meantime, a sizable force of Union cavalry struck the Confederates who were guarding the wagons they had captured at Brentwood. The Federals succeeded in recapturing some of the wagons before Forrest rode up with enough men to drive them off with some loss. The Southerners continued their march without further aggravation.[7]

The experiences of one Confederate during the Brentwood raid illustrate one of the reasons for Forrest's military success. Just prior to the operation, Newton Cannon volunteered for scouting duty. He recalled that Forrest asked him to infiltrate the area around Brentwood, taking "notes of all roads and creeks of any size that [I] crossed and where I saw army boddies [units] of the enemy and report back." Cannon fulfilled his mission and hastened back to camp where the general laid out a crude map and "told me to mark out my trip going and coming stop at the crossing of road or creek and explain." During the raid, he served as one of the pilots, or guides, for the main column. When Forrest released Cannon from his special assignment, he remarked to his adjutant "that he had sent several of the best men he had and that damned little boy had made him the only sensible report."[8] Another of Forrest's scouts recalled that he would send out squads "in every direction ... constantly reporting to Forrest's Headquarters movement or no movement." He explained that the general considered it "just as important for him [using his own language] 'To know where they aint—as to know where they are.'"[9]

The Confederate victories at Thompson's Station and Brentwood had at least one unexpected side effect, involving Generals Forrest and Van Dorn. Accounts differed as to what factor precipitated the disagreement and who acted first to end it, but the two officers lost their tempers and nearly had a violent confrontation. According to one version, Van Dorn became irritated by newspaper reports that tended to magnify Forrest's role in the two recent Southern victories and that he believed were authored by one of Forrest's staff members. In both of the other accounts the generals quarreled over the distribution of captured military supplies. In all three versions, tempers flared, until Van Dorn, in one, and Forrest, in the other two, made dramatic gestures toward reconciliation that allowed both men to save face.[10]

Forrest's Confederates settled back into their routine until April 10, when they took part in a heavy reconnaissance in the direction of Franklin. General Van Dorn believed that the Federals had evacuated the town, but wanted to confirm his belief. To that end, Forrest's men drove up the Lewisburg Turnpike and by midmorning encountered Union pickets. The Confederates moved along in column, with Armstrong's men in the lead, easily pushing the pickets before them. Colonel James W. Starnes came next and was so lulled by the ease with which General Armstrong was moving that he neglected to put enough outriders on his flanks. This omission proved costly. Union cavalry suddenly swooped down upon him, striking his command in the flank and capturing Captain Freeman, his battery, and thirty men before anyone could respond. As soon as he realized what had happened, Starnes turned to fight. The first minutes were chaotic. The caissons from Freeman's battery managed to escape, but scattered the nearest friendly regiments in the process. Staff officers raced back along the lines to bring other units to the front. Following a brief struggle, the Confederates succeeded in recapturing their artillery pieces, but failed to liberate Captain Freeman. Their failure cost him his life. As he ran along in the hands of his captors, they apparently did not believe that he was running fast enough, so one of the Union cavalrymen shot him through the head and rode away.[11]

As Forrest rode back to retrieve the situation, he also began to consolidate his command. He sent a courier out looking for Morton, then on the Columbia Turnpike with his battery. The courier rode along the column, frequently stopping to inquire where he could find the artilleryman. When he finally reached the head of the column and saw how young the man leading it appeared to be, he paused a final time, explaining to the cannoneer, "I don't want to make a mistake and give the message to the wrong person. If I give this order to that boy, Forrest'll give me hell."[12] The courier knew his commanding officer well.

The Southerners ran into increasingly stubborn resistance the closer they came to Franklin. From the nature of the fighting, General Van Dorn determined that the town had not been abandoned. Having attained the object of his reconnaissance, he ordered the men to fall back. The losses on both sides were relatively minor, although Forrest and his men mourned the loss of their extremely popular artillery chieftain. Freeman's death particularly affected Bedford. When he had finished driving off the Federal cavalry, he rode to the spot where Freeman lay. Seeing the body, the cavalry commander jumped from his horse and knelt beside the fallen artilleryman. Taking Freeman's hand, Forrest paused, tears welling in his eyes, and in a voice choked with feeling, quietly observed, "Brave man; none braver!"[13] It was the most complimentary statement he knew how to make.

As usual, the war provided little time for mourning such losses. By the end of April, a new threat emerged that required Forrest and his troopers to exert their maximum efforts to overcome. This threat began as an attempt by the Federals to raid deep into Southern territory and disrupt the Confederates' supply lines. The primary target for this raid was the Western and Atlantic Railroad, over which supplies flowed to General Braxton Bragg in Tennessee. The raid was to be carried out by a select body of men riding mules—animals thought to be perfectly suited for the rough terrain they would be traversing. Furthermore, these troops would be moving through territory inhabited largely by Unionists, when it was inhabited at all. This movement through a Union region would ensure reliable local guides, trustworthy information, and a friendly reception as the raiders moved toward Georgia and Bragg's lengthy supply lines.

Colonel Abel D. Streight provided the inspiration for and the leadership of this expedition. Once he received official approval, he immediately began the lengthy preparations. While occupied with this business, a large consignment of mules arrived from Nashville. But when Streight saw the animals for the first time, he was shocked and dismayed. For the most part, they were "nothing but poor, wild, and unbroken colts," many of which suffered from "the horse distemper." Some of the unfortunate animals died en route, others "were too near dead to travel," and even the relatively healthy mules "were so wild and unmanageable that it took us all day and a part of the next to catch and break them before we could move out across the country."[14] The beginning did not augur well for the stalwart Union colonel and his raiders.

Union General Grenville M. Dodge was supposed to prepare the way for Streight's raid by launching a diversionary attack against Tuscumbia. But while the two officers met to synchronize their plans, disaster, in the form of Confederate cavalrymen, struck. Streight had painstakingly gathered 1,250 mules in a corral at Eastport. During the night of April 19, some of Confederate

Colonel Philip D. Roddey's troopers broke into the corral and stampeded the mules. Streight later observed that they had run off "nearly four hundred of our best animals" and that he spent the better part of the next two days "scouring the country to recover them." Eventually recovering only about half the mules, Streight lost valuable time.[15]

On April 21, Colonel Streight finally moved out in tandem with General Dodge, pushing Roddey's troopers before them and arriving at Tuscumbia on April 24. In the meantime, Forrest received orders from Bragg to march to Alabama, unite with Roddey, and stop the Federals' advance. Forrest immediately set his command in motion, crossed the Tennessee River, and joined Roddey's exhausted horsemen in holding off Dodge. While Dodge kept Forrest occupied, Streight swung his command to the south and began his march to Georgia. Word did not reach the Confederate commander until April 28 of Streight's 1,500 to 2,000 man "mule brigade" and although he hurried his command in pursuit, the Union colonel was already well ahead of him, approaching Moulton, Alabama.[16]

At first Forrest did not know what to make of this new force. Accordingly, he left Roddey and a portion of his command to watch Dodge while he prepared to race after the mysterious column with the rest of his men, approximately 1,200 horsemen. Knowing that the pursuit could be long and undoubtedly would be grueling, the Confederate cavalry commander personally supervised the preparations. He wanted to know what he was working with, what he could call upon in an emergency. So, he doubled the teams of horses that would be pulling his artillery pieces; inspected the horses and the men; and supervised the distribution of ammunition, rations, and forage. At 1 A.M. on April 29 everything was finally ready. The focus of events shifted from Dodge and Roddey as Forrest moved out in pursuit of Streight.[17]

Forrest was confident that he could stop the Union raiders short of their destination. He planned to maintain pressure upon the Federals with at least a portion of his command, resting the others as much as possible. Heavy rains and muddy roads made for little progress as the raiders pressed on through the night in the direction of Moulton. Despite impressing animals from the

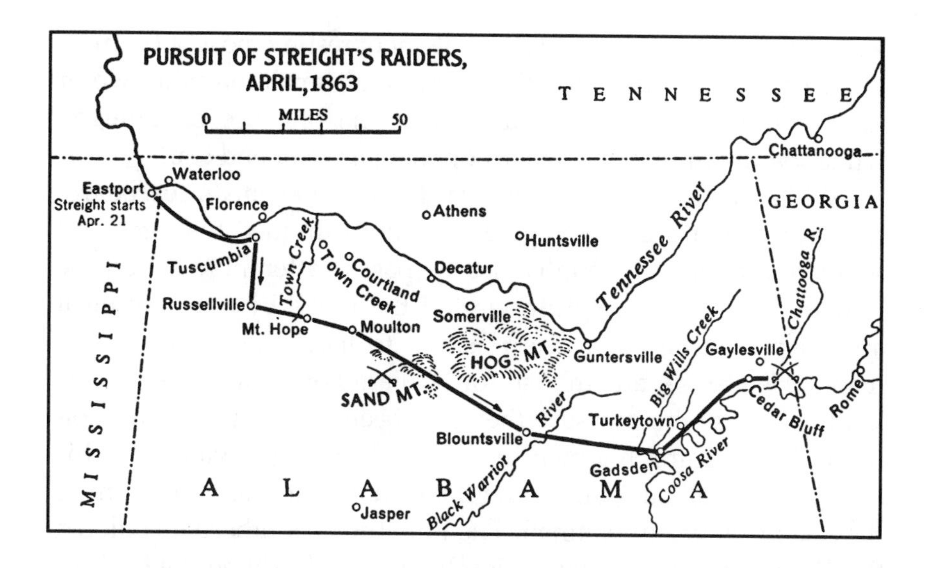

countryside for his men to ride, Streight still could not replace the number of mules that had been made unserviceable by distemper. The fact that part of his command had to march on foot slowed the progress of the entire expedition, a luxury that they simply could not afford.

Leaving Moulton at midnight on April 28, Streight made thirty-five miles over the poor, muddy roads, camping for the night at Day's Gap, at the foot of Sand Mountain. By scouring the route as they went, the Federals finally obtained enough animals for every soldier to have a mount. That fact, and the promise of fair weather, which might dry the roads, suggested that better luck might have come Streight's way at last. The colonel had no idea yet that Forrest was on his trail, although he had heard of small squads of conscript agents roaming the region. Streight's ignorance of Forrest's pursuit would all change quickly—too quickly for the Union raiders.

Early the next morning, Streight and his saddle-sore soldiers broke camp and headed through Day's Gap. As the column spread out, Forrest and his men struck its rear. It was not Bedford Forrest but his brother Captain William Forrest who dashed out of the underbrush to harass the Federals. William and his men had crept close to Streight's camp during the night, under orders from his older brother, while the bulk of the Southern command rested. It was all part of Forrest's twofold strategy of resting most of his men, while continually harassing the enemy with small forces of two or more companies. This maneuver kept the pressure on Streight, while sparing most of his own troops similar wear and tear.

While William Forrest's scouts drove the enemy's rearguard, capturing a handful of stragglers, Bedford divided his force and sent two regiments through a nearby pass to attempt to cut off the raiders. However, Streight thwarted the move by anticipating it and disposing his men in a position to meet the flanking regiments. He also set an ambush for William Forrest's Confederates, hoping to ease the pressure they had been exerting upon his column. Thus, hiding his men in the brush, Streight waited for his rearguard to fall back and draw the Confederates toward them as they had previously planned. The impetuous Southerners obliged the Union colonel, following closely and recklessly on the heels of the retreating Federals.

As soon as the Northerners passed, their comrades rose from the underbrush and poured a deadly fusillade into the unsuspecting Southern ranks. The plan worked marvelously. The Confederate attack broke in confusion, sustaining several casualties, including William Forrest, who fell when a minié ball crushed his thigh bone. Bedford soon came up, dismounted the men, and launched a fresh assault. The new attack withered under the severe fire, and Streight used the opportunity to launch a counterattack. Streight's counterstroke proved successful, capturing two pieces of artillery, which the Confederates had brought up to the front, and some forty prisoners. The fighting cost the Federals approximately thirty killed and wounded of their own, including one of the staff officers Streight considered indispensable. The loss of the two fieldpieces infuriated Forrest. He stormed about, rallying the men for a charge to retake the guns, raging at those who did not move fast enough to satisfy him. But by the time he had the men organized, the enemy was gone—with his guns. An embarrassment, more than anything else, the capture of these two pieces of artillery would have more serious consequences later.[18]

Having momentarily checked the pursuit, Streight disengaged and resumed his march, leaving a strong rearguard to hold off the Southerners. Just before dark, the Union colonel turned to fight the Confederates at Hog Mountain. There he used the captured artillery pieces to fend off Forrest's attacks. Streight still hoped to press on without more interference, and at 10 P.M. he broke off the fight to march again. As the Federals pulled back, they spiked and abandoned the two captured cannons, having no more ammunition for them.[19] Forrest was incensed. For the remainder of the chase he demanded that his men pursue the Federals with complete abandon or, as he explained: "Whenever you see anything blue, shoot at it, and do all you can to keep up the scare."[20]

Forrest's troopers continued to nip at the heels of Streight's men until the latter again turned to set an ambush. The Federals hid in thickets, within sight of the road along which the Southerners would come. In the bright moonlight, the Confederate horsemen made fair targets. "The head of his column passed without discovering our position," Streight explained. "At this moment the whole regiment opened a most destructive fire, causing a complete stampede of the enemy." The Union colonel moved on: "I had hopes that by pushing ahead we could reach a place where we could feed before the enemy would come up with us, and, by holding him back where there was no feed, compel him to lay over a day at least to recuperate." Streight knew that his Confederate pursuers had endured forced marches and fighting of their own. He hoped to take advantage of their exhaustion to compensate for that of his own troops.[21]

Streight's respite was short. The Southerners soon regrouped and pressed his column so vigorously that between 2 and 3 A.M. he had to turn and fight once more. Again the Union cavalryman set his trap, but this time the more cautious Confederates refused to fall victim to it. An outrider suspected the ploy and raced back to warn the advance units. Forrest responded with a ploy of his own. He sent three scouts forward to flush out the ambush, one way or another. They did so by drawing fire, avoiding the volley by leaning against their horses' necks, and running for safety. The Confederate commander brought up two artillery pieces and shelled the brush, driving off the ambushers.[22]

By ten o'clock on May 1, Streight's weary column reached Blountsville, forty-three miles from Day's Gap. In the meantime, Forrest rested his men briefly before pushing on after the Federals.

At Blountsville, the Union column also paused to eat and rest. Streight ordered the ammunition distributed, with the remainder packed on mules, and burned his wagons. This action would lighten the load and enable the column to move a bit faster. But the Federals would not enjoy their rest for long. Forrest and his escort rode into Blountsville in time to skirmish with the Federals, extinguish some of the fires, and salvage some of the contents.

Forrest had yet to bring Streight to bay, but he was increasingly getting the best of him. To stay on top of the situation, he relied heavily upon his own scouts, scattered throughout the region. These scouts kept him informed and allowed him to set plans and implement strategy. Occasionally, some of them ran afoul of Forrest's temper, particularly when the information they brought their commander was faulty. One such instance occurred near Blountsville, and Bedford's reaction was typical.

The incident occurred when one of William Forrest's usually reliable scouts wandered off the main road, looking for a blacksmith to shoe his horse. At some point during the visit, a civilian raced up to say that a heavy force of Union cavalry was moving along a parallel road, preparing to confront the Confederates' main column. The scout hurried back to find Forrest and inform him of what he had heard. "Did you see the Yankees?" Forrest wanted to know. "No; I did not see them myself," he replied, adding that "a citizen ... told me he had seen them." At that, Bedford reached up, pulled the man from the saddle, and smashed him against a nearby tree. Before the astounded scout could recover, Forrest pounded him against the tree trunk repeatedly, angrily spouting, "Now, damn you, if you ever come to me again with a pack of lies, you won't get off so easily!"[23]

Forrest and his troopers continued to harry the raiders as they left Blountsville. Streight tried dispatching small detachments to set ambushes and slow the pursuit, but the Confederates followed closely until the Federals reached the Black Warrior River. There Streight turned to fight the Southerners once more and succeeded in driving off the handful of pesky Confederates before beginning to cross the river. Streight left his skirmish line in place while he pushed the major part of the command across, withdrawing them as well, under cover of the artillery. The Federals pressed on, still continually pestered by small parties of Confederates. Streight repeated the sequence at the crossing of Big Will's Creek, where a substantial amount of ammunition got wet during the crossing and was thereafter useless to the Federals.[24]

Forrest's continual effort to flank Streight's force had been to no avail until now. The Union raiders, tired of defending every river and creek crossing, marched "all night" to avoid a Confederate flanking movement, "though the command was in no condition to do so."[25] Then, at eight o'clock the next morning, May 2, Forrest paused in his pursuit long enough to dash off a message "to the authoritys of Rome Georgia[.]" He noted his position as "20 Miles west of Gadson [Gadsden, Alabama]" and warned "theirs is a Federal Force of fifteen Hundred cavalry Marching on your place I am pressing them Prepare your selves to Repuls them—they have 2 Mountain Howitsers I will be clost on them I have kild 300 of their men they air runing for their lives[.]"[26] A courier raced off with the message Forrest hoped would seal Streight's fate. An hour later the Confederate pursuit struck Streight's column as it prepared to cross Black Creek. The Federals held their pursuers off until they had the wooden bridge crossing the creek well engulfed in flames. It looked like Streight had finally gotten the better of Forrest, perhaps significantly reducing the harassment his column had endured since the pursuit began.

But always resourceful, Forrest found help from an unlikely source. He and his men arrived too late to cross or extinguish the flaming bridge, but a young girl had watched them dash up from a nearby farmhouse. She called out to the exasperated Confederate cavalryman, and he rode over to her. In their brief exchange the sixteen-year-old told Forrest that she knew of a nearby ford through which the cows crossed in low water. She offered to show it to him if someone would saddle her horse. Forrest held his hand out to her, saying: "There is no time to saddle a horse; get up here behind me." At that she hopped up onto his horse to point it out, as the general assured her mother, "Don't be uneasy; I will bring her back safe."

There was still firing coming from across the creek as Forrest and his guide dismounted and crept to the site of the ford. Bedford studied it briefly before returning his young guide to her home. Within a short while, he had the ford cleared and his command crossing, ready to renew the pursuit. As the operation proceeded, Forrest rode back to the house and left a note, thanking Emma Sansom for her assistance:

> Hed Quaters in Sadle
> May 2, 1863
>
> My highest regardes to Miss Ema Sansom for hir gallant conduct while my posse was skirmmishing with the Federals a cross Black Creek near Gadsden Allabama
>
> N. B. Forrest
> Brig. Genl
> Comding N. Ala—[27]

Once across Black Creek, the Confederates continued to harass the Union column. At Gadsden, Streight halted his men briefly, destroying some supplies stored there before leaving. By now, even the brief rests and a strong rearguard failed to prevent severe straggling. As Streight later pointed out, "Many of our animals and men were entirely worn out and unable to keep up with the column; consequently they fell behind the rear guard and were captured."[28] Finally, at about 4 P.M., the raiders simply stopped at Blount's plantation, a dozen or so miles outside Gadsden. Streight realized that he was allowing Forrest to catch up, but his men could go no farther without some rest and food. The Union colonel formed most of his men in a line of battle, while others fed the animals. Soon the Confederates drove in the rearguard and attacked the main line. In brief but furious fighting, the Southerners smashed against the Northern line, but could not break it, although they succeeded in mortally wounding another important Union subaltern, Colonel Gilbert Hathaway. Hathaway's death, the worthless condition of much of their remaining ammunition, and the general weariness of the men combined to dampen their spirits even more.[29]

In the meantime, Streight realized that his final hope to save the expedition lay in capturing and holding the bridge over the

Oostanaula River leading into Rome, Georgia. "It now became evident to me," he observed, "that our only hope was in crossing the river at Rome and destroying the bridge, which would delay Forrest a day or two and give us time to collect horses and mules, and allow the command a little time to sleep, without which it was impossible to proceed." Accordingly, he detailed two hundred men on the best mounts in the command to ride under Captain Milton Russell to push on to Rome with all speed, to seize and hold the bridge.[30]

It was a good plan, and it might have worked except for a forty-three-year-old mail carrier named John Wisdom. Sometime around 3:30 P.M. on May 2, while performing his usual rounds, Wisdom approached the Coosa River and found the ferry sunk. The presence of Union soldiers in Gadsden, across the river, prompted him to take off in his buggy to warn the people of Rome, sixty-seven miles away, to prepare to defend their town. In the course of a grueling night of riding that required him to abandon the buggy and change horses frequently, Wisdom reached Rome about midnight, six or more hours before Russell arrived with his band.[31]

As Russell's men dashed toward Rome, Streight pushed his men toward a crossing over the Chattooga River. Again bad luck plagued the Union commander. Russell's troops had passed over hours before, but Russell forgot to leave a guard to hold the ferry. Once his men were gone, local citizens, sympathetic to the South, hid the boat and forced Streight's troops to turn upriver for a bridge several miles away. As he marched his men toward the new crossing, Forrest dispatched some men to "devil them all night" and rested the remainder. By dawn, Streight's troops had crossed and burned Dyke's Bridge, but Forrest's men were well rested for the final pursuit.[32]

Time was running out for Abel Streight. His men were exhausted. When he finally halted at 9 A.M. on May 3 near the Alabama-Georgia line, some twenty-five miles short of Rome, many of the Federals were so tired that they could not muster enough energy to feed their animals or themselves. Forrest was soon upon them, having dragged his artillery through the Chattooga River, using ropes and double teams of horses. Streight succeeded in forming a line of battle, but as he observed: "A large portion of my best troops actually went to sleep while lying in line of battle under a severe skirmish fire."[33] Only the numerical weakness of the equally weary Confederates (about 600 to Streight's 1,466) prevented Forrest from finishing off his worthy opponent with a last charge. Instead, he decided to rely on bluff to win the day and end the race.

Suspecting that his opponents had finally reached their limit, General Forrest sent in a flag of truce. He softened the terms of surrender somewhat, leaving out the Murfreesboro-style threat of "no quarter," asking only for the surrender of the Union command, "to avoid the further effusion of blood."[34] Streight replied that he would meet with him, fully aware that he could not resist any substantial force of Confederates. The Union commander realized by this time that Russell's detachment had failed to secure the Rome bridge. With the command "so exhausted from fatigue and loss of sleep that it was almost impossible to keep them awake long enough to feed," Streight's subordinates all counseled surrender.[35]

The groundwork thus laid, Forrest had only to convince Streight to listen to his subordinates and to reason and yield to the Confederates' demand for surrender. He sweetened the demand by offering to allow the officers to retain their side arms and personal property. Still the Union officer appeared openly reluctant to accept this final turn of events. Forrest realized that Streight, who so stubbornly refused to be stopped short of fulfilling his mission, might prove reluctant to surrender even now, so he planned to convince him that he was surrounded by overwhelming numbers.

The Confederate commander's scheme involved the bluff that Forrest, the gambler, so thoroughly enjoyed. He knew that bluff, properly applied, could succeed, having used it liberally in the past with gratifying results. So now, with only his small number of weary troopers to help him pull it off, Forrest created phantom units and artillery pieces, displaying the only men and guns he had, time and again. He chided couriers for bringing him the news that such units had arrived and found no place in line on a field already too crowded to give them room. And when a section of Southern guns appeared during the negotiations, Forrest sent a staff officer to get them to "drop back a little," to appease Colonel Streight. The section commander complied and then instantly went to "action front" to present as hostile an appearance as possible. The subsequent arrival of another gun helped Forrest bluff his Union counterpart with the number of artillery pieces he had on hand.[36]

Forrest later recalled this final act in the race for Rome with the exuberant embellishment of a victor: "I seen him all the time we was talking, looking over my shoulder and counting the guns. Presently he said: 'Name of God! How many guns have you got? There's fifteen I've counted already!'" Undoubtedly pleased that his deception was having the desired effect, Forrest turned in that direction and calmly observed, "I reckon that's all that has kept up." Streight still clung to his refusal to surrender until he knew the number of men he faced, to which Forrest replied matter-of-factly, "I've got enough to whip you out of your boots." When Streight rejected this answer, Forrest played his final card. He turned to the bugler and instructed him to "Sound to mount!"[37] Streight could afford to delay no longer and agreed to surrender. A relieved General Forrest ordered the 1,466 Federals to stack their guns and assemble in a nearby field.[38] He revealed the small number of his troops only after the Union soldiers had complied with his wishes. As he concluded: "When Streight saw they were barely four hundred,* he did rear! demanded to have his arms back and that we should fight it out. I just laughed at him and patted him on the shoulder, and said: 'Ah, Colonel, all is fair in love and war you know.'"[39]

*Forrest's statement was an exaggeration—downward.

CHAPTER 7

Nothing to Bragg About

(May–November 1863)

It's nothing but a damned little pistol ball!

—FORREST AFTER BEING SHOT
BY LIEUTENANT A. W. GOULD

I wish old Forrest was here, he'd make you fight!

—UNKNOWN WOMAN TO FORREST

You have played the part of a damned scoundrel, and are a coward, and if you were any part of a man I would slap your jaws and force you to resent it.... I say to you that if you ever again try to interfere with me or cross my path it will be at the peril of your life.

—FORREST TO GENERAL BRAXTON BRAGG

THE CITIZENS OF ROME POURED into the streets to greet Forrest and his victorious cavalrymen. The Confederates' exhausted quarry rode grimly alongside their equally weary captors. Colonel Abel Streight had hoped to enter the little Southern community under different circumstances, but fate and Forrest had decreed differently. Then, in the midst of the celebrations, the column of fatigued riders nearly fell victim to a tragedy. In their excitement over the favorable turn of events, some of the citizens fired the two old cannons that had been dusted off to intimidate Russell's squadron, as a sort of salute. The guns, still loaded with shot, boomed their salute and fortunately missed their unintended targets.[1]

The whole town wanted to express their appreciation to Forrest, but the cavalry commander preferred to have them lavish their attentions on his tired troopers and their prisoners.[2] However, Forrest and his Confederate horsemen did not remain long in Rome. During the night of May 5, Forrest received word of a new Union raiding party headed toward Jasper and Elyton (present-day Birmingham). By dawn the Confederates were moving toward Gadsden to meet the new threat, but when they arrived there the next day, they found that the raid had not actually materialized. Forrest called off the pursuit and headed for his old lines in Tennessee.[3]

On the way back into his native state, Forrest left the column to report directly to General Braxton Bragg at Shelbyville. The commander met his subordinate with unaccustomed cordiality, even assuring Forrest of his desire to obtain a promotion to major general for him. Bragg's appreciation of Forrest was at its zenith; it was so high, in fact, that Bragg offered to place Forrest in command of all the cavalry attached to the army when his promotion came through. But Bedford demurred. Aside from his long-standing preference to act independently, Forrest felt inadequate for the task. Nevertheless, when he left Shelbyville to rejoin his command at Spring Hill, it was as commander of the cavalry on the left wing of the Army of Tennessee, recently made available by the death of General Earl Van Dorn.[4]

Forrest immediately set about reorganizing his new command. He established two divisions under Generals William H. Jackson and Frank C. Armstrong. However, the new arrangement did not last long, for Jackson's division soon transferred to Mississippi, leaving Forrest divisional commander of two brigades—Armstrong's and Starnes's. Throughout the next several weeks, the Confederates performed the ordinary duties of picketing and scouting. Then on June 3, sensing that the Federals were moving the major portion of their forces out of Franklin, Forrest took his division to reconnoiter.

In the ensuing skirmishing, Forrest saw what he took to be a flag of truce waving from a nearby fortification. Calling for his men to cease firing, he sent in his own flag, following closely behind it to participate in the parley. As the Southern commander approached the fortification, a Union officer stood up on the parapet, waving his arms to catch Forrest's attention, and shouted: "General Forrest! That isn't a flag of truce. It's a signal flag. Go back, sir, go back!" Bedford paused, raised his hat in a salute of thanks, and rode back to his own lines. The skirmishing resumed, briefly but vigorously, in and around Franklin. Then, having obviously determined that the Federals remained there in strength, Forrest withdrew his command.[5]

Ironically, while Bedford Forrest escaped harm at the hands of his enemies, his temper, quick judgment, and harsh actions toward his friends nearly cost him his life. This affair came about as a result of the battle, on April 30, at Sand Mountain, when Streight first turned and ambushed Forrest's pursuing men. During the fighting, Lieutenant Andrew Wills Gould pushed his section of guns to the front, as Forrest always insisted his artillerymen do. However, when the Federals succeeded in surprising the Confederates, wounding William Forrest in the process and launching a counterattack in the ensuing confusion, the two artillery pieces could not be withdrawn. As John Morton, Forrest's artillery commander and friend to both men, remembered, "Gould thought it best to abandon them, as nearly all the horses had been shot and had become entangled in the gearing." To Forrest, who, in a similar situation, once ordered four cavalrymen to throw the harness of a gun over their horses and pull it to safety behind them, such inaction "seemed an unforgivable offense." Forrest's subsequent failure to recapture the weapons made him even angrier at having lost them in the first place.[6]

Thus, when General Forrest assumed command of the cavalry on Bragg's left flank and reorganized his forces, he put in for a transfer of Lieutenant Gould to another command. He had not been satisfied with the handling and loss of those guns, which, in the heat of the moment, he had attributed to Gould's cowardice. Gould could not allow such an affront to his Southern honor to go without challenge. Morton recalled that "quick of temper and remembering the statements made in the excitement of the loss on the battlefield, [Gould] contrived this as a reflection on his personal honor, and sought an interview with General Forrest." Knowing both men well, Morton tried to meet with them individually and settle the rift between them, but he failed to see either one before they met in the Masonic Building in Columbia, Tennessee, on the afternoon of June 13, 1863.[7]

When Gould arrived at the Masonic Building, he found his commander already there in the quartermaster's office, fiddling with a penknife as he talked. The two men stepped into the vast hallway to speak more privately, and the tone of the conversation quickly became heated. Gould believed he had ample reason to be angry. He wanted the transfer order rescinded or, at the least, an explanation of why the general had acted as he had in the matter, but Forrest was in no mood to discuss the issue. He had already acted and would not reconsider what he had done. It did not matter much what Gould's interpretation of the facts was. He had lost his guns, and there could be no more room for discussion.

Gould could scarcely find this conclusion satisfactory. The meeting that the two men might have hoped would provide peaceful satisfaction had turned into a heated impasse. One officer was determined to assuage his honor; the other was unwilling to alter his opinion. Neither could back down or allow the other to save face. Adding the hair-trigger temper both men possessed, confrontation was virtually inevitable. And it came in short order.

Four boys who had followed the general, excited at the prospect of seeing a well-known figure so closely, stood on the stone steps of the Masonic Building. They were the only other witnesses of what happened next. Forrest had his back to the door (and the boys), while Gould stood facing them but totally involved in the conversation with his superior. One of the boys heard Gould say "it's false," or "that's all false," when Forrest apparently thought the junior officer was going to attack him. He thrust his left hand into his pants pocket and whipped out the penknife, throwing out his right hand to protect himself, all the while watching Gould intently. In the meantime, the lieutenant fumbled with a pistol he had in the right pocket of his long linen coat, attempting to pull it out. The seconds stretched interminably as he struggled to free the weapon. At the same time, the general lunged at Gould, opening the knife with his teeth. The gun caught in the lieutenant's pocket momentarily, firing through the pocket as Forrest closed in on him. The general grimaced as the ball struck him just above his left hip. In another instant Gould pulled the pistol out, but Forrest grabbed his wrist and pushed the gun into the air to prevent the lieutenant from hitting him with another shot. Then, with a swift motion, he thrust the knife into Gould's right side. The look on the lieutenant's face told that the blade had run true. Gould broke free and ran through the hall into the street.[8]

Hearing the commotion, several officers appeared as an enraged Forrest tried to follow Gould; instead, they ushered the stricken general into a nearby doctor's office so the wound could be examined. The doctor who looked at the wound worked under a couple of disadvantages. He had to perform the examination hastily and do so under the gaze of an infuriated and restless patient who had his mind bent more on revenge than anything else. He thought the wound possibly fatal and was counseling Forrest to seek better treatment when the latter stood up and roared, "No damned man shall kill me and live!" For the moment it must have seemed to him that he was back in the square at Hernando, with the bullets flying. He burst from the doctor's office, seething with anger. Spotting a horse tied to the railing nearby, Forrest walked over to it, found a pistol, and stalked after Gould.[9]

In the meantime, the lieutenant had burst into the street, followed shortly by the quartermaster who dashed out of the building shouting, "Stop that man! Stop that man! He's shot General Forrest!" By chance, two doctors, one of whom was related to Gould, saw the wounded man stagger across the street, and ran to his assistance. They grabbed him and pulled him through the nearest open door, a tailor shop. Once inside, one of the doctors went out to get the surgical equipment he would need, and the other helped Gould onto a table, got him undressed, and examined his wound. The knife wound was visible to the crowd now gathered at the door of the tailor shop. Located between the ribs, the wound spurted blood with each breath he took. The doctor attempted to stop the bleeding with his fingers while they waited precious moments for the other doctor to return.

Forrest's quartermaster had seen Gould, still standing, in the tailor shop and raced back to tell him: "General, that damned scoundrel is not much hurt." At that, Bedford left the doctor's office, his clothes still in disarray from the examination, promising: "By God, he has mortally wounded me, and I'll kill him dead before I die." By now Forrest was in the street looking for Gould. A local resident, who had seen the lieutenant's condition, ran over to the general to persuade him to stop the search. "I think you need not pursue Gould," the man explained, "for I think he is fatally wounded; he is bleeding profusely and losing blood with every breath." But the citizen's analysis did not impress Bedford Forrest: "Get out of my way. I am fatally wounded and will kill the man who has wounded me."[10]

Not to be stopped, Forrest stormed down the street. Learning that Gould had sought refuge in the tailor shop, Bedford headed for it, grabbing another pistol on the way, still determined to seek vengeance. Suddenly, the general appeared in the doorway, shouting, cursing, and waving the pistols. He saw Gould as the latter rolled off the table and into the back alley. Forrest fired a shot as he went, missing Gould, but slightly wounding a bystander in the leg. The lieutenant fell into some high weeds nearby as Forrest emerged from the tailor shop to follow him. According to one witness, the general walked over to where Gould lay, pushed him with his foot to see if he was dead, and returned to the tailor shop.[11]

As he made his way back, General Forrest saw the two doctors who had attended Gould and demanded that they assist him. Both observed that they should see about the condition of the man they had been attending, but Forrest, "with an oath," ordered them to go with him instead. Now attended by an entourage of doctors, Bedford rode in a carriage to the house in which he and his family boarded. With the appearance of his wife, her sister, and his son, Forrest's language became "more guarded [although] his passion was terrible."

Here Forrest finally calmed somewhat. As one biographer noted, "His rage fading as rapidly as it had flamed, Forrest submitted to treatment of his own wound." The doctors probed the wound and found that the ball had missed the intestines and lodged into muscle where it would do no real harm. Informing him of their finding, the doctors observed that they could easily cut it out and that he would be back in the saddle in a few days. Now realizing that he was not going to die, Forrest changed his whole demeanor toward the young lieutenant. Arguing against any further effort on his behalf—"It's nothing but a damned little pistol ball!"—he instructed the doctors, "Let it alone and go get Lieutenant Gould. Take him to the Nelson House and make him as comfortable as you can. Spare nothing to save him." According to one account, Forrest offered to pay for all expenses and wanted Gould to have the best room and care available. He punctuated the order with, "By God Ridley, when I give such an order, I mean it."[12]

Forrest was in a much better mood and insisted upon telling his version of the story to those who remained. He had not expected any difficulty, he explained, and only when the angry young officer reached into his pocket to pull out a pistol did he act to defend himself. He had gone after Gould, he admitted, but stopped when a doctor informed him that the lieutenant was mortally wounded. Only after the quartermaster told him that the wound apparently was not so serious did he stalk after Gould again. Forrest paused in the narrative to show the blade to one of the doctors who was still attending him and observed that if the lieutenant had demonstrated as much courage on the battlefield, the entire incident would not have occurred. The doctor washed the blood from the knife and gave it back to the general.

Having successfully outlasted Forrest's tirade, Gould indeed went to the Nelson House to receive treatment. While there, according to the widely accepted version by Forrest's biographer John Allan Wyeth, a remorseful Lieutenant Gould, "rapidly sinking from septic peritonitis, which followed a perforation of the intestine," sent his general word that he wished to talk with him before he died. The still bedridden General Forrest had to be carried to his stricken subordinate's side. Wyeth noted that an unnamed "eyewitness" told him that a weakened Gould took Forrest's hand and remarked, "General, I shall not be here long, and I was not willing to go away without seeing you in person and saying to you how thankful I am that I am the one who is to die and that you are spared to the country. What I did, I did in a moment of rashness, and I want your forgiveness." Forrest then leaned over, expressed his regret that the wound had proved fatal, and gave the lieutenant his forgiveness.[13] John Morton, friend and comrade in arms to both men, observed that the same eyewitness who related the story to Wyeth told it to him.[14]

While this incident certainly might have happened, it is unlikely that it did in the manner described. One of Gould's relatives sat with the dying man throughout the period and denied that such a meeting, much less such a conversation, ever took place. Dr. Wilkes contended that Gould died from pneumonia, not "septic peritonitis," since the wound occurred in the lung, not in the intestines. His contention appears to be supported by the accounts that Forrest plunged his knife into Gould's ribs, not his abdomen.[15] A few days after the incident, Bedford told a visitor that he had been mistaken about the lieutenant; he now thought him brave and intended to tell him so personally, but he may well have been unable to fulfill his good intentions. Indeed, had the general played a more noble role in the affair, even at the end of it, his earliest biographers, Thomas Jordan and J. P. Pryor, would have surely included it in their account. Instead they conspicuously avoided the entire subject.[16]

Whatever role Forrest may have assumed in the Gould affair, events forced him into a speedy recuperation. On June 24, Union General William S. Rosecrans decided to push General Bragg out of middle Tennessee. Bragg determined not to fight it out with his adversary on that line and ordered his army to pull back. The order included Forrest's cavalry command at Columbia. Thus, the general left his bed to direct his men toward Shelbyville and a rendezvous with General Leonidas Polk's infantry and the rest of the Confederate cavalry. Subsequent movements by the enemy required Polk to pull out earlier than planned, although Forrest still expected to unite with General Joseph Wheeler's cavalry command and cross the Duck River at Shelbyville.

As Forrest's troopers approached the town, even that junction appeared in jeopardy. The sound of heavy fighting suggested that the Federals had followed Wheeler's command closely and would contest the river crossing there. Forrest pushed his command forward to help Wheeler, who was waging a desperate rearguard

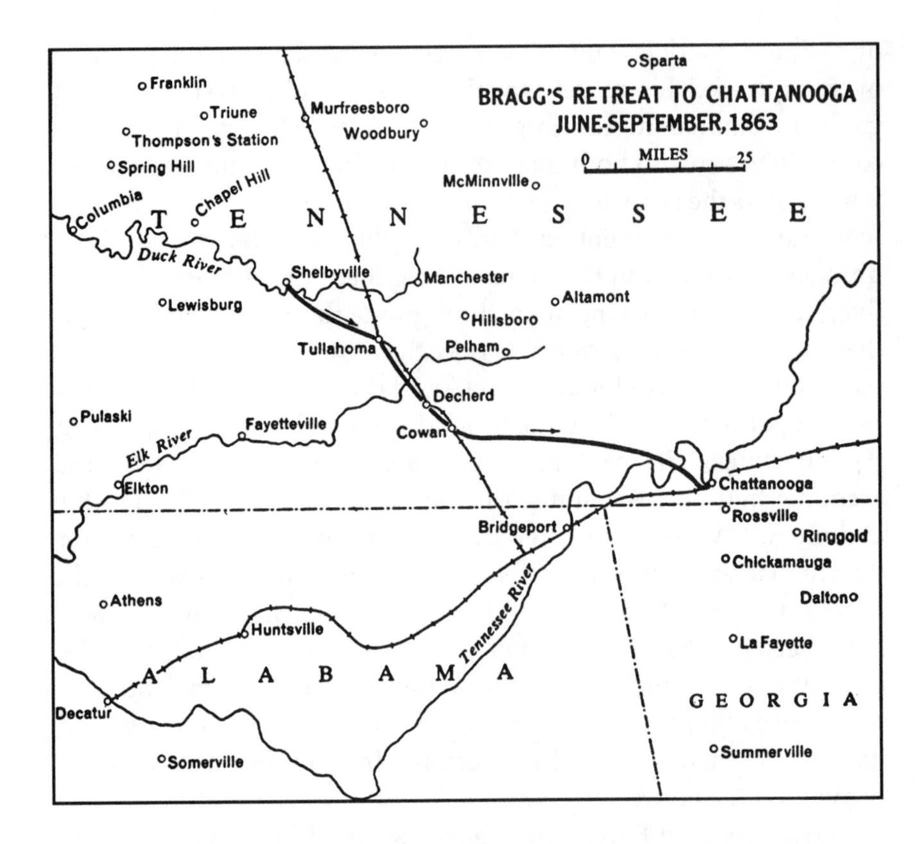

action to hold the Federals off while the vast Southern supply train plodded toward Tullahoma and safety. Ironically, Wheeler also fought to hold the bridge so that Forrest's men, should they arrive, could cross there. Just as Wheeler's men were about to burn the bridge, a small force of Forrest's men burst through to say that he was coming up as fast as possible and wanted to cross the river at the bridge before it was destroyed.

Wheeler pulled together a scratch force of four or five hundred men and threw them back across the river to fight the Federals, now pouring into Shelbyville. Many of the men belonged to Colonel A. A. Russell's Alabama troops, who had fought previously under Forrest. The fighting became fierce, quickly turning into individual hand-to-hand combat, as the Federals ran through and over Wheeler's line. With his line broken, Wheeler called for his men to cut their way out as best they could. Slashing their way to the bank, Wheeler and most of his men plunged their horses into the water and swam to safety. Although unable to hold the bridge, Wheeler had gallantly tried his best to do so, for the officer who had vowed six months earlier never to serve under his command again.[17]

Forrest was now in a tight spot. He could not know how desperately Wheeler struggled to keep his escape route open, but with it closed, he had to attempt to cross the river somewhere else. According to Wyeth, "General Forrest, who had the science and art of running—when it was the thing to do—as well in mind as that of fighting, took to his heels when he learned that Wheeler's men had been driven across Duck River, and sought safety in the crossing of this stream four miles east of Shelbyville."[18] Following this new route of escape, Forrest and his men arrived safely at Tullahoma on the next day, June 28. Still, Bragg had no intention of remaining. Federal movements already threatened to make his position at Tullahoma untenable. Thus, he promptly threw the cavalry out on the roads to shield his army while it retreated further toward Chattanooga. During this screening action, Forrest lost an officer, Colonel James W. Starnes, whom he valued so highly that he had given Starnes command of his old brigade.[19]

Bragg continued to pull back toward Chattanooga. Always the cavalry followed the main army, protecting it and screening its movements. Forrest's troopers frequently clashed with their Union opposites, firing and falling back repeatedly. During one of these delaying actions, Forrest raced into a little mountain village with his rearguard. As they passed one of the houses, the general noticed a woman standing on the porch yelling at his men. Turning her attentions to him, she shook her fist and raged at him: "You great big cowardly rascal; why don't you turn and fight like a man, instead of running like a cur? I wish old Forrest was here, he'd make you fight!" Forrest accepted her reproach goodnaturedly, laughing as he rode off.[20]

Bragg settled with the bulk of his army at Chattanooga, while cavalry under Wheeler and Forrest guarded the army's left and right flanks, respectively. General Forrest established his headquarters at Kingston, forty-five miles southwest of Knoxville. General Simon Bolivar Buckner occupied Knoxville for the Confederacy and kept watch on the Union troops under General

Ambrose E. Burnside. Forrest sent men, under Colonel George G. Dibrell, as far out as Sparta to recruit new men and watch the enemy. Yet, while Dibrell and his men remained in their home region, the Federals were also watching them. Finally, Colonel Robert H. G. Minty marched after them with his brigade of Union cavalry. Minty's horsemen managed to dash in among Dibrell's pickets and stampede his regiment out of its camp, but the Confederates took a strong position across Wild Cat Creek, which they successfully defended against several enemy attacks, inflicting heavy losses.[21]

Despite the excitement some of his men experienced, Forrest chafed at this outpost duty. He much preferred to be turned loose in Mississippi or Tennessee, where he could operate independently and remain relatively free to control his own actions. No doubt with this thought in mind, he submitted a plan to Adjutant General Samuel Cooper in which he would go to the region along the Mississippi River in northern Mississippi and western Tennessee with a select group of four hundred men and a four-gun battery, raise other troops, and with them "harass and destroy boats on the [Mississippi] river," and thus "seriously, if not entirely, obstruct ... navigation" on that waterway.

Forrest supported his capacity to close the river to Union transport, except to those boats "heavily protected by gunboats," by observing: "I have resided on the Mississippi River for over twenty years. Was for many years engaged in buying and selling negroes, and know the country perfectly from Memphis to Vicksburg on both sides of the river; and am well acquainted with all prominent planters in that region, as well as above Memphis." And if that were not enough to convince Cooper that he knew what he was saying in this regard, Forrest added: "I also have officers in my command and on my staff who have rafted timber out of the bottom, and know every foot of ground from Commerce to Vicksburg." He stated plainly that he would leave his men "with many regrets," noting that "nothing but a desire to destroy the enemy's transports and property, and increase the strength of our army, could for a moment induce me voluntarily to part with them."

Bragg forwarded the proposal to Richmond, observing in his endorsement: "I know of no officer to whom I would sooner assign the duty proposed, than which none is more important, but it would deprive this army of one of its greatest elements of strength to remove General Forrest." Forrest suspected that "it was likely" that his proposal "would not be forwarded by the general commanding the department," so he sent another directly to Confederate President Jefferson Davis, believing "the matter of sufficient importance to warrant the President's consideration." By the end of the month, the president decided to postpone the plan indefinitely, leaving Forrest to assume that Bragg had thwarted him once again.[22]

Whatever Forrest thought, President Davis had more on his mind than Bragg's reluctance to part with his cavalry commander. In July 1863, the Confederate States of America endured its "second great morale crisis" with the defeat of Robert E. Lee's invasion of Pennsylvania at Gettysburg, on July 3, and the loss of the fortress of Vicksburg, Mississippi, and an army of 30,000 men, on July 4. Historian Bell I. Wiley noted, "The effect on public morale of these two disasters was tremendous. In their wake a cloud of gloom such as the Confederacy had never known settled over the land and the Southern spirit suffered an injury from which it never recovered."[23]

On August 16, Rosecrans broke out of his six-week lethargy. Minty's tangle with Dibrell near Sparta was a prelude. By August 21, Rosecrans had reached the opposite side of the Tennessee River from Chattanooga. But although the Union commander shelled the city and feinted to his left and front, he unexpectedly crossed the Tennessee River with most of his army at several points to his right, below the city. His 60,000 men completed the crossing on September 4, virtually unopposed and a day after General Burnside and his 24,000 men entered Knoxville without firing a shot.

Bragg made this bloodless occupation of Knoxville possible when he ordered Forrest and Buckner to fall back toward Chattanooga. The cavalry commander recalled his men from their outposts, joined Buckner, and both pulled back closer and closer to the major portion of the army. On September 3, Bragg augmented Forrest's command with a division under General John Pegram and put the former in command of all Confederate cavalry north of Chattanooga.

Rosecrans continued to elude Bragg, slowly moving through the mountains toward the Confederate commander's lifeline—the Western and Atlantic Railroad—which Streight had tried unsuccessfully to reach earlier in the year. Finally aware of where Rosecrans was, Bragg had no choice but to evacuate Chattanooga and move back along his supply line to avoid being cut off. Once again, "Old Rosy" had outmaneuvered Bragg, and his prize was the Federal occupation of Chattanooga.

Despite his success, Rosecrans increased his vulnerability to attack as he continued to march eastward. By moving as it did through the mountain passes, the Union army became separated into three widely scattered columns, each too far away from the others to cooperate in the event of an attack. General Thomas L. Crittenden moved northward around Lookout Mountain to occupy Chattanooga. General George H. Thomas marched through Steven's Gap, eighteen miles to the south, and General Alexander McCook moved through Winston Gap, twenty-four miles away. As one historian put it, Rosecrans was "accepting the risk of dispersion for the sake of speed," and all with the hope of finishing off Bragg's demoralized army, whether it remained in Chattanooga or raced southward.[24] But Bragg had finally stopped retreating and was concentrating his forces to strike at the Federals. The moment seemed perfect for the entire Army of Tennessee to attack each column of the Union army in detail, destroy it, and turn on the next until the Army of the Cumberland ceased to exist.

Only Bragg's incompetence or Rosecrans's sudden awareness of his situation could prevent utter disaster for the Union cause in the west. And Jefferson Davis was determined to prevent his commander from throwing away this opportunity. He directed reinforcements to come to Bragg from General Joseph E. Johnston's command in Mississippi and from Robert E. Lee's Army of Northern Virginia. The first of Lee's men, under General James Longstreet, embarked on September 9 for their nine-hundred-mile train ride to Bragg's army.

When Bragg, steeled by orders and reinforcements, turned to fight, he found himself in an extraordinary position. His left rested at La Fayette, Georgia, guarded by Wheeler's cavalry, and his right lay at Lee & Gordon's Mill, watched over by Forrest's cavalry. As General Thomas's Federals poured into McLemore's Cove, west of Chickamauga Creek, Bragg was in the unique position to strike him with twice his numbers. The outcome could hardly be in doubt.

What happened next was typical of Bragg and his ill-fated Army of Tennessee. Issuing elaborate orders to attack and destroy Thomas before he could obtain help or withdraw to safety, Bragg waited as his subordinates dallied, only to squander their golden opportunity. He was enraged by the performance, and both the commander and his subordinates hurled blame at each other, while the Federals, at last aware of their desperate situation, attempted to concentrate.

Ironically, this effort to concentrate presented Bragg with a second chance for success, when Crittenden left Chattanooga in the wake of the Confederate retreat to join the other Union columns. The Southern commander, still fuming, ordered General Polk to turn northward and destroy this Federal column. At dawn, September 13, the time set for the offensive, Polk still nervously occupied his defensive position. More furious than before, Bragg attempted to rectify the situation, only to find that Crittenden, like Thomas before him, had slipped out of the trap.

For the next several days, both commanders concentrated, or attempted to concentrate, their units and determine what the other was planning to do. Rosecrans finally understood that he could not complacently plod after a Confederate army in retreat because that army was not only not retreating, it was being heavily reinforced. Affairs would soon come to a head, resulting in the bloody engagement west of the creek whose Indian name translated to "River of Death."[25]

Forrest was at the northern end of the army to watch Crittenden's advance from Chattanooga. It was he who had sent word of the Union column's dangerously exposed position. In sharp fighting near Ringgold and again at Tunnel Hill, Forrest did what Polk was unwilling to do. But his force was too small to accomplish much more than a delaying action. And during his stand at Tunnel Hill, Forrest suffered another wound "near the spine," apparently similar though far less dangerous and debilitating than the one he had received at Shiloh.[26] He remained in the field despite having "become faint with pain and loss of blood"; he broke his vow of abstinence and took a drink of whiskey at the behest of his surgeon.[27]

By September 17, hard marching by Rosecrans's men and Bragg's indecision had the opposing armies facing each other across Chickamauga Creek. The Confederate commander, finally determined to attack, issued orders that night for his troops to cross to the west side of the creek early the next morning, face south (or left), and drive the enemy before them. Since the Confederates were already positioned closer to Chattanooga than was Rosecrans, this move would cut the Federals off completely from their supply lines. Then, with an eye to what had occurred in this vicinity earlier, Bragg closed his instructions with a firm admonition to his subordinate commanders: "The above movements will be executed with the utmost promptness, vigor and persistence."[28]

Perhaps sensing what Bragg planned to do, and certainly aware of the activity across the creek (though unsure of exactly what it meant), Rosecrans shifted his troops northward through the night. The shift put him two miles farther north and more tightly concentrated than he had been when Bragg formulated his plan. Thus, at dawn on September 18, the Union army was not exactly where it was supposed to be, and it was in a better position to fend off attacks made against any of its components. Inevitable delays that constantly seemed to plague the Army of Tennessee's operations again slowed the Southern army's movements, and the Confederate offensive appeared doomed to failure.

Despite all these developments, the Southern assault finally got under way about 11 A.M. when General Bushrod Johnson's infantry deployed in line of battle near Reed's Bridge. Forrest covered Johnson's front and right flank with a battalion of Kentuckians, formerly under the command of General John Hunt Morgan, and his own escort. He ran into enemy cavalry under Colonel Minty at Pea Vine Creek and skirmished with them steadily until Johnson came up to help drive the Union horsemen across the Chickamauga at Reed's Bridge. About three in the afternoon, with the Federals pushed beyond the Chickamauga, General John Bell Hood arrived on the field, fresh from the railroad cars that had

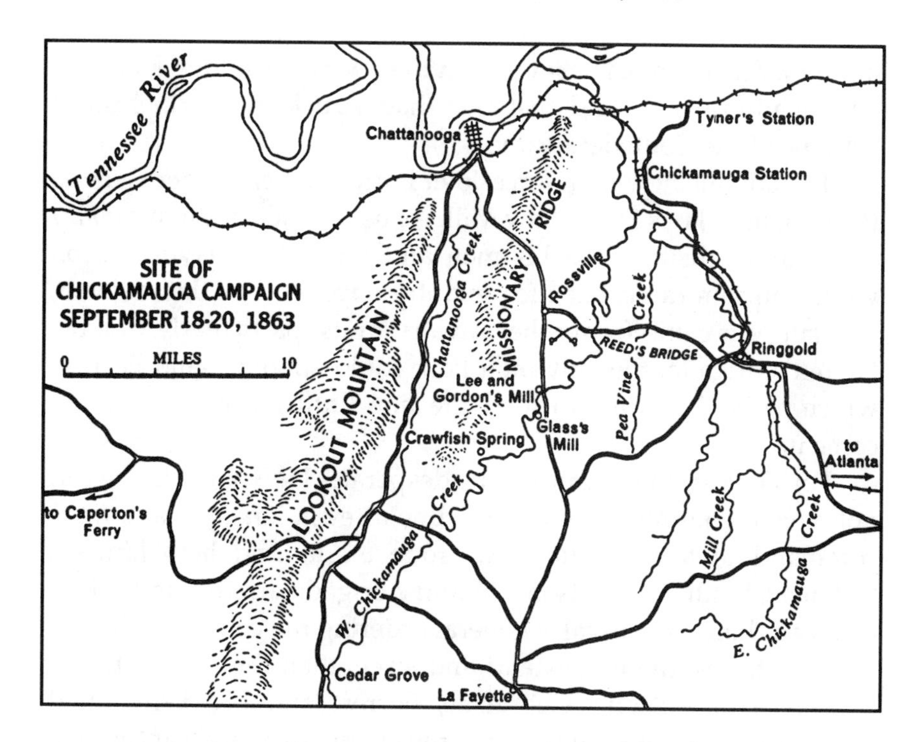

brought him from Virginia. Hood assumed command on the Confederate right flank and within an hour had pushed as far as Jay's Steam Saw Mill and faced his command to the south, ready to drive upstream as ordered. By the end of the day, Forrest was as far south as Alexander's Bridge, where he bivouacked for the night, directly in the rear of Hood's line. Bragg's offensive had hardly been smashing, but at least it was fully under way.[29]

Throughout the night, Rosecrans again shifted to the north, moving his battle line another two miles closer to his supply and communications lines. The Union left flank now extended farther to the north than did the Confederate right. Thus, instead of outflanking Rosecrans, Bragg was himself outflanked and had no idea that it had happened. Forrest had bivouacked near the center of the Southern line and ridden with Hood to Bragg's headquarters about 9 P.M. on September 18, where he received orders to reconnoiter early the next morning. In compliance with those orders, Forrest moved out on the morning of September 19 to find that instead of cavalry, he faced a formidable array of Union infantry. The Federals believed that they were assaulting an isolated brigade only to find that they had struck the northernmost extreme of the Confederate line.

The advancing Union forces met Forrest's men, under General Pegram, near Jay's Steam Saw Mill. As usual, the Southern cavalry commander dismounted his men and fought a delaying action while couriers raced back for infantry support. For the moment, that support came from other cavalry units, particularly Colonel Dibrell's brigade, the only men Polk could spare to send Forrest, which arrived in time to hold the line until the infantry could come up.

For Forrest, the situation was desperate. He knew that he did not have the numbers to hold the line forever. Finally, leaving the command to a subordinate, he rode off to find help himself. Colonel Claudius C. Wilson's infantry brigade arrived under Forrest's guidance, the cavalry general ordering the colonel to deploy on his left and thereby extend and strengthen the line. With the assistance of Wilson's Georgians, Forrest and his dismounted troopers surged forward "driving the enemy back and capturing a battery of artillery." Forrest led the way, wearing a long linen overcoat, his weapons strapped on over it.[30]

Despite the initial success Forrest and Wilson enjoyed, the superior numbers of the enemy began to tell. On his own initiative, having "assumed temporary command of the infantry," Bedford brought General Matthew D. Ector's brigade up to relieve his cavalrymen. Taking their place on Wilson's right, these men helped to stabilize the situation momentarily.[31] But Ector became increasingly concerned with his flanks, adding to Forrest's worries. In the heat of the battle, the infantry commander's plaintive inquiries tested Forrest's control, eventually unleashing his furious temper. "Tell General Ector that he need not bother about his right flank," Forrest first assured a courier. "I'll take care of it." But when the courier returned a short while later, interrupting the general while he directed the fire of one of his artillery batteries, this time expressing Ector's concern about his other flank, Forrest exploded: "Tell General Ector that by God I am here, and will take care of his left flank as well as his right!"[32]

After fiercely contesting the ground, the Confederate line again was subjected to an enfilading fire from the flanks, and the Southern foot soldiers had to fall back, resuming the position from which Forrest and his cavalrymen first fought the enemy that morning. In the meantime, General W. H. T. Walker arrived and assumed command. The fighting continued in this manner for the rest of the day. Each side gained a temporary advantage as it poured in fresh troops, only to lose that advantage when the other side responded in the same way.

Watching as new units entered the fray, Forrest became involved a final time in the fighting on September 19, when Union troops threatened to flank General George Maney's brigade. Forrest "hastened to his relief" with a battery and Dibrell's dismounted cavalry.[33] The combat was so close that Maney had to ride to the battery, where he found "General Forrest in person," and request that Forrest redirect the fire farther away from his lines.[34] The cavalry commander complied and "continued firing." Forrest noted that his artillery "kept up a constant and destructive fire upon the enemy until they were within 50 yards of the guns," happily adding that his artillerymen left the field with all the guns, "notwithstanding the loss of horses" they had sustained.[35]

After the effort to relieve Maney's infantry, Forrest retired from the front ranks to give his men a chance to rest from the day's rigorous fighting. The combat became increasingly severe to the south as Generals Alexander Stewart's, Hood's, and Patrick Cleburne's Southerners hurled themselves at Rosecrans's Federals. But Forrest remained on the Confederate right flank, where the rest of General Armstrong's brigade joined him that night.

About 11 P.M. General Longstreet arrived on the field, immediately going to Bragg's headquarters, where the commander informed him of the Confederates' plan of attack for the next day. Bragg explained that he wanted the offensive to begin on the right and move successively to the left, with the extreme left of the Confederates' line acting as a pivot. In this way, he expected to force Rosecrans southward and interpose the Army of Tennessee between the Union army and its supply lines. It was the same strategy that Bragg had attempted from the beginning. But to make the movement more efficient, Bragg decided to reorganize his army in the middle of the battle, giving the new right wing to Polk and the left to Longstreet.

Of course, Bragg faced enormous obstacles as he attempted to implement his new scheme, particularly in communicating the new structure to all his field commanders in one night in the face of an active enemy army. Bragg needed a miracle for nothing to go wrong. General D. H. Hill was just one of the significant Confederate commanders who had no concept of what was expected of him in the new arrangement. When Hill could not find his superior, Polk, he returned to his command, unaware that he was supposed to open the attack at dawn. He learned of his assignment only after Bragg rode to his lines and informed him personally. Furthermore, the entire length and breadth of the Confederate line lay where it had ceased to fight the night before. There was little order, and often units overlapped other units or halted in places where they required some readjustment before they could undertake a concerted offensive. Apparently Bragg knew he was going to attack the next morning at dawn, as did a few of his senior commanders, but he shared that knowledge with precious few others in his army. In any event, the Army of Tennessee was in no shape to launch a coordinated attack on the Army of the Cumberland at dawn on September 20.[36]

As for Rosecrans, he also had a meeting with his generals to coordinate the army's activities for the next day. Generals Thomas, McCook, and Crittenden all attended. Only Thomas could think of anything constructive to say, and then only when he awoke from a nap he took while the others talked. He calmly observed, "I would strengthen the left," and went back to sleep when Rosecrans asked where he would find the men to do that. Once the council broke up, Thomas returned to find that he really did need more men. Before he went to sleep for the night, he dashed off a message to that effect to headquarters and received word that help would come in the morning.[37]

While the Union generals talked (or slept), their men spent the night digging in their positions. By morning, they confronted the Confederates with breastworks of logs, fence rails, and dirt. But the Southerners did not advance against these new defenses until

9:30 A.M., well after they should have launched their assault. Bragg later recalled: "With increasing anxiety and disappointment, I waited until after sunrise without hearing a gun," which would hardly seem adequate to describe the frame of mind of the volatile general who had given explicit orders "to assail the enemy on our extreme right at day-dawn of the 20th."[38] And when the attack finally came, after prodding from Bragg himself, it was no better coordinated than was the attack of the day before. Contrary to the plan, the entire Southern line did not swing into action until nearly midday. Forrest, still on the Confederate right flank, did not receive any instructions until after sunrise.

As the fighting on the Confederate right intensified and the Southern troops hurled themselves against Thomas's breastworks, Forrest dismounted his men and sent them forward with Breckinridge's infantry. Their primary task was to hold off the Union reserve under General Gordon Granger as it marched toward the fighting. The Confederate cavalrymen did so for two hours, before Granger finally united with Thomas in time to help Thomas earn his sobriquet as the Rock of Chickamauga. General Hill, who watched Forrest's dismounted troopers in action, asked a staff officer, "What infantry is that?" Learning that it was Forrest's cavalry, he subsequently met Forrest riding along the line, and told him, "General Forrest, I wish to congratulate you and those brave men moving across that field like veteran infantry upon their magnificent behavior." Then remarking that he had made himself unpopular with the cavalry in Virginia by saying that he "had not seen a dead man with spurs on," Hill concluded, "No one can speak disparagingly of such troops as yours." Forrest thanked him and rode on.[39] Hill later included a similar comment in his official report, noting that Forrest, "though not of my command, most heartily co-operated throughout the day and rendered the most valuable service." He closed his remark on the cavalry commander by observing, "I would ask no better fortune if again placed on a flank, than to have such a vigilant, gallant, and accomplished officer guarding its approaches."[40]

The crowning moment of Southern arms at Chickamauga came by accident, when Rosecrans pulled a division from his right center to plug a gap that did not exist, creating one instead. At just this opportune moment, Confederates under General Longstreet crashed through the hole, pouring over the empty breastworks and widening the break as they went. The Union center dissolved; the Union right collapsed with it. Badly demoralized Federals began to race ignominiously toward Chattanooga, taking Generals Rosecrans, McCook, and Crittenden with them. Longstreet turned north to help destroy Thomas.[41] Bragg was on the verge of a smashing victory.

With fully one-third of his comrades running toward Chattanooga, General Thomas continued to hang on at Snodgrass Hill. He gathered about him such remnants of the Union right as he could, established a new line, and braced himself for the onslaught he knew Longstreet would unleash upon him at any moment. For the rest of the day, he stood this ground doggedly, finally withdrawing his forces, one division at a time. Thomas's cool determination to leave the field in an orderly fashion prevented an even greater disaster for the Federals at Chickamauga, though they had suffered disaster enough. Even so, Bragg could not fathom that he had won.

Longstreet halted his men for the night and prepared to pursue the Federals at first light. Even the usually reluctant General Polk sent scouts into the country before him, and when they returned to report that the Union army was in full retreat, rode to headquarters to persuade his commander to follow them. He woke Bragg from his sleep and informed him of the scouts' report, but the victorious general seemed strangely uninterested.[42]

Daylight brought confirmation of the victory and its costs. Casualties for Rosecrans's Army of the Cumberland stood at 16,170: 1,657 killed, 9,756 wounded, and 4,757 missing. Bragg's Army of Tennessee lost 18,454: 2,312 killed, 14,674 wounded, and 1,468 missing.[43] Bragg needed no more information than the number of dead men on the battlefield to convince him that any further pursuit would be pointless—his army being too exhausted and beaten—if not impossible. He had won at Chickamauga, and that would have to do.

But some Confederates were unwilling to let the battle go at that. Early on September 21, Forrest and some four hundred of his troopers hoisted themselves into their saddles and picked up the chase. They collected stragglers and skirmished with some Union outposts, working their way to the crest of Missionary Ridge, overlooking Chattanooga. The Confederate cavalry officer scaled a nearby oak tree, used by the Federals as a signal tower. From that vantage point, he could peer into Chattanooga. What he saw, and did not see, greatly disturbed him. He could make out the chaos still prevalent in the Union ranks. He could also see no Southern columns marching toward the city to renew the attack. Hoping to take advantage of one and to encourage the other, Forrest hastily dispatched a note to General Polk: "We are in a mile of Rossville—Have been on the point of Missionary Ridge. Can see Chattanooga and everything around." All he could see below him was a demoralized enemy, still reeling from defeat. He wanted to convey the sense of what he saw to his superiors, quickly and succinctly. "The Enemy's trains are leaving, going around the point of Lookout Mountain. The prisoners captured report two pontoons thrown across [the Tennessee River] for the purpose of retreating. I think they are evacuating as hard as they can go. They are cutting timber down to obstruct our passage." Now, he could get to the heart of the matter: "I think we ought to press forward as rapidly as possible."[44]

Forrest wanted Polk to send the message on to Bragg and perhaps to urge him to act before it was too late. He knew the value of pressing a beaten foe, of not allowing that enemy to regroup and live to fight another day. Earlier at Sand Mountain, he had said, "Whenever you see anything blue, shoot at it, and do all you can to keep up the scare."[45] Now, the entire Army of Tennessee had a chance to put that simple axiom into practice, with the promise of a tremendous payoff if they did. While he waited for the rest of the army to come up, Forrest did his best to "keep up the scare" by employing another of his theories of success in waging war: "Whenever you meet the enemy, no matter how few there are of you or how many of them, show fight."[46] Then, when no one seemed to respond to his first dispatch, he sent a second, warning Polk that the Federals "are evidently fortifying, as I can distinctly hear the sound of axes in great numbers." Even so, Forrest explained, "The appearance is still as in [the] last dispatch, that he is hurrying on toward Chattanooga."[47] Finally the cavalryman implored his tardy comrades to hurry, as "every hour is worth 10,000 men."[48]

But General Bragg remained reluctant to move. When an escaped Southern prisoner came back into the lines with tales of the chaos in the Union army, his commanders sent him to Bragg. The general listened, but remained unconvinced. "Do you know what a retreat looks like?" Bragg wanted to know. Perhaps angered at the skeptical tone of his question, the soldier replied, "I ought to General, I've been with you during your whole campaign."[49] An equally exasperated Forrest, realizing that the army commander simply was not going to press his victory with anything approaching celerity, returned to headquarters to try his hand at persuading Bragg to act. He need not have bothered. Bragg had an excuse for not doing whatever Forrest suggested that he do. Finally, the thoroughly frustrated cavalryman left, muttering, "What does he fight battles for?"[50]

Bragg eventually followed up his victory at Chickamauga, but in a way that hardly satisfied his more aggressive subordinates. His army occupied Missionary Ridge and Lookout Mountain and settled in for a long stay in which they hoped to starve the Federals in Chattanooga into submission. In the meantime, Bragg instructed Forrest to ride for Harrison, in eastern Tennessee, where General Burnside was reported to be, and to watch Burnside's movements. On the way, Forrest received new orders to proceed to Charleston, Tennessee, where he encountered and fought the Union forces located there. Then engaging in a running battle with them, he pushed on until he was only thirty miles outside Knoxville. Clearly, Burnside was not marching to Chattanooga, as Bragg feared, Rosecrans hoped, and Lincoln expected.[51]

While Forrest was engaged in driving off the Federal cavalry toward Knoxville, a dispatch arrived from Bragg, dated September 28, advising him that "the general commanding desires that you will without delay turn over the troops of your command, previously ordered, to Major-General Wheeler."[52] The note sent Forrest into a towering rage. The order originated from Bragg's desire to send General Wheeler on a grand raid, across the Tennessee River and into the Sequatchie Valley, where he could harass

Rosecrans's tenuous and tortuous remaining line of supply. To augment Wheeler's command, Bragg pared Forrest's force to a mere brigade. Forrest issued the necessary orders, but with the men short of rations, the horses in need of shoeing, and all in need of rest, Bedford advised Wheeler that they were "in no condition to cross the mountains."[53] When the men joined Wheeler's command, Wheeler saw that his comrade's judgment was correct. "The three brigades from General Forrest were mere skeletons," he observed, "scarcely averaging 500 effective men each." Furthermore, they "were badly armed, had but a small supply of ammunition, and their horses were in horrible condition, having been marched continuously for three days and nights without removing saddles. The men were worn out, and without rations." Wheeler had no choice but to press on, and he did, leaving behind the worst of the lot.[54]

Bragg had great difficulty choosing an officer to lead this expedition. According to one officer, who encountered the general during one of his tirades, Bragg angrily paced his room, lamenting, "I have not a single general officer of cavalry fit for command—look at Forrest; [he] has allowed himself to be drawn off toward Knoxville in a general rampage, capturing villages and towns, that are of no use whatever to me.... The man is ignorant, and does not know anything of cooperation. He is nothing more than a good raider."[55]

It may have been in this frame of mind that Bragg reassigned the greater portion of Forrest's command to Wheeler for the Sequatchie Valley operation. At any rate, Bragg's action infuriated Forrest, who dashed off a strongly worded message, remarking to an aide, "Bragg never got such a letter as that before from a brigadier." Forrest followed his letter with a personal visit, in which he received assurances that his men would be returned to him at the completion of Wheeler's operation. Having settled this issue to his satisfaction, Bedford requested and received a ten-day furlough to travel by rail to LaGrange, Georgia, where he saw his wife for one of the few times since he convalesced in Memphis from the wound he received at Shiloh, eighteen months earlier.[56]

However, Forrest's peace of mind would not last for long. On October 3, Bragg placed Forrest under the command of General

Wheeler. Forrest received the notice two days later. Perhaps he remained calm while still in the presence of his wife, out of deference to her, but he was sure to lambaste Bragg when next he saw him. Appearing to thrive on the chaos he created among his general officers, Bragg had, with this order, provoked a firestorm of protest, the likes of which he had not seen before and doubtless would never see again.

Forrest biographer Robert S. Henry observed of the deteriorating relationship between Forrest and Bragg as the Chickamauga campaign ended: "Forrest was to grow so outdone with the fatal fumblings of his commanding general that the restraining power of military subordination, never too strong with him in any case, was to give way entirely. It was not that Forrest was inherently insubordinate or intractable," Henry suggested, noting his generally pleasant personal and official relationships with Generals Stephen Dill Lee, Dabney Maury, and Richard Taylor, "but that he was intolerant and impatient at what seemed to him to be official incompetence and stupidity, regardless of rank."[57] Henry's assessment was accurate, and certainly not limited to Bragg. Forrest had previously demonstrated limited patience and control in his relationships with Generals Wheeler and Van Dorn, Lieutenant Gould, and others. He simply could not tolerate actions or behavior of which he did not approve. Longtime staff officer and friend David C. Kelley wrote candidly of Forrest: "The truth may as well be told—he was unfit to serve under a superior; he was like a caged lion on the field of battle where he was not himself commanding."[58] This tendency toward independence and self-reliance was also true of Forrest in situations other than battle, particularly if he had lost confidence in his superior.

To his own men, Forrest was a strict disciplinarian and a demanding leader. He willingly applied the harshest penalties for insubordination, desertion, or dereliction of duty. Many of the men of Colonel Thomas G. Woodward's Kentucky regiment refused to serve under his command because, as a member of the unit explained, "at the time Forrest was as much feared and despised as he was afterward appreciated and beloved."[59] Occasionally, would-be troopers objected to Forrest as their commander for other reasons. As one disgruntled soldier confided in his journal, in 1864: "The dog's dead: finally we are under N. Bedford Forrest." Observing that he had feared this would happen, "since the death of the noble Van Dorn," the unhappy trooper continued with undisguised disgust: "'The Wizzard' now commands us ... and I must express my distaste to being commanded by a man having no pretension to gentility—a negro trader, gambler,—an ambitious man, careless with his men so long as preferment be en prospectu." Then, noting that his new commander "may be & no doubt is, the best Cav officer in the West," he nevertheless concluded, "but I object to a tyrannical, hotheaded vulgarian's commanding me."[60]

An Alabama trooper wrote his father that he had "called upon old Forrest & Chalmers" for a furlough and "shewed them my ragged plight"; however, he "got no satisfactory reply then." He concluded, "Forrest is a hardened old dog, & has little of the gentleman about him. He dislikes our regt. because it is not composed of Tennesseans, & is mad because we outfought them."[61] Another Confederate suffered a similar fate, but made the mistake of persisting in his request until Forrest finally scribbled across the application, "I have tole you twict goddamit No!"[62]

Hotheaded Forrest could be. And when he rode to Bragg's headquarters, having hurried back from LaGrange with the news of his reassignment to Wheeler's command still burning in his mind, there was little reason to believe that he could control his emotions or his temper when he saw Bragg next. Accompanied only by his chief surgeon, Dr. J. B. Cowan, he rode in silence, seething with anger. He had reached the end of his rope with his commander and was fully prepared to tell him so.

Forrest stalked past the sentry in front of General Bragg's tent without saluting and burst into Bragg's presence unannounced. The general rose to greet the unexpected arrival, apparently not sensing the fury of emotion his subordinate was about to unleash. Forrest ignored his commander's outstretched hand and launched forth, as Cowan recalled, "emphasizing each expression of contempt with a quick motion of the left index-finger, which he thrust almost into Bragg's face," while his stunned superior officer dropped into a camp chair.

"I am not here to pass civilities or compliments with you,"

Forrest began, "but on other business." He was in no mood to mince words:

> You commenced your cowardly and contemptible persecution of me soon after the battle of Shiloh, and you have kept it up ever since. You did it because I reported to Richmond facts, while you reported damned lies. You robbed me of my command in Kentucky, and gave it to one of your favorites—men whom I armed and equipped from the enemies of our country. In a spirit of revenge and spite, because I would not fawn upon you as others did, you drove me into west Tennessee in the winter of 1862, with a second brigade I had organized, with improper arms and without sufficient ammunition, although I had made repeated applications for the same. You did it to ruin me and my career. When in spite of all this I returned well equipped by captures, you began again your work of spite and persecution, and have kept it up; and now this second brigade, organized and equipped without thanks to you or the government, a brigade which has won a reputation for successful fighting second to none in the army, taking advantage of your position as the commanding general in order to further humiliate me, you have taken these brave men from me. I have stood your meanness as long as I intend to. You have played the part of a damned scoundrel, and are a coward, and if you were any part of a man I would slap your jaws and force you to resent it. You may as well not issue any orders to me, for I will not obey them, and I will hold you personally responsible for any further indignities you endeavor to inflict upon me. You have threatened to arrest me for not obeying your orders promptly. I dare you to do it, and I say to you that if you ever again try to interfere with me or cross my path it will be at the peril of your life.

Bragg was dumbfounded. Cowan was astounded. Forrest turned and abruptly left the tent, having nothing further to say. As the two men rode off, the surgeon, still overwhelmed by his commander's temerity, exclaimed, "Now you are in for it!" Forrest looked over at his staffer, his temper abated, and quietly observed, "No, he'll never say a word about it; he'll be the last man to men tion it; and mark my word, he'll take no action in the matter. I will ask to be relieved and transferred to a different field, and he will not oppose it."[63]

Forrest's actions toward Bragg reflected the interesting way in which the influences of honor, control, and the frontier interacted. Forrest resented Bragg's alleged persecutions, and honor demanded that he confront the miscreant. Yet, he could hardly treat his superior officer in the manner that he felt he deserved. Furthermore, Forrest's entrance into the ranks of planters in the years just before the war had encouraged him to moderate his conduct. Gentlemen fought duels, not gouging matches. But he could not dismiss or ignore that heritage. Therefore, he lost control and angrily confronted Bragg, as honor demanded. Nevertheless, he refused to exact punishment on the spot, as he might have done in Hernando and Memphis. He also refused to treat Bragg as an equal: "If you were any part of a man, I would slap your jaws and force you to resent it." Despite the tone and rhetoric, the implication was that Bragg was not a "man" in the frontier sense of that word. If Forrest had ever had any respect for his commanding officer, he had none now, and that was the worst insult he could hurl at him.

CHAPTER 8

The War Hits Home

(November 1863–February 1864)

Is that all you know? Then, I will go and see myself.

—FORREST TO GENERAL JAMES CHALMERS

Forrest must fight or run. I think we shall cure him of his ambition to command West Tennessee.

—GENERAL STEPHEN A. HURLBUT

Forrest is a rash man and fond of going into danger.

—ROBERT E. CORRY

BEDFORD FORREST WAS NOT THE only officer with whom Braxton Bragg was having trouble. In fact, the situation was so bad that President Jefferson Davis felt compelled to leave Richmond and travel by special train to sort out the quarrels and settle them. Beginning on October 9, when he arrived, the Confederate president spent the next five days listening to the complaints of Bragg's disgruntled subordinates. During Davis's visit, Bragg finally agreed that it was time to let the hot-tempered cavalryman go. Noting that he had been reluctant to lose the services of "that distinguished soldier" because they were "necessary to this army," Bragg thought that he could now dispense with those services and grant Forrest's request for a transfer "without injury to the public interests in this quarter."[1] Finally free from the ill-starred commander and his arbitrary decisions, Forrest met with President Davis two weeks later and obtained his consent to transfer to the west, where he would be free to operate in and around the Union lines in northern Mississippi and western Tennessee.

When he left the Army of Tennessee to take his new command to Mississippi, Forrest did not have all the men he requested, and what he did have on hand was little more than a nucleus around which to build a respectable force. He carried with him a little over three hundred men, included in his escort; Charles McDonald's battalion; and John Morton's four-gun battery. He was supposed to take Tom Woodward's Kentucky Battalion with him, as he had originally requested in his August letter to the president, but at the last minute that unit got orders to remain with the Army of Tennessee.[2]

Forrest set out with his small band of horsemen, once again to create a new command. He reached Okolona, Mississippi, and his new field of operations in mid-November, arriving there as the commander of western Tennessee, with specific orders from General Joseph E. Johnston to "proceed to raise and organize as many troops for the Confederate service as he [found] practicable."[3] Even the Federal commanders in the region anticipated his arrival. On November 3, General Stephen A. Hurlbut, based in Forrest's onetime hometown of Memphis, wired Grant, "It is currently believed that Forrest has been assigned to this department. If so, there will be more dash in their attacks."[4]

However, Forrest was not yet ready to attack, with or without dash. He expected to find cavalry under Colonel Robert V. Richardson to add to his command. He found Richardson, but, as he explained to Johnston on November 21, "I think two hundred and fifty will cover all the troops Colonel Richardson has." Forrest noted that his new subordinate wanted a brigade, "but as I shall have only about a thousand men with which to cross the Memphis and Charleston railroad, I shall take direct and immediate command of all the troops myself."[5] Richardson would just have to wait.

To these men, Forrest added 150 more under the command of his youngest brother, Colonel Jeffrey E. Forrest. Jeffrey had been wounded and captured in fighting before Bedford left the Army of Tennessee, and presumed killed, so that when the regiment joined the others at Okolona, he was still recuperating. Forrest lacked a great deal in the way of men and equipment, but he surrounded himself with good officers, among them Colonel Tyree H. Bell, whom he had lured away from Bragg's army with the promise of a promotion to brigadier general if he could raise the troops to fill a brigade. Forrest also finally had a sympathetic immediate superior in Stephen Dill Lee. However, initial appearances suggested that Forrest had left one awkward command situation only to plunge straight into another. According to S. D. Lee's biographer, "Many observers felt that Forrest—older, unorthodox, and not a West Pointer, would be unable to function under a man like Lee. Their backgrounds could not have been more different." Nevertheless, Lee "handled the situation beautifully."[6]

In a letter to Forrest, which the cavalryman could not avoid appreciating, Lee assured him, "Whether you are under my command or not, we shall not disagree, and you shall have all the assistance and support I can render you." Then, in the spirit of generosity and respect that would mark their friendship thereafter, he observed, "I would feel proud either in commanding or co-operating with so gallant an officer as yourself and one who has such an established reputation in the cavalry service to which I have been recently assigned."[7]

Forrest first had to create a command, and the best place to find recruits was in western Tennessee and Kentucky. This task would not be easy, since the territory from which Forrest would be drawing his men had long since been under Federal control. Union garrisons and fortifications dotted the region, and Union gunboats roamed its waters. Yet, whether he could convince the people he found to volunteer or had to conscript them, Forrest was determined to build his command under the very nose of the enemy.

It was important that Forrest construct his command as rapidly as possible, for Ulysses S. Grant, having replaced Rosecrans, had routed the Army of Tennessee and lifted Bragg's siege of Chattanooga in a series of engagements from November 23 to November 25, 1863. Undoubtedly, the Federals would renew their operations into Georgia when the spring campaign season arrived. Forrest would likely be called upon to help thwart the Union advance with whatever forces he had on hand.

The general made his intentions clear to the men he would take with him. On November 21, one Alabama trooper wrote his wife that Forrest "says that our field of operations will be between the Miss. & Tenn. Rivers and that he don't want any man to go with him unwillingly[.]" Forrest had no reason to doubt his leadership abilities, but he offered such inducements as he had to encourage his men further to follow him in the dangerous undertaking. He sent word "that everything that will add to our Comfort Shall be Supplied—Blankets, Shoes, and all that is necessary for a Soldier and also that all we Capture will be ours."[8] Nevertheless, these troopers understood the risks. In a subsequent letter, the Alabamian explained, "Tomorrow we have to start with I suppose about 1500 men and we will be lucky if some of us don't pay a visit to Alton [Illinois] or some other miserable Prison for I know that our leader the *great go ahead* Forrest is a *rash* man and fond of going into danger."[9]

With the help of a demonstration by General S. D. Lee, Forrest passed over the heavily guarded Memphis and Charleston Railroad on December 2. Despite Lee's efforts, Union General Hurlbut was aware of Forrest's movements. But to his announcement of the Confederate cavalryman's appearance in western Tennessee, General William Tecumseh Sherman responded, "[I] am rather indifferent to Forrest's reported expedition. He may cavort about the country as much as he pleases. Every conscript they now catch will cost a good man to watch."[10]

Forrest established his headquarters at Jackson, Tennessee, and slowly built a command. He wrote Johnston that he still needed "arms and money" to operate successfully, plaintively noting, "I hope, general, that you will be able to supply me with both." For the time being, he drew on his own money, spending "$20,000 of my private funds to subsist the command thus far." At the same time, Forrest kept his subordinates busy collecting absentees and deserters and watching for the enemy.[11]

Forrest may have excited little initial interest from Sherman, but by mid-December he had that general's attention, and others'

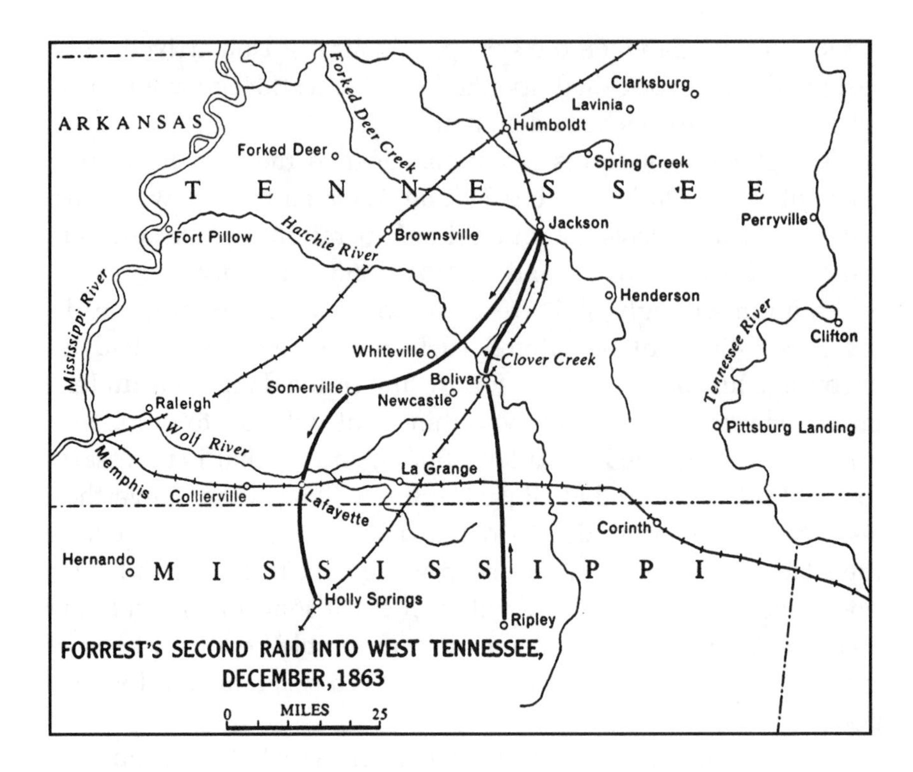

FORREST'S SECOND RAID INTO WEST TENNESSEE, DECEMBER, 1863

as well. He began to worry, correctly as it turned out, that the Federals were massing forces to move against him. Consequently, he deemed the removal to safety of his new, unarmed recruits a precaution he had to undertake as soon as possible. On the thirteenth, the same day that President Davis wired Johnston that Forrest had been promoted, the new major general sent a recently formed and unarmed regiment under Colonel R. M. Russell toward the safety of Confederate lines. In the meantime, his men continued to collect and enlist recruits, some of whom had recently eluded the Union conscript agents.[12]

Thus far, the cavalry commander had managed to avoid a fight. By December 18, it looked as if the only way he could continue to do so would be for him to leave western Tennessee. Strong columns of Federals marched toward him from nearly every direction: A. J. Smith's from the north, starting at Columbus, Kentucky; William Sooy Smith's from the east, out of middle Tennessee; Joseph Mower's from the southeast, out of Corinth, Mississippi; George Crook's from the east, from his base at Huntsville,

Alabama; and Benjamin Grierson's from the southwest, coming from La Grange, Tennessee. If any two or more of these forces converged on Forrest at the same time, it could spell trouble for the Confederate cavalryman. If all of them did, with some fifteen thousand Federals all told, it would assuredly mean disaster. In Memphis, General Hurlbut gloated, "Forrest must fight or run. I think we shall cure him of his ambition to command West Tennessee."[13] Indeed, discretion seemed to suggest that running, in this case, would be the better part of valor.

In the meantime, Forrest issued several calls for assistance, and fortunately for him, they did not go unheeded. On December 22, General James R. Chalmers launched a diversionary attack near Memphis. Even so, Hurlbut sensed it, and signaled Grierson to keep a "close watch" that Forrest "does not slip by you on some of the roads."[14] That Union cavalry officer knew something of raiding behind enemy lines himself and immediately set to work destroying bridges and ferries over the Hatchie River, beginning at Bolivar, Tennessee, and moving westward to the Mississippi River. With the rivers swollen by winter rains, this strategy could effectively close the door on any attempt Forrest might make to run for safety.

But Bedford Forrest was one step ahead of them. Expecting the Federals to apply such a strategy, he had already ordered the ferryboat at Bolivar moved and sunk in shallow water near Estenaula. When the time came, he could have it raised and use it to cross the Hatchie. That time, and the Union columns, were rapidly coming. On December 23, with scouts racing to and fro to keep him apprised of enemy movements, Forrest started his command southward toward the Confederates' lines. He dispatched a small force to race ahead and secure the crossing at Estenaula. This detachment, under recently promoted General R. V. Richardson, succeeded in beating the Federals to the town and crossed to the south side, pushing out from the river for several miles.

The next day, some of Grierson's men arrived to carry out their orders to destroy bridges and ferries, only to find the Southerners already across. Although they drove Richardson's men, many of whom still did not have guns, back against the river, the timely assistance of other Confederates, under Colonel J. J. Neely, stabilized the situation, and the bridgehead remained intact.

Meanwhile, as he moved with his main column of 2,500 men, 40–50 wagons loaded with food and other supplies, 200 beef cattle, and 300 hogs, Forrest took the further precaution of sending out detachments to watch roads along which other Federals might be coming. One of these detachments, consisting of 500 men under Colonel D. M. Wisdom, ran into a Union column moving north at dawn on December 24. For the remainder of the day, he bluffed and battled the Federals, buying Forrest the time he needed to cross the Hatchie unmolested. Finally, after dark, Wisdom pulled out, rejoining the main Confederate column early on Christmas morning.

Forrest rode out of Jackson, Tennessee, with the rearguard, composed of his escort, at six o'clock on Christmas Eve. He skirmished briefly outside Jackson with Union troops coming from Corinth and moved on to the crossing. Arriving at Estenaula about 10 P.M., Forrest immediately crossed the river with his escort and helped to disperse the Federals who had worried Richardson earlier. His way now clear, at least for the moment, he hastened back to the river to supervise the crossing of the remainder of his men and supplies.[15]

Forrest was watching the crossing when suddenly the lone ferryboat capsized, dumping a wagon and its team into the icy waters. The current swept the teamster away and under the water, the only man lost during the operation. Forrest plunged into the river without a second thought and waded to where the animals were still struggling with their harness. As he cut the great leather straps that held the mules to the wagon, Forrest heard the loud complaint of a recent conscript on the bank behind him. The erstwhile soldier was saying that he had no intention of going in the water himself, and he was saying so loudly and repeatedly. The veterans knew better than to sound off in such a way, particularly within earshot of the general, and they waited for the response they knew was coming. However, Forrest finished the task at hand before he turned back to shore. Without saying a word, the dripping cavalry general walked over to the soldier, still insisting that "he wasn't goin' to get down in that water, no sir, not for nobody he wasn't." He picked the soldier up off the ground, carried him over to the bank, and unceremoniously dumped him into the cold water.[16]

By midday, all of Forrest's men were finally across the Hatchie River. But they were not home free yet. There was still the Wolf River, also swollen by rain, its bridges and ferries destroyed, to cross. Or he could turn eastward, to go around the Wolf and run headlong into Union forces that had gathered to prevent him from doing just that. None of the choices looked particularly appealing. Forrest was in another "tight spot," or so it seemed.

Then he received another stroke of good fortune that always seemed to come his way in such situations. A colonel, on detached duty to recruit for his regiment, had learned of Forrest's operation and knew that he would need a place to cross the Wolf River. As it happened, he found that the Union detachment that had been sent to destroy the bridge over the river near Lafayette, Tennessee, had done a poor job of their assignment, having removed only the floorboards from the structure. This benefactor sent word of his discovery to Forrest, who, in turn, rushed Colonel Bell and three hundred men forward to hold it.[17]

Early on December 26, as the main Confederate column marched toward the Wolf River, they ran into the same Federal detachment that Forrest had dispersed previously. Once again, they had to fight. Using his poker experience to his advantage, Forrest threw both his armed and his unarmed men into the engagement, making his number of effectives appear greater than they actually were. After some bitter fighting, he finally succeeded in forcing the Federals, in the words of their commander, "to retire ... in considerable disorder."[18]

The Confederates pushed on to Lafayette and ran off the small guard in an earthwork on the south bank. Finding the floorboards neatly stacked near the earthwork, the Southerners relaid them and fanned out to secure this new bridgehead. In a heavy downpour, Forrest sent detachments to the east and west to hold off the Union columns that were advancing against him, while he hurried the bulk of his men across the river. By nightfall on December 27, the men were well on their way to Holly Springs, while Forrest toyed with nearby Federal garrisons, causing the Union commander at Colliersville to request reinforcements to resist the attack he expected at daylight. In the meantime, Forrest turned south.[19]

Forrest left behind him a mass of Federals trying to sort out where he was and what he might do next. They slowly began to realize, as one Union officer forlornly admitted, that "Forrest is certainly far away."[20] On December 29, Forrest reported to the new commander of the department, General Leonidas Polk, who had replaced Johnston when he succeeded Bragg as commander of the Army of Tennessee. He expressed regret at leaving western Tennessee so quickly, remarking that if he could return, he could bring out three thousand more recruits and thus virtually double the number of men who recently came out with him.[21]

Despite the satisfaction he had in once again eluding the combination of forces sent to catch him, Forrest complained that the expedition had left him "unwell and much fatigued."[22] Even so, there was still a great deal for him to do. He had to organize the new recruits, a process that required special authority from the War Department, since so many of the men he had enlisted (or conscripted) had ties to other active units in the Confederate service. By late January, the War Department granted the authorization Forrest needed to complete his reorganization.[23] In the meantime, he also effected a small-scale exchange of prisoners with General Hurlbut.[24] Forrest may have been "unwell and much fatigued," but he remained busy, and a subsequent visit to departmental headquarters in Meridian, Mississippi, made him even more so.

General Forrest's journey to Meridian, on January 13, 1864, proved eventful for him. Aside from the opportunity to present Generals Polk and S. D. Lee with a complete report of his excursion into western Tennessee, he hoped to discuss and obtain remedies for the various administrative difficulties that were burdening him. The result of these conversations was the creation of a new department, Forrest's Cavalry Department, which consisted of all mounted troops in western Tennessee and northern Mississippi.[25]

Returning to his headquarters at Como, Mississippi, Forrest issued the first of his general orders announcing the scope of his department, the composition of his staff, and the reorganization of his forces into four brigades under General R. V. Richardson and Colonels Tyree Bell, Robert McCulloch, and Jeffrey Forrest, the last two forming a division under General James R. Chalmers.[26] No doubt these were heady times for the man who had entered the war a private, and all too frequently, it seemed to him, labored under the doubtful leadership of others who were less competent at waging war than he was.

Despite these arrangements, Forrest was having his share of troubles. Sherman had not been entirely incorrect when he asserted that hauling conscripts into the service would require "good" men to watch them. Indeed, desertion plagued Forrest, as it did other commanders, but it proved to be a most vexing problem for this commander who required the strictest discipline from his soldiers. Typically, Forrest reacted to the difficulty with directness and firmness. For him, no punishment was too severe for men who deserted their comrades, regardless of their reasons or their willingness to return at some later point. For the morale of his "good" men and the fact that desertion reflected negatively on his generalship (and thus was a question of honor), he had to stop the outflow while it was a trickle and not yet a flood.

This state of affairs finally came to a head in early February, when nineteen of the new recruits left camp as a group, without authorization. Forrest sent out a detachment to run them down and bring them back to face disciplinary measures. Such measures, for desertion in time of war, meant death. Thus, when the posse returned with the offenders, an extremely angry Forrest had them paraded through camp, which served the double function of shaming them and warning others, and then declared that they would all be shot in front of the entire command. Apparently the general had decided to make an example of these men.

As the preparations for this mass execution proceeded, people from the nearby town of Oxford came into camp to beg Forrest to show compassion and spare the men. Some of the officers in his command also requested that he call off the executions, since they might provoke a mutiny. The general showed no sign of complying with these requests. His course was firm, his mind made up. Apparently he could not be moved by such emotional appeals.

On the day of the execution, Forrest assembled his command in a field. Bell's brigade, to which the deserters had belonged, formed three sides of a square facing the condemned men, who were sitting on their coffins in front of their freshly dug graves. With the final aspects of the ceremony complete and the men blindfolded, the firing squads stepped up to carry out the sentence. All that remained was the command to "fire!" Then one of Forrest's staff officers rode up with a reprieve, to which the command responded with a cheer.[27]

Even with such a demonstration of compassion or, more accurately, because of it, Forrest had made his point. As one officer explained, "There were no more desertions and the men learned that General Forrest was not cruel, nor necessarily severe, but they also learned that he would not be trifled with."[28] Forrest had once again proved to be a master of human nature. As much as he despised desertion, for which he compelled other violators later to suffer the full penalty, he understood the need to handle new recruits with some sensitivity until he could mold them into a fighting force with the cohesion that only working, fighting, and dying together would bring. Pride in the unit and the esteem of riding with Bedford Forrest would come with time.

In the meantime, the experience left understandable concerns in Forrest's mind as he prepared to break camp and march against the Federal forces that were reported to be moving into Mississippi from several directions. The largest and most formidable of these columns was to come out of Vicksburg (which had been captured by the Federals on July 4, 1863) under General Sherman. Plans called for this force of twenty thousand foot soldiers to strike across the state and unite at Meridian with a cavalry command of approximately half that size moving south from Memphis. A third column would go by gunboat up the Yazoo River and march overland to Greenwood, Mississippi, acting primarily as a diversion for the other two forces. Sherman then expected to seize Selma, Alabama, with its arsenals and foundaries, before proceeding to Mobile, Alabama.[29]

Sherman set out on his part of this coordinated operation on February 3 and was in Meridian by the afternoon of February 14. At the same time, General William Sooy Smith concentrated an enormous number of men, horses, and equipment at Colliersville, out of which he would select seven thousand for his march southeastward to meet Sherman. Although he declared himself anxious "to pitch into Forrest wherever I find him,"[30] Smith dallied while waiting for the arrival of a veteran brigade of cavalry from Kentucky, losing valuable time and virtually assuring that he would not reach Meridian when Sherman arrived there. Finally, on February 11, Smith's column set out with his seven thousand well-armed horsemen and twenty pieces of artillery.

Forrest was well aware of the Federals' activity, but he could not be sure of Smith's intentions, so he had to disperse his command to watch the Federals. He expected that the Union cavalry column was on its way to join Sherman and kept the bulk of his two forces between the two Union generals. Forrest also suspected that the Federals would march for their destination along the Mobile and Ohio Railroad and thus through the enormously rich agricultural prairie region around Okolona, Mississippi. Even so, owing to the scattered nature of his command, the Southern general could bring only twenty-five-hundred men, at best, against Smith's invasionary force.[31]

Realizing this disparity in numbers, the Confederate cavalryman steadily fell back as the Federal horsemen approached. That approach was slow, but seemed inexorable. By February 14, Smith was across the Tallahatchie River at New Albany. He had expected Forrest to fight before he could cross, but did so "without firing a shot."[32] Despite the apparent lack of opposition, except for small brushes with Mississippi state troops, Smith did not reach Okolona until February 18. Forrest was still spread thin, to watch for any sudden movement east or west, but he was about to present the Federals with some opposition.

Sherman had warned Smith about Forrest. And as he moved farther south, Smith began to inflate the number of men facing him. Nevertheless, the Union column and its followers, liberated slaves eventually numbering in the thousands, began a systematic destruction of the region. One Union officer remarked that "during two days, the sky was red with the flames of burning corn and cotton." Of the former slaves, the same man observed that they were "driven wild with the infection, set the torch to mansion houses, stables, cotton gins, and quarters," coming "en masse to join our column, leaving only fire and absolute destruction behind them."[33]

While Smith marched to and then down the Mobile and Ohio, Forrest transferred his headquarters to Starkville, Mississippi, and began to set his strategy for stopping the Federals. He sent his youngest brother, Jeffrey, northward to harass the enemy's advance near West Point, while he concentrated the forces on hand to present more formidable opposition and perhaps even set an ambush. The Confederate cavalry commander still feared a sudden change in the enemy's movements, and one came, although certainly not the one Forrest might have anticipated.

Smith was growing increasingly unsure of himself and his part of the operation. He faced a swampy region ahead in which lay a Confederate force whose size he had vastly overrated. He was severely behind schedule and worried what his lateness might mean to his rendezvous with Sherman. Indeed, it was well that he worried about it, for on February 21, Sherman gave up on Smith and started back to Vicksburg. At any rate, Smith explained, "Under the circumstances, I determined not to move my encumbered command into the trap set for me by the rebels."[34] He left a strong rearguard to give the impression that he was still moving southward and began the return march.

Forrest had remained ahead of Smith, determining to watch him closely, but "desiring to delay a general engagement as long as possible," while he awaited assistance from General S. D. Lee.[35] In the meantime, the Union rearguard struck the Confederates at Ellis' Bridge, as part of their feint to keep Forrest busy while the main part of the force started northward. According to Chalmers, who was directing the fighting there, Forrest had been expected, but by nine o'clock still had not arrived. "Suddenly, out of a cloud of dust, accompanied only by an orderly, he came dashing up the road towards the bridge." Chalmers saw that "his face was greatly flushed," a trait of Forrest in the heat of battle, "and he seemed very much ... excited." Forrest asked Chalmers for a report on the fighting, and when Chalmers repeated what the commander on the front had reported, as could be expected through the chain of command, Forrest snapped impatiently, "Is that all you know? Then, I will go and see myself."[36] For Bedford, the only place to gain accurate information was the battlefront.

Chalmers followed his commander (more out of curiosity than

anything else, since this was their first fight together). As the two generals rode toward the front line, on the opposite bank a panic-stricken Southern soldier broke for the rear. Discarding everything in his desperate attempt to get away, the hapless Confederate ran headlong into his commander. Forrest leapt from his horse and grabbed the trooper. Dragging the man to the side of the road, Forrest broke off a branch and began to administer, in Chalmers's words, "one of the worst thrashings I have ever seen a human being get." When he had finished flailing the soldier, Forrest yanked him to his feet, turned him toward the front, and pushed him that way with the stern admonition: "Now, God damn you, go back to the front and fight; you might as well be killed there as here, for if you ever run away again you'll not get off so easy." When the northern press got news of the incident, they made light of it. *Harper's Weekly* published an illustration entitled "Forrest Breaking in a Conscript."[37]

Along with his disciplinary actions, Forrest directed the fighting and soon began to realize that he was dealing with a diversion. Then, "being unwilling [that] they should leave the country without a fight," the Confederate commander determined to give the Federals one.[38] Union Colonel George E. Waring attested to the effectiveness of Forrest's leadership. "No sooner had we turned tail, than Forrest saw that his time had come, and he pressed us sorely all day and until nightfall."[39] After driving their rearguard through West Point, Forrest met the Federals, who were strongly posted four miles north of the town. He sent a strike force around the flank, to get into their rear if possible, while he dismounted the rest of his command for a frontal assault.

Remaining at the front, Forrest led the assault and broke the Union line. The Southerners returned to their horses and sped after the fleeing enemy. Forrest continued to "press" the Union column until nightfall rendered pursuit too dangerous, a fact he learned when his troopers mistakenly fired into his party as it rode ahead of them, killing one man. Forrest's Confederates bivouacked for the night in camps left vacant by their retreating foes. Smith's Federals rode on toward Okolona, finally stopping for the night at 2 A.M., four miles south of the town.

Two hours later, Forrest roused his men and resumed the pursuit. As usual, the general and his escort outraced the rest of the troops and made contact with the Union rearguard first, early that morning.[40] Forrest's idea was to give Smith, as he had earlier given Streight, no rest or ease from a relentless pursuit by at least a portion of his command. This strategy forced Smith to break camp early and form his troops into a line of battle just north of town. When Forrest chased the Federals through Okolona, he came upon the line Smith had drawn up. Despite the bravery of his escort, the Confederate cavalryman realized that his men were not yet up in sufficient numbers to drive his opponents out of their position.

At the same time, Bell's brigade, led during this campaign by Colonel Clark S. Barteau, followed the Union troopers to the east of Forrest's column, having been on the march since 7 A.M. Bedford spotted them and left his men to maintain their fire against the Union line as he dashed across the plain to Bell's position. Riding up to Barteau, Forrest inquired, "Where is the enemy's whole position?" Barteau pointed at the line visible before them. "You see it, General, and they are preparing to charge."

Never one to accept an assault when he could deliver one, Forrest immediately answered, "Then we will charge them."[41] He was peculiarly aware of the relatively small number of men he could bring to bear against the Federals and knew that by being aggressive, he could mask his weakness, instill courage in the men, and perhaps even win the day with a show of bravado. Despite his willingness to "show fight," the superior weaponry of the Union cavalrymen enabled them to repulse the Confederate attack and keep the Southerners at bay.[42]

Again, Forrest decided to call upon a familiar tactic to break the impasse. Maintaining some of his men at the front to keep the Federals busy, he took others under his personal command to strike the enemy's flank. This maneuvering and the timely appearance of McCulloch's brigade arriving from the south had the desired effect. Smith's line broke in confusion. In their haste, the Federals "became entirely disorganized," their units so badly entangled in the dash northward that Smith lost six artillery pieces.[43]

For the next four or five miles, pursued and pursuers engaged in a running fight. Both sides rapidly lost cohesion and became scattered along the road. In the meantime, Colonel Waring, whose brigade occupied the advance of the Union column, formed his men in an effort to stem the rout and slow the pursuit. As the Federals streamed through the line, Waring opened his ranks to allow them to pass behind him and then closed his formation to present a formidable front to the Confederates. He fell back another mile and took up a strong position on a high ridge. Here Smith planned to fight; he placed his artillery, deployed men on the front and flanks as skirmishers, and settled in to resist the Confederates when they attacked.[44]

Forrest formed Jeffrey Forrest's and McCulloch's brigades on either side of the road, as his men approached the Union position, allowing Bell's exhausted troopers to act as the reserve for the command. The two brigades swept forward in the face of a steady explosion of Union artillery and small arms. Then Jeffrey Forrest, leading his men against the Federal position, fell from his horse, shot through the neck. The fire hit McCulloch as well, wounding him in the hand. With both commanders down and the charge broken by the steady stream of fire from the Union lines, the way lay open for Smith to counterattack and punish the soldiers who had so relentlessly pursued him. But the Federals chose to remain behind their breastworks.[45]

In the meantime, Bedford Forrest rushed over to where his youngest brother lay. Leaping from his horse, the general knelt beside him, cradling Jeffrey's head in his arms and calling his name repeatedly. He had earlier thought his brother dead, only to hear that he was wounded and captured and to have him return to the service. Now, there could be no doubt that Jeffrey was gone.[46]

Jeffrey's death symbolized the sacrifice that Bedford Forrest had been willing to undergo for the Southern war effort. Because of the unusual circumstances of his youngest brother's birth (four months after the death of their father) and the difference in their ages, Bedford had raised Jeffrey almost as a son. Nevertheless, he had never held his brother back from the fighting; instead, he had insisted that Jeffrey take an active part. The general had enjoyed the confidence that when he issued a command, this subordinate knew what he meant by it and how best to implement it.

But Bedford Forrest was a realist and a soldier, and when he understood that Jeffrey was dead, he left Jeffrey's remains to a staff officer and returned to the fighting, bent upon vengeance for the loss he had suffered. The general rode to an open point in the field from which he could view the current state of affairs. With bullets flying around him, Forrest calmly directed Colonel W. L. Duckworth, now commanding Jeffrey Forrest's brigade, to take his troopers to the left and hit the Union line in its flank and rear. At the same time, he called for his bugler, formed the rest of his Confederates into a line, and renewed the charge.[47]

The vehemence with which Forrest led the attack upon the Union line so shook Major J. P. Strange, of the general's staff, that he thought his commander had gone mad with grief and was racing to his own death. Since he could not follow, having been left the task of watching over Colonel Forrest's body, he anxiously looked around for someone. Spotting Forrest's surgeon, Dr. J. B. Cowan, Strange called out to him, "Doctor, hurry after the general; I am afraid he will be killed."[48]

In the meantime, the charge had the effect that Forrest had hoped it would have. The Union line melted, and the rush to get away began again. Forrest kept riding after the retreating enemy, firing and slashing as he went. Cowan had to go almost a mile before he caught up with Forrest, but when he did, he "came upon a scene which made my blood run cold." Forrest and part of his escort had plunged into a line of Federals who were attempting to form as a rearguard of sorts. Cowan could see them in the road "in a hand-to-hand fight to the death." The concerned doctor looked around for troops to assist his leader and caught sight of McCulloch's men, with "Black Bob" still in command, despite suffering a wound in the charge that had killed Jeffrey.

Cowan rushed over to McCulloch and informed him of the desperate situation. As the doctor recalled, "the position occupied by the Federals at this time was a strong one, and the number of Federals engaged with the general and his escort seemed so large, and the undertaking to drive them off so great, that for a moment McCulloch's men hesitated." In a gesture of Napoleonic high drama, McCulloch stripped the bloody bandage from his wounded hand, waved it over his head for his men to see, and called out, "My God, men, will you see them kill your general? I will go to his rescue if not a man follows me!"[49] Forrest may have been in no need of assistance, although he undoubtedly appreciated receiving it, for according to one account he personally dispatched three men in the few moments of close-hand fighting.[50]

In any case, the Union troopers again broke off the fighting and withdrew, still pursued by their relentless foes. The running fight continued for another mile when the firing became fairly severe. Dr. Cowan, who by this point had reached the general, remembered Strange's words and remarked, "General, I think you should get out of the road; it is not right unnecessarily to expose yourself." Forrest looked at him blankly for a moment and calmly replied, "Doctor, if you are alarmed, you may get out of the way; I am as safe here as there." The words had no sooner left his lips when a Union artillery shell killed Forrest's horse, shattering the saddle beneath him. Still unimpressed with the danger of his position, Forrest searched for a replacement for his dead animal. He declined to take the surgeon's horse, instead taking one from a member of his escort. Before the day was out, that horse would also be dead.[51]

The surgeon's presence had little effect on the Confederate general, but it proved useful to several individuals who were caught up in the reality of war. One group was a family, seeking shelter from fighting raging near their home. Just after Forrest found a new horse, he noticed a woman and her children huddled next to the chimney behind their little log house. The general called his surgeon's attention to the terrified family. "Dr. Cowan," he called out, pointing to the chimney, "please put that woman and her children in that hole. In there they will be perfectly safe." With that he rode off to resume the chase.[52]

About the same time, after Forrest had driven the Union troopers out of another stand, he was distracted by piteous cries from a nearby hut that was flying a hospital flag. He dismounted and went in to investigate, finding a Union soldier lying on a makeshift operating table, abandoned in the midst of an amputation. Fortunately, Forrest found a bottle of chloroform, doused a cloth with it, and used it to put the soldier out of his misery, at least temporarily. He then sent for Dr. Cowan to finish the surgery and left. Although described as "an authentic occurrence" by Forrest's biographers Thomas Jordan and J. P. Pryor, the story is most likely apocryphal. The Confederate general had too many other concerns and was still too overwrought by his younger brother's death to attend to such details in the midst of fighting and chasing the Federals. Forrest was two months away from the slaughter at Fort Pillow, and the authors may have wanted to put him in a sympathetic light in anticipation of the controversies that surrounded his behavior there.[53]

Whatever he might have done for such people in distress, Forrest had to maintain the pressure on a thoroughly demoralized General William Sooy Smith. "Ten miles from Pontotoc" (Mississippi), the Confederate commander noted that the Federals made "one last and final effort to check pursuit." Forrest knew that he had the best of his enemy, but he also knew that his men were low on ammunition, badly scattered, and virtually exhausted from "clambering the hills on foot and fighting almost constantly for the last 9 miles." Even so, he wanted to press on with those he had on hand, lest the Union troopers rally and turn on him with their superior numbers.[54]

Forrest's instincts were not unfounded, for the Federals were determined to break the stranglehold the Confederates seemed to have on them. Thus, when they turned to fight this last time, they did so with boldness and reckless abandon. Forrest, with evident gratification, later reported, "As we moved up, the whole force charged down at a gallop, and I am proud to say that my men did not disappoint me. Standing firm, repulsed the grandest cavalry charge I have ever witnessed."[55]

The Federals came more than once, and each time the Southerners repulsed them with a sheet of fire, using their rifles, carbines, and pistols to deadly effect. One of Forrest's troopers described this style of fighting effectively: "When you were near enough for our rifles to do good work we commenced pumping lead." Then as the Federal horsemen closed in, "we dropped our carbines (which were strung by a strap across the shoulder), drew the navy sixes, one in each hand—we had discharged sabres as fighting weapons—then we fed you on lead so fast and furious you whirled your backs to us." Yet, even in the moments before the Union troops' withdrawal began again, not to stop until they had reached Memphis, the fighting was at its fiercest and most intensely personal. Forrest saved the life of one Southerner who had exhausted his ammunition by striking a blow that "nearly severed the Federal officer's head from his shoulders." Then, as the officer fell from his horse, his would-be victim grabbed the pistol from his hand and vaulted into the saddle to chase after other opponents.[56]

There would be no more stands. As Union Colonel Waring admitted, "The retreat to Memphis was a weary, disheartening, and almost panic-stricken flight, in the greatest disorder and confusion."[57] As darkness descended upon a day filled with bitter fighting, both sides seemed too exhausted to continue. Forrest's scattered command began to concentrate, and General S. J. Gholson's Mississippi State troops joined as well. These latter were the same soldiers Smith had blithely "brushed aside" on his way south earlier in the campaign. Now they would be the ones Forrest used to harass the retreating Federals the rest of the way, his own command finally too broken down to follow the fleeing enemy.[58]

In three days of severe fighting, in various encounters and running fights, the Confederates suffered 27 killed, 97 wounded, and 20 missing, among the most lamented being Colonel Jeffrey Forrest and Lieutenant Colonel James A. Barksdale, both killed. In his after action report, General Forrest allowed himself only the briefest official notice of his intensely personal loss. "The death of my brother, Colonel Jeffrey E. Forrest, is deeply felt by his brigade as well as by myself, and it is but just to say that for sobriety, ability, prudence, and bravery he had no superior of his age." The Federals, at the same time, lost 54 killed, 179 wounded, and 155 missing.[59]

Forrest had thwarted this Union drive into Mississippi, and now he returned to his headquarters to attend to the refitting of his command for future action. His commanders reacted favorably to his accomplishments, but the failure of the Union campaign incensed and frustrated Generals William Tecumseh Sherman and Ulysses S. Grant. In his *Memoirs* Sherman recalled, still somewhat bitterly, "I wanted to destroy General Forrest, who was constantly threatening Memphis and river above, as well as our route to supplies in middle Tennessee. In this we failed utterly, because General Smith, when he did start, allowed General Forrest to head him off and to defeat him with an inferior force near West Point, below Okolona." He angrily and frankly admitted, "I had set so much store on his part of the project that I was disappointed, and so reported officially to General Grant."[60]

Grant attributed the Southern success to the experience of Forrest's men, perhaps without realizing that the Confederate commander had entered the campaign unsure of what to expect from the majority of his men, who were just entering their first combat under him. But the Union general also placed much of the credit on "the way troops are officered; and for the peculiar kind of warfare which Forrest had carried on neither army could present a more effective officer than he."[61]

Forrest *(right)* and Major D. C. Kelley as they watched the unsuccessful Union naval assault on Fort Donelson. The ferocity of the attack caused Forrest to shout to Kelley: "Parson! For God's sake, pray; nothing but God Almighty can save that fort!" *(From the* Life of General Nathan Bedford Forrest*)*

Described by one trooper as "a rash man and fond of going into danger," Forrest usually led his men from the front lines. His favorite command on the battlefield was, "Forward, men, and mix with 'em." Here he directs the movement of his men in an attack on Fort Donelson. *(From the* Life of General Nathan Bedford Forrest*)*

Forrest's presence on the front lines cost him twenty-nine horses killed by hostile fire, but he could claim that he had slain thirty Union opponents in personal combat. Here Forrest steps over a horse just killed beneath him at Fort Donelson. *(From the* Life of General Nathan Bedford Forrest*)*

When the Confederate commanders decided to surrender the fort, Forrest got permission to attempt an escape. Leading his men out along a flooded road, he told them, "Boys, these people are talking about surrendering, and I am going out of this place before they do or bust hell wide open." *(From the* Life of General Nathan Bedford Forrest*)*

Streight valiantly tried every device to delay Forrest's pursuing Confederates. At Black Creek the Federals burned the bridge, but timely assistance from young Emma Sansom enabled Forrest to find a crossing and continue trailing the Union raiders. *(From the* Life of General Nathan Bedford Forrest*)*

Emma Sansom (from a photograph taken after the war). *(From the* Life of General Nathan Bedford Forrest*)*

Forrest used various devices to encourage Union commanders to surrender their troops without bloodshed. Here, he attempts to convince the garrison of Fort Pillow, Tennessee, to surrender by promising "no quarter" if they resisted. *(From the* Life of General Nathan Bedford Forrest*)*

During Forrest's pursuit of Colonel Abel D. Streight's raiders, the Federals staged a surprise counterattack and captured two Confederate artillery pieces. The incident led to a deadly confrontation between Forrest and a subordinate, Lieutenant A. W. Gould, shortly thereafter. *(From the* Life of General Nathan Bedford Forrest*)*

Forrest's sharpshooters kept Union defenders close to Fort Pillow's defenses while the bulk of the Confederate forces stormed over the parapet and into the main works. Questions remain concerning Forrest's role in the events that followed the collapse of resistance. *(From the* Life of General Nathan Bedford Forrest*)*

The "Fort Pillow Massacre" provided Northern newspapers with considerable propaganda and pursued Forrest for the remainder of his life. (*From* Harper's Weekly, *April 30, 1864*)

Much of the fighting around Brice's Cross Roads was hand-to-hand combat as units of both sides struggled amid the black-jack thickets. (*From the* Life of General Nathan Bedford Forrest*)*

Forrest ordered Morton to take his artillery into the thick of the fighting, observing, "Well, artillery is made to be captured, and I wanted to see them take yours." *(From the* Life of General Nathan Bedford Forrest*)*

After a hard day of combat, Forrest's Confederates finally succeeded in breaking the Union lines at Brice's Cross Roads. The retreat became a rout when overturned wagons blocked the bridge over Tishomingo Creek, resulting in one of Forrest's greatest victories of the war. *(From the* Life of General Nathan Bedford Forrest*)*

Wearing the badge of Fort Pillow, brandishing the knife of the Lost Cause, and carrying the whip of slavery in his pocket, Forrest stands with other elements of a "White Man's Government" in this Thomas Nast cartoon of a Democratically controlled South during Reconstruction: "This Is a White Man's Government" in *Harper's Weekly*, September 5, 1868. *(Library of Congress)*

The presidential election of 1868 was particularly heated. In this Thomas Nast cartoon, Forrest stands with other supporters of the Democratic party beneath a flag touting "slavery," "Fort Pillow," "mob law," and "the Ku Klux Klan," while the party strips a recently freed black Samson of his strength—the vote: "The Modern Samson," in *Harper's Weekly*, October 3, 1868.

CHAPTER 9

War Means Fighting, and Fighting Means Killing

(March–April 1864)

War means fighting, and fighting means killing.

—NATHAN BEDFORD FORREST

War is an act of violence pushed to its utmost bounds.

—CARL VON CLAUSEWITZ

EVEN IN HIS MOMENT OF VICTORY, Bedford Forrest began to plan how he would return to western Tennessee to augment his command and harass the Federals there. When new units, consisting of fragments of three Kentucky regiments under General Abraham Buford, joined his cavalry command, Forrest expanded his plans for a raid to include Kentucky as well. Then, on March 7, 1864, the general reorganized his forces into two divisions (four total brigades) under Generals James R. Chalmers and Buford. Chalmers's division would include brigades under General R. V. Richardson and Colonel Robert M. McCulloch; Buford's would consist of brigades under Colonel Tyree Bell and Colonel A. P. Thompson.[1]

Almost immediately there was trouble. Within two days after the reorganization, an angry General Forrest relieved Chalmers and ordered him to report in person to General Leonidas Polk. Chalmers complied, but under protest. The whole affair emanated from a trivial argument that reflected larger matters of personality. Bedford Forrest simply could not operate in an atmosphere in which his authority was questioned or even appeared to be questioned. He would brook no interference with the prerogatives of command, especially from a subordinate.[2]

For his part, Chalmers felt ill-used by Forrest. He wrote Polk and Adjutant General Samuel Cooper that "General Forrest took my only tent from me and gave it to his brother." Hidden beneath this statement was the fact that Chalmers had commanded cavalry before Bedford Forrest even joined the service and achieved the rank of brigadier general before Shiloh. He was used to command and, indeed, had been in command of the cavalry in northern Mississippi before Forrest transferred there. He had cooperated with General Forrest in the latter's recent foray into western Tennessee, not as a subordinate, but as an equal. Chalmers probably believed that he had as much, if not more, reason to be Forrest's commander rather than his subordinate.[3]

However trivial the matter over which the break between the two Confederate cavalry generals finally came may have been, it threatened to have serious repercussions. On March 10, Forrest informed General Polk that he had relieved the officer, "satisfied that I have not and shall not receive the co-operation of Brigadier-General Chalmers, and that matters of the smallest moment will continue, as they have heretofore done, to be a source of annoyance to myself and detrimental to the service." And since Forrest considered himself "responsible to the proper authority for all orders I have or may hereafter issue, I deem it both necessary and beneficial that we should separate."[4]

Although Forrest subsequently wrote that he "regretted the necessity of relieving Brigadier-General Chalmers," he felt he had no other choice. Chalmers had written a letter to which Forrest took exception and which the commander remarked "speaks for itself." The cavalry chieftain reiterated: "He has never been satisfied since I came here, and being satisfied that I have not had and will not receive his support and co-operation, deemed it necessary that we should separate." In essence this was a power struggle between a general who had commanded the cavalry in the region and another who now exercised the same command. Forrest was determined to have division and brigade commanders he could trust implicitly. "I must have the cordial support of my subordinate officers," he explained to Polk, "in order to succeed and make my command effective." In the end, Forrest tried to sound benevolent: "I hope you may be able to place him where he will be better satisfied than with me."[5]

Polk took the matter under advisement. He knew Forrest well enough not to challenge his actions, but thought the measure excessive. On March 14, Polk informed Adjutant General Cooper of Forrest's actions, adding, "My decision is that the former [Forrest] has exceeded his authority, notwithstanding the precedents quoted." Cooper replied that he agreed with Polk's assessment and restored Chalmers to command.[6]

Nor was Chalmers the only officer under Forrest to face charges and the relief of his command. At about the same time, Forrest relieved General Richardson "on account of charges preferred against him by Colonel [J. U.] Green," commanding one of the regiments in Richardson's brigade. Unlike Chalmers, Richardson failed to return to Confederate service under Forrest. Colonel J. J. Neely succeeded him in command of the brigade.[7]

In the meantime, Forrest anxiously continued to plan his return to western Tennessee. Then in mid-March, with internal discord as an irritating backdrop, he started Buford's division northward. He left Chalmers's division, under Colonel McCulloch, behind in Mississippi, to stand watch there, to sweep the area clean of absentees and deserters, and to act as police for the region. He warned McCulloch: "Impress upon the officers commanding the regiments sent out to scour and breast the country to do the work thoroughly and catch, if possible, the men who are going through the country and impressing and stealing horses without authority."[8]

Bedford Forrest was not one who was easily surprised, but as he marched northward, he could see the effect the war was having on the region. He noted, "The whole of West Tennessee is overrun by bands and squads of robbers, horse thieves and deserters, whose depredations and unlawful appropriations of private property are rapidly and effectually depleting the country."[9] He had been there during the previous winter and probably expected to confront desolation at that time of year, but this was spring, the area should be coming back to life, and it was not.

Compounding this desolation was the news Forrest received when he reached Jackson, Tennessee. The citizens there told him horror stories of the actions of Colonel Fielding Hurst and other Union or pro-Union soldiers in the area. On March 21 and 22, Forrest sent strongly worded dispatches to his superiors and to the Union commander at Memphis outlining the "outrages committed by the commands of Col. Fielding Hurst and others of the Federal Army" and appointed an investigator to determine the validity of the charges. In Forrest's telling assessment, these men were "renegade Tennesseans" and should be held accountable for their actions against their defenseless neighbors.

Forrest spelled out these "outrages" to the Union commander at Memphis and demanded "restitution" and the release of political prisoners. "I respectfully demand that restitution be made by the U.S. authorities in the sum of $5,139.25 to the citizens of Jackson, Tenn., the amount extorted from them by Col. Fielding Hurst, on or about the 12th day of February, 1864, under threats of burning the town." The catalog of wrongs included murder as well. "It appears that within the past two months seven cases of deliberate murder have been committed in this department, most of them known and all believed to have been perpetrated by the command of Colonel Hurst." For these offenses Forrest demanded "the surrender of Col. Fielding Hurst and the officers and men of his command guilty of these murders, to be dealt with by the C.S. authorities as their offenses require." Finally, he noted that the Federals had detained "many citizens of this portion of the State" without bringing charges against them. He "demanded" that one of them, Rev. G. W. D. Harris, "be granted a fair trial before a competent tribunal, or else unconditionally and promptly [be] released, or otherwise I shall place in close confinement 5 Federal soldiers, now in my hands, as hostages for his protection." And should the minister die while in confinement "from ill treatment," then "these men" would be "duly executed in retaliation."[10]

Forrest's appointed inspector, Lieutenant Colonel W. M. Reed, carried the demands to Memphis and compiled his own report. He detailed the "facts of the recent tax levied by Col. Fielding Hurst upon the citizens" of Jackson and the murders Forrest had alluded to in his report. The most heinous of these murders was the "death by torture" of Lieutenant Willis Dodds, late of Forrest's command. Dodds had been in the area collecting absentees and deserters when he was captured "at the residence of his father in Henderson County, Tenn." One witness reported seeing Dodds's body "very soon after his murder." The body "was most horribly mutilated, the face having been skinned, the nose cut off, the under jaw disjointed, the privates cut off, and the body otherwise barberously lacerated and most wantonly injured, and that his death was brought about by the most inhumane process of torture." Accompanying Reed was Forrest's threat, should the Federals reject his demands concerning Hurst and the others, to "declare the aforesaid Fielding Hurst, and the officers and men of his command, outlaws, and not entitled to be treated as prisoners of war falling into the hands of the forces of the Confederate States."[11]

Forrest felt strongly about the Hurst business. He wanted some form of retribution and wrote Polk, seeking it from him. "I desire," he explained, "if it meets with the approval of the lieutenant-general commanding, that this report may be sent to some newspaper for publication. Such conduct should be made known to the world."[12] What had been and was continuing to happen in Missouri and Kansas on a grand scale was happening in western Tennessee on a smaller scale. Scores were being settled, as they had been in the prewar days, with blood.[13]

The war had taken on a more "modern" aspect by 1864, with soldiers waging war on whole populations, including civilians. Although Forrest's subsequent actions demonstrated his understanding of that fact, he could not completely free himself from his past. Thus, when the people of Jackson complained that they had been victimized and harassed by men claiming the protection of the Federal uniform for their deeds, Forrest was inclined to reject that claim and revert to the methods he had used in the backcountry to deal with persons who violated the commonly held sense of honor. Already hardened by his frontier heritage, his prewar slave dealings, and his wartime experience, Bedford Forrest was hardened even more by such acts. Never one to shy away from spilling blood, he became even less so in his quest to punish violators of his code of ethics.

In the meantime, Forrest determined to accomplish the tasks for which he had returned to western Tennessee. He marched off on March 22 to Trenton to set up a recruiting office there. The next day he sent Colonel W. L. Duckworth with some five hundred men to capture Union City. When they arrived there early on March 24, the Confederates found the Federals well entrenched. They tested the Union position with several charges, driving the Union troops into the earthworks, but making no further inroads. Duckworth deployed his men to harass the garrison, but had no artillery to compel them to surrender.

Aware of his predicament, Duckworth called upon one of Forrest's stratagems—bluff. Forrest had earlier victimized this Union commander, Colonel Isaac R. Hawkins, in 1862. Thus, Duckworth decided to send in a typical "Forrest" demand for the immediate surrender of the garrison. Hawkins, knowing Forrest from their earlier acquaintance, asked for time to consider the demand and insisted upon meeting with Forrest personally in the interim. Duckworth was equal to the challenge and sent back word, again under the name of Bedford Forrest, that "I am not in the habit of meeting officers inferior to myself in rank under a flag of truce, but I will send Col. Duckworth, who is your equal in rank, and who is authorized to arrange terms and conditions with you under instructions."[14]

To assist him in the ruse, Duckworth took various measures to make his command look larger than it actually was and to fool the Federals into believing that he had artillery with him. This latter maneuver may have won the day, for as the Union officers discussed their options, a telegraph operator warned them that the Southerners "had two pieces of artillery; that he had seen them." The presence of artillery sealed the garrison's fate in Hawkins's mind; as he explained, "it would save a great many lives if we surrender." Hawkins then met with Duckworth and around 11:00 A.M. the garrison surrendered. Duckworth knew his man, and the Confederates later joked that they would willingly parole Hawkins to

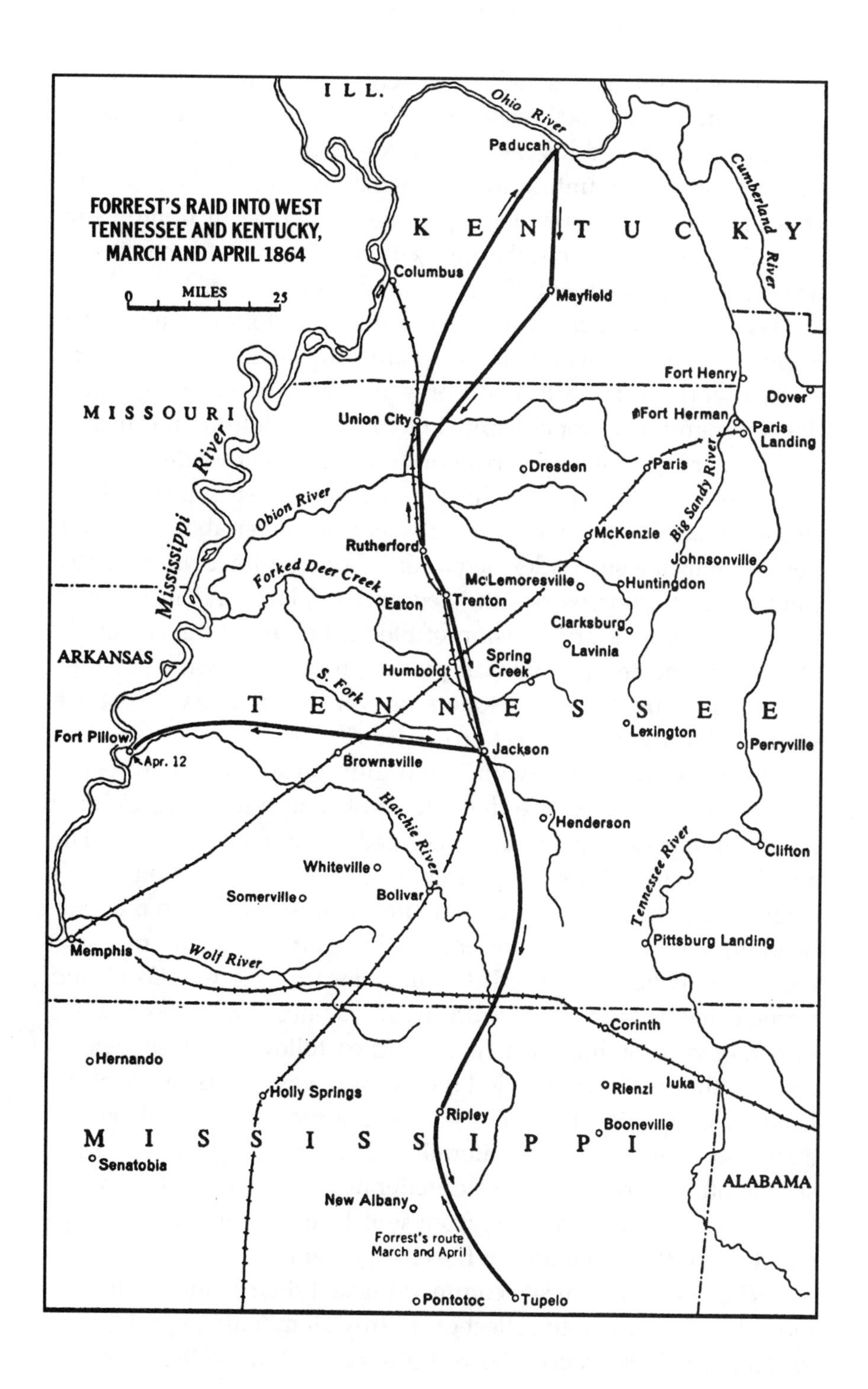
FORREST'S RAID INTO WEST TENNESSEE AND KENTUCKY, MARCH AND APRIL 1864
0 MILES 25
ILL.
Ohio River
Paducah
KENTUCKY
Cumberland River
Columbus
Mayfield
Fort Henry
Dover
MISSOURI
Union City
Fort Herman
Paris Landing
Mississippi River
Dresden
Paris
Big Sandy River
Obion River
McKenzie
Rutherford
Johnsonville
Forked Deer Creek
McLemoresville
Huntingdon
Eaton
Trenton
Clarksburg
Lavinia
ARKANSAS
Humboldt
Spring Creek
S. Fork
TENNESSEE
Fort Pillow
Apr. 12
Lexington
Brownsville
Jackson
Perryville
Hatchie River
Henderson
Clifton
Tennessee River
Whiteville
Somerville
Bolivar
Memphis
Wolf River
Pittsburg Landing
Corinth
Hernando
Rienzi
Iuka
Holly Springs
Ripley
Booneville
MISSISSIPPI
Senatobia
ALABAMA
New Albany
Forrest's route March and April
Pontotoc
Tupelo

obtain even more horses and equipment. In this case, the Southerners captured some 500 men and 300 horses. To make matters worse, Hawkins and his men had recently drawn pay for "over a year's service" amounting to approximately $60,000. The Confederates later lined the prisoners up at the courthouse in Trenton and, according to one of the unhappy Federals, "searched each man as he went in, robbing them of their money, blankets, etc."[15]

While Duckworth led his small force to victory at Union City, Forrest proceeded farther north to Paducah, which he and his men reached early in the afternoon of March 25. The Federals, under the command of Colonel Samuel G. Hicks, withdrew into nearby Fort Anderson, a strong earthwork on the western side of town. Hicks held the fort with over 650 men, and Forrest contented himself with harassing fire from nearby houses. After about an hour, Forrest sent in a surrender demand: "Having a force amply sufficient to carry your works and reduce the place, and in order to avoid the unnecessary effusion of blood, I demand the surrender of the fort and troops, with all public property. If you surrender, you shall be treated as prisoners of war; but if I have to storm your works, you may expect no quarter."[16]

But Hicks was no Hawkins, and unimpressed by the threat of "no quarter," rejected the demand. Not long afterward, Colonel A. P. Thompson led an unauthorized assault on the fort. The attack was ill advised, apparently prompted by Thompson's desire to achieve success in his hometown. According to one participant, the colonel so confidently believed that he could race into the fort that he announced, "I am going to take that fort" and formed his men for "a wild rush" against it.[17] Thompson's impetuosity cost him dearly. A soldier following close behind recalled that as the colonel led the assault, waving his cap over his head to encourage his men, "he was struck by a shell, which exploded as it struck him, literally tearing him to pieces and the saddle off his horse."[18] The Confederates retreated to the protection of some nearby houses, from which they operated as sharpshooters for the remainder of the engagement.[19]

While part of Forrest's command licked their wounds, the rest moved into the town to collect or destroy all military supplies they found there. In his report, Forrest observed, "I drove the enemy to their gunboats and fort, and held the town for ten hours; captured many stores and horses; burned sixty bales of cotton, one steamer [the *Dacotah*], and a drydock, bringing out fifty prisoners." As some of the men cleaned out the town and others harassed the garrison from long range, still other Confederates fired at the portholes of the gunboats. This annoyance drove the vessels under the shelter of the fort, but did not prevent the Federal boats from shelling the town and causing it considerable damage.[20]

With nothing left to accomplish in Paducah, Forrest and his men rode out of the town. Forrest spent the remainder of the month granting brief furloughs, particularly to the Kentuckians in his command, with orders to return with new clothes, mounts, and recruits. In the meantime, the Federals remained active. General Benjamin Grierson sent Colonel Hurst after Forrest with orders "to hang upon, harass, and watch the movements of the enemy." In doing so, Grierson kept in mind Forrest's threat to declare Hurst and his men outlaws. He warned the officer, "You are particularly cautioned against allowing your men to straggle or pillage. Issue and enforce the strictest orders upon this subject, as a deviation from this rule may prove fatal to yourself and command."[21]

Ironically, the Confederates got an opportunity to punish Hurst, although not in a court of law. On March 29, while pushing northward, Southern cavalry under Colonel J. J. Neely, in the words of General Chalmers, "met the traitor Hurst at Bolivar, after a short conflict, in which we killed and captured 75 prisoners of the enemy, drove Hurst hatless into Memphis." Chalmers noted that aside from "leaving in our hands all his wagons, ambulances, [and] papers," the Tennessee Unionist left behind "his mistresses, both black and white."[22]

Despite Hurst's abortive effort to harass Forrest, the Federals did not march out of Memphis until April 3. Even then the advance was so cautious that a small battalion of 150 Confederates turned back a much larger force of Federals, losing only 2 men wounded while killing 6, wounding 15 to 20, and capturing 3 of the enemy.[23] The next day, Forrest assessed his entire operation in a dispatch to departmental headquarters. He placed his total casualties at 15 killed and 42 wounded, and those of the Federals at 79 killed, 102 wounded, and 612 captured. In this dispatch Forrest also hinted at his future plans. "There is a Federal force of 500 or 600 at Fort Pillow," he noted almost nonchalantly, "which I shall attend to in a day or two, as they have horses and supplies which we need."[24]

In conjunction with his plan to take Fort Pillow, Tennessee, Forrest ordered various demonstrations against Paducah, Kentucky, and Memphis, Tennessee. He sent General Buford's brigade in the direction of Paducah, to create a diversion well away from the fort, located on the Mississippi, north of Memphis. In addition, the brigade would continue to scour the area for horses and supplies. Neely's men, fresh from their victory over Hurst, would conduct similar operations in the direction of Memphis. With the help of other units in the area, they would attempt to keep the sizable Union force garrisoned there occupied.

Forrest was at least partially aware of his place in the broader context of the war east of the Mississippi. In his April 4 dispatch to departmental headquarters he observed, "It is clear that they are concentrating all their available force before Richmond and at Chattanooga."[25] For him the advantage of remaining in western Tennessee was immediate: more horses, more men, and more equipment and supplies. The more Federal troops he kept busy in western Tennessee and Kentucky, the less the enemy could throw against Generals Joseph E. Johnston and Robert E. Lee. General William Tecumseh Sherman was even more aware of these implications. On April 9, he wrote General Stephen A. Hurlbut in Memphis, "The object of Forrest's move is to prevent our concentration as against Johnston, but we must not permit it."[26]

On his way to Paducah, Buford detached a small force to carry out a demonstration against Columbus, Kentucky. The Confederates had already profited from bluff and bluster and perhaps could again. Buford rode on to Paducah, while Captain H. A. Tyler and 150 men toyed with the garrison at Columbus. Tyler sent in a note, under the name "A. Buford," which contained the usual demand for surrender to avoid bloodshed, but added, "Should you surrender, the negroes now in arms will be returned to their masters. Should I, however, be compelled to take the place, no quarter will be shown to the negro troops whatever; the white troops will be treated as prisoners of war."[27] Of course, Tyler knew that he did not have the means to carry out his threat. By using such language, he clearly hoped to intimidate the commander of the Union garrison and stall for time while Forrest (and Buford) carried out the more substantial aspects of the Confederate strategy.

Buford was miles away, nearing Paducah, which he reached on April 14, the day after Tyler used his name to deceive the Federals at Columbus. He also sent in a demand for surrender, again to Colonel Hicks, under the name "Buford." In the note, Buford expressed his reluctance "to endanger the lives of women and children and non-combatants," granting them an hour's grace to leave town. Hicks responded with gratitude for the "act of humanity on your part." He agreed to order the evacuation of civilians, insisting, "After that time come ahead; I am ready for you." Buford's scheme was largely bluff. He wanted to hold the garrison in the fort, while his men scoured through Paducah looking for supplies, particularly 140 horses that the Northern newspapers had bragged the Confederates missed on their first raid of the town. This time the Southerners found their quarry and, having gotten what they wanted, they left a small rearguard to continue the deception and started back toward Tennessee.[28] By this time, Bedford Forrest and his men were also well on their way back from the scene of their recent activities at Fort Pillow.

Fort Pillow was situated on a high bluff on the eastern bank of the Mississippi, overlooking that river. Originally constructed by the Confederates in 1861 to assist in defending the water approaches to Memphis, the fort eventually consisted of three distinct lines of entrenchments. The innermost of these earthworks consisted of a ditch 8 feet deep, with the dirt thrown on the inside to form a parapet, or bank, 6 to 8 feet high and 4 to 6 feet across. The fort lay in the shape of a half circle, approximately 125 yards long, and faced the east, or landward side, its rear open to a bluff that dropped off sharply to the river below. Ravines split the landscape surrounding this inner earthwork.[29]

The Confederates evacuated the fort in 1862, and it became part of the chain of isolated garrisons the Federals employed to protect their communications and supply lines. In 1864, a garrison variously estimated at between 557 and 580 black and white Union troops, more or less evenly divided, manned Fort Pillow. The black units consisted largely of former slaves, the white units of Tennessee Unionists, some of whom had deserted from Forrest's command, all under the command of Major Lionel F. Booth. In addition, Booth had six pieces of artillery and the promise of assistance from the gunboat *New Era,* lying just off the shore, to defend his position.[30]

Forrest knew about Fort Pillow and its garrison, as his dispatch of April 4 indicated.[31] He did not expect much resistance, if any, from a force of soldiers composed of humanity he did not respect. Forrest simply did not believe that the fort's garrison was capable of behaving like soldiers. He had already bluffed Hawkins into a surrender, and a mere fraction of his men had routed Hurst, both commanders of "renegade Tennesseans." There was also the opportunity to expose the fallacy of placing guns in the hands of blacks by demonstrating their inferiority as soldiers.[32]

In his attitude toward the members of the Union fort's garrison, Forrest exposed his deepest prejudices. As a white Southerner, he considered the white Southerners in Fort Pillow to be traitors and examples of humanity at its worst. To Forrest, it was such "renegade Tennesseans" who violated the norms of warfare and civilization. They were the cold-blooded savages who waged war on civilians, tortured prisoners, and compounded their sins by fighting beside former slaves. And the black troops were little better. They were deluded miscreants, coerced from the fields by their new masters. But their current behavior, as misguided as it might be, could not be tolerated.

Bedford Forrest's past experience with black Southerners led him to develop several generalizations. He could not think of such people as people and certainly refused to take them seriously as soldiers. Black Southerners were commodities to be bought and sold and made to work, not human beings who might wish to control their lives by carrying weapons and wearing uniforms. That they carried weapons and wore uniforms could only be attributed to interference from Northern whites, who threatened what many Southern whites saw as the proper social order. Furthermore, widespread rumors of depredations by the garrison against local civilians sympathetic to the South circulated through the Confederate camps, further enflaming the sentiments against the soldiers in Fort Pillow.[33] Thus, when Forrest's men rode against it in April, Fort Pillow offered a tempting target for a number of reasons.

The first Confederates arrived before the fort in the early morning of April 12, under the command of General Chalmers. Forrest had directed Chalmers to "invest" the Union position and await his arrival. Chalmers followed Forrest's orders to the letter, advancing slowly and cautiously, but steadily driving the Federals into their innermost earthwork. That achieved, he deployed his men, McCulloch's brigade to the left and Bell's brigade to the right.[34]

Forrest arrived on the scene at 10 A.M. to find the fort virtually surrounded. He carefully surveyed the situation and acquainted himself with the lay of the land and the enemy's position. In the course of this particular reconnaissance, Union fire hit Forrest's horse, causing the animal to rear and fall, badly bruising the general in the process. When he had collected himself enough to mount another horse, his aide suggested that he reconnoiter on foot instead. Forrest replied that he was "just as apt to be hit one way as another, and that he could see better where he was." Before the day was through, he would lose two more horses, shot from beneath him.[35]

Despite his painful fall, Forrest gained valuable information from his examination. He discovered two assets that would place the fort within his grasp. The first asset was the ravines surrounding the Union position, the possession of which would place his troops within easy reach of the fort and protect them from the enemy's fire. The second was the high ground outside the fort, from which sharpshooters could take most of the interior of Fort Pillow under fire. Some of these men already occupied this ground, but Forrest added substantially to their numbers.[36]

Confederate marksmen had already made an impact upon the Union garrison. Lieutenant Mack J. Leaming reported that the Union troops "suffered pretty severely in the loss of commissioned officers by the unerring aim of the rebel sharpshooters."[37]

One of the officers killed by this fire, unbeknownst to the Southerners, was Major Booth, shot through the chest as he stood near porthole number two, sometime around 9 A.M.[38] As some of the men carried Booth away, Major William F. Bradford assumed command of the fort.

Returning from his reconnaissance, Forrest asked McCulloch what he "thought of capturing the barracks and houses which were near the fort and between it and my position." McCulloch told his chief that if he took them, he could "silence the enemy's artillery." Without hesitating, Forrest told him to "go ahead and take them."[39] Already the Federals had attempted to burn the structures, but succeeded in destroying only the row nearest the fort before Confederate fire drove them back. Leaming attested to McCulloch's subsequent success in taking the buildings and using them to the attackers' advantage: "From these barracks the enemy kept up a murderous fire on our men despite all our efforts to dislodge him."[40]

Forrest also ordered the remaining troops in his command to seize the abandoned rifle pits outside the fort. The success of these actions convinced him that he was now in a position to storm the fort. But, as was typical of Forrest, he preferred to send in a surrender demand first. There was no need to fight for something that ought to be gained in a less bloody fashion. And with this thought in mind, Forrest displayed a flag of truce and sent in a demand at 3:30 P.M. that read: "The conduct of the officers and men garrisoning Fort Pillow has been such as to entitle them to being treated as prisoners of war. I demand the unconditional surrender of this garrison, promising you that you shall be treated as prisoners of war." Explaining that his men had just received "a fresh supply of ammunition," Forrest observed that "from their present position," they could "easily assault and capture the fort." He closed with the warning: "Should my demand be refused, I cannot be responsible for the fate of your command."[41] This last "threat" was part of Forrest's psychological arsenal, by which he hoped to encourage his enemy, here and elsewhere, to give up without further struggle.

Bradford did not realize it, but he was in no position to argue. He responded to the demand with a request, under Booth's name, for one hour to consult with his subordinates. Forrest worried that the delay would allow reinforcements to arrive, and when he saw a transport vessel "apparently crowded with troops" nearing the fort and "the smoke" of several others "ascending the river," he shortened the time to twenty minutes.[42]

As the boats continued to approach Fort Pillow, without any signal from the fort that they should stop as long as the truce was in force, Forrest dispatched his adjutant, Captain Charles W. Anderson, and Colonel Clark S. Barteau to take two hundred men each to the riverbank below to ward off any attempt to land reinforcements. He specifically instructed Anderson to "hold my position on the bluff, prevent any escape of the garrison by water, to pour rifle-balls into the open ports of the *New Era* when she went into action, and to fight everything blue betwixt wind and water until yonder flag comes down [referring to the flag inside Fort Pillow itself]."[43] To the members of the garrison who saw it, this movement constituted a breach of ethics, a violation of the flag of truce. Likewise, the Confederate commander viewed the actions of the steamer as a violation of the truce.[44]

Meanwhile, Forrest grew impatient and rode to the scene of the negotiations between the truce parties. Ironically, as he came up to them, they were arguing over whether Forrest was actually on the field. The general assured the Federals that he was Bedford Forrest and that he wanted to know from Booth "in plain and unmistakable English. Will he fight or surrender?"[45] Undoubtedly still skeptical about the Confederate officer's identity, the Union party returned to the fort, got an answer, and rode back. Forrest took the paper, unfolded it, and quietly read the succinct reply, "I will not surrender." He saluted and went back to his lines. There was nothing left to do but fight.[46]

While the truce parties traded notes, some members of the garrison, apparently feeling secure within the confines of their earthworks, taunted their opponents. Confederate Colonel Barteau later recalled, "During the truce they openly defied us from the breastworks to come and take the fort."[47] Some of the participants attributed this and later behavior to the presence of alcohol in the fort, and no doubt many of the Confederates determined to punish the fort's defenders for their temerity.[48]

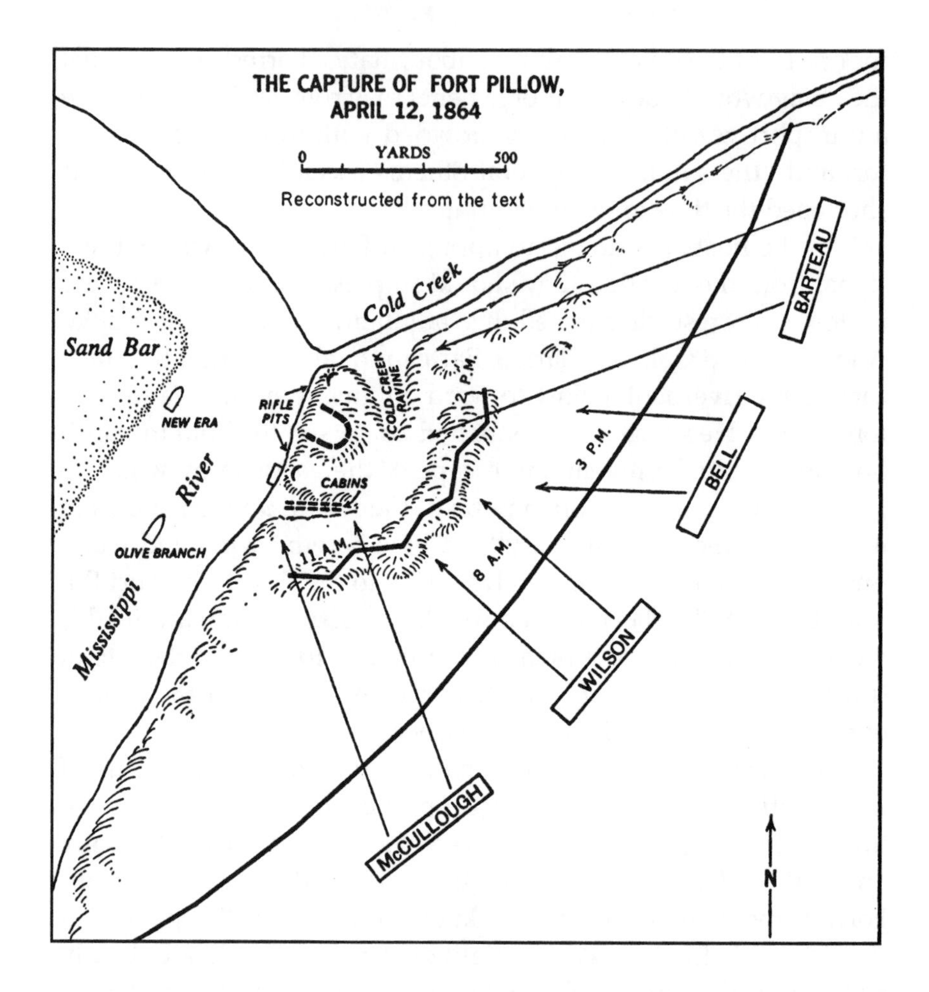

Forrest rode back to his earlier position in the lines, four hundred yards from the fort, fully determined to carry the works by assault, and began issuing orders to that effect. In his April 26 report, he observed, "I dispatched staff officers to Colonels Bell and McCulloch, commanding brigades, to say to them that I should watch with interest the conduct of the troops; that Missourians, Mississippians, and Tennesseans surrounded the works, and I desired to see who would first scale the fort."[49] This application of loyalty to and pride in states would ensure that the men fought even harder as they sought to compete with each other. Having been compelled to assault the fort, Forrest obviously wanted the work completed as quickly and effectively as possible.

Any Southern life lost at this juncture would be a life squandered.

Finally, with the arrangements and instructions complete, Forrest ordered his bugler to sound the "charge." Significantly, he remained at his post four hundred yards away and did not lead the assault, as was his custom. Perhaps he still ached from his earlier fall, or he might have sensed what was about to happen and wished to distance himself from it. Nevertheless, it is important to note that had Forrest planned to massacre the garrison, he most assuredly would have led the charge himself and waded wholeheartedly into the bloodletting without hesitation. In any event, what happened next became almost immediately the subject of bitter debate between Confederates (and their partisans) and Federals (and their partisans).[50]

The Confederates rushed across the relatively short distance between their lines and the fort. They plunged into the ditch and helped each other scale the parapet. Almost before the Federal garrison could react, the Southerners were atop the earthworks, firing into the fort itself. By all reports, this turn of events was too much for the defenders, and many of them began to run.[51] As Forrest explained in one of several reports issued on April 15, "The victory was complete, and the loss of the enemy will never be known from the fact that large numbers ran into the river and were shot and drowned." Then, after describing the makeup of the garrison, he explained, "The river was dyed with the blood of the slaughtered for 200 yards. There was in the fort a large number of citizens who had fled there to escape the conscript law. Most of these ran into the river and were drowned." Erroneously establishing the number of Federals at 700, the Confederate commander thought that 500 of them must have been killed, and concluded from this: "It is hoped that these facts will demonstrate to the Northern people that negro soldiers cannot cope with Southerners."[52]

In another dispatch, Forrest repeated what he had said earlier, speculating, "The enemy attempted to retreat to the river, either for protection of gun-boats or to escape, and the slaughter was heavy."[53] There was something to Forrest's speculation about a plan for the gunboat to assist the garrison. One man inside the fort wrote in a letter to the "folks at home" in Minnesota, "After our men had been fighting about four hours and were pretty well tired out, the smoke of a steamboat was seen by the river. The commander came around & said, 'You have done well my boys.' 'Hold out a little longer for there is a boat coming with reinforcements & if we can hold the place a little longer we will have plenty of help as there is a thousand soldiers on the boat.'"[54]

Of course, Bedford Forrest had no intention of letting this happen, even if there had been "a thousand soldiers on the boat." Captain James Marshall, commanding the gunboat *New Era,* told a congressional committee that investigated the Fort Pillow affair, "Major Bradford signalled to me that we were whipped. We had agreed on a signal that, if they had to leave the fort, they would drop down under the bank, and I was to give the rebels canister."[55] Information contained in the logbook of the *New Era* also substantiated the level of cooperation between the fort and the gunboat. The record noted that after the steamer *Liberty* passed the fort, the *New Era* "continued firing from a Signal from the fort."[56]

Despite the plan the Union officers had prepared to implement in such an eventuality, they were unable to execute it. The sudden turn of events, as victorious Confederates swarmed into the fort, firing point-blank into them, caused the garrison to retreat, regardless of any strategy their commanders had devised. Bradford may have abandoned the plan himself, for according to one witness, "During the last attack, when the rebels entered the works, I heard Major Bradford give the command, 'Boys, save your lives.'"[57]

In any case, as the garrison broke for the riverbank, the fighting became chaotic and confusing. Many tried to surrender. Others ran for their lives. Some fired as they fell back. Naturally, General Forrest summarized events as he saw them from a vantage point of four hundred yards away. The scene from the garrison's point of view was different and considerably more frightening and deadly. One member of the garrison recalled, in a letter on April 17, "As soon as the rebels got to the top of the bank there commenced the most horrible slaughter that could possibly be conceived. Our boys when they saw they were overpowered threw down their arms and held up, some their handkerchiefs & some their hands in token of surrender, but no sooner were they seen than they were shot down, & if one shot failed to kill them the bayonet or revolver did not."[58]

Almost immediately, the Federal government took a special interest in Fort Pillow. A joint Congressional investigating committee, under Senator Benjamin F. Wade and Representative Daniel W. Gooch, called witnesses and participants, listened to their testimony, and concluded that Forrest's Southerners "treacherously gained" the positions from which they assaulted the fort during a flag of truce and then "commenced an indiscriminate slaughter, sparing neither age nor sex, white or black, soldier or civilian." Furthermore, the Confederates committed atrocities of the most heinous character, including burning and burying men alive. "No cruelty which the most fiendish malignity could devise was omitted by these murderers." In addition, the investigating committee observed that "the atrocities committed at Fort Pillow were not the result of passions excited by the heat of conflict, but were the results of a policy deliberately decided upon and unhesitatingly announced." Finally, committee members referred readers to the "voluminous testimony herewith submitted" of "eyewitnesses and sufferers" who had fallen victim "to the malignity and barbarity of Forrest and his followers."[59] Gathered in the midst of the last full year of the war and issued for public consumption, it would have been virtually impossible for the committee to conclude otherwise.

Although some evidence has pointed to Bedford Forrest as the perpetrator of the systematic massacre of the garrison of Fort Pillow, it was either circumstantial or questionable. Participants or victims had used his name or heard it mentioned; they had not seen him carrying out the killings himself, which Forrest, in his highly personalized style of fighting, would not have hesitated to do.[60] And if they claimed to have seen him ordering others to do his killing for him, the testimony, as in the case of Jacob Thompson, was extremely dubious. Thompson insisted that Forrest was one of the officers present during the killings. When asked if he knew the general, he replied, "Yes, sir," and described the six foot two inch Southerner as "a little bit of a man."[61]

While certainly it would be tempting and, to some, appealing to accuse Forrest of such official misconduct, the record simply does not substantiate this charge. What the evidence conclusively supports would have angered Bedford Forrest even more. One Southerner, Samuel H. Caldwell, wrote his wife on April 15, "It was decidedly the most horrible sight that I have ever witnessed." He observed, "They refused to surrender—which incensed our men & if General Forrest had not run between our men & the Yanks with his pistol and sabre drawn not a man would have been spared."[62] A black Union soldier, Ellis Falls, testified that the "rebels" had killed black and white men "after they had surrendered." Then, when asked if black and white were killed equally, he responded, "Yes, sir, till he gave orders to stop fighting." Asked, "Till who gave orders?" Falls replied, "They told me his name was Forrest."[63] Later, Private Major Williams, of the Sixth U.S. Colored Heavy Artillery, recalled that when one officer yelled, "Kill the niggers," another protested, "No, Forrest says take them and carry them with him to wait upon him and cook for him, and put them in jail and send them to their masters."[64] Confederate Colonel D. M. Wisdom later explained that after he "entered the fort, and while the Federal flag was still flying, General Forrest rode up on horseback and ordered me to go down the bluff and stop any and all firing by the Confederates on the retreating garrison." He observed that "General Forrest was exceedingly anxious to check any undue slaughter."[65]

Yet Dr. Charles Fitch, a Massachusetts-born surgeon who signed on with the Union army in Iowa, may have best captured Bedford Forrest's mood during the battle of Fort Pillow. On April 30, 1864, Dr. Fitch drafted a report on what he had seen at Fort Pillow. He had been tending the wounded below the bluff when the Southerners attacked and overwhelmed the fort. As the garrison fled down the bluff, many of whom Fitch saw throw their weapons to the ground "as they came," the victorious Confederates followed closely. Fitch avoided being killed in the melee, but felt threatened as the enemy swarmed around him. "I formed lock step with a Rebel Soldier who was leading a horse up the Bluff," he explained. As he ascended the hill, the surgeon asked:

> Who [is] in command? a soldier replied Genl Forrest. I asked where is he? he pointed to Forrest saying that is him sighting the

> Parrott Gun on the Gun boat, the breech of the gun was not over forty feet from me. I sprang instantly to Forrest addressing him, are you Genl. Forrest? He replied yes sir, What do you want? I told him I was the Surgeon of the Post, and asked protection from him that was due a prisoner. He said, you are Surgeon of a Damn Nigger Regiment. I replied, I was not. You are a Damn Tenn. Yankee then. I told him I was from Iowa. Forrest said what in hell are you down here for? I have a great mind to have you killed for being down here. He then said if the North west had staid home the war would have been over long ago, then turning to a Soldier told him to take charge of me and see that I was not harmed. For which I thanked him.

The guard took Fitch to the fort, where he "saw" some of the Southern soldiers "kill every negro that made his appearance dressed in Federal uniform." Other white Union soldiers, seeing him with a guard, "rushed to him claiming protection." The number of prisoners swelled to the point that "there was a Guard detailed under the command of a Lieut. and placed over us." Even with such efforts by some of the Confederates to safeguard the prisoners, "it was but a short time before some drunken Rebel soldiers came up and fired in among the Prisoners with their Revolvers, wounding some four or five. General Chalmers riding up and seeing such conduct, ordered a strong Guard to be mounted in double file, forming a hollow square around us, after which we were not molested."[66]

In his appreciation for Chalmers's actions, Dr. Fitch went so far as to compose, in 1879, a defense of the general that appeared in the *Southern Historical Society Papers.* In his letter, the doctor recounted the basic facts that he had reported in April 1864. The "greatest slaughter" had occurred "under the bluffs next to the river." While he was there, Fitch recalled that he had seen "few officers among Forrest's soldiers under the bluffs—none above the ranks of lieutenant and captain." He did not see Forrest until he had climbed the bluffs and reentered the fort. "Forrest was up there," he explained, "sighting a piece of artillery on the little gunboat up the river." The Confederate commander was so preoccupied with what he was doing that, Fitch surmised, "I do not think Forrest knew what was going on under the bluffs." When the doctor subsequently left the fort, some Confederate soldiers harassed him, until Chalmers appeared. "You cursed them, and put a guard over me, giving orders to the guard to shoot down the first one that molested me." He concluded, "I have always thought that neither you nor Forrest knew anything that was going on at the time under the bluffs. What was done was done very quickly."[67]

Union Lieutenant Leaming supported Dr. Fitch's account through his testimony that when he heard firing, accompanied by the cry, "They are shooting the darkey prisoners," an officer rode up ordering, "Stop the firing; arrest that man."[68] And Captain John Woodruff offered the telling confession of General Chalmers when asked if most of the blacks who died were killed after the fort had been taken. "Chalmers replied that he thought they had been, and that the men of General Forrest's command had such hatred toward the armed negro that they could not be restrained from killing the negroes after they had captured them. He said they were not killed by General Forrest's or his orders, but that both Forrest and he stopped the massacre as soon as they were able to do so." Then the Union officer noted that the Confederate general closed his remarks on the subject with the observation that "it was nothing better than we [the Union] could expect so long as we persisted in arming the negro."[69]

This attitude was widespread among Confederate soldiers in all theaters of the war. Students of the Civil War soldier have agreed with Bell I. Wiley's contention that "the mere thought of a Negro in uniform was enough to arouse the ire of the average Reb."[70] Nor were dramatic events like those at Fort Pillow the most commonplace expressions of such racism. Reid Mitchell explained that the "Confederate soldiers' virulent hatred of black troops ... was revealed in unspectacular day-to-day hostilities as well."[71] Even so, Southern racism's most vicious expression came in conjunction with combat. As James I. Robertson, Jr., observed, "Southern troops often reacted with cold fury when they encountered former slaves fighting against them."[72] This reaction led to excesses and brutalities in confrontations between black and white troops from Arkansas to Virginia—at places like Milliken's Bend, Poison Spring, Saltville, Petersburg, and Fort Pillow. Perhaps one Confederate summarized the prevailing racial attitudes best when he confided to his mother, "I hope I may never see a Negro Soldier ... or I cannot be ... a Christian Soldier."[73]

Nor was racism confined solely to Southern whites. Robertson noted that "blacks wearing Federal uniforms brought forth the deep-rooted prejudices of Billy Yank."[74] And in his study of the United States Colored Troops, Joseph T. Glatthaar ably demonstrated that racial attitudes died hard, if they died at all. He concluded that "in a society with such widespread and deep-seated prejudice as the North, rare indeed was the individual untainted by racism."[75] Indeed, there was much to overcome, for as a member of one Pennsylvania regiment explained after inquiring about "them dam niger Regiments," the army "had better not send any of them out here fore if they do our own Soldiers will kill more of them than the Rebs would fore a Soldier hates a niger more than they do a Reb."[76]

To be sure, Nathan Bedford Forrest had many opportunities to express his racism and did so with a vehemence seldom matched, but he was not alone in possessing such attitudes. Of course, this does not excuse Forrest's behavior; it merely places that behavior in perspective. In any case, James McPherson was quite correct when he asserted that the Confederate cavalry commander "possessed a killer instinct toward Yankees and toward blacks in any capacity other than slave."[77]

It is worth mentioning that even given his hostility toward the troops in Fort Pillow, Forrest had demonstrated no desire to "massacre" other units he found unsavory. In one of his Fort Pillow reports, he gloated over his recent string of victories over the white Tennessee Unionists, but seemed satisfied with the bloodless capture of Union City: "I am gratified in being able to say that the capture of Hawkins at Union City, and Bradford at Fort Pillow, with the recent defeat (by Richardson's brigade, of my command) of Colonel Hurst, has broken up the Tennessee Federal regiments in the country."[78]

Such evidence suggests several important conclusions. Although never averse to shedding blood and sincerely loathing black Union troops and white "renegade Tennesseans," Forrest did not march against Fort Pillow to obliterate its garrison. Obtaining the garrison's surrender would have sufficed for his purposes. Even having failed to convince the garrison to surrender, General Forrest did not send his men into the fort to exact punishment in blood through murder for their choice. He rode into the fort as soon as it appeared to him to be taken and took steps to stop the fighting or firing he still heard on and below the bluff, but his attention also centered upon the gunboats and transports in the river from which he still expected trouble. Regardless of the reasons, the evidence clearly demonstrates that Forrest had lost control. He lost control of the battle and, more important, he lost control of his men. The exertions he and other Confederate officers had to take to prevent "undue slaughter" are the most telling testimony that such slaughter took place and that, for however long, Forrest was powerless to prevent it. This was what made Fort Pillow so distasteful to Forrest, not the deaths of defenseless Union soldiers there.

There were many causes for the "massacre" at Fort Pillow. Booth and Bradford clearly thought they could hold the fort until help arrived and had, in the back of their minds at least, the promise of assistance from the *New Era*. Forrest had come to Fort Pillow to take out an isolated garrison and capture horses and supplies, but he obviously was willing to "demonstrate" the inferiority of black troops and their white Tennessee Unionist comrades. Dr. Fitch correctly observed, "There seemed to be a great hatred on the part of Forrest's men towards" the Tennessee Unionists—"personal feeling—as I heard many of Forrest's men charge the soldiers of the Thirteenth regiment with doing many things that were mean towards their friends since they had deserted Forrest and joined the Thirteenth Federal regiment."[79] Given the feelings the opposing sides harbored against each other; the chaotic nature of the fighting once the fort fell; and, as one historian put it, the "combination of race hatred, personal animosity, and battle fury" present, it would have been shocking if no excesses had taken place there.[80] Even Forrest's well-known success with bluff elsewhere contributed to the tragedy at Fort Pillow. A fellow prisoner later asked Bradford why he did not surrender the fort. "I am not Hawkins," he replied, referring to the Union commander who twice fell victim to Forrest's bluff.[81]

Historian Lonnie Maness disagreed with the application of the term *massacre* to describe the events at Fort Pillow, citing many of the same defenses that Forrest's apologists employed through the years.[82] Indeed, many people used the term *slaughter* to describe the aftermath of combat. Both sides used the same word in reference to the fighting at Fort Pillow. In and of itself, the use of the word *slaughter* did not mean that a *massacre* occurred there. Nor did Forrest's use of hyperbole in his demands for surrender and dispatches amount to a "policy deliberately decided upon and unhesitatingly announced." But historian Albert Castel's assertion that a massacre of Union troops at Fort Pillow occurred, "in the sense that they were shot down in great numbers without being able to offer effective resistance or to inflict casualties commensurate to their own losses," seems to be borne out.[83]

In any event, at least one Confederate soldier left Fort Pillow unsure of how to describe his service there. On April 19, Sergeant Achilles V. Clark wrote his sisters "a few hurried lines to inform you that I am quite well and have just passed safely through the most terrible ordeal of my whole life." Portraying subsequent events in far more detail than his opening line implied he intended, Clark left his letter's recipients "to judge whether or not we acted well or ill." He proceeded to describe the fort, the dispositions, and the fighting. Then focusing upon the action following the successful assault on the fort, he observed:

> Our men were so exasperated by the Yankee's threats of no quarter that they gave but little. The slaughter was awful—words cannot describe the scene. The poor deluded negros would run up to our men, fall upon their knees and with uplifted hands scream for mercy but they were ordered to their feet and then shot down. The white men fared but little better. Their fort turned out to be a great slaughter pen—blood, human blood stood about in pools and brains could have been gathered up in any quantity. I with several others tried to stop the butchery and at one time had partially succeeded but Gen. Forrest ordered them shot down like dogs and the carnage continued. Finally our men became sick of blood and the firing ceased.[84]

Whether Sergeant Clark's assertion that "Gen. Forrest ordered them shot down like dogs" actually reflects Forrest's instructions, at least some of his men acted under that belief. And nothing in their commander's past conduct indicated that he thought this phase of war and fighting meant any less killing.

There is ample evidence that black troops suffered disproportionately heavy losses at Fort Pillow. The casualty figures certainly corroborate this view. But, given Bedford Forrest's personal brand of racism, built on his experience as a slave trader and Southern planter, it is unlikely that he authorized or sanctioned the "indiscriminate slaughter" of blacks. One simply did not slaughter such "deluded" people who had been led astray by others. To be sure, Forrest noted, almost as an afterthought, that he believed Fort Pillow would demonstrate the inferiority of black troops and the stupidity of a policy that made soldiers of them. He simply could not conceive of blacks as soldiers and thought of them as the commodities or laborers he had always understood them to be.

The Reverend David C. Kelley, Forrest's friend and aide, recalled that the two of them talked about the fighting at Fort Pillow shortly after it occurred. In the course of the conversation, Kelley remembered that Forrest said "that he was opposed to the killing of negro troops; that it was his policy to capture all he could and return them to their owners."[85] He had followed this policy before and would continue to do so, believing that the value of black Americans was as a force of laborers.

In his subsequent correspondence with Union General Cadwallader C. Washburn in June 1864, Forrest betrayed this attitude repeatedly. On June 23, he responded to Washburn's earlier query of whether the Confederates intended to treat captured blacks as prisoners of war. "I regard captured negroes as I do other captured property," he observed, "and not as captured soldiers." This was typical of Forrest's racial attitudes. Black Southerners were "property," not "soldiers." To destroy such property wantonly made no sense. The best disposition would be to return these runaways to their rightful owners, if those owners could be determined. Yet, if black Southerners wearing Federal uniforms had the gall to act like more than they were, Confederates, from Forrest to the private soldiers in the ranks, would view it as nothing less than insufferable and overbearing behavior. The same Forrest who could not accept "insubordination" from his own lieutenants would certainly not tolerate "insolence" from the occupants of the fort.

In his communications with Washburn, Forrest attempted to cast his position in as favorable a light as possible. He noted that he would leave the "disposition" of black prisoners to "my Government," and added, "It is not the policy nor the interest of the South to destroy the negro—on the contrary, to preserve and protect him—and all who have surrendered to us have received kind and humane treatment."[86] However, if, as historian Reid Mitchell noted, "white soldiers saw black [military] service as a threat," then this was especially true of white Confederate soldiers.[87] Thus, while it is probably true that most of those Federals whom the Confederates allowed to surrender received reasonable treatment, others, whom some of the Southerners either refused to let surrender or failed to recognize as having surrendered, were shot down in cold blood.

Later, Forrest explained his views of the black Union troops in his typically clear style: "You ask me to state whether 'I contemplate either their slaughter or their return to slavery.' I answer that I slaughter no man except in open warfare, and that my prisoners, both white and black, are turned over to my Government to be dealt with as it may direct." He knew that such dealings meant a return to servitude for men whom he and his "Government" recognized only as wayward servants. He concluded that the apparent acquiescence of the Union army to a policy of "no quarter" by its black soldiers would "visit its terrible consequences alone upon that ignorant, deluded, but unfortunate people, the negro, whose destruction you are planning in order to accomplish ours." Forrest particularly wanted the Federals to know that "the negroes have our sympathy, and so far as consistent with safety will spare them at the expense of those who are alone responsible for the inauguration of a worse than savage warfare."[88] To destroy these "deluded" people would be to waste valuable resources and to punish a "people" that were not responsible, in his opinion, for their actions. Following Fort Pillow, Forrest's provost marshal demonstrated the practical application of his commander's policy toward captured black troops: "I accompany herewith [a] list of prisoners captured by Major-General Forrest at Fort Pillow, as also one containing the names and owners and residences of the negroes captured at [the] same place."[89]

Through painstaking research, two scholars, John Cimprich

and Robert C. Mainfort, Jr., have studied the "Fort Pillow massacre" in great detail. These men found that the garrison of 585 to 605 men suffered deaths or mortal wounds of between 277 and 297, or 47 to 49 percent. They further determined that the black units lost considerably more men, in deaths, than did the white troops—64 percent to 31–34 percent, and concluded that a massacre occurred at Fort Pillow on April 12, 1864.[90] Indeed, casualties among the 1,500 Confederates, which amounted to only 14 killed and 86 wounded, were comparatively light, considering the fact that the Southerners were the attacking party.[91]

The final death toll at Fort Pillow was a heavy one for the Federals. There was no wholesale or premeditated massacre there, for had Bedford Forrest wanted to annhilate the garrison, he could have easily done so and would certainly have supervised the operation personally. Nevertheless, there was brutal slaughter, beyond what should have occurred. People died who were attempting to surrender and should have been spared. Although these deaths were widespread, they appear to have been the acts of individuals—men who were angry because blacks had taken up arms against them, that some of their neighbors had chosen to don Union uniforms, that they had been forced to attack a fort that should have surrendered.

Even so, these men acted as they believed their general would want them to act. In a sense, the men became extensions of their commander. They caught the bloodlust of battle in much the same way that Forrest did on virtually every other battlefield. And if it disturbed Forrest that many of his men carried their bloodlust too far, he felt remorse only because he had lost control over their actions, not because they had killed blacks and white "renegade Tennesseans." In his eyes they probably got what they deserved. Although he lost control over the fighting at Fort Pillow, the Confederate cavalry commander clearly did not disapprove of the results.

For a variety of reasons, Fort Pillow became a collective release of pent-up anger and hatred. It became, in clinical terms, a group catharsis. And as the overall commander of the troops on the scene, some of whom carried out these acts, Nathan Bedford Forrest was responsible.

CHAPTER 10

Forrest's Finest Moment

(April–June 1864)

I regret very much that I could not have the pleasure of bringing you his hair, but he is too great a plunderer to fight anything like an equal force.

—GENERAL SAMUEL D. STURGIS TO
GENERAL WILLIAM TECUMSEH SHERMAN

For God's sake, if Mr. Forrest will let me alone, I will let him alone.

—GENERAL SAMUEL D. STURGIS

BEDFORD FORREST RODE AWAY from Fort Pillow on the night of April 12. Still sore from his fall, he made only nine miles that night. He subsequently fared better when he, his staff, and the escort spent the evening of April 13 and the morning of April 14 enjoying the hospitality of the people of Brownsville, Tennessee.[1] In the meantime, the general sent his aide, Captain Charles W. Anderson, back to the fort to "make some disposition of the wounded Federals, and to see that the dead were buried, etc." Anderson caught the attention of Acting Master William Ferguson, commanding the *Silver Cloud*, and sent him a note explaining Forrest's intentions. "I am authorized by Major-General Forrest to say that he desires to place the badly wounded of your army on board of your boat, provided you will acknowledge their paroles. I shall send all, white or black, who desire to go."[2] Ferguson accepted the terms and drew up an agreement with Anderson that "would put me in possession of the fort and the country around until 5 P.M. for the purpose of burying our dead and removing our wounded, whom he [Forrest] had no means of attending to." Ferguson reported, "Details of rebel soldiers assisted us in this duty."[3] Union surgeon Fitch noted that although Forrest had regretfully held him as a prisoner on April 12 against the parole of a Confederate surgeon held as a prisoner at Paducah, Chalmers released him the next day, at the behest of "two Rebel Surgeons [who] came and dressed the wounded Prisoners in Camp after which they went with me to General Chalmers Head Quarters, and urged him to Parole me."[4]

One more episode resulting from Forrest's capture of Fort Pillow was yet to be resolved. Shortly after his capture at the fort, Major Bradford died while in the hands of his captors. As Forrest's biographer R. S. Henry summarized, "The circumstances are obscure and the testimony contradictory."[5] It is not surprising that two versions of Bradford's fate circulated. One version, with which General Cadwallader C. Washburn confronted Forrest in a post–Fort Pillow letter, was obviously based upon the testimony of W. R. McLagan, who stated that he witnessed Bradford's murder. According to McLagan's statement, he was part of a group of conscripts rounded up by Forrest's men. Major Bradford joined their group "under guard, as a prisoner of war, and was reported as such," although he "had tried to conceal his identity as much as possible, by putting on citizen's clothes." Then, on the subsequent march to Brownsville, five soldiers who "seemed to have received special instructions about something" at the headquarters of Confederate Colonel W. L. Duckworth "took Major Bradford out about fifty yards from the road" and deliberately shot and killed him.[6]

Forrest responded to Washburn's allegations, observing: "As to the death of Major Bradford, I knew nothing of it until eight or ten days after it is said to have occurred." But, in any case, he had heard a different report of the affair. According to the second version, "Bradford requested the privilege of attending the burial of his brother [Captain Theodorick Bradford, who was killed at Fort Pillow], which was granted, he giving his parole to return; instead of returning he changed his clothing and started for Memphis."

Forrest noted that some of the men he had "hunting deserters" caught and "arrested him." The general reiterated that he "knew nothing of the matter until eight or ten days afterward" and understood that Bradford had "attempted to escape, and was shot." Forrest concluded, "If he was improperly killed nothing would afford me more pleasure than to punish the perpetrators to the full extent of the law, and to show you how I regard such transactions I can refer you to my demand upon Major-General Hurlbut (no doubt upon file in your office)" concerning Colonel Fielding Hurst. In either case, Major William Bradford's death was another element of the tragedy of Fort Pillow.[7]

At some point after his return from the campaign, Forrest received the news that his brother Aaron had died of pneumonia.[8] This was the second brother he had lost to Confederate service, but Bedford could not afford the luxury of a lengthy period of mourning. His success generally, as well as in the last raid, demonstrated the need for changes in the Federal command structure in western Tennessee, especially to William Tecumseh Sherman, who was anxious to be rid of the Forrest nuisance. To that end, Sherman relieved Hurlbut, replacing him on April 18 with General Washburn. He also sent a new cavalry commander to Memphis, observing that this new man would "assume command of all the cavalry, and [was] to move out and attack Forrest wherever he can be found."[9] General Samuel D. Sturgis was the commander upon whom Sherman now pinned his hopes for Bedford Forrest's destruction. Sturgis gave every appearance of being able to get the job done. A West Pointer with considerable military experience, he had commanded cavalry in the eastern and western theaters. "I have sent Sturgis down to take command of that cavalry and whip Forrest," Sherman explained to General Ulysses S. Grant's chief of staff.[10] Then to Washburn, he wryly noted, "I know there are troops enough at Memphis to whale Forrest if you can reach him."[11]

Although Sherman's words were still fresh when Washburn and Sturgis reached Memphis on April 22 and 23, respectively, the new commanders thought that their forces were woefully inadequate against the Confederate cavalryman. Sherman had to be perplexed by the continual delay that plagued the efforts to defeat

Forrest. Perhaps with that in mind, he warned Washburn not to "exaggerate the forces of the enemy or your own weakness" and implored, "Don't let Forrest insult you by passing in sight almost of your command."[12]

Sherman had considerably more on his mind than one Southern cavalry officer, but he worried about the damage that officer could do if allowed to roam free. He asked Admiral David D. Porter to "keep a bright lookout up the Tennessee that Forrest don't cross and cut my [rail]roads when I am in Georgia." And to Washburn, Sherman stated, "We are now all in motion for Georgia. We want you to hold Forrest ... until we strike Johnston. This is quite as important as to whip him."[13] General James McPherson echoed these sentiments to Washburn: "It is of the utmost importance ... to keep his forces occupied, and prevent him from forming plans and combinations to cross the Tennessee River and break up the railroad communications in our rear."[14]

Finally, on April 30, Sturgis left Memphis with a combined force of over six thousand cavalrymen and infantrymen and twenty pieces of artillery "in pursuit of Forrest."[15] On the afternoon of May 2, portions of the opposing cavalry commands clashed near Bolivar. Forrest, who had recently left Jackson, was near enough to join the fighting with his escort. Arriving on the scene, the Confederate cavalryman led a charge that initially drove the Federals back. Owing to the enormous disparity in numbers (two thousand to three hundred), he withdrew to an old line of defenses west of the town. Then as darkness fell, Forrest pulled out of his precarious position, destroying the bridge behind him.[16]

Sturgis complained that Forrest had managed to "elude our most strenuous exertions," adding that "it was with the greatest reluctance that I resolved to abandon the chase." He closed with a lame attempt to make his superiors happy with the lackluster results of his expedition: "Although we could not catch the scoundrel we are at least rid of him, and that is something."[17]

A week later, Sturgis sent Sherman the same disappointing news. "My little campaign is over," he remorsefully began, "and I regret to say that Forrest is still at large." Sturgis disparaged his counterpart for being "so disposed to run," instead of willing to fight, adding in a tone that was designed to please his hard-hitting superior, "I regret very much that I could not have the pleasure of bringing you his hair, but he is too great a plunderer to fight anything like an equal force, and we have to be satisfied with driving him from the State." Unfortunately, this inability to destroy Forrest probably meant that he would "turn on your communications ... but I see no way to prevent it from this point with this force."[18]

In the meantime, Forrest reorganized his command once more. The structure remained essentially the same, with two divisions under Generals James R. Chalmers and Abraham Buford. Chalmers's division consisted of the brigades of Colonels Robert McCulloch, J. J. Neely, and Edmund W. Rucker. Buford's division consisted of General Tyree Bell's and Colonel Hylan B. Lyon's brigades. The artillery, under the overall command of Captain John Morton, consisted of four four-gun batteries. Forrest continued to keep his men scattered, both to keep them properly supplied and to allow them to watch the enemy's movements from several quarters.[19]

Ironically, Forrest's penchant for waging war on practical, realistic terms, rather than by strict adherence to the rules, threatened to undo much of his recruiting work. In the course of his operations, he had netted significant numbers of absentees, deserters, and other conscripts. To his mind, these men served the public interest and his, of course, as long as they wore the uniform and performed their duties as cavalrymen, regardless of their prior service records or obligations. However, the War Department refused to ignore their earlier service and wanted the absentees and deserters returned to their original commands. Forrest knew that many of these men had been enrolled or were currently enrolled in other units, but he incorporated them into his command as if they were now his own.

As much common sense as the practice may have seemed to have to Forrest, it was viewed as an unlawful infringement of authority by others. The cavalry commander was certainly aware of this other view, for he wrote of the problem to General Stephen Dill Lee, on May 15. "There are about 1,000 men in my command who left the army at its reorganization in the spring of 1862," he observed. "Orders are here to return these men to their command." He worried that such orders would "break up Bell's and

Neely's brigades, and lead to desertion." Instead, he proposed that the orders be suspended for sixty days, which would allow him time to compile a list, secure the deserters, and "safely effect their return without injury to my command or detriment to the public service."[20]

Later the same day Forrest again informed Lee of the problem. "Some officers are here from infantry to identify and get their men," he reported. Although he "had given them free access to the muster rolls," he preferred to wait "until such times as all the regiments who have absentees here can be represented." Obviously, Forrest was hoping to buy some time, but he also greatly feared that if the few officers on hand dragged off their men, he would lose far more, "for, as soon as you commenced arresting, the balance, anticipating a similar fate, will take to the woods with arms, equipments, and horses"—all property that he could ill afford to lose. Thus, for a second time, he requested a sixty-day stay.[21]

Despite his best efforts, Forrest apparently failed to win his argument. On May 21, he gave orders for the division commanders to hold a dress parade the next day with "their entire commands on foot" for the purpose of arresting 653 absentees from the Army of Tennessee found on his rolls. These men were to be "forwarded under guard," as soon as they turned in their horses, weapons, and other equipment.[22] And as if to confirm the general's prediction, 126 men subsequently slipped out of the camps of Neely's brigade, on May 22, undoubtedly to filter back into western Tennessee, from where they had been so recently recruited.[23]

The advance of Union forces under William Tecumseh Sherman was largely responsible for this attention to absentees and deserters. Joseph E. Johnston, now commanding the Army of Tennessee following Bragg's resignation the previous November, wanted every man he could have to stop Sherman. The Union general maintained the pressure in heavy fighting through the latter part of May 1864, at Resaca, Georgia, and in the area of New Hope Church–Dallas, Georgia.

Finally, on June 1, Sturgis deemed himself ready to reemerge to confront Forrest. He led an impressive mixed column of infantry and cavalry, 8,300 strong, with 22 pieces of artillery and 250 wagons to carry supplies for the expedition. An officer well versed in mounted raids and with experience pursuing Forrest, General Benjamin H. Grierson, commanded Sturgis's 3,300 cavalrymen. Furthermore, 1,200 of the 5,000 infantrymen who were marching in the expedition under the overall command of Colonel William L. McMillen were black troops who had sworn to avenge Fort Pillow by showing the Confederates no quarter.[24] All in all, General Sturgis gave every assurance of keeping Forrest busy, if not actually crippling or destroying him.

Over roads turned to quagmires by the rain, Sturgis and his mighty column slowly trudged southward. They reached the town of Ripley on June 8. Sturgis had no idea how many men the Confederates were gathering to oppose him. He was inclined to turn back to Memphis, but McMillen chided him into continuing by noting that he "would rather go on and meet the enemy, even if we should be whipped, than to return again to Memphis without having met them." Sturgis knew that Sherman had selected him because of his aggressiveness. To abandon this second expedition might prove fatal to his career. Sherman expected results. With a force of over eight thousand, Sturgis knew that he would have to deliver.[25]

As for Sherman, still deftly maneuvering General Joseph E. Johnston farther into Georgia toward Atlanta, he could not stop worrying about his vulnerable supply lines and what Forrest might do to them. "I cannot hear of Forrest," Sherman noted warily on June 9, "though I believe the expedition which left Memphis June 1 ... will give him good employment."[26] In a manner of speaking, Sherman was right.

While the Federal column slogged through the mud near the Tennessee-Mississippi border, Forrest rode into Tupelo, Mississippi, having raced back from an abortive raid into middle Tennessee. He immediately took steps to determine the enemy's intentions. On the afternoon of June 6, General Stephen D. Lee arrived, and the two Confederate commanders began to make plans for the concentration of sufficient forces to confront the Union column if it headed southward toward Tupelo and Okolona or to follow and harass it if it continued to move eastward, possibly to link up with Sherman in Georgia, as they mistakenly believed.[27]

Neither Forrest nor Lee yet knew what Sturgis planned to do.

Accordingly, Forrest disposed his men widely to watch the Federals and attempt to determine which way they would go in time to respond. When word finally reached the two commanders, on June 9, of Union activity near Ripley, Mississippi, they agreed that the enemy's target was the rich "breadbasket" of Mississippi near Okolona. Lee immediately prepared to return on the train to that town and ordered Forrest to follow. Although Lee hoped to lure the Federals even farther from their supply base at Memphis, he left the cavalryman with discretion to act as he saw fit, according to the enemy's movements.[28]

While Lee traveled southward to gather the forces with which he hoped to defeat Sturgis, Forrest called a council of war. Buford, Rucker, and Morton met with him, and Forrest explained that he had information that Sturgis was encamped with his entire force at Stubb's farm (ten miles from Brice's Cross Roads) and that he, Forrest, intended to attack the Federals as soon as possible.[29]

Forrest realized that he was gambling against heavy odds. He knew that he could bring only 4,800 men, at best, against a Federal force he believed to number at least 10,000. He also knew that half his men were at Rienzi, twenty-five miles from the point at which he planned to intercept the Union column, while the entire enemy force rested only ten miles from the same point. It looked as if Forrest had overreached himself this time.[30] But he had a plan, and on the morning of June 10 as he rode with Colonel Rucker, he explained it plainly.

Rain had fallen for several days, not stopping until early on June 10. Consequently, the roads were awash with mud, and the day promised to be hot and muggy. "I know they greatly outnumber the troops I have on hand," he calmly told Rucker, "but the road along which they will march is narrow and muddy; they will make slow progress." Then, betraying the extent to which he had calculated his plans and the enemy's movements, Forrest remarked, "The country is densely wooded and the undergrowth so heavy that when we strike them they will not know how few men we have. Their cavalry will move out ahead of the infantry, and should reach the cross-roads three hours in advance. We can whip their cavalry in that time." But this was only the first part of his plan. "As soon as the fight opens," he predicted, "they will send back to have the infantry hurried up. It is going to be as hot as hell, and coming on a run for five or six miles over such roads, their infantry will be so tired out we will ride right over them." And even though his own men would be moving over the same roads, he had the confidence that they would do so far more efficiently than their opponents. "I want everything to move up as fast as possible," he instructed. "I will go ahead with Lyon and the escort and open the fight."[31]

The area in which Forrest expected to meet the Federals was indeed "densely wooded," consisting of thick blackjack and scrub-oak forests dotted only occasionally by small cleared fields. At the crossroads, formed by the juncture of the Ripley–Fulton Road and the Wire Road leading from Booneville to Pontotoc, stood the two-story Brice home and William Brice's store, northwest and northeast of the intersection, respectively. Below the intersection the road crossed over Tishomingo Creek on a small wooden bridge and continued through the bottom land to Ripley. This was the road along which the Union forces would come from Stubb's farm while Forrest's men approached the crossroads on the Wire Road.[32]

Although Forrest had hoped to reach Brice's Cross Roads first, Grierson, up since 5:30 A.M., got there ahead of him. Lead elements of Grierson's cavalry, under Colonel Robert C. Waring, drove off a small patrol near the crossroads and fanned out along the road toward Baldwyn. In the meantime, perhaps not wishing to plunge down the churned-up roads just yet, Sturgis allowed the infantry to prepare for the day at a much more leisurely pace. While their commanders, Sturgis and McMillen, shared an early dram of liquor, the men prepared and ate their breakfast. Finally, about 7 A.M., the infantry formed to follow their comrades. This slow deployment played directly into Forrest's hands.[33]

Waring's 1,400 Federal troopers proceeded about a mile before they ran into the first of Forrest's men, two companies under Captain H. A. Tyler. Tyler's men ran into a withering sheet of fire, wheeled, and raced back to the main column of Confederates. They had done their job. The enemy was there in force. Although Waring had his opponents vastly outnumbered, thick woods and tangled growth helped to hide the disparity, as Forrest had predicted. By this time, both commands were fighting on foot. As the two sides sparred with each other, Forrest arrived at the scene and assumed command. He hastily sent word back to Buford, with his largest brigade, "to move up with the artillery and Bell's brigade as rapidly as the condition of the horses and roads would permit," or as Forrest said it, "Tell Bell to move up fast and fetch all he's got."[34]

Forrest knew that he could not count on the natural obstacles that hid his men to hold Waring's Federals for long. With his troops scattered along the road behind him, the Confederate cavalry commander knew that he had to act boldly, lest the enemy discover his numerical weakness. The disparity of numbers was growing minute by minute as Colonel Edward Winslow brought his Federals across Tishomingo Creek and into position on Waring's right, about 10:30 A.M.[35]

With all this in mind, Forrest called upon his tested tactic: "show fight." Aggressiveness would confuse his enemy, hide his small numbers, and allow him to maintain the initiative. He knew well that passing the momentum to his enemy at this point could prove disastrous. As Forrest put it, a man "in motion was worth two standing."[36] Lyon's dismounted Confederates tore through the trees and undergrowth and struck Waring's men with such effect that the Union officer reported, "We were immediately met by a strong advance of the enemy and were compelled to fall back."[37] The advance was hardly as "strong" as Waring suspected, and the Southerners soon fell back and dug in. "Desiring to avoid a general engagement," as the Southern commander later explained, "until the balance of my troops and the artillery came up, Colonel Lyon was not pushed forward."[38]

Meanwhile, Grierson sent word to Sturgis, riding at the head of the infantry column, that he had met the enemy at Brice's Cross Roads, "had an advantageous position and could hold it if the infantry was brought up promptly."[39] Again, this was just what Forrest had planned. And Sturgis obliged him still more. The infantry had halted "some five miles from camp" at Stubb's farm because of the horrible road conditions, both to allow the wagons to catch up with the rest of the force and to give the pioneer units (military engineers) time to work on the road. This was where Sturgis received Grierson's dispatch, and he soon set out for the

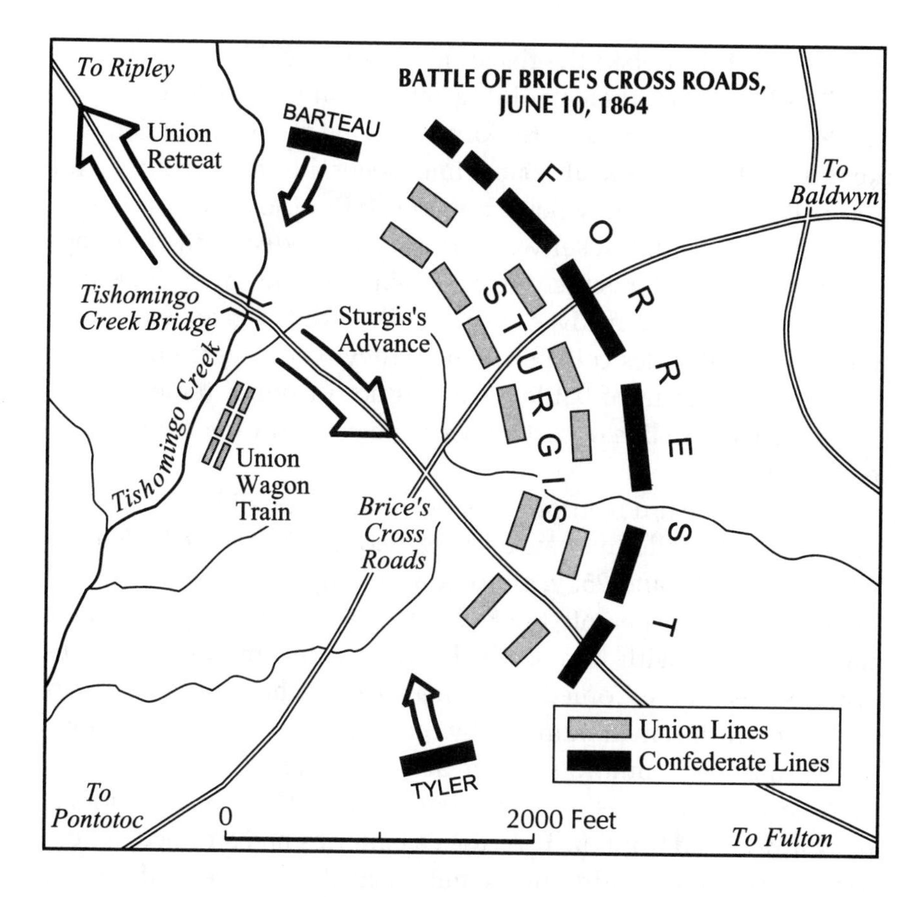

crossroads. He had not gone far when he realized that he had better instruct McMillen how to proceed with the infantry. McMillen was "to move up his advanced brigade as rapidly as possible without distressing his troops."[40]

Back at Brice's Cross Roads, Lyon's assault had achieved its goal. As one Union officer noted, the Confederates "retired with but little disorder to the edge of the woods and kept up a skirmish fire at long range for some time."[41] Then Rucker appeared with his seven hundred troopers. Forrest dismounted them and threw them into line on Lyon's left. Until now, Waring's men had actually held positions beyond the Confederates' left flank, although he did not realize it. With Rucker's men and Colonel William A. Johnson's five hundred, also freshly arrived on the field and sent to Lyon's right flank, Forrest thought of the offensive once more.

He sent his men forward, still hoping to buy time with boldness. Forrest described the fierce fighting in lackluster terms, seeing it as little more than a holding action that had worked according to plan. "We had a severe skirmish with the enemy, which was kept up until 1 o'clock, at which time General Buford arrived with the artillery, followed by Bell's brigade."[42] But the contest was savage while it lasted. Rucker was seriously wounded in the fighting, but remained with his men. A gap opened in the Union lines that the Confederates quickly exploited. They did not go far before men from both sides collapsed where they were, overcome by the heat and the strain of battle. One Southern trooper remembered, "Our men still in line of battle lay on the ground for a much needed rest."[43]

At the same time, Buford was pushing on for all he was worth. At Old Carrollville, he paused long enough to dispatch Colonel Clark S. Barteau and 250 men to move along the farm lanes in the area to attempt to get into the Federals' rear.[44] Barteau was not taking many men with him, but if he arrived in time to coordinate with the rest of the Confederates in an assault, he could more than make up for the small numbers by the confusion he would create.

With General Buford's arrival at 1 P.M., Forrest had all the men at Brice's Cross Roads he was going to have. The men and horses of Morton's and Captain T. W. Rice's batteries had strained almost to the end of their endurance to get the artillery there, and Forrest was not about to squander their efforts. He ordered them to unlimber and deploy in order to "develop the enemies batteries and his lines."[45] Morton did well just to find a place amid the blackjack from which to fire, and when his guns opened, their aim was uncanny. As he directed the fire of his own guns, Sturgis recalled, "The enemy's artillery soon replied, and with great accuracy, every shell bursting over and in the immediate vicinity of our guns."[46]

Throughout the early stages of the battle, the Federal infantrymen pushed along through the mire as best they could. As the distance over which they traveled grew longer and the sun climbed higher, some of the men began to fall out of the column. Finally, Colonel George B. Hoge, commanding the lead brigade, had to slow the pace. After resting briefly, the column resumed its race to the crossroads at the urging of couriers, who steadily dashed up to bring the latest news of the fighting. At the same time, Sturgis was doing everything he could to hold Brice's Cross Roads until his infantry could come up, even to the point of sending his escort to help shore up the Union left.[47]

McMillen rode ahead of the infantry, using his staff to set the pace, and reached the battlefield to find "everything at the cross roads ... going to the devil as fast as it possibly could."[48] The cavalrymen were exhausted from their holding action and wanted to be relieved. McMillen rode back to push his lead brigade along. Hoge's men picked up the pace, but paid dearly for it, as more men dropped from the effects of the heat and the sun, while the rest staggered over the creek and up the hill to the intersection.[49]

Therefore, not long after Buford rode to the head of his Confederate brigade to reinforce Forrest, the Federal infantry began to arrive on the scene. Hoge's Federals reached the battlefield about 1:30 P.M. and immediately began replacing Waring's exhausted cavalrymen. In the sweltering June heat, the pace that events required Hoge's foot soldiers to undertake was grueling. He later observed, "It was impossible to keep up the rapid gait. I received a peremptory order to move forward rapidly, as the enemy was gaining ground, and the only thing that would save us was the infantry."[50]

Sturgis was desperate, indeed. He had no real idea how many enemy soldiers he faced. Despite his best efforts to keep the column concentrated, Forrest seemed to have picked the one time they were badly strung out to attack. Instead of forcing the Confederates to fight for their lives, he felt as if he was fighting for his, and just barely holding on at that. Betraying a sense of the urgency and fear that he felt, Sturgis noted in his after-action report, "Frequent calls were now made for re-enforcements, but until the infantry should arrive I had, of course, none to give."[51]

As McMillen's infantrymen came panting up, they slowly began to replace the cavalry on the front lines. By the time Sturgis completed shuffling units, the Union battle line formed an arc with the crossroads behind and at its center. Then, for about half an hour, the battlefield fell strangely quiet as both sides positioned themselves for the onslaught they knew would be coming shortly. Forrest had probably preferred not to allow even that long a lull in the action. But he needed to position his men, too. To that end, he left Buford in command of the Confederates' right, consisting of Johnson's and Lyon's brigades, while Rucker held the center and Bell the left under Forrest's personal supervision.[52]

Forrest was now about ready to unleash Bell against the Union right. He rode toward the center of his lines, calling for the men to "get up" and get ready to go in to support that attack. "I have ordered Bell to charge on the left," he told them. "When you hear his guns, and the bugle sounds, every man must charge, and we will give them hell."[53] At some point during the day's action, he had succumbed to the heat, pulled off the jacket of his uniform, and draped it across the pommel of his saddle. He thundered these instructions in his shirtsleeves, his face flushed as it usually was during battle. The image was one that few men ever forgot, once they had seen it.[54]

The sounds of Bell's advance soon filled the air. His men moved forward to hit the Union line. In some cases they got within thirty yards of the Federals before the two sides even saw each other. Bell's men pushed their opponents back under the force of the assault, although reinforcements quickly stabilized the situation. The lines swayed back and forth as each side lost ground and won it back.[55]

Forrest continued to ride along his lines exhorting his men. But his patience was thin and, as one soldier remembered, his exhortations took many forms: "Our movement was too slow to suit Forrest, he would curse, then praise and then threaten to shoot us himself, if we were so afraid the Yanks might hit us.... He would praise in one breath, then in the next would curse us and finally said, 'I will lead you.'" Whatever the trooper might have thought of his general's methods, he could attest that they worked. "We hustled," he noted, "and across that narrow field was a race."[56]

No doubt influenced by Forrest's urging, Rucker's men surged forward and battled fiercely with their opponents in close-hand fighting. Rucker avoided trouble on his section of the lines by calling out to his men with practical instructions: "Kneel on the ground men, draw your six-shooters, and don't run."[57] But having stabilized the left and seeing the center engaged, Forrest worried that the right, under Buford, had not yet gone forward. He jumped back into the saddle and dashed off in that direction. And when he got there, Forrest ordered the guns to be pushed up to the front and double-shotted with canister for the greatest effect at such short range. He also instructed Buford to get Lyon's and Johnson's brigades into the fight. With this order, the fighting soon erupted in that sector. On the extreme left flank, Tyler's men, Forrest's escort, and Captain Henry Gattrell's Georgians threatened the Union right. And by now, Barteau was on the scene as well, arriving from his cross-country march just where Forrest had expected him to appear, on the Union left flank and rear.[58]

The fighting continued relentlessly for more than two hours. Men fought and collapsed and rose to fight again. Even Forrest felt the strain. Like the rest of the men on the battlefield, he was tired. At one point, Forrest dismounted and walked up to watch Morton's battery in action. Morton greeted him with a warning to drop back out of the line of fire. Then, in a moment of realization, he blurted, "Please excuse me, General. I don't mean to say where you shall go." Uncharacteristically, Forrest put up no fight at his subordinate's suggestion. He sensed that the enemy was about to crack, and as he stretched out beneath an oak for a brief rest, he told the artilleryman that he believed one final push would do the trick. Forrest asked Morton to be ready to throw his artillery as near the enemy as possible so the double canister would have its deadliest effect.

Approximately fifteen minutes later, Forrest summoned Morton. Pointing to a column of troopers just appearing on the road, the general explained his plans to "strike" the enemy and "double 'em up on that road." When the attack began, he wanted Morton to "charge right down the road, and get as close as you can. Give 'em hell right yonder where I'm going to double 'em up."[59] The artilleryman later confessed to his commander that the unorthodox strategy "scared me pretty badly when you pushed me up so close to their infantry and left me without protection," concluding, "I was afraid they might take my guns." Forrest wryly answered, "Well, artillery is made to be captured, and I wanted to see them take yours."[60]

Forrest remounted and shortly ordered the assault he felt sure would win the day. The Confederates surged forward, and Lyon's men achieved a breakthrough that caused the Federal regiments to retreat in succession as each found itself outflanked. McMillen, directing the Union right, received word that the left and center were retreating "in considerable confusion."[61] As McMillen dashed off to bring order out of the chaos, Rucker and Bell hit the Union right, and it slowly began to give way, too. The Confederates continued to press home their assaults with the vigor of men who knew the day was nearly theirs, and the Union line constricted even more.

As the Union line tightened, Forrest could shorten and concentrate his own lines, allowing him to mass his firepower still more. Whatever advantage the Federals might have gained in shortening their lines they lost in the confusion and chaos of a battle that was slipping out of their control. Many of the men were low on ammunition or out of it, others were demoralized and staggered toward the rear, and the remainder were dispirited and exhausted from the exertions of the day. Forrest realized their condition, indeed, had anticipated it, and came on relentlessly. He sent a staff officer to tell Tyler, on the far left of his line, to "hit 'em on the e-e-end."[62]

McMillen began to pull his men back, using the artillery as cover. But in the confusion of battle and under constant pressure from the Confederates, any hope of organized retreat disappeared. The fighting continued in this unrelenting manner for hours. Finally, between 4 and 5 P.M., the Union line gave way, and "the retreat or rout," as Forrest called it, began.[63] For Sturgis, the situation confirmed his worst fears. Caught far from his base, encumbered by wagons, and whipped by the enemy, he could think of little else than saving as many of his men as possible. "Order soon gave way to confusion and confusion to panic," he recalled. "For seven hours these gallant officers and men had held their ground against overwhelming numbers," Sturgis recounted, "but at last, overpowered and exhausted, they were compelled to abandon ... the field." He looked around to determine what to do next, but saw little to encourage him. "Everywhere the army now drifted toward the rear, and was soon altogether beyond control."[64]

To make matters worse, some of the wagons had crossed the

bridge and parked on the east side of Tishomingo Creek. Thus, when the Union line gave way, only a few wagons were facing in the proper direction to escape, and the teamsters who attempted to cross the stream succeeded only in tangling the teams and wagons and blocking the bridge. Thus, as the Union soldiers retreated, a bottleneck formed at the bridge.[65] This bottleneck added to the general confusion and terror of the mob of soldiers who were now fleeing back along the road to Ripley.

Confederate Captain Tyler recalled that as he came into a clearing near the Brice house, he saw Lyon and Morton pushing their way forward. "Then, too, I saw Colonel Rucker and Colonel Bell both leading their brigades up to the cross-roads and General Forrest. It was but a few minutes when we all met at the cross-roads." Having finally won the hard-fought contest, they were "a happy and enthusiastic band," but there was other work to do as the broken Union column clogged the bridge over Tishomingo Creek and poured down the road along which they had come that morning.[66]

At the height of this final phase of the fighting, Colonel Edward Bouton arrived with a portion of his brigade. These men, black soldiers wearing patches that read "Remember Fort Pillow," either went into battle against Barteau's Confederates or crossed the bridge to form a line to cover the retreat of their comrades. While deploying his men, Bouton ran into McMillen, who wanted to know what he was doing. Bouton patiently explained his dispositions and promised to "fight the enemy as long as I ... have one man left." He must have been astounded when McMillen replied, "That's right, if you can hold this position until I go to the rear and form on the next ridge, you can save this entire command. It all depends on you now."[67]

Forrest was never one to relax the pressure once he had won a victory. He firmly believed that having gotten the "skeer" into them, you had to keep it there. Forrest's Confederates pressed home their advantage, forcing the Federals to abandon their wagons, artillery, and other war materiel. Sturgis reported, "The road became crowded and jammed with troops, the wagons and artillery, sinking into the deep mud, became inextricable, and added to the general confusion that now prevailed. No power could now check or control the panic-stricken mass as it swept toward the rear."[68]

The next day, General Stephen D. Lee wired Richmond, "The battle of Tishomingo Creek, fought yesterday by Major-General Forrest, is one of the most signal victories of the war for [the] forces engaged.... The rout was complete."[69] Indeed, it was. He set his own losses, based on the chief surgeon's report, at 96 killed and 396 wounded (losses proportionately heavier than Sturgis suffered in those categories).[70] But Forrest had inflicted far worse overall losses upon the Federals—223 killed, 394 wounded, and 1,623 missing—and he captured 16 artillery pieces, 176 wagons, 1,500 stands of small arms, and vast quantities of ammunition.[71]

The Confederates spent the next two days hounding the Federals as they retreated to Memphis. One Southerner wrote his wife that the defeated Northerners fled "in Such great Confusion and in Such a fright that our men killed and wounded them all along the road."[72] Another remembered that when his regiment took up the pursuit at 2 A.M., "Much of our way was lighted up by wagons and other abandoned property." In some cases, the wheels of these vehicles had entangled or smashed into trees, and numerous Union stragglers, "thoroughly exhausted" and "sleeping by the roadside," surrendered to their pursuers without a struggle. The trooper noted, "I saw much of General Forrest that night, who was in great good humor in regard to the results of the previous day's battle."[73]

About the same time, another Confederate saw the cavalry commander in a different frame of mind. "Don't you see the damned Yanks are burning my wagons?" Forrest stormed, when his men failed to prevent the Union soldiers from burning some of the wagons to keep them from falling into the Southerners' hands. "Get off your horses and throw the burning beds off!" Every man complied, except a lieutenant, protesting that he was an officer and should not have to do such work. Forrest drew his saber and started toward the malcontent, shouting, "I'll officer you." The lieutenant tumbled from his horse and began to help the others save the wagons.[74]

A local resident recalled seeing "hundreds of shoes and articles of clothing of every description" on the road when his family returned to their home near Brice's Cross Roads.[75] Much of this discarded clothing belonged to Bouton's black troops, who, fearing a recurrence of the slaughter at Fort Pillow, discarded their uniforms and badges that read "Remember Fort Pillow." Even so, in too many cases, this symbolic action was not enough to appease the anger of their Confederate pursuers. One witness explained that the badges, in particular, "incensed the Southern soldiers, and they relentlessly shot them down."[76] Forrest's men were aware that Sturgis's command included black troops, and both during and after the battle, they anxiously sought to confront "the damned negroes."[77] Once again, black soldiers suffered inordinately when Forrest, who was busy directing the pursuit of organized bodies of the retreating enemy, lost control of the actions of many of the individuals under his command.

Forrest followed the shattered Union forces as long as he could, until the hours in the saddle overwhelmed his enormous physical stamina. Faint from exhaustion and fatigue, he finally had to be helped from his horse. Buford continued the pursuit. Eventually, he also had to end the chase, when, as he told a staff officer, "Every damn man with me is sound asleep." One of Buford's troopers agreed. "The fact is," the man admitted, "we had about reached the limit of endurance for man and horse."[78]

The relentless Confederate pursuit, much to Sturgis's chagrin, rendered an organized withdrawal virtually impossible. At one point, during the retreat, the exasperated Union commander remarked to one of his subordinates, "For God's sake, if Mr. Forrest will let me alone, I will let him alone. You have done all you could, and more than expected of you, and now all you can do is to save yourselves."[79]

CHAPTER 11

There Will Never Be Peace in Tennessee

(June – October 1864)

... follow Forrest to the death if it costs 10,000 lives and breaks the Treasury. There will never be peace in Tennessee till Forrest is dead.

—GENERAL WILLIAM T. SHERMAN

Is Forrest surely dead?

—GENERAL WILLIAM T. SHERMAN

They removed me from command because I couldn't keep Forrest out of West Tennessee, and now [General] Washburn can't keep him out of his own bedroom.

—GENERAL STEPHEN A. HURLBUT

THE DEFEAT AT BRICE'S CROSS ROADS mystified General William Tecumseh Sherman. On June 14, he wrote Secretary of War Edwin M. Stanton, "I cannot understand how he could defeat Sturgis with 8,000 men."[1] A day later he still had no answer. "I will have the matter of Sturgis critically examined," he warned, "and, if he be at fault, he shall have no mercy at my hands." The expedition puzzled him. "I cannot but believe he had troops enough," Sherman observed. "I know I would have been willing to attempt the same task with that force." But General Samuel D. Sturgis was no Sherman, and besides, he ventured, "Forrest is the very devil, and I think he has got some of our troops under cower." But if the fiery Union commander could suspect the problem, he could also offer a solution. "I have two officers at Memphis that will fight all the time—[Andrew Jackson] Smith and [Joseph] Mower.... I will order them to make up a force and go out and follow Forrest to the death if it costs 10,000 lives and breaks the Treasury. There will never be peace in Tennessee till Forrest is dead."[2]

Bedford Forrest had little opportunity to enjoy the fruits of his spectacular victory at Brice's Cross Roads. Sherman was doing everything in his power to prod his people at Memphis into striking at Forrest again, as soon as possible. He had high expectations for a new Smith-Mower expedition from Memphis; as he noted in a June 20 telegram to the Union commander at Nashville, "I propose to keep him [Forrest] occupied from Memphis. He whipped Sturgis fair and square, and now I have got against him ... Smith and Mower, and will let them try their hands."[3]

While Sherman plotted, Forrest's superiors and other high-ranking officials in the Confederacy argued over how best to use his talents. General Joseph E. Johnston, battling against Sherman's inexorable drive into Georgia, recalled in his *Memoirs* that on at least seven separate occasions during June and July, he wrote either President Jefferson Davis or his military adviser, General Braxton Bragg, to release "an adequate force to destroy the railroad communications of the Federal army ... under an officer fully competent to head such an enterprise—General Forrest." Thinking on a strategic level, Johnston insisted that he "made these suggestions in the strong belief that this cavalry would serve the Confederacy far better by contributing to the defeat of a formidable invasion [in Georgia], than by waiting for and repelling raids." Johnston maintained that he "was confident" that "the Administration would see the expediency of employing Forrest and his cavalry to break the enemy's railroad communications, by which he [Sherman] could have been defeated."[4]

Georgia Governor Joseph E. Brown made the same request of President Davis, hoping to find some means to ease the pressure on his state. In late June, he implored Davis, "Could not Forrest ... do more now for our cause in Sherman's rear than anywhere else?"[5] Fellow Georgian Howell Cobb despaired of affairs in his state to the Confederate Secretary of War, John Seddon: "I see no end to the slow process of Sherman's advance through Georgia." Then optimistically predicting that much of the Southern territory being threatened could be saved if Sherman's lines of communication could be cut for ten days, he pointedly inquired, "To effect such a result could we not afford to uncover for a short time the country protected by Forrest?"[6]

President Davis replied to the worried governor that "Forrest's command is now operating on one of Sherman's lines of communication [though Brown might have justifiably asked to which line Davis was referring], and is necessary for other purposes in his present field of service."[7] To which Brown immediately responded that "ten thousand good cavalry under Forrest [should] be thrown in Sherman's rear," adding, perhaps with an eye to other political pressures the president might be experiencing, "The whole country expects this though points of less importance should be for a time overrun.... We do not see how Forrest's operations in Mississippi ... interfere with Sherman's plans in this State as his supplies continue to reach him."[8] Of course, Governor Brown was right, but Davis was hardly inclined to listen to one of his worst critics.

President Davis angrily thundered back at the governor: "Your dicta cannot control the disposition of troops in different parts of the Confederate States. Most men in your position would not assume to decide on the value of the service to be rendered by troops in distant positions." He sarcastically invited Brown to forward his "reliable statement of the comparative strength of the armies," caustically noting, "I will be glad also to know the source of your information as to what the whole country expects, and posterity will judge."[9]

Resigned to the president's obvious unwillingness to entertain his suggestion, Brown fired one parting shot. He regretted the "exhibition of temper with which I am met in your dispatch" and warned that "if you continue to keep our forces divided and our cavalry raiding and meeting raids while the enemy's line of communication, nearly 300 miles long, is uninterrupted," the results could be devastating. "If Atlanta is sacrificed and Georgia overrun while our cavalry are engaged in distant raids," he explained with a twinge of sarcasm himself, "you will have no difficulty in ascertaining from correct sources of information what was expected of you by the whole people, and what verdict posterity will record."[10]

Posterity has judged the failure to utilize Forrest as a raider against Sherman's supply lines in Tennessee in a timely fashion. Most recently, Steven Woodworth blamed the failure upon "the rapidly degenerating Confederate departmental system." Commanders with vested interests in a given department, such as Stephen D. Lee in Mississippi, were loathe to release troops or sacrifice their departments for the greater good of the Confederacy. Woodworth concluded that holding Forrest in Mississippi "may have made sense for S. D. Lee ... but it was sheer folly for the Confederacy, for whom Mississippi had become a backwater and Georgia the scene of life-and-death struggle."[11] Despite Sherman's advance toward Kennesaw Mountain in Georgia, Forrest's attentions remained fixed, for the most part, upon his immediate field of operations. He had enjoyed his greatest successes in this region and all too frequently seemed to become entangled with the Army of Tennessee when he moved eastward.

While Brown's and Davis's vituperative exchange heated the telegraph wires, Forrest remained oblivious to the debate raging over his strategic usefulness and kept active. Correctly anticipating another invasion of Mississippi, the Confederate cavalry commander strove to pull together what troops he could to meet it. His scouts warned that a formidable force was preparing to march against him at any moment.

Indeed, the force that General Andrew Jackson Smith, fresh from service in the Red River campaign, compiled in Memphis was formidable. When he marched out of Memphis in late June, he led a combined force of fourteen thousand infantry and cavalry, and twenty-four pieces of artillery. Smith remained at La Grange attending to last-minute preparations until July 5, when he started south in search of Bedford Forrest. The cavalry, under General Benjamin Grierson, who was already well acquainted with Forrest, initially moved eastward to Saulsbury before turning south to join the main column north of Ripley.[12]

In the meantime, the Southern cavalry commander was doing his utmost to scrape together as large a force as possible. He established a camp for men who either had no mounts or whose mounts were in no condition to withstand the strains of a campaign. Out of these men, some of whom "ran away rather than come to the dismounted camp," the general hoped to create a force the size of a "good brigade of infantry." He also took steps to augment his command by adding to the camp "attaches, employes, and detailed men"—men who were normally exempt from such service. If he could press into duty the vast number of individuals who roamed the region on a variety of pretenses, he felt he could swell this dismounted command to as many as two thousand men.[13]

Even though he was making every effort to prepare his men for the fighting to come, Forrest felt in no condition to participate in it himself. On June 28, he wired S. D. Lee congratulations on the promotion that made Lee the youngest lieutenant general in either army. But the news was not all good; Forrest was suffering badly from boils. "If the enemy should move out," he advised the new lieutenant general, indicating his level of distress, "I desire you to take command of the forces."[14] Artilleryman John Morton observed that his chief's ailment "depleted even his iron constitution."[15] Nevertheless, the Union invasion force was finally on the march and had to be stopped. Whatever his discomfort, Forrest could not leave the field now, although he would be strangely reticent in the fighting to come.

Smith suffered none of the physical discomfort of his counterpart, but even so, the Union advance moved slowly and deliberately. Passing through Ripley on July 8, the Federals paused long enough to burn the principal buildings in the town. On the ninth, they crossed the Tallahatchie River at New Albany, and on the tenth, the column camped some five miles north of Pontotoc. The next day they encountered Colonel Clark S. Barteau's Second Tennessee, forcing them out of a strong position astride the road. Barteau deployed his men in successive lines, each line supporting the other as they fell back toward Pontotoc. Colonel Robert McCulloch's brigade relieved Barteau's men and took up defensive positions in and around the town, but the Federals had little difficulty pushing them out.[16]

Forrest made little effort to impede his opponents' progress. He expected to be in no position to fight until he reached Okolona. Therefore, he sent General Abraham Buford explicit orders "to develop the enemy's strength, not to bring on a general engagement, but keep in the enemy's front and on his flanks and gradually fall back to Okolona."[17] Likewise, Forrest instructed General James R. Chalmers to "skirmish with the enemy, and make him develop his strength, but not to bring on a general engagement."[18]

The two sides clashed briefly on July 12, near Pontotoc, with the Confederates easily turning the Federals back. But the apparent strength of the Southern position gave Smith a better idea. "As they had a very strong position on a hill on the other side of the bottom," he later explained, "I did not deem it prudent to attack the position from the front if it could be flanked."[19] Thus, early the next day, he left part of his cavalry to carry out demonstrations while he moved the bulk of his forces on the road toward Tupelo, eighteen miles to the east.

The maneuver caught Lee and Forrest by surprise. They had bent their efforts toward luring A. J. Smith toward Okolona, which lay to the south. Even so, they might have had greater success against the Federals had they firmly determined a course of action. Instead, they first sent Chalmers orders to "let the enemy come on if he would, as everything was ready to receive him" at Okolona, and then abruptly canceled those orders when they decided to fight near Pontotoc.[20] In the ensuing confusion, the Confederates left the road from Pontotoc to Tupelo virtually unguarded. Smith swept aside the few Southerners he found in his way and marched on down that road.[21]

Realizing the mistake, Forrest made every effort to rectify it by promptly attacking the rear of the Union's column. Again using his escort as the catalyst, the Confederate cavalry commander pushed the last Federals out of Pontotoc, relentlessly pursuing them. "I made a vigorous assault on the enemy's rear for ten miles," he reported. And while Forrest harassed the enemy's rearguard, Lee maneuvered "with a view of attacking the enemy's flanks at every vulnerable point." Having pressed the Union column for ten miles without hearing any action from the attack S. D. Lee was supposed to deliver, Forrest began to worry that he had "driven" the enemy "too rapidly." He called a halt for about an hour to await the attack. Then, hearing fighting in the distance ahead of him at Burrow's Shop, he raced ahead to find that Chalmers had "dashed into the road, surprised the enemy, and

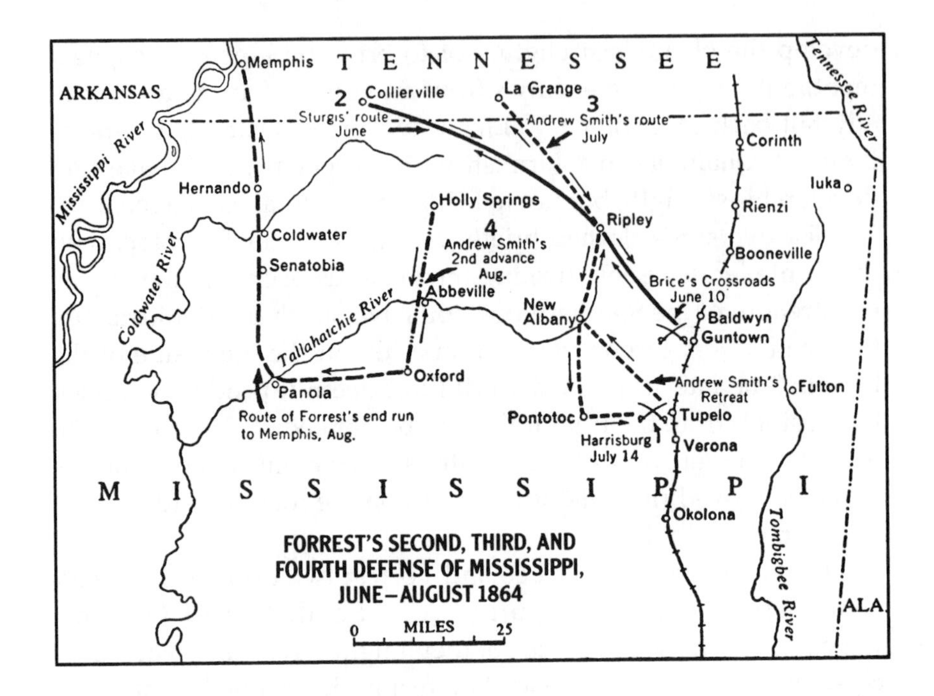

FORREST'S SECOND, THIRD, AND FOURTH DEFENSE OF MISSISSIPPI, JUNE–AUGUST 1864

took possession of his wagon train."[22] Smith reacted almost immediately and sent a sufficient number of men to drive Chalmers away, but not before the Southerners had killed some of the mules, forcing the Federals to abandon and burn seven of their supply wagons.[23]

Grierson's horsemen set to work destroying the railroad in the vicinity of Tupelo and waited for the infantry. Despite the harassment, Smith had suffered little real damage. He finally marched into the neighboring village of Harrisburg and settled down for the night. There was little rest for the weary Federals as they worked through the night constructing defenses from everything on hand. By dawn the next day, July 14, Smith's men were poised to receive whatever Lee and Forrest might send their way.[24]

Forrest reached the area of Harrisburg about the same time as Smith did. He had spent most of the day trailing the Union column, striking where and when he could. He accomplished little except to force the enemy to deploy occasionally and thereby to slow their progress. Forrest was probably angry that he had failed to make any real impression upon the enemy. He was also tired, for the day had been another hot, dusty one. Again as he had after

Brice's Cross Roads, the cavalryman dismounted, perhaps gingerly considering his boils, and stretched out on the ground for a few minutes' rest.[25] Some of Forrest's enormous reservoir of energy seemed to be gone.

But the Confederate cavalryman was soon up and about. He wanted to know as much as he could of the situation, and as usual he sought the information himself. Thus, he and one of his staff officers rode off into the darkness, heading in the direction of the Union lines. They had not gone far when the general realized that he had left his pistols behind. The aide offered him his own weapon, but Forrest declined it, remarking, "It doesn't matter much anyway. I don't think we will have any use for them." They moved on, surveyed a portion of the Union encampment, and turned to go back. The two officers had not gone far when a voice called out in the darkness for them to "halt." Although he might have regretted not having the pistols now, Forrest rode forward and peremptorily demanded, "What do you mean by halting your commanding officer?" Having thrown the pickets temporarily off guard, the general and his companion calmly rode past, fully expecting the darkness to assist them. They were past the post before the pickets realized that they were the enemy and fired into the darkness. Bending forward in the saddle, the horsemen dashed to safety, enabling Forrest to joke later that a bullet might have eased his pain by lancing one of the boils.[26]

Forrest may have been in the mood to joke, but what he had seen left him with a sobering reality. In his report he noted that "at a late hour in the night, accompanied by one of my staff officers, I approached Harrisburg and discovered the enemy strongly posted and prepared to give battle the next day."[27] He wrote from the benefit of hindsight, but the enemy was indeed "prepared to give battle," and the whole experience must have reminded him of the ill-fated attack against the entrenchments at Dover in early 1863.

Unfortunately, the record is unclear about whether Forrest found the situation as potentially disastrous as the repulse at Dover had been. He was not feeling well, his energy was low, and he openly expressed the desire for S. D. Lee to assume full authority over the campaign. Whether, as Lee wrote years later, the two men "were in perfect accord as to delivering battle" or Forrest, in his distracted state of mind and health, acquiesced may never be known. Lee also explained that in light of Forrest's victory at Brice's Cross Roads, he "insist[ed] on his commanding the field, but he [Forrest] said no; that the responsibility was too great, and that his superior in rank should assume and exercise the command; that he considered the Confederate troops inadequate to defeat Smith."[28]

There may have been something to this last statement, for Major Charles W. Anderson, Forrest's friend and aide, observed that Lee and Forrest discussed the attack in his presence early on July 14. According to Anderson, Forrest pointedly remarked to Lee, "The enemy have a strong position—have thrown up defensive works and are vastly our superior in numbers and it will not do for us to attack them under such conditions." Instead, he proposed that they wait Smith out. "One thing is sure," Forrest explained, "the enemy cannot remain long where he is. He must come out, and when he does, all I ask or wish is to be turned loose with my command." Obviously, General Forrest had in mind the devastating pursuit he had so recently administered to General Sturgis, and not so long ago to Colonel Abel D. Streight. But Smith was not yet defeated and in retreat, nor was he out in the open anymore. Even so, Forrest promised that when Smith came out in the open again, he would "be on all sides of him, attacking day and night," no matter which direction the Union commander chose to go. "He shall not cook a meal or have a night's sleep and I will wear his army to a frazzle before he gets out of the country."[29]

But S. D. Lee was under pressure of his own. He received frequent calls for assistance from Mobile.[30] He also had seen the rather lackluster results from the attacks made against Smith as he marched to Tupelo. The potential for the much quicker and more decisive results that a grand assault might bring was undoubtedly more promising and tempting than were the long harassing cut, slash, and run operations Forrest proposed. Forrest could always pursue Smith once the Federals were defeated and retreating from Tupelo back to Memphis.

In any case, by the time the battle opened on July 14, Forrest was either won over or resigned to Lee's plan to fight there, on the ground of the enemy's choosing. He answered General Buford's gloomy prediction that "we are going to be badly whipped" with bravado: "You don't know what you are talking about; we'll whip 'em in five minutes." Buford, who ordinarily had no reason to doubt his chief, may have sensed that the sudden, defensive reply was for show and belied what was in Forrest's heart. "I hope you may be right," the subordinate wistfully noted, "but I don't believe it."[31]

When two scouts rode up to report that the Federals appeared about to retreat, S. D. Lee recalled years later, Forrest called for an immediate assault. His "blood was up," Lee remembered of his subordinate, "the fire of battle was in his eye. He said that if he was in command, he would not hesitate [to attack] a moment."[32] And so, Forrest took the right wing and Lee took the left, and both set out to engage Smith's Federals. Together, the two Confederates had approximately 6,000 to 7,000 men (excluding horseholders who did not participate in the fight), facing 11,000 well-entrenched Federals, supported by 6 batteries of artillery. Buford's division, 3,200 strong, occupied the left; Chalmers's division of 2,300, the center; and General P. D. Roddey's division of 1,500, the right.[33]

Almost from the start, even discounting the apparent disagreement over the propriety of making the attack at all, there was confusion. John Morton advised Lee to mass his firepower by concentrating all the Confederates' artillery in one place. Instead, Lee, in a move his biographer called "so unlike himself," rejected the advice and divided the twenty field pieces among his brigades.[34] Then, at about 7:30 A.M., Forrest rode off "with all possible speed" to find Roddey. Giving that officer "the necessary orders in person," Forrest "dashed across the field in a gallop for the purpose of selecting a position in which to place his troops."[35] Forrest's biographer R. S. Henry noted critically that these were "all things which should have been done, it would seem, before the order to advance was given."[36]

As Forrest rode to the front to "find a place" for Roddey's men, he heard firing off to his left, where Buford's three brigades, under Generals Hinchie Mabry and Tyree Bell and Colonel Edward Crossland, dashed forward prematurely. The Federals watched as these Confederates came on, all the while holding their fire. As the Southerners closed in, Smith observed that "they lost all semblance of lines and the attack resembled a mob of huge magnitude." He described the assault as "a footrace to see who should reach us first," with the Southerners "yelling and howling like Comanches." As soon as they got within canister range, the Union artillery erupted, and the Confederate attack melted away. Smith reported that the assault "was gallantly made, but without order, organization, or skill. They would come forward and fall back, rally and [come] forward again, with the like result."[37]

Forrest was a large part of the reason these men rallied at all. He explained in his report, "On reaching the front I found the Kentucky brigade [Crossland's] had been rashly precipitated forward, and were retiring under the murderous fire concentrated upon them." Indeed, these men took a tremendous beating and suffered severe casualties, some men reaching as close as twenty steps from the Union line before being cut down. A Confederate trooper, Henry E. Hord, graphically described the bloody fighting at the line of Federal earthworks:

> One of the Yankee officers jumped up on the works, waving his sword. I was standing a little to the right of him. He caught me with an empty gun; but I struck him over the head with it, and he tumbled off on our side. His company rose *en masse* to rescue him. As I struck him something hit me in the side. I lost my balance, and fell on our side of the works. Glancing back to see what it was that had pushed me off, I saw a Yank with his throat cut from ear to ear. He had dropped his gun and had both hands clasped around his throat, trying in vain to check the blood that was gushing through his fingers. They were crowding over the works ... it was clubbed gun against bayonet....

Hord fought desperately, and when he found a moment to reach back for a gun from the wounded comrade who was reloading for him, he saw that the man was dead. The Union officer Hord had struck with his gun lay there, the dead Confederate's hands clutching his throat, his face "as blue as his uniform."[38] Under the punishing fire storm, the Southerners broke and fell back in disorder. Seeing this disorder, Forrest rushed up. "I seized their colors," he explained, "and after a short appeal ordered them forward to form a new line."[39]

Because of the poorly coordinated assault, Roddey's men had been in no position to support Crossland's advance. And when Forrest saw the effect of the enemy's fire on "the gallant Kentucky brigade" and "wishing to save my troops from the unprofitable slaughter I knew would follow any attempt to charge his [the enemy's] works, I did not push forward General Roddey's command when it arrived, knowing it would receive the same concentrated fire which repulsed the Kentucky Brigade."[40]

Forrest was not the only officer who saw the trouble the Kentuckians were having in their premature attack. Buford saw the situation and rushed forward Mabry's and Bell's brigades. Mabry's Mississippians appeared first and caught the brunt of the enemy fire. Even so, they surged to within sixty yards of the Union works before the charge dissolved, and the men sought cover. In the meantime, Bell's Tennesseans came up and fared little better than did their predecessors. These Confederates briefly held their own under "a furious cannonade and terrific fire of small-arms."[41] With Bell to support him, Mabry withdrew his shattered brigade, meeting the advance of Colonel Edmund W. Rucker's brigade as they fell back.[42]

Rucker's appearance on the field typified the tactical failures of the Confederates in this battle. Chalmers, Rucker's division commander, received three separate orders from three distinct sources, requiring him to do three different things. Only when S. D. Lee rode up and personally ordered him to send Rucker in "at a double-quick and with a shout" did he move to assist Buford's hard-pressed division.[43] Following this order, Chalmers rode forward with Rucker, passing Mabry's men as they retreated, and charged the Union lines. They also fell victim to the heavy enemy fire, with Rucker himself being seriously wounded. These men, like their comrades before them, could stand to brave the fire only briefly before retreating from the deadly barrage.[44]

With the Confederate attacks broken, the Union infantry, under General Mower, surged forward from its defenses. The infantrymen easily drove off or captured the remnants they encountered, but the vicious Southern sun took its toll. Mower had two officers and "several" men collapse from sunstroke. The exhausted state of the men and the fact that the enemy was already gone led Mower to conclude that there was no point to pressing the counterattack any further. The Union infantrymen remained on the field to count the Confederate dead (270 on the field immediately in front of Mower), gather the prisoners and wounded, and collect and smash the abandoned weapons they found. This accomplished, Mower returned to the main Union defenses. For the most part, the fighting was over for the day.[45]

S. D. Lee had watched with dismay as the Confederate attacks failed to crack the Union right. His dismay turned to anger when he realized that there was no assault against the Union left. He rode off to find out why. When Lee found Forrest, he wanted to know, "Why did you not carry out the plan of attack?" Forrest replied that having seen the brutal repulse the Kentucky brigade had suffered, he "exercised" his "discretion," and held Roddey's men back. Lee could not believe what he had heard and sharply observed, "In doing as you did, you failed to carry out the plan of battle agreed on." Perhaps with a sigh of resignation, the lieutenant general plainly stated that it "was too late to remedy the matter" now.[46] In later years, Lee spoke of the poorly managed battle, generously concluding of Forrest, "I am sure he did the best as he saw it. I am sure I did my best as I saw it."[47]

Widely dispersed skirmishing and sharpshooting characterized the fighting for the rest of the day. That night, some of the Federals began to burn buildings in Harrisburg. Ironically, the Confederates used the light of these fires to shell them. Forrest edged forward with Rucker's brigade and goaded the enemy into what he described as "one of the heaviest fires I have heard during the war." Fortunately for the battered Southerners, the pyrotechnics were harmless, for in the darkness the Federals overshot their intended targets.[48]

The cost of the day for the Southerners was exceptionally heavy. They reported 1,249 killed and wounded and another 49 captured or missing. Buford set his losses for the entire campaign, most of which came in this one battle, at 153 killed and 798 wounded, for a total of 951.[49] Buford's division had numbered 3,200 before it assaulted the Union works at Tupelo. General Buford was so affected by the losses suffered by his division that when Forrest asked him where his command was, he replied: "They are dead and wounded."[50] Forrest later observed that his men had driven the enemy from Mississippi, "but this achievement cost the best blood of the South."[51] Much of that blood was spilled at Harrisburg.

General A. J. Smith's losses were considerably lighter than his opponent's, his worst loss being the death of Colonel Wilkin, who commanded the Second Brigade. Smith was in possession of the battlefield with a superior force, having won a decisive victory. Even so, he found himself in a bad way. He discovered that much of his supply of food had spoiled in the heat, his ammunition was low, and his men were exhausted. So, rather than exploit his success, the Union commander decided to return to Memphis.

The decision must have been painful. Because he lacked sufficient wagons and ambulances, Smith had to leave forty of his most severely wounded men in Tupelo.[52] Then he began the slow process of withdrawing his men. The Confederates sparred with Mower's infantry and part of the cavalry. Although the fighting was relatively light, the heat again had its effect upon the men. Buford had "eighty men carried off the field that morning perfectly exhausted, many of whom were insensible."[53] Forrest found his path "strewn with men fainting under the oppressive heat, hard labor, and want of water."[54] But at least he now had the retreat and the opportunity to pursue that he had wanted earlier, and he would make the most of it.

Forrest took up his familiar task of harassing the enemy's rearguard. Buford pushed on to Tupelo to deal with the remaining Federals there. Lee met with Forrest at Harrisburg and gave him command of the pursuit. The cavalry commander coordinated the pursuit and rode out a few miles on the Ellistown Road, when he heard firing in the distance in front of him. He raced up to find Buford and Chalmers heavily engaged with the Federals at Old Town Creek. At first, they encountered mostly Union cavalry and drove them off easily, but when the infantry doubled back to help, it was the infantry's turn to drive the Confederates back. Chalmers came up behind Buford and threw his men into action as they arrived. But even this stopgap measure failed, and the Southerners fell back in disorder.

By now Forrest was also on the scene. He directed the placement of troops and was "riding across the field and endeavoring to press forward" when he received "a painful wound" in the right foot. He sent a courier to inform Lee of the situation and turned the command over to Chalmers, whose task it became to extricate the Confederates.[55] During the same day's fighting, both Colonels McCulloch and Crossland also were severely wounded.[56]

Amid the chaos, rumors began to circulate almost immediately that Forrest was dead. Washburn wrote Sherman with the happy news on August 2, 1864: "Forrest [has] not been able to resume command by reason of [a] wound in [the] fight with Smith. I have a report to-day that he died of lockjaw some days ago."[57] An incredulous Sherman responded, "Is Forrest surely dead?" Then, remembering his promise, he added, "If so, tell General Mower I am pledged to him for his promotion, and if Old Abe don't make good my promise then General Mower may have my place."[58] Finally, on August 11, Washburn had to break the news that regrettably, "General Forrest is not dead, but was in Pontotoc four days ago."[59]

When the news of his demise reached Forrest, who was receiving treatment in a Tupelo hospital, he knew that however discomforting, he had to make an appearance to squelch those rumors. To that end, he left his bed, mounted his horse, and like El Cid in Spanish lore, "rode in his shirt-sleeves at a gallop along the line of troopers, cheering them not only by his presence, but with encouraging words, among them that it was only a flesh wound, and [he] was still able and ready to lead them."[60] The effect of this dramatic act was everything he hoped it would be, for as one soldier explained, "They seem[ed] wild with joy at seeing their great leader still with them."[61] Through his various exploits, Forrest had already established a sort of personality cult among those who rode with him. Like the Desert Fox (Erwin Rommel) in World War II, "that Devil" Forrest had also established a reputation with his foes that was well beyond his capacity to affect the outcome of the war.

Despite chastising his opponents again and wounding their leader, Smith still had his mind and heart set upon returning to Memphis. Thus, early the next morning he moved out, camping that night at Ellistown. Chalmers remained in pursuit, but kept a respectable distance and contented himself with long-range skirmishing. Smith had little further harassment as he led the Union column through New Albany and Salem, where he found supplies waiting for him from Memphis. By July 21, the Union commander was back in La Grange with his weary soldiers. The campaign was over.[62]

General Smith's expedition had achieved a great deal. He kept Forrest fully occupied and away from Sherman's supply lines while the latter bore down upon Atlanta. He inflicted severe losses upon the enemy and damaged or destroyed the combat effectiveness of some of the Confederate units. He even put a scratch on Forrest, who listed his losses for the campaign as 210 killed and 1,116 wounded. Smith put his own casualties at 77 killed, 559 wounded, and 38 captured or missing. Smith had not destroyed the Confederate cavalry leader, but he had badly pummeled his command.[63]

Sherman greeted the news of Smith's achievements halfheartedly. He wanted Forrest dead, not just hurt. Almost immediately he began to design another expedition. Apparently, Smith took the lukewarm response to heart, for his superior informed Sherman that the expedition's commander "thinks you have a wrong impression in regard to his fight," adding, "That he whipped the enemy very badly there is no doubt."[64] All this was well and good, but Sherman clearly wanted more. "I have ordered General Smith to put his command in order to again move against Forrest," he explained. "He will so move as soon as he can get ready."[65]

Although neither the setback at Tupelo nor the wound he received during the pursuit caused Forrest any irreparable harm, both were symptomatic of the slow erosion of the Confederate cavalryman's titanic energy and spirit. Forrest's wound also forced him to undertake his duties in an undignified (and embarrassing) style. Instead of riding with his troops on horseback, his injury kept him out of the saddle and confined to a buggy. The buggy had to be outfitted with a board to allow him to keep his foot elevated. Although Forrest probably failed to see much humor in the situation, one of his biographers did. John Allan Wyeth, himself a doctor and sympathetic to the general's plight, nonetheless seemed bemused by the "novel sight" of the fearless cavalryman "seated in a dilapidated 'war-time' buggy, guiding a spiritless nag among the trees and along the highways of Mississippi, carefully dodging stumps and roots and stones, or anything which might jolt the crippled foot!"[66]

Even if General Forrest found his circumstances humorous or at least ironic, he had far more to worry about, and these concerns kept him from convalescing properly. The enemy seemed intent upon giving him another "try." Late on July 22, Washburn informed Smith that he (and Sherman) expected Smith to go out after Forrest once more. The next day, Smith passed the word to his subordinates, and all adjourned to make ready for their assignments.[67]

About this same time, Forrest learned that S. D. Lee had transferred to the Army of Tennessee, and the Department of Alabama, Mississippi, and East Louisiana came under the command of General Dabney H. Maury. The new commander seemed particularly appreciative of Forrest's talents and achievements, graciously writing him, "I intrust to you the operations against the enemy threatening an invasion of North Mississippi." Maury assured his independently minded subordinate that he did not intend to "interfere with your plan for conducting these operations," but would "confine myself to the duty of sending you the means, as far as I can, of accomplishing the successful results it has been your good fortune [and presumably the Confederacy's] to achieve." Noting the limits to his "means," Maury wrote, "But we must do the best we can with what little we have, and it is with no small satisfaction I reflect that of all the commanders of the Confederacy you are accustomed to accomplish the very greatest results with small means when left to your own untrammeled judgment. Upon that judgment I now rely."[68] The tone was similar to the one that S. D. Lee used when he first communicated with Forrest. Clearly, Maury calculated his approach to appeal to the maverick cavalryman, and it undoubtedly did.[69]

Forrest knew that he was shorthanded following the recent campaign with Smith, but he promised Maury, "I will do all that can be done to drive the enemy back." However, he warned, "At the same time I have not the force to risk a general engagement, but will resort to all other means in my power to harass, annoy and force the enemy back."[70] Although he may not yet have known what those means would be, he would have to come up with them soon, for General A. J. Smith was about to move, in his own slow but steady pace, with a force that was even more "formidable" than the one with which he had mauled Lee and Forrest at Tupelo. From Memphis, General Washburn triumphantly predicted that Smith's eighteen-thousand-man force of infantry and cavalry would be enough "to whip the combined force of the enemy this side of Georgia and east of the Mississippi."[71]

In the face of this new threat, Forrest was again able to "take the saddle," although he could keep only "one foot in the stirrup."[72] He was unsure of what Smith intended to do and had to scatter his men once more to be in a position to respond to any eventuality. He kept Buford at Okolona, ordered Colonel J. J. Neely's brigade to Pontotoc, sent Mabry's brigade to Grenada, and instructed Chalmers to fortify and guard the crossings of the Tallahatchie.[73]

Then, in the face of a threatened invasion, the petty problems of the Confederate War Department's bureaucratic rules regarding administration and organization returned to plague him. On August 7, Forrest wrote directly to President Davis concerning the election of officers in his command. The issue dated from the complaints Forrest received from various commanders that some of his men were absentees or deserters from their units. The general complied with his orders to turn them over, despite his request for a sixty-day suspension. As a result, 653 men were arrested and transported back to their original commands, while others, fearing the same action, deserted.

About the same time, Colonel George W. Brent, the assistant adjutant general, conducted a thorough inspection of Forrest's command with that general's full cooperation. In his report, dated June 10, 1864, the day Forrest fought at Brice's Cross Roads, Colonel Brent noted that the cavalry commander arrived in Mississippi to find only one "organized command." All the others "were either in a chaotic, disorganized condition or incomplete, and claiming to be followers of different leaders." Furthermore, Brent observed, "Their commanders found it impossible to keep their commands together." As an example, he cited one brigade that had only 826 and 330 men present, at two respective roll calls, out of 2,954 men.

Into this state of affairs came Forrest, who, Brent explained, recognized the "necessity for reconstruction and reorganization of all these scattered, disorganized, and fragmentary bodies.... General Forrest accordingly informed the commanders that unless by the 5th of February, 1864, they could reassemble their commands he would assume the power of reconstructing them." Brent noted that when these officers "failed to reassemble their commands," Forrest fulfilled his promise and did it for them. In getting these results, Brent observed, Forrest "assumed and exercised the power of appointing both field and staff for many of these commands."

Some thought General Forrest's actions practical; others did not. Forrest had consolidated units to the point that, as Brent maintained, "it is impossible to trace out the origin and subsequent history of all these organizations. It is equally so to reinstate them in their original condition." Some officers believed that Forrest's actions were arbitrary infringements upon their authority. They demanded satisfaction, at least to the point of recognizing their authority and reconstituting their commands. However, Brent concluded, "To do so would produce endless confusion and controversy. To avoid such calamity, the good of the service would be best promoted by accepting the existing organization." Furthermore, the colonel suggested that "even if individual wrong were inflicted by so doing, the action of the Government would be justified by the principle that private interest should be subordinated to great public considerations in times like the present."[74]

Now, Forrest faced new challenges because of the way he had reorganized these commands, despite the glaring need to do so. He received a War Department communique citing the "irregularities and illegalities" in the manner by which he reconstituted some of the regiments in his command, along with orders to hold elections for new field officers for those regiments. Forrest went to great lengths to justify his actions and to appeal for a suspension of the order. He summarized the conditions that made his actions necessary in the first place and reminded President Davis of the situation in Mississippi when he arrived. He had accomplished a great deal and was concerned that the actions of people in Richmond would set back his work.

Forrest made every argument he could in support of his position. He had understood "that elections for field-officers could not be held" in the case of the western Tennessee units, since they came "from the odds and ends of some twelve or fifteen reputed commands and of unattached companies and squads raised inside the enemies lines." Furthermore, he had made the selections largely on "their ability and merits as officers."

Forrest stressed to the president that "with great labor, and under many difficulties and disadvantages, I succeeded in bringing order out of confusion, and organized and placed in the service a majority of the troops now constituting my command." Then, in an effort to demonstrate that the regiments in question were both happy with their appointed commanders and well-officered by them, he contradicted himself, "They are all contented, and everything is moving along harmoniously, and an election will surely result in the loss of the best field-officers I have, who by strict discipline have kept the men together." These officers had proved themselves "by gallantry" in recent fighting. However they had come to command, they had demonstrated competence, and with the enemy approaching, change could spell disaster.

As for himself, the general "distinctly disavow[ed] any assumption of any power or authority to make these appointments, but selected the very best men in the commands for the positions, and in doing so believed I was acting properly and legally." What he had done had been "for the best," and he expressed the "hope" concerning his command, "that nothing will now be done to destroy its effectiveness or weaken my influence and control over it." Somewhat defensively he explained, "I regarded the commands as detached, raised under various authorities, at different times and by different parties, and that field-officers could only be made by appointment from the War Department."

With his own control (and honor) challenged, he wanted to make it clear that he had "no desire to see the rights of any one disregarded." Believing that he had acted responsibly and noting that the appointments were accomplished facts that had "proved satisfactory to all parties," he hoped that "the appointments will be made as per roster forwarded to the department." He would not have troubled the president with the matter, he observed, "but for the fact that the good of the service and the efficiency of my command, and justice to the officers who have served so faithfully, require that I should lay this matter before you."[75]

These were important words for Forrest, words filled with powerful meanings. He wanted to maintain his "influence and control." He had brought "order out of confusion." He had "organized and placed" these men "in the service." His selections for officers had "kept the men together." Written by a staff officer, these were nevertheless Forrest's words, in spirit if not in style. Although possessing limited education, the general took great care with his official correspondence, unless he was hastily scribbling a note in the field. Staff officer D. C. Kelley observed, "Forrest, though writing but little himself, was very exacting as to what was written by his order."[76] The cavalry commander dictated to members of his staff, but had them read back to him what they had written. If he did not like the wording, he had it changed, remarking, "That hasn't got the right pitch."[77]

Davis read the letter and referred it to the adjutant general for a recommendation. On September 15, General Samuel Cooper advised that the units in question appeared not to have been independent at the time "they were originally mustered into service.... Hence the decision that the field officers must be elected according to the usage of the Department." He added that Forrest's instructions made it clear "that the necessary changes might not be made until such time as they could be done without detriment to the service." Then, in a postscript, Cooper asked the president to note the "remarks respecting deserters from the infantry arm being taken into these newly-created cavalry corps" on the "fifth page" of "the report [Brent's] marked No. 7."[78] Four days later, President Davis concluded, "I cannot delegate the power; indeed, do not possess it, if, as appears, these were not independent companies which the Executive could organize into regiments, etc."[79] And in a final endorsement, the secretary of war wrote, "Note President's indorsement; inform General Forrest."[80] Ironically, in a marvelous example of bureaucratic logic, the Confederate Assistant Secretary of War J. A. Campbell wrote an opinion to the secretary of war on September 21 that stated, in effect, that Davis had such authority. He concluded, "It seems to me, therefore, if it be deemed expedient to appoint officers under the circumstances mentioned herein, the order of the Department accepting these commands might discriminate the acts of Congress which are to be applied to them, and that the acts cited furnish authority for the action proposed by the commanders."[81]

The question went deeper than Forrest's authority to appoint commanders; it was a matter of control. Forrest's concern was his control over his men. He worked well with Lee and Maury because they respected that control and left it to him to exercise it as he saw fit. They allowed him the power to control his internal organization, to punish violators in his own manner, to fight battles in his own way, to exercise his "own untrammeled judgment." Wheeler did not, and Forrest denounced him for it. Bragg did not repeatedly, and Forrest excoriated him viciously for it. Now he was writing the Confederate president because Davis was the one man whose authority could ensure his own.

While Forrest grappled with this irritating issue, General A. J. Smith finally marched out of Holly Springs on August 8. He forced his way across the Tallahatchie, giving Forrest a clear indication of his line of march. The Confederate cavalry commander promptly ordered Chalmers to "contest every inch of ground," while he readied his men to respond to Smith's incursion.[82]

Chalmers tried to "contest every inch of ground," but the Union forces outflanked or forced him out of each defensive position he took. The Union troops used a ferryboat to cross the Tallahatchie, and although the Confederates attempted a night attack to eliminate the bridgehead, they failed to do so. Following some more maneuvering the next day, the Federals constructed a makeshift bridge and secured the structure against counterattack. Chalmers subsequently withdrew to Hurricane Creek to avoid being cut off by the enemy, and then to Oxford, Mississippi, when that line collapsed.[83]

Chalmers made a brief stand at Oxford, on August 10, before withdrawing so rapidly that he abandoned several artillery caissons and some camp equipment. The Federals rode into town to find little of value to them. Even so, they were content with what they had accomplished. Chalmers dropped below the rain-swollen Yocona River, rather than risk being trapped in front of it.

But the news was not all bad for the Confederates. The Federals soon evacuated Oxford, leaving it for Forrest, recently arrived from Pontotoc, to enter the town unchallenged sometime around 11 P.M. Thus, when the people awoke the next morning, they found Southerners where Northerners had been the night before.[84]

Forrest immediately sent word to Chalmers to move back up to Oxford and unite with his command. The Confederate commander spent most of August 11 reorganizing his men into two divisions under Chalmers and himself and establishing a defensive position behind Hurricane Creek. The Federals reacted slowly but firmly to Forrest's efforts. On August 13, Union General Mower marched against the Confederate's defense line, only to find that Forrest was as ready as he could be for them. According to one historian, the Southern commander skillfully employed "an elastic defense," or "a defense in depth."[85] This defense forced the Federals to spend several hours driving relatively small enemy forces back across Hurricane Creek. Having failed in his original plan to flank the Confederates, General Mower opted to attack the center of their line. The pressure of the Federal attacks forced Mabry, on the left of Forrest's line, to retreat. Forrest now had no choice but to follow and pull the rest of his men out of the line. For the next several days, little else happened as the two sides adjusted themselves in the midst of a pelting rain. Finally on August 18, Smith marched out of Holly Springs, slogging through the mud.[86]

In the meantime, Forrest became justifiably concerned that he would do no better against the Union's advance than Chalmers had done earlier. The Federals were repairing the railroad behind them, which would facilitate the movement of supplies and reinforcements. Smith was slow and cautious, but there appeared to be no way to stop him from pushing ever southward. But in the ponderous movement of the Union column and its dependence upon a single line of supply and communication, Forrest saw a possible solution to his dilemma. If he could sweep around Smith and cut that line, the deliberate Union commander might decide to retreat.

With this plan in mind, Forrest called for detachments of the best men from Bell's and Neely's brigades to meet at his headquarters at Oxford at 5 P.M. on August 18. When these men assembled, Forrest personally inspected them, "weeding out" men and horses that were too weak to engage in the arduous and dangerous operation he had in mind. With the two thousand men he selected and a battery of Morton's artillery, Forrest set out for Panola, leaving Chalmers behind with a similar number to hold the line, or at least the attention of the formidable Union column that was bearing down on him.[87]

The men in Forrest's raiding party had their work cut out for them. The rains continued to fall, raising the level of every body of water they would have to cross. The raiding party finally reached Panola at 7 A.M. on August 19 following a night battling rain and mud. The march thus far had been so strenuous that the Confederate cavalryman had to send back half his artillery and one hundred of his men whose mounts showed signs of breaking down. To ensure that the remaining artillery pieces kept pace, he put ten horses to each gun. He crossed the Tallahatchie with the remainder and pushed on toward Memphis.[88]

The sun broke out that day, but the roads remained in fearful condition. Although Forrest knew that time was of the essence, he halted for the night at Senatobia to let his men and horses rest before making their final dash to Memphis. And the next day, Forrest awoke to find that the Hickahala Creek, a mile north of the town, was badly swollen from the rain. Despite this unsettling news, the general later explained, "I had no idea of giving up my visit to Memphis, nor did I intend to lay around the creek waiting for it to fall."[89]

Ever the man of action, Forrest divided his men into patrols to gather planks from nearby gin houses, telegraph poles, and grapevines. With these items, the Confederates constructed a makeshift pontoon bridge, using a flatboat as the center pontoon for stability and the telegraph poles, tied together with grapevines, for the remaining pontoons. Once they had thrown planks across, the Southerners had their bridge. Then, in order not to overburden it, the Confederate troopers dismounted and walked their horses across. The cannoneers also unlimbered their two remaining artillery pieces and carried the teams and ammunition, as well as the guns, across by hand.[90]

No doubt, much to their disappointment, the men had to

repeat the entire process six miles farther down the road at the next crossing over the Coldwater. But by dark on August 20, they arrived at Forrest's old hometown of Hernando. There, Forrest stopped the raiding column to allow the men and animals to eat and rest before continuing to Memphis, now twenty-five miles away. Both at Hernando and at other points along the way, Forrest obtained additional information about the city and its garrison.

The column left Hernando and arrived in the southern suburbs of Memphis around 3 A.M. Understanding the need to operate quickly and efficiently, Forrest divided his force into detachments, assigning each a particular task. Since he and his brothers, Captain William H. and Lieutenant Colonel Jesse Forrest, had lived in Memphis before the war, he knew they could find their way around the city streets. Therefore, he selected them to lead details to capture the principal Union commanders in the city. He instructed William to seize the pickets on the road into Memphis, race into the city, and capture General Stephen A. Hurlbut at his headquarters in the Gayoso House Hotel. He designated Jesse to ride to the Union Street residence that General Cadwallader C. Washburn reportedly occupied and capture him. Other detachments were to capture transports and steamers at the landing or engage troops garrisoning the city. The Confederate cavalry commander had no intention of remaining in Memphis long or attacking nearby Fort Pickering.[91]

Bedford Forrest had ample confidence in his brother William and selected him to lead the column. One Confederate soldier described Captain Forrest as "a powerful man, five feet eleven inches tall [with] broad shoulders, weighing about two hundred pounds." Like his oldest brother, William also had a tremendous temper. The same soldier labeled him "brave to [the point of] recklessness," noting, "He did not fear one man, nor did he fear a hundred men.... He never provoked a quarrel, but, when disturbed, would shoot a man on the slightest provocation." Bedford apparently recognized and respected this aspect of his younger brother's character, for the soldier recalled, "It has been often said that General Forrest never feared but one man, and that man was his brother William."[92] Another contemporary reported in an obituary of the general that of all the Forrests, only this brother "turned out to be what we might really term a desperado." Furthermore, he observed, William was "the only man General Forrest used to say that he ever felt afraid of," quoting the eldest Forrest: "'No one living,' said the General, 'can tell when Bill's going to get mad.'" And the writer added, "whenever Bill got mad he shot, and he never missed his man."[93]

Implicit faith in his brothers, his command, himself, and the thoroughness of his plans gave Forrest the confidence to ride into a major fortified Union post with the full expectation that he could accomplish his goals and ride out again at his pleasure. Even some of the men the raid victimized gave Forrest and his men their grudging admiration. Shortly after it occurred, General Ralph P. Buckland, commander of the District of Memphis, summarized the reasons for Forrest's success in the daring raid. "His plan was well laid and the moment propitious." He also observed, "The parties sent into the city were led by officers and others well-acquainted with the city."[94]

Captain William Forrest moved out with a small patrol in the vanguard. They had not gone far when they ran into a sentry. William responded to the traditional question, "Halt! Who comes there?" by saying that he led a "detachment with rebel prisoners." The sentry called for him to dismount and approach, but he stayed on his horse, and just as he emerged from the darkness and the fog, he spurred the animal and dropped the sentry with a blow from his pistol as he dashed by. His patrol easily captured the remaining pickets at this post and continued along the road.[95]

At the next post, they were not so fortunate. This set of pickets fired a volley, thereby warning their comrades, before the Southerners scattered them. Undoubtedly thinking that there was no more reason for silence, the men began to yell as they rode into Memphis. Believing that the order for silence was nullified by all their noise, Forrest decided to make the most of it by ordering his bugler to sound the charge. Perhaps he could bluff the groggy Federals into thinking that a much greater mass of Southern horsemen was riding down upon them.[96]

Captain Forrest's detail dispersed the gunners of a Wisconsin battery as they rode by, killing and wounding several, but no one thought to disable the guns themselves. They raced on to the

Gayoso House, where William rode his horse through the doorway and into the lobby with shouts to others to bar the doors and search the rooms. Despite their quick work, the Southerners could not find General Hurlbut, who had spent the night elsewhere. Other members of his staff were not so fortunate, and after a brief exchange of gunfire in which one of them was killed, the rest surrendered.[97] But not all was so grim in the Gayoso House that Sunday morning. One of the Southerners took the time to write the names of General Forrest "and party" in the hotel's registration book. Then, in the section for comments, he thanked the Union generals for their invitation to visit Memphis.[98]

Lieutenant Colonel Jesse Forrest's detachment fared no better in its attempt to capture General Washburn. A subordinate had warned Washburn of the danger, and he raced into the night to Fort Pickering. Even so, the Confederates captured some of Washburn's staff officers, as well as his uniform. This latter occurrence gave a still embittered General Hurlbut a chance to ridicule his successor with the observation, "They removed me from command because I couldn't keep Forrest out of West Tennessee, and now Washburn can't keep him out of his own bedroom."[99]

By this time the scene in Memphis was one of utter chaos. Confederate horsemen raced through the streets firing and yelling, as one Southerner wrote, "like Comanches." Startled Union soldiers, so suddenly awakened, dashed to their posts or ran for their lives. Civilians crowded windows and porches to see what was happening so early in the morning. Other Southern troopers dispersed to find friends and family or to raid stables and cupboards. Drum rolls, gunfire, shouts, and virtually every other sound imaginable filled the air.[100]

As Captain Forrest dramatically rode through the doors of the Gayoso House in search of General Hurlbut, other Confederate detachments, under Colonels Thomas H. Logwood and Neely, encountered serious opposition. They rode through the camps and streets, where the Federals, now roused to their presence, attempted to block their paths. In these encounters, the Southerners suffered some losses, but scattered the lines formed to stop them.

Colonel Neely and his men met the greatest difficulty. Near Elmwood Cemetery, they attacked an infantry camp, but incurred severe casualties. Bedford saw their situation and rode with the reserve to their assistance. As he pushed along, hoping to strike the Union infantry in the flank, he passed a cavalry encampment from which he received fire. He abruptly broke off the flanking attack, turned back, and drove off the Union cavalry. About the same time, Neely gained the upper hand in his fight and drove the Federals into the State Female College. From that stronghold, the Union soldiers fired upon their assailants. Bedford brought up a section of artillery and had several shells thrown into the building, but he had no intention of assaulting it.[101]

William Forrest soon left the hotel and rode to the Irving Block prison. Although he made every effort to free the prisoners, some of whom belonged to Forrest's command, the resistance proved too great and his force too small. He had to abandon the attempt and ride on, although his elder brother soon sounded the recall. With this, the various detachments and innumerable stragglers began to filter out of the city. Some of the Confederates loitered too long and became prisoners; others barely escaped as the Federals organized to resist and pursue them.

The last real fighting of the Memphis raid occurred when Union cavalrymen under Colonel Matthew H. Starr followed some of the stragglers out of the city. Again Bedford rode to the rescue and promptly came to close quarters with the Federals. Starr rode for him, and the two battled hand to hand. Forrest quickly got the better of his opponent, mortally wounding him with a saber thrust "entirely through his body."[102]

By 9 A.M., Forrest had most of his men reassembled, and with some six hundred prisoners, marched southward, toward Hernando. He could not go far before he realized that most of the prisoners lacked sufficient clothing, particularly shoes, to withstand the upcoming march, captured as many of them had been in their night clothes. The general sent word through his aide, Captain Anderson, for Washburn either to agree to exchange the prisoners or, failing that, at least to send them some suitable clothing. Washburn replied that he lacked the authority to make an exchange, but sent the clothing.

Forrest then had his surgeons examine the prisoners. He freed the weakest, about two hundred, on the promise that they would not take up arms against the Confederacy until they were properly exchanged. The Confederates and their remaining captives proceeded to Hernando, where Forrest encountered a second problem—he did not have enough rations to feed the prisoners—and once again turned to Washburn. The column camped for the night at Hernando and the next morning distributed the food from two wagons that had just arrived from Memphis. The prisoners received two days' rations, while the Southerners took the remainder for themselves.

As long as the Union detachment remained in the area, Forrest allowed his men to go about their work at a leisurely pace, hoping to give them the impression that he had no intention of leaving. But as soon as the Federals disappeared on the road back to Memphis, the Southern commander hastily broke camp and headed south. This strange sequence of events was part of Forrest's psychological arsenal. If the Federals thought he was merely regrouping to renew the attack, they might remain in their defenses in Memphis and not pursue him.[103]

The haste was also due to an exchange Forrest had with one of the Union officers whom Washburn had sent with the special request that he return the general's captured uniform. According to General Maury, to whom Forrest told the story, the officer also brought a promise to forward the Confederate general "a bolt of the finest gray cloth to be found in Memphis." The officer had one other message as well. "General W. desired me to say," he explained to Forrest, that "he will catch you before you get back." The Southerner quickly replied, "You may tell the general for me, that I am going back on the same road I came by, and if we meet, I promise to whip him out of his boots."

Forrest confided that he regretted making the boast. "When I told him that, I allowed he would not believe me, and would send all of his forces to intercept me on the other road." But, he added, "as soon as the major had gone off with the message, I began to think he might believe me and attack me on the same homeward road, and I got scared, and ran back as fast as I could."[104]

All the while Bedford Forrest and his men rode into and out of Memphis, Chalmers gamely held Smith's superior invasion force at bay. On August 19, he made such a bold attack on the Union line that the Federals not only failed to realize that Forrest was no longer in front of them, but thought he had been reinforced. Two days later, Chalmers retreated beyond the Yocona River, once again leaving Oxford in Union hands. This time the town suffered heavily when the Federals burned many of its buildings. But by 5 P.M. the Federals received the garbled and confusing news of Forrest's dash into Memphis and began to recoil.[105]

The next day, August 23, Chalmers recrossed the Yocona and pursued General A. J. Smith's retiring column. The Confederates struck the Union rearguard at Abbeville and battled with them for a few hours before breaking off the attack under duress. Chalmers might have been brave, but he lacked the numbers to fight head on. The Federals got the better of the battle, losing only 1 man killed and 15 wounded to the Confederate casualties of 7 killed, 15 wounded, and 12 missing. Even so, one of Chalmers's Mississippians, angry at the enemy's destruction of Oxford, summed up the mood of these men best. "Damn them." Colonel William Wade exclaimed to his commanding general "They ran us for two or three days. I wanted them to know we are not afraid of them."[106]

In the meantime, Washburn tried unsuccessfully to coordinate with Smith to trap Forrest on his return ride. He later blamed Smith for their failure to catch the Confederates, but the Southerners were too far ahead, and Smith was too concerned with the fate of Memphis, which he believed remained in doubt. Forrest and his raiders returned safely to middle Mississippi, leaving the Federals to determine how they had come and gone so easily.[107]

Casualties for the affair were relatively light. As usual, reports varied. Washburn placed his losses at 15 killed, 65 wounded, and 112 missing and put the Confederates' casualties at 22 killed and 40 captured.[108] Forrest reported capturing many more men than the Union commander admitted losing, 600 (200 of whom he released near Memphis). He placed his own losses at 9 killed and 24 wounded.[109] As for the larger goals of the raid, the Southerners failed to capture any of the three principal Union generals in Memphis, but succeeded in convincing General Smith to break off his invasion of Mississippi.

Sherman thought the whole operation daring, but pointless. On August 24, he wrote Washburn and asked him, "If you get a chance send word to Forrest I admire his dash but not his judgment. The oftener he runs his head against Memphis the better."[110] In this case, the Union general might have been wise to remember that Forrest lost little in forcing Smith to give up the primary objective of his campaign: to kill the Confederate cavalryman. Nevertheless, Sherman had the satisfaction of knowing that for a while longer, at least, Forrest remained occupied well away from his supply lines.

CHAPTER 12

Making Havoc among the Gunboats

(September–November 1864)

I began to think he had no stomach for the work.

—GENERAL RICHARD TAYLOR ON FORREST

There is no doubt we could soon wipe old Sherman off the face of the earth, John, if they'd give me enough men and you enough guns.

—FORREST TO CAPTAIN JOHN MORTON

That devil Forrest was down about Johnsonville, making havoc among the gunboats and transports.

—GENERAL WILLIAM T. SHERMAN

ONE OF THE MOST UNUSUAL EVENTS of Forrest's life occurred in September 1864, almost as a postscript to the raid on Memphis. The grand jury of the newly established Federal Circuit Court for the District of West Tennessee returned an indictment for treason against eighty Memphians, including Bedford Forrest and his brothers William and Jesse, who were engaged in the Confederate service. The grand jury noted that "an open and public rebellion, insurrection was with force and arms existing and is existing and prosecuted and carried on" against the United States, observing, in part,

> that Nathan B. Forrest, late of the said district being an inhabitant of and resident within the United States of America and owing allegiance and fidelity to the said United States of America, well knowing the promise but not weighing it regarding the duty of his allegiance and fidelity ... was a traitor ... [and] withdrew the allegiance and fidelity and obedience which every citizen of the United States of America ought to bear toward his Government ... by conspiring, contriving and intending by all the means in his power to aid and assist ... the said Confederate States of America by the prosecution of said rebellion, insurrection and war, to wit:
>
> On August 21, 1864, and divers other days and times before as well as after that day at the county of Shelby within the jurisdiction of this court ... wickedly devising and invading the peace and tranquility of the United States of America to disturb and to stir, move, excite, aid and assist in the rebellion ... with force and arms unlawfully, falsely, maliciously, and traitorously did raise and levy war ... and the said Nathan B. Forrest on August 21, 1864 at the County of Shelby with a great multitude of persons ... [did] arm and arrange and appear in a war like manner, that is to say with guns, swords, pistols and other war like weapons ... contrary to the form of the Statutes in such cases and against the peace and dignity of the United States of America.[1]

Ironically, at least one of the grand jurors who signed the indictment knew Bedford Forrest long before he rode into Memphis in August 1864, and belonged to the lodge of the Independent Order of Odd Fellows with Forrest. The Confederate knew D. C. Trader well enough to write him in his own hand on May 23, 1862, from Corinth, "Sir your note of 21 Ins [of the present month] is to hand I did not fully understand the contents and ask for Information the amount you ask for is it for a publick contrabution or is it my dues due the lodge I wish you to give me the amt due the log [lodge] from me as you did not State it in your notice[.]"

This business done, Forrest passed the war news on to the

future grand juror. "I had a small brush with the Enamy on yesterday I Suceded in gaining thir rear and got in to thir entrenchments 8 miles from ham burg and 5 behind farmington and Burned a portion of thir camp at that place," adding gleefully, "they wair not looking for me I taken them by Surprise they run like Suns of Biches I captured the Rev Dr Warin from Ilanois and one fin Sorel Stud[.]" Forrest expected the Federals to follow up their recent victory at Shiloh, observing with an eye to posterity: "This army is at this time in front of our Entrenchments I look for a fite soon and a big one when it coms off Cant you come up and take a hand this fite wil do to hand down to your childrens children I feel confident of our sucess[.]"[2]

But even as he faced this indictment and the prospects of a new enemy campaign, Bedford Forrest had to rest and refit his command; disperse them to various points, such as Mobile, where General Dabney Maury desperately wanted his assistance; and reorganize the remainder. He retained the two-division structure, with General James R. Chalmers in command of one (composed of Colonels Robert McCulloch's and Edmund W. Rucker's brigades) and General Abraham Buford in charge of the other (consisting of Colonel Hylan B. Lyon's and General Tyree Bell's brigades).[3]

Forrest made every effort to comply with Maury's appeal, but by September 3 the immediate crisis had passed and help was no longer needed in Mobile. Even so, some evidence points to the general's presence in the city, as one biographer postulated, "some time between August thirtieth and September third."[4] Maury recalled Forrest's apparent visit in his memoirs: "My wife wished to entertain him, and gave him a dinner, inviting some lady friends who were desirous of meeting this great hero." He noted that Forrest's "natural deference to the sex gave them all much pleasure." Then noting that "under all circumstances he was their defender and protector from every sort of wrong," Maury observed, "his wife was a gentle lady, to whom he was careful in his deference."[5]

However long he remained in Mobile, Forrest soon met with the new commander of the Department of Alabama, Mississippi, and East Louisiana, General Richard Taylor. Taylor had never met the cavalryman before, and when he saw him, described him as "a tall, stalwart man, with grayish hair, mild countenance and slow and homely of speech." The new departmental commander expressed his intention to send his subordinate into Tennessee to operate on the enemy's supply lines. "To my surprise," Taylor recalled years later, "Forrest suggested many difficulties and asked numerous questions: how he was to get over the Tennessee; how he was to get back if pressed by the enemy; how he was to be supplied; what should be his line of retreat in certain contingencies; what he was to do with prisoners if any were taken, etc." Undoubtedly Taylor had heard of the cavalryman's reputation as a fighter, but the barrage of questions unnerved him. "I began to think he had no stomach for the work," General Taylor confessed, "but at last, having isolated the chances of success from causes of failure with the care of a chemist experimenting in his laboratory, he rose and asked for ... the superintendent of the railway."

When that man arrived, Taylor observed, "Forrest's whole manner now changed." The cavalryman rattled off "a dozen sharp sentences" explaining his needs, offered to "leave a staff officer to bring up his supplies, asked for an engine to take him back north twenty miles to meet his troops, informed me he would march with the dawn, and hoped to give an account of himself in Tennessee." Although he would not invade middle Tennessee "with the dawn," Forrest sprang to action to march into that region as rapidly as he could.[6]

Forrest now set his sights upon carrying out the task that Georgia's Governor Brown had pleaded with President Davis to allow him to do. As usual, he became totally absorbed in his plans. One soldier recalled that in these cases he sat motionless in his chair, transfixed by thought, "chin sunk on his chest," or paced with his head down and his hands clasped behind him.[7] At such times, the staff knew well that he was best left undisturbed. And when someone failed to heed this common practice, the result was usually swift and summary. When one soldier made the mistake of disturbing the general repeatedly while he was pacing and could not see the trouble he was creating for himself, Forrest reminded him with a quick blow. The general continued to pace, still lost in thought, stepping over the unconscious man each time he reached him.[8]

By September 19, the Confederate cavalry commander had his force assembled at Cherokee Station on the Memphis and Charleston Railroad. The troops remained there until early on September 21, completing the last-minute preparations. Then the Confederate horsemen crossed the Tennessee River amid the tremendous shoals and rocks and camped for the night a few miles outside Florence. General P. D. Roddey joined them the next day, bringing the total of Forrest's raiders to approximately 4,500.[9]

At sunset on September 23, the Southern column arrived in the vicinity of Athens, Alabama, on the Nashville and Decatur Railroad. They encountered a strong earthwork, manned by 469 men from the 106th U.S. Colored Infantry and the 111th U.S. Colored Infantry and another 150 men from the Third Tennessee Cavalry. Forrest immediately surrounded the place and waited out the night. He spent part of the morning shelling the fort and arranging his forces to attack it, and by 10:30 A.M. was ready. As usual, once he was prepared to fight, Forrest sent in a flag of truce in the hopes that he might not have to do so. The demand contained the typical promise of sufficient force to take the works and dispensation of "responsibility of the consequences" should an attack prove necessary. Undoubtedly with Fort Pillow still fresh in his mind, Forrest concluded, "Should you, however, accept the terms, all white soldiers shall be treated as prisoners of war and the negroes returned to their masters."[10]

The Federal commander sent back word that he would not surrender, to which Forrest replied by asking to meet with him personally. Once more relying on bluff, the Confederate general met with his counterpart, Colonel Wallace Campbell, and told him that he did not wish to shed blood unnecessarily. He was sure that he could take the fort without difficulty—so sure, in fact, that he would take the unorthodox step of showing Campbell his command, which he placed at eight thousand, to convince the Union officer of the hopelessness of his position. Campbell agreed that if his adversary had the numbers he claimed, a defense would be useless. Forrest had him halfway there.

The Confederate general graciously led the Union colonel on a review of his lines. Forrest referred to his dismounted men as infantry. In the distance, the horse holders gave the impression of large bodies of cavalry. To add to the deception, batteries shifted from place to place, inflating the number of guns the Confederates could claim to have. And Campbell could see clearly that his position was surrounded.[11] Indeed, General Forrest and his men did so well that by the time the review ended, Colonel Campbell was ready to surrender his men and save their lives from an attack by such overwhelming numbers. He rode back into the fort and reported the state of affairs. "The jig is up; pull down the flag," a large number of his officers reported him stating.[12]

While Colonel Campbell was reviewing Forrest's command, a relief force of 360 men approached the area from Decatur. These Federals attempted to break through, but could not do so before the fort surrendered. Although their effort proved unsuccessful, even Forrest attested that they "fought with great gallantry and desperation."[13] But the odds were against them, and after losing 106 of their men killed and wounded, they also had to yield.[14]

This left one final obstacle to the complete success of the operation at Athens. One of the blockhouses guarding the railroad refused to surrender. Forrest ordered up his artillery and sent two rounds into the fortification, killing two men and wounding another. This convinced the Union commander that further resistance would lead to needless slaughter, since the Confederates could blast the blockhouse with artillery and avoid making an assault.[15]

The fighting at Athens now complete, Forrest could turn his attention to the destruction of the railroad and public property. His men burned the blockhouses and the wooden structures in the fort. They destroyed two locomotives and their train of cars. The Federals had already burned a great deal the night before, when they retreated into the fort itself. Soon Forrest started the prisoners and the captured stores back toward Cherokee and pressed on with the rest of his command.[16] Within four miles they encountered another blockhouse and quickly captured it with thirty occupants. Forrest reported, "The trestle, railroad, and block-house at this point were all in blazing ruins twenty minutes after we reached them."[17] The tired Confederates rode another four miles and halted for the night.

Long after the war, Forrest's artillery chief, Captain John Mor-

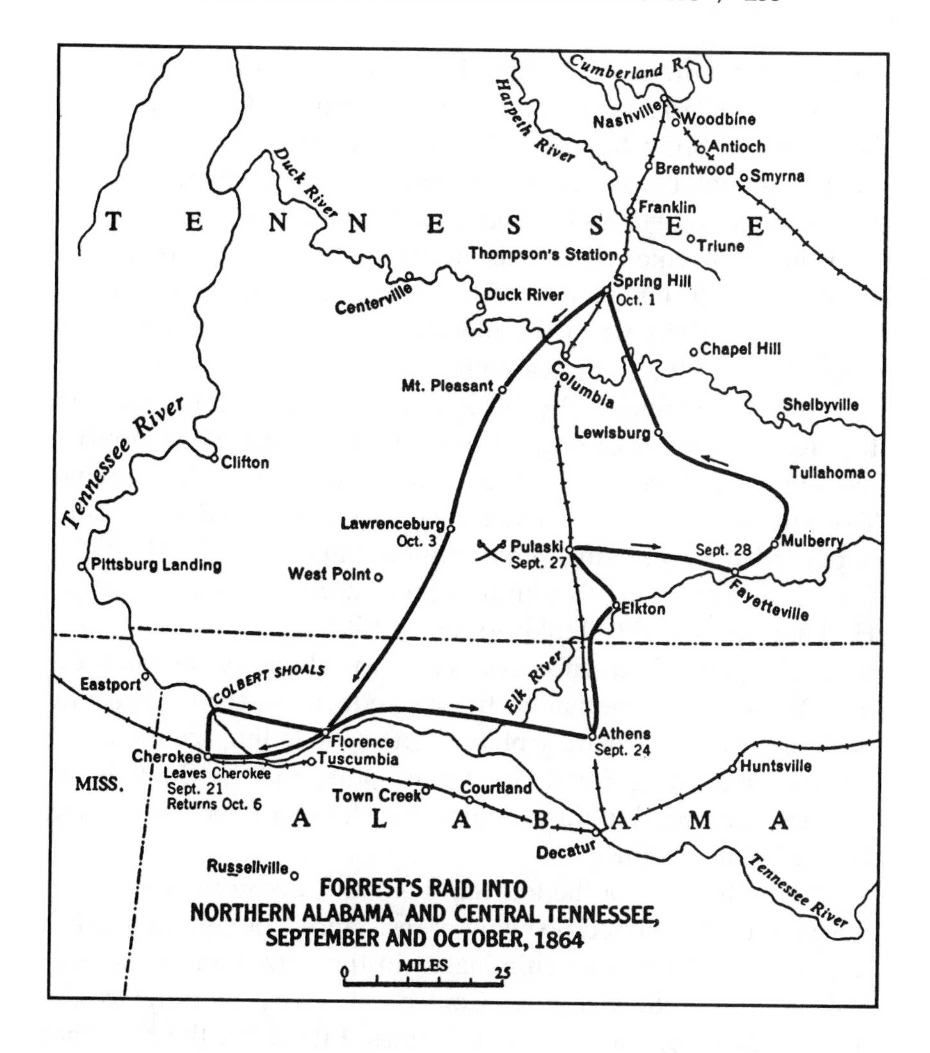

FORREST'S RAID INTO NORTHERN ALABAMA AND CENTRAL TENNESSEE, SEPTEMBER AND OCTOBER, 1864

ton, recalled that the commander of one of the blockhouses Forrest captured during this phase of the campaign was "a Dutch officer." This "Dutchman" greatly angered the general by refusing to surrender when called upon to do so, despite the visible odds against him holding out. Forrest "made the atmosphere blue for a while" with his curses and finally yelled, "Does the damned fool want to be blown up?" Then turning to Morton, he added emphatically, "Well, I'll blow him up, then. Give him hell, Captain Morton—as hot as you've got it, too."

Morton recalled that he went into action in obedience to his general's command and needed only two shots to convince the garrison to show a white flag. He promptly ordered the firing stopped, but Forrest called for him to continue: "Go on, John, go on. That was bully. Keep it up!" Morton pointed at the stockade. "Why, General, I see a white cloth from a porthole; look yonder!" Forrest glanced over and glared back, "Well, I don't see any. Keep on firing. It'll take a sheet to attract my eye at this distance." Knowing well his commander's mood and temper, Morton obeyed. The Federals in the blockhouse quickly found a larger white flag, and the firing ceased for good.[18]

Early on September 25, the Southerners moved two miles farther to the Sulpher Springs. The trestle there stood seventy-two feet high and three hundred feet across, spanning a deep ravine. Two strong blockhouses and an earthwork guarded the trestle, with garrisons consisting of four hundred men from the 111th U.S. Colored Infantry and six hundred cavalry, under Colonel William H. Lathrop. Forrest deployed his artillery and his men and ordered a general advance to drive all the Union pickets into the fort. At the same time that his troopers edged closer to the Federal positions, Morton's battery blazed forth with telling accuracy. The long-range shelling lasted about two hours, and the Confederate gunners succeeded in dismounting the Union artillery pieces and killing Colonel Lathrop.[19]

When the guns of the fort fell silent and, according to Forrest, the garrison "exhibited no show of resistance," he sent in another flag of truce.[20] This one culminated in the surrender of the fort, and once more the victorious Confederates consigned the trestle, the blockhouses, and the fort to flames. Just about the time that the fort was surrendering, Union Colonel George Spalding rode up with eight hundred men in an attempt to reinforce the beleaguered garrison. He skirmished with the Confederates for about twenty minutes when he learned that the earthwork had capitulated and retreated to the Elk River, leaving Forrest unmolested.[21]

Forrest sent back a new batch of prisoners, some one thousand, and the captured equipment. He was enjoying enormous success and suffering comparatively few losses, but he faced a serious dilemma. Along with the captured Union artillery, he had to send back four of his own guns because of the lack of ammunition. In addition, every time he sent prisoners and equipment back to the Tennessee River, he had to send his own men to guard them. Ironically, success was draining his manpower.[22]

Even so, Forrest and his troopers started early on September 26 for the Elk River. Colonel Spalding had determined to hold on to the blockhouses and bridges there, but he wanted to keep his cavalry command free to strike Forrest at a time and place of his own choosing. Therefore, he consolidated the garrison troops at hand, about one hundred, and put them into two of the blockhouses with the admonition to hold the blockhouses "at all hazards." Assured by the garrison commanders that they would "hold the block-houses until they were knocked to pieces," Spalding slowly rode off with his cavalry, in the direction of Pulaski.[23]

Despite these assurances, when General Buford and his men arrived on the scene, they found the blockhouses abandoned and the bridge unguarded. Buford's Confederates set to work destroying everything of military value, while Spalding was shocked to find that the men who were supposed to be holding the blockhouses behind him "had abandoned the stockade and been in advance of my cavalry all the morning, having evacuated the stockades without firing a shot."[24]

Spalding proceeded with his cavalry to the railroad crossing at Richland Creek, where he found the commander and the garrison packing to evacuate to Pulaski, Tennessee. The Union colonel "immediately sent directions to the captain in command of the blockhouses to make a stubborn resistance, and also stated that I would support him and shoot every officer and soldier I found deserting his post." Then Spalding rode off again, this time toward Elkton, where reports placed part of the Southern raiding force.[25] The Union colonel's iron hand was enough to keep this garrison in the blockhouses until Forrest arrived. And when Forrest appeared and fired a few rounds, the fifty-man garrison surrendered, preferring to walk away as prisoners than to die in the blockhouses they had earlier tried to evacuate.[26]

After destroying the bridge and works at Richland Creek, Forrest's column pushed on, camping for the night within ten miles of Pulaski. Then on the morning of September 27, the Confederates moved up the road toward that town. They encountered resistance, which Forrest characterized as "most obstinate." The

Federals "contested every inch of ground and grew more stubborn the nearer we approached the town, but my troops drove them steadily back." Finally, three miles short of Pulaski, the Union forces made a stand. Forrest had to deploy his men in line of battle, with Colonel David C. Kelley on the left, Colonel William A. Johnson in the center, and General Buford on the right.[27]

Despite the Federals' obstinacy, the Confederates drove the Federals the remainder of the way into town, reaching Pulaski about 1 P.M. Here Forrest conducted a personal reconnaissance, accompanied by his escort, and determined that any attack against the Union works would be suicidal. He made a great show, particularly after dark, when the men built camp fires along the lines "for the purpose of deceiving the enemy." Then, he established a picket line to add to the deception. Before he rode off to the east with the main force to break up the Nashville and Chattanooga Railroad, Forrest sent a detachment northward "to destroy the railroad and the telegraph line between Pulaski and Columbia." This action might also divert the Federals' attention and pursuit while he raced for his real target.[28]

Forrest reached Fayetteville on September 28 and camped five miles east of there for the night. Rain had rendered the roads almost impassable. The ordnance train and artillery slogged along at a crawl, frequently miring in the mud, while splattered men and animals struggled to free them. At one point, Forrest rode up to find one of the captured caissons hopelessly caught in a deep rut. Thinking that the men might succeed with a bit of encouragement, the general called out, "Who has charge here?" An officer replied, "I have, sir." Forrest eyed him a moment and launched into him with a string of oaths and epithets, beginning, "Then why in hell don't you do something?" Perhaps he had meant the language to urge the men to work harder, or he might just have been angry, wet, and tired. But the officer, Captain Andrew McGregor, apparently felt no better about the situation than did his commander. "I'll not be cursed out by anyone, even a superior officer," he shouted as he grabbed a torch and thrust it into the caisson's ammunition chest.

Forrest sat stunned for a moment, then jerked his horse

around, put spurs to the animal, and dashed away for all he was worth, calling out a warning to everyone nearby. When he reached his staff, he breathlessly asked, "What infernal lunatic is that just out of the asylum down there? He came near blowing himself and me up with a whole caisson full of powder." Undoubtedly they tried to keep from laughing too loudly at their sensitive commander, but the matter was simply too humorous to contain. They knew that the men had emptied the caisson, trying to lighten it sufficiently to free it from the mud, and that McGregor was playing a joke at Forrest's expense. Finally, the general joined in the good-natured laughter. The joke had one effect, according to artillery chief Morton: "He never used profanity to Captain McGregor after that."[29]

Forrest became increasingly concerned that his command had become too weak and the enemy too strong for him to do any great harm to the Nashville and Chattanooga Railroad without allowing the Federals the opportunity to do even greater harm to him. As he later explained his subsequent actions, "Under these circumstances I deemed it hazardous and unwise to move upon the enemy, who was prepared to meet me with overwhelming numbers."[30] Although Forrest sent a small detachment that caused minimal damage to that railroad and the telegraph line running alongside it, he could not disable Sherman's main line of communication and supply with anything approaching the precision he had used against the Nashville and Decatur.[31]

And so, Forrest turned south, where "there was a prospect of accomplishing some good."[32] Deep in Union-occupied territory, with large concentrations of enemy troops preparing to find and annihilate him, Forrest split his small force. By dispatching Buford and fifteen hundred men to attack Huntsville, Alabama, and destroy the Memphis and Charleston Railroad from there to Decatur, Alabama, while he and the remainder of his men marched westward through Lewisburg and then northward to Spring Hill, the Confederate cavalryman hoped to confuse his pursuers and finish the work he had started on the Nashville and Decatur line.[33]

On September 30, Buford appeared before Huntsville. Using a familiar ploy, he demanded the garrison's surrender, signing his correspondence, "N. B. Forrest, Major General." The Union commander, General Gordon Granger, called for him "to come and take it as soon as you get ready." Granger's men worked feverishly through the night preparing to repulse an attack that would not come. Early the next day, instead of attacking "from every rock, house, tree and shrub in the vicinity," as he promised, Buford quietly slipped away and wrecked the railroad tracks.[34]

Later on October 1, Buford reappeared before Athens, now reoccupied by two hundred men and a battery. He deployed his men and waited through a night filled with torrents of rain to strike early the next day. Again, Buford had no desire to sacrifice his command in frontal assaults against a well-entrenched enemy. He shelled the position, sent in a demand for surrender, and when it was rejected, rode off as quietly as he had arrived. There was little else for him to do except to recross the Tennessee River and wait for his commander.[35]

Forrest had also been busy since he divided his command. He reached Lewisburg by September 30 and turned northward, arriving at Spring Hill at noon on the next day. By turning south to follow the railroad and wreck it as he went, he compelled three more blockhouses to surrender and burned the bridges they had guarded. However, later on the same day, Forrest ran into a stubborn Union officer, whom he labeled a "Dutchman," who refused his demand. Since he had no artillery with which to treat this "Dutchman," as he had the one he encountered earlier in the campaign, he waited for night. Under the cover of darkness, he sent several volunteers to the truss bridge, which they succeeded in burning. The task completed, despite his stubborn opponent, Forrest proceeded south.[36]

On October 2, Forrest demonstrated before Columbia, while his men took out several small bridges. He had no intention of attacking the town and pulled out to push toward the Tennessee River. On all sides of him, larger commands than his closed in to prevent him from crossing the river. In fact, General George H. Thomas, coordinating the pursuit, was so confident that he wrote one subordinate, "I do not think we shall ever have a better chance at Forrest than this."[37] Sensing the opportunity to trap the pesky Confederate raider, Thomas told his commanders in the pursuing columns to "press Forrest to the death."[38]

Forrest reached Florence by October 5, to find that the river was badly flooded from the rain. He deployed units to hold off the pursuit while he attempted to get his command across. The operation took two days and a night of grueling, dangerous work. Late on October 6, his rearguard began to show signs of breaking down. "At this critical juncture," he observed, "I ordered all troops on the north side of the river, with the exception of one regiment, to mount their horses and swim across a slough about seventy yards wide to a large island, which would afford them ample protection and from which they could ferry over at [comparative] leisure." The sole regiment, Colonel C. C. Wilson's, had the unenviable task of fighting with the Federals while the others crossed to the island. With obvious satisfaction, Forrest reported, "This strategy was successful. Every man reached the island in safety." As for Wilson, his men harassed the Union forces with hit-and-run strikes that cost him only two killed and four missing and eventually crossed the river himself.[39]

During the long and hazardous process, General Forrest kept his men going through his strong will and personal example. It was how he operated best as a commander. And as the boats shuttled back and forth from the island for two more days, he gave every aspect of the operation his close attention. Then, when the last boat was about to leave the island, he disappeared into the cane. Coming upon four stragglers, oblivious to their situation, he bellowed at them, "I thought I would catch some of you damned fools loafing back here in the cane as if nothing was going on. If you don't want to get left all winter on the island you had better come along with me; the last boat is going over right away." The four men scurried along after their commander and jumped into the boat with him.

On the way, Forrest had another opportunity to illustrate his idea of discipline. Already worn from the campaign and the crossing, Forrest was in a foul mood and cursed everything that did not please him. His level of control was extremely low, and it snapped as he helped to pole the vessel and noticed a young lieutenant at the bow doing nothing to help. He shouted out to the officer, "Why don't you take hold of an oar or pole and help get this boat across?" The lieutenant shrugged off the question, arrogantly insisting that he was an officer and thought that there were privates enough to do the chore. This was the wrong thing to say to the tired and temperamental general, as the officer quickly learned when Forrest pulled the pole he was using out of the water and smashed it across the man's face. The blow knocked him into the water and only the timely offer of a pole prevented him from drowning. As the others pulled him into the boat, the soaked and stunned soldier looked into the angry glare of his general, who pointed at him and said, "Now, damn you, get hold of the oars and go to work! If I knock you out of the boat again I'll let you drown." Everyone, including the haughty lieutenant, quickly returned to work.[40]

"Forrest has escaped us," General James D. Morgan informed Nashville.[41] General Thomas advised the commander of one of the pursuing columns, "If you are sufficiently near to Forrest to lead you to hope you can capture him by crossing the river, you can do so and pursue him, but you must not venture too far from the river or so as to endanger your command."[42] But Forrest was now safe, and "hopes" of his capture were just that.

The Union telegraph wires filled with the bad news and with explanations why the pursuit had failed to snare the Confederates. In any case, all these Federals could do now was to express their disappointment. "Forrest did slip out past [our] gun-boats," one officer wrote to another, "and escape[d] over the Tennessee without serious loss, much to General Thomas' chagrin, who expected better results as a large portion of our force was mounted, and ought to have crowded that rebel into the river."[43]

The Federals had one more plan in mind for Bedford Forrest. Sherman told Thomas that he was "sorry that Forrest escaped" and subsequently arranged to "dispose of" the Confederate cavalryman and his command.[44] But plans to use a combined strike of 1,300 infantrymen under Colonel George B. Hoge, via the water, and 3,000 cavalrymen by land went awry when Confederate Colonel Kelley ambushed the infantry as they disembarked from the transports at Eastport. In what Hoge called a "scene of confusion," the transports sustained hits from the Southern artillery and, he said, "in spite of all I could do, the boats backed out, parting their lines [and] leaving about two-thirds of the command on the shore."[45] The naval commander reported that the infantry "broke and fled pell-mell down the river. The battery of four guns was abandoned. The transports cut their lines and drifted downstream."[46] In either case, the abortive expedition against Forrest was over almost before it had begun, leaving seventy-five of the Federal infantrymen in Southern hands. And the success the Confederates enjoyed against the Union gunboats gave them the confidence to engage them again.[47]

This latest Confederate expedition had mixed results. Forrest experienced great success in his efforts to destroy the Nashville and Decatur Railroad, but he failed to disrupt the Nashville and Chattanooga line. He captured 2,360 Union soldiers and numerous supplies. He harassed and aggravated the Federals, but his efforts were far too late to impair Sherman's ability to remain in Georgia.[48] After long and bloody fighting, Atlanta fell to the Union at the beginning of September, before Forrest even began his expedition against Sherman's supply lines. Now, no matter what the Confederate cavalryman might concoct, there seemed to be little that anyone could do to prevent William Tecumseh Sherman from carrying out his threat to "make Georgia howl."[49]

There was no doubt that Forrest was worn out. He wrote to General Taylor that he planned to "make the trip to West Tennessee," but hoped that "as soon thereafter as you can do so you will relieve me from duty for twenty or thirty days, to rest and recruit." "I have been constantly in the field," he explained to Taylor without a great deal of exaggeration. "I have never asked for a furlough of over ten days in which to rest and recruit, and except when wounded and unable to leave my bed have had no respite from duty." His reservoir of energy was declining even more, and he needed to recoup it. "My strength is failing," he admitted, "and it is absolutely necessary that I should have some rest."[50]

Although the army and this war were his life, he still had concerns that predated the war and occupied at least some of his attention. He insisted that he had "never given a day's attention at any one time since the war began" to his personal and business affairs, implying that he wanted to do so now.[51] Some members of his family, including his mother, remained near Memphis and thus behind Union lines. Having served as protector and defender of his family following the death of his father, Forrest had a paternal concern for their welfare. For Forrest, as indeed for many others, the war disrupted the family structure and support system. As capable of looking after her own affairs as he knew his mother to be, he was too dutiful a son and too conscientious a soldier not to worry about her welfare and to fear that some harm might come to his family if his enemies sought to strike at him through them. Besides, he knew quite well that she feared for her family's safety as well. Thus, when Forrest wrote to General Chalmers, operating somewhere near Memphis, it was not surprising that he exposed such concerns by asking that officer to deliver a personal message, "Say to my mother we are all well."[52]

Whatever his apprehensions, Forrest had the great comfort of having most of his family in the army with him, as in the case of his son and most of his brothers, or close by, as in the case of his wife. Since the beginning of the war, he had seen her only briefly, usually when recovering from a wound. But, following his ten-day furlough with her in LaGrange, Georgia, Mary Ann Forrest remained as close to her husband and son as the conditions of war would permit. Described as "an amiable, ladylike, religious woman," Mrs. Forrest remained "about headquarters."[53]

However badly he might need to rest, Forrest had no time for it, and the demands of duty outweighed personal concerns. He was just vain enough to believe that his presence in the field was vital to the Confederates' chances of success. The Confederacy needed him, as it had before, to strike a blow against the Union supply lines in Tennessee. To this end, he responded to Taylor that he would do what he could to gather conscripts and supplies and understood that the "great, predominating, absorbing desire is to cut Sherman's line of communication." He had already done "something toward accomplishing that result" and was "anxious" to return and "renew the effort."[54]

Forrest knew from his previous activities that, as he explained to Taylor, "the enemy derives much of his supplies from the northwestern railroad, which are shipped up the Tennessee River to Johnsonville and thence to Nashville." Consequently, he wanted to strike his blow there. And although Forrest's entire command was "greatly jaded by the recent raid ... and need more rest than I am able to give them at the present," he planned to "take possession of Fort Heiman, on the west bank of the Tennessee River below [north of] Johnsonville, and thus prevent all communication with Johnsonville by transports. It is highly important that this line be interrupted if not entirely destroyed."[55] He called for Chalmers to join him at Jackson, Tennessee, "with all the available men you have except enough to picket your front, fetching the two batteries with you." If he was going to blockade the Tennessee, he would need all the firepower he could muster.[56]

Forrest began his operation on October 16, when the first of his men, under General Tyree Bell, started north toward western Tennessee. By October 21, he was back in his old headquarters at Jackson, with Chalmers up from Memphis and Buford nearby in the vicinity of Lexington. His command was in woeful condition. Many of the horses were badly worn out or lacked shoes, circumstances that required remedy before he embarked on another campaign. Therefore, Forrest dispersed a large number of the men he had recruited from western Tennessee, with orders to replace their worn-out mounts and return to the command as soon as possible. This action seriously depleted his numbers. If Forrest attempted to fulfill his plans now, he would have to do so with fewer than three thousand men.[57]

Finally, on October 24, Forrest headed north. Buford held the vanguard and Chalmers the rearguard. By October 28 the former had reached the Tennessee River near Fort Heiman. He immediately set to work emplacing his batteries on the river. He put two guns (Lieutenant Edwin S. Walton's) in the fort, and placed the other section (Morton's) a few hundred yards downstream. Five miles upstream, at Paris Landing, Bell put the other section of Morton's battery into place and completed the blockade of the river.[58]

Just before nightfall, the Southerners watched as four small vessels steamed northward (downstream) from Johnsonville. Both the direction in which they were heading and the way they rode high in the water told Buford that they were empty. However much his men might wish to blast the steamboats as they floated complacently past, he had to convince them to forgo the temptation. He passed the word for the men to "keep quiet, don't fire a gun." He assured them, "These are empty boats going down after more supplies for Sherman's army. I want a loaded boat, a richer prize. Just wait until one comes up the river, then you may take her if you can." Buford knew that these boats, or others like them, would return, loaded with supplies. For once the rowdy troopers remained disciplined.[59]

Early on October 29, the Confederates got the opportunity for which they had been waiting when the steamer *Mazeppa* came into view with a barge in tow, headed for Johnsonville. Astutely, the Southerners allowed her to pass the guns in Fort Heiman. Already pushing against the current and towing a barge, the *Mazeppa* entered the gauntlet. The guns opened upon her, and after three salvos the pilot headed her bow into the opposite bank, and the crew abandoned ship. Not having thought to bring any kind of a boat with them, the Southerners had to send a swimmer across to board the vessel, bring a skiff back with a rope, and pull her to their side of the Tennessee. But once they had done so, they discovered a rich prize, indeed, for the ship's consignment consisted of shoes, blankets, heavy winter clothing, hardtack, and a jug of French brandy. Since Forrest did not drink, Buford decided to take the brandy for himself, telling his disappointed men, "Plenty of meat, boys, plenty of hard-tack, plenty of shoes and clothes for the boys, but just enough brandy for the General." The troopers quickly unloaded the supplies, since they could expect other vessels at any moment. Even before they had finished unloading the ship, three gunboats appeared above them on the river. Although Confederate artillery fire drove the boats off, the Southerners burned the *Mazeppa* to prevent her recapture.[60]

The next day, the steamer *Anna* appeared in the river, having left Johnsonville to go downstream for more supplies. This time Buford did not let the ship pass. As soon as she steamed past the upper section of guns, they blazed forth. The *Anna* ran up a white flag, promising to land at the lower landing. The Confederates relaxed, many of them gathering on the bank to watch her come to the landing. Suddenly the captain hit full steam, and the *Anna* shot by the lower guns. As she pulled away, the Southerners opened upon the steamer, damaging but not sinking or disabling her. She steamed into Paducah to warn of the Confederates' trap. Ironically, this warning sealed the blockade, since the Federals stopped any further transportation of supplies to Johnsonville.[61]

The gunboat *Undine* had accompanied the *Anna* for most of her voyage downriver, but before she entered the trap, the *Undine* left her to return to Johnsonville. Then, hearing the artillery fire in the distance, the captain of the gunboat changed course and steered back downstream. By the time the *Undine* arrived, the *Anna* was gone, and the Confederates had faded into the brush. The gunboat moved cautiously, but as they had done before, the Southerners let the *Undine* run past their upper battery before blasting her with artillery. The gunboat stubbornly returned their fire before drifting against the west bank of the river to seek shelter.

In the meantime, the steamer *Venus* appeared, towing two barges. Inexplicably, she ignored signals from the *Undine* to turn back and entered the Confederates' gauntlet. The unfortunate captain paid for his decision with his life as his boat ran by the batteries to anchor under the *Undine*'s heavy guns. And twenty minutes later the scene virtually repeated itself when the *J. W. Cheeseman* steamed up, also ignoring the warning signals. The Confederates quickly disabled her, and the Union vessel drifted to the bank and her crew surrendered. Although the Southerners hoped to use the captured boat, they subsequently found the *J. W. Cheeseman* too badly damaged and set fire to her.

While some of the Confederate artillerymen blasted the steamer into submission, others manhandled two guns within close range of the *Undine* and *Venus,* under cover of heavy small-arms fire. A little after 3 P.M., these guns opened fire. Within an hour the Union gunboat weighed anchor and drifted to the east bank, where the crew abandoned her. A short time later, without the gunboat to protect her, the *Venus* surrendered. The Southerners took possession of her and crossed the Tennessee to seize the *Undine* as well. During this period, another gunboat, the *Tawah,* made a brief appearance before steaming away.[62]

Thus far, the Confederates had destroyed two Union steamboats and captured another, as well as a gunboat. They also took forty-three Federal prisoners and inflicted losses of eight killed and eleven wounded, while losing only one man wounded in the process. The Southerners intended to do much more. Almost immediately they took steps to repair the two Union vessels in

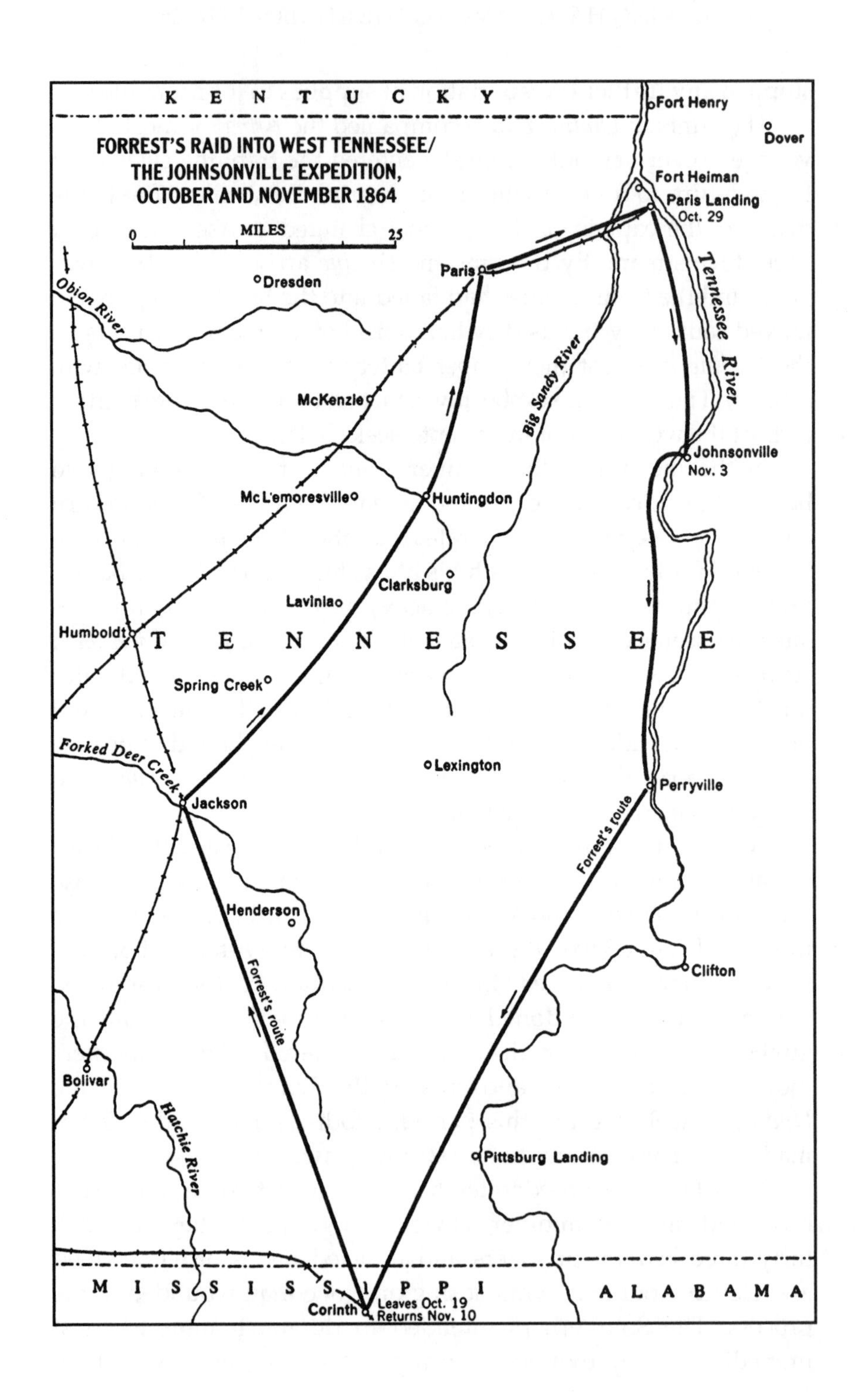
FORREST'S RAID INTO WEST TENNESSEE/
THE JOHNSONVILLE EXPEDITION,
OCTOBER AND NOVEMBER 1864
MILES
0
25
K E N T U C K Y
T E N N E S S E E
M I S S I S S I P P I
A L A B A M A
Fort Henry
Dover
Fort Heiman
Paris Landing
Oct. 29
Tennessee River
Paris
Dresden
Obion River
Big Sandy River
McKenzie
Johnsonville
Nov. 3
Mc L'emoresville
Huntingdon
Clarksburg
Lavinia
Humboldt
Spring Creek
Forked Deer Creek
Lexington
Perryville
Jackson
Forrest's route
Henderson
Clifton
Forrest's route
Bolivar
Hatchie River
Pittsburg Landing
Corinth
Leaves Oct. 19
Returns Nov. 10

their hands. Forrest, who arrived at the scene on October 31, formulated a plan to launch his own flotilla—albeit a small one—in the Tennessee River.[63]

Forrest's mind raced as he surveyed the *Undine* lying against the opposite bank. He looked at his chief of artillery and asked, "John, how would you like to transfer your guns to these boats and command a gunboat fleet?" Morton wanted no part of Forrest's scheme. "Not at all, General," he replied to the inquiry. "My whole knowledge is of land batteries. I know nothing of water, and I prefer to stay on *terra firma*." At his suggestion, Forrest chose Captain Frank M. Gracey, a former steamboat captain, to take command of the *Undine*. As for the *Venus*, he selected Lieutenant Colonel William A. Dawson, but not without first giving some assurances. Dawson knew his general's temper could be fierce and he did not want it turned upon him should circumstances become bad for the tiny Confederate fleet. "Now, General," he stated plaintively, "I will go with these gunboats wherever you order, but I want to tell you now that if I lose your fleet and come in afoot you will not curse me out about it."

Forrest gave his worried subordinate his assurances. "No, Colonel, you will do the best you can; that is all I want. I promise not to haul you over the coals if you come home wet." He ordered both commanders to keep their vessels between the land batteries, with which he expected to protect the boats in case of contact with the enemy, but told Dawson, "I want you and Gracey, if you see you are going to be caught, to run your boats into the bank, let your men save themselves as best they can, and then set the steamers on fire."[64] No doubt, Forrest had in mind using the gunboats to shell the depot and storage facilities at Johnsonville, in tandem with the land-based artillery. However, when the expedition began on November 1, rains made the going on land extremely difficult. The units attempting to move along the bank dropped farther and farther behind as they slogged through the mud. By the end of the day, the exhausted cavalry and artillerymen rode into Danville, while their naval comrades moored offshore.[65]

They set out in the same manner the following day, with similar results. The flotilla gradually moved ahead while the land column fell behind. For the novice sailors, steaming complacently along in the *Venus,* this situation invited trouble. And trouble soon came in the form of two Union gunboats that suddenly appeared in the river about 3:30 P.M. This was the moment that Colonel Dawson had feared as his vessel came head to head with the *Key West* and the *Tawah.* The lightly armed *Venus* had no chance with only two twenty-pounder Parrotts as her armament and her inexperienced crew. The Federals overpowered the boat, forcing her skipper to run her bow into the bank. The crew abandoned ship so hastily that no one made any effort to scuttle her, and both the ship and the guns fell into Union hands. Ironically, in losing the *Venus,* the Confederates also lost a portion of the supplies they had captured with the *Mazeppa* that they had put aboard "for convenience of transportation."[66]

The *Undine* came up to assist the much-distressed *Venus,* but to no avail. With the *Venus* driven ashore, the *Undine*'s crew fought to save themselves and their vessel from a similar fate. The crew managed to pull the *Undine* out of the fight and back under the protection of the land batteries.[67] Even so, Forrest had lost half his fleet, and the prospects were grim for him to keep the other boat in the Confederates' service for much longer.

Forrest's brush with Union ships prompted the Federals to dispatch gunboats from Paducah to travel up the Tennessee. Six of these gunboats shelled the area near Paris Landing on November 3. On the same day, Forrest put his artillery into strong positions on either end of Reynoldsburg Island, only a few short miles from Johnsonville. This time the Confederate naval vessel cooperated closely with the land-based guns. Forrest attempted to use it to lure the Union gunboats from Johnsonville within range of those guns, but they refused to take the bait.[68] Nevertheless, the Federals had great difficulty bringing this flotilla of gunboats, with their heavy artillery, to bear against the Southerners. Forrest's gun emplacements commanded the river at Reynoldsburg Island. The river there was navigable on only one side (the western), which narrowed sharply and came directly under the Southern guns.[69]

Some of the guns had to remain to protect the Northern flank and the *Undine* from the Paducah gunboats. Forrest also began to deploy his troops and artillery across from the massive Union depot and storage facility at Johnsonville. He and Morton spent the latter part of November 3 reconnoitering the area and deciding where to place the Southern batteries. After nightfall, the cannoneers manhandled the guns through the bottomland, cut embrasures into the natural embankment, and matted vines and branches to conceal the batteries. As Forrest later explained, "I planted most of my guns during the night, and while completing the work the next morning my men worked behind ambushcades [screens], which obscured everything from the enemy."[70]

Forrest placed Captain J. C. Thrall's guns above, Morton's opposite, and Hudson's (commanded by Walton) just below Johnsonville, eleven pieces in all. Throughout, the Confederates worked without arousing suspicions across the river.[71] They had assistance in this endeavor from the Federals themselves, who for whatever reason seemed to have allowed the Venus's recapture and the *Undine*'s subsequent destruction to lull them into believing that they had run Forrest off and that Johnsonville was now safe from attack. The Confederate general may even have still thought to use the captured Union gunboat to supplement his firepower, although the Federal gunboats at the depot would have made it difficult and were about to make it impossible for him to do so.

At 8 A.M. on November 4, Lieutenant Commander LeRoy Fitch and his six gunboats joined with Lieutenant Edward M. King's Johnsonville flotilla of three gunboats in blasting the *Undine* and the Confederates' land batteries. Gracey became increasingly concerned for the fate of his ship and crew. Caught between the Union gunboats, he reluctantly decided to abandon the vessel and destroy her. Using oil-soaked mattresses to start fires on board, Gracey left the *Undine* to burn. When the fire reached the magazine, the resulting explosion ripped her apart.[72] Thus, the flirtation of Forrest's cavalrymen with naval service came to an abrupt and inglorious conclusion.

Despite the loss of the *Undine*, the Confederates' land batteries held the Paducah gunboats at bay. Fitch refused to attempt the risky passage through the narrow strait between Reynoldsburg Island and the western bank, where his vessels, forced to run through in single file, would be easy prey for the Southern artillery. He knew that the Confederates would have to disable only one of his boats to block the channel and rightly feared that if they did so, he might lose part of his fleet. Of course, he could not know that Forrest had withdrawn most of his guns for the attack on Johnsonville. Therefore, the Union naval commander contented himself with bombarding the enemy positions from long range.[73]

At the same time, Fitch's colleague, Lieutenant King, took even more direct fire at the other end of the island. He had half the number of gunboats and the responsibility of helping to guard the depot. He could not afford to lose one or more of his ships to the Southern artillery. Even so, one of his vessels sustained nineteen hits from the Confederates' fire. King reported that the fire was "too much for us" and quickly turned his flotilla around and headed back upriver to Johnsonville.[74]

Despite the fighting that had just occurred several miles farther down the Tennessee, the depot remained active and oblivious to the Confederates' presence. Captain Morton crawled to the top of the embankment and looked over the water at Johnsonville. He did not like the location of some of the embrasures and wanted to have another look at the target to decide how to place his guns better. He watched the feverish activity with great interest, later writing, "A number of barges and transports clustered around; negroes were loading them, officers and men were coming and going." In addition, there were clear signs of the accumulation of stores and supplies. "The river banks for some distance back were lined with quantities of stores and two freight trains were being made up. It was an animated scene, and one which wore an air of complete security."[75]

Part of the reason for this complacency was the existence of a strong Union earthwork that overlooked Johnsonville from a hill behind the depot. Approximately two thousand soldiers manned the fort, and a dozen artillery pieces, including the two captured Parrotts taken from the *Venus,* bristled from the fort's parapet. Furthermore, the three Union gunboats that had recently forced the Confederates to destroy the *Undine* stood just off the bank, boasting the additional firepower of twenty-eight guns.[76]

Forrest had chosen the general sites for his artillery well, but Morton, with his gunner's eye, improved the placement by asking his commander to allow him to put a section of guns at the spot from which he had viewed Johnsonville.[77] Forrest was reluctant to give his approval, thinking the position too vulnerable. "No, that's getting too close," he told Morton, explaining, "They'll knock you all to pieces there from the fort and the gunboats too." But Morton had been on the levee, and he knew the situation even better than did Forrest. The trick was to make his point without making his commander angry. "No, General, I have examined the location well," he ventured, pointing out the position's many advantages. It gave the Southern cannoneers clear targets at excellent range, while virtually prohibiting enemy fire from reaching them. "The fort is so elevated that they can't depress their guns sufficiently to affect me, and the gunboats are so much below in the river that they will fire over me, and I'll be in an angle of comparative safety." In effect, the Union shells would sail harmlessly over Morton's position.

Forrest listened attentively. He had long since come to trust his artillery chief. "Well, you may carry two guns," he replied, promising to postpone the start of the bombardment until Morton was in position.[78] By about 2 P.M., all the artillery was in place and ready to open fire. From the close range and having already had ample time to aim their weapons accurately, the Confederate gunners made their shots with devastating effectiveness. One Union gunboat, the *Key West,* tried to back out into the channel and damaged her machinery when she ran over her cable. Another gunboat, the *Tawah,* came to the *Key West's* assistance, towing her into the river but coming under concentrated fire. The Southern batteries quickly disabled both gunboats, and Lieutenant King gave orders to abandon and burn them. Before long, all three gunboats (including the *Elfin*) were ablaze.[79]

Shells from the Confederate guns burst over the twenty-eight steamboats and barges and among the stacks of supplies, setting fires all along the shoreline. The Union post commander added to the destruction by ordering the remaining vessels burned as well, ostensibly to prevent them from falling into Southern hands. Johnsonville burned fiercely, the smoke and smells of burning equipment and food filling the air.[80] Forrest watched with barely disguised satisfaction, later observing, "By night the wharf for nearly one mile up and down the river presented one solid sheet of flame."[81]

The Confederate cavalry commander remained with Morton's

guns opposite Johnsonville during the bombardment. The effectiveness of their work elated him, and in his jubilation he tried his hand as an artillery commander. Morton recalled that Forrest gleefully directed the firing of one of the guns, with the help of Generals Buford and Bell. When a shot fell short, he yelled out, "I'll hit her next time!" And to improve his aim, he would instruct the gunners to "elevate the breech of that gun lower." They followed the confusing instructions and the weapon blazed forth, each time the generals assisting in rolling back the gun after it had recoiled from the shot.[82]

Forrest subsequently reported, "Having completed the work designed for the expedition, I moved my command six miles during the night by the light of the enemy's burning property."[83] The next day, he returned to survey the scene of destruction. He stood on the west bank looking over at the wreckage that had been a major supply depot and storage facility. Charred ruins still smoldered. The outlines of vessels, burned to the waterline, showed where they had been moored when the Southern gunners had found their marks. Morton joined him for a moment, and they both examined what they had worked so hard the previous day to accomplish. Suddenly, Forrest turned to his artilleryman, remarking, "There is no doubt we could soon wipe old Sherman off the face of the earth, John, if they'd give me enough men and you enough guns."[84]

The Southerners had done good work, and at virtually no cost to themselves. In the entire raid Forrest put his losses at only 2 men killed and 9 wounded. He placed the final tally for the expedition at "4 gunboats, 14 transports, 20 barges, 26 pieces of artillery, and $6,700,000 worth of property" destroyed, and 150 Federals captured.[85] The Union post commander confessed, "In the fight which ensued the gunboats were abandoned and burned, and all the transports were destroyed by fire, the fire extending to the large pile of stores on the levee, and from that to the warehouse, which was destroyed."[86] Another Union officer set the monetary loss at "about $2,200,000."[87]

Rumors quickly circulated about the Confederates' intentions. One farfetched report had Forrest much farther north. The provost marshal at Danville, Illinois, sent word to General Joseph Hooker in Cincinnati: "Forrest has been in disguise alternately in Chicago, Michigan City, and Canada for two months; has 14,000 men mostly from the draft, near Michigan City." And with the widely accepted belief that a northwestern conspiracy existed, awaiting only the right time and perhaps the right leader to spring forth, the officer ominously predicted, "On 7th of November, midnight [they] will seize telegraph and rail at Chicago, release prisoners there, arm them, sack the city, shoot down all Federal soldiers, and urge concert of action with southern sympathizers."[88] Hooker thought that "the wires have never been put to worse use" and curtly condemned the message: "It is all stuff."[89]

Sherman was also disinclined to believe such hysteria, but Forrest had once again proved an irritant, and with a touch of exasperation, the Union general wired General Ulysses S. Grant on November 6, "That devil Forrest was down about Johnsonville, making havoc among the gunboats and transports."[90] Nevertheless, the Confederate cavalryman would not remain in that area much longer. General John Bell Hood had determined to make a final bid to force Sherman out of Georgia by striking into Tennessee to threaten the Union commander's line of communication and supply. For this operation, Hood wanted Forrest to unite his command with the Army of Tennessee.

CHAPTER 13

Advancing and Retreating with Hood

(November–December 1864)

They was in there sure enough, wasn't they, Chalmers?

—FORREST'S RESPONSE TO HEAVY SKIRMISHING

If you are a better man than I am, General Cheatham, your troops can cross ahead of mine.

—NATHAN BEDFORD FORREST

BEDFORD FORREST WAS uncharacteristically slow to join Hood for the latter's invasion of Tennessee. The weather and the confusing signals Forrest received from his superiors had much to do with his tardiness, but one suspects that he marched with a sense of foreboding. His previous connections with the Army of Tennessee had provided him with none of the spectacular successes he had achieved on his own, such as Brice's Cross Roads and Johnsonville. However, those victories had little material affect upon the course of the war. Once more he was being called upon to relinquish a good bit of the control he had enjoyed over his actions in Mississippi, but the field of operations and the stakes were bigger.

As with virtually everything connected with Hood's invasion of Tennessee, the circumstances around which he chose Forrest to command the cavalry of the Army of Tennessee were somewhat muddled. Apparently, General Hood and General P. G. T. Beauregard, now commanding the new Military Division of the West, met in Gadsden, Alabama, on October 21 and decided to replace General Joseph Wheeler's cavalry with Forrest's. Of course, Forrest was already in the midst of his Johnsonville expedition and received his first indication about Hood's plans on October 30.[1]

Even then, this news came from General Richard Taylor, who conveyed Beauregard's orders by advising Forrest, "As soon as you have accomplished the objects of your present movement your course will be directed toward Middle Tennessee, where you will put yourself in communication with General Hood and be governed by his orders relative to future movements."[2] Perhaps Taylor still acted with his customary policy in relation to Forrest and left the orders sufficiently vague to allow that general to interpret them as he wished. Whatever Taylor intended, the orders gave Forrest leeway to march to join Hood after he had "accomplished the objects" of his "present movement." The cavalryman accepted the discretion and continued his current operation.

For some reason, no one seemed to know what Hood expected of him or how to convey those expectations to his own subordinates. On October 22, Beauregard prompted Taylor's dispatch to Forrest by writing, "In order to save time, I desire you to attend as soon as possible to the following matters." One of these "matters" was the need for Forrest "to enter as soon as practicable into communication, by letter or otherwise, with Hood, at some point between Guntersville and Decatur, Ala., and to remain subject to his orders for the present."[3] It may have been that Taylor interpreted the acceptability of communicating "by letter" to mean that Hood, who had already called upon him to send Forrest to break up the Nashville and Chattanooga Railroad, was only urging that same course once more. Under such circumstances, Taylor could let Forrest finish his expedition before he sent him to join Hood.[4]

In any case, Hood grew anxious to have Forrest. From Tuscumbia, Alabama, on November 2, he sent the cavalryman a plaintive message. "When can I expect you here or when can I hear from you? I am waiting for you."[5] The next day, he informed the War Department that he would move the army "on Saturday morning next" and wanted Forrest "to be informed of the time and certainty of the movement."[6] Finally, on November 12, Hood explained to President Davis the reasons for his delay in advancing. "Before leaving Gadsden I urged on General Beauregard to send General Forrest across the Tennessee River," the army commander observed, but when he arrived at Gunter's Landing, he found "that Forrest had not yet crossed [and] I could not without his co-operation pass the river there." The usually combative general concluded, "This circumstance, high water, and the fact that I had to draw supplies from and through a department not under my command, involving the delay in their reaching me, have retarded my operations." But, he promised, "As soon as Forrest joins me, which will be in a few days, I shall be able to move forward. Without the assistance of Forrest's cavalry I cannot secure my wagon trains when crossing the river. You may rely upon my striking the enemy wherever a suitable opportunity presents, and that I will spare no efforts to make that opportunity."[7]

Although apparently unaware of the urgency of Hood's request, Forrest set out to comply with those orders as soon as he had finished with Johnsonville. He encountered some difficulty with high water and the poor condition of the roads. The flooded Tennessee River proved the greatest obstacle. Forrest arrived with his command at Perryville late on November 5, hoping to cross there. He had thought to bring some boats from the *Undine* to ferry his command across, and these, with planks taken from nearby buildings, were sufficient to push a small portion of his men across. Although the general "was as busy as anybody" throughout the night, the rain fell incessantly, and the water level rose, rendering the crossing more and more difficult and dangerous. Driftwood filled the churning waters, making further attempts to cross hazardous. Forrest finally gave up the effort and instructed the men on the east bank, about four hundred, to proceed southward along the bank and reunite with the main force farther down.[8]

Forrest noted, "I succeeded, however, in throwing across a portion of [Colonel Edmund W.] Rucker's brigade, while I moved to Corinth with the balance of my command." Forrest's succinct assessment glossed over the tremendous difficulty the Confederates had in their march southward. The roads were now in abysmal condition. In one day of exhausting work, Morton managed to drag his battery through only two and a half miles of mud. Battered by rain and weakened by the exertions of the campaign, the horses struggled vainly in the mire. Forrest had the teams increased from twelve to sixteen per gun and finally had to impress oxen from the local farmers for the grueling task. Even then it took eight of the massive and sturdy animals to pull each gun.[9]

Having finally reached Corinth, Forrest paused on November 12 long enough to send a friendly note to his recent departmental commander, General Taylor. The dispatch points to the high esteem he had for some of his superiors, especially those who left him alone to fight as he saw fit. Noting that he would be forwarding reports on his recent activities, Forrest speculated that these "documents will, I presume, for the present terminate my official connection with you—an event which I deeply deplore." Although they had not worked together for long and it was his "duty" to respond to the "call" wherever that call sent him, he observed, "but in leaving you I shall carry with me a sincere friendship, made so by your kindness and official courtesy."[10] The cavalry commander genuinely admired General Taylor. James R. Chalmers later wrote, "Forrest admitted that he was more awed by Dick Taylor's power of will than any man he ever met, or, as he expressed it, 'I lost my charm when I met Dick Taylor.'"[11] Obviously, he felt it important to express these sentiments before he embarked upon a new campaign. Forrest then turned the main command toward Florence, where he tried again to cross the Tennessee.

The Confederate cavalry finally crossed the river, reaching Florence, Alabama, on November 18, where they united with Hood and the army. Hood placed Forrest in command of all the cavalry associated with the Army of Tennessee. This command gave him an additional division under General William H. Jackson and a portion of Colonel George G. Dibrell's brigade under Colonel Jacob Biffle. Even so, the Confederate cavalry over which Forrest would exercise command suffered from badly depleted numbers and worn-out horses. Many of the men Forrest had sent on furloughs into western Tennessee to replenish their mounts had not yet returned when he abruptly left middle Tennessee to join

Hood. As Forrest rode toward Nashville, his entire cavalry command of three divisions amounted to no more than six thousand effectives.[12]

On the morning of November 21, Forrest received orders from Hood to take the lead. This day, on which Hood finally began his invasion, portended badly for the expedition. An early snowstorm buffeted the troopers and foot soldiers as they swung into saddles or formed their ranks. Hood arranged his infantry in three columns, with Forrest and his three divisions operating in front. Forrest reported that the Confederate horsemen "had several engagements with the enemy, and were almost constantly skirmishing with him, but drove him in every encounter." At Henryville, General Chalmers captured forty-five prisoners.[13]

Then at Fouche Springs, the southern cavalry commander ordered Chalmers "to throw forward Rucker's brigade and to keep up a slight skirmish with the enemy until I could gain his rear." He next sent Colonel David C. Kelley around the left flank and moved with his escort around the right. Forrest planned to combine with Kelley and hit the Union rear, but had to make "the charge upon the enemy with my escort alone," when Kelley failed to arrive in time. Even so, the attack was successful, "producing a perfect stampede," in which the Confederates captured "about 50 prisoners, 20 horses, and 1 ambulance." With the coming of night, Forrest set an ambush with his escort. Rucker had been driving the Federals slowly backwards, and, according to Forrest, "as they rushed into the ambushcade my escort fired into them, producing the wildest confusion." At the same time, the other column of Confederate cavalrymen, under Generals Abraham Buford and William H. Jackson, moved toward Pulaski.[14]

Reports of Forrest's activities warned Union General James Schofield of his predicament. Early on November 24, Schofield sent a frantic message to General Jacob D. Cox to advise him of the situation. "All information indicates," he explained, "that Hood is nearer Columbia than I am." If this were true, then Hood could block Schofield's line of retreat. Schofield ordered Cox to move as quickly as possible to Columbia and hold the town for the Federals, concluding, "The question is to concentrate the entire force at Columbia in time."[15]

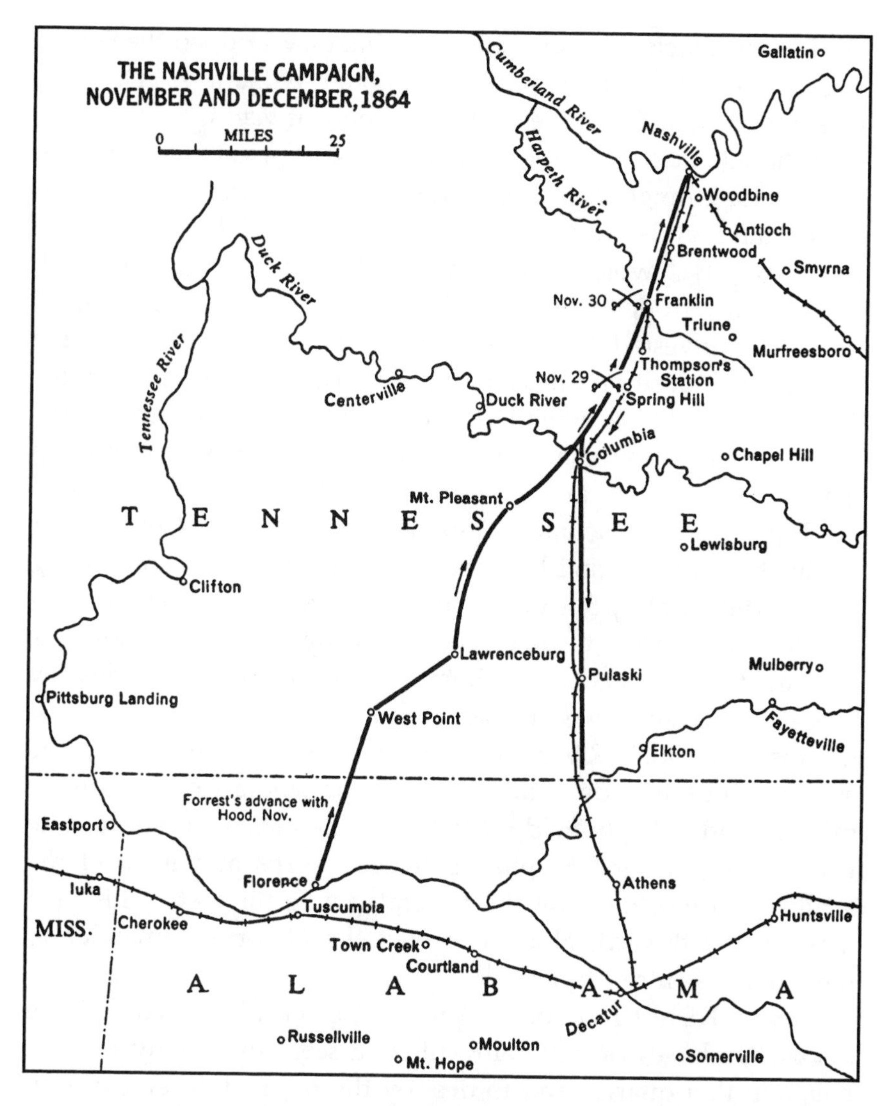

Forrest's cavalry was doing all they could to harass Schofield and disrupt his plans. Buford and Jackson pushed General Edward Hatch's Union cavalry division in a series of brief but fierce fights. Chalmers was back in the saddle in the early morning hours of November 24, driving for Columbia via Mount Pleasant. But Cox reached Columbia in time to check the Confederates' advance, although he found the Union cavalry "in hasty retreat" when he arrived there. Cox deployed his infantry across the road from Mount Pleasant, three miles from the town, and secured his hold on the Duck River crossings. His infantry stopped the Southern pursuit, mortally wounding Colonel William A. Dawson, recently commander of the converted gunboat *Venus*.[16]

Schofield had won the race. Although Forrest's cavalrymen kept up long-range skirmishing, they could not prevent Cox from entrenching while the rest of the Federals arrived. For Forrest, the next few days' work was unspectacular. As he later reported, "Most of my troops having reached Columbia on the evening of the 24th I invested the town from Duck River to the extreme north, which position I held until the arrival of the infantry on the morning of the 27th, when I was relieved." But as soon as Hood's infantry arrived to replace the cavalrymen, Forrest's men took up new duties as pickets and scouts along the Duck River.[17]

The Federals evacuated Columbia on the night of November 27, in the midst of swirling snow and intense cold, completing their withdrawal by 5 A.M. on November 28. Also that night, Forrest met with Hood to determine the army's next move and his part in it. Hood had an elaborate plan and hoped to destroy Schofield's twenty-five-thousand-man army. He ordered Forrest to cross the Duck River early on November 28 and drive the enemy from the fords. If all went well, he would follow with his infantry and cut Schofield off from his line of retreat. Because he was leaving General Stephen Dill Lee's corps and most of the artillery behind to decoy the Federals while the rest of his men marched northward, Hood expected the Union commander to remain in his entrenchments.[18]

Before Forrest rode out to seize the Duck River crossings, he dispatched his escort to Shelbyville to discern the enemy's movements in that quarter and to destroy the railroad. Then early on November 28, he started his cavalry toward the fords. Although Schofield was already pulling out of Columbia, the Southern horsemen encountered resistance, some of it heavy, as they attempted to carry out their assignments. Chalmers crossed at Carr's Mill, seven miles from Columbia; Jackson, at Holland's Ford; and Forrest, with part of Biffle's regiment, at Owen's Ford.[19]

Chalmers and Forrest reunited about eight miles north of Columbia on the road to Spring Hill. But Jackson's division met more serious opposition and had great difficulty forcing passage of the river. Forrest noted, "At 11 o'clock at night I received a dispatch from General Buford informing me that the enemy had made such a stubborn resistance to his crossing that he could not join the command until the morning of the 29th."[20]

In the meantime, Jackson's opponent, General James Harrison Wilson, fresh from service in the East and recently turned twenty-seven years old, urgently called for Schofield to "get back to Franklin without delay, leaving a small force to detain the enemy."[21] Although the Union commander resented the cavalryman's tone, which sounded like an order, the advice was sound. Once again the Confederates' movements were threatening to isolate him, and when he received the message at 7:30 A.M., while still near Columbia, Schofield wisely rushed units ahead to secure his line of retreat.[22]

The Confederate cavalrymen continued to push their counterparts ahead of them, opening the river crossings to their own infantrymen. As Forrest observed, "The enemy gradually fell back, making resistance only at favorable positions. After waiting a short time for my troops to close up, I moved rapidly toward Spring Hill with my entire command."[23] Within a couple of miles of the town, Forrest's horsemen ran into the enemy's pickets and engaged in heavy skirmishing. Constantly hoping to determine Union strength, Forrest sent Chalmers against an unknown number of Federals in some nearby woods. But when those same woods erupted with fire, forcing the Confederates to fall back rapidly, Forrest remarked to his subordinate, "They was in there sure enough, wasn't they, Chalmers?"[24]

Next he ordered General Frank C. Armstrong, a portion of the Kentucky brigade, and the Fourteenth Tennessee Regiment to charge the Federals, but they also fell back. Forrest reported, "I then dismounted my entire command to push the enemy's right flank with all possible vigor." Understanding the importance of his cavalryman's position, Hood ordered him to "hold" his "position at all hazards, as the advance of the infantry column was only two miles distant and rapidly advancing." To do so, Forrest applied his standard tactical thinking, that the best defense is a good offense, and ordered General Tyree Bell's brigade to attack. Finally, about 4 P.M., the leading elements of Hood's infantry arrived, under Patrick Cleburne. They formed on Forrest's left and joined the attack. But by this time the Confederate cavalrymen were nearly out of ammunition and daylight. However, Cleburne's veteran infantry and Bell's battle-tested troopers charged the Federals and drove them from their rifle pits back toward Spring Hill. Yet, this moment of success proved the Southerners' undoing, for at least three Union batteries poured their fire into the suddenly exposed Confederate ranks and forced them back to regroup.[25]

Back at the crossing, General Benjamin Cheatham was rushing the rest of his division forward to assist Cleburne in obstructing the turnpike from Columbia. But, as any corps commander might wish to do, he wanted to put each division in support of the next. Consequently, he gave General William C. Bate instructions to make contact with his right to Cleburne's left, which would place Bate parallel to the road. At the same time, Hood wanted Bate to advance to the pike and turn south.[26] Cheatham's third division commander, General John C. Brown, received orders to move up on Cleburne's right, which would put Cheatham's entire corps in position to move against the vital turnpike. Brown attempted to carry out these orders, but found that his right was vulnerable to a flank attack from the Federals. He explained that his right became vulnerable because "Forrest's cavalry, which I had been assured would protect my right, had been ordered to another part of the field," forcing him to draw back, away from the road.[27]

Confused and contradictory orders involved several Confederate generals on the field. Cheatham sought out Hood for instructions, which he could pass on to his subordinate commanders. Hood seemed to believe that he had stolen a march on Schofield and therefore could afford to let his men rest before attacking the turnpike the next day and destroying the Union forces that were isolated by his movements. He told Cheatham that he had "concluded to wait until the morning and directed me to hold my command in readiness to attack at daylight."[28]

General Alexander P. Stewart, coming up with his corps, and Forrest also decided to ride to Hood's headquarters and ask the commanding general just what they should do. Hood was all for letting the infantry rest, while employing the cavalry to block the northward route along which Schofield was pushing his men as hastily as possible. Hood asked Forrest if he could do the job, and although his men were virtually out of ammunition and tired themselves, Forrest thought he could. Jackson's men had captured enough ammunition from the Federals to make the effort, and Forrest promised he "would do the best he could in the emergency."[29]

In the meantime, Bate could hear the Federals march northward along the main pike toward Franklin. He, too, wanted more precise instructions from the army commander. But when he arrived at headquarters, Bate got the same story from Hood. Everything would be fine, the commander assured his subordinate, "for General Forrest, as you see, has just left and informs me that he holds the turnpike with a position of his forces north of Spring Hill, and will stop the enemy if he tries to pass toward Franklin, and so in the morning we will have a surrender without a fight. We can sleep quiet tonight."[30] Of course, everything that Hood said might have been true. But Forrest knew that he was low on ammunition, and his promise to "do the best he could in the emergency" hardly suggests that he was confident of long-term success. If Schofield moved his army northward, all Forrest's men, much less a fraction of them, could not stop it.[31]

The road that Hood wanted and Schofield feared would be blocked remained open, and the Federals moved unmolested past several Confederate divisions to the works at Franklin. Hood later lamented that the "best move in my career as a soldier, I was thus destined to behold come to nought." Although he attributed the lost opportunity to his army and its apparent unwillingness to fight, Hood had blundered. And worse, he seemed intent upon "eradicating the evil" on the next available occasion. The next day, Hood compounded his blunder at Spring Hill by hurling his men against the fortified Union lines at Franklin.[32]

Whoever or whatever was to blame, Schofield had slipped away once more. But, true to his promise, Forrest attempted to block the road north of Spring Hill and cut off a portion of the Union column by sending Jackson toward Thompson's Station. Forrest later reported that the division partially succeeded in its objective, when it struck the pike some four miles from Spring Hill at 11 P.M., "just as the front of the enemy's column had passed. This attack was a complete surprise, producing much panic and confusion." Even so, Jackson's cavalry division was simply too small to obstruct the Union line of retreat. "General Jackson had possession of the pike and fought the enemy until near daylight, but receiving no support, he was compelled to retire, after killing a large number of horses and mules and burning several wagons." For once, Forrest's reputation could not outweigh his exhausted ammunition, and although he tried to obtain more ammunition in time to help Jackson hold the road, his supply trains were not near enough to the point of fighting and the infantry had but little to lend.[33]

By daylight on November 30, Forrest managed to borrow enough ammunition to send Chalmers in pursuit. Forrest had reports that some of the Federals were still isolated, and he wanted to determine if these reports were true. However, a subsequent report confirmed the Confederates' worst fears—the Federals had, as Forrest put it, "passed unmolested on the main pike during the night."[34] The cavalryman knew that recriminations would do no good now. His concern was to conduct an effective pursuit. With that in mind, he unleashed his other divisions to join Chalmers's in harassing the Union column as it retreated toward Franklin.[35]

General Hood did not react to events as dispassionately as did his cavalry commander. He had an elaborate plan; his subordinates and the enemy failed to cooperate. Thus, when Hood arrived at Franklin, he had one thing on his mind to redeem himself and his army's reputation—attack. But attacking was something Forrest's men had been doing all morning. Buford and Jackson quickly overtook the Union's rearguard and drove it on to Winstead's Hill, just south of Franklin. The pursuit halted when the Confederate horsemen ran into well-positioned Federal infantrymen.[36]

When Stewart's Confederate corps finally reached the field, Forrest redeployed his cavalry units to cover the infantry's flanks. He placed Buford's and Jackson's divisions to the right, which extended to the Harpeth River, and ordered Chalmers to take up positions on the left. The Union rearguard soon fell back from Winstead's Hill to their main line of fortifications. Forrest could clearly see that the Federals occupied strong positions, and at roughly 1 P.M., he went to find out what Hood planned to do.[37]

From his position atop Winstead Hill, the fiesty army commander shocked everyone present with the announcement that he would launch a frontal assault. He believed that Schofield had no intention of holding the line here, but was using it to secure a retreat. Forrest advised him not to attack frontally because the Union position was quite strong, whatever Schofield's intentions might be. He said to Hood, "Give me one strong division of infantry with my cavalry, and within two hours' time I can flank the Federals from their works."[38] This was precisely what the Union commander feared. Schofield confided to Thomas in a dispatch, "I have no doubt Forrest will be in my rear tomorrow, or doing some greater mischief."[39] But Hood had determined to throw his army against the lines at Franklin, and nothing would dissuade him.

Consequently, at about 4:30 P.M., Hood sent his infantry into a cauldron of artillery and small-arms fire that decimated their ranks and cost the lives of some of his best commanders, including Patrick Cleburne. Forrest supported the assault with Chalmers's men on the left and Buford's on the right, "covering the ground from the Lewisburg pike to Harpeth River," but they came under only a fraction of the fire that the Federals concentrated upon the Confederate infantry. When the smoke cleared over the carnage at Franklin, the Army of Tennessee had over 6,000 casualties, 1,750 of whom were killed. For the Federals, who retreated from their positions that night, the cost was much less, totaling 2,326, of whom only 189 were dead. Hood had dealt a serious blow; he had all but destroyed his own army.[40]

That night, Schofield began the last leg of his retreat to Nashville. The next morning, Forrest took up the pursuit once more. He moved across the Harpeth River, Chalmers to the west of Franklin, from his position on the Confederate left flank, and Buford and Jackson to the east of the town, where they had anchored the Southern right. Forrest's troopers harassed the Union rear, capturing some prisoners, but not materially affecting the retreat. Forrest reunited his horsemen at Brentwood and followed the Federal retreat closely.[41]

Forrest still hoped to cut off at least a portion of the Union column and took steps, as he later explained, to accomplish that goal.

"Ordering Chalmers to proceed with his division up the Franklin and Hillsborough pike, and to cross over and intercept, if possible, the enemy retreating toward Nashville, I moved with Buford's and Jackson's divisions toward the Nashville pike." But Forrest failed to make any serious impression upon the Federals, "and, learning the enemy had reached Nashville, I camped for the night."[42] Indeed, Schofield had been marching his men into the works at Nashville since noon. He had won the race and bloodied Hood badly in the process.

The next day, December 2, Forrest deployed his command, "in sight of the capitol at Nashville." Again he pushed Chalmers out on the left, while he, Buford, and Jackson moved to the right, and everyone waited for the infantry to come up. When the main force arrived, Hood sent Forrest new instructions, apparently hoping to utilize his skills against the Union rail lines, but weakening the force with which he hoped to besiege Nashville at the same time. Forrest reported, "My command being relieved by the infantry I commenced operating upon the railroad, blockhouses, and telegraph lines leading from Nashville to Murfreesborough. I ordered Buford's division on the Nashville and Chattanooga Railroad for the purpose of destroying stockades and block-houses."[43]

Chalmers remained behind with Hood to serve as the cavalry arm for the Army of Tennessee while Forrest was away. Part of his force established a blockade of the Cumberland River, several miles below the city. In work they no doubt found reminiscent of the recent Johnsonville expedition, these Confederates, under Colonel Kelley, captured two Union transports and fifty-six men, and battled with several ironclads and gunboats. Through it all, the Southerners managed to hold their positions. And once again, the Federals aided them by halting traffic on the river in the vicinity.[44]

In the meantime, Forrest and his detached divisions enjoyed considerable success against the blockhouses and stockades guarding the Nashville and Chattanooga Railroad. For two days they compelled or convinced several of these strong points to surrender, capturing their garrisons and a train coming from Chattanooga. They burned bridges and wrecked tracks, before receiving orders to march on the sizable garrison, under Union General Lovell Rousseau, at Murfreesboro, the scene of one of Forrest's earliest triumphs as a Confederate cavalry raider.[45]

On the way to Murfreesboro, Forrest made short work of the blockhouse and fortifications at La Vergne. Following the "usual demand for surrender," the garrison of eighty men capitulated, with "2 pieces of artillery, several wagons, and a considerable supply of stores." Then, after burning everything of military value, Forrest moved four miles farther along, to join General Bate, "who had been ordered to report to me with his division for the purpose of operating against Murfreesborough."[46]

With his reinforced command, Forrest drove the Federal pickets back into their main lines at Murfreesboro, deployed his men along a broad front, Buford to the left and Jackson to the right, and waited for the infantry to catch up. Bate's foot soldiers finally arrived the next day, December 6, and Forrest immediately pushed them forward to test the Union lines. The opposing forces skirmished for two hours until, Forrest observed, "the enemy ceased firing, and showed no disposition to give battle." The Confederate commander then conducted "a careful reconnaissance of the enemy's position and works," determining that a frontal assault would be too costly. Later that day, two additional brigades arrived, with 1,600 men, bringing the total in Forrest's command to about 6,500.[47]

Early the next morning, Rousseau sent a combined detachment of over three thousand on a reconnaissance in force to determine Forrest's strength. The Confederates withdrew to new lines, hoping to draw the Federals farther from their works. In the ensuing fight, Forrest noted, "the enemy moved boldly forward, driving in my pickets, when the infantry ... from some cause which I cannot explain, made a shameful retreat, losing two pieces of artillery." An enfuriated Forrest tried everything to stem the rout. "I seized the colors of the retreating troops and endeavored to rally them," he observed, "but they could not be moved by any entreaty or appeal to their patriotism. Bate did the same thing, but was equally as unsuccessful as myself." In the crisis, Forrest sent a staff officer "to Generals Armstrong and [Lawrence S.] Ross, of Jackson's division, with orders to say to them that everything depended on their cavalry. They proved themselves equal to the emergency by charging on the enemy, thereby checking his farther advance."[48]

Even before the Union attack hit his lines, Forrest must have sensed that there would be trouble. One infantry officer recalled that he rode up to where they were standing and told them, "Men, all I ask of you is to hold the enemy back for fifteen minutes, which will give me sufficient time to gain their rear with my cavalry, and I will capture the last one of them."[49] That may have been his plan, but when the infantry broke, Forrest's plan went with them. And so did Forrest, who, one witness recalled, "rode in among the infantry, ordering the men to rally, and doing all in his power to stop the retreat." When this tactic failed, the cavalry commander tried a new one. "Rushing towards a color-bearer who was running for dear life, he ordered him to halt. Failing to have his command obeyed, he drew his pistol and shot the retreating soldier. Dismounting, Forrest took the colors, remounted his horse, and riding in front of the soldiers, waved the colors at them and finally succeeded in rallying them to their duty."[50] Another participant had Forrest flailing about with the flat of his saber and then using the flagstaff to pummel the frightened soldiers.[51] Of course, whether they rallied at the sight of the flag or because their commander was willing to shoot them did not matter much to Forrest.

Having finally stopped the panic-stricken withdrawal of his infantry, Forrest received timely assistance from his cavalry, both in his immediate front, under Armstrong and Ross, and on his left, under Buford. The latter, acting on his own initiative, lessened the pressure against Forrest by riding directly into Murfreesboro. Although he had to retreat from the position, Buford's actions caused the Union attacking column to fall back to Murfreesboro and allowed Forrest the time to stabilize his battle line.[52] The cavalry general had ample reason to be as pleased with his horsemen as he was furious at his foot soldiers.

On December 9, Hood made some rearrangements in Forrest's force when he recalled Bate's division and replaced it with a brigade under the command of Colonel Charles Olmstead. Forrest remained in the area for another week, content to wreck nearby tracks and hold Rousseau's force within their works at Murfreesboro. On December 13, Jackson ranged south of the town and captured a seventeen-car train, carrying sixty thousand rations to the town and guarded by a regiment of soldiers. The Confederates burned the train and supplies and took two hundred prisoners.[53]

The next day, Forrest began a movement to strike the Union forage train, east of Murfreesboro, but the arrival of news of "a general engagement" at Nashville on December 15 preempted the effort. Hood wanted Forrest "to hold" himself "in readiness to move at any moment."[54] One infantry officer with Forrest noted that the cavalry commander "kept in touch with Gen. Hood by a stream of couriers with dispatches reporting on the progress of the battle."[55] If Hood won at Nashville, then Rousseau's people were doomed. If Hood lost, the capture of the entire garrison at Murfreesboro would not matter. And the next night, after Forrest had moved his entire command to the Wilkinson Cross Roads, six miles from Murfreesboro, he received word from one of Hood's staff officers "informing me of the disaster at Nashville and ordering me to fall back via Shelbyville and Pulaski."[56] Union commander George H. Thomas had struck the Army of Tennessee, driving it back the first day and routing it the second.

In response to this new development, Forrest "immediately dispatched orders to Buford to fall back from the Cumberland River, via La Vergne, to the Nashville pike, and to protect my rear until I could move my artillery and wagon train." Forrest soon shifted Buford's men to the Nashville and Columbia pike, where they were in position to act as the rearguard for Hood's retreating army.[57] A little later, he sent Armstrong to the same point for the same purpose. In the meantime the cavalryman, acting on his own initiative, altered his route and marched with his sick, wounded, and wagon train in the direction of Lillard's Mills, on the Duck River. His force was in poor condition, with many of the infantry barefoot in December. But, although the march was painfully slow, the command finally reached Lillard's Mills, where Forrest attempted to push his troops and wagon train across the swollen and rapidly rising waters. Despite his best effort, the cavalry commander could put only a small part of his wagon train across the river before it became too hazardous to cross. He then turned toward Columbia, reaching the vicinity late on December 18.[58]

Forrest could now help defend Hood's shattered army. He immediately began to get his men in position to prevent the Federals from crossing. "Everything being across Duck River," he explained, "I was ordered by General Hood to withdraw my command at 3 o'clock, which I did, and went into camp at Columbia."[59] But during the crossing, the frustrations of a hard campaign and the bitterness of defeat combined to produce a confrontation between two Southern officers. As Forrest approached the Duck River, hoping to cross after his failure to do so earlier, Cheatham's battered infantry corps also arrived at the ford with the same intention. Both men expected to cross first. And when Forrest insisted upon his right to do so, Cheatham angrily answered, "I think not, sir. You are mistaken. I intend to cross now, and will thank you to move out of the way of my troops."

For an instant, Forrest must have stared at the infantry commander. At one time in his life, he would have treated this kind of public display with the response he felt all such actions deserved—abject contempt. But this was a brother officer in the midst of a retreat with the enemy in pursuit. It was a moment in which Forrest's personal struggle between control and passion came to a head and passion won. The furious cavalryman drew his pistol and rode over to Cheatham. "If you are a better man than I am, General Cheatham," the irate officer exclaimed, taking the infantryman's comments personally, "your troops can cross ahead of mine." Behind this scene of Southern honor played out in wartime, soldiers within hearing distance raised their weapons to defend their respective commanders. The scene could have been tragic. Fortunately, General S. D. Lee happened upon the affair, stepped in to mediate, and soon the two commanders apologized and the crossing proceeded.[60] Ironically, reports differed as to which command crossed first, although one suggested that Lee sent Forrest, while pacifying Cheatham.[61]

Hood was virtually in a stupor about the future. He thought about defending a line along the Duck River in Tennessee and considered falling back still farther. According to one witness, Forrest arrived at army headquarters with a definite opinion. Hood should dispel any thoughts of remaining and fighting on some line in Tennessee. Even as Hood pondered his alternatives, the sound of firing underscored Forrest's advice. He had no choice but to retreat.[62]

As Hood marched out of Columbia, he issued Forrest instructions "to hold the town as long as possible, and when compelled to retire to move in the direction of Florence, Ala., via Pulaski, protecting and guarding his rear."[63] Realizing that Forrest would need assistance, he ordered General Edward C. Walthall to report to the cavalryman with about 1,900 infantry.[64] However, to save the Army of Tennessee from further mauling, Forrest needed luck, as well as men. He received it from an unlikely source, when a Union officer sent the pontoon train that Wilson needed to cross the Duck River to Murfreesboro instead of Columbia by mistake. The blunder gave Forrest a brief respite. Nevertheless, the Federals, under General Edward Hatch, appeared before Columbia late on December 20 and began shelling the town.[65]

Forrest had evacuated the town and knew that there was no reason to bombard it. To relay that fact to Hatch, he sent out a flag of truce, explaining to the Union officer "that his shelling would only result in injury to the women and children and his own wounded, after which interview the shelling was discontinued."[66] Yet, even with such civilities, the Federals remained dogged in their pursuit. They finally succeeded in crossing the Duck River early on December 22. Ironically, Colonel Abel Streight commanded the men who constructed the pontoon over the river that enabled the Federals to continue their pursuit of Forrest. The Union movement forced the Confederate rearguard to fall back toward Pulaski. From here, Forrest pushed his men along, stopping periodically to slow the pursuit before moving farther southward, halting for the night of December 23 near Lynnville.[67]

Colonel Charles Olmstead, one of the infantry commanders serving with Forrest during the retreat, recalled the general's usual tactics. Olmstead noted that while a portion of the Southerners engaged the enemy, the rest "detached to select and hold a position still farther to the rear to which our first line retreated when the increased intensity of the skirmishing seemed to indicate that an assault was about to be made." The Confederates employed this tactic repeatedly, each time forcing the pursuing Federals "to halt, reconnoitre and deploy and then feel our lines before advancing to the attack." Olmstead explained the strategy succinctly: "It all took time and time was what we were fighting for."[68]

The next morning, Forrest "ordered the infantry back toward

Columbia on the main pike and my cavalry on the right and left flanks." The Southerners proceeded "about three miles," when they encountered their pursuers, "where a severe engagement occurred and the enemy was held in check for two hours." Under the weight of Federal counterattacks, Forrest retreated to Richland Creek. He put Armstrong in front, Ross on the right, and Chalmers and Buford on the left. He placed his six artillery pieces on the pike, behind Armstrong "and on a line with Buford's and Chalmers' divisions and Ross' brigade, of Jackson's division." The two sides traded artillery fire, Forrest's gunners succeeding in dismounting two of the Union guns. But when the Federals attempted to flank the Confederates on either side of the creek, Forrest acted to block the move and began to pull out of his increasingly untenable position. He placed his loss in this rearguard action at one killed and six wounded, including General Buford, and noted that the Federals "lost heavily." In any event, Forrest achieved his purpose: "I reached Pulaski without further molestation."[69]

Forrest spent Christmas morning "destroying all the ammunition which could not be removed from Pulaski by General Hood and two trains of cars" and ordered Jackson "to remain in town as long as possible and to destroy the bridge at Richland Creek after everything had passed over." Jackson tried, but the pursuers reached Pulaski and saved the burning bridge. Thus, Forrest was forced to entrench at King's Hill, some seven miles out of Pulaski, where he drove off the Union troops following him, "with a loss of 150 killed and wounded, besides capturing many prisoners and one piece of artillery." Once again the effort was temporarily successful, allowing Forrest to move on to Sugar Creek, where he bivouacked for the night.[70]

The next morning, December 26, the Federals were again hot on Forrest's trail. A dense fog rendered visibility poor and helped to shield the Confederates' position from their opponents' view. The Federals advanced slowly and cautiously, but still failed to detect the Southern presence close by. Their failure proved costly, for as Forrest later reported, "The enemy therefore advanced to within fifty paces of these works, when a volley was opened upon him, causing the wildest confusion." Forrest added to the confusion by ordering two regiments of cavalry and two brigades of infantry to "charge upon the discomfited foe, which was done, producing a complete rout." The Southerners pursued their opponents for some two miles and then fell back. "In this engagement he sustained a loss of about 150 in killed and wounded; many prisoners and horses were captured and about 400 horses killed." Forrest held his ground briefly, but worrying that the Federals might try another flanking movement under cover of the fog, he fell back with everyone except a thin picket line.[71]

Even in the trying circumstances of Hood's retreat from Tennessee, Forrest continued to place enormous confidence in the abilities of his men. Just before the fight at Sugar Creek, Forrest told his field commanders, "The Yankees are coming. We are going to have a fight, and when the infantry break their lines, I'll throw in Ross's Cavalry on them." One of the officers misunderstood and expressed confidence that the Southern infantry would hold the line. Forrest answered good-naturedly, "I don't mean when they break our lines, but when we break theirs."[72]

It was also during this encounter that a Confederate who was standing near Forrest watched the general direct the battle. He could see staff officers receive orders and dash off to implement them. "Tell Walthall to come down from the hill and form his line so that the end of it will reach this road," Forrest told one. "Tell Morton to take his guns up that hill and put them so that they will swipe down this road," he ordered another. And to a third, "Tell Jackson to go back to the creek and begin fighting them fellows like the very devil."[73] This was Forrest at his best—in command of himself and in control of the situation—his mind working furiously, his orders delivered clearly, and his commands carried out precisely.

This final confrontation sated the Union appetite for pursuing the Army of Tennessee's rearguard. Forrest proceeded to the Tennessee River, "which stream," he noted, "I crossed on the evening of the 27th of December." From that point, his cavalry command left their infantry companions and moved on to Corinth.[74] Hood's Tennessee Campaign was finally over.

CHAPTER 14

I'm A-going Home

(January–May 1865)

Well, General, you have beaten me badly, and for the first time I am compelled to make such an acknowledgment. I have met many of your men, but never before one I did not get away with, first or last.

—FORREST TO GENERAL JAMES H. WILSON

Such men as Wade Hampton, Forrest, Wirt Adams, etc., never will work and nothing is left for them but death or highway robbery.

—GENERAL WILLIAM T. SHERMAN

Men, you may all do as you damn please, but I'm a-going home.

—NATHAN BEDFORD FORREST

Any man who is in favor of a further prosecution of this war is a fit subject for a lunatic asylum, and ought to be sent there immediately.

—NATHAN BEDFORD FORREST

DURING GENERAL JOHN BELL HOOD'S TENNESSEE CAMPAIGN, Bedford Forrest demonstrated that he had learned a great deal about cooperating with others in an army. He generally performed his duties well. Even so, at Spring Hill he also demonstrated that when acting as part of a team, he usually reverted to strict obedience of orders.

To be sure, he tried to slow the Union column to allow the Confederate infantry time to arrive and he worked reasonably well with individual commanders, but he failed to convince Hood of the need for immediate action to close the road to Franklin and vainly believed he could block that road with a portion of his cavalry.

Forrest simply worked better on his own. Thus, when he conducted the rearguard operation protecting the Army of Tennessee as it retreated, he achieved greater success. In such a position he could act in a relatively independent manner, exercising control over his affairs virtually without any interference from his superiors. But whatever Forrest had accomplished or failed to accomplish for Hood, he now had other concerns.

Following the punishing ordeal of protecting Hood's retreat, Forrest withdrew his command into Mississippi, to rest and refit them. A broken Hood asked to be relieved of his command, and President Davis complied.[1] In Corinth, Forrest tried to put the command back together that he had been "compelled almost to sacrifice to save the Army in its retreat from Nashville." It was no easy task. Men and horses needed everything from food to shoes to arms and equipment. Once again, he had to send some of the men home to replenish them, even offering an inducement of a twenty-day furlough for every man who returned with a recruit or a conscript.[2]

In the wake of Hood's campaign, Forrest demonstrated that he understood the psychology of war quite well. He had just completed a year that tested his energies, his stamina, his abilities, and his control to the fullest. Beginning, as he had in late 1863, with virtually no command, he had created one from the disparate units and the mass of absentees and deserters on hand. He had done so "for the good of the service," and yet the bureaucrats constantly interfered with him over these efforts. Despite this interference, he conducted raids; turned back invasions; destroyed vast amounts of Union property; and, he believed, saved the Army of Tennessee in its greatest moment of crisis. Forrest was deeply proud of all that he felt he had accomplished, and he wanted his men to be proud, too.

Now safely back in the region he had ruled almost as a private fiefdom for the past year and where he had enjoyed his greatest military feats, Forrest issued an address designed to regenerate and rejuvenate his battered and exhausted command. "Soldiers—The old campaign is ended," he began, "and your commanding general deems this an appropriate occasion to speak of the steadiness, self-denial, and patriotism with which you have borne the hardships of the past year." He was thinking of himself here, as well as the men, but since he shared their hardships and endured what they endured, the distinction between them was negligible. He believed, as a proud father who rattles off the accomplishments of his children, that this cavalry command deserved fame and honored memory: "The marches and labors you have performed during that period will find no parallel in the history of the war."

The general recounted the exploits of his men, but behind each feat was the unmistakable presence of Forrest himself. He had led these men from their "unorganized and undisciplined" state through "battles which will enshrine your names in the hearts of your countrymen and live in history [as] an imperishable monument to your prowess." He named each battle, "fields upon which you have won fadeless immortality," notably including Fort Pillow on the list.

Ostensibly, Forrest's reason for issuing this address was "the recent campaign into Middle Tennessee." Yet, even then, when the command "constantly engaged with the enemy, and endured the hunger, cold, and labor incident to that arduous campaign without murmur," they had "sustained the reputation so nobly won." Also unspoken, yet clearly present, was the blight the Army of Tennessee had suffered, but that Forrest was determined would not blemish his command. And as if to prove that the army's defeat had not blemished his command's reputation, the proud cavalry commander lay the sum total of the accomplishments of the command before them in raw numbers: 50 battles, 16,000 Union casualties, and the capture or destruction of 67 artillery pieces, 38 vessels of various types, 300 wagons, 40 blockhouses, 36 railroad bridges, 200 miles of railroad, and so on, all at a cost to the United States of some $15 million. Furthermore, he noted, this had come at a cost to his troops, their comrades, of 2,200 killed, wounded, and captured. He recognized the demoralizing effect of losing comrades, but assured the men, "If your course has been marked by the graves of patriotic heroes who have fallen by your side, it has, at the same time, been more plainly marked by the blood of the invader." While he understood their need to "sympathize with the friends of the fallen," there was great solace in knowing that "they fell as brave men battling for all that makes life worth living for."

Forrest closed his address to the men with a long, patriotic call to arms, sprinkled with references to obedience and discipline:

> Soldiers! you now rest for a short time from your labors. During the respite prepare for future action. Your commanding general is ready to lead you again to the defense of the common cause, and he appeals to you, by a remembrance of the glories of your past career; your desolated homes; your insulted women and suffering children; and, above all, by the memory of your dead comrades, to yield a ready obedience to discipline, and to buckle on the armor anew for the fight. Bring with you the soldier's safest armor—a determination to fight while the enemy pollutes your soil; to fight as long as he denies your rights; to fight until independence shall have been achieved; to fight for home, children, liberty, and all you hold dear. Show to the world the superhuman and sublime spirit with which a people may be inspired when fighting for the inestimable boon of liberty. Be not allured by the siren song of peace, for there can be no peace save upon your separate, independent nationality. You can never again unite with those who have murdered your sons, outraged your helpless families, and with demoniac malice wantonly destroyed your property, and now seek to make slaves of you.... Be patient, obedient, and earnest, and the day is not far distant when you can return to your homes and live in the full fruition of freemen around the old family altar.[3]

These were the words of someone who was trying to convince himself to continue fighting.

Forrest's biographer John Allan Wyeth observed that by this point, the general "was fully impressed with the hopelessness of the struggle, but as a soldier he was in honor bound to fight to the bitter end." He cited the testimony of an officer to whom Forrest asked what he planned to do when the war was over. The surprised man responded, "I do not exactly understand what you mean." The commander then patiently replied, "To my mind it is evident that the end is not far off; it will only be a question of time as to when General Lee's lines at Petersburg will be broken, for Grant is wearing him out; with unlimited resources of men and money, he must ultimately force Lee to leave Virginia or surrender."[4] Even Forrest's most recent opponent, General James Harrison Wilson, noted in his memoirs that Forrest "had evidently begun to despair of the Confederacy from the time he took command of Hood's rear guard," although "he betrayed no weakness, but put forth ceaseless energy and activity in the reorganization of his own corps and for the defenses of the great stretch of country committed to his care."[5]

If this were so, then why did Forrest go to such lengths to persuade his men (and himself) to keep going? Why expend so much effort recounting their exploits through the past year? The answer is deceptively simple. This address was part of his effort to restore his control over his men, over himself, and over this war (or at least Forrest's part in it). He had seen the mortality of the army and of the cause; it reminded him of his own mortality. Did he really believe that such patriotic puffing would stir his men? Did he really still hope for the "separate, independent nationality" of the Confederate States of America? Probably not. He had never been a rabid secessionist or Southern nationalist. Moreover, the record suggests that he realized the end was only a matter of time. And Bedford Forrest was too shrewd and too practical to ignore the visible signs of defeat. Then why write all of this now, when the struggle was, for all intents and purposes, finished?

Forrest had delivered the address for posterity as much as for the purposes of the present crisis. He had seen enough tired and defeated men who refused to rally, once they had been broken, by appeals to their patriotism. If words worked, so much the better, and he was more than willing to shoot a few of them if that would help. But the key thing here, he felt, was to remind the men that until now, they had not "tarnished" their "reputation," even in the darkest hours of Hood's Tennessee campaign, and that they must not tarnish it now in the darkest hours of the Confederacy's death throes. To do so would stain their honor and threaten the "imperishable monument" and the "fadeless immortality" of their (and his) part in the lost cause. They, and he, must fight to the end, not to secure a past they no longer had, but to ensure an honorable place in the future.

Like Forrest, the Federals also needed time to recuperate from the exertions of the recent campaign. But by early January, they began to show signs of striking into Southern territory. To watch their movements in northern Alabama, the Confederates had General P. D. Roddey's brigade. However, a detachment of the increasingly aggressive Union cavalry, under Colonel William Palmer, crossed the Tennessee, surprised and drove off Roddey, and captured Hood's pontoon train in the process. After destroying the pontoon train, they faded back across the river. An exasperated General P. G. T. Beauregard understood that this was just the beginning of such operations, and he wanted a unified cavalry command to respond. Informing Adjutant General Samuel Cooper of the loss of the pontoon train and Roddey's failure to protect it, he ventured, "I wish to substitute another brigade in its place, and put all the cavalry of this department under one commanding officer, Forrest."[6]

Beauregard promptly got his wish when General Richard Taylor named Forrest the commander of the cavalry in the Department of Alabama, Mississippi, and East Louisiana on January 24.[7] In assuming his new role, Forrest distributed a circular, detailing his expectations. The circular revealed his thinking during the period, noting that in assuming the position, "it is due both to myself and the troops thus placed under my command, to see that every effort will be made to render them thoroughly effective." This effectiveness could be achieved only through "strict obedience to all orders" that "must be rigidly enforced by subordinate commanders, and prompt punishment inflicted for all violations of law and of orders." Forrest was clearly prepared to use an iron fist of regulations and punishment in tandem with the velvet glove of patriotic appeal.

He called upon everyone to respect and protect the rights and property of civilians, promising swift justice for crimes committed against them. Such crimes, Forrest sternly warned, "demand a remedy, which I shall not hesitate to apply, even to extermination." As for the soldiers themselves, he noted the appropriateness of the maxim, "Kindness to bad men is cruelty to the good," and observed that "all agree, without obedience and strict discipline troops cannot be made effective, and kindness to a bad soldier does great injustice to those who are faithful and true." Determined to gain and exercise control over his men, Forrest added, "and it is but justice to those who discharge their duties with promptness and fidelity that others who are disobedient, turbulent, and mutinous, or who desert or straggle from their commands, should be promptly and effectively dealt with, as the law directs."[8]

As further evidence of his desire to enhance the effectiveness of his command and his control over it, he immediately reorganized the structure. Undoubtedly hoping to use loyalty to states to advantage, Forrest put all the Mississippians under General James R. Chalmers, the Alabamians and Kentuckians under General Abraham Buford, the Tennesseans under General Tyree Bell, and the Texans under General William H. Jackson. The rest of the men were to act independently under the general's personal direction.[9] The total number of cavalrymen in the department was approximately ten thousand. Forrest received one final boon to his control over cavalry affairs in the department when he received a promotion to lieutenant general on February 28, 1865.[10] The recognition had come late, but it had at least finally come.

By the end of February, the new lieutenant general had considerably more on his mind than deserters and marauders. The Federals had shown an interest in renewing their campaign to penetrate Confederate territory, and Selma, Alabama, with its vast factories and foundries, was the apparent target. General Wilson was accumulating a vast array of cavalry in two camps along the north bank of the Tennessee River, at Waterloo and Gravelly Springs. Forrest shifted his headquarters from Verona (where he had moved it in late January) to West Point, Mississippi, near the border of that state and Alabama, to be in a better position to respond to any moves Wilson might make.[11]

As both sides gathered forces and jockeyed for position in the next campaign, they each actively sought information concerning the other. Both sides used scouts and spies extensively. As part of his intelligence-gathering effort, General George H. Thomas sent his provost marshal, Colonel John G. Parkhurst, to meet with Forrest in mid-February regarding supplies and the exchange of prisoners. A young captain from Wilson's cavalry, Lewis Hosea, accompanied Parkhurst, with instructions to "keep his eyes open."[12] They met with the Confederate cavalry leader on the evening of January 23. The meeting took place in Rienzi and lasted well into the night.[13] Wilson observed that Forrest received Hosea "politely and entertained him with true Southern hospitality."[14]

Hosea was careful in his description of Forrest. He noted the general's uniform and manner. He confessed to be "particularly impressed with a becomingly aristocratic mien which he undoubtedly possesses." They talked briefly about the exchange, and the young officer was "again impressed with the mental power [Forrest] displayed, and his quickness of perceptive comprehension in seizing at once the entire idea intended to be conveyed from the first introductory expressions." The young captain concluded, "He seems to think quickly and to decide likewise. A certain soldierly simplicity and engaging frankness was observable, and I confess that I was frequently lost in real admiration."

Hosea described Forrest in great detail, remarking that his "habitual expression seemed rather subdued and thoughtful." The Union officer could not help but notice the Confederate's colloquial speech. "His language indicates a very limited education, but his impressive manner conceals many otherwise noticeable defects.... He invariably omits the final 'g' in the termination 'ing'; and many words are inexcusably mispronounced; and he always uses the past participle in place of the past tense of 'see' ['I seen' instead of 'I saw']. 'Help tote' is his expression for assisting to carry. In a very short time however these pass unnoticed."

The young Federal commented upon the Confederate cavalry leader's obvious pride in his achievements. "He speaks of his success with a soldierly vanity, and expresses the kindliest feelings toward prisoners and wounded." And when Hosea presented General Wilson's "compliments" with the hope that they might meet "upon some future occasion," Forrest accepted the greeting as a friendly challenge, responding "jist tell Gin'ral Wilson that I know the nicest little place down below here, in the world, and whenever he is ready, I will fight him with any number from one to ten thousand cavalry and abide the issue. Gin'ral Wilson may pick his men and I'll pick mine. He may take his sabres and I'll take my six shooters." Then, with characteristic zest and exaggeration, Forrest added, "I don't want nary a sabre in my command—haven't got one."[15]

However, if Forrest expressed the "kindliest feelings towards prisoners and wounded," in the course of the discussions, he felt less kindly toward the marauders, explaining his desire "to rid the country of guerrillas" and noting "that he would esteem it a favor if General Thomas would hang every one caught."[16] He was also interested to learn more about Wilson, the commander he had faced earlier during the rearguard actions in Tennessee and would soon confront again. On the basis of Hosea's report, the Union cavalry commander later wrote that Forrest "talked freely on all subjects except numbers and plans. He seemed curious to learn what he could about me and my career." Since Wilson had only recently arrived in this theater of operations, Forrest knew little about him and wanted to know "whether I was a regular or a volunteer, a young man or an old one," and "when Hosea told him that I was a West Pointer, an officer of engineers, had recently commanded a division in Sheridan's cavalry, and had some knowledge of tactics, strategy, and military organization, he seemed to be greatly interested."[17]

For his part, General Forrest remarked, "I ain't no graduate of West Point, and never rubbed my back up against any college."[18] His tactics were those he "had learned in actual campaigning." Forrest then proceeded to note, probably for effect, rather than as the expression of the reality he had known in four years of war, "But I always make it a rule to get there first with the most men." Then, summarizing his theory on tactics, he remarked, "But you can tell your General that I will give more for fifteen minutes of the bulge on him than for three days of tactics."[19] He expressed a belief in the pistol over the saber—"Wilson may take his sabres and I'll use my six-shooters and agree to whip the fight with any cavalry he can bring"—and in "personal gallantry." In true frontier fashion, Forrest observed that "he was afraid of no man with the sabre & would fight any individual singlehanded & agree to 'whip the fight.'"[20] Forrest did not realize that when Wilson "came down," he would bring with him a force as large and far better armed than any the Southern cavalryman had seen before.

Whatever force Wilson might bring against him and however armed that force might be, Forrest had to be prepared to meet it. Apparently, some Southerners doubted whether he would be ready or even available to meet any threatened incursion into his department. Greensboro's *Alabama Beacon* assured its readers, who "would like to know the whereabouts of the 'Wizard of the Saddle' we suggest to them to be quiet for a few days only." They should soon hear from Forrest "as he is now getting ready for the move, and when he does move he will make the sound of his roaring heard among the Negroes and Yankees in the West."[21] Indeed, Forrest sent his scattered subordinates urgent messages to prepare themselves. The dispatch he sent Chalmers, on February 19, was typical: "Spare no time, hasten to reorganize and fit up your command. We have no time to lose."[22] Forrest knew that time was of the essence and that the discipline and combat effectiveness he needed to instill in the command would have to come quickly.

Perhaps with this need for a speedy infusion of discipline in mind, and knowing that he would need all the resources to defeat any new Union invasion, Forrest distributed a comprehensive set of General Orders, Number 99, prescribing regulations affecting the command in camp, on the march, and on the battlefield. The bulk of these orders concerned the more efficient regulation of camp life and activity from the layout of the camp itself to the daily routine, including roll calls, drills, reviews, and inspections. Forrest issued orders for officers and men to "remain in camp habitually" and restricted leave or absence from camp, obviously hoping to curb desertions. To increase the available manpower, he ordered white teamsters to return to their commands and replaced them with black teamsters.

Of all the orders, perhaps Number V proved most unpopular with the common soldiers. In an attempt to conserve the quality of their mounts and the quantity of their ammunition and powder, Forrest explicitly ordered: "Galloping and other unnecessary use of horses about camps, or on the march, is positively forbidden." The "discharging of fire-arms about camp, or on the march" was also prohibited, except by special order.[23] Some of the feistiest soldiers in his command resented these prohibitions and determined to ignore them. Many of the irritated Southerners fired their weapons through the night following the announcement of the orders, thereby demonstrating their dissatisfaction.

The next day, the boldest of them went as far as to lay out a quarter-mile course in front of the general's command headquarters. They were actively and loudly engaged in racing and betting when Forrest and some of his staff officers appeared. However, instead of berating the participants, Forrest joined in the festivities himself, betting on this or that horse and enjoying himself to the fullest. When the men tired of the entertainment, they assembled before the general to offer him three cheers for so obviously having seen the error of his ways. They started back to their respective camps when an armed guard rode in front of them, placed them under arrest, and took them back to face the general they had just cheered. Forrest reminded them of the seriousness of his orders and had them court-martialed. As punishment the court ordered them to carry fence rails through camp for a specified period, leaving each of them, including the general's son William, with sore shoulders and a greater willingness to obey the letter of Forrest's law.[24]

Forrest was doing everything in his power to exercise his authority and control over these men, as the conclusion to "General Orders No. 99" suggests: "Finally, there must be system, order, and discipline in every department of the command; promptness and precision on the part of all in the performance of every duty, and in the execution of all orders. No straggling or depredation, and, above all, respect to private property and citizens; and no [unauthorized] impressments of property will be made."[25]

While Forrest molded his command, heavy rains and swollen rivers bought him more time to prepare and played havoc with Wilson's plans. Then, on March 22, Wilson started south on his long-awaited expedition.[26] One Union artilleryman observed in his journal, "Finally we have started—after so long a time to equip."[27] Wilson's compact force of fourteen thousand enjoyed remarkably good fortune from the start. Just before his horsemen began their expedition, another threatened Union movement, from Pensacola, Florida, diverted Forrest's attention long enough to give Wilson several days' unmolested travel before the Confederate cavalry realized the danger. Then Forrest had to concentrate widely scattered forces, which, at best, could bring roughly only half the numbers together that Wilson was bringing with him. Forrest hoped to converge his disparate forces at or near Selma and understood the necessity of delaying Wilson while he did so.[28]

On his march eastward into Alabama, Forrest had one final opportunity to demonstrate his willingness to apply the iron fist to matters of discipline and desertion. Near the bridge crossing over the Sipsey River, the Confederates detained two men they believed to be deserters. Both men insisted upon their innocence, although neither had passes, furloughs, or other official documents to substantiate their claims. The command hastily convened a court-martial, listened to the testimony, and condemned them to military justice. A firing squad formed and carried out the sentence. Then, as a final gesture to remind others of the fate that deserters could expect to meet, Forrest had the bodies laid out alongside the road with a sign looming over them that read SHOT FOR DESERTION. Ironically, Forrest's biographer Wyeth maintained that the men, claiming to be too old and too young for the service, had told the truth.[29]

This distasteful duty behind him, Forrest left an officer and two men to bury the two soldiers and to arrest and execute any other deserters they found. Then he pressed on toward central Alabama. Finally, on March 26, he learned about Wilson's column and immediately sought to concentrate his forces against it. But the Union commander moved with a swiftness that had not characterized other generals' movements against Forrest. On March 29, Wilson crossed the Black Warrior River, which one soldier described as "a wild, rough, swift stream" in which he "saw many men and mules drowned before my eyes."[30] By March 30, Wilson was in Elyton, while Chalmers and Jackson were still on the west side of the Cahaba River. From that point, Wilson dispatched 1,100 men, under General John Croxton, to march to Tuscaloosa, where they were to burn anything of supposed military value, including the University of Alabama. This expedition took Croxton's men out of the remainder of the Selma campaign.[31]

Forrest attempted to use Roddey's cavalry and General Daniel Adams's Alabama state troops to delay the Federals north of Montevallo. However, Wilson's men, with General Emory Upton in the lead, had little trouble brushing these forces aside. Only when Colonel Edward Crossland's Confederate brigade arrived to reinforce their beleagured comrades were they able to throw the Union troops back. Even then, the Federals regrouped and counterattacked, catching Crossland's men as they were trying to remount. The sudden attack threw Crossland's brigade into a confused retreat, in which they lost one hundred men killed, wounded, or captured, or about one-sixth of the small brigade's strength.[32]

At the same time, Forrest scored one of the few Confederate triumphs of the entire campaign when he suddenly appeared on the scene as the victorious Federals dispersed Crossland's men. His timing in this case was impeccable. Forrest arrived with his seventy-five-man escort and some two hundred troopers under General Frank C. Armstrong in time to hit the rear of the force that had just hit Crossland. The resulting attack came as a total surprise and netted Forrest some prisoners and the wounded Confederates left on the field during the hasty retreat. Forrest then left the main road to swing around the bulk of Wilson's force and found the rest of the Confederates near Randolph later that night. He still hoped to carry out his plan, but an untoward and unknown circumstance had occurred that would give Wilson a tremendous advantage.[33]

In the meantime, Forrest developed an elaborate plan to thwart the Union invasion. He hoped to bring Jackson's men across the Cahaba River behind Wilson's column. Then, if he could gather enough troops in front to force the Federals to retreat, they would be trapped between two forces, front and rear. In the panic that would inevitably follow, he could virtually annihilate the Union invasion force. But until he could carry out that plan, he had to use the men at hand to slow Wilson's progress to give his plan time to come to fruition.[34]

At some point late on the night of March 31 or early in the morning of April 1, Wilson received the most important stroke of good fortune he would get in the campaign, when some of Upton's cavalrymen captured a courier shuttling messages between Forrest and his subordinates. The captured dispatches gave Wilson vital information concerning Forrest's plans. Through these messages, Wilson determined that Forrest was in front of him with only a

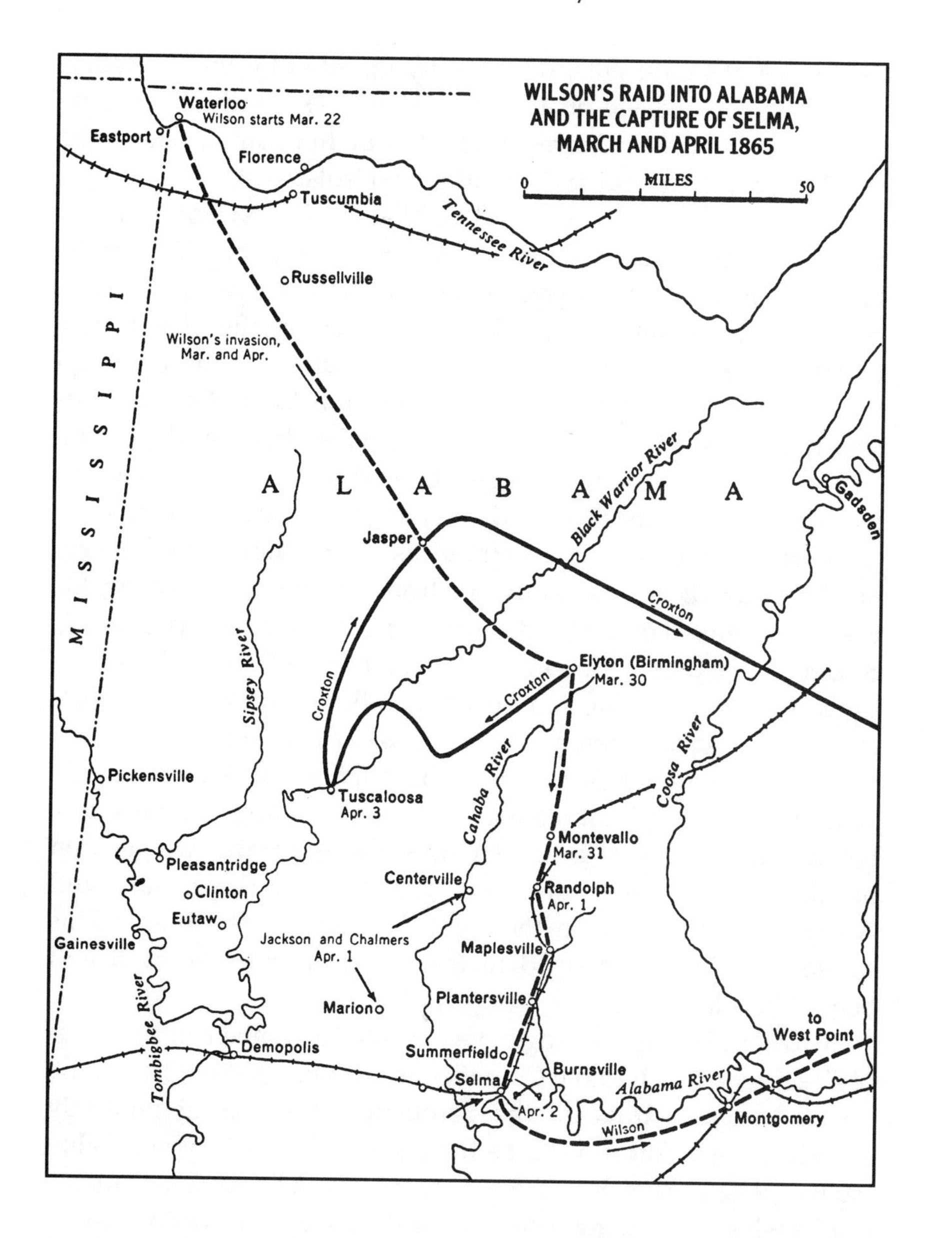

small portion of his forces, awaiting the arrival of Jackson and Chalmers. As part of his plan, the Confederate general had ordered Jackson to fall in behind Wilson's column and "follow down after them, taking the road behind them from Montevallo."[35] Wilson also learned that these two commands had not yet crossed the rain-swollen Cahaba River, with the key to crossing it, the bridge at Centerville, only lightly guarded by the Confederates. If he could drive off that guard and destroy the bridge, he could not only thwart Forrest's plan to trap him, but also keep the Southern cavalry commands divided and isolated.

Wilson dispatched General Edward M. McCook with a brigade to find Croxton and hold or destroy the Centerville bridge. The two Union commands failed to connect, but each played a role in preventing Jackson from crossing the river in time to assist Forrest. Croxton's men engaged Jackson's, and although they eventually had to retreat, delayed the Confederates sufficiently to allow McCook to reach Centerville, drive off the guard, and seize and destroy the bridge. These actions denied Forrest the use of Jackson's three thousand veterans in the ensuing combat.[36]

Wilson could now concentrate his efforts almost exclusively on defeating the Confederates in front of him and pushing his way into Selma. Forrest made a final stand in a strong position at Bogler's Creek, near Ebenezer Church, a small Baptist church. In preparing that position, he received excellent support from Crossland, who used alternately retiring lines to slow Wilson's advance. By 4 P.M., when the first Union soldiers arrived at Bogler's Creek, Forrest was as well situated as his circumstances would allow behind rail breastworks—Crossland's troopers taking up position on the Confederates' left, Roddey's men in the center, and Adams's state militia on the right. Forrest and the bulk of his available artillery remained in the center, astride the road and behind Roddey.[37]

Crossland's leapfrogging gave the initial advantage of the battle of Ebenezer Church to the Confederates, when some of General Eli Long's troopers drove in the Southern pickets. Long promptly ordered a small force to charge the position, apparently not realizing its strength. However, the impetuous attack bore some valuable results when a trooper at the head of the Union line lost control of his horse and careened into a Confederate artillery piece with such force that they knocked off the wheel and disabled the gun. The blow killed the horse; a Southern cannoneer killed the rider.[38]

In the ensuing close-hand fighting, a Union captain chose Forrest as his target. He raced up to the Confederate general and hacked at him with his saber. The slashing blows fell mostly on

Forrest's arm and quickly covered him with blood. Struggling to protect himself, Forrest finally got his pistol free and killed his assailant.[39] After the battle of Selma, when he met with Wilson, Forrest spoke of the affair: "A young captain of yours singled me out at Ebenezer Church and rained such a shower of saber strokes on my head and shoulders that I thought he would kill me." Then he candidly admitted, "While warding them off with my arm I feared that he would give me the point of his saber instead of its edge, and, had he known enough to do that, I should not have been here to tell you about it."[40]

Although this small force penetrated the Confederates' line, the Southerners drove them back with some loss. Long then launched a more serious assault, aided by Upton, who had advanced along another road, heard the sound of fighting, and emerged on the Confederates' right. Again the state militia broke under the weight of the Union offensive, and Forrest's entire force retreated to the works at Selma, eighteen miles away. The battle of Ebenezer Church had cost Wilson 12 killed and 40 wounded; it cost Forrest 300 or more, mostly captured, and three artillery pieces. But, more important, the Confederate cavalryman failed to delay or damage his opponent before Wilson reached Selma.[41]

Forrest then attempted to create a creditable defense of the city from the resources on hand. By putting every available man in three and a half miles of earthworks surrounding the city, Forrest succeeded in compiling a mixed force of about three thousand men. But he had to spread the men thinly to cover the length of the works. Doing so not only greatly reduced his firepower, but meant that he had to rely on militia who had already broken twice before the enemy or upon impressed civilians who had never before faced the Federals. If they broke this time, all would be lost. Chalmers, with his numbers and his artillery, had still not joined Forrest's force in Selma, later attributing his failure to do so to high waters and conflicting orders.[42]

Forrest worked to shorten the lines by constructing a second set of entrenchments closer to the city, but Wilson gave no indication that he would wait for the Confederates to finish it. Indeed, by 2 P.M. on April 2, the first of Wilson's troopers arrived before Selma. On their way to the city, the Federals received one last piece of good fortune, when they brought in one of the designers of Selma's defenses. The man willingly drew a sketch of the works, giving Wilson and his subordinates a clear idea of how to approach and attack the city.[43] Given the condition of Forrest's defenders and the confidence the Union troopers had after repeatedly beating them, the intelligence was probably not even necessary.

Pressing his advantage with precision, Wilson promptly prepared to attack Selma. At approximately 5 P.M., Long and Upton charged across the plain. Although the Southern fire was heavier and more effective than might have been expected, the Federals soon drove their opponents out of the first line of works and into the second. A renewed attack succeeded in forcing that line as well, when the militia broke for the final time. For Forrest and the rest of his men, the battle degenerated into hundreds of individual combats as the Confederates struggled to escape or gave in and surrendered. By the end of the day, Wilson securely held the industrial center and some 2,700 Confederate prisoners, at a cost of 46 killed, 300 wounded, and 13 missing.[44]

There was little left for Forrest to do except to complete his escape, fall behind the Cahaba River, and pull together the scattered remnants of his command. As the last line disintegrated, Forrest dashed up to General Taylor to warn him to flee as quickly as possible. Taylor recalled the scene years after: "Forrest appeared, horse and man covered with blood, and announced the enemy [was] at his heels, and that I must move at once to escape capture. I felt anxious for him, but he said he was unhurt and would cut his way through, as most of his men had done, whom he had ordered to meet him west of the Cahawba." Taylor promptly fired up the engine he had standing by and "started toward Meridian." He "barely escaped" under fire.[45]

As night fell Forrest and his companions made their way around the eastern side of the city. They cut their way through a force of Union troopers who were attempting to block their escape. In this fighting, Forrest killed the last Federal soldier attributed to him—the thirtieth man he killed in personal combat during the war.[46] As the beaten Southerners continued their escape from Selma, they captured a picket from the Fourth United States Cavalry. Learning that other Federal troopers occupied a nearby house, the Confederates decided to strike a final blow at Wilson's cavalry. But the men refused to attack until Forrest agreed to stay with the horse holders, where he would not put his life at risk in the night fighting. Atypically, the tired general complied.

When the Confederates burst upon their sleeping opponents, the startled Federals barely had time to awaken and defend themselves. Although only one Southerner suffered a wound, the Union detachment lost thirty-five men killed and wounded and five captured.[47] Wilson later wrote that the Confederates had "killed the last one of them," remarking, "Such incidents as this were far too frequent with Forrest. He appears to have had a ruthless temper which impelled him upon every occasion where he had a clear advantage to push his success to a bloody end, and yet he always seemed not only to resent but to have a plausible excuse for the cruel excesses which were charged against him."[48]

The next day, Forrest's entourage stumbled upon and captured the Union hospital at Plantersville. Afterwards they crossed the Cahaba River to rest and recover from their recent defeat. Several days later, on April 8, Wilson traveled to Cahaba to meet with Forrest. He was concerned mostly with Croxton's fate, but undoubtedly wanted to meet Forrest and assure himself of that commander's state of mind and command before he turned eastward for Montgomery. The Confederate general agreed to the meeting, arriving at the house where it was to occur about 1 P.M. The parties exchanged stiff greetings and sat down to dinner. Wilson later recalled that by the time the meal had ended, the atmosphere was somewhat lighter, and "we were treating each other like old acquaintances, if not old friends."

The two opponents naturally talked about their recent encounter. Wilson noted of his counterpart, "It was easy to see, however, that he was depressed. He carried his left arm in a sling and moved with cautious deliberation." In this state Forrest hardly presented the appearance he normally gave to others. Wilson admitted to being "somewhat disappointed" in finding the Confederate "stooping and slouchy." Indeed, some of his first words to the Union cavalryman demonstrated his frame of mind: "Well, General,you have beaten me badly, and for the first time I am compelled to make such an acknowledgment. I have met many of your men, but never before one I did not get away with, first or last."

Wilson generously replied, "Our victory was not without cost. You put up a stout fight, but we were too many and too fast for you." A subdued Forrest accepted his opponent's comments, but then realistically observed, "Yes, I did my best, but, if I now had your entire force in hand, it would not compensate us for the deadly blow you have inflicted upon our cause by the capture and destruction of ... Selma."[49]

In the aftermath of Selma and as the obvious end of the struggle approached, Bedford Forrest faced a serious dilemma. On the one hand, he could continue to fight and ignore the additional sacrifice it would mean. On the other hand, he could accept the verdict of four years of war and disband his troops. By this point in the conflict, neither choice offered much promise to the beleaguered Southern commander. The recent turn of events depressed him, and on April 15, some of that depression spilled onto the pages of a note Forrest wrote to his son William.

In the note Bedford observed, "Life, as you know, is uncertain at best, and occupying the position I do it is exceedingly hazardous. I may fall at any time, or I may, at no distant day, be an exile in a foreign land, and I desire to address you a few words, which I trust you will remember through life." Although Forrest had enjoyed great success in the army, he now faced ultimate failure and the accompanying insecurity of having fought on the losing side. He hoped to retain some element of control over his son's future, if only by means of advice given in a letter.

Bedford first wanted Willie to know that he and Mary Ann felt that their son had given them "little pain or trouble" over the years. Then Forrest explained that although they "had a full understanding" concerning the family's affairs "in the event the enemy overruns the country," Willie should be "a prop and support" to his mother, for she would "look to you in the hour of trouble." But if William was to act as his mother's protector and defender, as Bedford had done for his own mother, the elder Forrest hoped to discourage any further similarities between father and son. "Try to emulate her noble virtues," he advised, "and practice her blameless life." Then he confessed, "If I have been wicked and sinful myself, it would rejoice my heart to see you leading the Christian life which has adorned your mother."

As Bedford considered his son's future, he reflected upon his own past. He had made mistakes that he did not wish for Willie to make. "What I desire most of you, my son," the father admonished, "is never to gamble or swear. These are baneful vices." As if to confirm his point, Forrest candidly admitted, "As I grow older I see the folly of these two vices, and beg that you will never engage in them." He called upon the young man not to stain his name, adding, "Be honest, be truthful, in all your dealings with the world. Be cautious in the selection of your friends. Shun the society of the low and vulgar. Strive to elevate your character and to take a high and honorable position in society."

Bedford had high expectations for young William. "You are my only child, the pride and hope of my life," he observed, noting his son's "fine intellect" and "talent of the highest order." Willie had served on his father's staff, and the close proximity allowed Bedford to observe his boy in a variety of situations. "I have watched your entrance upon the threshold of manhood and life with all the admiration of a proud father, and I trust your future career will be an honor to yourself and solace to my declining years." Then the "proud father" closed the note by asking his son to "keep this letter prominently before you," particularly should they "meet no more on earth."[50]

The note reveals a great deal about Bedford Forrest as both father and human being. Forrest was aware of his own shortcomings and wanted his son to benefit from his experience—to be a better person than he felt himself to be. Yet, Forrest knew that he could not forsake his frontier heritage or his personality, and he did not try to do so. He saw Mary Ann as a more acceptable role model for their son, and in time, for himself as well.

D. C. Kelley, Forrest's fighting parson, knew Bedford's son well. After the war he wrote that William had assisted him in conducting religious services in the camps. He noted that William "blended the cool courage and active service of his father with the modesty and gentleness of his refined and beautiful mother." Kelley described Forrest's efforts to bring young men from well-respected families to headquarters so William would have suitable friends and companions. Such efforts became particularly important when Mary Ann's "health would no longer allow her to keep near headquarters, watching over this boy."[51] Mary Ann and Bedford had watched, as much as possible, their eighteen-year-old son grow to maturity in the midst of a war, with all the attendant hazards and risks.

If Forrest was uncertain about his future, others thought they understood his options clearly. General William Tecumseh Sherman believed that Forrest would continue fighting. In a letter to General Ulysses S. Grant, he hypothesized that organized Confederate resistance would dissolve into "numberless bands of desperadoes, headed by such men as Mosby, Forrest, Red Jackson, and others, who know not and care not for danger and its consequences."[52] Similarly, Sherman explained to his wife, "There is great danger of the Confederate armies breaking up into guerrillas, and that is what I most fear. Such men as Wade Hampton, Forrest, Wirt Adams, etc., never will work and nothing is left for them but death or highway robbery. They will not work and their negroes are all gone, their plantations destroyed, etc."[53]

General Thomas took the rumors that Forrest would continue to fight, either in the West or in Mexico, seriously. On May 2, he wired one of his subordinates, General Hatch, "Send under a flag of truce a summons to Forrest to surrender upon the terms given by General Grant to Generals Lee and Johnston. Inform him of the rumors which have reached you, and that you are prepared for him." Thomas suggested that Hatch assure the Confederate that "if he attempts such a reckless and bloodthirsty adventure he will be treated thereafter as an outlaw, and the States of Mississippi and Alabama will be so destroyed that they will not recover for fifty years."[54]

Forrest's actions suggest that he considered remaining in the field even as late as April 25, 1865, a few weeks after the Union victory at Selma. Forrest spent the intervening period consolidating and reorganizing his scattered command. Rumors soon sifted through the camp that the war had ended in Virginia. Forrest acted promptly to squelch those rumors. He issued a statement to his soldiers, saying, in effect, that he did not believe the reports of General Robert E. Lee's surrender and that, in any event, they should remain faithful. The general observed:

> It is the duty of every man to stand firm at his post and true to his colors. Your past services, your gallant and heroic conduct on many victorious fields, forbid the thought that you will ever ground your arms except with honor. Duty to your country, to yourselves, and the gallant dead who have fallen in this great struggle for liberty and independence demand that every man should continue to do his whole duty. With undiminished confidence in your courage and fortitude, and knowing you will not disregard the claims of honor, patriotism, and manhood, and those of the women and children of the country ... your commander announces his determination to stand by you, stay with you, and lead you to the end.

Finally, Forrest admonished his men, "Preserve untarnished the reputation you have so nobly won."[55] Even in defeat, honor remained a paramount concern.

In these final days of the war, Forrest attended to the needs of the men he had gathered at Gainesville, Alabama. A young clerk observed, "General Forrest is a hard worker." Although the war might be over, "Everybody about him must be busy. I think he calls for 'them clerks' a dozen times a day. He attends to everything himself, sits and talks to everyone, knows everyone by name, tells the same instructions over fifty times in half an hour. His brain, however, is as clear as crystal and he seems to think of a dozen things at once."[56]

Forrest later attested to a Congressional committee that when the war first broke out, he called his slaves together. "I said to forty-five colored fellows on my plantation that it was a war upon slavery, and that I was going into the army; that if they would go with me, if we got whipped they would be free anyhow, and that if we succeeded and slavery was perpetuated, if they would act faithfully with me to the end of the war, I would set them free." He then added: "Eighteen months before the war closed I was satisfied that we were going to be defeated, and I gave these forty-five men, or forty-four men of them, their free papers, for fear I might be killed."[57] As was common with the testimony he gave before the committee, Forrest remembered the events incorrectly. His desire for control over his affairs led him to manumit his slaves as he testified, but in the last days of the war—not eighteen months before it ended. The clerk who described Forrest so thoroughly in his daily routine at Gainesville drew up the papers for him there; Forrest sent each slave to him, one by one, until the task was complete.[58]

Shortly after Forrest issued his address urging his men "to stand firm," General Taylor confirmed the rumors when he met with Union General E. R. S. Canby, north of Mobile, to obtain the terms of surrender. Now that Generals Robert E. Lee, in Virginia; Joseph Johnston, in North Carolina; and Taylor, in Alabama, had determined to cease fighting, further resistance by Forrest and his cavalry would be both futile and foolish. Even so, some still refused to accept defeat.

In early May, Mississippi governor Charles Clark and former Tennessee governor Isham G. Harris met with Forrest. They strongly advocated linking his command with that of General Edmund Kirby Smith in the Trans-Mississippi theater of operations. Forrest would have none of it. By this point he had determined that further resistance would be senseless. Already he had explained to some of his troops, "Men, you may all do as you damn please, but I'm a-going home." Now, these politicians were attempting to persuade him to change his mind. Harris questioned his honor by asking, "Havn't you still a command?" It was the wrong tack to take with Forrest, who responded rather rationally, "Any man who is in favor of a further prosecution of this war is a fit subject for a lunatic asylum, and ought to be sent there immediately."[59]

Despite his protestations, Forrest remained privately ambivalent about his future course. Just before he surrendered his men, he rode out of camp with an aide. The two men traveled in silence until they reached a fork in the road. The staff officer broke the quiet to ask his commander which road to take. Forrest revealed the matters weighing upon his mind by responding, "Either. If one road led to hell and the other to Mexico, I would be indifferent as to which to take." The general and his subordinate debated the alternatives until the latter finally reminded his chief of his responsibility as a commander. Forrest looked at the aide and answered simply, "That settles it."[60]

Nathan Bedford Forrest issued one final address before he surrendered his command. In it he acknowledged: "That we are beaten is a self-evident fact, and any further resistance on our part would be justly regarded as the very height of folly and rashness." He instructed his men to return to their homes and reminded them, "You have been good soldiers, you can be good citizens." Forrest advised them to "blot out" any "neighborhood feuds, personal animosities, and private differences" that existed as a result of the war, and he appealed to their loyalty to him as their former commander. "I have never on the field of battle sent you where I was unwilling to go myself, nor would I now advise you to a course which I felt myself unwilling to pursue." Finally, in closing his address, the general exhorted, "Obey the laws, preserve your honor, and the government to which you have surrendered can afford to be and will be magnanimous."[61] At long last, Nathan Bedford Forrest was going home.

CHAPTER 15

Home Is Where the Hearth Was

(1865–68)

I did all in my power to break up the government, but I have found it a useless undertaking, and am now resolved to stand by the government as earnestly and honestly as I fought it.

—NATHAN BEDFORD FORREST

I am also aware that I am at this moment regarded in large communities, at the North, with abhorrence, as a detestable monster, ruthless and swift to take life.

—NATHAN BEDFORD FORREST

We have already lost all but our honor by the last war, and I must say, that in order to be men we must protect our honor at all hazards and we must also protect our wives, our homes and our families.

—NATHAN BEDFORD FORREST

BEDFORD FORREST MUST HAVE BEEN lost in thought as he rode the train back to Memphis. He was not used to failure. He now had time to reflect on the final, fatal campaign. General James Harrison Wilson had outgunned, outmaneuvered, and outfought him. He had to accept that. Nor could the former Confederate general know with any degree of certainty what awaited him in the days ahead as he sought to return to civilian life, restore his properties, and rebuild his fortune. But whatever his thoughts were, the sudden scraping of metal and the violent jerking of the cars told him that something was wrong. Fortunately, the train was not going fast when the wheels left the track, for ex-soldiers and refugees filled nearly every inch of available space.

One witness recalled that Forrest left the car in which he had been riding and immediately assumed command of the situation. "He ordered every one of us out of the cars," the man explained, "and soon had us at work with levers placed in position to lift the trucks and coach so that the displaced rails could be pushed back in proper line." Despite the effort to coordinate their activity, the first attempt failed to raise the cars. Forrest was about to try again when a man rushed up to him. "General, there are still some men in the car," he said, "and if they would get out we could lift it more readily."

As he had done so often before in similar circumstances when someone refused to do his share of the work or shirked his duty, Forrest lost his temper. He stormed onto the platform and yelled into the car: "If you damned rascals don't get out here and help get this car on the track I will throw every one of you through the windows." Then, as he stomped through the car to carry out his threat, a number of men stumbled out of the opposite end. The witness observed, "He soon had them swinging on the lever, and in a few minutes the car was in the air, the tracks adjusted to the rails, and we were again on our way."[1]

Before he left on his journey homeward, Forrest had remained in Gainesville long enough to ensure that the men in his command were paroled, fed, and started on their way home. Once this task was completed, he boarded the train. The editors of the Memphis *Bulletin* noted, "Gen. N. B. Forrest was at Grenada till the middle of last week." While there, they observed he "remarked that he was now as good a Union man as anybody—that the South was whipped and he was going to support the Federal government as heartily as any one could." He intended to try planting again, and some of the same men he manumitted were returning with him. "When Genl. Forrest left Grenada for his plantation on the Mississippi River about 20 of his former slaves started with him."[2]

General William Tecumseh Sherman believed that the loss of slaves and the damage to plantation property would be sufficient to force men like Forrest into lives of crime. Instead, Forrest returned home and quietly began to restore his properties. To be sure, he lost part of his land during the war when financial shortfalls required him to relinquish a 1,445-acre tract of land to its original owner, Henry C. Chambers, from whom he bought the tract just before the war and for which he traded property in Memphis.[3] And emancipation eliminated the "capital" investment he had made in slaves. Nevertheless, he still had the larger property, Green Grove (in southwestern Coahoma County, Mississippi), and it was this plantation that Forrest hoped to revive.[4] Although he had gone "into the army worth a million and a half dollars, and came out a beggar," Bedford Forrest was in no condition, physically or emotionally, to become a highwayman. By his own admission, he had come "out of the war pretty well wrecked ... completely used up—shot to pieces, crippled up."[5] He wished only to be unmolested while he sought to regain his prewar status as a successful planter.

Forrest and others like him needed laborers—significant numbers of them. To accommodate this need, state legislatures throughout the former Confederacy acted quickly to resurrect thinly veiled slave codes or other restrictions on laborers. These "black" codes often recognized the former slaves' new status only by substituting the word *freedmen* wherever the word *slaves* had appeared. Southern white planters feared the loss of their chief source of labor. Of course, these laborers were no longer slaves, whatever Southern white planters might think, and the United States government created a temporary Federal agency to assist them in making the transition from slavery to freedom. This agency, the Bureau of Refugees, Freedmen, and Abandoned Lands, was designed to play a crucial role in the reconstruction of the South, by providing the former slaves with relief, education, legal aid, and other forms of assistance.[6]

Bedford Forrest immediately set about the task of obtaining workers. In September 1865, a notice appeared in a local Mississippi paper in which "N. Bedford Forrest" announced, "Having thoroughly repaired my Steam Saw Mill, situated in the lower part of

Coahoma County, Mississippi, four miles back of Sunflower Landing, I can now furnish the public with lumber of every description."[7] On September 29, an advertisement appeared: "Wanted—Twenty good hands are wanted at the Saw Mill of Gen. N. B. Forrest. The highest prices paid."[8] Largely because of this effort to restart the sawmill, *The Coahomian* touted Forrest as an example to others. On November 10, 1865, the editors observed: "Gen. N. B. Forrest—It is an item worth stating that this distinguished gentleman is now running his Saw Mill in this county, and gives it his personal attention." Then they offered their readers a bit of advice: "His example should be followed by the many men who are standing a round grumbling about hard times, and they will discover that the times will improve."[9]

However, if one of the notices suggested that Forrest was short of labor for his plantations, he was in a relatively better position than were his neighbors. In attempting to return his lands to productivity, the former Confederate joined in a partnership with several former Union officers. As he later explained, "I carried seven Federal officers home with me, after the war was over, and I rented them plantations, some of my own lands, and some of my neighbors'. In 1866 those seven officers made a crop in my neighborhood. I assisted those men, and found great relief from them."[10] This was an incredibly astute move for a man who did not know what to expect from the victorious Federal government and who was known in the North as "Forrest of Fort Pillow." But his partnership had a practical side as well. Forrest successfully used his recent enemies to help satisfy his demand for laborers. One official of the Freedmen's Bureau reported that the general "employed the greatest number of hands of any place I visited.... General Forrest works about 140 hands on two plantations."[11] Of his Union Army associates, the ex-Confederate cavalryman later admitted, "They got me my hands, and they kept my hands engaged for me."[12]

The partners implemented a system of debt peonage. As the bureau officer noted of Forrest's own plantation and the contracts that bound the labor force to it: "I examined his accounts with his hands at his own request and found that almost every one of them are in his debt from $25. to $90. for clothing and articles which they needed." Nevertheless, he observed that Forrest's labor contracts "range higher than any others I found ... for 1st class hands he pays $20. per month," deducting the costs of the items he furnished them.[13] Forrest used the savvy of years of interstate slave trading to garner laborers from wherever he could find them. The same official noted, "The hands in this neighborhood were most of them brought from Georgia especially those on Forrest's place."[14] This practice opened him up to criticism from those who could not afford high contracts and thus lost their own laborers.[15] Nevertheless, self-interest allowed Forrest to ignore such criticisms.

But if some of his fellow Southerners criticized him and many Northerners castigated him for his prewar and wartime activities, others were quick to rush to his defense. After the editors of the local newspaper, the Friar's Point *Coahomian,* "noticed lately in several of the radical papers" statements to the effect that Forrest was "so odious to the citizens in the vicinity of his home, that his life is in constant danger," they felt compelled to respond on his behalf. "Now we know this to be utterly without truth," they assured, "for Gen. F's. residence is in this county, and not only his immediate neighbors, but the whole community entertain for him the strongest feelings of friendship and would rather protect than endanger his life."[16]

Bedford Forrest had the ability, largely through personal charisma, to win other allies as well. His partnership with his former enemies, his willingness to meet with Federal authorities, and his desire to be left alone, all benefited him considerably. In testimony before a Congressional committee, Union General Edward Hatch described Forrest's status in the region and the reason a former staff officer, B. F. Diffenbocker, gave for going into partnership with the ex-Confederate: "There is no more popular man in West Tennessee to-day than the late rebel General Forrest. The quartermaster of my old regiment is partner with Forrest on a plantation; he said he took the plantation because Forrest is popular, and will take care of him and his interests."[17]

Later, former Missouri Unionist and Union General Frank P. Blair, who assisted Forrest in communicating with President Andrew Johnson concerning his parole, noted that Forrest's "influence" was "more powerful than that of any man in West Tennessee," adding that it "has been wielded invariably in the maintenance of peace and amicable feelings." Blair thought that the former Confederate's "noble bearing since the war in accepting without complaint the result and using his powerful influence to make others accept it in the same spirit, have inspired me with a respect and admiration I have not felt for any other man." These qualities enabled him to state rather candidly, "I have conceived a very great personal attachment for Forrest."[18]

And following Forrest's meeting with former Union general and current commissioner of the Freedmen's Bureau Oliver O. Howard, that officer described Forrest as "disposed to do everything that is fair and right for the Negroes which might be employed."[19] Yet this was the same man who was heavily involved in the slave trade and was the instigator of the Fort Pillow "massacre." Self-interest enabled Forrest and his Northern partners to act in such an apparently contradictory fashion. By providing relatively good contracts and associating with Northern partners, on the one hand, and continuing to demonstrate a willingness to act as the intimidator on the other, Forrest was taking the action he believed was necessary, however drastic, to ensure desirable behavior from others. In this case, he not only acquired a labor force, but encouraged its docility.

Forrest was generally satisfied with the state of his personal affairs. In a letter to his friend and former commander Stephen Dill Lee, he explained, "I have Setled for the present at my plantation in Coahoma Co Miss have gone to hard work have a fine crop of corn if the Seasons hit wil make a fine crop Mrs F is making Buter & Rasing chickens[.]" And in a display of the high esteem in which he held Lee, Forrest invited him "to cum and Se us and Bring Mrs Lee with you[.]" Then, in case Lee was also thinking of getting into farming, Forrest advised, "if you go to planting the Miss River is the place to do so[.]"[20]

Bedford Forrest had become, for the moment at least, the model of reconciliation. But the threat of arrest menaced this position. Friends sent the general a letter of credit and advised him to flee to Europe until he could return safely. Forrest respectfully declined the offer, saying, "This is my country. I am hard at work upon my plantation, and carefully observing the obligations of my parole." With a touch of anger, the general added, "If the Federal government does not regard it they will be sorry. I shall not go away."[21]

Forrest's determination to remain was all the more important because of the unsettled state of affairs in Tennessee. The war left the state bitterly divided. Bushwhacking and other forms of internecine warfare plagued the eastern portion of the state, both during and following the war. Bedford Forrest's chief adversary was the current governor of Tennessee, "Parson" William Gannaway Brownlow. The former Methodist minister and eastern Tennessee Unionist encouraged all "active leading Rebels and bad men ... to sell out and go to a new country, take a new start in life."[22]

Forrest took two significant steps to ensure his security in the present circumstances. Locally, he met with the Union commander in Memphis, receiving assurances from that officer that he had nothing to fear from the Federal authorities.[23] Then, on July 1, 1865, he traveled to Jackson, Mississippi, "for the purpos of making application to the pres for a pardon[.]" Governor William Sharkey promised to forward the application, with the amnesty oath attached, to Washington as rapidly as possible. The general advised his friend Stephen D. Lee to do likewise, perhaps out of concern for his former commander's status.[24]

Despite the steps he undoubtedly took to maintain control of his Mississippi plantation lands, Forrest apparently encountered more financial difficulties. In November 1865, he lent his name to the "Commission, Grocery & Cotton Factorage Business" of Tate, Gill, Able, & Company. Through a broad circular in *The Coahomian*, Samuel Tate, George M. Gill, and Daniel Able announced that they had "associated with themselves, General N. B. Forrest." Boasting the "largest and best selected stocks of Groceries and Plantation Supplies," they now had the easily recognizable and popular name of Bedford Forrest to assist them.[25]

Rumors concerning his activities continued to plague Forrest as he tried unobtrusively to ply his trade and maintain his plantations. One rumor had the former Confederate in Mexico, ostensibly to raise troops to renew the war against the United States. In early 1866, a newspaperman sighted him on a steamer near Memphis and asked the general how he could be in both Mexico and Memphis at the same time. With a wry touch of humor, Forrest responded that he "was not responsible for his rapid locomotion." Then, in a more serious vein, the paper quoted him as saying, "'Tell all whom it may concern,' says the General, 'that FORREST may be found at any time on his farm, among his plows, hoes, and shovels, endeavoring to make a support, and that others would do well to settle down with like purposes.'" Then, seemingly for emphasis, given the rumors, the soldier-turned-farmer added, "'As for me, I did all in my power to break up the government, but I have found it a useless undertaking, and am now resolved to stand by the government as earnestly and honestly as I fought it.'"[26]

Then, in the spring of 1866, two events occurred that disturbed Forrest. The first was related to his indictment for treason just after the 1864 raid on Memphis. On March 13, Forrest went to Memphis to appear before the clerk of the circuit court to post a $10,000 bond.[27] Then, he began to prepare for a treason trial later in the year. In July, Forrest received an offer from General Braxton Bragg's former judge advocate, and current Holly Springs attorney, Harvey W. Walter, to join the defense. The general responded to the offer from Memphis on August 14, observing, "Since your favor of July is to hand offering your Services as one of my atys in my tresen case at this place in Sept it wil afford me much pleasure to have your assistance when the case cums up as no one knows me beter & Longer than your Self and no one has had a Beter opportunity to watch my milatary career than your Self[.]" Then he added, "I wil ascertain at what time the case wil cum up and let you know[.]"[28] Although Forrest had to renew the $10,000 bond in September, the trial for treason never took place.[29] But by this point, the general faced another serious trial, this one for the murder of Thomas Edwards, one of the freedmen on his plantations.

This second trial, in 1866, arose from a confrontation between Forrest and Edwards and led directly to the latter's death. Described by an officer of the Freedmen's Bureau as "a leading character employed on the home plantation of General Forrest," Edwards apparently had an explosive temper and a tendency to be cruel.[30] One fellow worker observed, "He was generally considered a bad man, frequently cruelly abusing mules and other stock. About four weeks ago he beat a mule to death." This same laborer noted that on one occasion, Edwards "whipped his wife so unmercifully that a Physician was called to attend her."[31]

In her affidavit, Mrs. Edwards denied that her husband ever beat or abused her, insisting that "he never abused me in his life in any way." She asserted that her husband "never struck me a blow in his life; he was always very kind to me and very pleasant" and maintained that he "was very mild in his disposition."[32] But another laborer who lived in the same quarters with the couple testified, "I saw him whip her twice last Christmas day and kick her in the stomach," adding, "She would sometimes cry out when he was whipping her."[33]

Edwards was fiercely defensive over what he saw as a personal prerogative, telling the white carpenter on Forrest's plantation, "I will whip my wife when I damn please." And when the man warned him that this behavior "was against General Forrest's orders for any man to whip his wife on the place," Edwards curtly dismissed the warning: "I do not care a God damn for General Forrest or any other God damn man. If Gen'l Forrest or any other man attempts to interfere with me in the privilege I enjoy as regards whipping her or beating [her], I'll cut his God damn guts out," all the while holding a knife in his hand.[34]

Matters escalated when one of Diffenbocker's assistants unwisely threatened to use corporal punishment against freedmen who refused "to work a proper number of hours each day" as stipulated by the contract. "At this," the bureau man noted, "they nearly all quit work and some one of them went over to the other place and got their chief Tom Edwards and some of his followers, who came back armed with a Spencer rifle and other warlike weapons, and joined the movement." Although nothing more serious than "cursing and threatening" occurred, such actions constituted "a spirit of insubordination" that challenged the white supervisor's and Forrest's power and control. Even so, Edwards's involvement partially stemmed from the fact that, according to the bureau official, he "was displeased with Diffenbacker for something which occurred while he was on the other place with reference to his (Edwards) abusing his wife, which he is reported to have been adicted to; and had threatened to shoot Mr. Diffenbacker for interfering."[35]

Finally, on March 31, 1866, matters came to a head between Edwards and Forrest. Having learned of an outbreak of cholera, the general went down to the quarters to get the freedmen to ditch the area for better drainage and to eliminate several pools of stagnant water. While Forrest supervised this work, Tom Edwards walked by, ignoring the general's calls for him to help with the work. Edwards proceeded into his cabin and, according to Forrest, "commenced cursing and abusing his wife about his dinner at the same time making threats that he intended to whip her."[36] Mrs. Edwards testified that her husband asked if dinner was ready, and when she replied it was "not quite ready," he did not react in any violent way.[37] But Hannah Powell, the woman living in the cabin with them, corroborated Forrest's version. "I was sitting in the entry way of Tom Edwards quarters," she recalled, "when Gen'l Forrest came along and told the hands we ought to clean up around the quarters on account of the colera. Tom Edwards came along into the quarters and commenced swearing at his wife about his dinner."[38]

Next, Forrest explained, "[I] slipped in and remarked to him that he had already abused his wife too much and that I had frequently requested him to cease his abuses to her, and that he could not whip her, that if he attempted to whip her again I would whip him." With that, Edwards "stepped back" and holding a knife in his hand, remarked, "Damn you, I ask you no odds." Forrest angrily told him that "you should not give me such impudence and I struck him with a broom handle." Edwards then lunged forward, wounding the general slightly with his knife. Both men simultaneously noticed an ax lying against a box. Forrest testified, "I saw him look at the ax, and move towards it as if to take hold of it when I immediately jumped for the ax and seized it." Having failed to grab the ax first, Edwards "made a lick at me with the knife, turning partly around, when I struck him behind the left ear with the pole of the ax, knocking him down, killing him instantly; which blow was the only one I struck."[39]

Sarah Edwards insisted that Tom had barely asked if dinner was ready, "when General Forrest came in and says Tom Edwards I want you to stop abusing your wife. Tom says General Forrest I am not abusing my wife I want her to get my dinner." At this point, Mrs. Edwards testified that the general, without any provocation, "struck Tom with his fist, then with a broom stick & then he grabed the ax and struck him on the head."[40] Hannah Powell noted that Forrest "came in and told him he must not abuse his wife any more, he had done it enough. Tom said he wanted his dinner and if she would not get it he would make her get it, and commenced swearing at the General; then the General struck Tom with a broom stick, and then hit him with the ax and killed him." When asked if she saw Edwards strike at Forrest with a knife, she answered, "No I did not, the General was between us and when they were fussing I went away."[41]

Whatever the exact sequence of events, Forrest was in a serious situation now. Word of what had transpired immediately spread throughout the plantation and surrounding area. The official of the Freedmen's Bureau had noticed the preponderance of weapons available to the freedmen, remarking that they were "in the habit of carrying pistols and bowie knives both in the field and while about their quarters."[42] The availability of weapons had led to some incidents between them and clearly meant that if they wished to avenge Edwards's death, they had the means to do so. In any event, a significant number of angry people gathered outside Forrest's house, demanding revenge.[43]

According to one fanciful account, Forrest suddenly appeared in the doorway, holding a pistol in each hand, and started barking orders at the mass of men, many of whom were former Union soldiers. As he yelled "halt!" "order arms," and "ground arms!" the laborers blindly obeyed. Then the general defiantly told them, "Now men, get out of this yard or I will shoot the heads off every one of you." At this, the freedmen, "crushed under the overmastering willpower ... slunk away to their work without a protest."[44]

Another account of these subsequent events, given to a local resident by Wirt Shaw, the man deputized to bring Forrest in to Friar's Point immediately after the killing, has a much more realistic ring. Noting that Forrest "had a personal difficulty with a negro on his plantation," Shaw recalled that he arrived at the Forrest place "about twelve o'clock midnight," where he "found that the negroes had built fires all around the General's house to prevent his escape." The deputy promptly spoke with the freedmen, assuring them that Forrest would be brought to trial and punished for the crime. As Shaw climbed the steps, Forrest called out from inside the house, asking who was there. "It's Wirt Shaw, General," he replied. Then the general wanted to know what brought him out so late at night. When Shaw answered that he was there "to arrest you General," Forrest responded, "It's alright you've got me. Come in." When the deputy got inside the door, he saw that Forrest had "some old guns and pistols which he had loaded, anticipating an attack from the negroes." Under the circumstances, they decided not to venture the journey to Friar's Point that night.

The next morning, Forrest suggested that they take a steamboat into Friar's Point. When the boat arrived at the landing, it was filled with Federal soldiers. Forrest advised Shaw not to divulge his identity "for fear of his being insulted." The deputy agreed, but when the soldiers pestered him repeatedly, wanting "to know if it wasn't General Forrest," they agreed to disclose the general's identity. The result was quite unexpected, as Shaw remembered. "Instead of being insulted by them he was very much honored and lionized. Nothing on the boat was too good for him. They were dined and champagned." In the meantime, Forrest explained how he had come to be on the boat in the first place. The Federals offered to toss the deputy "in the river" and take the general with them to Memphis, but Forrest demurred. "No, I prefer getting off at Friar's Point," he explained, noting his desire to have the entire affair "over with" and assuring his would-be benefactors that he "anticipated no trouble what-so-ever." And so, when they landed at Friar's Point, Forrest and Shaw left the boat.[45]

The Coahoma County Circuit Court subsequently issued an indictment for Forrest's arrest during its April term, noting that the "aforesaid feloniously wilfully and of malice aforethought did kill and murder a certain free man of color commonly known and called by the name of Thomas Edwards." Sheriff J. N. Allen arrested Forrest under this indictment on April 11, 1866, and brought him "into open court."[46] On April 20, *The Coahomian* reported, "General Forrest was arraigned for the homicide of a colored freeman on his plantation a few weeks before, and was admitted to bail in the sum of $10,000 for his appearance at the next term of [the] Circuit Court."[47]

Throughout the summer months, the court subpoenaed witnesses and summoned prospective jurors. Then, with the jury impaneled, the trial opened on October 8, 1866. Finally, having heard the testimony, the judge instructed the jury to find Forrest guilty of manslaughter if he, "in the heat of passion without malice, and by the use of a deadly weapon and without authority of Law, and not in necessary self-defense—killed the Deceased," or if Forrest "struck him the first blow at a time when he was in no immediate danger from the Deceased."

Apparently the jurors had some difficulty with these instructions, for they returned and required the judge to give them a new, modified set. The confusion may have arisen from the question of how to determine the issue of self-defense in their ruling, for the judge began his second instructions: "Every man has a right to Kill in defense of his own life, where there is either actual, present and urgent danger, or he has a reasonable ground to apprehend or believe there is a danger on the part of the person slain, to commit a felony as to do him some great bodily harm, and there is imminent danger of such design being accomplished, and he has reasonable grounds at the time of the Killing to apprehend or believe that such design would be executed."

Now the judge instructed the jury to find the defendant guilty of manslaughter "if he made the first assault upon the deceased and struck the first blow," even if he did so "in the heat of passion without malice," as long as there was "nothing to justify or show that such Killing was in self-defense or to avert great bodily harm impending at the time of the Killing." However, if the jury found that Forrest, "although he may have struck the first blow," had acted in self-defense in the belief that Edwards meant him "great bodily injury," then he should be acquitted. Under these new instructions, the jury retired to consider their verdict. When the jurors returned with their judgment, recorded on October 11, 1866, they found Forrest "not guilty in the manner and form as charged in the Indictment."[48] Bedford Forrest was free to go.

Nevertheless, the stress of recent events weighed heavily on his mind. Forrest's letter to Harvey Walter, in August, hinted at the tension brought on by events in his own life, as well as the life of the nation. By this point, Congress had passed a civil rights bill over President Johnson's veto. It must have galled Forrest to see former slaves receiving greater recognition of their concerns, while he faced trial for treason, merely, in his mind, for defending his family, his home, and his way of life. Furthermore, the defense of family appeared paramount, as disturbing rifts appeared in the new social fabric.

These tears were significant enough that in the spring and summer of 1866, the whole South seemed threatened with disintegration. Racial clashes occurred during April in Norfolk, Virginia; during May in Memphis, Tennessee; and during July in Charleston, South Carolina, and New Orleans, Louisiana.[49] The worst confrontations took place in Memphis and New Orleans. Forrest's hometown erupted in racial rioting on May 1, when white policemen and recently discharged black soldiers clashed, leading to three days of widespread violence against blacks in the city, carried out predominately by white policemen and firemen. Tensions related to the economic upheavals of war and the massive influx of blacks into the city helped to bring about this racial violence. Then, on July 30, the scene of violence shifted to New Orleans. Mobs of white citizens, again including large numbers of policemen, attacked blacks and Union men attempting to hold a political convention in that city. The violence in both places left approximately 80–90 blacks dead.[50]

What Forrest specifically thought about this violence is not known. However, he would not have been able to understand that such rioting occurred in part because the white policemen, many of whom in Memphis were Irish, had systematically brutalized black prisoners and harassed black citizens. Memphis was at least one instance in which two major ethnic groups in a Southern urban center clashed for economic and racial, as well as political, reasons. Nor would he have appreciated or sanctioned the desire of black Southerners to gain a significant level of participation in the South's political system. But a political undertone characterized all these confrontations. As historian William S. McFeely observed, "The 1866 riots, which occurred because Negroes were asserting themselves and white men were determined that no elevation take place, were quite as political as any later clash."[51] Ironically, the lower class as a whole lost the most. One Memphian thought that it did not matter much which group won, whether the Irish killed all the blacks or the blacks killed all the Irish.[52]

For men like Forrest, the violence in Memphis, New Orleans, and elsewhere in the South during 1866 suggested a society out of control. The times demanded law and order. White Southerners were prepared to restore what they believed to be law and order with brickbats, clubs, and guns, if necessary. But this sort of law and order meant that free blacks would return to virtually the same status they had maintained as slaves.

Bedford Forrest would have been particularly affected by the riots in Memphis, although since he had a voracious appetite for newspapers, he undoubtedly knew about the other incidents as well.[53] He had lived in Memphis before the war and was contemplating returning to live there. As he explained in August 1866, "I have Sold out my plantation in the Botom and if allowed think of making my home a gain in Memphis[.]"[54] Obviously, Forrest had failed to make his plantations work, despite assistance from his Northern partners. Having tried unsuccessfully to regain his prewar status by returning to his Mississippi plantation lands, the former Confederate cavalryman decided to go back to Memphis to find a solution to his financial woes. In the meantime, he may have briefly shuttled back and forth from Memphis to Mississippi, for the 1866 city directory contained an entry for him under "Forrest, N. Bedford gen.," and listed him as a boarder at the Gayoso House.[55]

While contemplating his future, Forrest also acted to safeguard his family and his military legacy. With the resurrection of his indictment for treason, his confrontation with Edwards and the resulting murder trial, and the violence that marked the early part of the year in mind, Forrest applied for $10,000 worth of life insurance on September 23, 1866. He listed himself as a "merchant" in Memphis, obviously referring to his connection with Tate, Gill, Able & Co., and named his wife as the sole beneficiary. Noting that he had never been addicted to alcohol or other drugs, he admitted, "Has been shot twice, in the field," but quickly added, "Does not suffer from any [wound] now."[56] Forrest probably lowered the number of wounds he had suffered in an effort to gain approval for the policy. Coincidentally, the general also wanted to exhibit his exploits by recording his wartime career for posterity. In early September he wrote former Mississippi governor and Confederate general Charles Clark: "I am collecting materials for the compilation of a correct history of the operations of the Cavalry serving under my orders during the late war, and would be pleased to receive from you any assistance your convenience may allow you to render."[57]

Near the end of the year, Forrest journeyed to Little Rock, Arkansas, with a contract for completing and grading the Memphis and Little Rock Railroad. His arrival generated great public interest. One man wrote his wife, "Gen'l Forrest reached town last evening. I am going up this morning to take a look at him."[58] And to those who gathered "to take a look at him," Forrest observed with a twist of humor that he had arrived "to reverse his general practice, and build up instead of destroying railroads."[59] He traveled between Memphis and the railroad construction site with some frequency, for a Confederate veteran remembered traveling and conversing with him aboard "a Memphis and St. Francis River steamboat from Memphis to Madison, a few miles from where his construction camp was"; another man wrote of Forrest's appearance in Little Rock twice in November.[60] Freedmen's Bureau chief Oliver O. Howard supplied some of the laborers Forrest subsequently used as construction crews on this line.[61] In any case, this was only the beginning of what would be Forrest's serious involvement with railroads.

In the meantime, Forrest continued to seek a pardon. Writing directly to President Andrew Johnson, on November 25, 1866, he observed, "It has been nearly eighteen months, since laying down my arms, I gave my parole, to cease war, against, and to submit to the constituted authority of the United States, with the determination to do so, in all loyalty, and with full recognition of the complete restoration of the Constitutional Supremacy of the federal union over all the States." Forrest assured the president that he had remained faithful to his parole, "in both spirit and letter."

The general decried the manner in which Northerners viewed him. "I am also aware," he explained, "that I am at this moment regarded in large communities, at the North, with abhorrence, as a detestable monster, ruthless and swift to take life, and guilty of unpardonable crimes in connection with the capture of Fort Pillow on the 12th of April 1864." No doubt recalling the recent racial violence in Memphis and New Orleans, he added, "Perhaps at a time of political excitement so fierce and high as at present, this misjudgment of my conduct and character should not surprise me."

Briefly, he betrayed his own political views in the same letter. Noting President Johnson's struggles "with an appalling army of forces hostile to Constitutional regulated liberty," Forrest expressed himself unwilling to ask for amnesty. Instead, he observed, "I have preferred to endure these private embarrassments rather than to give your vindictive enemies an opportunity to misrepresent your motives were you to grant my Amnesty." In closing, the former Confederate cavalry general offered the president one means by which he could mitigate the concerns of Northern Republicans, by agreeing to "waive all immunity from investigation into my conduct at Fort Pillow."[62]

By 1867, Bedford Forrest was no longer content to remain silent. He had decided to take action. Not coincidentally, he joined a secret organization called the Pale Faces about this time. Forrest later likened this organization to the Masons and explained that its purpose was to protect the "weak and defenseless" and to prevent disorder.[63] It is tempting to belittle Forrest's use of such terms, but they were important symbols to him. His life on the Southern frontier, his wartime experience, and his personality all conditioned Forrest's view of himself and his world. He was the Jacksonian man of action, the rough-and-ready defender and protector of family and self. This action was most often spontaneous and emotional, for it was usually the personal reaction of an intensely individualistic human being who was bound to the society in which he lived by the opinion others held of him. Thus, for Bedford Forrest, defense, order (in the society this meant white supremacy), control, honor, and violence were essential elements of life.[64]

The racial confrontations of 1866 and the stress of the times underscored the vulnerability many white Southerners felt as they attempted to make sense of their present. During this period of uncertainty, many former Confederates sought the comfort of their wartime associations. They saw a world in the throes of change—change they did not like. To compensate, they attempted to recast their world in familiar terms. In this way, they could make an active attempt to regain an element of control over affairs that they had not enjoyed since the end of the war. In a real sense, these men hoped to turn back the clock and return to their prewar world. To do so would mean a restoration of black subordination—in effect, a return of the "bottom rail" back to the bottom. Ironically, these white Southerners did not realize that it was no longer possible to return to the South as it had been in 1860. Yet, attempting to do so, they and the black Southerners who resisted that effort created, as Eric Foner described it, "a subtle dialectic of persistence and change, continuity and conflict." Although white conservative Democrats eventually thwarted the blacks' aspirations in the South, Foner maintained that "blacks continued to assert their claims, against unequal odds, to economic autonomy, political citizenship, and a voice in determining the consequences of emancipation."[65]

In addition to the elements of order, control, and defense in the existence of the secret organizations that sprang to life during this period, an even more fundamental factor was involved. Just as the soldier Forrest could not disregard or discard his prewar heritage, the civilian Forrest could not disregard or discard his wartime experience. Like his frontier heritage and his experience as a Southern planter, the war had come to define him, both to himself and to others.

The war had also come to define those who had served with him or under him in the Confederate armed forces. They all shared a bond of common experience in which they had endured hardships and defeat, and this bond continued long after the guns fell silent. This was the reason for the reunions and the parades, the celebration of the "lost cause"; it was also one of the reasons for the potency of such secret societies as the Ku Klux Klan as social and political manifestations of the desire that white Southerners felt to regain power and control over their lives and the affairs of their region.[66]

In April 1867, one such association of ex-Confederates met in

Nashville to organize. This budding organization was the Ku Klux Klan, and its popularity was increasing rapidly. At some point concurrent with this meeting, Bedford Forrest traveled to Nashville to attempt to join it. He visited with his former artillery chief, John Morton, who was Grand Cyclops of the Nashville Den. Morton apparently administered a preliminary oath to his former superior and directed him to return to the Maxwell House hotel for a more formal ceremony.[67] One of the original members of the Klan, James R. Crowe, wrote nearly forty years later, "After the order grew to large numbers we found it necessary to have someone of large experience to command. We chose General Forrest."[68] Another man who became a member of the Klan in Memphis later observed, "N. B. Forrest of Confederate fame was at our head, and was known as the Grand Wizard. I heard him make a speech in one of our Dens."[69]

While there is no doubt that Forrest joined the Klan, there is some question as to whether he actually was the Grand Wizard of the Ku Klux Klan. The widow of fellow Tennessean and Confederate veteran George W. Gordon asserted that her husband held that position.[70] Forrest denied even being a member of the organization, much less commander of it. Nevertheless, General Forrest told a Congressional committee, "I was getting at that time from fifty to one hundred letters a day, and had a private secretary writing all the time. I was receiving letters from all the Southern States, men complaining, being dissatisfied, persons whose friends had been killed, or their families insulted, and they were writing to me to know what they ought to do." When asked why people wrote to him, Forrest replied, "I suppose they thought I was a man who would do to counsel with."[71] They would particularly think so if they knew he was at the head of such a powerful organization.

According to the general, his efforts concerning the Klan had been "addressed to stop it, disband it and prevent it." Then with an air of finality and pride, he added, "I did suppress it."[72] Obviously, Forrest had to be in a position of significant influence with the Klan to be able to suppress it, as he claimed he did. Furthermore, in a newspaper interview, he expressed considerable knowledge of the Ku Klux Klan's activities, although he persisted in denying that he was a member. He noted that there "were some foolish young men who put masks on their faces and rode over the country, frightening negroes, but orders have been issued to stop that, and it has ceased." How would he have known of such orders unless, as a Klansman, he had heard them or, as a Klan leader, he had issued them? In addition, Forrest explained that three Klansmen had been "court-martialed and shot for violations of the orders not to disturb or molest people." Twice he admitted that he had either sent someone or ordered someone to investigate matters concerning the Klan's activities and report to him or arrest alleged violators.[73] If he did not actually command the Ku Klux Klan, Bedford Forrest certainly acted like a commander. He exercised the same stern discipline he had formally demanded of his soldiers, punished violators in a similar fashion, and attempted to maintain the same element of control over their actions.

Under Forrest's control, the Ku Klux Klan became a major force of counterrevolution in Tennessee and the rest of the South. The former Confederate officer believed that the Klan was organized as a protective and defensive mechanism and saw in it the potential for political benefits. There can be no doubt that the organization became affiliated with the Democratic party and depended upon intimidation and terrorism to achieve its goals.[74] Foner described the Klan's purposes as "political, but political in the broadest sense, for it sought to affect power relations, both public and private, throughout Southern society." If successfully implemented, the Klan's agenda would be tragically significant, for it would "reverse the interlocking changes sweeping over the South during Reconstruction." To Foner, this would mean that white conservative Democrats had succeeded in their aims "to destroy the Republican party's infrastructure, undermine the Reconstruction state, reestablish control of the black labor force, and restore racial subordination in every aspect of Southern life."[75]

The "reign of terror in Tennessee," as one historian described it, did not begin immediately. In the August 1867 elections, white Southern Conservatives tried to persuade black voters that by voting Democratic they were acting in their own best interests. Although attempts to convince former slaves that their former masters held the key to those "best interests" uniformly failed, there is evidence that Forrest "made an earnest attempt to keep Klansmen in line" during this election.[76] Such attempts apparently included the formation, in Memphis, of "a body of volunteer police who co-operated with the city police department on election day" to prevent violence at the polls.[77] Ironically, Forrest feared the possibility of violence enough to communicate his concern to the local Union commander that "the Irish people" of the city might interfere with the black voters.[78] Since he had only recently assumed leadership of the Klan, these efforts might have been a combination of his desire to prepare more thoroughly before acting or for propaganda purposes, but Forrest more likely genuinely believed that he and other prominent white Southerners could exert their influence over black Southerners through persuasion.

Biographer J. Harvey Mathes noted that during the election of 1868, "the colored people gave a grand barbecue at the [Memphis] fair-grounds," which Forrest attended. Although both blacks and whites had "some mental reservations" and Forrest "struggled through the ordeal with painful difficulty," all made "overtures of peace and good-will," and Forrest made a "strong common-sense talk" and graciously accepted a bouquet of flowers. Mathes observed that some of the anxiety passed when "the white visitors were invited down to the barbecue, given a separate table and a great feast, which they enjoyed more than all the oratory of the day."[79]

Clearly, many white Southerners, including Bedford Forrest, hoped to persuade black Southerners to return to the status quo antebellum, in which they would perform labor much as they had when they were slaves. When such attempts at persuasion demonstrably failed, the Klan turned to more violent means to control the new voters. Historian Wyn Craig Wade maintained, "By spring 1868, the Klan was fully launched throughout Tennesee as a vigilante army."[80] Yet, Forrest walked a tightrope. He wanted to return the old prewar leadership to power and he desired blacks to resume their "proper place" in the social order, but he also wanted to avoid overt activities that might bring down upon white Southerners even greater wrath from the Federal officials he was attempting to appease. However, he was willing to sacrifice subtlety, a trait he possessed in no great quantity in any event, to obtain control.

If Forrest saw the Klan as the strongest line of defense for his concept of Southern society, he also remained under the influence of the precepts of Southern honor and the desire to "make a support." These influences undoubtedly motivated him when he offered, in his letter to President Johnson in 1866, to waive immunity with regard to the Fort Pillow incident. Forrest still firmly believed that he had done nothing that a Federal court could use against him, regardless of the testimony unearthed by the 1864 congressional investigation or the charges that Northern newspapers persisted in placing before their readers. Even if he were arrested and charged, Forrest assumed that he could rely upon his testimony to counter that of the prosecution and that his testimony would lead, inevitably, to an acquittal. In any case, he hoped that merely by opening himself to indictment, he could improve his image and proceed with his life.

Ironically, his search for financial independence led him to involve himself in Memphis's attempts to improve its image and its viability as a regional trading center and marketplace. The river city retained elements of its frontier origins, even in its streets, which were still largely unpaved and thus condemned the flow of commerce to the extremes of the weather. Muddy roads made for the inefficient movement of goods. In the hopes of improving these conditions, Memphis merchants and city officials attempted to finance street improvements and thereby facilitate the shipment of raw materials, particularly cotton, through the city and into the market economy.[81]

Forrest's connection to this Memphis enterprise began in the summer of 1867, when he joined the firm of Hopper & Montgomery, to whom the city had awarded paving contracts as the lowest bidder. In July, after some wrangling over details, the City Council approved a request to drop A. J. Hopper's name from the contracts, "substituting N. B. Forrest, F. G. McGavock and Joseph Mitchel[l] in his stead." Thus, the paving contracts now belonged to the firm Forrest, Montgomery & Co. These contracts covered improvements on a large number of the roads running through Memphis, financed by the city through the sale of paving bonds.[82]

Forrest immediately set out to fulfill his new company's obligations, and the work proceeded apace. In October, the general's firm reported to the City Council that it had completed "more than 1/3 of our contract;" accomplishing in "30 working days" a task the city had given it a year to complete. The firm thought it could finish the work "in ninety working days." It reported, "The work just completed by us has cost an outlay of $95,000 cash: for this work we have received from the Mayor $138,000 in paving bonds." If Forrest's company (now Forrest, Mitchell & Co.) could sell the bonds, it stood to collect a sizable profit—but that was the problem.

The general encountered considerable snags in trying to find buyers for these paving bonds. Despite his extensive travels in this regard, his efforts were hampered by the city's inability to pay the significant back interest it owed on other bonds. Potential buyers in Louisville, St. Louis, and New York shied away from buying the bonds. Consequently, the firm sent a letter to the council observing that "in consequence of the City having failed to pay the past July interest which when we offered bids for the payment we were assumed would be promptly met together with ... interest past due amounting in the aggregate since January 1867 to nearly $300,000," Forrest had found the city's credit "so depreciated that it was impossible to hypothecate the bonds at any such price as would enable us to proceed with the work of paving Main Street." Thus, the report concluded, "Until something is done by the city to relieve her credit it is impossible to raise the money required to carry on the work."

Despite his dismal forecast, Forrest offered the City Council one possible solution. The "present low and comparatively worthless condition" of the paving bonds would not pay for the work, but if propertyholders along the streets paid cash in sums ranging from $3.89 to $3.95 per square yard for paving, and $1.60 for curbing, sufficient capital might become available to complete the project. Of course, under this arrangement, the city would continue to pay for its share of the work, such as the paving of intersections, with bonds, although it would allow the use of city engineers at no cost. The council already had such an arrangement with another paving company that was doing similar work. Again after some maneuvering, the Memphis City Council agreed to these terms, but the relief came too late. On October 15, Forrest, Mitchell & Co. submitted a request, which the council approved: "Having made arrangements with Taylor McBean & Baldwin to complete the work of paving the streets unfinished under our contract with the city we ask that your Board will substitute them for us both in the remaining original and modified contracts."[83]

Bedford Forrest lost no time finding and attaching himself to a new enterprise. He later explained, apparently forgetting his brief and unsuccessful experience with paving: "In 1867 I was in the insurance business, as president of a fire-insurance company, and I organized a life-insurance company. My business was principally in Tennessee and Alabama, but my health became so bad that I could not travel, and remained at home."[84] However, throughout the summer of 1868, Forrest's health was such that he could still leave Memphis, for he traveled extensively in connection with his insurance work. Several scholars have speculated that he did more than just discuss insurance on these trips. Wyn Craig Wade, Allen Trelease, and Stanley Horn all noted that soon after the general appeared in Atlanta, ostensibly to discuss insurance with former Confederate general and future Grand Dragon John B. Gordon, the first Klan notices appeared in local newspapers.[85] Certainly, Forrest could have been in the city exclusively on business, and meetings with former Confederate generals were hardly unusual (nor would such meetings require ulterior motives to take place). However, limited evidence indicates that there indeed was more going on than insurance at such times.

Huntsville attorney William M. Lowe, a former Confederate colonel, observed that when Forrest came to northern Alabama in early 1868, they met to discuss insurance. But once the men concluded this business, their conversation turned to the Klan, although Lowe expressed no interest in it.[86] Furthermore, as Trelease pointed out, "The easiest means of spreading the organization, and doubtless the most obvious to Forrest and other military men, was to confer personally with Confederate officers in the several states." These would be the most trustworthy men, and Lowe to the contrary, likely the most receptive to the Klan's message. These men had the necessary experience to help organize and run "a secret semimilitary society for the purpose of protecting Southern white society against the impending horrors of Radical Reconstruction."[87] Besides, Forrest enjoyed every opportunity to renew his wartime connections.

But even this new effort gave little immediate promise of better days for Southerners in general. In November 1867, Forrest wrote a former Confederate officer in his capacity as president of the Planters' Insurance Company, "I have no busines nor do I no of any by which you culd find Employment in this City at any price[.]" Then on an even more depressing note, he observed that he was "Setling up" his "affairs as rapidly as posable Beliving as I do that Eny thing under the laws that wil be Enaugerated by the milatary authoritys wil result in ruin to our people." Even so, the general had connections to two insurance companies and thought that something might be arranged. "probuly I culd make you an agent for the two companys," he speculated, "provided it wuld Suite you[.] we wil want agents that wil canvas the country and one that can Explain the Life polacys Satisfactury[.]"[88]

If Bedford Forrest sounded a negative note in his letter to the former colonel, it was because of the bleak aspect that surrounded his personal affairs and the affairs of his region. He was continuing to struggle with his finances, and it was a struggle he was rapidly losing. He also had little reason to hope that affairs would return to "normal" for the white South. Congress had spent a busy session overriding President Johnson's vetoes of the Reconstruction legislation. Congress divided the South into military districts. Long the scene of confrontation between the executive and legislative branches of the national government, the Washington stage was set for the impeachment of the president, an event that Forrest could not have looked upon with any satisfaction.

Forrest saw one glimmer of light in the midst of the seemingly endless barrage of failures he was enduring. This was a study of his military career and campaigns, together with a sketch of his early life, undertaken by two former Confederate officers, Thomas Jordan and John P. Pryor. As seen by his earlier letter to Charles Clark, governor of Mississippi, Forrest cooperated closely with the authors on the project. He not only encouraged his former commanders to participate, but gave the authors access to his papers and records and granted oral interviews. On October 3, 1867, he wrote an endorsement that the authors included in their preface when the book was published the next year. In this letter, Forrest called the work "an authentic account" of his wartime operations and stated his responsibility for "the greater part of the statements of the narrative."[89] Eight years later, in June 1875, the former general offered to send a gentleman a copy of the "history of my campains written by Thos Jourdan and supervised by myself, which I know to be true and correct with one exception." That exception, Forrest wrote with an element of vanity, was his acceptance of "the statement of the Federal authorities as to the number of men I had in the differant engagements, which often exceeded the number I really had."[90]

Forrest was at a point in his life in which he needed some reinforcement. Jordan and Pryor's study gave it to him by reminding him of the exploits of his early years and the glories of the recent war. For the moment, Forrest was a general again, leading valiant men in a desperate struggle against overwhelming odds. It was no coincidence that in later describing the membership of the Ku Klux Klan, Forrest observed that they were "worthy men who belonged to the southern army; the others were not to be trusted; they would not fight when the war was on them, and of course they would not do anything when it was over."[91] In this light, the account of Forrest's "rescue" of John Able in 1857 constitutes one of the most illustrative and symbolic aspects of Jordan and Pryor's biography. The authors gave no sources for their version of this feat, and thus, according to his statement, Forrest must have related it to them orally. As such, the story carries with it a clear indication of the general's state of mind during this period.

John Able was a gambler who lived in Memphis and killed another man during an argument (see chapter 2). Able's father had gone unpunished for a similiar crime earlier, and a mob gathered to prevent any further miscarriage of justice. Forrest thwarted the mob of vigilantes with a speech. But on the next night, the mob's thirst for vengeance arose once more, and this time, no speech would stop them. They promptly marched to the jail, dragged Able from his cell, and took him to the navy yard to hang him. Barely had the citizens finished their preparations when Forrest burst forth, pulled out a knife, and cut the rope. Having saved Able from the angry lynch mob, Forrest took him back to the jail. Once more the crowd gathered, calling for the prisoner and threatening to storm the place. Suddenly, Forrest appeared in front of them, brandishing a pistol and promising to shoot anyone who tried. The intrepid leader had taken "fully three thousand excited men, as it were, by the throats" and rescued young Able.[92]

According to one scholar, "the actual facts, as reported in the Memphis newspapers at the time, make an equally dramatic story, but, rather than making Forrest a hero, they barely mention him at all."[93] Apparently, Forrest had embellished the story of his "rescue" of John Able. In reality, he had been, at best, only a peripheral player in the drama. Why, then, did he relate these events to his biographers in such a fashion as to magnify his role from participant to central character and hero? Or did the authors practice the deception, as one historian suggested, to make the former slave trader look better (more heroic)?[94] Of course, there are other possibilities as well, but the evidence suggests that Forrest "remembered" playing a more significant role in the affair than he had actually played. Having met with such limited success in the postwar period, he hearkened back to an earlier, more glamorous time in his life. Now, he felt it necessary, even essential, to be the most heroic figure. He should have rescued John Able. And, in time, he did.

However, if Bedford Forrest could not really defend a gambler from a lynch mob in prewar Memphis, perhaps he could do much more. Thus, the former Confederate decided, not only to continue his association with the Klan, but to take a more active role in the political affairs of his state, region, and nation. One friend and associate, former Confederate general Basil Duke, later observed of Forrest, "After a fashion, he took much interest in politics, which was, I believe, purely impersonal.... His sole concern seemed to be to relieve his people from the terrible and oppressive conditions under which they so grievously suffered, and he went about that work with the same ardour and indifference to any personal hazard which characterized him in his military service."[95] But even as Forrest contemplated the role he would play in political affairs, he continued to face more personal battles in Tennessee.

The new year of 1868 brought Forrest no financial relief. By

February, the general filed for bankruptcy in the United States District Court in Memphis.[96] Forrest understandably became depressed. Again his mind shifted to happier times. If the publication of Jordan and Pryor's biography was not sufficient, perhaps he could return to the battlefield and thereby regain control of his life. Perhaps with that idea in mind, during a Sunday afternoon conversation in February, just after he declared bankruptcy, the general told two former Confederates, Norman Farrell and Thomas B. Smith, of a filibustering adventure he had been contemplating. Farrell recounted the conversation to his fiancée:

> He told us of a scheme of his for conquering Mexico, asked Tom if he could raise a regiment, and wanted to know if I would go with him.... Forrest said that he had been promised 20,000 muskets and that he would want 30,000 men, he could conquer the country in six months; that he would then confiscate the mines and the church property; that is about 1/3 of all the real estate of the country; hold possession of each state, as he advanced, by leaving four or five thousand men in each; take possession of all the offices for himself and his men, among which, of course [Farrell speculated], N.B. would get the lion's share with the title of King or President; while the private got his in bullets; and then he concluded: "I would open up the country to immigration, after I had given it a free government, and would get at least 200,000 people from the southern states, besides many from Europe and the north."

Finally, sounding incredibly like William Tecumseh Sherman, Forrest described where he expected to find the bulk of his conquering army. "He said that there are at least 50,000 young men in the south who won't plow, but who would fight or dig for gold. I asked him if he did not think the United States would interfere with his little arrangement, but he said they would be glad to get rid of him."[97]

Whether Forrest actually pursued the scheme beyond talk is unknown. But if he dismissed forcibly entering Mexican politics, he was ready to participate in the American political arena. He went to New York in July as a delegate to the Democratic National Convention. He later revealed that he had considered active political involvement imprudent while he awaited a pardon from the president. However, he observed, "My friends thought differently and sent me to New York, and I am glad that I went there."[98]

In May 1868, the *New York Times* reprinted a letter from Forrest in which the former Confederate observed, "Upon consultation with many of my late associates in the war, I have concluded to advise against any further emasculation of ourselves in the [Democratic] party movements of the State [of Tennessee]." The comment was in response to reports that some wished for the "late Confederate soldiers" to decline to attend the June 9 state convention at Nashville and the July national convention in New York in apparent hopes of making the Democratic party more attractive to Northern voters. Forrest thought that Southern veterans were "already sufficiently proscribed" by the "mendacious hostility of our legislative enemies" to the point that "until now we barely live under the accumulated weight of disfranchisement and oppression." Rather than dishonestly admit "ourselves unworthy to soil the deliberations of that Convention with our presence," he argued that former Confederates should fully participate in the process, since the "only hope of a restoration of a good government in this country is the success of the National Democracy." Considering the nature of the letter, Forrest closed rather disingenuously: "So far as I am personally concerned, I have no desire to take any part in politics, nor to occupy any political position whatever; but I do not wish to see my State represented by men whose only claim to public favor is the dexterity with which they took either side of the question in the late war, as interest dictated, and who bank upon it as their only capital for popular support."[99] This was a specious argument, for if Bedford Forrest rejected public office for himself, he clearly wanted people in office who supported his social and political views—white, conservative Democrats.

Having chosen to participate, delegate Forrest attracted considerable attention, both on the journey to New York and upon his arrival in the city. Along the way, the train approached a station where a crowd had gathered. From all indications, the scene promised trouble, and the conductor hastened to the passenger car to ask Basil Duke to advise his friend to remain on the train. According to Duke, Forrest accepted the warning without emotion. However, when the train reached the depot, the ringleader of the mob got aboard and pushed his way into the coach yelling, "Where's that damned butcher, Forrest? I want him." Forrest sprang from his seat, "his face the colour of heated bronze," and confronted him. "I am Forrest. What do you want?" The would-be assailant weighed his prospects and promptly vanished from the car. Duke remembered that "the humour of the thing struck Forrest and he burst into a great shout of laughter." Afterwards, the former Confederate cavalryman gave a brief speech and the train continued on its way.[100]

Forrest reached New York without further incident. He declined to tell one correspondent who he would support at the national party convention, saying, "We don't want to dictate to the party." Then after observing, "What we do want is the best man," he quickly added, "It aint because we hate GRANT that we are anxious to beat his ticket. It's because the Radicals won't give us a chance if they keep in power. Look at Tennessee. That's radicalism, and that's why I'm a Democrat."[101] At the convention, Forrest initially supported Andrew Johnson as the Democratic nominee, lobbying other Southerners to vote for the president, before eventually switching to the ticket of Horatio Seymour and Frank Blair. Apparently, Johnson took the vote seriously, for Forrest later asserted, "I have a letter in my pocket from Washington" containing news that the president was angry because "we of the South, who were delegates to the Convention, did not press his nomination." But, the general insisted, "I did press it and used all my influence with the Southern delegates ... and procured him fifty votes." Although Forrest's effort had failed to win the nomination for Johnson, it may have helped his own case. On July 17, 1868, Forrest finally received a pardon from the president, "for which," he told an audience, "I am truly thankful."[102]

But the pardon was not yet a reality when the former Confederate attended the convention, and given his notoriety, it is not surprising that New Yorkers exhibited "a very lively curiosity" to see him.[103] Forrest became the subject of numerous editorials and cartoons. He later observed, "there were a great many things said in regard to myself that I looked upon as gotten up merely to affect the elections in the North."[104] Ironically, the name and influence of Nathan Bedford Forrest became important factors for both the Democratic and Republican parties and their respective propaganda. One correspondent thought that any speech Forrest made while he was in New York would "serve as an excellent Democratic campaign document."[105]

However, Forrest's increased political involvement nearly resulted in a duel with Judson Kilpatrick. Now stumping for the Republican party, the fiery former Union general chose to direct his sharpest barbs at Forrest. For a time, the former Confederate chose to ignore Kilpatrick's comments, but eventually they became too excessive. In a blistering letter addressed to a third party who had written him about Kilpatrick's characterizations, Forrest slammed his attacker, employing such phrases as: "false and mendacious representations of me," "his criminal capacity for ribald invention," "his unprincipled and indecent libels," and so forth. He concluded by denouncing Kilpatrick as "a blackguard, a liar, a scoundrel and poltroon," and issued a thinly veiled challenge to him for a duel between them.[106]

Much to his surprise, Duke read the letter and learned that Forrest had named him "his friend in this affair" and offered him as the man to whom Kilpatrick should communicate. "I sympathized of course with Forrest," he wrote later, "but was somewhat amused at the indignation he expressed, for I supposed that he had become so much accustomed to such attacks as to regard them with indifference." Forrest wrote Duke belatedly, telling him that he might hear from Kilpatrick and expressing a preference to fight the duel with sabers on horseback, an appropriate choice for two ex-cavalrymen. Duke had to tread lightly in the matter because of laws against dueling, but selected "a suitable mount" and carried out the other arrangements as well as he could. However, Kilpatrick soon declared that he could not accept Forrest's challenge because he did not "regard him as a gentleman."[107]

Forrest returned from New York to find affairs in Tennessee in greater turmoil than before. Governor Brownlow threatened to organize the militia, fill its ranks largely with eastern Tennessee Unionists, and unleash the troops upon the Klansmen and other unregenerate conservatives. Forrest and his allies took the news seriously, and on August 1, 1868, they met in Nashville to determine their course. Dubbed the "Council of Peace," he and sixteen other former Confederate generals attended, hoping to preempt Brownlow's "militia bill." Forrest spoke briefly and was among those who signed the memorial pledging "to maintain the order and peace of the state with whatever of influence we possess, to uphold and support the laws."[108] The rhetoric was conciliatory, but neither side trusted the other, with good reason, and Forrest toured the middle and western parts of the state warning his friends and followers to prepare themselves for the worst.

At a subsequent meeting in Memphis, Forrest, after being "called for and cheered most enthusiastically," reportedly told the gathering that "he wanted peace," but if Brownlow carried through with his threat, he would call out "his old comrades." The newspaper article continued, "He knew that his old troops would answer as they had always done. He bade them arm themselves and be ready."[109] This may have been the instance in which a Memphis Klansman heard Forrest tell one den, "Brownlow says he will bring his militia down here and get us. I say, let him fetch 'em, and you boys be ready to receive 'em."[110]

Then, later at Brownsville, Tennessee, Forrest complained that he was "suffering from a sour throat" brought on by a "severe cold," but promised to "say a few words." However, his "few words" carried a powerful message. Forrest told the audience about the meeting at Nashville and the fears of violence, adding that the governor had called Klansmen outlaws:

> I believe that Gov. BROWNLOW thinks all Confederate soldiers, and, in fact, the whole Democratic Party in the South, belong to the Kuklux Klan. [Cheers and laughter.] All are declared outlaws, for the Governor says he has no doubt they belong to the Klan, if there is such a clan. The Legislature has passed some laws, I believe, on the subject, in which the militia are called on to shoot all Kukluxes they may find, and they need fear no prosecution for doing so. That is, simply, that they may call a Confederate soldier a Kuklux, shoot him down, and no harm shall befall any of the militia who shall commit such an outrageous act.... When this is done, I tell you, fellow-citizens, there will be civil war.... I can assure you, fellow-citizens, that I, for one, do not want any more war. I have seen it in all its phases, and believe

> me when I say so, that I don't want to see any more bloodshed, nor do I want to see any negroes armed to shoot down white men. If they bring this war upon us, there is one thing I will tell you—that I *shall not shoot any negroes so long as I can see a white Radical to shoot,* for it is the Radicals who will be to blame for bringing on this war.

Forrest reminded the audience that he did not want war and asked them first to "exhaust all honorable means before you do anything." He then added: "We have already lost all but our honor by the last war, and I must say, that in order to be men we must protect our honor at all hazards, and we must also protect our wives, our homes and our families." He continued to pound the theme of preparedness, calling upon white Southerners to unite. "We must be a unit on this grave question," he insisted. "The militia will be a unit, and we must be in the same position." As part of this push for unity and without any sense of the irony of what he was saying, Forrest called upon "the black men who are here before me ... to stand by the men who raised you, who nursed you when you were sick, and who took care of you when you were little children. I say, stand by them who are your real friends, and leave the Loyal Leagues, where you are taught to refuse the franchise to those who have always proved your friends."[111]

Of course, Forrest did not propose to shoot white Radical Republicans simply because they were not white conservative Democrats. His was not a "loyal" opposition. These "Radicals" represented the clearest threat since the Civil War to all he held dear. They proposed equality for former slaves; he did not. They advocated black suffrage; he found the idea preposterous, unless he could dictate the blacks' votes. They threatened the social and political fabric based upon white supremacy, segregation, and black disfranchisement that he supported.

Forrest sounded similar themes in a much more widely read interview with a reporter from the Cincinnati *Commercial.* Perhaps he wanted to capitalize upon the interest he had generated to explain his views on conditions in the South to Northern readers. In any event, he met with the correspondent at his office in Memphis. Later, he would argue that he had been ill throughout the course of the interview and thus could not have possibly said everything that was attributed to him. But the complaint has a distinctly hollow ring to it.[112]

Forrest began by emphasizing that he had honored his parole. "I have counselled peace," he explained, "in all the speeches I have made; I have advised my people to submit to the laws of the State, oppressive as they are, and unconstitutional as I believe them to be." He added that he had determined not "to take any active part until the oppressions of my people became so great that they could not endure it, and then I would be with them." Forrest noted that although the oppression was "growing worse hourly," still, he countenanced quiet submission until such time as the wrongs being perpetrated "might be righted peacefully." Furthermore, he felt no hatred toward the Federal government. Rather, he reserved his hostility for "the radical revolutionists who are trying to destroy it." For Forrest, the Republican party, particularly the branch of it in Tennessee, was the prime culprit for the South's woes. It was composed of "the worst men on God's earth—men who would hesitate at no crime."

Finally, the reporter came to the heart of his readers' interest. Would Forrest openly oppose Governor Brownlow if the latter called out the militia? The general hedged only briefly. If the militia interfered with no one, there would be no fight. But, Forrest declared, obviously warming to the subject, "If, on the contrary, they do what I believe they will do, commit outrages or even one outrage, upon the people, they and Mr. Brownlow's government will be swept out of existence; not a radical will be left alive. If the militia are called out," Forrest observed, "we cannot but look upon it as a declaration of war."[113]

The Ku Klux Klan was the object of Governor Brownlow's scorn and the reason he might feel compelled to call out the militia. It was also, by Forrest's definition, the instrument of defense for the Southern people. Forrest set the number of Klansmen in Tennessee at approximately 40,000 and the number throughout the South at 550,000. He described the Klan as "a protective political military organization" whose original purpose was "protection against Loyal Leagues and the Grand Army of the Republic." He noted that "after it became general it was found that political matters and interests could best be promoted within it, and it was then made a political organization, giving its support, of course, to the democratic party."[114]

Forrest made clear the fate Republicans would suffer if the Tennessee government attempted to take on the Klan. "I have no powder to burn killing negroes. I intend to kill the radicals.... I have told them that they are trying to create a disturbance and then slip out and leave the consequences to fall upon the negroes, but they can't do it." For Forrest, the real threat to the South emanated from the Republicans. The freedmen were simply dupes. Eliminate, or at the least neutralize, the radicals, and the freedmen would understand who were their true friends. As Forrest summarized, "I am not an enemy of the negro.... We want him here among us; he is the only laboring class we have, and more than that, I would sooner trust him than the white scalawag or carpetbagger."[115] Forrest thought that violent reactions to "insolence" among blacks were so banal as to be almost routine. However, violence toward the radicals took on a special significance. To Bedford, it was not a moral question of rights and wrongs; it was a matter of survival.

Clearly, Forrest had abandoned the attitude that prompted him to label as a lunatic any person who desired to continue fighting the war. He had done so because he wanted people like himself—white conservative Democrats—to regain power in the region and to restore peace and order in a South he could recognize. He did not want bloodshed for its own sake, but he was prepared to accept it as a necessary means to a desirable end. "But I want it distinctly understood," Forrest emphatically told the reporter who interviewed him, "that I am opposed to any war, and will fight only in self-defense. If the militia attack us, we will resist to the last, and, if necessary, I think I could raise 40,000 men in five days, ready for the field." Ironically, Forrest had attributed 40,000 Klan members to the state of Tennessee, the state over which he exercised the most control as Klan leader. And although he subsequently denied actually knowing that 40,000 such Klansmen existed in the state, he corrected the record by observing that even if there were, he could raise no such numbers in so short a time. Of course, during the war, General Forrest had displayed a phenomenal ability to raise troops in areas that both armies had already swept thoroughly. Obviously, he was prepared to obtain his goals by force, if necessary.

In testimony before a congressional committee that was investigating Klan activities in the South, Forrest compared the Klan to the Loyal Leagues and suggested that the former had originated as "a sort of offset" to the latter. He detailed the anxiety of white Southerners who feared a recurrence of the racial violence of Santo Domingo in the American South. Furthermore, this insecurity was prompted by a "great many northern men coming down there, forming Leagues all over the country." These outside agitators threatened the peace and stability of the South. Under their influence, freedmen "were holding night meetings; were going about; were becoming very insolent; and the southern people all over the State were very much alarmed." According to Forrest, blacks had "remained at home working and were quiet, and were not organized" during the war. Emancipation had changed them, and not, in Forrest's opinion, for the better. "When the war was over our servants began to mix with the republicans, and they broke off from the Southern people, and were sulky and insolent. There was a general fear throughout the country that there would be an uprising."[116]

The psychological trauma of war, defeat, and Reconstruction that the returning veterans suffered added to the tension. Survivors of the conflict attempted to redefine their world in familiar terms. They wanted to reestablish what they saw as a distinct way of life. Conversely, the victorious North expected to impose its own free-labor ideology upon the South to make the aberrant South into its own image. White Southerners balked. Black Southerners refused to submit quietly to the restoration of slavery in all but its name.[117]

Forrest suffered one final personal blow in the summer of 1868, when his mother died from blood poisoning. Following the war, she emigrated to Texas with the children from her second marriage. One of her sons became ill, which required her to travel to his bedside. As she climbed out of the buggy, she stepped on a nail, the wound became infected, and she lapsed into delirium. As she lay dying, Mariam Beck Forrest Luxton called repeatedly for her favorite and eldest son, Bedford.[118]

The death of his mother must have struck Forrest heavily, for by all accounts, he was extremely devoted to her. From his father's death, he had long assumed the role of defender and protector. During this period, Forrest suffered through an extended period of severe trials and personal struggles. Throughout he fought to defend all he held dear. He wrestled with the problems of business and finance. He publicly counseled peace and submission to Federal authority, while he privately determined to wage war against what he saw as the excesses of Brownlowism and radicalism. Forrest could neither understand nor appreciate the concerns of the former slaves, and he did not try to do so. He believed that the interests of the freedmen were best reflected in his own interests. Forrest would be willing to bestow citizenship upon the freedmen, but it would have to be the second-class citizenship of a "laboring class." He wanted a stable and docile labor force and eventually turned to Chinese laborers and Tennessee convicts in his search for one.[119]

Nathan Bedford Forrest fought to return rule in the South to the "proper" hands. An intimidating personality, he was willing to go to great lengths and to employ violence when he believed it was necessary to reconstruct a new South out of familiar building materials. But the element of control was essential to him, and the same growth that signified the success of the Ku Klux Klan also contained within it the seeds of the secret order's destruction, if Bedford Forrest, as Grand Wizard, ever reached the point that he no longer believed he could control it.

CHAPTER 16

Completely Used Up

(1869–October 29, 1877)

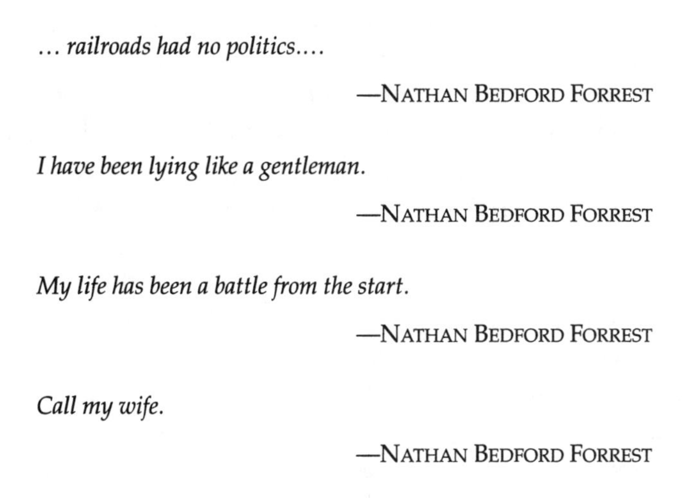

... railroads had no politics....

—NATHAN BEDFORD FORREST

I have been lying like a gentleman.

—NATHAN BEDFORD FORREST

My life has been a battle from the start.

—NATHAN BEDFORD FORREST

Call my wife.

—NATHAN BEDFORD FORREST

RAILROADS WERE POTENT SYMBOLS for mid-nineteenth century America. One scholar observed that "in the popular culture of the period the railroad was a favorite emblem of progress—not merely technological progress, but the overall progress of the race."[1] "Iron horses" belching smoke and spewing steam as churning wheels pushed people and produce faster and farther seemed to embody this concept of progress. During the war, victory for the Union "rode the rails," while for the Confederacy it sat on the sidings of the dilapidated rails of mixed-gauge lines.[2] William A. Williams noted that just as "railroads played an increasing role in northern logistics and troop movements, they also announced the coming of a new order. They extended and integrated the market place and so made it possible to specialize and consequently accelerate other economic activities."[3]

Thus, in the post–Civil War period, railroads represented the power and progress of a growing nation, mending itself from the severe wounds of civil war. As James M. McPherson observed of the South, "Democrats and Republicans alike recognized the crucial role of improved transportation for regional economic growth."[4] Undoubtedly owing in large part to this rare bipartisan interest, the South, in Gavin Wright's estimation, "shared fully in the national railroad building boom of 1865–75." Wright added that this phenomenon opened "previously isolated counties and towns" in the South, sponsored, not by outside interests, but by stocks in the hands of Southern individuals and municipalities.[5] And so railroad tracks increasingly tied the raw material-producing outer regions—the South and West—to the industrial might of the North.

Railroads interested Bedford Forrest. During the war, his cavalry had been effective in demolishing rail lines and rolling stock. Now, he liked to say, he planned to reverse that wartime trend and build them back up. He took one of the first steps in early 1868, when he bought a controlling interest in the Cahaba, Marion and Memphis Railroad. By the end of the year, the name of that road changed to the Selma, Marion and Memphis Railroad, and Nathan Bedford Forrest was its president.[6]

For the next five years of his life, Forrest devoted himself and his energies to this railroad. In the same personal style in which he had struggled to pull his family up from frontier semisubsistence and with which he fought the war, Forrest supervised nearly every aspect of the construction, maintenance, and daily operation of this rail line. To be sure, he acted primarily as the front man, with directors, engineers, and construction crews providing most of the technical knowledge and detailed work, but the former Confederate retained an interest and enthusiasm for his work that a born "railroad man" would have been hard pressed to match. Proud of the title of president, he often scribbled the letters "pres" or "prest" under his signature on official correspondence, even when a secretary wrote the body of the letter, just as he had written his rank under his name while in the army.[7]

In his capacity as president, Forrest attended subscription meetings, addressed audiences and crowds, lobbied civic leaders and politicians for money and favorable legislation, promoted the railroad in letters and newspaper interviews, worked strenuously to obtain laborers for the construction crews, and involved himself in virtually every phase of the work on the line. He later observed, without a great deal of exaggeration, that since going "into this railroad business ... my whole time has been occupied in that."[8]

Forrest unquestionably devoted himself to the railroad, with a strong business sense that had the best interests of the enterprise at heart. But he conducted his railroad business as he had his slave-trading interests and his military career—in his own headstrong, independent way. For instance, when he contacted a former army associate, Edmund W. Rucker, on September 18, 1869, to serve "as Supt of my Road," he sent the "comision or appoint ment" in his own handwriting and through a special courier and advised Rucker to "say nothing a bout your appointment to any one until I return[.]" Forrest specifically instructed his new superintendent "to take hold of things and push a hed as per [the] undistanding betwen us this morning[.]" Finally, in a note that sounded similar to the orders he might have given Rucker in wartime, Forrest ordered him to "make out the proper certificate for the completion of the Road and Send by Express to me at Chatanoga So as to reach me by the morning of 25 if my wife cums Send by hir[.]"[9]

While he was occupied with his railroad, Forrest received an unexpected boon from his old nemesis, "Parson" Brownlow, when the latter resigned as governor of Tennessee to become a United States senator. DeWitt Senter replaced him in February 1869, and quickly demonstrated a willingness to appease the Democrats in the state.[10] This conciliatory attitude surely pleased Forrest and undoubtedly hastened his decision to finish the task he had begun in January when he, as Grand Wizard, issued orders for Klan members to destroy their regalia and curtail their activities.

"General Order Number One," dated "Dismal Era, Fourth Green Day, Last Hour, C.A.R.N." (January, fourth Monday, 12 o'clock, 1869, or January 25), began with a statement detailing the reasons for the order and concluded with general instructions for implementing it and the threat of punishment for those who failed or refused to heed it.[11]

> WHEREAS, The Order of the K.K.K. is in some localities being perverted from its original honorable and patriotic purposes;
>
> AND WHEREAS, Such a perversion of the Order is in some instances defeating the very objects of its origin, and is becoming injurious instead of subservient to the public peace and public safety for which it was intended, and in some cases is being used to achieve personal benefit and private purposes, and to satiate private revenge by means of its masked features ...
>
> It is therefore ordered and decreed, that the masks and costumes of this Order be entirely abolished and destroyed. And every Grand Cyclops shall assemble the men of his Den and require them to destroy in his presence every article of his mask and costume and at the same time shall destroy his own. And every man who shall refuse to do so shall be deemed an enemy of this Order, and shall be treated accordingly. And every man who shall hereafter be seen in mask or costume, shall not be known or recognized as a member of this Order, but shall be deemed an enemy of the same.[12]

"General Order Number One" also included instructions for Klansmen to moderate some of their more unsavory excesses, such as conducting whippings, breaking into jails, or sending threatening letters under the auspices of the Ku Klux Klan.[13]

This order was unmistakably clear, but it affected only those dens or individuals who felt obliged to obey the dictates of the formal chain of command within the organization. Almost anyone who wished to ignore the order could do so with impunity. As one scholar explained, the order "merely dissociated Imperial Headquarters from responsibility for the behavior of rank-and-file Klansmen, which was probably all that Forrest hoped it would do."[14] Although frequently labeled a disbandment order, "General Order Number One" acknowledged the continued existence of the organization, ostensibly to watch over the implementation of the order and to punish its violators.[15]

Forrest reached this decision because he finally realized that as the Klan spread, he exercised less and less control over its disparate activities. Despite his selection of only the "best men" (that is, former Confederate officers and army associates) for positions of leadership, despite the speeches and addresses, despite the plethora of letters he daily received and sent, he had no real means to exert his authority as Grand Wizard over all areas where the Klan existed and over all people who claimed to be members. Historian Wyn C. Wade was largely correct in his assertion: "When Grand Wizard Forrest realized that his so-called 'honorable and patriotic' organization had become a sprawling, intractable monster, he too wanted no further part of it."[16] But Forrest issued the order less because the Ku Klux Klan had turned into a monster than because it was a monster that he no longer believed he could restrain or regulate as he saw fit.

However, at the same time that Forrest lost control of the Klan, exercising the last element of influence in ordering the membership to curtail their more blatant activities and destroy their regalia, he turned increasingly to his railroad activities. He still needed workmen, and in an interview with the Louisville *Courier-Journal*, he displayed a remarkable nonchalance about who they should be and from where they should come. As they passed through land left vacant since the war, the reporter asked Forrest "how it could ever be populated?" The general immediately responded, "With negroes. They are the best laborers we have ever had in the South."[17] Others like Forrest certainly shared this view. One of these men, a former subordinate of Forrest, James R. Chalmers, later used his military experience to disperse a large gathering of armed blacks in Coahoma County, Mississippi, during the "riot of 1875." As the former slaves fled, the man who had once helped Forrest take Fort Pillow yelled at his exuberant followers, "Don't shoot the negroes boys, we need cotton pickers."[18]

Forrest used the opportunity of the interview to reiterate his "kindly" feelings toward the freedmen. Without challenging the general's veracity, the reporter asked him how he would repopulate the land in this manner. "Get them from Africa," Forrest explained, detailing an elaborate scheme whereby prisoners taken in tribal wars would be "turned over to us, and emigrate and be freedmen here." Observing that Africans "are the most imitative creatures in the world," he suggested, "if you put them in squads of ten, with one experienced leader in each squad, they will soon revive our country." Since others—Northern men and Europeans—would not come, "then I say, let's get Africans." Forrest ironically concluded, "When prejudice gets over our Government will foster this scheme; there is no need of a war of races."[19] The irony is that in the wake of such racist expressions, Forrest probably meant the prejudice of the Republican "government" against white Southern Democrats.

In the summer of 1869, Forrest had in mind more than just a scheme to bring Africans to the American South. He also advocated using Chinese "coolies" as laborers. Memphis held a "Chinese Labor Convention" in July, at which leading Southern civic and business leaders debated the propriety of bringing large numbers of Chinese workers into the region. Forrest supported the proposal wholeheartedly, offering to "subscribe" $5,000 toward the effort "in the name of the Selma, Marion and Memphis Railroad, and [saying] that he would receive and employ one thousand Chinese, and pay them cash." In support of the idea, he produced a letter to him from Walter Gibson, formerly of South Carolina, who offered his services as agent for obtaining Chinese and Japanese laborers. Gibson listed the advantages of such workers, saying that he knew "how important a judicious Chinese immigration would be in the development and the restoration of the South." After citing the costs, he added, "You can work fabulous results with Chinese immigration. The mighty reservoir of labor is ready to flow into your rich lands."

Once the letter had been read, Forrest professed that "his object in producing this letter and having it brought before the Convention was to show the propriety of getting labor in China, the cost, etc." During the apparently lively debate, Forrest reportedly asserted to one speaker "that the people had come together there to get labor and not to talk politics, not to bring up the war, and to abuse and run down the negro." In his usual vein, the general protested that he "had seen a good deal of the war" and reminded everyone that he "had taken a very prominent part in it, and [that] he, for one, hoped that in future politics would be left alone, and to hear no more of it." When the speaker continued his discourse, observing that "the negroes and Chinese would be in emnity," Forrest interrupted to say that when he "announced that he intended to use Chinese labor in building his road" during a speech in Alabama, "he got $1,500 in subscriptions from negroes, at the meeting; and this morning he had received a letter from there announcing that there had been stock subscribed by the county, by a vote of sixty to one, and that by the negro vote."[20] Clearly, Bedford Forrest was doing all he could to persuade the convention attendees to support the idea of a Chinese labor force.

As part of this effort, Forrest was fond of observing "that railroads had no politics; that I wanted the assistance of everybody; that railroads were for the general good of the whole country."[21] And aside from attempting to procure laborers, for which the Memphis convention would subsequently prove to be a dismal disappointment, Forrest also spent most of the summer traveling throughout the counties over which his railroad would run, drumming up subscriptions. In June, the town of Greensboro, Alabama, voted 166 to 1 in favor of a $15,000 subscription. Then in July, Hale County, Alabama, voted 2,260 to 301 for a $60,000 subscription. By the second week in September, the railroad was completed just over two miles west of the town of Marion. Near the end of the year, one of the directors reported that 150 hands were now at work on the line.[22] It seemed that all was going well for Bedford Forrest and his railroad.

Then, on January 3, 1870, Forrest ran into some trouble with the probate judge of Hale County, William T. Blackford. Although the voters of the county had authorized the issuance of bonds for the railroad, Judge Blackford refused to sign them. The scene in the subsequent hearing was a mixture of farce and near-tragedy as Forrest's lawyer and the judge traded barbs, with the attorney rushing at the judge and the judge pulling a pistol on the attorney. Forrest had not become involved until that minute, when he sprang from his chair, grabbed the weapon from the judge, and scolded him. "Wal, Judge," he began, "I don't care a damn whether you sign them bonds nunc pro tunc, nolens volens or americus curi; you are going to sign 'em." Then, after a few private words in the judge's chambers, Blackford emerged to comply with Forrest's "request."[23]

This was not the last time that the former Confederate would have to deal with the Republican judge, although the circumstances of their next meeting would be different. Local Democrats had targeted Blackford for some time. But the judge wisely cultivated some of the more prominent Democrats, ironically including Forrest, while retaining his Republican connections. In fact, Blackford even assisted Forrest with some of his local subscription drives. The general later observed, "I had had a great deal to do with him; he and I had canvassed two counties together."[24]

Despite Forrest's friendship, local Klansmen continued to target the Republican judge for special attention. In early 1871, Blackford barely escaped when sixty or seventy masked riders surrounded his house. Warned of their approach in time to hide in the woods, the judge sought out Forrest, who had recently arrived at the county seat, Greensboro, on railroad business.[25] The former Confederate later explained that on this occasion "Judge Blackford came to me for protection, and I did protect him for a week." While protecting him, the general warned him not to tamper with the Klansmen and advised him to leave. The guardian noted that he protected the judge "until he went away; finally he left the country." Forrest described him as "a man who had given bad advice to the negroes, and kept them in confusion, and off the plantations." Aside from once being a Confederate soldier, Blackford had not endeared himself to many of his neighbors when he "had gone over to the radical party." Furthermore, the judge "had large meetings of the negroes at his house, firing around and shooting, and it had become very dissatisfactory to the people." Forrest attributed this behavior to Blackford's being "a drinking man," but added that he did not "believe there was any harm in him."[26]

Throughout 1870, the general continued to perform various functions as the president of the Selma, Marion and Memphis Railroad. In January he procured more iron for the road. In June he traveled to Greensboro to select a location for a depot. In July he went to New York to sell railroad bonds. In September he met with a party of Hale County officials who wanted to ensure that money raised in their county was being spent on the section of the road being built there.[27] However, for all the progress, Forrest still wrestled with control. His concern for "his" railroad was such that he felt honor bound to defend it. And so when reports reached him that one of the contractors had failed to fulfill his obligations as Forrest saw them, the general lost control, and his temper flared once more.

At the next encounter with the contractor, Colonel A. K. Shepherd, Forrest lashed out at the man without giving him the opportunity to speak on his own behalf. In fact, the colonel became so enraged at the general's tirade against him that he challenged Forrest to a duel. The general was all too willing to accept and chose pistols for the weapons. That night the general could not sleep. Feeling guilty that he had lost control and allowed his temper to put him in such a position, he tried to think of an honorable way out of the confrontation. A companion who happened to like both men noticed Forrest's discomfort and used it as a means to convince him that he should apologize. As always, Forrest had said things in the heat of anger that he did not mean, or certainly that he did not mean with such intensity. Once his temper had cooled and he had regained control, he felt bad. "I haven't slept for thinking about the trouble with Shepherd," Forrest admitted. "I feel sure I can kill him, and if I do I will never forgive myself. I am convinced that he was right in resenting the way I talked to him. I am in the wrong, and do not feel satisfied about it."

Forrest's companion handled the situation with tact. "General Forrest your courage has never been questioned," he began. "I have no reputation of being a brave man, but under the circumstances I should feel it to be my duty to apologize to Colonel Shepherd and openly tell him that I was wrong." Forrest looked back at his friend for a moment and replied, "You are right, I will do it." Before long the men were dressed and when they reached Shepherd's quarters, they found him preparing for the duel. Forrest marched up to Shepherd, thrust his hand out and calmly remarked, "Colonel, I am in the wrong in this affair and I have come to say so." Shepherd accepted the apology and called off the duel.[28]

On June 27, 1871, Bedford Forrest appeared before a joint congressional committee in Washington, D.C., that was investigating the Ku Klux Klan. He knew that he would have a lot of explaining to do. As "Forrest of Fort Pillow" and the reputed head of the secret organization, he understood the likelihood that he would be questioned extensively. And so he sat in his chair before the members of the committee and maneuvered, dodged, and evaded the barrage of questions, with surprising deftness. There is no doubt that all the while he knew far more than he was saying. Forrest later supposedly told a friend he saw shortly after the interrogation, "I have been lying like a gentleman."[29]

On one occasion, when asked if he took steps to organize under the Klan prescript, Forrest answered, "I do not think I am compelled to answer any question that would implicate me in anything. I believe the law does not require that I should do anything of the sort." But when that answer failed to force his questioner onto a different line, he responded, "I did not."[30] And when he thought it necessary, he failed to recall events or individuals. Many of his answers included sufficiently and safely vague phrases such as: "I reckon," "I presume," "I think," "I heard," "I believe," "I do not recollect," "I do not remember," and "I do not know."

Such sudden lapses of memory were clear demonstrations that Forrest was deceiving the committee. Friends and associates consistently noted the general's quick mind and remarkable memory.[31] Yet, when the congressional committee pressed him for specific names, he could offer only two. One of these names was a man named "Saunders," who had once resided in Mississippi, but moved to Asheville, North Carolina, sometime around 1867.[32] Ironically, Benjamin F. Saunders had been a slaveholder in Coahoma County, Mississippi, before the war and the commander of a company of scouts under Forrest's command during the war.[33] One resident of Coahoma County later recalled that, in 1866, Saunders "moved to Asheville North Carolina, and there, in 1867, he organized the Ku Klux Klan."[34] The committee could not have known all these facts, but Forrest did. At one point in his testimony, he alluded to this connection in response to questions on the extent of the Klan in the South: "Probably it was reported that it was in North Carolina, about where this man Saunders [lived], about Asheville."[35] Forrest hedged his answer, as he did throughout the proceedings, in an attempt to control his testimony by responding in specific detail only to those questions that he chose to answer.

From the start, the panel questioned Forrest about his interview in the Cincinnati *Commercial*. He obviously felt the need to distance himself from the statements attributed to him, claiming that the reporter "misrepresented me almost entirely." Forrest insisted that the correspondent had taken advantage of him while he was "suffering from a sick headache" and "was too unwell to talk with him." At first, he observed that he had talked with the reporter for "three or four minutes" and constantly maintained that they had not conversed long enough for him to have said all that was included in the interview. But later, when asked if he meant that he had spoken only "twenty words" to the newspaperman, Forrest replied, "I should have said twenty minutes, I reckon."[36]

All that he said was the truth, in part, but it was not the whole truth. The reporter had noticed that Forrest was in his office "hard at work, although complaining of an illness contracted at the New York convention."[37] The general's friends knew him to be "restless and impatient" when sick, but hardly so incapacitated as to be manipulated.[38] Forrest protested that he was "not accustomed to writing letters, or to be interrogated by reporters. That was something entirely new to me; I did not expect it."[39] Later, he contradicted this testimony when he offered a letter, saying that it was "one of hundreds that I wrote" counseling peace. Forrest asserted that he "wrote a great many letters," although he had to rely on a personal secretary to do "all the copying."[40] What the former Confederate clearly did not expect was that his words would come back to haunt him.

Bedford Forrest was not the only person who testified before the congressional committee in the summer of 1871. The investigators summoned scores of others—black and white—to appear before them and traveled into the South to gather testimony there as well. The committee compiled thirteen volumes of testimony cataloguing hundreds of examples of the Klan's violence and terror tactics, from whippings and beatings to shootings and killings. Still others had no one to articulate their experiences for them. Countless individuals died or suffered at the hands of the Klan's terrorism because they were unwilling to ignore the outcome of the war. Slavery had supposedly ended, and many died because they believed and acted as if it really had.

Forrest returned to his railroad line in Alabama. Although

marred by occasional accidents, exasperatingly slow progress, and an almost constantly weak financial condition, the construction and the daily operation of the line proceeded for the next three years under his leadership. The railroad president augmented the construction crews with convicts from the Alabama state penitentiary and continued his efforts to raise money. When the stockholders met in Memphis in March 1873, they reelected Forrest. Even so, he warned that the line suffered from such poor cash flow that further construction might have to be halted. He called for more capital to ease the situation.[41]

Forrest had good reason for his warning. A month earlier he had gone to New York and returned, as he explained to his associate, E. W. Rucker, having "entirely failed to raise a dollar for work done, or to *carry the work on further.*" He angrily admitted that he saw "no chance but to stop [work] until I can raise money, which I do not believe can be done *this year,*" with the market flooded as it was with railroad bonds. Thoroughly frustrated, Forrest advised Rucker to "endeavor to get work on other Roads" and suggested that he dismiss the workers, or contract them out to someone else, "as it would be folly under the present circumstances to attempt to work them longer on this road."[42] Unless he and the board could find another source for the necessary capital, the Selma, Marion, and Memphis Railroad was doomed.

It was probably in this frame of mind that Forrest had another tempestuous encounter with a subordinate on the railroad. When the road's civil engineer, Minor Meriwether, failed to certify a section of the line as completed, which would require pledges from subscribers for that section to be paid, Forrest exploded. The general believed that Meriwether's actions constituted an attack upon him. He needed the money to keep the railroad going, and the engineer's scrupulousness was an unnecessary obstacle. Meriwether later recalled that at some point in the meeting Forrest threatened "that he would make a personal attack upon me in the meeting the next day."[43] According to another account, the general's threat amounted to a warning that if Meriwether persisted, "one of us" would not get out of the meeting room "alive."[44]

Naturally everyone came to the meeting the next day waiting for the explosion. When the time came for his report, Meriwether stood up, laid a pistol on the table before him, and casually remarked, "I understand that some persons object to my speaking here tonight. If that is true, let the objections be made now. I do not wish to be interrupted after I begin my speech." All eyes flashed to Forrest, but to nearly everyone's relief, Forrest did nothing.[45] Meriwether less dramatically observed that he "went to the meeting next morning expecting the attack, but the day passed off & nothing was said or done, Genl F I suppose having thought better of the matter."[46] Nevertheless, the two former friends remained estranged for the next two years.

The Selma, Marion and Memphis Railroad's Board of Directors subsequently held a special meeting in July 1873 in which they expressed their confidence in Forrest's leadership. This expression came in the form of a resolution, which read: "Resolved: That we have implicit confidence in the ability, energy, and capacity of General Forrest, president, and feel that if he receives the earnest support of the friends of the enterprise, and the people on the line of the road, that he will carry it to a successful completion."[47]

With this vote of confidence, Forrest noted his belief that the railroad's financial condition was improving. He had liquidated $200,000 of its debt and planned to go to New York to raise more funds. Unfortunately, when Forrest traveled to that city in September 1873, he found a financial panic brewing that would hit the country in devastating proportions and unravel his plans for his railroad. When he returned on September 13, he noted that the resulting panic was greater than anything he had seen in his life, presumably including the evacuation of Nashville in 1862. At any rate, no money would be forthcoming from the financial institutions of the Northeast, and any work undertaken on the line would have to be funded locally.[48]

By October, Forrest was in desperate straits. He wrote Alabama Governor David P. Lewis to inform him of the financial difficulties plaguing the line. He explained that he had "visited New York before the financial panic for the purpose of arranging to comply with the Railroad Act to relieve the State from the endorsement of the State on the Road I represent, and was about completing the same when the financial crisis broke out, which has destroyed all hope of making any arrangements for the present." For the moment, Forrest noted despairingly, "I am endeavoring to run that part of the Road completed & am doing some work in repairing & keeping up the same." But the economic crisis might prove fatal, for the "earnings of the Road are barely paying running expenses with the closest economy I am able to bring to bear, having reduced the price of all labor & officers at least 33 1/3%, and yet we are hardly able to live." He had once viewed the railroad as a great salvation and undertaken its promotion and operation with every fiber of his being. Now the economy threatened to wipe out his railroad and himself. "I am more anxious," he confessed to the governor, "as I am the heaviest creditor on the Road."[49]

Nathan Bedford Forrest's tenure as president of the Selma, Marion and Memphis Railroad ended on April 1, 1874. Although he had held the office of president since the company first organized, he surrendered the presidency, according to one newspaper, "to relieve the company of any embarrassment it might suffer from his connection with the management." The paper added that the general's actions were "greatly commended by his friends and accepted by the public generally as an act of Self-sacrificing patriotism."[50]

For one of the few times in his life, Forrest felt out of touch. He could no longer control the activities of the railroad. On August 9, he wrote Rucker, who remained with the line as superintendent. The general was still clearly angry about giving up the presidency. Noting that he was "suprised you was in a hurry to return to your Road," Forrest told Rucker that he "wuld have liked to have Seen you and learned how maters was moving in Ala as I do not talk with [new president A. J.] white and of course can learn nothing of what is doing on the Road[.]" Although no longer "his Road," Forrest remained intensely interested in its progress and status.

Even so, the former railroad executive feared the worst now that the Selma, Marion and Memphis was no longer under his firm hand. "I presume nothing," he remarked after wondering what was "doing on the Road," adding, "the present Board will do nothing in my opinion and the Sooner the Stock Holders mete and Elect a new board the Beter for their Interest[.]" Forrest believed that he "culd have contracted ... to have completed the Road from Selma to Eutaw & from Memphis to Holly Springs ... but culd not Git the Board to move on the mater[.]" He expressed his "opinion" that the line "be completed as a narrow gauge Road but not as a broad gauge Road and the quicker the change is mad the Beter." He simply could not relinquish something that he had once considered "his," and warned Rucker, "I will remain quiet a while longer and Se if they will act [but] if they fail I will call a meting of the Stock Holders." Having vented his anger, Forrest turned to a more pleasant subject. "our Election paste off quiet and for the Democratic party," he observed, adding, "the Civil Rights Bil has Setled the Republican party[.]" Then in a final word of triumph, the former Grand Wizard remarked that "the white people" need "only do as we have dun all work to gether."[51]

Although no longer associated with the promotion of the railroad, the general remained in the public eye at reunions, decoration ceremonies, and other celebrations of the "lost cause." At one of these functions, a ceremony in May 1875, at Elmwood Cemetery near Memphis, Forrest and Meriwether patched up their differences and renewed their friendship. And in a subsequent exchange of letters, the two men expressed their satisfaction at the reconciliation, as Forrest explained, "that all diferances between us air Satisfactury Setled and I asure you that thair is no unkind feling to wards you from me." Then in a characteristic note of explanation, he added, "I have all wase cherished a high regard for your Self and good lady and have felt unkindly to wards your Self only when I felt you was using Your influence against My interest hoping we may live and be as here to fore good friends[.]"[52]

Despite all that had happened to him, including the latest blow from the railroad and the falling out with Meriwether, Forrest retained his sense of humor. On August 3, 1875, he responded to a request from a former Confederate for a cannon. He observed that he had been "looking around the city this morning, but am unable to procure one. Am promised one by a friend from Cincinnati. I will ship it on arrival." Forrest then ventured, "Would it not be as well to employ a brass band to accompany the cannon; if so, I can order it from the same place." Whether or not Forrest meant for the band comment to be taken seriously, he clearly meant the next statement more humorously. "If you had applied 12 or 14 years ago, I could have furnished you with almost any sort of a cannon." Then he noted reflectively and nostalgically, "There is nothing like fighting at the front."[53]

Regardless of the varying circumstances in Bedford's life, Mary Ann Forrest remained a strong constant for him. Through the years, her mellowing influence increasingly affected her rough-hewn husband. Despite their differences or, more correctly, because of them, Mary Ann and Bedford complemented each other. She represented the "values of the home," as historian Tom Ownby termed them: "harmony, self-control, and moderation."[54] She provided the moderating influence for Bedford's forceful personality and could calm him when others dared not approach. Mary Ann symbolized what her husband hoped to be, but could not be. As Bedford had once explained to her guardian when he asked for permission to marry her, he knew that she was not like him and that was why he wanted her to be his wife.

The dichotomies of Southern society, as Ownby expressed them, appeared within the Forrest household as well. "Where evangelicalism demanded self-control, humility in manner, and harmony in personal relations, Southern honor demanded self-assertiveness, aggressiveness, and competitiveness."[55] Bedford Forrest was certainly different from his wife in personality. Nevertheless, he recognized the flaws in his own character. He often overcompensated for his failings by explaining away his behavior after the fact. As Union General James Harrison Wilson noticed, Forrest "always seemed ... to have a plausible excuse" for his actions.[56] But Forrest also demonstrated his recognition of his personal shortcomings through his devotion to Mary Ann. To be sure, he lived, worked, and fought hard; struggled for control over himself and others; lived by the tenets of Southern honor; and remained shaped by his heritage and personality—and Forrest obviously could not discard these factors—but he increasingly showed signs of assimilating some of Mary Ann's characteristics.

The habits of a lifetime proved hard to break. Forrest continued to wrestle with his temper. As one contemporary observed, "His temper during the last few years of his life was just as ungovernable as ever." On one occasion, Forrest became so enraged when moths damaged a suit of clothes he had ordered and apparently forgot to pick up for a time that he stormed into the tailor shop. After enduring a stream of invective, the tailor tried to calm his irate customer, "General, I am very sorry this thing happened," he explained. "We did not know the clothes were moth eaten, and are willing to make all reparation possible." But, much to the tailor's chagrin, Forrest waved a pistol at him. "Why, General, you would not shoot me for such a trifle as that!" he cried. "God damn you, yes," Forrest replied. "I'd shoot you like a rat."

The incensed general did not shoot and, in fact, felt so badly about his behavior that the next day he went back to the shop and apologized with great sincerity and flourish. "But then he was often doing just such things, and apologizing for them," the narrator of this account explained; a victim of one of Forrest's tirades once asked, "Good gracious! General, can you do nothing with that temper of yours?" And Forrest honestly replied, "No; I'll be damned if I can."[57]

Forrest also loved to play cards for money. Mary Ann deplored the habit, and tried repeatedly in her way to get him to stop. For much of their married life, she failed. This impulse sometimes led to embarrassment—as it did in the spring of 1861, when the Grand Jury of Coahoma County, Mississippi, returned an indictment against him for gambling. Noting that on February 25, 1861, Forrest "unlawfully then and there did play at and bet upon a certain game of cards for money, contrary to the form and Statute in such cases ... and against the peace and dignity of the State of Mississippi," the Grand Jury instructed the sheriff to arrest him and hold him for trial. Twice the sheriff reported that he could not find Forrest in the county because he was away at war, and the court eventually dropped the charges.[58]

However, neither the war nor Mary Ann's influence could cool Forrest's ardor for gambling. As John Morton noted, "After the war, when very needy, he won $3,000 gambling, although his wife, to whom he was devoted, tried to persuade him to live on half rations rather than play cards." He recalled an instance when he met Forrest on the streets of Nashville. "John, can you tell me where I can find a gambling saloon?" the general asked. Morton looked at his former chief quizzically. He did not know where to find one and wanted to know why Forrest was asking. "Well,"

Forrest explained, "I found one to-night, broke the bank and have $2,500 of their money. I thought I had time to tackle another before I went to bed."[59]

Eventually, Mary Ann seemed to have won her battle with Bedford over gambling. According to one account, Forrest came home one night, while living in Memphis, and told his wife he was going out that night to play cards. Undoubtedly having debated the merits of this activity with her before, he tried to convince her that he had no choice but to go out and gamble. He explained that a friend had defaulted on a bond that he had agreed to back. "And you know, Mary Ann, I haven't the money to pay this debt." She replied, "Well, if you will go remember I will be here praying that you give up this evil habit, and I will be waiting for you, too."

Thinking that he had won the argument, Forrest happily went on to the game, where, in a short time, he won the money he needed. With guilt nagging at him and knowing that his luck could turn bad, he stood up and dramatically announced that he was "through." The rest of his companions groaned. "Forrest, you mustn't leave now," they protested, explaining that if he stayed he might win even more (although they were undoubtedly more concerned with winning some of their money back). The towering figure looked down at them and resolutely responded, "No. I am through. My wife is sitting at home with a Bible on her knee. I told her I would quit as soon as I had enough money to pay my debt of honor. I am never going to gamble again." With that, he turned and walked out.[60] Whether Forrest lived up to that promise is not known. However, as he grew older and his health became worse, he surrendered greater control of his life to Mary Ann and her influence.

Forrest also turned to the church. Mary Ann had long been a member of the First Cumberland Presbyterian Church, or Old Court Avenue Church. For much of his life, the general found religion intriguing. As minister and former staff officer David C. Kelley remarked, Forrest's interest in religious services and ceremonies was genuine, but "his religion was a superstition rather than a principle." Nevertheless, Kelley observed that both Forrest's mother and wife encouraged Bedford to accept the tenets of

"Christian faith," and he finally "accepted the obligations of the Church to which his wife belonged ... and died in peace."[61]

Forrest's religious conversion occurred in 1875, when he met a former subordinate, Raleigh R. White, on the streets of Memphis. Forrest asked White what he had been doing since the war, and White replied, "Preaching the Gospel of the Son of God." The answer surprised the general, who then inquired about White's work. Shortly thereafter, the two men stepped into a bank parlor, where they could escape the noise of the street. Forrest turned to the minister and asked White to "pray for him." The two former comrades knelt in prayer.[62] Then, on November 14, 1875, Forrest, with his wife at his side, publicly professed his conversion in the Cumberland Presbyterian Church.[63]

Even as Forrest turned increasingly to other sources of support and strength, he retained his role as the breadwinner of the family for as long as he was able. In the wake of the railroad disaster, he returned to planting. Having long since divested himself of his Mississippi plantation properties, he had to look for new land and new laborers to work that land. He solved the first problem by leasing President's Island, in the Mississippi River just outside Memphis. For the second, he turned to Shelby County, which provided him with convict laborers.[64] Forrest had experience with convict lease, having employed state prisoners on some of his railroad construction crews.[65] At President's Island, he established an elaborate system, complete with military-style barracks and heavily regimented working and living schedules.

On May 4, 1876, a correspondent for the Memphis *Daily Appeal* accompanied the Grand Jury of the Shelby County Criminal Court on a "raid of President's Island." Since Forrest was "at home," he greeted the party at the landing and escorted them to his house, "a small but very comfortable old-fashioned double log house, improvised from two cabins that he found on the island." The reporter thought the general "had that easy air characteristic of the old-time Southern planter." The jury proceeded to inspect the prisoners' quarters. Within the main building, Forrest had 117 convicts segregated into "five apartments": "First, female prisoners [18 black and four white]; second, [35] white males; third, the office and guard-room; fourth, [60] black males; fifth, store-room."

Forrest had 1,300 acres, 800 of which were "cleared and in cultivation"—550 in cotton; 150 in corn; and the rest in potatoes, millet, and garden vegetables. He contracted with the county for the use of the convict laborers for five years, paying the county "ten cents a day for all who are sent to him." The reporter, a vocal proponent of the convict-lease system, pronounced Forrest's "workhouse" "an admirably conducted institution." Of the general himself, the correspondent observed, "There is a magnetism in his superb presence even in his shirt sleeves and slouch hat that impels obedience and makes everything move like clockwork."[66]

Nevertheless, Forrest's health was rapidly deteriorating. At one time he admitted that he had "not been in good health since the war." And on September 21, 1876, as Forrest attended a reunion of the Seventh Tennessee Cavalry, he confessed, "Soldiers, I was afraid that I could not be with you today, but I could not bear the thought of not meeting with you." Although he promised, "I will always try to meet with you in the future," Forrest hoped that the veterans and their families would "continue to meet from year to year" in any case.

Forrest's connection with the Seventh Tennessee dated from June 1861, when he first entered Confederate service as a private. As the glories of his past flashed before him, Forrest began his impromptu speech: "Soldiers of the Seventh Tennessee Cavalry, Ladies, and Gentlemen: I name the soldiers first because I love them best. I am extremely pleased to meet you here to-day. I love the gallant men with whom I was so intimately connected during the war." Then he proudly added, "You can hardly realize what must pass through a commander's mind when called upon to meet in reunion the brave spirits who, through four years of war and bloodshed, fought fearlessly for a cause that they thought right, and who, even when they foresaw as we did, that we must soon close in disaster, and that we must all surrender, yet did not quail, but marched to victory in many battles, and fought as boldly and persistently in their last battles as they did in their first." These men had sustained their honor and thereby sustained his as their leader.

Then recalling the dead who had left families behind, he implored the veterans, "Comrades, I have remembered their wives and little ones, and have taken care of them, and I want every one of you to remember them too, and join with me in the labor of love." Finally, he called upon his old "comrades" to remain as "good citizens" as they had been "tried and true soldiers." Forrest defended Confederate reunions and other ceremonies as "right and proper" and promised that such activities would "show our country-men by our conduct and dignity that brave soldiers are always good citizens and law-abiding and loyal people."[67]

During the spring of 1877, Forrest realized that his health was failing rapidly. In an effort to stem the deterioration, he determined to "take the waters" at Hurricane Springs during the summer heat. Not wishing to remain the whole summer away from the many associations he enjoyed in Memphis, Forrest wrote to some of his acquaintances, including former staff officer Charles Anderson, asking them to visit with him for a brief time while he was at the Springs.

In early July, Forrest traveled to Hurricane Springs and renewed his request to Anderson to visit him there. Anderson replied that he would leave immediately. The old comrades met at the stage. Anderson was surprised to find his former commander much more subdued than he remembered him having been before. "There was a mildness in his manner, a softness of expression, and a gentleness in his words that appeared to me strange and unnatural. At first I thought his bad health had brought about this change, but then I remembered that when sick or wounded he was the most restless and impatient man I ever saw."

As they walked toward Forrest's quarters, Anderson could not resist observing that Forrest did not appear to be the man whom he had known so well. The general pondered for a moment, stopped abruptly, and turned toward his subordinate. "Major," the old officer explained, "I am not the man you were with so long and knew so well—I hope I am a better man. I've joined the Church and am trying to live a Christian life." Anderson promptly replied, "General, that's it, and you are indebted to Old Mistress (as we called Mrs. Forrest), and to no one else, for this great change." Forrest then quietly reflected, "Yes, you are right. Mary has prayed for me night and day for many years, and I feel now that through her prayers my life has been spared, and to them am I indebted for passing safely through so many dangers."

Anderson was tired from his trip. He asked the general to give him a few minutes to get "the dust brushed off." But Forrest, who had waited so impatiently for his friend and comrade to arrive, was loathe to let him go just yet. "No, you must come right up to my room," Forrest told him, "Mary is waiting to see you. I have already selected a good room for you, and we have seen you many a time far dustier than you are now."

Anderson remained at Hurricane Springs for "several days," in which Forrest "spoke hopefully of recovering his health." Mary Ann Forrest did not share her husband's optimism, telling Anderson that she based her fears on Bedford's "unnatural appetite," for he "seemed always to crave food unsuited for him." And the former staff officer saw proof of Mary Ann's assertion, and her influence over Bedford. Anderson recalled that "the General, with knife and fork in hand, started to help himself from one of the dishes brought in by the waiter. Mrs. Forrest laid her hand gently on his arm and said, 'Please don't eat that. Your breakfast has been prepared, and will be here in a few minutes.'" Forrest dropped his knife and fork and looked plaintively at his friend. "Major, I know Mary is the best friend I have on earth," he dejectedly explained, "but sometimes it does seem that she is determined to starve me to death."[68]

Anderson was not the only former colleague who noticed the change in Forrest's disposition and health. Joseph Wheeler saw Forrest during this period and remarked that the once-strong features had softened considerably. "It so happened that I had not seen General Forrest for several years until a few months before his death," he recalled, "and I could [not help] but notice the startling change which had come over him." To Wheeler, Forrest appeared "greatly emaciated," and he attributed it to "an exhausting diarrhoea from which he was hopelessly suffering." Forrest's face, heightened in anger or battle to bronze, now seemed "pale" and "thin." He was no longer the man who had promised to be "in my coffin," rather than serve under Wheeler again after the disaster at Dover in 1863.[69]

By the end of August, reports were extremely negative. The Memphis *Avalanche* noted: "Gen. N. B. Forrest is lying in a hopeless condition at Bailey Springs, Ala.... He has for months past been afflicted with chronic diarrhea, and a malarial impregnation has brought on a combination of diseases which makes his case hopeless." Explaining that Forrest's "life has been one wherein he became inured to exposure," the writer speculated that overconfidence "in his powers of physical endurance" and overwork had led to the point that "he lies now a shattered man on the verge of the grave." Forrest's inability to eat made recovery unlikely. "Beef tea is the only nourishment he can take, and he is gradually growing weaker and weaker."[70]

On September 15, 1877, Forrest recovered sufficiently to write a letter to an old friend and wartime comrade, G. W. Adair, from Bailey Springs. In the letter he admitted, "I have been lying here flat on my back for a month, unable to get up without help," but added, "I feel now that I am just passing out of a most terrible case of sickness, which has lasted me about twelve months. My disease has been inflammation of the stomach and bowels. I am too weak to walk about without help—only weigh about one hundred and twenty pounds." This physical weakness was as severe a blow as his earlier financial helplessness had been. Forrest could no longer rely upon his remarkable strength and stamina to pull him through. The deterioration of his body was the last, crucial assault on Forrest's ability to control his destiny.

Even so, he could not give up. In an effort to bolster his morale, Bedford noted hopefully, "My symptoms now are all gone, and the doctor thinks I will soon recover." He turned his thoughts from his own physical condition, observing that Mary Ann's health was "unusually good." Then, with a measure of pride and an eye to his future and to posterity, Forrest mentioned his son and grandchildren. "Willie has four fine children, and is planting with me just below Memphis. We have 800 acres of cotton and 400 in corn. The crop looks very promising. I am endeavoring to raise all kinds of stock."[71]

As he approached death, Forrest sought to settle his affairs in hopes of leaving his son free of the litigation that had plagued him generally since the war and particularly since the railroad failed. He summoned his legal adviser, John T. Morgan, and instructed him to discontinue all legal actions then pending. "General, I am broken in health and spirit, and have not long to live," he confessed. Then, in a moment of reflection over the toils of his life, Forrest added, "My life has been a battle from the start. It was a fight to achieve a livelihood for those dependent upon me in my younger days, and independence for myself when I grew up to manhood, as well as in the terrible turmoil of the Civil War." His words suggested the grip that the desire for control had on him throughout his life. And in this last struggle, he looked to his wife's example for guidance.

"I have seen too much of violence," the man whose name carried with it a reputation for a terrible temper and ferocious fighting wearily admitted, "and I want to close my days at peace with all the world, as I am now at peace with my Maker." Morgan must have been astounded as much by the words he heard as by the physical state of the broken ex-soldier who uttered them. But Forrest told him of his conversion to the church and gave that as one reason for breaking off any further legal actions.[72]

Forrest continued to "take the waters," but there was increasingly little chance for his recovery. By the time he returned to Memphis, the formerly robust cavalryman was reduced to little more than a mere skeleton. He had to be carried from his carriage to his residence, where he remained to wait for death. On October 28, Forrest moved from his plantation on President's Island to his brother Jesse's house on Union Street. While he remained there, October 28 and 29, he received a number of visitors, although he was barely strong enough to lift himself up in bed. Among the more distinguished visitors was a fellow planter and ex-Confederate, Jefferson Davis. Forrest feebly greeted his former chief and talked with him briefly. But his strength was fading quickly. According to his friend and railroad associate Meriwether, his "last coherent words ... uttered about 15 minutes before death, were 'Call my wife [.]'"[73] By 7:30 P.M., on October 29, 1877, Nathan Bedford Forrest was dead.[74]

Epilogue

A Statue in Memphis

Old citizens of Memphis mildly described him to me as "a terror."

—LAFCADIO HEARN

Let the historians and all those who are so fond of the general take him and do what they want with him.

—MAXINE SMITH, EXECUTIVE SECRETARY, NAACP, MEMPHIS

THE FUNERAL PROCESSION STRETCHED OUT along the three miles from Jesse Forrest's home to Elmwood Cemetery. Twenty thousand people lined the streets or followed the casket. Former comrades, subordinates, and superiors came to pay homage to the fallen warrior.[1] The ex-president of the Confederate States, Jefferson Davis, served as one of the pallbearers, and Forrest was laid to rest "with Odd-fellows' rites and military honors."[2] At his request, Forrest wore his Confederate general's uniform for the last time.[3] But even as they sought to render these final honors to the mortal remains of Nathan Bedford Forrest, they began to transform him into the legend that would encase him as surely as any tomb.

Ironically, the writer Lafcadio Hearn, chronicling the funeral for a Cincinnati newspaper, understood what others did not about this complex man. Under the pen name Ozias Midwinter, he wrote of Forrest, "Old citizens of Memphis mildly described him to me as 'a terror,'" adding, "He was, further, one of the most arbitrary, imperious and determined men that it is possible to conceive of as holding a high position in a civilized community. Rough, rugged, desperate, uncultured, his character fitted him rather for the life of the borderer than the planter; he seemed by nature a typical pioneer, one of those fierce and terrible men, who form in themselves a kind of protecting fringe to the borders of white civilization."[4]

As the correspondent suggested, Bedford Forrest could not discard his frontier heritage. Conditioned by life in the Southern backcountry, subject to the demands of Southern honor, and constantly beset by the desire for control and the struggle with his passions that desire generated, Forrest faced each phase of his life with an energy and zest that few others could match. Yet, the same factors that characterized him—honor, violence, control, and passion—also brought out the best and the worst in him as a human being. As Midwinter observed, "his ferocity and reckless temper—faults not incompatible with fine qualities as a soldier"—made him many enemies as well.[5] Forrest's need for control over his life and affairs pushed him from semisubsistence to planter status before the Civil War. During the war, he achieved remarkable successes, but his need for independence limited his effectiveness as a soldier when working in conjunction with others. Following the war, he struggled to regain control over his life through the trauma, as he saw it, of Reconstruction and in the face of a series of devastating business failures. Forrest was never completely able to adjust to the new realities.

In 1905, the city of Memphis unveiled an equestrian statue of Forrest, in a park named in his honor, amid great pomp and circumstance. Both Bedford and Mary Ann, who died fifteen years after her husband, were reinterred at its base.[6] About seventy-five years later, the executive director of the Memphis chapter of the Congress of Racial Equality called for the removal of the statue.[7] The National Association for the Advancement of Colored People issued the same demand nine years after that, also asking the city to transfer the bodies of Forrest and his wife and to rename the park. The executive secretary of the Memphis branch of the NAACP explained, "The presence of this park is a daily slap in the face to blacks throughout the city, and we intend to see that it's removed." She pointedly concluded, "Let the historians and all those who are so fond of the general take him and do what they want with him."

Southern historian Shelby Foote responded to these complaints by observing, "While I can understand why blacks might see that statue as a symbol of racism, I think they've overlooked the facts about Bedford Forrest. He was certainly not the villain they perceive him to be."[8] In one sense it was true. Bedford Forrest was neither the incarnation of evil his detractors have described him as being nor the paragon of Southern virtue some of his apologists have maintained. He was a man, living in the context of his times and shaped by forces over which he ultimately had no control. Perhaps it is only fitting that Forrest continues to generate controversy, for he certainly did nothing to avoid it while he lived.

Notes

INTRODUCTION: GIT THAR FUSTEST WITH THE MOSTEST

1. Quoted in W. H. Whitsitt, "A Year With Forrest," *Confederate Veteran* 25 (August 1917), p. 362 see also Robert Selph Henry, *"First With the Most" Forrest* (Indianapolis: Bobbs-Merrill Co., 1944), p. 462, and Andrew Nelson Lytle, *Bedford Forrest and His Critter Company* (New York: G. P. Putnam's Sons, 1931), p. 357.

2. Quoted in Henry, p. 15; Lytle, p. 357.

3. Richard Taylor, *Destruction and Reconstruction: Personal Experiences of the Late War* (New York: Longmans, Green & Co., 1955), p. 244.

4. Quoted in John Allan Wyeth, *Life of General Nathan Bedford Forrest* (New York: Harper & Bros., 1899), p. 605; see also Paul E. Steiner, *Medical-Military Portraits of Union and Confederate Generals* (Philadelphia: Whitmore Publishing Co., 1968), p. 297.

5. By 1902, three biographies of Forrest had appeared: Thomas Jordan and J. P. Pryor, *The Campaigns of Lieut. Gen. N. B. Forrest, and of Forrest's Cavalry* (New Orleans: Blelock & Co., 1868); Wyeth; and J. Harvey Mathes, *General Forrest* (New York: D. Appleton & Co., 1902), as well as numerous sketches and tributes in such publications as the *Confederate Veteran* and the *Southern Historical Society Papers.* Four more biographies have appeared since: H. J. Eckenrode, *Life of Nathan B. Forrest* (Richmond, Va.: B. F. Johnson Publishing Co., 1918); Eric William Sheppard, *Bedford Forrest: The Confederacy's Greatest Cavalryman* (New York: Dial Press 1930), Lytle; and Henry. Jordan and Pryor's study of Forrest comes closest to being an autobiography. On more than one occasion, the general acknowledged his cooperation with and approval of the work. The close proximity to the events and the access to Forrest are both the book's strongest and weakest qualities. The most authoritative biographies are Wyeth's, Mathes's, and Henry's. Lytle's study is highly readable, but emphasizes Forrest as a folk hero. Eckenrode's biography, which is written for children, and Sheppard's, which includes composite fictional

characters and invented dialogue, are the least useful to scholars.

6. For a listing of these references, see Thomas E. Dasher, *William Faulkner's Characters: An Index to the Published and Unpublished Fiction* (New York: Garland Publishing, 1981), pp. 412–13. Cleanth Brooks (*William Faulkner: Toward Yoknapatawpha and Beyond* [New Haven, Conn.: Yale University Press, 1978], p. 375) noted that Forrest was "the special Confederate hero ... of a number of Faulkner's own Civil War stories." One explanation for William Faulkner's interest in Bedford Forrest is the popular belief that the author's grandfather, Colonel William C. Falkner (spelled without the "u"), fought for a time during the war with Forrest. There is no evidence that he did, although a Colonel W. W. Faulkner (whose last name is spelled the same as the writer's) served under the cavalry commander. See Joseph Blotner, *Faulkner: A Biography* (New York: Random House, 1974), vol. 1, p. 28, and Frederick R. Karl, *William Faulkner: American Writer* (New York: Weidenfeld & Nicolson, 1989), p. 42.

7. Malcolm Cowley, "Introduction to *The Portable Faulkner*," in *Faulkner: A Collection of Critical Essays*, ed. by Robert Penn Warren (Englewood Cliffs, N.J.: Prentice-Hall, 1966), p. 39; Robert Penn Warren, "Faulkner: The South, the Negro, and Time," in *Faulkner: A Collection of Critical Essays*, p. 265.

8. William Faulkner, *Go Down, Moses* (New York: Modern Library, 1955), pp. 263–64.

9. George Marion O'Donnell, "Faulkner's Mythology," in *Faulkner: A Collection of Critical Essays*, pp. 23–24; Cleanth Brooks, "Faulkner's Ultimate Values," in *Faulkner and the Southern Renaissance: Faulkner and Yoknapatawpha*, ed. by Doreen Fowler and Ann J. Abadie (Jackson: University Press of Mississippi, 1982), pp. 278–81. For an extensive analysis of the Snopes family, see James Gray Watson, *The Snopes Dilemma: Faulkner's Trilogy* (Coral Gables, Fla.: University of Miami Press, 1968).

10. William Faulkner, *Sartoris* (New York: Random House, 1956), p. 174. See also William Faulkner, *Flags in the Dust* (New York: Random House, 1973), p. 155.

11. Faulkner, *Sartoris*, p. 224; Faulkner, *Flags*, p. 212.

12. William Faulkner, *Light in August* (New York: Random House, 1959), p. 423.

CHAPTER 1: YOUNG BEDFORD

1. Ralph Waldo Emerson, *Essays and Lectures* (New York: Viking Press, 1983), pp. 51–71.

2. Ralph Waldo Emerson, *Journals of Ralph Waldo Emerson*, ed. by Edward Waldo Emerson and Waldo Emerson Forbes (Boston: Houghton Mifflin Co., 1910), vol. 4, pp. 312–13.

3. Lewis P. Simpson, *Mind and the American Civil War: A Meditation on Lost Causes* (Baton Rouge: Louisiana State University Press, 1989), p. 50.

4. Ibid., pp. 49–50, 61–63; see also Daniel Aaron, *The Unwritten War: American Writers and the Civil War* (Oxford: Oxford University Press, 1973), pp. 34–38.

5. George E. Woodberry, *Edgar Allan Poe* (Boston: Houghton Mifflin Co., 1885), pp. 156–57; Joseph Wood Krutch, *Edgar Allan Poe: A Study in Genius* (New York: Russell & Russell, 1926), pp. 138–39.

6. Edgar Allan Poe, *Collected Works of Edgar Allan Poe,* ed. by Thomas Ollive Mabbott (Cambridge, Mass.: Belknap Press of Harvard University Press, 1978), vol. 2, p. 620.

7. Ibid., pp. 619–34.

8. Dickson D. Bruce, Jr., *Violence and Culture in the Antebellum South* (Austin: University of Texas Press, 1979), pp. 233, 234, 236.

9. Thomas Jordan and J. P. Pryor, *The Campaigns of Lieut.-Gen. N. B. Forrest, and of Forrest's Cavalry* (New Orleans: Blelock & Co., 1868), pp. 17–18; John Allan Wyeth, *Life of General Nathan Bedford Forrest* (New York: Harper & Bros., 1899), pp. 2–6; Henry, pp. 22–23; Lytle, pp. 9–13.

10. Wyeth, p. 13.

11. Ibid.; Andrew Nelson Lytle, *Bedford Forrest and His Critter Company* (New York: G. P. Putnam's Sons, 1931), p. 13.

12. Wyeth, p. 14; Lytle, pp. 13–14.

13. Wyeth, pp. 14–15; Lytle, p. 14.

14. Lytle, pp. 14–15.

15. Jordan and Pryor, pp. 18–19; Wyeth, p. 5; and Robert Selph Henry, *"First With the Most" Forrest* (Indianapolis: Bobbs-Merrill Co., 1944), p. 23.

16. Wyeth, p. 15.

17. Malcolm J. Rohrbough, *The Trans-Appalachian Frontier: People, Societies, and Institutions 1775–1850* (New York: Oxford University Press, 1978), p. 199.

18. Wyeth, p. 15.

19. Rohrbough, p. 199.

20. Wyeth, p. 15.

21. Lytle, p. 14.

22. Wyeth, p. 626.

23. Ray Allen Billington, *America's Frontier Heritage* (Albuquerque: University of New Mexico Press, 1967).

24. Ibid., p. 626; Jordan and Pryor, pp. 19–20; Henry, p. 23.

25. Jordan and Pryor, p. 21.

26. John Hope Franklin, *The Militant South, 1800–1861* (Cambridge, Mass.: Harvard University Press, 1956), pp. 12–13, 17, 21. For a thorough study of Southern honor, see Bertram Wyatt-Brown, *Southern Honor: Ethics and Behavior in the Old South* (Oxford: Oxford University Press, 1982). See also Elliott J. Gorn, "'Gouge and Bite, Pull Hair and Scratch': The Social Significance of Fighting in the Southern Backcountry," *American Historical Review* 90 (February 1985), pp. 18–32. Sheldon Hackney, "Southern Violence," *American Historical Review* 74 (February 1969), pp.

906–25, offers a wide-ranging analysis of a "southern pattern of violence." John Shelton Reed, "To Live—and Die—in Dixie: A Contribution to the Study of Southern Violence," *Political Science Quarterly* 80 (September 1971), pp. 429–43, examines private ownership and use of guns and corporal punishment of children in relation to the "Southern reputation for violence."

27. J. Harvey Mathes, *General Forrest* (New York: D. Appleton & Co., 1902), pp. 5–6; Wyeth, pp. 8–10; Lytle, pp. 3–7.

28. Jordan and Pryor, pp. 20–21; Wyeth, p. 16; Mathes, pp. 6–7; Lytle, p. 18.

29. Franklin, p. 35.

30. Billington, pp. 143–144, 147.

31. David G. Pugh, *Sons of Liberty: The Masculine Mind in Nineteenth-Century America* (Westport, Conn.: Greenwood Press, 1983), p. xv.

32. Quoted in Bruce, p. 98. See also James C. Curtis, *Andrew Jackson and the Search for Vindication* (Boston: Little, Brown & Co., 1976). As presented by Curtis, Andrew Jackson and Bedford Forrest shared numerous character traits, attitudes, and experiences, including early life on a frontier marked by violence and bloodshed (pp. 3–4); limited educational opportunities (p. 7); a violent temper (p. 8); a love of horses, horse racing, and gambling (pp. 7–8, 34–35); the desire for control (p. 14); the importance of the code of honor (p. 17); slaveholding (p. 18); the struggle for economic survival and the desire for financial independence (pp. 32–35); violent personal confrontations (p. 48); boldness as a military tactician (p. 51); the threat of bankruptcy and financial ruin (pp. 111–113); and the threat of chaos and disorder (p. 144).

33. W. J. Cash, *The Mind of the South* (New York: Vintage Books, 1969), p. 44.

34. Frank Lawrence Owsley, *Plain Folk of the Old South* (Baton Rouge: Louisiana State University Press, 1949), is the classic study of the "plain folk" of the Antebellum South. Andrew Lytle's role in the "Agrarian School" heavily influenced his interpretation of Forrest. See Lytle, "The Hind Tit," in *I'll Take My Stand: The South and the Agrarian Tradition By 12 Southerners* (New York: Harper & Bros., 1930), pp. 201–45; and Benjamin B. Alexander, "Nathan Bedford Forrest and Southern Folkways," *Southern Partisan* 7 (Summer 1987), pp. 27–32.

35. Emory M. Thomas, *The Confederate Nation: 1861–1865* (New York: Harper & Row, 1979), p. 20.

36. Bruce, pp. 98–99.

37. Franklin, p. 21.

38. Curtis, p. 31.

39. Bruce, pp. 11–12, 17, 74–75.

40. Ibid., p. 75.

41. Wyeth, pp. 629–30.

42. Ozias Midwinter, "Notes on Forrest's Funeral," *Cincinnati Com-*

mercial, November 6, 1877. See also Lafcadio Hearn, *Occidental Gleanings* (New York: Dodd, Mead & Co., 1925), vol. 1, p. 147.

43. Gorn, pp. 21, 39.

44. Bruce, p. 74.

45. Cash, p. 39.

46. Bruce, pp. 74–75.

47. Wyeth, p. 629.

48. Mathes, p. 357; Lytle, p. 20.

49. James R. Chalmers, *Southern Historical Society Papers* 7, no. 10 (October 1879), p. 455; Henry, p. 24.

50. Jordan and Pryor, pp. 21–22; Wyeth, p. 17; Lytle, pp. 18–19; Henry, p. 24.

51. Wyeth, p. 6; Henry, p. 22; H. W. Evans, "The Mother of General Forrest," *Confederate Veteran* 33 (October 1925), p. 369.

CHAPTER 2: THE MAKING OF A PLANTER

1. Robert Selph Henry, *"First With the Most" Forrest* (Indianapolis: Bobbs-Merrill Co., 1944), p. 24.

2. John Allan Wyeth, *Life of General Nathan Bedford Forrest* (New York: Harper & Bros., 1899), p. 17.

3. Ibid., pp. 17–18; Henry, p. 24; Thomas Jordan and J. P. Pryor, *The Campaigns of Lieut.-Gen. N. B. Forrest, and of Forrest's Cavalry* (New Orleans: Blelock & Co., 1868), pp. 22–24.

4. *The Phenix*, Hernando, Mississippi, March 15, 1845.

5. *Final Record Book*, Probate Court, 1845–46, Hernando, DeSoto County, Mississippi, pp. 105–106; *Final Record*, August term, 1845, pp. 574–576.

6. Jordan and Pryor, pp. 24–25.

7. *Final Record Book*, Probate Court, 1845–46, Hernando, DeSoto County, Mississippi, pp. 190, 218–219; *The Phenix*, August 9, 1845, November 8, 1845.

8. Wyeth, pp. 21, 629.

9. Quoted in ibid., p. 629.

10. Ibid., p. 21.

11. Ibid., pp. 19–20; Henry, pp. 24–25.

12. Quoted in Henry, p. 25.

13. William S. Speer, *Sketches of Prominent Tennesseans* (c. 1888; reprint, Easley, S.C.: Southern Historical Press, 1978), p. 79.

14. *The Phenix*, Hernando, Mississippi, September 27, 1845; Henry, p. 25.

15. *Final Record Book*, Probate Court, 1845–46, Hernando, DeSoto County, Mississippi, pp. 218–19.

16. *Subpoena and Witness Docket*, May term, 1846, p. 74.

17. *Register of Military Appointments, 1841–1848*, Series K., vol. A,

p. 327, Mississippi Department of Archives and History, Jackson.

18. Henry, p. 26; *U.S. Census, Population and Slave Schedules, DeSoto County, Mississippi*, 1850.

19. Henry, p. 24; Wyeth, p. 20. According to Forrest's obituary in the *New York Times*, he was also "for some time" the "Captain of a boat which ran between Memphis and Vicksburg," although the writer gave no dates for either the beginning or the duration of the enterprise. See "Death of Gen. Forrest," *New York Times*, October 30, 1877.

20. J. Harvey Mathes, *General Forrest* (New York: D. Appleton & Co., 1902), p. 15.

21. *U.S. Census Population and Slave Schedules, DeSoto County, Mississippi*, 1850.

22. Frederic Bancroft, *Slave-Trading in the Old South* (Baltimore: J. H. Furst Co., 1931), p. 250.

23. *Memphis City Directory*, 1855, p. 205.

24. Jordan and Pryor, pp. 27–28.

25. Bancroft, p. 258.

26. *Memphis Daily Appeal*, April 7, 1858.

27. John Forrest had suffered "a gun-shot wound through the lower part of the spinal cord" in the Mexican War that resulted in partial paralysis. According to Wyeth (pp. 6–7), he "could neither walk nor stand without the aid of crutches." See also Henry, p. 23.

28. Bancroft, p. 265.

29. Quoted in ibid., p. 258; *Memphis Eagle & Enquirer*, January 4, 1854.

30. *Memphis Daily Appeal*, July 15, 1855.

31. Ibid., July 24, 1855.

32. *Memphis City Directory*, 1855, p. 251.

33. Horatio J. Eden memoirs, Tennessee State Library and Archives, Nashville, Tenn.

34. Michael Tadman, *Speculators and Slaves: Masters, Traders, and Slaves in the Old South* (Madison: University of Wisconsin Press, 1990), p. 187.

35. Jordan and Pryor, pp. 25–26; Wyeth, pp. 20–21; Mathes, p. 16; Andrew Nelson Lytle, *Bedford Forrest and His Critter Company* (New York: G. P. Putnam's Sons, 1931), pp. 27–28; Henry, p. 26.

36. Bancroft, pp. 258–259.

37. *Memphis Daily Appeal*, July 15, 1855.

38. Ibid., June 3, 1857.

39. James Oakes, *The Ruling Race: A History of American Slaveholders* (New York: Alfred A. Knopf, 1982), p. 171.

40. Ibid., p. 122; *Memphis City Directory*, 1855, p. 251.

41. Oakes, p. 194.

42. Tadman, pp. 8, 47.

43. Ibid., p. 133.

44. Oakes, p. 123.

45. Tadman, p. 205.

46. Oakes, p. 134.

47. This economic model stems from the work of Immanuel Wallerstein, Eugene D. Genovese, and Elizabeth Fox-Genovese. For more information on world-systems analysis and American slavery, see Immanuel Wallerstein, "American Slavery and the Capitalist World Economy," *The Capitalist World-Economy* (Cambridge, England: Cambridge University Press, 1979), pp. 202–21. See also Eugene D. Genovese, *The World the Slaveholders Made: Two Essays on Interpretation* (New York: Vintage Books, 1971); Elizabeth Fox-Genovese and Eugene D. Genovese, *Fruits of Merchant Capital: Slavery and Bourgeois Property in the Rise and Expansion of Capitalism* (Cambridge, England: Cambridge University Press, 1983).

48. Tadman, p. 192.

49. Ibid., p. 200.

50. Ibid., p. 83.

51. Ibid., p. 203.

52. Oakes, p. 124.

53. *Memphis Daily Appeal*, June 3, 1857.

54. Joe Gray Taylor, *Negro Slavery in Louisiana* (Baton Rouge: Louisiana Historical Association, 1963), p. 50.

55. Bill of sale, Memphis Pink Palace Museum, Memphis, Tenn.

56. *Memphis Daily Appeal*, May 7, 1857.

57. James Sheppard Papers, William R. Perkins Library, Duke University, Durham, N.C.; Orville W. Taylor, *Negro Slavery in Arkansas* (Durham, N.C.: Duke University Press, 1958), p. 64. There is some discrepancy in the name of one of the slaves. Forrest's receipt listed the name as Emanuel, whereas the captain's receipt used the name Edmund, as did Taylor.

58. Wyeth, p. 22; Henry, p. 27.

59. Harry Abernathy, "Famous General Retired to Coahoma County Plantation," *Clarksdale Press Register*, July 21, 1984.

60. Ozias Midwinter, "Notes on Forrest's Funeral," *Cincinnati Commercial*, November 6, 1877; Lafcadio Hearn, *Occidental Gleanings* (New York: Dodd, Mead & Co., 1925), vol. 1, p. 148.

61. J. H. Sherard interview, Carnegie Public Library, Clarksdale, Coahoma County, Miss.

62. *U.S. Census, Population and Slave Schedules, Coahoma County, Mississippi, and Memphis, Shelby County, Tennessee*, 1860.

63. Raimondo Luraghi, *The Rise and Fall of the Plantation South* (New York: New Viewpoints, 1978).

64. Bancroft, pp. 253–55.

65. *Memphis Daily Appeal*, April 7, 1858.

66. Shields McIlwaine, *Memphis Down in Dixie* (New York: E. P. Dutton, 1948), p. 106.

67. Bancroft, p. 262.

68. William S. Fitzgerald, "Did Nathan Bedford Forrest Really Rescue John Able?" *Tennessee Historical Quarterly* 39 (Spring 1980), pp. 16–26; Jordan and Pryor, pp. 29–33; Wyeth, pp. 21–22; Henry, p. 27.

69. *Memphis Daily Appeal,* August 4, 1859.

70. Ibid.

71. Jordan and Pryor, pp. 33–34.

72. Mathes, pp. 19–21.

73. Quoted in Jordan and Pryor, p. 34.

74. Ibid.; Henry, p. 27.

75. N. B. Forrest testimony, *Ku Klux Conspiracy: Report of the Joint Select Committee to Inquire into the Condition of Affairs in the Late Insurrectionary States,* to the two Houses of Congress, February 19, 1872, 42nd Cong., 2d sess., Senate Report no. 41, vol. 13, p. 24.

CHAPTER 3: A CHANCE FOR ACTIVE SERVICE

1. Thomas Jordan and J. P. Pryor, *The Campaigns of Lieut.-Gen. N. B. Forrest, and of Forrest's Cavalry* (New Orleans: Blelock & Co., 1868), p. 40.

2. For more on the ideology of the Republican party, see Eric Foner, *Free Soil, Free Labor, Free Men: The Ideology of the Republican Party Before the Civil War* (New York: Oxford University Press, 1970).

3. Jordan and Pryor, p. 40; Robert Selph Henry, *"First With the Most" Forrest* (Indianapolis: Bobbs-Merrill Co., 1944), p. 30.

4. Henry, p. 31.

5. John Allan Wyeth, *Life of General Nathan Bedford Forrest* (New York: Harper & Bros., 1899), p. 24.

6. Ibid., pp. 24–25; Jordan and Pryor, pp. 41–43; Henry, pp. 32–33. See also Charles W. Button, "Early Engagements With Forrest," *Confederate Veteran* 5 (September 1897), p. 478.

7. Quoted in Wyeth, p. 26.

8. *Memphis Daily Appeal,* August 29, 1861.

9. Tate to A. S. Johnston, November 4, 1861, *The War of the Rebellion: A Compilation of the Official Records of the Union and Confederate Armies,* 128 vols. (Washington, D.C.: U.S. Government Printing Office, 1880–1901), Series I, 4, p. 513 (cited hereafter as *OR.* All references are to Series I unless otherwise noted).

10. Button, p. 479.

11. James H. Hamner to mother and brother, December 19, 1861, Hamner-Stacy Papers, West Tennessee Historical Society, Memphis State University, Memphis, Tenn.

12. Ibid.

13. Forrest report, December 5, 1861, *OR,* 7, p. 5.

14. Jordan and Pryor, pp. 48–49.

15. Hamner to mother and brother, January 7, 1862.

16. Forrest report, December 30, 1861, *OR,* 7, p. 65.

17. Button, p. 479.
18. Hamner letter, January 7, 1862.
19. Wyeth, pp. 32–33.
20. Hamner letter, January 7, 1862.
21. Forrest report, December 30, 1861, *OR*, 7, p. 65.
22. Hamner letter, January 7, 1862.
23. Jordan and Pryor, pp. 52–53; Wyeth, p. 32; Henry, p. 45.
24. Forrest report, December 30, 1861, *OR*, 7, p. 66.
25. Hamner letter, January 7, 1862.
26. Crittenden to Buell, December 30, 1861, *OR*, 7, p. 63.
27. Hamner letter, January 7, 1862. See also H. T. Gray, "Forrest's First Cavalry Fight," *Confederate Veteran*, 15 (March 1907), p. 139.
28. J. C. Blanton, "Forrest's Old Regiment," *Confederate Veteran* 3 (February 1895), p. 41.
29. Richard Taylor, *Destruction and Reconstruction: Personal Experiences of the Late War* (New York: Longmans, Green & Co., 1955), p. 244.

CHAPTER 4: RIDERS ON THE STORM

1. Thomas Jordan and J. P. Pryor, *The Campaigns of Lieut.-Gen. N. B. Forrest, and of Forrest's Cavalry* (New Orleans: Blelock & Co., 1868), p. 55.
2. Jordan and Pryor, pp. 62–63; John Allan Wyeth, *Life of General Nathan Bedford Forrest* (New York: Harper & Bros., 1899), pp. 42–43; Robert Selph Henry, *"First With the Most" Forrest* (Indianapolis: Bobbs Merrill Co., 1944), pp. 49–50; Tilghman reports, February 7, February 12, 1862, *OR*, 7, pp. 136, 136–44; James J. Hamilton, *The Battle of Fort Donelson* (South Brunswick, N.J.: Thomas Yoseloff, 1968), pp. 24–28; Benjamin Franklin Cooling, *Forts Henry and Donelson: The Key to the Confederate Heartland* (Knoxville: University of Tennessee Press, 1987), pp. 101–09.
3. Henry, pp. 51–53; Hamilton, pp. 59, 63, 66, 69–72; Cooling, p. 123.
4. Wyeth, pp. 44–45; Hamilton, 114; Cooling, p. 140.
5. Thomas J. Riddell, "Western Campaign: Movements of the Goochland Light Artillery—Captain John H. Guy," *Southern Historical Society Papers* 24 (1896), p. 318.
6. Wyeth, p. 45.
7. Henry, p. 53; Cooling, pp. 122, 138.
8. Cooling, pp. 153–59.
9. Quoted in Wyeth, pp. 46–47.
10. Forrest report, February, 1862, *OR*, 7, p. 384.
11. Ibid., p. 385.
12. Wyeth, pp. 53–54.
13. Forrest report, February, 1862, *OR*, 7, p. 385; Henry, pp. 55–56.
14. Cooling, p. 202.
15. Spot F. Terrell journal, Tennessee State Library and Archives, Nashville.

16. Forrest report, March 15, 1862, *OR*, 7, p. 295.

17. Forrest report, February, 1862, *OR*, 7, p. 386.

18. Forrest reports, March 15, November 7, 1862, *OR*, 7, pp. 295–96; 387.

19. Bruce Catton, *Terrible Swift Sword* (Garden City, N.Y.: Doubleday & Co., 1963), p. 150.

20. Henry, p. 59; Cooling, p. 205.

21. John S. Wilkes, "First Battle Experience—Fort Donelson," *Confederate Veteran* 14 (November 1916), p. 501.

22. Jordan and Pryor, pp. 92–93; Henry, p. 59.

23. Forrest report, February, 1862, *OR*, 7, p. 386; Jordan and Pryor, p. 93; Henry, pp. 59–60.

24. Forrest report, February, 1862, *OR*, 7, p. 386; Henry, p. 63.

25. Stanley F. Horn, "Nashville During the Civil War," *Tennessee Historical Quarterly* 4 (March 1945), p. 9.

26. Henry, p. 67.

27. Horn, p. 9.

28. Forrest report, n.d., *OR*, 7, pp. 429–31.

29. Jordan and Pryor, p. 106; Wyeth, p. 74; Henry, p. 71.

30. James M. McPherson, *Battle Cry of Freedom: The Civil War Era* (New York: Oxford University Press, 1988), p. 327.

31. Jordan and Pryor, p. 106; Wyeth, p. 74; Henry, p. 71.

32. Henry, p. 77.

33. Ibid., p. 79; see also Wyeth, p. 77; James Lee McDonough, *Shiloh—In Hell Before Night* (Knoxville: University of Tennessee Press, 1977), p. 194.

34. William T. Sherman, *Memoirs of General William T. Sherman* (New York: Charles L. Webster & Co., 1892), Vol. 1, p. 243.

35. Jordan and Pryor, pp. 146–48; Wyeth, pp. 78–79; Henry, p. 81.

36. Jordan and Pryor, p. 158.

37. Quoted in Henry, p. 82.

38. Abstract from return of the Central Army of Kentucky, March 31, 1862, *OR*, 10, pt. 2, p. 377; abstract from morning report of the Cavalry Brigade, April 28, 1862, *OR*, 10, pt. 2, p. 459.

39. Ibid., p. 83; Jordan and Pryor, p. 159; Wyeth, p. 84.

40. Brent to Forrest, June 9, 1862, *OR*, 10, pt. 2, p. 602.

41. Jordan and Pryor, p. 160; Wyeth, p. 84; Henry, p. 83.

42. Quoted in Wyeth, pp. 639–40.

43. Tennessee Cavalry, Regiment Fourth, Folder 13, Military Units, Confederate Collection, Civil War Collection, Box 17, Tennessee State Library and Archives, Nashville (hereafter called Fourth Tennessee Cavalry, TSLA).

44. Crittenden report, n.d., *OR*, 16, pt. 1, pp. 794–95; Findings of a Court of Inquiry, January 24, 1863, *OR*, 16, pt. 1, p. 797; Duffield report, July 234, 1862, *OR*, 16, pt. 1, p. 801; Parkhurst report, n.d., *OR*, 16, pt. 1, p. 804; Henry, pp. 86–87.

45. Forrest Report,—, 1862, *OR*, 16, pt. 1, pp. 810–11; see also Henry, pp. 88–89; Lytle, p. 97; Charles F. Bryan, "'I Mean to Have Them All': Forrest's Murfreesboro Raid," *Civil War Times Illustrated* 12 (July 1974), p. 31. See also Frank Battle, "Gen. Forrest's Order to Col. Baxter Smith," *Confederate Veteran* 7 (February 1899), p. 70.

46. Parkhurst report, n.d., *OR*, 16, pt. 1, p. 805; Henry, p. 89.

47. Forrest report,—, 1862, *OR*, 16, pt. 1, p. 811.

48. Fourth Tennessee Cavalry, TSLA.

49. Forrest to Washburne, June 23, 1864, *OR*, 32, pt. 1, pp. 590, 591; Wyeth, p. 390; J. Harvey Mathes, *General Forrest* (New York: D. Appleton & Co., 1902), p. 231.

50. Jordan and Pryor, pp. 169–70.

51. Wyeth barely mentioned the incident, and did so without reference to race (p. 88). Mathes referred to the incident in two lines, essentially summarizing Wyeth's version (p. 66). Lytle devoted two sentences to the incident (p. 96), while Henry did not mention the affair.

52. D. S. Stanley, "Is Forrest a Butcher?—A Little Bit of History," *New York Times*, September 14, 1868.

53. Fourth Tennessee Cavalry, TSLA.

54. George Richard Browder, *The Heavens Are Weeping: The Diaries of George Richard Browder 1852–1886*, ed. by Richard L. Troutman (Grand Rapids, Mich.: Zondervan Publishing House, 1987), p. 125.

CHAPTER 5: CHARGE THEM BOTH WAYS

1. Bragg to Kirby Smith, July 20, 1862, *OR*, 17, pt. 2, p. 652.

2. Nelson to Buell, July 24, 1862, *OR*, 16, pt. 2, pp. 208–09.

3. Forrest report, July 24, 1862, *OR*, 16, pt. 1, p. 819.

4. Nelson report, July 24, 1862, *OR*, 16, pt. 1, p. 816.

5. Buell to Nelson, August 10, 1862, *OR*, 16, pt. 2, p. 304.

6. Nelson to Buell, July 30, 1862, *OR*, 16, pt. 2, p. 234.

7. Buell to Miller, August 15, 1862, *OR*, 16, pt. 2, p. 340.

8. Forrest to Garner, August 6, 1862, Nathan Bedford Forrest Collection, Chicago Historical Society, Chicago.

9. Thomas Lawrence Connelly, *Army of the Heartland: The Army of Tennessee, 1861–1862* (Baton Rouge: Louisiana State University Press, 1967), pp. 221–22.

10. D. C. Kelley, "General Nathan Bedford Forrest," *Methodist Review* 49 (March–April 1900), p. 226.

11. John Allan Wyeth, *Life of General Nathan Bedford Forrest* (New York: Harper & Bros., 1899), p. 101.

12. Ibid., pp. 101–02.

13. Forrest to Garner, September 3, 1862, EG Box 19, Henry E. Huntington Library, San Marino, Calif.

14. Forrest to Bragg, September 4, 1862, Braxton Bragg Papers, Western Reserve Historical Society, Cleveland, Ohio.

15. Forrest to Garner, September 10, 1862, Braxton Bragg Papers.

16. Thomas Jordan and J. P. Pryor, *The Campaigns of Lieut.-Gen. N. B. Forrest, and of Forrest's Cavalry* (New Orleans: Blelock & Co. 1868), pp. 184–86; Wyeth, p. 103; Robert Selph Henry, *"First With the Most" Forrest* (Indianapolis: Bobbs-Merrill Co., 1944), pp. 100–01; John P. Dyer, *"'Fightin' Joe" Wheeler* (Baton Rouge: Louisiana State University Press, 1941), p. 56. Dyer speculates that Bragg "rid himself" of Forrest "ostensibly to cope with Federal raiding parties sent out from Nashville."

17. Dan W. Baird, "Forrest's Men with Bravest of Brave," *Southern Historical Society Papers* 37 (1909), p. 364.

18. Forrest to Breckinridge, October 20, 1862—9 P.M., John Cabell Breckinridge Collection, Chicago Historical Society, Chicago (hereafter Breckinridge Collection).

19. Forrest to Breckinridge, October 21, 1862, Breckinridge Collection.

20. Forrest to Breckinridge, two telegrams, November 4, 1862, Breckinridge Collection.

21. Henry, p. 105.

22. Forrest report, December 24, 1862, *OR,* 17, pt. 1, p. 593; Jordan and Pryor, pp. 195–96; Wyeth, pp. 110–14; Henry, pp. 109–10. See also V. Y. Cook, "Forrest's Capture of Col. R. G. Ingersoll," *Confederate Veteran* 15 (February 1907), pp. 54–55; J. C. Steger, "The Cavalry Fight at Lexington, Tenn.," *Confederate Veteran* 15 (May 1907), p. 226; Dan W. Beard, "With Forrest in West Tennessee," *Southern Historical Society Papers* 37 (1909), pp. 304–05.

23. John Watson Morton, *The Artillery of Nathan Bedford Forrest's Cavalry* (Nashville, Tenn.: Publishing House of the M. E. Church, South, 1909), pp. 46–47.

24. Sullivan to Grant, 7:10 P.M., December 18, 1862, *OR,* 17, pt. 1, p. 551; Henry, p. 110.

25. Morton, p. 49.

26. Henry, p. 113.

27. Dibrell report, January 6, 1863, *OR,* 17, pt. 1, p. 598.

28. Sullivan to Grant, December 19, 1862, *OR,* 17, pt. 1, p. 551.

29. Henry, p. 112.

30. Englemann report, December 29, 1862, *OR,* 17, pt. 1, p. 556.

31. Forrest report, December 24, 1862, *OR,* 17, pt. 1, pp. 593–94; Fry report, January 17, 1863, *OR,* 17, pt. 1, pp. 560–62.

32. Henry, p. 113.

33. Ibid., p. 114; Forrest report, December 24, 1862, *OR,* 17, pt. 1, p. 594; Jordan and Pryor, p. 203; Wyeth, p. 119; Beard, pp. 306–07.

34. Logan report, December 27, 1862, *OR,* 17, pt. 1, pp. 562–68.

35. Forrest report, December 24, 1862, *OR,* 17, pt. 1, p. 594.

36. Davies report, January 9, 1863, *OR*, 17, pt. 1, pp. 548–49.
37. Fisk to Grant, December 27, 1862, *OR*, 17, pt. 2, pp. 494–95.
38. Sullivan to Grant, *OR*, 17, pt. 2, p. 505.
39. Wyeth, p. 121.
40. Dunham report, December 31, 1862, *OR*, 17, pt. 1, p. 580.
41. Quoted in Wyeth p. 132; see also Henry, p. 118.
42. Forrest report, January 3, 1863, *OR*, 17, pt. 1, p. 596.
43. Cummings report, December 31, 1862, *OR*, 17, pt. 1, p. 589.
44. Forrest report, January 3, 1863, *OR*, 17, pt. 1, p. 596.
45. Ibid.
46. "Reunion of Forrest's Escort," *Confederate Veteran* 2 (October 1894), p. 308.
47. Ibid.
48. Quoted in Henry, p. 118. See also Andrew Nelson Lytle, *Bedford Forrest and His Critter Company* (New York: G. P. Putnam's Sons, 1931), p. 134; Dan Kennerly, "The Dawn of Lightning War—General Forrest and Parker's Crossroads" (Houston: Dan Kennerly, 1982), p. 15; Lonnie E. Maness, "Forrest and the Battle of Parker's Crossroads," *Tennessee Historical Quarterly* 34 (Summer 1975), p. 163.
49. Quoted in Wyeth, pp. 134–35; see also, Kennerly, p. 16.
50. Henry, p. 120; see also A. J. Lacy to father and mother, January 1863, Andrew Jackson Lacy Papers, Tennessee State Library and Archives, Nashville, for an excellent summary of the campaign by a participant.
51. Sylvanus Cadwallader, *Three Years With Grant: As Recalled by War Correspondent Sylvanus Cadwallader* (New York: Alfred A. Knopf, 1955), p. 39.
52. Sullivan to Grant, December 31, 1862, *OR*, 17, pt. 1, p. 552.
53. Sullivan to Grant, January 2, 1863, *OR*, 17, pt. 1.
54. Grant to Sullivan, January 2, 1863, *OR*, 17, pt. 1, p. 553.
55. Sullivan to Grant, January 2, 1863, *OR*, 17, pt. 1, p. 552.
56. Return of Casualties, n.d., *OR*, 17, pt. 1, p. 553.
57. Forrest report, January 3, 1863, *OR*, 17, pt. 1.
58. Wheeler report, February, 1863, *OR*, 23, pt. 1, p. 40.
59. Jordan and Pryor, pp. 225–26.
60. Quoted in Wyeth, pp. 146–47.
61. Henry, p. 124, J. Harvey Mathes, *General Forrest* (New York: D. Appleton & Co., 1902), p. 97, and Lytle, pp. 141–42, noted Forrest's objections to the operation.
62. Harding to Wheeler, February 3, 1863, *OR*, 23, pt. 1, p. 39.
63. Wheeler report, February, 1863, *OR*, 23, pt. 1, p. 40.
64. Harding report, February 6, 1863, *OR*, 23, pt. 1, pp. 36–37.
65. Wyeth, pp. 148–149.
66. Wheeler report, February, 1863, *OR*, 23, pt. 1, p. 40.
67. Ibid., pp. 40–41.

68. Harding report, February 6, 1863, *OR*, 23, pt. 1, pp. 38–39.
69. Wyeth, pp. 151–52; Henry, p. 126; Dyer, pp. 94–96.

CHAPTER 6: A STREIGHT BLUFF

1. John Allan Wyeth, *Life of General Nathan Bedford Forrest* (New York: Harper & Bros., 1899), p. 154; see also Forrest to Wheeler, February 18, 1863, *OR*, 23, pt. 2, p. 638.
2. Forrest report, March, 1863, *OR*, 23, pt. 1, pp. 120–21.
3. John Watson Morton, *The Artillery of Nathan Bedford Forrest's Cavalry* (Nashville, Tenn.: Publishing House of the M. E. Church, South, 1909), p. 82.
4. Forrest report, March, 1863, *OR*, 23, pt. 1, p. 121.
5. Bloodgood report, May 23, 1863, *OR*, 23, pt. 1, pp. 183–84; Forrest report, April 1, 1863, *OR*, 23, pt. 1, pp. 187–88; Wyeth, pp. 168–69; Robert Selph Henry, *"First With the Most" Forrest* (Indianapolis: Bobbs-Merrill Co., 1944), pp. 132–33.
6. Thomas Jordan and J. P. Pryor, *The Campaigns of Lieut.-Gen. N. B. Forrest, and of Forrest's Cavalry* (New Orleans: Blelock & Co., 1868), pp. 242–43.
7. Ibid., pp. 243–45.
8. Newton Cannon memoir, p. 9, Newton Cannon Papers, Tennessee State Library and Archives, Nashville.
9. J. L. Weaver to Mr. and Mrs. J. A. Clark, April 5, 1917, Joseph Dent Clark Papers, Tennessee State Library and Archives, Nashville.
10. Wyeth, pp. 176–177; Edward Dillon, "General Van Dorn's Operations between Columbia and Nashville in 1863," *Southern Historical Society Papers* 7 (1879), pp. 144–146; Robert G. Hartje, *Van Dorn: The Life and Times of a Confederate General* (Nashville, Tenn.: Vanderbilt University Press, 1967), pp. 301–04.
11. Ibid., p. 247; Morton, pp. 87–88; Wyeth, p. 183; Henry, p. 137. See also Thomas R. Tullos, "When Capt. Sam Freeman was Killed," *Confederate Veteran* 21 (August 1913), p. 407.
12. Morton, pp. 88–89.
13. Wyeth, pp. 183–184.
14. Streight report, August 22, 1864, *OR*, 23, pt. 1, p. 286. For assessments of Streight's raid, see Edward G. Longacre, "All Is Fair in Love and War," *Civil War Times Illustrated* 8 (June 1969), pp. 32–40; William Barton McCash, "Colonel Abel D. Streight's Raid, His Capture, and Imprisonment" (master's thesis, University of Georgia, 1959); James F. Cook, "The 1863 Raid of Abel D. Streight: Why It Failed," *Alabama Review* 22 (October 1969), pp. 254–69.
15. Streight report, August 22, 1864, *OR*, 23, pt. 1, p. 286; see also Longacre, p. 34.
16. Longacre, pp. 35–36.

17. Ibid., p. 36.
18. Jordan and Pryor, pp. 257–59; Wyeth, pp. 197–201; Henry, p. 147.
19. Wyeth, p. 202; Henry, p. 148.
20. Quoted in Wyeth, p. 198.
21. Streight report, August 22, 1864, *OR*, 23, pt. 1, p. 289.
22. Wyeth, pp. 203–04.
23. Ibid., p. 206.
24. Ibid., p. 207.
25. Streight report, August 22, 1864, *OR*, 23, pt. 1, p. 290.
26. Charles W. Crawford, "A Note on Forrest's Race for Rome," *Georgia Historical Quarterly* 50 (September 1966), pp. 289–90. Crawford speculated that this message never reached Rome, which, in any event, was warned when mail carrier John Wisdom rode into town.
27. Jordan and Pryor, pp. 267–69; see also Wyeth, pp. 207–12; Henry, pp. 150–51.
28. Streight report, August 22, 1864, *OR*, 23, pt. 1, p. 290.
29. Jordan and Pryor, pp. 270–71; Wyeth, p. 214; Henry, p. 152.
30. Streight report, August 22, 1864, *OR*, 23, pt. 1, p. 290.
31. Henry, pp. 153–54, George Magruder Battey, Jr., *A History of Rome and Floyd County* (Atlanta: Web & Vary Co., 1922), provided a detailed description of Wisdom's dramatic ride and likened it to that of Paul Revere (pp. 171–74).
32. Jordan and Pryor, p. 272; Wyeth, pp. 214–16.
33. Streight report, August 22, 1864, *OR*, 23, pt. 1, p. 292.
34. Jordan and Pryor, p. 273; Wyeth, pp. 217–18; Henry, p. 156.
35. Streight report, August 22, 1864, *OR*, 23, pt. 1, p. 292.
36. Wyeth, p. 218.
37. Quoted in Jordan and Pryor, pp. 273–74; see also Henry, pp. 156–57; Dabney Herndon Maury, *Recollections of a Virginian in the Mexican, Indian and Civil Wars* (New York: Charles Scribner's Sons, 1894), p. 209.
38. Henry, p. 157.
39. Quoted in Maury, p. 209; see also Longacre, p. 40.

CHAPTER 7: NOTHING TO BRAGG ABOUT

1. Robert Selph Henry, *"First With the Most" Forrest* (Indianapolis: Bobbs-Merrill Co., 1944), p. 158.
2. Ibid.
3. Thomas Jordan and J. P. Pryor, *The Campaigns of Lieut.-Gen. N. B. Forrest, and of His Cavalry* (New Orleans: Blelock & Co., 1868), pp. 280–81; John Allan Wyeth, *Life of General Nathan Bedford Forrest* (New York: Harper & Bros., 1899), pp. 221–22.
4. Jordan and Pryor, p. 282.

5. Jordan and Pryor, p. 286; Wyeth, pp. 226–27; Henry, p. 161.

6. John Watson Morton, *The Artillery of Nathan Bedford Forrest's Cavalry* (Nashville, Tenn.: Publishing House of the M. E. Church, South, 1909), p. 101.

7. Ibid.

8. Frank H. Smith, "The Forrest-Gould Affair," *Civil War Times Illustrated* 9 (November 1970), p. 32. Henry H. Smith described the Forrest-Gould affair differently. He had been having a meal with the general in a local home when Gould came to the door. Forrest postponed their meeting until 3 P.M. While Smith sat in "the clerk's office" smoking a cigar, Gould "sprang out" at an unsuspecting Forrest, "drew his pistol, and shot the General in the thigh." Forrest then used the knife Smith had given him earlier to defend himself. See Henry H. Smith, "Reminiscences of Capt. Henry H. Smith," *Confederate Veteran* 8 (January 1900), p. 14.

9. Henry, p. 162.

10. Quoted in Frank Smith, pp. 32–33.

11. Ibid., pp. 33–34; see also Henry Smith, pp. 14–15.

12. Quoted in Frank Smith, pp. 34–35; see also Henry, p. 163.

13. Wyeth, pp. 225–26.

14. Morton, p. 104.

15. Frank Smith, p. 36.

16. Jordan and Pryor.

17. Henry, pp. 165–66.

18. Wyeth, p. 233.

19. Ibid., p. 234; Henry, p. 167.

20. Morton, p. 110; Wyeth, p. 628; Henry, p. 168.

21. Wyeth, pp. 236–37; Henry, p. 173.

22. Forrest to Davis, August 19, 1863; Forrest to Cooper, August 9, 1863, *OR*, 30, pt. 4, pp. 507–11.

23. Bell Irvin Wiley, *The Road to Appomattox* (New York: Atheneum, 1977), pp. 61, 65.

24. Henry, pp. 172–73; Thomas Lawrence Connelly, *Autumn of Glory: The Army of Tennessee, 1862–1865* (Baton Rouge: Louisiana State University Press, 1971), pp. 166–75.

25. Henry, pp. 173–81; Connelly, pp. 175–96.

26. By a Confederate, *The Grayjackets: And How They Lived, Fought and Died, for Dixie* (Richmond, Va.: Jones Bro. & Co., n.d.), pp. 356–357. This collection of war stories includes "A Thrilling Event," which appears to be the only account that indicated the location and nature of Forrest's wound in this engagement. "The ball struck General Forrest near the spine, within an inch of the wound he received at Shiloh, inflicting a painful but not dangerous wound." No source is listed for this information.

27. Wyeth, p. 240.

28. Brent circular, September 18, 1863; see also Bragg report, December 28, 1863, *OR,* 30, pt. 2, p. 31.

29. Henry, pp. 181–82.

30. Ibid., pp. 182–83; Wyeth, p. 250; A. B. Clay, "On the Right at Chickamauga," *Confederate Veteran* 19 (July 1911), p. 329.

31. Forrest report, October 22, 1863, *OR,* 30, pt. 2, p. 524.

32. Wyeth, p. 250.

33. Forrest report, October 22, 1863, *OR,* 30, pt. 2, p. 524.

34. Maney report, October 6, 1863, *OR,* 30, pt. 2, p. 95.

35. Forrest report, October 22, 1863, *OR,* 30, pt. 2, p. 525.

36. Glenn Tucker, *Chickamauga: Bloody Battle in the West* (Indianapolis: Bobbs-Merrill Co., 1961), pp. 211, 213–15, 222–24.

37. Ibid., pp. 195–96, 202; see also Freeman Cleaves, *Rock of Chickamauga: The Life of General George H. Thomas* (Norman: University of Oklahoma Press, 1948), pp. 162–63.

38. Bragg report, December 28, 1863, *OR,* 30, pt. 2, p. 33.

39. Quoted in Wyeth, pp. 252–53.

40. D. H. Hill report, n.d., *OR,* 30, pt. 2, p. 146.

41. Tucker, pp. 252–59; Cleaves, pp. 166–67.

42. Tucker, pp. 332, 358–59, 362–75, 377–78; Cleaves, pp. 171–75; Joseph H. Parks, *General Leonidas Polk CSA: The Fighting Bishop* (Baton Rouge: Louisiana State University Press, 1962), p. 340.

43. Tucker placed Bragg's total casualties higher, at 20,950.

44. Forrest to Polk, September 21, 1863, *OR,* 30, pt. 4, p. 681; Forrest to Polk, September 21, 1863, James Longstreet Papers, Georgia Department of Archives and History, Atlanta.

45. Quoted in Wyeth, p. 198.

46. Quoted in ibid., p. 644.

47. Forrest to Polk, September 21, 1863, 11:30 A.M., *OR,* 30, pt. 4, p. 675.

48. Quoted in Tucker, p. 382; see also, Daniel H. Hill, "Chickamauga—The Great Battle of the West," *Battles and Leaders of the Civil War* (New York: Thomas Yoseloff, 1956), vol. 3, p. 622; B. L. Ridley, "Daring Deeds of Staff and Escort," *Confederate Veteran* 4 (October 1896), p. 359.

49. James Lee McDonough, *Chattanooga—A Death Grip on the Confederacy* (Knoxville: University of Tennessee Press, 1984), p. 23.

50. Quoted in Henry, p. 193. Although undoubtedly motivated by the exhaustion and disorganization of his army in his decision not to pursue the defeated Union forces after Chickamauga, Bragg may also have been influenced by the spate of messages he had received the previous year from Forrest concerning Union activities in Nashville. Forrest believed in 1862, as vehemently as he believed now, that the Federals were evacuating the city and urged vigorous action by his superiors. In the case of Nashville, he was incorrect.

51. Ibid., pp. 194–95; Forrest report, October 22, 1863, *OR,* pt. 2, p. 526.

52. Brent to Forrest, September 28, 1863, *OR*, 30, pt. 4, p. 710.

53. Quoted in Henry, pp. 196–97; see also Forrest to Wheeler, September 28, 1863, *OR*, 30, pt. 4, p. 711.

54. Wheeler report, October 30, 1863, *OR*, 30, pt. 2, p. 723.

55. Quoted in McDonough, p. 32.

56. Wyeth, p. 264; Henry, p. 198.

57. Henry, p. 175.

58. D. C. Kelley, "General Nathan Bedford Forrest," *Methodist Review* 49 (March–April 1900), p. 226.

59. Quoted in ibid., p. 171.

60. Harry St. John Dixon diary, November and December 1864 entries, Harry St. John Dixon Papers, Southern Historical Collection, University of North Carolina, Chapel Hill. See also Bell I. Wiley, *The Life of Johnny Reb: The Common Soldier of the Confederacy* (Baton Rouge: Louisiana State University Press, 1978), p. 338.

61. John W. DuBose to father, January 22, 1865, John W. DuBose Papers, Alabama Department of Archives and History, Montgomery.

62. Quoted in Henry, p. 14.

63. Quoted in Wyeth, pp. 264–66.

CHAPTER 8: THE WAR HITS HOME

1. Bragg to S. D. Lee, October 13, 1863, *OR*, 31, pt. 3, p. 604.

2. Robert Selph Henry, *"First With the Most" Forrest* (Indianapolis: Bobbs-Merrill Co., 1944), pp. 200–01.

3. Special Orders, No. 245, November 14, 1863, *OR*, 31, pt. 3, p. 694.

4. Hurlbut to Grant, November 3, 1863, *OR*, 31, pt. 3, p. 31.

5. Forrest to B. S. Ewell, November 21, 1863, *OR*, 31, pt. 3, p. 730.

6. Herman Hattaway, *General Stephen D. Lee* (Jackson: University Press of Mississippi, 1976), p. 104.

7. Ibid., pp. 104–05; S. D. Lee to Forrest, November 7, 1863, *OR*, 31, pt. 3, p. 646.

8. R. E. Corry to wife, November 21, 1863, Robert E. Corry Papers, Auburn University Library, Auburn, Ala.

9. R. E. Corry to Lizzie, November 25, 1863, Corry Papers, Auburn.

10. Sherman to Hurlbut, November 18, 1863, *OR*, 31, pt. 3, p. 187.

11. Forrest to Johnston, December 13, 1863, *OR*, 31, pt. 3, pp. 789–90.

12. Davis to Johnston, December 13, 1863, *OR*, 31, pt. 3, pp. 816–17; Forrest to B. S. Ewell, December 13, 1863, *OR*, 31, pt. 3, p. 817.

13. Hurlbut to Grant, December 19, 1863, *OR*, 31, pt. 3, p. 449.

14. Hurlbut to Grierson, December 23, 1863, *OR*, 31, pt. 3, p. 478.

15. John Allan Wyeth, *Life of General Nathan Bedford Forrest* (New York: Harper & Bros., 1899), pp. 281–86; Henry, pp. 207–09.

16. Quoted in Henry, p. 209.

17. Ibid., p. 210; Wyeth, pp. 286–87.

18. Quoted in Thomas Jordan and J. P. Pryor, *The Campaigns of Lieut.-Gen. N. B. Forrest, and of Forrest's Cavalry* (New Orleans: Blelock & Co., 1868), pp. 375–76; Henry, p. 210.

19. Henry, pp. 210–11.

20. Morgan to Grierson, December 29, 1863, *OR*, 31, pt. 3, p. 534.

21. Forrest to Polk, December 29, 1863, *OR*, 31, pt. 1, p. 621.

22. Forrest to Chalmers, December 28, 1863, *OR*, 31, pt. 3, p. 877.

23. Forrest to Cooper, January 2, 1864, *OR*, 32, pt. 2, pp. 512–13; Seddon endorsement, January 24, 1864, *OR*, 32, pt. 2, p. 513.

24. Wyeth, p. 289; Henry, pp. 213–14.

25. General Orders No. 1, January 26, 1864, *OR*, 32, pt. 2, p. 617.

26. Ibid.; General Orders No. 2, January 24, 1864, *OR*, 32, pt. 2, p. 609; General Orders No. 3, January 25, 1864, *OR*, 32, pt. 2, p. 614.

27. Jordan and Pryor, pp. 384–85; Wyeth, pp. 295–96; Henry, p. 215; James Dinkins, *1861 to 1865 Personal Recollections and Experiences in the Confederate Army. By an Old Johnnie* (Cincinnati: Robert Clarke Co., 1897), pp. 129–31.

28. Dinkins, p. 131.

29. Sherman to Halleck, January 12, 1864, *OR*, 32, pt. 2, p. 75; Grant to Halleck, January 15, 1864, *OR*, 32, pt. 2, pp. 100–01; Grant to Sherman, January 15, 1864, *OR*, 32, pt. 2, p. 105.

30. Henry, p. 219; see also W. S. Smith to Sherman, January 28, 1864, *OR*, 32, pt. 2, p. 251.

31. Henry, pp. 222–23; Forrest to Polk, February 10, 1864—1 P.M., *OR*, 32, pt. 1, p. 347; Forrest to Polk, February 11, 1864, *OR*, 32, pt. 1, p. 348; Forrest to Polk, February 26, 1864, *OR*, 32, pt. 1, p. 350; Forrest to Chalmers, February 9, 1864—5:40 P.M., *OR*, 32, pt. 2, p. 703; Anderson to Chalmers, February 10, 1864, *OR*, 32, pt. 2, p. 706.

32. W. S. Smith reports, February 26, March 4, 1864, *OR*, 32, pt. 1, pp. 251–52, 255–56.

33. Quoted in Henry, p. 224; see also W. S. Smith reports, February 26, March 4, 1864, *OR*, 32, pt. 1, pp. 252, 256–57; Waring report, March 7, 1864, *OR*, 32, pt. 1, p. 267.

34. W. S. Smith Reports, February 26, March 4, 1864, *OR*, 32, pt. 1, pp. 252, 256–57.

35. Forrest report, March 8, 1864, *OR*, 32, pt. 1, p. 352.

36. Quoted in Wyeth, pp. 301–02.

37. Quoted in ibid., pp. 302–03.

38. Forrest to Polk, February 26, 1864, *OR*, 32, pt. 1, p. 350.

39. Quoted in Wyeth, p. 303; Henry, p. 227.

40. Forrest report, March 8, 1864, *OR*, 32, pt. 1, p. 353.

41. Quoted in ibid., Henry, pp. 227–29.

42. Forrest report, March 8, 1864, *OR*, 32, pt. 1, p. 353.

43. Ibid., p. 353; see also W. S. Smith reports, February 26, March 4, 1864, *OR*, 32, pt. 1, pp. 252–53, 257.

44. Forrest report, March 8, 1864, *OR*, 32, pt. 1, p. 353; W. S. Smith reports, February 26, March 4, 1864, *OR*, 32, pt. 1, pp. 253, 257–58.

45. Jordan and Pryor, p. 395; Wyeth, p. 312; Henry, pp. 229–30; Forrest report, March 8, 1864, *OR*, 32, pt. 1, p. 353.

46. Jordan and Pryor, pp. 395–96; Wyeth, pp. 313–14; Henry, pp. 229–30.

47. Jordan and Pryor, p. 396; Wyeth, p. 314; Henry, p. 230.

48. Quoted in Wyeth, pp. 314–15.

49. Quoted in ibid., pp. 315–16.

50. Ibid., p. 316.

51. Quoted in ibid.

52. Quoted in ibid.

53. Jordan and Pryor, p. 398.

54. Forrest report, March 8, 1864, *OR*, 32, pt. 1, p. 354.

55. Ibid.

56. Quoted in Henry, pp. 231–32; see also William Witherspoon, *Reminiscences of a Scout, Spy and Soldier of Forrest's Cavalry* (Jackson, Tenn.: McCowat-Mercer Printing Co., 1910), pp. 34–36; *As They Saw Forrest: Some Recollections and Comments of Contemporaries*, ed. Robert Selph Henry (Jackson, Tenn.: McCowat-Mercer Press, 1956), pp. 98–99.

57. George E. Waring, Jr., "The Sooy Smith Expedition (February, 1864)," *Battles and Leaders of the Civil War* (New York: Thomas Yoseloff, 1956), vol. 4, p. 418.

58. Forrest report, March 8, 1864, *OR*, 32, pt. 1, p. 354.

59. Ibid., pp. 354–55.

60. William T. Sherman, *Memoirs of General William T. Sherman* (New York: Charles L. Webster & Co., 1892), vol. 1, pp. 422–23.

61. Ulysses S. Grant, *Personal Memoirs of U.S. Grant* (New York: Charles L. Webster & Co., 1886) vol. 2, pp. 108–09.

CHAPTER 9: WAR MEANS FIGHTING, AND FIGHTING MEANS KILLING

1. Robert Selph Henry, *"First With the Most" Forrest* (Indianapolis: Bobbs-Merrill Co., 1944), pp. 235–36.

2. Ibid., p. 236; Forrest to Jack, March 10, 1864, *OR*, 32, pt. 3, pp. 609–10.

3. Chalmers to Jack, March 10, 1864, *OR*, 32, pt. 3, p. 610; Chalmers to Cooper, March 10, 1864, *OR*, 32, pt. 3, p. 610.

4. Forrest to Jack, March 10, 1864, *OR*, 32, pt. 3, p. 609.

5. Forrest to Polk, March 12, 1864, *OR*, 32, pt. 3, p. 616.

6. Polk to Cooper, March 14, 1864, *OR*, 32, pt. 3, p. 622.

7. Forrest to Polk, March 12, 1864, *OR*, 32, pt. 3, p. 616.

8. Strange to McCulloch, March 12, 1864, *OR*, 32, pt. 3, p. 617.

9. Forrest to Jack, March 21, 1864, *OR*, 32, pt. 3, p. 664.

10. Forrest to Buckland, March 22, 1864, *OR*, 32, pt. 3, p. 117.

11. Reed to Strange, March 21, 1864, *OR*, 32, pt. 3, pp. 118–19; Forrest report, March 22, 1864, *OR*, 32, pt. 3, p. 119.

12. Forrest to Jack, March 21, 1864, *OR*, 32, pt. 3, p. 663.

13. For a recent study, see Michael Fellman, *Inside War: The Guerrilla Conflict in Missouri During the American Civil War* (New York: Oxford University Press, 1989).

14. Henry, p. 239; Wyeth, p. 328.

15. Beatty report, April 12, 1864, *OR*, 32, pt. 1, p. 543.

16. Hicks report, April 6, 1864, *OR*, 32, pt. 1, p. 547.

17. John Allan Wyeth, *Life of General Nathan Bedford Forrest* (New York: Harper & Bros., 1899), p. 330.

18. J. V. Greif, "Forrest's Raid on Paducah," *Confederate Veteran*, 5 (May 1897), p. 212.

19. Quoted in Wyeth, p. 330.

20. Henry, pp. 240–41; Forrest report, March 27, 1864, *OR*, 32, pt. 1, p. 607.

21. Grierson to Hurst, March 24, 1864, *OR*, 32, pt. 3, pp. 145–46.

22. Chalmers address, April 20, 1864, *OR*, 32, pt. 1, p. 623.

23. Thomas Jordan and J. P. Pryor, *The Campaigns of Lieut.-Gen. N. B. Forrest, and of Forrest's Cavalry* (New Orleans: Blelock & Co., 1868), pp. 420–21; Henry, p. 243.

24. Forrest report, April 4, 1864, *OR*, 32, pt. 1, pp. 608–09.

25. Ibid., p. 609.

26. Sherman to Hurlbut, April 9, 1864,

27. Lawrence report, April 13, 1864, *OR*, 32, pt. 1, p. 553.

28. Hicks report, April 20, 1864, *OR*, 32, pt. 1, pp. 549–50.

29. Wyeth, p. 337; Albert Castel, "The Fort Pillow Massacre: A Fresh Examination of the Evidence," *Civil War History* 4 (1958), pp. 38–39.

30. Wyeth, p. 337; Henry, p. 249.

31. Forrest report, April 4, 1864, *OR*, 32, pt. 1, p. 609.

32. Henry, pp. 249–50.

33. Forrest report, April 15, 1864, *OR*, 32, pt. 1, p. 610; Chalmers circular, April 20, 1864, *OR*, 32, pt. 1, p. 623.

34. Wyeth, pp. 339–41.

35. Quoted in ibid., p. 342; see also Henry, p. 252.

36. Jordan and Pryor, pp. 429–30.

37. Leaming report, January 17, 1865, *OR*, 32, pt. 1, p. 559.

38. Revelle testimony, April 17, 1864, *OR*, 32, pt. 1, p. 528; Gaylord testimony, April 28, 1864, *OR*, 32, pt. 1, p. 535.

39. Wyeth, p. 341.

40. Leaming report, January 17, 1865, *OR*, 32, pt. 1, pp. 559–60.

41. Anderson report, n.d., *OR*, 32, pt. 1, p. 596.

42. Forrest report, April 26, 1864, *OR*, 32, pt. 1, p. 616.

43. Quoted in Wyeth, p. 351; see also Charles W. Anderson, "The

True Story of Fort Pillow," *Confederate Veteran* 3 (November 1895), p. 323.

44. Wyeth, pp. 344–50; Castel, pp. 40–41.

45. Quoted in Jordan and Pryor, p. 435; Forrest report, April 26, 1864, *OR*, 32, pt. 1, p. 614; Statement of John T. Young, May 16, 1864, *OR*, 32, pt. 1, pp. 594–95.

46. Anderson report, n.d., *OR*, 32, pt. 1, p. 597.

47. Quoted in Wyeth, p. 385.

48. Ibid., pp. 384, 389.

49. Forrest report, April 26, 1864, *OR*, 32, pt. 1, p. 615.

50. Ibid.

51. Ibid.; Leaming report, January 17, 1865, *OR*, 32, pt. 1, p. 561.

52. Forrest report, April 15, 1864, *OR*, 32, pt. 1, p. 610.

53. Forrest to Davis, April 15, 1864, *OR*, 32, pt. 1, p. 612.

54. Charles Robinson letter, April 17, 1864, "Fort Pillow 'Massacre' Observations of a Minnesotan," ed. George Bodnia, *Minnesota History* 43 (Spring 1973), p. 188.

55. Marshall testimony, April 25, 1864, *"Fort Pillow Massacre," House Report No. 65.*, 38 Cong., 1 sess. (Washington, D.C.: U.S. Government Printing Office, 1864), p. 86. Cited hereafter as Fort Pillow report.

56. Log of the *New Era*, "Fort Pillow Revisited: New Evidence About an Old Controversy," eds. John Cimprich and Robert C. Mainfort, Jr., *Civil War History* 28 (December 1982), p. 294.

57. Lamberg reports, April 20, April 27, 1864, *OR*, 32, pt. 1, pp. 566, 567.

58. Robinson letter, April 17, 1864, p. 188.

59. Report of Sub-Committee, Fort Pillow Report, pp. 1–7. See also testimony in *Freedom: A Documentary History of Emancipation, 1861–1867*, ed. Ira Berlin, Joseph P. Reidy, and Leslie S. Rowland (Cambridge, England: Cambridge University Press, 1982), pp. 542–48.

60. Falls testimony, April 22, 1864, Fort Pillow Report, p. 15; Hunter testimony, April 22, 1864, Fort Pillow Report, p. 18; Stamps testimony, April 23, 1864, Fort Pillow Report, p. 45; Mays testimony, April 23, 1864, Fort Pillow Report, p. 47.

61. Thompson testimony, April 22, 1864, Fort Pillow Report, p. 30.

62. Samuel H. Caldwell letter, April 15, 1864, "Fort Pillow Revisited," pp. 300–301.

63. Falls testimony, April 22, 1864, Fort Pillow Report, p. 15.

64. Williams testimony, April 22, 1864, Fort Pillow Report, p. 27.

65. Quoted in Wyeth, p. 386.

66. Quoted in John Cimprich and Robert C. Mainfort, Jr., "Dr. Fitch's Report on the Fort Pillow Massacre," *Tennessee Historical Quarterly* 44 (Spring 1985), pp. 36–37.

67. C. Fitch, "Capture of Fort Pillow—Vindication of General Chalmers by a Federal Officer," *Southern Historical Society Papers* 7 (1879), pp. 440–41.

68. Leaming testimony, April 22, 1864, *OR*, 32, pt. 1, p. 40.

69. Woodruff report, April 15, 1864, *OR*, 32, pt. 1, p. 558.

70. Bell I. Wiley, *The Life of Johnny Reb: The Common Soldier of the Confederacy* (Baton Rouge: Louisiana State University Press, 1978), p. 314.

71. Reid Mitchell, *Civil War Soldiers* (New York: Viking Penguin, 1988), pp. 174–75.

72. James I. Robertson, Jr., *Soldiers Blue and Gray* (Columbia: University of South Carolina Press, 1988), p. 35.

73. Quoted in Wiley, p. 314.

74. Robertson, p. 32.

75. Joseph T. Glatthaar, *Forged in Battle: The Civil War Alliance of Black Soldiers and White Officers* (New York: Free Press, 1990), p. 81.

76. Quoted in Robertson, p. 32.

77. James M. McPherson, *Battle Cry of Freedom: The Civil War Era* (New York: Oxford University Press, 1988), p. 402.

78. Forrest to Davis, April 15, 1864, *OR*, 32, pt. 1, p. 612.

79. Fitch, p. 441.

80. Castel, p. 50.

81. Cimprich and Mainfort, "Dr. Fitch's Report," p. 38; Charles L. Lufkin, "'Not Heard From Since April 12, 1864:' The Thirteenth Tennessee Cavalry, U.S.A.," *Tennessee Historical Quarterly* 45 (Spring 1986), p. 142.

82. Lonnie E. Maness, "The Fort Pillow Massacre: Fact or Fiction?" *Tennessee Historical Quarterly* 45 (Spring, 1986), pp. 287–315.

83. Castel, p. 46.

84. Clark to sisters, April 14, 1864, Achilles V. Clark Letters, Confederate Collection, Tennessee State Library and Archives, Nashville; "Fort Pillow Revisited," pp. 279–99.

85. Quoted in Wyeth, p. 390.

86. Forrest to Washburn, June 23, 1864, *OR*, 32, pt. 1, p. 590.

87. Mitchell, p. 195.

88. Forrest to Washburn, June 23, 1864, *OR*, 32, pt. 1, pp. 591, 593.

89. Goodwin report, April 21, 1864, *OR*, 32, pt. 1, p. 619.

90. John Cimprich and Robert C. Mainfort, Jr., "The Fort Pillow Massacre: A Statistical Note," *Journal of American History* 76 (December 1989), pp. 835–37.

91. Castel, p. 46; Wyeth, p. 361; Chalmers report, May 7, 1864, *OR*, 32, pt. 1, p. 361. Forrest put his dead at 20 and his wounded at 60. Forrest to Polk, April 15, 1864, *OR*, 32, pt. 1, p. 609; Forrest reports, April 15, pp. 610, 612.

CHAPTER 10: FORREST'S FINEST MOMENT

1. R. R. Hancock, *Hancock's Diary: or, a History of the Second Tennessee Confederate Cavalry, with Sketches of First and Seventh Battalions; also Por-*

traits and Biographical Sketches (c. 1877; reprint, Dayton, Ohio: Press of Morningside Bookshop, 1981), p. 365.

2. Anderson report, April 17, 1864, *OR,* 32, pt. 1, pp. 598–99; Anderson to Ferguson, April 13, 1864, *OR,* 32, pt. 1, p. 599.

3. Ferguson report, April 14, 1864, *OR,* 32, pt. 1, p. 571.

4. Quoted in Cimprich and Mainfort, "Dr. Fitch's Report," p. 39.

5. Robert Selph Henry, *"First With the Most" Forrest* (Indianapolis: Bobbs-Merrill Co., 1944), p. 269.

6. Washburn to Forrest, June 19, 1864, *OR,* 32, pt. 1, p. 589; McLagan statement, n.d., *OR,* 32, pt. 1, p. 557; McLagan testimony, pp. 101–103.

7. Forrest to Washburn, June 23, 1864, *OR,* 32, pt. 1, p. 592.

8. Henry, pp. 22–23, 271; John Allan Wyeth, *Life of General Nathan Bedford Forrest* (New York: Harper & Bros., 1899), p. 7. Aaron died sometime in spring 1864, near Dresden, Tennessee. William and Jesse, like their eldest brother, received wounds but survived the war.

9. Sherman to Rawlins, April 19, 1864, *OR,* 32, pt. 3, p. 411; McPherson to Hurlbut, April 19, 1864, *OR,* 32, pt. 3, p. 415; Edwin C. Bearss, *Forrest at Brice's Cross Roads and in North Mississippi in 1864* (Dayton, Ohio: Press of Morningside Bookshop, 1979), offers a comprehensive examination of these campaigns.

10. Sherman to Rawlins, April 19, 1864, *OR,* 32, pt. 3, p. 411.

11. Sherman to Washburn, April 21, 1864, *OR,* 32, pt. 3, p. 441.

12. Sherman to Washburn, April 24, 1864, *OR,* 32, pt. 3, p. 485.

13. Sherman to Washburn, April 28, 1864, *OR,* 32, pt. 3, p. 527.

14. McPherson to Washburn, April 29, 1864, *OR,* 32, pt. 3, p. 536.

15. Washburn to Rawlins, April 23, 1864, *OR,* 32, pt. 3, pp. 462–463.

16. Thomas Jordan and J. P. Pryor, *The Campaigns of Lieut.-Gen. N. B. Forrest, and of Forrest's Cavalry* (New Orleans: Blelock & Co., 1868), pp. 457–58; Henry, p. 275.

17. Sturgis to Washburn, May 7, 1864, *OR,* 32, pt. 1, p. 697.

18. Sturgis to Sherman, May 13, 1864, *OR,* 32, pt. 1, p. 698.

19. John Watson Morton, *The Artillery of Nathan Bedford Forrest's Cavalry* (Nashville, Tenn.: Publishing House of the M. E. Church, South, 1909), pp. 161–67.

20. Forrest to S. D. Lee, May 15, 1864, *OR,* 39, pt. 2, p. 601.

21. Forrest to S. D. Lee, May 15, 1864, *OR,* 39, pt. 2, p. 601.

22. Special Orders No. 63, May 21, 1864, *OR,* 39, pt. 2, p. 614.

23. Field returns, Chalmers Division, May 23, 1864, *OR,* 39, pt. 2, p. 618.

24. Henry, pp. 282–83.

25. Sturgis report, June 24, 1864, *OR,* 39, pt. 1, p. 91; Hoge testimony, Proceedings of Board of Investigation, July 5, 1864—2 P.M., *OR,* 39, pt. 1, p. 162; Grierson testimony, Proceedings of Board of Investigation, July 23, 1864—2 P.M., *OR,* 39, pt. 1, p. 200; McMillen testimony, Proceedings of Board of Investigation, July 26, 1864—2 P.M., *OR,* 39, pt. 1, p. 207.

26. Sherman to Thomas, June 9, 1864, *OR*, 38, pt. 4, p. 442.

27. S. D. Lee to Cooper, June 6, 1864, *OR*, 39, pt. 2, p. 637. See also "Forrest's Guntown Victory," *Confederate Veteran* 13 (October 1905), p. 463.

28. Forrest report, July 1, 1864, *OR*, 39, pt. 1, p. 222.

29. Wyeth, p. 398; Bearss, p. 63.

30. Henry, p. 286; Bearss, p. 64.

31. Quoted in Wyeth, p. 400; Wyeth to Rucker, February 6, 1896, March 9, 1896, March 16, 1896, March 23, 1896, Edmund Winchester Rucker Papers, Birmingham Public Library, Birmingham, Ala. Various contemporaries insisted that the battle was less premeditated than the Wyeth-Rucker account indicated. In these accounts, Forrest's actions implied that he was only attempting to carry out S. D. Lee's directions to march to Tupelo and fight there, until circumstances caused Forrest to commit to battle at Brice's Cross Roads. See also Bearss, pp. 63–64; and William W. Luckett, "Bedford Forrest in the Battle of Brice's Cross Roads," *Tennessee Historical Quarterly* 15 (June 1956), pp. 102–103.

32. Bearss, p. 65; Samuel A. Agnew, "Battle of Tishomingo Creek," *Confederate Veteran* 8 (1900), pp. 401–02.

33. *OR*, 39, pt. 1, pp. 92, 103, 119, 125, 129,141, 168, 172; Bearss, p. 66; H. A. Tyler to Rucker, June 22, 1908, Rucker Papers; Henry Ewell Hord, "Brice's X Roads From a Private's View," *Confederate Veteran* 12 (November 1904), p. 529.

34. Quoted in Wyeth, p. 409; see also Henry, p. 289.

35. Bearss, pp. 70–71.

36. Quoted in ibid., p. 71; see also Wyeth, p. 404.

37. Waring report, June 17, 1864, *OR*, 39, pt. 1, p. 132.

38. Forrest report, July 1, 1864, *OR*, 39, pt. 1, p. 223.

39. Grierson report, June 21, 1864, *OR*, 39, pt. 1, p. 129.

40. Sturgis report, June 24, 1864, *OR*, 39, pt. 1, p. 92.

41. Quoted in Jordan and Pryor, p. 470; see also Wyeth, pp. 404–05; Bearss, p. 72; Forrest report, July 1, 1864, *OR*, 39, pt. 1, p. 223.

42. Hord, p. 529; Forrest report, June 17, 1864, *OR*, 39, pt. 1, p. 223.

43. John Milton Hubbard, *Notes of a Private* (St. Louis: Nixon-Jones Printing Co., 1911), p. 110.

44. Henry, p. 291; "Forrest's Guntown Victory," p. 464; Forrest report, July 1, 1864, *OR*, 39, pt. 1, pp. 223–24.

45. Hord, p. 529; Forrest report, June 17, 1864, *OR*, 39, pt. 1, p. 223.

46. Sturgis report, June 24, 1864, *OR*, 39, pt. 1, p. 92.

47. Ibid.; Hoge report, June 14, 1864, *OR*, 39, pt. 1, p. 119.

48. McMillen testimony, July 26, 1864—2 P.M., *OR*, 39, pt. 1, p. 208.

49. Hoge report, June 14, 1864, *OR*, 39, pt. 1, p. 119.

50. Ibid.

51. Sturgis report, June 24, 1864, *OR*, 39, pt. 1, p. 92.

52. Forrest report, July 1, 1864, *OR*, 39, pt. 1, p. 223.

53. Hubbard, pp. 110–11.
54. Ibid., p. 110.
55. Wyeth, pp. 413–14.
56. Quoted in Henry, p. 292.
57. Quoted in Wyeth, p. 414.
58. Henry, pp. 291–93; Hord, pp. 529–30.
59. Morton, p. 178; Wyeth, pp. 415–16; "Reunion of Forrest's Cavalry Corps," *Confederate Veteran* 8 (July 1990), p. 301.
60. Wyeth, p. 416.
61. McMillen report, June 22, 1864, *OR*, 39, pt. 1, p. 105.
62. Quoted in Henry, p. 293.
63. Forrest report, July 1, 1864, *OR*, 39, pt. 1, p. 224; Hord, p. 530; "Forrest's Guntown Victory," p. 464; William Witherspoon, "Tishomingo Creek or Bryce's Cross Roads," in *As They Saw Forrest: Some Recollections and Comments of Contemporaries*, ed. by Robert Selph Henry (Jackson, Tenn.: McCowat-Mercer Press, 1956), pp. 122, 126.
64. Sturgis report, June 24, 1864, *OR*, 39, pt. 1, p. 93.
65. Morton, pp. 176–77.
66. Bearss, p. 100. For more on Tyler's activities before the Union retreat, see H. A. Tyler to Edmund H. Rucker, June 22, 1908, Rucker Papers.
67. Bouton testimony, July 28, 1864, *OR*, 39, pt. 1, p. 213.
68. Sturgis report, June 24, 1864, *OR*, 39, pt. 1, p. 94.
69. S. D. Lee to Cooper, June 11, 1864, *OR*, 39, pt. 1, p. 221.
70. Return of casualties, C. S. forces, *OR*, 39, pt. 1, pp. 230–31.
71. Bearss, p. 133; Henry, p. 300.
72. R. E. Corry to wife, June 17, 1864, Robert E. Corry Papers, Auburn University, Auburn, Alabama.
73. Hubbard, pp. 116–17.
74. Witherspoon, pp. 126–27.
75. Agnew, p. 402.
76. Ibid.
77. Witherspoon, pp. 123–25.
78. Henry Ewell Hord, "Pursuit of Gen. Sturgiss," *Confederate Veteran* 13 (January 1905), p. 18.
79. Bouton testimony, July 28, 1864, *OR*, 39, pt. 1, p. 214.

CHAPTER 11: THERE WILL NEVER BE PEACE IN TENNESSEE

1. Sherman to Stanton, June 14, 1864, *OR*, 38, pt. 4, p. 474.
2. Sherman to Stanton, June 15, 1864—6:30 P.M., *OR*, 39, pt. 2, p. 121.
3. Sherman to Rousseau, June 20, 1864, *OR*, 38, pt. 4, p. 542.
4. Joseph E. Johnston, *Narrative of Military Operations, Directed, During the Late War Between the States by Joseph E. Johnston* (New York: D. Appleton & Co., 1874), pp. 318, 359–60.

5. Brown to Davis, June 28, 1864, *OR*, 52, pt. 2, pp. 680–81.

6. Quoted in John Allan Wyeth, *Life of General Nathan Bedford Forrest* (New York: Harper & Bros., 1899), pp. 433–34.

7. Davis to Brown, June 29, 1864, *OR*, 52, pt. 2, p. 681.

8. Brown to Davis, July 5, 1864, *OR*, 39, pt. 2, p. 688.

9. Davis to Brown, July 5, 1864, *OR*, 39, pt. 2, p. 688.

10. Brown to Davis, July 7, 1864, *OR*, 52, pt. 2, p. 687.

11. Steven Woodworth, *Jefferson Davis and His Generals: The Failure of Confederate Command in the West* (Lawrence: University Press of Kansas, 1990), p. 278. See also Thomas Lawrence Connelly and Archer Jones, *The Politics of Command: Factions and Ideas in Confederate Strategy* (Baton Rouge: Louisiana State University Press, 1973), pp. 166–67. Connelly and Jones argued that Davis "overestimated the threat presented by the Federal forces based at Memphis." This overestimate resulted in Davis allocating "too many resources to S. D. Lee's department."

12. Robert Selph Henry, *"First With the Most" Forrest* (Indianapolis: Bobbs-Merrill Co., 1944), p. 313; General Orders No. 6, July 4, 1864, *OR*, 39, pt. 2, p. 671.

13. Thomas Jordan and J. P. Pryor, *The Campaigns of Lieut.-Gen. N. B. Forrest, and of Forrest's Cavalry* (New Orleans: Blelock & Co., 1868), p. 496; Forrest to Elliott, July 3, 1864, *OR*, 39, pt. 2, p. 682.

14. Forrest to S. D. Lee, June 28, 1864, *OR*, 39, pt. 2, p. 671.

15. John Watson Morton, *The Artillery of Nathan Bedford Forrest's Cavalry* (Nashville, Tenn. Publishing House of the M. E. Church, South, 1909), p. 203.

16. Jordan and Pryor, p. 498; James Dinkins, *1861 to 1865 Personal Recollections and Experiences in the Confederate Army. By an Old Johnnie* (Cincinnati: Robert Clarke Co., 1897), p. 166; Henry, p. 314; S. D. Lee to Bragg, July 8, 1864, *OR*, 39, pt. 2, p. 694; A. J. Smith report, August 5, 1864, *OR*, 39, pt. 1, p. 250.

17. Forrest report, August 1, 1864, *OR*, 39, pt. 1, p. 320.

18. Chalmers report, July 23, 1864, *OR*, 39, pt. 1, p. 325.

19. A. J. Smith report, August 5, 1864, *OR*, 39, pt. 1, pp. 250–51.

20. Chalmers report, July 23, 1864, *OR*, 39, pt. 1, p. 325.

21. Henry, p. 315.

22. Forrest report, August 1, 1864, *OR*, 39, pt. 1, p. 321.

23. Smith report, August 5, 1864, *OR*, 39, pt. 1, p. 251. See also Theodore G. Carter, "Reply to 'Experiences at Harrisburg,'" *Confederate Veteran* 14 (July 1906), p. 310.

24. Henry, pp. 315–16.

25. Ibid., p. 316.

26. Ibid., p. 316; Morton, pp. 204–05.

27. Forrest report, August 1, 1864, *OR*, 39, pt. 1, p. 322.

28. Henry, p. 318; Stephen D. Lee, "Battle of Harrisburg, or Tupelo," *Publications of the Mississippi Historical Society* (1902), Vol. 6, pp. 38–52.

29. Quoted in Edwin C. Bearss, *Forrest at Brice's Cross Roads and in North Mississippi in 1864* (Dayton, Ohio: Press of Morningside Bookshop, 1979), p. 199; Henry, p. 317.

30. Bearss, p. 198.

31. Quoted in James R. Chalmers, "Forrest and His Campaigns," *Southern Historical Society Papers* 7 (October 1879), pp. 476–77.

32. Lee, "Battle of Harrisburg," p. 45.

33. Bearss, pp. 200–01.

34. Herman Hattaway, *General Stephen D. Lee* (Jackson: University Press of Mississippi, 1976), pp. 120–21.

35. Forrest report, August 1, 1864, *OR*, 39, pt. 1, p. 322.

36. Henry, p. 320.

37. Smith report, August 5, 1864, *OR*, 39, pt. 1, p. 252.

38. Henry Ewell Hord, "Personal Experiences at Harrisburg, Miss.," *Confederate Veteran* 13 (August 1905), p. 362.

39. Forrest report, August 1, 1864, *OR*, 39, pt. 1, p. 322.

40. Ibid.; Buford report, July 22, 1864, *OR*, 39, pt. 1, p. 331; Crossland report, July 21, 1864, *OR*, 39, pt. 1, p. 336.

41. Forrest report, August 1, 1864, *OR*, 39, pt. 1, p. 322; Bell report, July 23, 1864, *OR*, 39, pt. 1, p. 347; Mabry report, July 20, 1864, *OR*, 39, pt. 1, p. 349.

42. Bearss, p. 208; Bell report, July 23, 1864, *OR*, 39, pt. 1, p. 347; Mabry report, July 20, 1864, *OR*, 39, pt. 1, pp. 326–27.

43. Bearss, p. 208; Chalmers report, July 23, 1864, *OR*, 39, pt. 1, pp. 326–27.

44. Bearss, pp. 208–09; Chalmers report, July 23, 1864, *OR*, 39, pt. 1, p. 327.

45. Smith report, August 5, 1864, *OR*, 39, pt. 1, p. 252; Mower report, July 27, 1864, *OR*, 39, pt. 1, pp. 257–58.

46. Henry, p. 323.

47. Quoted in ibid., p. 324.

48. Forrest report, August 1, 1864, *OR*, 39, pt. 1, p. 323.

49. Ibid., p. 324; Buford report, July 22, 1864, *OR*, 39, pt. 1, p. 333.

50. Quoted in Bearss, p. 323; see also R. R. Hancock, *Hancock's Diary*.... (c. 1877; reprint, Dayton, Ohio: Press of Morningside Bookshop, 1981), p. 435.

51. Forrest report, August 1, 1864, *OR*, 39, pt. 1, p. 324.

52. Smith report, August 5, 1864, *OR*, 39, pt. 1, pp. 252–53.

53. Buford report, July 22, 1864, *OR*, 39, pt. 1, pp. 331–32.

54. Forrest report, August 1, 1864, *OR*, 39, pt. 1, p. 323.

55. Ibid., pp. 323–24; Chalmers report, July 23, 1864, *OR*, 39, pt. 1, p. 327.

56. Wyeth, pp. 454–55.

57. Washburn to Sherman, August 2, 1864, *OR*, 39, pt. 2, p. 219.

58. Sherman to Washburn, August 7, 1864, *OR*, 39, pt. 2, p. 233.

59. Washburn to Sherman, August 11, 1864—4 P.M., *OR,* 39, pt. 2, p. 242.

60. Bearss, p. 228; Wyeth, pp. 454–55.

61. Bearss, p. 228; Wyeth, p. 455.

62. A. J. Smith report, August 5, 1864, *OR,* 39, pt. 1, p. 253; Chalmers report, July 23, 1864, *OR,* 39, pt. 1, p. 328.

63. Bearss, p. 232; return of casualties, U.S. forces, *OR,* 39, pt. 1, pp. 254–56.

64. Washburn to Sherman, July 23, 1864, *OR,* 39, pt. 2, p. 201.

65. Ibid.

66. Wyeth, p. 461.

67. Bearss, p. 238.

68. Maury to Forrest, July 27, 1864, *OR,* 39, pt. 2, p. 731; Maury to Forrest, August 2, 1864, *OR,* 39, pt. 2, pp. 748–49.

69. Dabney Herndon Maury, *Recollections of a Virginian in the Mexican, Indian and Civil Wars* (New York: Charles Scribner's Sons, 1894), p. 213.

70. Forrest to Maury, August 5, 1864, *OR,* 39, pt. 2, p. 756.

71. Washburn to Sherman, August 2, 1864, *OR,* 39, pt. 2, p. 219.

72. Forrest to Maury, August 5, 1864, *OR,* 39, pt. 2, p. 756.

73. Ibid.; Henry, p. 330.

74. Forrest to Davis, August 7, 1864, *OR,* 39, pt. 2, pp. 760–761; Brent to Cooper, June 10, 1864, *OR,* 39, pt. 2, pp. 640–42.

75. Forrest to Davis, August 7, 1864, *OR,* 39, pt. 2, pp. 760–61.

76. "Group of Officers of Forrest's Cavalry," *Confederate Veteran* 16 (April 1908), p. xxvi. Although the article was compiled by the editors of the *Confederate Veteran,* D. C. Kelley wrote the substance of this piece as a tribute to the recently deceased Charles W. Anderson and William Montgomery Forrest.

77. Wyeth, p. 627.

78. Cooper endorsement, September 15, 1864, *OR,* 39, pt. 2, p. 762.

79. Davis endorsement, September 19, 1864, *OR,* 39, pt. 2, p. 762.

80. Seddon endorsement, n.d., *OR,* 39, pt. 2, p. 762.

81. Campbell to secretary of war, September 21, 1864, *OR,* 39, pt. 2, pp. 762–63.

82. Forrest to Chalmers, August 8, 1864, *OR,* 39, pt. 2, p. 765; Forrest to Chalmers, August 8, 1864, *OR,* 39, pt. 2, p. 766.

83. Chalmers to Forrest, August 8, 1864—6 P.M., *OR,* 39, pt. 2, p. 766; Henry, p. 332.

84. Henry, p. 332; Bearss, pp. 268–69.

85. Bearss, p. 274.

86. Jordan and Pryor, p. 532; Wolfe report, August 27, 1864, *OR,* 39, pt. 1, p. 382; Mattocks report, August 26, 1864, *OR,* 39, pt. 1, p. 385; Hatch report, August 30, 1864, *OR,* 39, pt. 1, p. 389; Horton report, September 1, 1864, *OR,* 39, pt. 1, pp. 390–91.

87. John Milton Hubbard, *Notes of a Private* (St. Louis: Nixon-Jones

Printing Co., 1911), p. 139; Bearss, pp. 333–34; Henry, pp. 333–34. See also W. B. Stewart, "Forrest's Raid into Memphis," *Confederate Veteran* 11 (November 1913), pp. 503–04.

88. Henry, p. 334; Forrest to Chalmers, August 19, 1864, *OR*, 39, pt. 2, p. 783.

89. Dinkins, pp. 179–80; Hancock, pp. 446–47; Jordan and Pryor, pp. 535–36; Wyeth, p. 471; Henry, p. 334.

90. Dinkins, pp. 179–81; Hancock, p. 446; Jordan and Pryor, pp. 535–36; Wyeth, pp. 470–71; Bearss, p. 283.

91. Hancock, pp. 446–48; Jordan and Pryor, pp. 536–38; Henry, pp. 334, 337; Bearss, pp. 283–85.

92. Dinkins, p. 181.

93. Ozias Midwinter, "Notes on Forrest's Funeral," *Cincinnati Commercial*, November 6, 1877; Lafcadio Hearn, *Occidental Gleanings* (New York: Dodd, Mead & Co., 1925), p. 146. Hearn noted that "Bill killed men almost at regular intervals, both before and after the war.... Since the war he slew men in Mississippi, and Alabama, and Georgia, and had to leave various cities in those various States because of these things. Where known he was feared." Mercer Otey agreed that "the only man in the world that Gen. Bedford Forrest feared was his brother Bill." Mercer Otey, "Story of Our Great War," *Confederate Veteran* 9 (March 1901), p. 107.

94. Buckland report, August 24, 1864, *OR*, 39, pt. 1, p. 474.

95. Dinkins, pp. 181–82; Hancock, pp. 448–49; Jordan and Pryor, pp. 538–39; Wyeth, pp. 472–73; J. Harvey Mathes, *General Forrest* (New York: D. Appleton Century Co., 1902), p. 271; Bearss, p. 286.

96. Dinkins, p. 182; Hancock, pp. 449–50; Jordan and Pryor, pp. 539–40; Wyeth, p. 473.

97. Dinkins, pp. 183–84; Hancock, pp. 450–51; Jordan and Pryor, pp. 540–41; Wyeth, p. 473; Bearss, pp. 287–88; Henry, p. 338; Stewart, p. 503.

98. Jack D. L. Holmes, "Forrest's 1864 Raid on Memphis," *Tennessee Historical Quarterly* 18 (December 1959), p. 308.

99. Bearss, p. 289; Henry, p. 338.

100. Dinkins, p. 187.

101. Hancock, pp. 451–54; Bearss, pp. 289–90; Henry, pp. 339–40.

102. Hancock, p. 456; Jordan and Pryor, p. 545; Wyeth, p. 476; Bearss, pp. 291, 294–95; Henry, pp. 339–40.

103. Hancock, pp. 456–58; Jordan and Pryor, pp. 545–47; Bearss, pp. 295–97; Henry, p. 340.

104. Maury, pp. 214–15.

105. Grierson report, September 6, 1864, *OR*, 39, pt. 1, p. 387; Hatch report, August 30, 1864, *OR*, 39, pt. 1, p. 389; Biser report, August 31, 1864, *OR*, 39, pt. 1, p. 400; Jordan and Pryor, pp. 549–52; Bearss, pp. 302, 309–10; Henry, p. 341; Howard Bahr and William Duke, "The Wet August: Andrew J. Smith's Mississippi Campaign," *Civil War Times Illustrated* 16 (November 1977), pp. 17–18.

106. Bahr and Duke, p. 19.

107. Washburn report, September 2, 1864, *OR*, 39, pt. 1, pp. 469–71; Bearss, pp. 315, 317; Wyeth, pp. 479–81.

108. Smith report, September 2, 1864, *OR*, 39, pt. 1, p. 471.

109. Forrest report, August 21, 1864, *OR*, 39, pt. 1, p. 484.

110. Sherman to Washburn, August 24, 1864—8:45 P.M., *OR*, 39, pt. 2, p. 296.

CHAPTER 12: MAKING HAVOC AMONG THE GUNBOATS

1. Robert Selph Henry, *"First With the Most" Forrest* (Indianapolis: Bobbs-Merrill Co., 1944), pp. 343–44; Monroe Cockrell Papers, Tennessee State Library and Archives, Nashville (hereafter Cockrell Papers, TSLA).

2. Cockrell Papers, TSLA.

3. Henry, p. 345.

4. Ibid., p. 348.

5. Dabney Herndon Maury, *Recollections of a Virginian in the Mexican, Indian and Civil Wars* (New York: Charles Scribner's Sons, 1894), p. 215.

6. Richard Taylor, *Destruction and Reconstruction: Personal Experiences of the Late War* (New York: Longmans, Green & Co., 1955), pp. 242–43.

7. Henry, p. 350.

8. Ibid.

9. Thomas Jordan and J. P. Pryor, *The Campaigns of Lieut.-Gen. N. B. Forrest, and of Forrest's Cavalry* (New Orleans: Blelock & Co., 1868), p. 559.

10. John Allan Wyeth, *Life of General Nathan Bedford Forrest* (New York: Harper & Bros., 1899), p. 490; Wallace report, November 24, 1864, *OR*, 39, pt. 1, p. 521; Forrest report, October 17, 1864, *OR*, 39, pt. 1, p. 543.

11. Jordan and Pryor, pp. 562–63; Wallace report, November 24, 1864, *OR*, 39, pt. 1, p. 522; Forrest report, October 17, 1864, *OR*, 39, pt. 1, p. 543.

12. Addendum to Wallace report, October 17, 1864, *OR*, 39, pt. 1, pp. 524–25.

13. Forrest report, October 17, 1864, *OR*, 39, pt. 1, pp. 543–44.

14. Granger report, October 10, 1864, *OR*, 39, pt. 1, pp. 513–14.

15. Forrest report, October 17, 1864, *OR*, 39, pt. 1, p. 544.

16. Ibid.

17. Ibid.

18. John Watson Morton, *The Artillery of Nathan Bedford Forrest's Cavalry* (Nashville, Tenn.: Publishing House of the M. E. Church, South, 1909), pp. 231–32.

19. Jordan and Pryor, pp. 566–70; Wyeth, pp. 494–95; Henry, pp. 355–56; Granger report, October 10, 1864, *OR*, 39, pt. 1, p. 514.

20. Forrest report, October 17, 1864, *OR*, 39, pt. 1, p. 544.

21. Spalding report, September 29, 1864, *OR*, 39, pt. 1, p. 537.

22. Henry, p. 356.
23. Spalding report, September 29, 1864, *OR*, 39, pt. 1, p. 537.
24. Ibid.; Forrest report, October 17, 1864, *OR*, 39, pt. 1, p. 545.
25. Spalding report, September 29, 1864, *OR*, 39, pt. 1, p. 537.
26. Henry, p. 357; Forrest report, October 17, 1864, *OR*, 39, pt. 1, p. 545.
27. Forrest report, October 17, 1864, *OR*, 39, pt. 1, p. 545.
28. Ibid., pp. 545–46.
29. Morton, pp. 239–40.
30. Forrest report, October 17, 1864, *OR*, 39, pt. 1, p. 546.
31. Henry, p. 358.
32. Forrest report, October 17, 1864, *OR*, 39, pt. 1, p. 546.
33. Ibid.; Henry, pp. 359–60.
34. Granger report, October 10, 1864, *OR*, 39, pt. 1, pp. 516–17.
35. Henry, p. 360.
36. Ibid., pp. 360–61; Forrest report, October 17, 1864, *OR*, 39, pt. 1, p. 547.
37. Thomas to Croxton, October 4, 1864, *OR*, pt. 3, p. 82.
38. Thomas to Rousseau, October 4, 1864—11:50 A.M., *OR*, 39, pt. 3, p. 81; Thomas to Croxton, October 4, 1864, *OR*, 39, pt. 3, p. 82.
39. Forrest report, October 17, 1864, *OR*, 39, pt. 1, pp. 547–48.
40. Wyeth, pp. 506–08; Henry, pp. 362–63.
41. Morgan to Ramsey, October 7, 1864—7 A.M., *OR*, 39, pt. 3, p. 140.
42. Thomas to Rousseau, October 7, 1864—10 P.M., *OR*, 39, pt. 3, p. 142.
43. Van Duzer to Eckert, October 8, 1864—10:30 P.M., *OR*, 39, pt. 3, p. 153.
44. Sherman to Thomas, October 9, 1864, *OR*, 39, pt. 3, p. 170.
45. Jordan and Pryor, pp. 584–86; Hoge report, October 14, 1864, *OR*, 39, pt. 1, p. 540; "Battle of Eastport," *Confederate Veteran* 5 (January 1897), p. 13.
46. Henry, p. 364; "Battle of Eastport," p. 13.
47. Henry, p. 365.
48. Ibid.
49. Sherman to Grant, October 9, 1864—7:30 P.M, *OR*, 39, pt. 3, p. 162.
50. Forrest to Taylor, October 8, 1864, *OR*, 39, pt. 3, p. 807.
51. Ibid.
52. Forrest to Chalmers, October 10, 1864, *OR*, 39, pt. 3, pp. 815–16.
53. Henry, p. 367.
54. Forrest to Taylor, October 12, 1864, *OR*, 39, pt. 3, pp. 815–16.
55. Ibid., p. 815.
56. Forrest to Chalmers, October 12, 1864, *OR*, 39, pt. 3, p. 817.
57. Henry, pp. 369–70.

58. Ibid., pp. 371–72; Forrest report, January 12, 1865, *OR*, 39, pt. 1, p. 870.

59. R. R. Hancock, *Hancock's Diary....* (c. 1877; reprint, Dayton, Ohio: Press of Morningside Bookshop, 1981), p. 495.

60. Ibid., p. 496; Jordan and Pryor, pp. 592–93; Morton, pp. 246–47; James Dinkins, *1861 to 1865 Personal Recollections and Experiences in the Confederate Army. By an Old Johnnie* (Cincinnati: Robert Clarke Co., 1897), p. 201; Sinclair report, January 7, 1865, *OR*, 39, pt. 1, p. 860; Forrest report, January 12, 1865, *OR*, 39, pt. 1, p. 870. See also Julien F. Gracey, "Capture of the Mazeppa," *Confederate Veteran* 13 (December 1905), pp. 566–70; J. F. Orr, "The Capture of the Undine and Mazeppa," *Confederate Veteran* 18 (July 1910), p. 323. After the war there was considerable debate as to who actually deserved credit for capturing the *Mazeppa*. Henry, p. 546, note 27, offers a summary.

61. Jordan and Pryor, p. 593; Morton, pp. 247–48; Forrest report, January 12, 1865, *OR*, 39, pt. 1, p. 870.

62. Jordan and Pryor, p. 594; Morton, p. 248; Forrest report, January 12, 1865, *OR*, 39, pt. 1, p. 870; Sinclair report, January 7, 1865, *OR*, 39, pt. 1, p. 860; Finding of the Court, November 7, 1864, *Official Records of the Union and Confederate Navies in the War of the Rebellion*, 30 vols. (Washington, D.C.: U.S. Government Printing Office, 1894–1922), 26, pp. 601–02 (hereafter NOR); Bryant testimony, n.d., *NOR*, 26, pp. 602–03; Donaldson report, November 1, 1864, *NOR*, 26, pp. 604–05; Howland report,—, 1864, *NOR*, 26, pp. 620–21.

63. Henry, p. 374.

64. Morton, pp. 248–49. See also Gracey, p. 566.

65. Henry, pp. 374–75.

66. Morton, pp. 250–51; Fitch to Lee, November 5, 1864, *NOR*, 26, p. 613; King to Shirk, November 2, 1864—6:30 P.M., *NOR*, 26, p. 615; Howland report,—, 1864, *NOR*, 26, p. 621; Sinclair report, January 7, 1865, *NOR*, 26, p. 624.

67. Howland report,—, 1864, *NOR*, 26, p. 621; Henry, p. 375.

68. Henry, p. 375.

69. Fitch to S. P. Lee, November 9, 1864, *NOR*, 26, p. 630.

70. Forrest report, January 12, 1865, *OR*, 39, pt. 1, p. 871.

71. Morton, p. 254; Jordan and Pryor, pp. 600–601; Henry, pp. 376–77; Forrest report, January 12, 1865, *OR*, 39, pt. 1, p. 871.

72. Shirk to S. P. Lee, November 5, 1864, *NOR*, 26, p. 610; King to Shirk, November 4, 1864—4 P.M., *NOR*, 26, pp. 610–11; Fitch to Lee, November 5, 1864, *NOR*, 26, pp. 612–13; Howland Report,—, 1864, *NOR*, 26, p. 622.

73. Fitch to S. D. Lee, November 5, 1864, *NOR*, 26, pp. 613–14.

74. King to Shirk, November 4, 1864—4 P.M., *NOR*, 26, pp. 610–11.

75. Morton, p. 253.

76. Edward F. Williams, III, "The Johnsonville Raid and Nathan Bedford Forrest State Park," *Tennessee Historical Quarterly* 28 (Fall 1969), p. 242.

77. Morton, pp. 253–54; Edmund W. Rucker to Jas. R. Chalmers, March 4, 1896; Rucker to Jno. A Wythe [Wyeth], March 5, 1869; Rucker to Chalmers, March 9, 1896; Wyeth to Rucker, March 9, 1896; Chalmers to Rucker, April 4, 1896; Edmund Winchester Rucker Papers, Birmingham Public Library, Birmingham, Alabama; E. G. Cowen, "Battle of Johnsonville," *Confederate Veteran* 22 (April 1914), p. 175. The participants engaged in a lengthy debate over the role, or even presence, of Captain John Morton during the placement of the Confederate guns and the initial moments of the bombardment of the Union depot. At one point, Rucker observed to Chalmers, "The Captain's memory is bad."

78. Morton, p. 254.

79. Howland report,—, 1864, *NOR,* 26, pp. 622–23; Sinclair report, January 7, 1865, *NOR,* 26, pp. 625–26.

80. Morton, p. 256; Henry, pp. 377–78; Williams, p. 244.

81. Forrest report, January 12, 1865, *OR,* 39, pt. 1, p. 871.

82. Morton, pp. 255–56.

83. Forrest report, January 12, 1864, *OR,* 39, pt. 1, p. 871.

84. Morton, pp. 257–58.

85. Forrest report, January 12, 1864, *OR,* 39, pt. 1, p. 871.

86. Wyeth, p. 528.

87. Sinclair report, January 7, 1865, *OR,* 39, pt. 1, p. 862.

88. Fithian to Hooker, November 7, 1864, *OR,* 39, pt. 3, p. 694.

89. Hooker to Potter, November 7, 1864, *OR,* 39, pt. 3, p. 695.

90. Sherman to Grant, November 6, 1864, *OR,* 39, pt. 3, p. 659.

CHAPTER 13: ADVANCING AND RETREATING WITH HOOD

1. Robert Selph Henry, *"First With the Most" Forrest* (Indianapolis: Bobbs-Merrill Co., 1944), p. 379; Forrest report, January 24, 1865, *OR,* 45, pt. 1, p. 751; Thomas L. Connelly and James Lee McDonough, *Five Tragic Hours: The Battle of Franklin* (Knoxville: University of Tennessee Press, 1983), p. 17.

2. Surget to Forrest, October 26, 1864, *OR,* 31, pt. 3, p. 853.

3. Beauregard to Taylor, October 22, 1864, *OR,* 31, pt. 3, p. 843.

4. Hood to Taylor, October 16, 1864, *OR,* 31, pt. 3, p. 823.

5. Hood to Forrest, November 2, 1864, *OR,* 31, pt. 3, p. 879.

6. Hood to Brent, November 3, 1864, *OR,* 31, pt. 3, p. 880.

7. Hood to Davis, November 12, 1864, *OR,* 39, pt. 3, p. 913.

8. John Allan Wyeth, *Life of General Nathan Bedford Forrest* (New York: Harper & Bros., 1899), pp. 531–32; Henry, p. 379.

9. John Watson Morton, *The Artillery of Nathan Bedford Forrest's Cav-*

alry (Nashville, Tenn.: Publishing House of the M. E. Church, South, 1909), pp. 267–68; Thomas Jordan and J. P. Pryor, *The Campaigns of Lieut.-Gen. N. B. Forrest, and of Forrest's Cavalry* (New Orleans: Blelock & Co., 1868), pp. 606–07; Forrest report, January 24, 1865, *OR*, 45, pt. 1, pp. 751–52.

10. Forrest to Taylor, November 12, 1864, *OR*, 39, pt. 3, p. 915.

11. James R. Chalmers, "Forrest and His Campaigns," *Southern Historical Society Papers* 7 (October 1879), p. 479.

12. Forrest report, January 24, 1865, *OR*, 45, pt. 1, p. 752.

13. Ibid.; Mason to Forrest, November 21, 1864, *OR*, 45, pt. 1, p. 1236.

14. Forrest report, January 24, 1865, *OR*, 45, pt. 1, p. 752.

15. Schofield to Cox, November 24, 1864, *OR*, 45, pt. 1, p. 1020.

16. Jordan and Pryor, pp. 616–17; Wyeth, pp. 537–38; Henry, p. 386; Cox report, December 29, 1864, *OR*, 45, pt. 1, p. 400.

17. Forrest report, January 24, 1865, *OR*, 45, pt. 1, p. 752.

18. Jordan and Pryor, p. 619; Henry, pp. 386–87.

19. Forrest report, January 24, 1865, *OR*, 45, pt. 1, p. 752.

20. Ibid., 753.

21. Wilson to Schofield, November 29, 1864—1 A.M., *OR*, 45, pt. 1, p. 1143.

22. Henry, p. 388; McDonough and Connelly, p. 42.

23. Forrest report, January 24, 1865, *OR*, 45, pt. 1, p. 753.

24. Henry, p. 389.

25. Forrest report, January 24, 1865, *OR*, 45, pt. 1, p. 753.

26. Henry, p. 391.

27. Ibid., p. 392.

28. Ibid.

29. Jordan and Pryor, pp. 622–24.

30. Henry, pp. 393–94.

31. Forrest report, January 24, 1865, *OR*, 45, pt. 1, p. 753.

32. John Bell Hood, *Advance and Retreat: Personal Experiences in the United States and Confederate States Armies* (Bloomington: Indiana University Press, 1959), p. 290.

33. Forrest report, January 24, 1865, *OR*, 45, pt. 1, p. 753.

34. Ibid.

35. Ibid.

36. Ibid., pp. 753–54; Ross report, January 12, 1865, *OR*, 45, pt. 1, p. 770; Wilson report, February 1, 1865, *OR*, 45, pt. 1, pp. 559–60. The reasons given for Hood's decision to attack the Union works at Franklin are as many and varied as they are speculative. See McDonough and Connelly, pp. 63–64; Richard M. McMurry, *John Bell Hood and the War for Southern Independence* (Lexington: University Press of Kentucky, 1982).

37. Henry, p. 397.

38. Ibid.; Wyeth, p. 544.

39. Schofield to Thomas, November 30, 1864—3 P.M., *OR*, 45, pt. 1, p. 1170.

40. Forrest report, January 24, 1865, *OR*, 45, pt. 1, p. 754; Henry, pp. 399–400; McDonough and Connelly, pp. 157–68.

41. Forrest report, January 24, 1865, *OR*, 45, pt. 1, p. 754.

42. Ibid.

43. Ibid.

44. Henry, pp. 402–03.

45. Ibid., p. 403; Forrest report, January 24, 1865, *OR*, 45, pt. 1, pp. 754–55.

46. Forrest report, January 24, 1865, *OR*, 45, pt. 1, p. 755.

47. Ibid.; Henry, p. 403.

48. Forrest report, January 24, 1865, *OR*, 45, pt. 1, p. 755.

49. Wyeth, p. 551.

50. Ibid., pp. 551–52; Forrest report, January 24, 1865, *OR*, 45, pt. 1, p. 755.

51. Henry, pp. 404–05.

52. Forrest report, January 24, 1865, *OR*, 45, pt. 1, pp. 755–56; Rousseau report, December 8, 1864, *OR*, 45, pt. 1, p. 613; Milroy report, December 10, 1864, *OR*, 45, pt. 1, p. 618.

53. Forrest report, January 24, 1865, *OR*, 45, pt. 1, p. 756; Henry, p. 405; Jordan and Pryor, pp. 633–34.

54. Forrest report, January 24, 1865, *OR*, 45, pt. 1, p. 756.

55. Charles H. Olmstead, "Rear Guard Service in Tennessee," p. 1, Charles H. Olmstead Papers, Georgia Historical Society, Savannah.

56. Ibid.

57. H. A. Tyler, "Forrest Covers Hood's Retreat," *Confederate Veteran* 12 (September 1904), p. 436; F. G. Terry, "Buford's Division in Hood's Rear," *Confederate Veteran* 13 (April 1905), p. 161.

58. Ibid.; Jordan and Pryor, pp. 635–36.

59. Forrest report, January 24, 1865, *OR*, 45, pt. 1, p. 756.

60. Christopher Losson, *Tennessee's Forgotten Warriors: Frank Cheatham and His Confederate Division* (Knoxville: University of Tennessee Press, 1989), p. 240. One of Cheatham's infantrymen recalled that Forrest appeared when the pontoon his men had used to cross the river "broke loose." Brandishing a pistol, the angry cavalryman threatened to shoot, first a teamster and then General Cheatham, if he could not cross ahead of the infantry's ordinance wagons. The witness explained that "Forrest's adjutant plunged between the two generals and pulled Forrest down toward the bridge," thereby averting a violent confrontation. *Reminiscences of a Private: William E. Bevans of the First Arkansas Infantry*, ed. Daniel E. Sutherland (Fayetteville: University of Arkansas Press, 1991), pp. 264–67.

61. "An Incident of Hood's Campaign," *Southern Bivouac* (November 1884), pp. 131–32.

62. Losson, pp. 240–41; McMurry, p. 180.

63. Forrest report, January 24, 1865, *OR*, 45, pt. 1, p. 757.

64. D. W. Sanders, "Hood's Tennessee Campaign," *Confederate Veteran* 15 (September 1907), pp. 401–02.

65. Wilson report, February 1, 1865, *OR*, 45, pt. 1, p. 566; Henry, pp. 412–13.

66. Forrest report, January 24, 1865, *OR*, 45, pt. 1, p. 757; Jordan and Pryor, p. 646.

67. Forrest report, January 24, 1865, *OR*, 45, pt. 1, p. 757.

68. Olmstead, p. 5.

69. Forrest report, pp. 757–58.

70. Ibid., p. 758.

71. Ibid.

72. W. J. Milner, "The Ku-Klux Klan in Alabama," *Confederate Veteran* 26 (August 1918), p. 339.

73. Luke W. Finlay, "Another Report on Hood's Campaign," *Confederate Veteran* 15 (September 1907), p. 407.

74. Forrest report, p. 758.

CHAPTER 14: I'M A-GOING HOME

1. Beauregard, Special Field Orders, January 23, 1865, *OR*, 45, pt. 2, p. 805; Hood address, January 23, 1865, *OR*, 45, pt. 2, p. 805.

2. Forrest to Taylor, January 2, 1865, *OR*, 45, pt. 2, p. 756; Strange to Chalmers, January 1, 1865, *OR*, 45, pt. 2, pp. 751–52.

3. Forrest address, n.d., *OR*, 45, pt. 2, pp. 759–60.

4. Wyeth, p. 578.

5. James Harrison Wilson, *Under the Old Flag: Recollections of Military Operations in the War for the Union, the Spanish War, the Boxer Rebellion, etc.*, Vol. 2 (New York: D. Appleton & Co., 1912), p. 183.

6. Beauregard to Cooper, January 22, 1865, *OR*, 45, pt. 2, p. 804.

7. Forrest circular, January 24, 1865, *OR*, 49, pt. 1, pp. 930–31.

8. Ibid.

9. Henry, p. 422.

10. Thomas Jordan and J. P. Pryor, *The Campaigns of Lieut.-Gen. N. B. Forrest, and of Forrest's Cavalry* (New Orleans: Blelock & Co., 1868), p. 657.

11. Ibid., p. 658.

12. Wilson, p. 184.

13. Robert Selph Henry, *"First With the Most" Forrest* (Indianapolis: Bobbs-Merrill Co., 1944), p. 423; Lewis M. Hosea letter, February 26, 1865, Monroe Cockrell Papers, William R. Perkins Library, Duke University, Durham, North Carolina (hereafter Hosea letter, Duke).

14. Wilson, p. 184.

15. Hosea letter, February 26, 1865, Duke.

16. Henry, p. 423.
17. Wilson, p. 184.
18. Hosea letter, February 26, 1865, Duke.
19. Wilson, pp. 184–85.
20. Hosea letter, February 26, 1865, Duke.
21. Quoted in James Pickett Jones, *Yankee Blitzkrieg: Wilson's Raid Through Alabama and Georgia* (Athens: University of Georgia Press, 1976), p. 47.
22. Forrest to Chalmers, February 19, 1865, *OR*, 49, pt. 1, p. 994.
23. General Orders No. 99, March 3, 1865, *OR*, 49, pt. 1, pp. 1024–26.
24. J. Harvey Mathes, *General Forrest* (New York: D. Appleton & Co., 1902), p. 364.
25. General Orders No. 99, March 3, 1865, *OR*, 49, pt. 1, p. 1026.
26. Wilson, p. 189; Wyeth, p. 586; Wilson reports, May 3, June 29, 1865, *OR*, 49, pt. 1, pp. 350, 356; James L. Conrad, "Forrest's Great Gamble: The Battle of Ebenezer Church," *Civil War Times Illustrated* 20 (April 1982), p. 31.
27. March 22, James Nourse Papers, William L. Perkins Library, Duke University, Durham, North Carolina (hereafter James Nourse Papers, Duke).
28. Henry, pp. 427–28; Jones, pp. 50–52.
29. Wyeth, pp. 588–89.
30. March 29, James Nourse Papers, Duke.
31. Henry, p. 429.
32. Ibid.; Conrad, pp. 32–33.
33. Henry, p. 430; Conrad, pp. 33–34.
34. Henry, p. 430.
35. Ibid.
36. Wilson reports, May 3, June 29, 1865, *OR*, 49, pt. 1, pp. 350–51, 358.
37. Wilson report, June 29, 1865, *OR*, 49, pt. 1, p. 359.
38. Jordan and Pryor, pp. 667–68; Wyeth, p. 600; V. Y. Cook, "Forrest's Efforts to Save Selma," *Confederate Veteran* 26 (April 1918), p. 152.
39. Cook, "Selma," p. 152; E. N. Gilpin, *The Last Campaign: A Cavalryman's Journal* (Leavenworth, Kans: Press of Ketcheson Printing Co., n.d.), p. 637. See also E. C. Faulkner, "The Last Time I Saw Forrest," *Confederate Veteran* 5 (February 1897), p. 83.
40. Wilson, p. 244.
41. Wilson reports, May 3, June 29, 1865, *OR*, 49, pt. 1, pp. 351, 359; Long report, April 7, 1865, *OR*, 49, pt. 1, p. 437; Vail report, April 6, 1865, *OR*, 49, pt. 1, pp. 455–56; Upton report, May 30, 1865, *OR*, 49, pt. 1, p. 473; Jones, p. 73.
42. Henry, pp. 431–32. See also T. F. Pinckney, "At the Fall of Selma, Ala.," *Confederate Veteran* 40 (February 1932), p. 53.

43. Wilson, pp. 220–22.

44. Wilson, pp. 227–36; Wilson reports, May 3, June 29, 1865, *OR*, 49, pt. 1, pp. 351, 361; Long report, April 7, 1865, *OR*, 49, pt. 1, pp. 438–39; Upton report, May 30, 1865, *OR*, 49, pt. 1, p. 473; Jones, p. 91; Edward G. Longacre, *From Union Stars to Top Hat: A Biography of the Extraordinary General James Harrison Wilson* (Harrisburg, Pa.: Stackpole Co., 1972), pp. 206–08. See also Gilpin, pp. 637–40.

45. Richard Taylor, *Destruction and Reconstruction: Personal Experiences of the Late War* (New York: Longmans, Green & Co., 1955), pp. 268–69; Wilson, pp. 231–32.

46. Wyeth, p. 605.

47. Ibid., pp. 607–08; Salter report, n.d., *OR*, 49, pt. 1, p. 406; Wilson, pp. 239–40; Jordan and Pryor, pp. 676–77; Jones, p. 97.

48. Wilson, p. 240.

49. Ibid., pp. 241–43; Longacre, *From Union Stars to Top Hat*, pp. 209–10.

50. Quoted in Hamilton J. Eckenrode, *Life of Nathan B. Forrest* (Richmond, Virginia: B. F. Johnson Publishing Co., 1918), pp. 169–70.

51. "Group of Officers of Forrest's Cavalry," *Confederate Veteran* 16 (April 1908), pp. xxvi–xxvii.

52. Sherman to Grant, April 25, 1865, *OR*, 47, pt. 3, p. 303.

53. William T. Sherman, *Home Letters of General Sherman*, ed. by M. A. DeWolfe Howe (New York: Charles Scribner's Sons, 1909), p. 346.

54. Thomas to Hatch, May 2, 1865, George H. Thomas Papers, William R. Perkins Library, Duke University, Durham, N. C., pp. 2–3.

55. Wyeth, pp. 610–11.

56. "George W. Cable's Recollections of General Forrest," edited by Arlin Turner, *Journal of Southern History* 21 (May 1955), pp. 224–25.

57. Forrest testimony, pp. 20, 32–35.

58. "George W. Cable's Recollections," pp. 227–28.

59. Jason Niles Diary, Southern Historical Collection, University of North Carolina, Chapel Hill; Dan T. Carter, *When the War Was Over: The Failure of Self-Reconstruction in the South, 1865–1867* (Baton Rouge: Louisiana State University Press, 1985), p. 9.

60. Henry, p. 437; "Group of Officers," p. xxvi. Kelley noted the role that Anderson played in dissuading Forrest from going to Mexico and in drafting the general's farewell address.

61. Jordan and Pryor, pp. 680–82; Mathes, pp. 351–53.

CHAPTER 15: HOME IS WHERE THE HEARTH WAS

1. Quoted in John Allan Wyeth, *The Life of General Nathan Bedford Forrest* (New York: Harper & Bros., 1899), pp. 615–16.

2. Robert Selph Henry, *"First With the Most" Forrest* (Indianapolis: Bobbs-Merrill Co., 1944), p. 439. See also W. R. Hackley to wife, May 28, 1865, which noted, "Forrest has been paroled and is on his farm." "The Letters of William Beverley Randolph Hackley: Treasury Agent in West Tennessee, 1863–1866," ed. Walter Fraser, Jr., and Mrs. Pat C. Clark, *West Tennessee Historical Society Papers* 25 (1971), p. 104.

3. Harry Abernathy, "Famous General Retired to Coahoma Country Plantation," *Clarksdale Press Register,* July 21, 1984.

4. Linton Weeks, *Clarksdale & Coahoma County: A History* (Clarksdale, Mississippi: Carnegie Public Library, 1982), p. 76.

5. Forrest testimony, p. 24.

6. For a thorough discussion of black codes, the Freedmen's Bureau, and other aspects of Reconstruction, see Eric Foner, *Reconstruction: America's Unfinished Revolution, 1863–1877* (New York: Harper & Row, 1988).

7. Friar's Point *Coahomian,* September 29, 1865.

8. Ibid.

9. Ibid., November 10, 1865.

10. Forrest testimony, p. 24.

11. George Corliss to Lt. Stuart Eldridge, April 9, 1866, MF roll 13, Records of the Bureau of Refugees, Freedmen and Abandoned Lands (hereafter BRFAL), National Archives, Washington, D.C.

12. Forrest testimony, p. 24.

13. Corliss to Eldridge, April 9, 1866, BRFAL.

14. Ibid.

15. Allen W. Trelease, *White Terror: The Ku Klux Klan Conspiracy and Southern Reconstruction* (New York: Harper & Row, 1971), pp. 211–12.

16. Friar's Point *Coahomian,* February 23, 1866.

17. Hatch Testimony, January 25, 1866, *Report of the Joint Committee on Reconstruction, at the First Session Thirty-Ninth Congress* (Washington, D.C.: U.S. Government Printing Office, 1866), p. 106.

18. Quoted in Henry, pp. 440–41.

19. William S. McFeely, *Yankee Stepfather: General O. O. Howard and the Freedmen* (New Haven, Conn.: Yale University Press, 1968), p. 264.

20. Forrest to S. D. Lee, July 1, 1865, S. D. Lee Papers, Southern Historical Collection, University of North Carolina, Chapel Hill.

21. Dabney Herndon Maury, *Recollections of a Virginian in the Mexican, Indian and Civil Wars* (New York: Charles Scribner's Sons, 1894), pp. 222–23; Wyeth, pp. 616–17.

22. E. Merton Coulter, *William G. Brownlow: Fighting Parson of the Southern Highlands* (Chapel Hill: University of North Carolina Press, 1937), p. 273.

23. Maury, p. 223; Wyeth, p. 617.

24. Forrest to Lee, July 1, 1865, Southern Historical Collection, University of North Carolina, Chapel Hill; Wyeth, pp. 616–17.

25. Friar's Point *Coahomian*, November 17, 1865.

26. Ibid., February 23, 1866.

27. Henry, p. 442.

28. Forrest to Walter, August 14, 1868, Harvey W. Walter Papers, Southern Historical Collection, University of North Carolina, Chapel Hill.

29. Henry, p. 442.

30. Corliss to Eldridge, April 9, 1866, BRFAL.

31. Statement of Lewis G. Jones, Corliss to Eldridge, April 9, 1866, BRFAL.

32. Statement of Mrs. Sarah Jane Edwards, Corliss to Eldridge, April 9, 1866, BRFAL.

33. Statement of Hannah Powell, Corliss to Eldridge, April 9, 1866, BRFAL.

34. Statement of Lewis G. Jones, Corliss to Eldridge, April 9, 1866, BRFAL.

35. Corliss to Eldridge, April 9, 1866, BRFAL.

36. Statement of N. B. Forrest, Corliss to Eldridge, April 9, 1866, BRFAL.

37. Statement of Mrs. Sarah Jane Edwards, Corliss to Eldridge, April 9, 1866, BRFAL.

38. Statement of Hannah Powell, Corliss to Eldridge, April 9, 1866, BRFAL.

39. Statement of N. B. Forrest, Corliss to Eldridge, April 9, 1866, BRFAL.

40. Statement of Mrs. Sarah Jane Edwards, Corliss to Eldridge, April 9, 1866, BRFAL.

41. Statement of Hannah Powell, Corliss to Eldridge, April 9, 1866, BRFAL.

42. Corliss to Eldridge, April 9, 1866, BRFAL.

43. Henry, p. 442.

44. J. Harvey Mathes, *General Forrest* (New York: D. Appleton & Co., 1902), pp. 359–60.

45. Sherard interview, July 22, 1936, Carnegie Public Library, Clarksdale, Mississippi, pp. 15–17.

46. Coahoma County Circuit Court, *Final Record,* Book E, pp. 453–54.

47. Friar's Point *Coahomian,* April 20, 1866.

48. Coahoma County Circuit Court, *Final Record,* Book E, pp. 454–55.

49. McFeely, pp. 273–74; Foner, pp. 261–63; Dan T. Carter, *When the War Was Over: The Failure of Self-Reconstruction in the South, 1865–1867* (Baton Rouge: Louisiana State University Press, 1985), pp. 248–49; George C. Rable, *But There Was No Peace: The Role of Violence in the Politics*

of Reconstruction (Athens: University of Georgia Press, 1984), pp. 33–54; John Hope Franklin, *Reconstruction After the Civil War* (Chicago: University of Chicago Press, 1961), pp. 62–64.

50. Rable, pp. 33–58; Wyn Craig Wade, *The Fiery Cross: The Ku Klux Klan in America* (New York: Simon & Schuster, 1987), pp. 24–25. At least one Federal government agent in Memphis anticipated violence between returning Confederates and their former battlefield opponents a year before these riots occurred. In May 1865, W. R. Hackley predicted to his wife that when the Southerners returned home "there will be many murders. The Confederates have the same feeling they ever had and have only given up their arms because they cannot longer fight but they hate the men who have staid at home and will fight them upon small provocation." W. R. Hackley to wife, May 28, 1865.

51. McFeely, p. 274.

52. Rable, p. 35.

53. Wyeth, pp. 626–27.

54. Forrest to Walter, August 14, 1866, Harvey W. Walters Papers, Southern Historical Collection, University of North Carolina, Chapel Hill.

55. *Memphis City Directory*, 1866, p. 114.

56. Forrest Life Insurance Policy application, on display at Fort Pillow State Park, Tennessee.

57. Forrest to Clark, September 4, 1866, Clark Papers, Mississippi Department of Archives and History, Jackson.

58. F. R. Earle to Amanda Buchanan Earle, November 30, 1866, "The Earle-Buchanan Letters of 1861–1876," edited by Robert E. Waterman and Thomas Rothrock, *Arkansas Historical Quarterly* 33 (Summer 1974), p. 158.

59. Quoted in William W. White, *The Confederate Veteran* (Tuscaloosa, Ala.: Confederate Publishing Co., 1962), p. 54; "Change of Tactics," *Macon Telegraph*, November 28, 1866.

60. Albert Theodore Goodloe, *Confederate Echoes: A Soldier's Personal Story of Life in the Confederate Army From the Mississippi to the Carolinas* (Washington, D.C.: Zenger Publishing Co., 1983), p. 178; F. R. Earle to Amanda Earle, November 8 and November 30, 1866.

61. McFeely, pp. 263–64.

62. Forrest to Johnson, November 25, 1866, N. B. Forrest Papers, William R. Perkins Library, Duke University, Durham, N. C.

63. Forrest testimony, pp. 22–23. A contemporary student of the Klan, Albion W. Tourgée, listed The Society of the Pale Faces as one of the "various orders" associated with the name "The Ku-Klux." Albion Winegar Tourgée, *The Invisible Empire* (Baton Rouge: Louisiana State University Press, 1989), p. 26.

64. Dickson D. Bruce, Jr., *Violence and Culture in the Antebellum South* (Austin: University of Texas Press, 1979); Bertram Wyatt-Brown, *Southern Honor: Ethics and Behavior in the Old South* (Oxford: Oxford University

Press, 1982; John Hope Franklin, *The Militant South, 1800–1861* (Cambridge, Mass.: Harvard University Press, 1956); and Elliott J. Gorn, "'Gouge and Bite, Pull Hair and Scratch': The Social Significance of Fighting in the Southern Backcountry," *American Historical Review* 90 (February 1985), pp. 18–32, provide excellent discussions of such factors in the lives of Southerners.

65. Eric Foner, *Nothing But Freedom: Emancipation and Its Legacy* (Baton Rouge: Louisiana State University Press, 1983), p. 73.

66. Charles Reagan Wilson, *Baptized in Blood: The Religion of the Lost Cause, 1865–1920* (Athens: University of Georgia Press, 1980), explores the attempt Southerners made to preserve their Confederate heritage through a "civil religion." For an examination of "the lost cause" and its influence and persistence, see Thomas L. Connelly and Barbara L. Bellows, *God and General Longstreet: The Lost Cause and the Southern Mind* (Baton Rouge: Louisiana State University Press, 1982).

67. Morton, p. 344.

68. Henry, pp. 22–23; Wade, pp. 40–41; Morton, pp. 334, 344–45.

69. Stanley F. Horn, *Invisible Empire: The Story of the Ku Klux Klan, 1866–1871* (Boston: Houghton Mifflin Co., 1939), p. 96.

70. Enoch L. Mitchell, "The Role of General George Washington Gordon in the Ku Klux Klan," *West Tennessee Historical Society Papers* 1 (1947), pp. 72–80.

71. Forrest testimony, pp. 9, 27.

72. Ibid., p. 12; Henry, pp. 446–47.

73. Horn, *Invisible Empire*, p. 413.

74. Wade, p. 41; Trelease, pp. 50, 74, 82.

75. Foner, *Reconstruction*, pp. 425–26.

76. Wade, pp. 43–44.

77. Horn, *Invisible Empire*, p. 76.

78. Wade, p. 44.

79. Mathes, pp. 366–68. Apparently this was not the only such ceremony Forrest attended. On July 4, 1875, he gave a speech at a barbecue in Memphis, where he accepted "a bouquet in token of reconciliation." "Reconciliation Between Gen. Forrest and the Colored People," *New York Times*, July 6, 1875. For the text of the speech Forrest gave on this occasion, see "The Fourth in the South," *New York Times*, July 9, 1875.

80. Wade, p. 46.

81. Lynette B. Wrenn, "'Get the City Out of the Mud and Mire,' Financing Street Improvements in Post–Civil War Memphis," *Tennessee Historical Quarterly* 47 (Spring 1968), pp. 17–26.

82. Memphis City Council minutes, July 10, 1867, *Record* Book 12, pp. 508–09, Memphis-Shelby County Archives, Cossitt-Goodwyn Library, Memphis, Tenn.

83. Ibid., October 10, October 11, October 15, 1867, pp. 644–46, 647, 651–52; Wrenn, p. 20.

84. Forrest testimony, p. 25.

85. Wade, p. 51; Trelease, pp. 50, 74; Horn, *Invisible Empire*, p. 172.

86. Horn, *Invisible Empire*, pp. 115–16.

87. Trelease, p. 50.

88. Forrest to Andrews, November 5, 1867, Garnett Andrews Papers, Southern Historical Collection, University of North Carolina, Chapel Hill.

89. Forrest letter, October 3, 1867, Jordan and Pryor, p. viii.

90. Forrest to Jno. R. Nicholson, June 26, 1875, N: 750, Henry E. Huntington Library, San Marino, Calif.

91. Forrest testimony, p. 29.

92. Jordan and Pryor, pp. 29–33.

93. William S. Fitzgerald, "Did Nathan Bedford Forrest Really Rescue John Able?" *Tennessee Historical Quarterly* 39 (Spring 1980), p. 16.

94. Frederic Bancroft, *Slave-Trading in the Old South* (Baltimore: J. H. Furst Co., 1931), pp. 259–62.

95. Basil W. Duke, *Reminiscences of General Basil W. Duke, C.S.A.* (Garden City, N.Y.: Doubleday, Page & Co., 1911), p. 346.

96. Cockrell Papers, bankruptcy ruling, March 29, 1868, District Court of the United States, District of West Tennessee, TSLA.

97. Quoted in Henry, pp. 452–53.

98. Ibid., p. 453; Forrest testimony, p. 33.

99. "Tennessee Politics," *New York Times*, May 24, 1868.

100. Duke, pp. 348–49.

101. "Forrest as a Delegate," *New York Times*, June 22, 1868.

102. "A Speech by Gen. Forrest in Tennessee—His Views of the Next War," *New York Times*, August 17, 1868.

103. Duke, pp. 349–50.

104. Forrest testimony, p. 13.

105. "Forrest as a Delegate," *New York Times*, August 14, 1868.

106. "Fort Pillow Forrest's Independent Challenge to Gen. Kilpatrick," *New York Times*, November 3, 1868.

107. Duke, pp. 351–54.

108. Henry, p. 449; Horn, *Invisible Empire*, pp. 102–103.

109. "Meeting of Ex-Rebels in Memphis," *New York Times*, August 14, 1868.

110. Horn, *Invisible Empire*, p. 96.

111. "A Speech by Gen. Forrest in Tennessee."

112. Forrest testimony, pp. 4, 5, 19, 21.

113. Ibid., p. 33.

114. Ibid.

115. Ibid., p. 34.

116. Ibid., pp. 6–7, 14, 24, 28–29, 34.

117. Foner, *Free Soil, Free Labor, Free Men: The Ideology of the Republi-*

can Party Before the Civil War (New York: Oxford University Press, 1970).

118. Henry, p. 456.

119. Ibid., p. 459; Jones to Watson, September 4, 1870, Jones Family Papers, William R. Perkins Library, Duke University, Durham, N.C.; Lucy M. Cohen, *Chinese in the Post-Civil War South: A People Without a History* (Baton Rouge: Louisiana State University Press, 1984), p. 68; William C. Harris, *The Day of the Carpetbagger: Republican Reconstruction in Mississippi* (Baton Rouge: Louisiana State University Press, 1979), pp. 356–57; John C. Jay, "General N. B. Forrest as a Railroad Builder in Alabama," *Alabama Historical Quarterly* 24 (Spring 1962), p. 27.

CHAPTER 16: COMPLETELY USED UP

1. David G. Pugh, *Sons of Liberty: The Masculine Mind in Nineteenth-Century America* (Westport, Conn.: Greenwood Press), p. 122.

2. George E. Tucker, *Victory Rode the Rails* (Indianapolis: Bobbs-Merrill Co., 1953).

3. William Appleman Williams, *The Contours of American History* (New York: W. W. Norton & Co., 1988), p. 303.

4. James M. McPherson, *Ordeal by Fire: The Civil War and Reconstruction* (New York: Alfred A. Knopf, 1982), p. 582.

5. Gavin Wright, *Old South, New South: Revolutions in the Southern Economy Since the Civil War* (New York: Basic Books, 1986), p. 39.

6. John C. Jay, "General N. B. Forrest as a Railroad Builder in Alabama," *Alabama Historical Quarterly* 24 (Spring 1962), p. 17.

7. Forrest to Lewis, October 11, 1873, Forrest file, Hargrett Rare Book and Manuscript Library, University of Georgia Libraries, University of Georgia, Athens.

8. Forrest testimony, p. 25; Jay, pp. 17, 22, 23.

9. Forrest to Edmund W. Rucker, September 18, 1869, facsimile in Wyeth.

10. Allen W. Trelease, *White Terror: The Ku Klux Klan Conspiracy and Southern Reconstruction* (New York: Harper & Row, 1971), pp. 181–82.

11. Stanley F. Horn, *Invisible Empire: The Story of the Ku Klux Klan, 1866–1871* (Boston: Houghton Mifflin Co., 1939), pp. 356–57.

12. Wyn Craig Wade, *The Fiery Cross: The Ku Klux Klan in America* (New York: Simon & Schuster, 1987), p. 59.

13. Trelease, pp. 179–80.

14. Wade, p. 59.

15. Trelease, p. 180.

16. Wade, p. 59.

17. Quoted in "An Interview With Gen. Forrest," *Memphis Daily Appeal*, March 12, 1869.

18. "Outlaw Days," Mrs. Mary Fisher Robinson interview, "Riot of 1875," Mrs. Geo. S. Robinson interview, Carnegie Public Library, Clarksdale, Miss.

19. "An Interview With Gen. Forrest," *Memphis Daily Appeal*, March 12, 1869.

20. "Chinese Labor Convention," *Memphis Daily Appeal*, July 15, July 16, 1869.

21. Forrest testimony, p. 17.

22. Jay, p. 18.

23. Ibid., pp. 20–22.

24. Forrest testimony, p. 17.

25. Ibid., p. 16.

26. Ibid., pp. 16–17.

27. Jay, pp. 22–23.

28. Ibid., pp. 23–24; Wyeth, pp. 617–19.

29. Horn, *Invisible Empire*, p. 316.

30. Forrest testimony, p. 10.

31. For example, see "George W. Cable's Recollections of General Forrest," ed. by Arlin Turner, *Journal of Southern History* 21 (May 1955), pp. 224–25. As a clerk on Forrest's staff, Cable had the opportunity to observe the general closely. "He attends to everything himself, sits and talks to everyone, knows everyone by name.... His brain ... is as clear as crystal and he seems to think of a dozen things at once."

32. Forrest testimony, pp. 6, 12, and 22. The other name Forrest gave the committee was Jones (p. 29), although he did not give the first name for either man.

33. 1860 U.S. Census, Coahoma County, Mississippi; Dunbar Rowland, *Military History of Mississippi, 1803–1898* (Spartanburg, S.C.: Reprint Co., 1978), pp. 538–39.

34. "Benjamin F. Saunders," George F. Maynard, Sr., interview, Carnegie Public Library, Clarksdale, Miss.

35. Forrest testimony, p. 22.

36. Ibid., pp. 4, 5, 19, 21.

37. Ibid., p. 32.

38. Charles W. Anderson, "My Last Meeting With Gen. Forrest," *Confederate Veteran* 4 (November 1896), p. 387.

39. Forrest testimony, p. 6.

40. Forrest testimony, p. 26.

41. Jay, p. 27; William C. Harris, *The Day of the Carpetbagger: Republican Reconstruction in Mississippi* (Baton Rouge: Louisiana State University Press, 1979), pp. 356–57, noted that Forrest used Mississippi convicts on the railroad as well.

42. Forrest to Rucker, February 10, 1873, Nathan Bedford Forrest Papers, Lionel Baxter Collection, *Civil War Times Illustrated* Collection, U.S. Army Military History Institute, Carlisle Barracks, Penn.

43. Explanation, April 1886, attached to Meriwether to Forrest, May 25, 1875, and Forrest to Meriwether, April 26, 1875, Meriwether Family Papers, West Tennessee Historical Society, Memphis State University, Memphis.

44. Henry, p. 458.

45. Ibid., pp. 458–59.

46. Meriwether explanation, April 1886, Meriwether Family Papers, West Tennessee Historical Society, Memphis State University, Memphis.

47. Jay, p. 28.

48. Ibid.

49. Forrest to Lewis, October 11, 1873, Nathan Bedford Forrest File, Hargrett Rare Book and Manuscript Library, University of Georgia, Athens.

50. Jay, p. 29.

51. Forrest to Rucker, August 9, 1875, E. W. Rucker Papers, Southern Historical Collection, University of North Carolina, Chapel Hill.

52. Forrest to Meriwether, May 26, 1875, Meriwether Family Papers, West Tennessee Historical Society, Memphis State University, Memphis.

53. Forrest to Reuben Davis, August 30, 1875, Reuben Davis Papers, West Tennessee Historical Society, Memphis State University, Memphis.

54. Ted Ownby, *Subduing Satan: Religion, Recreation, and Manhood in the Rural South, 1865–1920* (Chapel Hill: University of North Carolina Press, 1990), p. 12.

55. Ibid.

56. Wilson, p. 240.

57. Ozias Midwinter, *Cincinnati Commercial*, November 6, 1877; Lafcadio Hearn, *Occidental Gleanings* (New York: Dodd, Mead & Co., 1925), pp. 151–52.

58. Coahoma County Circuit Court, *Final Record*, Book E, pp. 355–56, Clarksdale, Miss.

59. "Two Confederate Heroes," *Sunday News*, Charleston, S.C., September 27, 1903.

60. Florence Wilson, "Forrest, the Matchless Rider," Nashville *Banner*, July 7, 1935.

61. D. C. Kelley, "General Nathan Bedford Forrest," *Methodist Review*, p. 235.

62. Mathes, p. 374.

63. Henry, p. 459; Fred T. Wooten, Jr., "Religious Activity in Civil War Memphis," *Tennessee Historical Quarterly* 3 (September 1944).

64. "President's Island," *Memphis Daily Appeal*, May 5, 1876.

65. Jay, p. 27.

66. "President's Island," *Memphis Daily Appeal*, May 5, 1876.

67. Mathes, pp. 374–75; "Last Speech of General Forrest," *Confederate Veteran* 29 (January 1921), p. 25.

68. Anderson, p. 387.

69. Wyeth, pp. 621–22.

70. Quoted in "General Forrest's Illness," Atlanta *Daily Constitution*, September 3, 1877.

71. "Gen. N. B. Forrest," Atlanta *Daily Constitution*, September 20, 1877.

72. Ibid., pp. 622–23.

73. Ibid., p. 623; Henry, p. 460; Note of Minor Meriwether, Forrest to Meriwether, May 26, 1875, Meriwether Family Papers, West Tennessee Historical Society, Memphis State University, Memphis.

74. Henry, pp. 460–61; Meriwether observed that Forrest died at 7:15 P.M.

EPILOGUE: A STATUE IN MEMPHIS

1. Robert Selph Henry, *"First With the Most" Forrest* (Indianapolis: Bobbs-Merrill Co., 1944), pp. 461–62.

2. Lafcadio Hearn, *Occidental Gleanings* (New York: Dodd, Mead & Co., 1925), pp. 145–46.

3. Ibid.

4. Ozias Midwinter, "Notes on Forrest's Funeral," *Cincinnati Commercial*, November 6, 1877; "Death of Gen. Forrest's Wife," *Confederate Veteran* (February 1893), p. 63.

5. Ibid.

6. "Forrest Monument Unveiled Amid Cheering Thousands," *Memphis News-Scimitar*, May 16, 1905.

7. David Dawson, "Another Skirmish for N. B. Forrest," *Southern Magazine*, August 1988, p. 16.

8. Ibid.

Bibliography

PRIMARY SOURCES

Manuscripts

Andrews, Garnett. Papers. Southern Historical Collection, University of North Carolina, Chapel Hill.

Bragg, Braxton. Papers. Western Reserve Historical Society, Cleveland, Ohio.

Breckinridge, John Cabell. Collection. Chicago Historical Society, Chicago.

Cannon, Newton. Papers. Tennessee State Library and Archives, Nashville.

Cartmell, Robert H. Papers. Tennessee State Library and Archives, Nashville.

Clark, Charles. Papers. Mississippi Department of Archives and History, Jackson.

Clark, Joseph Dent. Papers. Tennessee State Library and Archives, Nashville.

Cockrell, Monroe. Papers. Tennessee State Library and Archives, Nashville.

Cockrell, Monroe. Papers. William R. Perkins Library, Duke University, Durham, North Carolina.

Corliss. Report. Records of the Bureau of Refugees, Freedmen and Abandoned Lands, National Archives, Washington, D.C.

Corry, Robert E. Papers. Auburn University Library, Auburn, Ala.

Davis, Reuben. Papers. West Tennessee Historical Society, Memphis State University, Memphis.

Dixon, Harry St. John. Papers. Southern Historical Collection, University of North Carolina, Chapel Hill.

DuBose, John W. Papers. Alabama Department of Archives and History, Montgomery.

Eldridge, James William. Collection. Henry E. Huntington Library, San Marino, Calif.

Forrest, Nathan Bedford. Collection. Chicago Historical Society, Chicago.

Forrest, Nathan Bedford. File. Hargrett Rare Book and Manuscript Library, University of Georgia, Athens.

Forrest, Nathan Bedford. File. Memphis Room, Memphis Public Library, Memphis, Tenn.

Forrest, Nathan Bedford. Papers. Henry E. Huntington Library, San Marino, Calif.

Forrest, Nathan Bedford. Papers. Lionel Baxter Collection, *Civil War Times Illustrated,* U.S. Army Military History Institute, Carlisle Barracks, Pa.

Forrest, Nathan Bedford. Papers. William R. Perkins Library, Duke University, Durham, N.C.

Govan, Daniel C. Papers. Southern Historical Collection, University of North Carolina, Chapel Hill.

Hamner-Stacy. Papers. West Tennessee Historical Society, Memphis State University, Memphis.

Harris, George Carroll. Papers. Tennessee State Library and Archives, Nashville.

Jackson, Francis. Papers. Tennessee State Library and Archives, Nashville.

Lacy, Andrew Jackson. Papers. Tennessee State Library and Archives, Nashville.

Lee, Stephen D. Papers. Southern Historical Collection, University of North Carolina, Chapel Hill.

Longstreet, James. Papers. Georgia Department of Archives and History, Atlanta.

Maynard. George F., Sr. Interview. Carnegie Public Library, Clarksdale, Miss.

Meriwether Family. Papers. West Tennessee Historical Society, Memphis State University, Memphis.

Nicholson, John Page. Collection. Henry E. Huntington Library, San Marino, Calif.

Niles, Jason. Diary. Southern Historical Collection, University of North Carolina, Chapel Hill.

Nourse, James. Papers. William L. Perkins Library, Duke University, Durham, N.C.

Nutt, Leroy Moncure. Papers. Southern Historical Collection, University of North Carolina, Chapel Hill.

Olmstead, Charles H. Papers. Georgia Historical Society, Savannah.

Robinson, Mrs. Geo. S. Interview. Carnegie Public Library, Clarksdale, Miss.

Robinson, Mrs. Mary Fisher. Interview. Carnegie Public Library, Clarksdale, Miss.

Rucker, Edmund Winchester. Papers. Birmingham Public Library, Birmingham, Ala.

Rucker, E. W. Papers. Southern Historical Collection, University of North Carolina, Chapel Hill.

Sheppard, James. Papers. William R. Perkins Library, Duke University, Durham, N.C.

Sherard, J. H. Interview. Carnegie Public Library, Clarksdale, Miss.

Tennessee Cavalry, Regiment Fourth, Folder 13, Military Units, Confederate Collection, Civil War Collection, Box 17. Tennessee State Library and Archives, Nashville.

Terrell, Spot F. Journal. Tennessee State Library and Archives, Nashville.

Thomas, George H. Papers. William R. Perkins Library, Duke University, Durham, N.C.

Walter, Harvey W. Papers. Southern Historical Collection, University of North Carolina, Chapel Hill.

Published Records of the U.S. Government

Ku Klux Conspiracy: Report of the Joint Select Committee to Inquire into the Condition of Affairs in the Late Insurrectionary States, made to the two Houses of Congress, February 19, 1872, 42nd Cong., 2d sess., Senate Report No. 41, Vol. 13.

Official Records of the Union and Confederate Navies in the War of the Rebellion. 30 vols. Washington, D.C.: U.S. Government Printing Office, 1894–1922.

Reports of the Committee on the Conduct of the War: Fort Pillow Massacre. House Report No. 65. 38th Cong., 1st sess., Washington, D.C.: U.S. Government Printing Office, 1864.

Report of the Joint Committee on Reconstruction, at the First Session Thirty-Ninth Congress. Washington, D.C.: U.S. Government Printing Office, 1866.

U.S. Census Office. *7th Census of the United States, 1850: Population and Slave Schedules.* DeSoto County, Miss.

———. *8th Census of the United States, 1860: Population and Slave Schedules.* Coahoma County, Miss.; Memphis, Shelby County, Tenn.

The War of the Rebellion: A Compilation of the Official Records of the Union and Confederate Armies. 70 vols. in 127 and index. Washington, D.C.: U.S. Government Printing Office, 1880–1901.

Public Records

Coahoma County Circuit Court. *Final Record,* Book E, Clarksdale, Miss.
Final Record Book. Probate Court, 1845–46, Hernando, DeSoto County, Miss.

Memphis City Council. Minutes, *Record Book 12*, Memphis-Shelby County Archives, Cossitt-Goodwyn Library, Memphis, Tenn.
Memphis City Drectories. Memphis Public Library, Memphis, Tenn.
Register of Military Appointments, 1841–1848. Series K, Volume A. Mississippi Department of Archives and History, Jackson.

Newspapers

Atlanta *Daily Constitution*
Coahomian, Friar's Point, Mississippi
Cincinnati Commercial
Macon *Telegraph*
Memphis Daily Appeal
Memphis Eagle & Enquirer
Memphis News-Scimitar
Nashville *Banner*
New York Times
The Phenix, Hernando, Mississippi
Sunday News, Charleston, South Carolina

Published Memoirs and Personal Papers

Bevans. William E. *Reminiscences of a Private: William E. Bevans of the First Arkansas Infantry*. Edited by Daniel E. Sutherland. Fayetteville: University of Arkansas Press, 1991.
Browder, George Richard. *The Heavens Are Weeping: The Diaries of George Richard Browder 1852–1886*. Edited by Richard L. Troutman. Grand Rapids, Mich.: Zondervan Publishing House, 1977.
Cadwallader, Sylvanus. *Three Years With Grant: As Recalled by War Correspondent Sylvanus Cadwallader.* New York: Alfred A. Knopf, 1955.
Dinkins, James. *1861 to 1865 Personal Recollections and Experiences in the Confederate Army. By an Old Johnnie*. Cincinnati: Robert Clarke Co., 1897.
Duke, Basil W. *Reminiscences of General Basil W. Duke, C.S.A.* Garden City, N.Y.: Doubleday, Page & Co., 1911.
Duncan, Thomas D. *Recollections of Thomas D. Duncan: A Confederate Soldier.* Nashville, Tenn.: McQuiddy Printing Co., 1922.
Freedom: A Documentary History of Emancipation, 1861–1867. Edited by Ira Berlin, Joseph P. Reidy, and Leslie S. Rowland. Series 2. Cambridge, England: Cambridge University Press, 1982.
Gilpin, E. N. *The Last Campaign: A Cavalryman's Journal*. Leavenworth, Kans: Press of Ketcheson Printing, Co., n.d.
Goodloe, Albert Theodore. *Confederate Echoes: A Soldier's Personal Story of Life in the Confederate Army From Mississippi to the Carolinas*. Washington, D.C.: Zenger Publishing Co., 1983.

Grant, Ulysses S. *Personal Memoirs of U.S. Grant.* New York: Charles L. Webster & Co., 1886.

The Grayjackets: And How They Lived, Fought and Died, For Dixie. By a Confederate. Richmond, Va.: Jones Brothers & Co., n.d.

Hancock, R. R. *Hancock's Diary: or, a History of the Second Tennessee Confederate Cavalry, with Sketches of First and Seventh Battalions; also Portraits and Biographical Sketches.* Dayton, Ohio: Press of Morningside Bookshop, 1981.

Hood, John Bell. *Advance and Retreat: Personal Experiences in the United States and Confederate States Armies.* Bloomington: Indiana University Press, 1959.

Hubbard, John Milton. *Notes of a Private.* St. Louis: Nixon-Jones Printing Co., 1911.

Johnston, Joseph E. *Narrative of Military Operations, Directed, During the Late War Between the States by Joseph E. Johnston.* New York: D. Appleton & Co., 1874.

Maury, Dabney Herndon. *Recollections of a Virginian in the Mexican, Indian and Civil Wars.* New York: Charles Scribner's Sons, 1894.

Morton, John Watson. *The Artillery of Nathan Bedford Forrest's Cavalry.* Nashville, Tenn.: Publishing House of the M. E. Church, South, 1909.

Sherman, William T. *Home Letters of General Sherman.* Edited by M. A. DeWolfe Howe. New York: Charles Scribner's Sons, 1909.

———. *Memoirs of General William T. Sherman.* New York: Charles L. Webster & Co., 1892.

Taylor, Richard, *Destruction and Reconstruction: Personal Experiences of the Late War.* New York: Longmans, Green & Co., 1955.

Wilson, James Harrison. *Under the Old Flag: Recollections of Military Operations in the War for the Union, the Spanish War, the Boxer Rebellion, etc.* New York: D. Appleton & Co., 1912.

Witherspoon, William. *Reminiscences of a Scout, Spy and Soldier of Forrest's Cavalry.* Jackson, Tenn.: McCowat-Mercer Printing Co., 1910.

Other Works

Emerson, Ralph Waldo. *Essays & Lectures.* New York: Viking Press, 1983.

———. *Journals of Ralph Waldo Emerson.* Edited by Edward Waldo Emerson and Waldo Emerson Forbes. Boston: Houghton Mifflin Co., 1910.

Faulkner, William. *Go Down, Moses.* New York: Modern Library, 1955.

———. *Flags in the Dust.* New York: Random House, 1973.

———. *Light in August.* New York: Random House, 1959.

———. *Sartoris.* New York: Random House, 1956.

Hearn, Lafcadio. *Occidental Gleanings.* New York: Dodd, Mead & Co., 1925.

Poe, Edgar Allan. *Collected Works of Edgar Allan Poe.* Edited by Thomas Ollive Mabbott. Cambridge, Mass.: Belknap Press of Harvard University Press, 1978.

Articles

Agnew, Samuel A. "Battle of Tishomingo Creek." *Confederate Veteran* 8 (1900), pp. 401–03.

Anderson, Charles W. "My Last Meeting With Gen. Forrest." *Confederate Veteran* 4 (November 1896), p. 387.

———. "The True Story of Fort Pillow." *Confederate Veteran* 3 (November 1, 1895), p. 323.

"An Incident of Hood's Campaign." *Southern Bivouac* (November 1884), pp. 131–32.

Baird, Dan W. "Forrest's Men With Bravest of Brave." *Southern Historical Society Papers* 37 (1909), pp. 364–68.

"Battle of Eastport." *Confederate Veteran* 5 (January 1897), p. 13.

Beard, Dan W. "With Forrest in West Tennessee." *Southern Historical Society Papers* 37 (1909), pp. 304–08.

Blanton, J. C. "Forrest's Old Regiment." *Confederate Veteran* 3 (February 1895), pp. 41–42, and 3 (March 1895) pp. 77–78.

Button, Charles W. "Early Engagements With Forrest." *Confederate Veteran* 5 (September 1897), pp. 478–80.

Cable, George W. "George W. Cable's Recollections of General Forrest." Edited by Arlin Turner. *Journal of Southern History* 21 (May 1955), pp. 224–28.

Carter, Theodore G. "Reply to 'Experiences at Harrisburg'" *Confederate Veteran* 14 (July 1906), pp. 309–11.

Chalmers, James R. "Forrest and His Campaigns." *Southern Historical Society Papers* 7 (October 1879), pp. 449–86.

Clay, A. B. "On the Right at Chickamauga." *Confederate Veteran* 19 (July 1911), pp. 329–30.

Cook, V. Y. "Forrest's Capture of Col. R. G. Ingersoll." *Confederate Veteran* 15 (February 1907), pp. 54–55.

———. "Forrest's Efforts to Save Selma." *Confederate Veteran* 26 (April 1918), pp. 151–52.

Cowen, E. G. "Battle of Johnsonville." *Confederate Veteran* 22 (April 1914), pp. 174–75.

"Death of Gen. Forrest's Wife." *Confederate Veteran* 1 (February 1893), p. 63.

Dillon, Edward. "General Van Dorn's Operations between Columbia and Nashville in 1863." *Southern Historical Society Papers* 7 (1879), pp. 144–46.

Earle, F. R. "The Earle-Buchanan Letters of 1861–1876." Edited by Robert

E. Waterman and Thomas Rothrock. *Arkansas Historical Quarterly* 33 (Summer 1974), pp. 99–174.

Evans, H. W. "The Mother of General Forrest." *Confederate Veteran* 33 (October 1925), pp. 369–71.

Faulkner, E. C. "The Last Time I Saw Forrest." *Confederate Veteran* 5 (February 1897), p. 83.

Finlay, Luke W. "Another Report on Hood's Campaign." *Confederate Veteran* 15 (September 1907), pp. 404–07.

Fitch, C. "Capture of Fort Pillow—Vindication of General Chalmers by a Federal Officer." *Southern Historical Society Papers* 7 (1879), pp. 439–41.

"Forrest's Guntown Victory." *Confederate Veteran* 13 (October 1905), pp. 463–65.

Gracey, Julien F. "Capture of the Mazeppa." *Confederate Veteran* 13 (December 1905), pp. 566–70.

Gray, H. T. "Forrest's First Cavalry Fight." *Confederate Veteran* 15 (March 1907), p. 139.

Greif, J. V. "Forrest's Raid on Paducah." *Confederate Veteran* 5 (May 1897), pp. 212–13.

"Group of Officers of Forrest's Cavalry." *Confederate Veteran* 16 (April 1908), pp. xxvi–xxvii.

Hackley, W. R. "The Letters of William Beverley Randolph Hackley: Treasury Agent in West Tennessee, 1863–1866." Edited by Walter Fraser, Jr., and Mrs. Pat C. Clark. *West Tennessee Historical Society Papers* 25 (1971), pp. 90–107.

Hill, D. H. "Chickamauga—The Great Battle of the West." In *Battles and Leaders of the Civil War*, pp. 638–62. New York: Thomas Yoseloff, 1956.

Hord, Henry Ewell. "Brice's X Roads From a Private's View." *Confederate Veteran* 12 (November 1904), pp. 529–30.

———. "Personal Experiences at Harrisburg." *Confederate Veteran* 13 (August 1905), pp. 361–63.

———. "Pursuit of Gen. Sturgiss." *Confederate Veteran* 13 (January 1905), pp. 17–18.

Kelley, D. C. "General Nathan Bedford Forrest." *Methodist Review* 49 (March–April 1900), pp. 220–35.

"Last Speech of General Forrest." *Confederate Veteran* 29 (January 1921), p. 25.

Lee, Stephen D. "Battle of Harrisburg, or Tupelo." *Publications of the Mississippi Historical Society* 6 (1902), pp. 38–52.

Milner, W. J. "The Ku-Klux Klan in Alabama." *Confederate Veteran* 26 (August 1918), pp. 337–40.

Orr, J. F. "The Capture of the Undine and Mazeppa." *Confederate Veteran* 18 (July 1910), p. 323.

Otey, Mercer. "Story of Our Great War." *Confederate Veteran* 9 (March 1901), pp. 107–10.
Pinckney, T. F. "At the Fall of Selma, Ala." *Confederate Veteran* 40 (February 1932), p. 53.
Reed, John C. "What I Know of the Ku Klux Klan." *Uncle Remus Magazine* (January–October, 1908).
"Reunion of Forrest's Escort." *Confederate Veteran* 2 (October 1894), p. 308.
"Reunion of Forrest's Cavalry Corps." *Confederate Veteran* 8 (July 1900), pp. 301–02.
Riddell, Thomas J. "Western Campaign. Movements of the Goochland Light Artillery—Captain John H. Guy." *Southern Historical Society Papers* 24 (1896), pp. 316–23.
Ridley, B. L. "Daring Deeds of Staff and Escort." *Confederate Veteran* 4 (October 1896), pp. 358–59.
Robinson, Charles. "Fort Pillow 'Massacre' Observations of a Minnesotan." Edited by George Bodnia. *Minnesota History* 43 (Spring 1973), pp. 186–90.
Sanders, D. W. "Hood's Tennessee Campaign." *Confederate Veteran* 15 (September 1907), pp. 401–04.
Smith, Frank H. "The Forrest-Gould Affair." *Civil War Times Illustrated* 9 (November 1970), pp. 32–37.
Smith, Henry H. "Reminiscences of Capt. Henry H. Smith." *Confederate Veteran* 8 (January 1900), pp. 14–15.
Steger, J. C. "The Cavalry Fight at Lexington, Tenn." *Confederate Veteran* 15 (May 1907), p. 226.
Stewart, W. B. "Forrest's Raid into Memphis." *Confederate Veteran* 11 (November 1913), pp. 503–504.
Terry, F. G. "Buford's Division in Hood's Rear." *Confederate Veteran* 13 (April 1905), p. 161.
Tullos, Thomas R. "When Capt. Sam Freeman Was Killed." *Confederate Veteran* 21 (August 1913), p. 407.
Tyler, H. A. "Forrest Covers Hood's Retreat." *Confederate Veteran* 12 (September 1904), p. 436.
Waring, George E., Jr. "The Sooy Smith Expedition (February, 1864)." In *Battles and Leaders of the Civil War*, Vol. 4, pp. 416–18. New York: Thomas Yoseloff, 1956.
Whitsitt, W. H. "A Year With Forrest." *Confederate Veteran* 25 (August 1917).
Wilkes, John S. "First Battle Experience—Fort Donelson." *Confederate Veteran* 14 (November 1916), pp. 500–01.

SECONDARY SOURCES

Aaron, Daniel. *The Unwritten War: American Writers and the Civil War.* Oxford: Oxford University Press, 1973.

Bailey, Fred Arthur. *Class and Tennessee's Confederate Generation*. Chapel Hill: University of North Carolina Press, 1987.
Bancroft, Frederic. *Slave-Trading in the Old South*. Baltimore: J. H. Furst Co., 1931.
Battey, George Magruder, Jr. *A History of Rome and Floyd County*. Atlanta: Webb & Vary Co., 1922.
Bearss, Edwin C. *Forrest at Brice's Cross Roads and in North Mississippi in 1864*. Dayton, Ohio: Press of Morningside Bookshop, 1979.
Beringer, Richard E., Herman Hattaway, Archer Jones, and William N. Still, Jr. *Why the South Lost the Civil War*. Athens: University of Georgia Press, 1986.
Billington, Ray Allen. *America's Frontier Heritage*. Albuquerque: University of New Mexico Press, 1967.
Blotner, Joseph. *Faulkner: A Biography*. 2 vols. New York: Random House, 1974.
Brooks, Cleanth. *William Faulkner: Toward Yoknapatawpha and Beyond*. New Haven, Conn.: Yale University Press, 1973.
Bruce, Dickson D., Jr. *Violence and Culture in the Antebellum South*. Austin: University of Texas Press, 1979.
Carter, Dan T. *When the War Was Over: The Failure of Self-Reconstruction in the South, 1865–1867*. Baton Rouge: Louisiana State University Press, 1985.
Cash, W. J. *The Mind of the South*. New York: Vintage Books, 1969.
Catton, Bruce. *Terrible Swift Sword*. Garden City, N.Y.: Doubleday & Co., 1963.
———. *Never Call Retreat*. Garden City, N.Y.: Doubleday & Co., 1965.
Cleaves, Freeman. *Rock of Chickamauga: The Life of General George H. Thomas*. Norman: University of Oklahoma Press, 1948.
Cohen, Lucy M. *Chinese in the Post-Civil War South: A People Without a History*. Baton Rouge: Louisiana State University Press, 1984.
Connelly, Thomas Lawrence. *Army of the Heartland: The Army of Tennessee, 1861–1862*. Baton Rouge: Louisiana State University Press, 1967.
———. *Autumn of Glory: The Army of Tennessee, 1862–1865*. Baton Rouge: Louisiana State University Press, 1971.
———, and Barbara L. Bellows. *God and General Longstreet: The Lost Cause and the Southern Mind*. Baton Rouge: Louisiana State University Press, 1982.
———, and Archer Jones. *The Politics of Command: Factions and Ideas in Confederate Strategy*. Baton Rouge: Louisiana State University Press, 1973.
———, and James Lee McDonough. *Five Tragic Hours: The Battle of Franklin*. Knoxville: University of Tennessee Press, 1983.
Cooling, Benjamin Franklin. *Forts Henry and Donelson: The Key to the Confederate Heartland*. Knoxville: University of Tennessee Press, 1987.
Coulter, E. Merton. *William G. Brownlow: Fighting Parson of the Southern*

Highlands. Chapel Hill: University of North Carolina Press, 1937.
Curtis, James C. *Andrew Jackson and the Search for Vindication*. Boston: Little, Brown & Co., 1976.
Dasher, Thomas E. *William Faulkner's Characters: An Index to the Published and Unpublished Fiction*. New York: Garland Publishing, 1981.
Dyer, John P. *"Fightin' Joe" Wheeler*. Baton Rouge: Louisiana State University Press, 1941.
Eckenrode, H. J. *Life of Nathan B. Forrest*. Richmond, Va.: B. F. Johnson Publishing Co., 1918.
Fellman, Michael. *Inside War: The Guerrilla Conflict in Missouri During the American Civil War*. New York: Oxford University Press, 1989.
Foner, Eric. *Free Soil, Free Labor, Free Men: The Ideology of the Republican Party Before the Civil War*. New York: Oxford University Press, 1970.
———. *Nothing But Freedom: Emancipation and Its Legacy*. Baton Rouge: Louisiana State University Press, 1983.
———. *Reconstruction: American's Unfinished Revolution, 1863–1877*. New York: Harper & Row, 1988.
Foote, Shelby. *The Civil War, A Narrative*. 3 vols. New York: Random House, 1958.
Fowler, Doreen, and Ann J. Abadie, eds. *Faulkner and the Southern Renaissance: Faulkner and Yoknapatawpha*. Jackson: University Press of Mississippi, 1982.
Fox-Genovese, Elizabeth, and Eugene D. Genovese. *Fruits of Merchant Capital: Slavery and Bourgeois Property in the Rise and Expansion of Capitalism*. Cambridge, England: Cambridge University Press, 1983.
Franklin, John Hope. *The Militant South, 1800–1861*. Cambridge, Mass.: Harvard University Press, 1956.
———. *Reconstruction After the Civil War*. Chicago: University of Chicago Press, 1961.
Genovese, Eugene D. *The World the Slaveholders Made: Two Essays on Interpretation*. New York: Vintage Books, 1971.
Glatthaar, Joseph T. *Forged in Battle: The Civil War Alliance of Black Soldiers and White Officers*. New York: Free Press, 1990.
Hamilton, James J. *The Battle of Fort Donelson*. South Brunswick, N.J.: Thomas Yoseloff, 1968.
Hartje, Robert G. *Van Dorn: The Life and Times of a Confederate General*. Nashville: Vanderbilt University Press, 1967.
Hattaway, Herman. *General Stephen D. Lee*. Jackson: University Press of Mississippi, 1976.
Henry, Robert Selph. *As They Saw Forrest: Some Recollections and Comments of Contemporaries*. Jackson, Tenn.: McCowat-Mercer Press, 1956.
———. *"First With the Most" Forrest*. Indianapolis: Bobbs-Merrill Co., 1944.

Horn, Stanley F. *Invisible Empire: The Story of the Ku Klux Klan, 1866–1871.* Boston: Houghton Mifflin Co., 1939.

Jones, James Pickett. *Yankee Blitzkrieg: Wilson's Raid Through Alabama and Georgia.* Athens: University of Georgia Press, 1976.

Jordan, Thomas, and J. P. Pryor. *The Campaigns of Lieut.-Gen. N. B. Forrest, and of Forrest's Cavalry.* New Orleans: Blelock & Co., 1868.

Karl, Frederick R. *William Faulkner: American Writer.* New York: Weidenfeld & Nicolson, 1989.

Kennerly, Dan. *The Dawn of Lightning War—General Forrest and Parker's Crossroads.* Houston: Dan Kennerly, 1982.

Krutch, Joseph Wood. *Edgar Allan Poe: A Study in Genius.* New York: Russell & Russell, 1926.

Longacre, Edward G. *From Union Stars to Top Hat: A Biography of the Extraordinary General James Harrison Wilson.* Harrisburg, Pa.: Stackpole Co., 1972.

Losson, Christopher. *Tennessee's Forgotten Warriors: Frank Cheatham and His Confederate Division.* Knoxville: University of Tennessee Press, 1989.

Luraghi, Raimondo. *The Rise and Fall of the Plantation South.* New York: New Viewpoints, 1978.

Lytle, Andrew Nelson. *Bedford Forrest and His Critter Company.* New York: G. P. Putnam's Sons, 1931.

Mathes, J. Harvey. *General Forrest.* New York: D. Appleton & Co., 1902.

McDonough, James Lee. *Chattanooga—A Death Grip on the Confederacy.* Knoxville: University of Tennessee Press, 1984.

———. *Shiloh—In Hell Before Night.* Knoxville: University of Tennessee Press, 1977.

McFeely, William S. *Yankee Stepfather: General O. O. Howard and the Freedmen.* New Haven, Conn.: Yale University Press, 1968.

McIlwaine, Shields. *Memphis Down in Dixie.* New York: E. P. Dutton, 1948.

McMurry, Richard M. *John Bell Hood and the War for Southern Independence.* Lexington: University Press of Kentucky, 1982.

McPherson, James M. *Battle Cry of Freedom: The Civil War Era.* New York: Oxford University Press, 1988.

———. *Ordeal by Fire: The Civil War and Reconstruction.* New York: Alfred A. Knopf, 1982.

Mitchell, Reid. *Civil War Soldiers.* New York: Viking Penguin, 1988.

Oakes, James. *The Ruling Race: A History of American Slaveholders.* New York: Alfred A. Knopf, 1982.

Ownby, Ted. *Subduing Satan: Religion, Recreation, and Manhood in the Rural South, 1865–1920.* Chapel Hill: University of North Carolina Press, 1990.

Owsley, Frank Lawrence. *Plain Folk of the Old South.* Baton Rouge: Louisiana State University Press, 1949.

Parks, Joseph H. *General Leonidas Polk CSA: The Fighting Bishop*. Baton Rouge: Louisiana State University Press, 1962.

Pugh, David G. *Sons of Liberty: The Masculine Mind in Nineteenth-Century America*. Westport, Conn.: Greenwood Press, 1983.

Rable, George C. *But There Was No Peace: The Role of Violence in the Politics of Reconstruction*. Athens: University of Georgia Press, 1984.

Roark, James L. *Masters Without Slaves: Southern Planters in the Civil War and Reconstruction*. New York: W. W. Norton & Co., 1977.

Robertson, James I., Jr. *Soldiers Blue and Gray*. Columbia: University of South Carolina Press, 1988.

Rohrbough, Malcolm J. *The Trans-Appalachian Frontier: People, Societies, and Institutions 1775–1850*. New York: Oxford University Press, 1978.

Rowland, Dunbar. *Military History of Mississippi, 1803–1898*. Spartanburg, S. C.: Reprint Co., 1978.

Sheppard, Eric William. *Bedford Forrest: The Confederacy's Greatest Cavalryman*. New York: Dial Press, 1930.

Shore, Laurence. *Southern Capitalists: The Ideological Leadership of an Elite, 1832–1885*. Chapel Hill: University of North Carolina Press, 1986.

Simpson, Lewis P. *Mind and the American Civil War: A Meditation on Lost Causes*. Baton Rouge: Louisiana State University Press, 1989.

Speer, William S. *Sketches of Prominent Tennesseans*. Easley, S.C.: Southern Historical Press, 1978.

Steiner, Paul E. *Medical-Military Portraits of Union and Confederate Generals*. Philadelphia: Whitmore Publishing Co., 1948.

Tadman, Michael. *Speculators and Slaves: Masters, Traders, and Slaves in the Old South*. Madison: University of Wisconsin Press, 1990.

Taylor, Joe Gray. *Negro Slavery in Louisiana*. Baton Rouge: Louisiana Historical Association, 1963.

Taylor, Orville W. *Negro Slavery in Arkansas*. Durham, N. C.: Duke University Press, 1958.

Thomas, Emory M. *The Confederate Nation: 1861–1865*. New York: Harper & Row, 1979.

Tourgée, Albion Winegar. *The Invisible Empire*. Baton Rouge: Louisiana State University Press, 1989.

Trelease, Allen W. *White Terror: The Ku Klux Klan Conspiracy and Southern Reconstruction*. New York: Harper & Row, 1971.

Tucker, George E. *Victory Rode the Rails*. Indianapolis: Bobbs-Merrill Co., 1953.

Tucker, Glenn. *Chickamauga: Bloody Battle in the West*. Indianapolis: Bobbs-Merrill Co., 1961.

Wade, Wyn Craig. *The Fiery Cross: The Ku Klux Klan in America*. New York: Simon & Schuster, 1987.

Wallerstein, Immanuel. *The Capitalist World-Economy*. Cambridge, England: Cambridge University Press, 1979.

Warren, Robert Penn, ed. *Faulkner: A Collection of Critical Essays.* Englewood Cliffs, N. J.: Prentice-Hall, 1966.

Watson, James Gray. *The Snopes Dilemma: Faulkner's Trilogy.* Coral Gables, Fla.: University of Miami Press, 1968.

Weeks, Linton. *Clarksdale & Coahoma County: A History.* Clarksdale, Miss.: Carnegie Public Library, 1982.

White, William W. *The Confederate Veteran.* Tuscaloosa, Ala.: Confederate Publishing Co., 1962.

Wiley, Bell Irvin. *The Life of Johnny Reb: The Common Soldier of the Confederacy.* Baton Rouge: Louisiana State University Press, 1978.

———. *The Road to Appomattox.* New York: Atheneum, 1977.

Williams, William Appleman. *The Contours of American History.* New York: W. W. Norton & Co., 1988.

Wilson, Charles Reagan. *Baptized in Blood: The Religion of the Lost Cause, 1865–1920.* Athens: University of Georgia Press, 1980.

Woodberry, George E. *Edgar Allan Poe.* Boston: Houghton Mifflin Co., 1885.

Woodworth, Steven. *Jefferson Davis and His Generals: The Failure of Confederate Command in the West.* Lawrence: University Press of Kansas, 1990.

Wright, Gavin. *Old South, New South: Revolutions in the Southern Economy Since the Civil War.* New York: Basic Books, 1986.

Wyatt-Brown, Bertram. *Southern Honor: Ethics and Behavior in the Old South.* Oxford: Oxford University Press, 1982.

Wyeth, John Allan. *Life of General Nathan Bedford Forrest.* New York: Harper & Bros., 1899.

Articles and Unpublished Works

Abernathy, Harry. "Famous General Retired to Coahoma County Plantation." *Clarksdale Press Register,* July 21, 1984.

Bahr, Howard, and William Duke. "The Wet August: Andrew J. Smith's Mississippi Campaign." *Civil War Times Illustrated* 16 (November 1977), pp. 10–19.

Brooksher, William R., and David K. Snider. "Devil on the River." *Civil War Times Illustrated* 15 (August 1976), pp. 12–19.

Bryan, Charles F. "'I Mean to Have Them All': Forrest's Murfreesboro Raid." *Civil War Times Illustrated* 12 (July 1974), pp. 26–34.

Castel, Albert. "The Fort Pillow Massacre: A Fresh Examination of the Evidence." *Civil War History* 4 (1958), pp. 37–50.

Cimprich, John, and Robert C. Mainfort, Jr. "Dr. Fitch's Report on the Fort Pillow Massacre." *Tennessee Historical Quarterly* 44 (Spring 1985), pp. 27–39.

———. "The Fort Pillow Massacre: A Statistical Note." *Journal of American History* 76 (December 1989), pp. 830–37.

———, eds. "Fort Pillow Revisited: New Evidence About an Old Controversy." *Civil War History* 28 (December 1982), pp. 293–306.

Conrad, James L. "Forrest's Great Gamble: The Battle of Ebenezer Church." *Civil War Time Illustrated* 20 (April 1982), pp. 30–39.

Cook, James F. "The 1863 Raid of Abel D. Streight: Why It Failed." *Alabama Review* 22 (October 1969), pp. 254–69.

Crawford, Charles W. "A Note on Forrest's Race for Rome." *Georgia Historical Quarterly* 50 (September 1966), pp. 288–90.

Dawson, David. "Another Skirmish for N. B. Forrest." *Southern Magazine*, August 1988, p. 16.

Fitzgerald, William S. "Did Nathan Bedford Forrest Really Rescue John Able?" *Tennessee Historical Quarterly* 39 (Spring 1980), pp. 16–26.

Gorn, Elliott J. "'Gouge and Bite, Pull Hair and Scratch': The Social Significance of Fighting in the Southern Backcountry." *American Historical Review* 90 (February 1985), pp. 18–32.

Holmes, Jack D. L. "Forrest's 1864 Raid on Memphis." *Tennessee Historical Quarterly* 28 (December 1959), pp. 295–321.

Horn, Stanley F. "Nashville During the Civil War." *Tennessee Historical Quarterly* 4 (March 1945), pp. 3–22.

Jay, John C. "General N. B. Forrest as a Railroad Builder in Alabama." *Alabama Historical Quarterly* 24 (Spring 1962), pp. 16–31.

Jordan, John L. "Was There a Massacre at Fort Pillow?" *Tennessee Historical Quarterly* 6 (1947), pp. 99–133.

Longacre, Edward G. "All Is Fair in Love and War." *Civil War Times Illustrated* 8 (June 1969), pp. 32–40.

Luckett, William W. "Bedford Forrest in the Battle of Brice's Cross Roads." *Tennessee Historical Quarterly* 15 (June 1956), pp. 99–110.

Lufkin, Charles L. "'Not Heard From Since April 12, 1864:' The Thirteenth Tennessee Cavalry, U.S.A." *Tennessee Historical Quarterly* 45 (Spring 1986), pp. 287–315.

Maness, Lonnie E. "Forrest and the Battle of Parker's Crossroads." *Tennessee Historical Quarterly* 34 (Summer 1975), pp. 154–67.

———. "The Fort Pillow Massacre: Fact or Fiction." *Tennessee Historical Quarterly* 45 (Spring 1986), pp. 287–315.

McCash, William Barton. "Colonel Abel D. Streight's Raid, His Capture, and Imprisonment." Master's thesis, University of Georgia, 1959.

Mitchell, Enoch L. "The Role of General George Washington Gordon in the Ku Klux Klan." *West Tennessee Historical Society Papers* 1 (1947), pp. 72–80.

Williams, Edward F., III. "The Johnsonville Raid and Nathan Bedford Forrest State Park." *Tennessee Historical Quarterly* 28 (Fall 1969), pp. 225–51.

Wilson, Florence. "Forrest, the Matchless Rider." *Nashville Banner*, July 7, 1935.

Wooten, Fred T., Jr. "Religious Activity in Civil War Memphis." *Tennessee Historical Quarterly* 2 and 3 (June and September, 1944), pp. 131–49, 248–72.

Wrenn, Lynette B. "'Get the City Out of the Mud and Mire,' Financing Street Improvements in Post-Civil War Memphis." *Tennessee Historical Quarterly* 47 (Spring 1968), pp. 17–26.

Index